THE ILIAD

The publisher gratefully acknowledges the generous support of the Joan Palevsky Literature in Translation Endowment Fund of the University of California Press Foundation.

HOMER

THE ILIAD

A NEW TRANSLATION BY

PETER GREEN

University of California Press

University of California Press, one of the most distinguished university presses in the United States, enriches lives around the world by advancing scholarship in the humanities, social sciences, and natural sciences. Its activities are supported by the UC Press Foundation and by philanthropic contributions from individuals and institutions. For more information, visit www.ucpress.edu.

University of California Press
Oakland, California

First Paperback Printing 2016

Library of Congress Cataloging-in-Publication Data
Homer, author.
[Iliad. English]
The Iliad / Homer; a new translation by Peter Green.
p. cm.
Includes bibliographical references.
ISBN 978-0-520-28143-1 (pbk.: alk. paper) — ISBN 978-0-520-96132-6 (electronic)
1. Achilles (Greek mythology)—Poetry. 2. Trojan War—Poetry. 3. Epic poetry, Greek. I. Green, Peter, translator I. Title.
PA4025.A2G75 2015
883'.01—dc23 2014038401

Manufactured in the United States of America

21 20 19 18 17 16
10 9 8 7 6 5 4 3 2 1

In keeping with a commitment to support environmentally responsible and sustainable printing practices, UC Press has printed this book on Natures Natural, a fiber that contains 30% post-consumer waste and meets the minimum requirements of ANSI/NISO Z39.48-1992 (R 1997) (*Permanence of Paper*).

For Carin M. C. Green (1948–2015)
amicae uxori collegae
in loving memory

Τυφλὸς ἀνήρ, οἰκεῖ δὲ Χίῳ ἔνι παιπαλοέσσῃ.
τοῦ πᾶσαι μετόπισθεν ἀριστεύσουσιν ἀοιδαί.

He is a blind man, and lives on rocky Chios:
All his songs will be supreme, now and forever.

Homeric Hymn to Delian Apollo, 172–73

Contents

Preface

This book is the improbable fulfillment of a dream that has haunted me ever since the middle of the twentieth century, when I was one of the team Donald Carne-Ross assembled to produce some new versions of Homer's *Iliad* on the (now long defunct) BBC Third Programme. Creative outreach was our watchword; we were targeting a postwar generation, mostly ex-service, that knew no Greek but was hungry for the classics. But in my case the magic went far further back: to Andrew Lang's marvelous *Tales of Troy and Greece* read in childhood; to the Greek I began to learn when I was ten years old; to the well-thumbed India-paper red cloth volume of Monro and Allen's third edition of the *Iliad*, which I had read from cover to cover by the time I was fifteen, and which went with me through three monsoons in India and Burma during World War II (and sits by me as I write these words, its pages crinkled from oppressive humidity and still smelling of the Arakan). When I finally got to Cambridge in 1947 it was a piece of providential luck that in the year I took Part II of the Classical Tripos, the annual revolving sequence of genres had reached Epic. I still have my ancient, battered copy of Walter Leaf's commentary, annotated throughout with my (mostly embarrassing) undergraduate comments. When, a few years later, with a Ph.D. in hand, I joined Carne-Ross's team, I saw the translations I did then as preparation for a full version of my own.

Of course, it didn't happen. A mass of other work got in the way. I married, had children, was caught up in endless responsibilities. The best part of a decade in Greece saw me productive in many ways, but not regarding Homer. Even when, at long last, I gravitated back by a somewhat circuitous route to teaching at university level, and became a professor of classics, other passions, mostly historical, monopolized what little spare time I had. From time to time—not least when I saw yet another version of the *Iliad* or the *Odyssey* collecting tribute in the headlines—a sad twinge of regret, a sense of opportunity lost, would nag at me, to be dismissed as self-indulgent romantic nostalgia. Even when I retired, the old dream still seemed a classic case of the *If only* syndrome.

I suspect, though, that my subconscious may have been quietly at work: I was aware, for example, when in 1996 I translated Apollonius Rhodius's *Argonautika,* that in tackling the myth of Jason and the Golden Fleece I was responding to a passion first ignited, like that for the Trojan War and the subsequent adventures of Odysseus, by Andrew Lang's retelling of both: his words had fired my imagination, as a child, in an unforgettable way. What that experience also gave me was a fresh lesson, and an extremely useful one, in how to deal, as a translator, with the unrelentingly tricky problem of the epic hexameter. But it was only a year ago, when I realized that on my next birthday I was going to be ninety, that I asked myself what I had to lose, even now, by tackling the *Iliad;* and in a curiously relaxed mood sat down and tried my hand at book 1. What, of course, I eventually discovered was the reason I had waited so long. In one way and another, my whole career had been a preparation for this moment. What would work for Homer in translation? Of all that I had done over half a century earlier for the Third Programme, I kept a grand total of three lines. When it came to presenting the *Iliad* to a modern, Greekless audience confronting ancient epic for the first time, Homer proved a more challenging taskmaster than I could ever have imagined: and yet to meet that challenge was something I found continually enjoyable and exciting. Preserving the strangeness, yet in an acceptable way; finding the *mot juste* for difficult and often alien concepts; matching the wonderful linear rhetoric, both in speeches and descriptive passages; keeping the simplicity while always acknowledging the emotional subtleties; writing rhythms that could, like the original, be declaimed aloud, and hold the attention of a listening audience; perhaps, above all, resisting the temptation to make nonexistent equations with easily recognizable English patterns—all this tested my skills to the utmost, and too often defeated my best efforts, forced me to settle for a compromise. Perhaps that is the best any translator can hope for.

To one nagging minor problem, the spelling of Greek proper names, I have found no altogether satisfactory solution, and probably none exists. The problem itself is one legacy of Rome's complete cultural domination of the European classical tradition from the Renaissance until well into the nineteenth century, which dictated (among much else), not only that Greek names be Latinized, but that the gods of the Greek pantheon should be replaced in translation by their nearest Roman equivalents. The second practice was reluctantly abandoned only after about 1880; the first is still very much with us. It is not just a matter of replacing *–os* and *–on* terminations with *–us* and *–um*; *k* with *c;* short *u* with *y*; and the diphthongs *–oi* with *–oe,* *– ei* with *ī*, and *–ou* with *ū*. The Latin *–er* termination is also imposed, so that

"Aléxandros" becomes "Alexander", and "Teukros" "Teucer". For the most part (but not invariably: for example, I use "Achilles" rather than "Akhilleus"), I have gone back to the Greek spelling. In a majority of cases this does not make for a wrenching unfamiliarity. But the shift from Roman "Hecuba" to Greek "Hekabē" or from Roman "Ajax" to Greek "Aias" can be disconcerting, and there are some Hellenisms—for example, "Oidipous" for "Oedipus", "Mykēnai" for "Mycenae", "Krētē" for "Crete—that take some getting used to. But one has to start getting rid of this wretched Latin legacy somewhere.

Now the work is done, and out of my hands, I suppose I should be relaxing; but the truth is, I find myself getting more and more involved in the not quite identical problems confronting a translator of the *Odyssey:* I suspect my tussle with doing Homer justice is not over yet. Meanwhile I would like to take this opportunity of thanking my publishers at the University of California Press for their confidence in supporting yet another version of the *Iliad;* the students who, over long years, most often without realizing it, sharpened my sense of how to look at Homer; my copy editor and old friend Peter Dreyer for, once again, his lynx-eyed common sense; and another good friend, Barbara Hird, for not only so generously agreeing at very short notice to execute a most complex index for me but also for spotting a number of errors that had got past all the rest of us. I am likewise extremely grateful to my in-house editors, Eric Schmidt and Cindy Fulton, whose professional aplomb when dealing with a challenging manuscript has been beyond all praise. Finally and above all, I thank my wife Carin, who put up so patiently with being a sounding board for my ideas as the translation progressed, and invariably came up with perceptive comments and shrewd professional ideas of her own. My translation is dedicated to her, and never was a dedication more richly deserved. μάλιστα δέ τ' ἔκλυον αὐτοί.

I am grateful to Richard Jenkyns for suggesting a perfect translation at 24.772, and to Charles Drace-Francis for pointing out an embarrassing slip that we had all missed on p. 474. I have left my tribute to my wife as originally written; sadly, it is now a memorial.

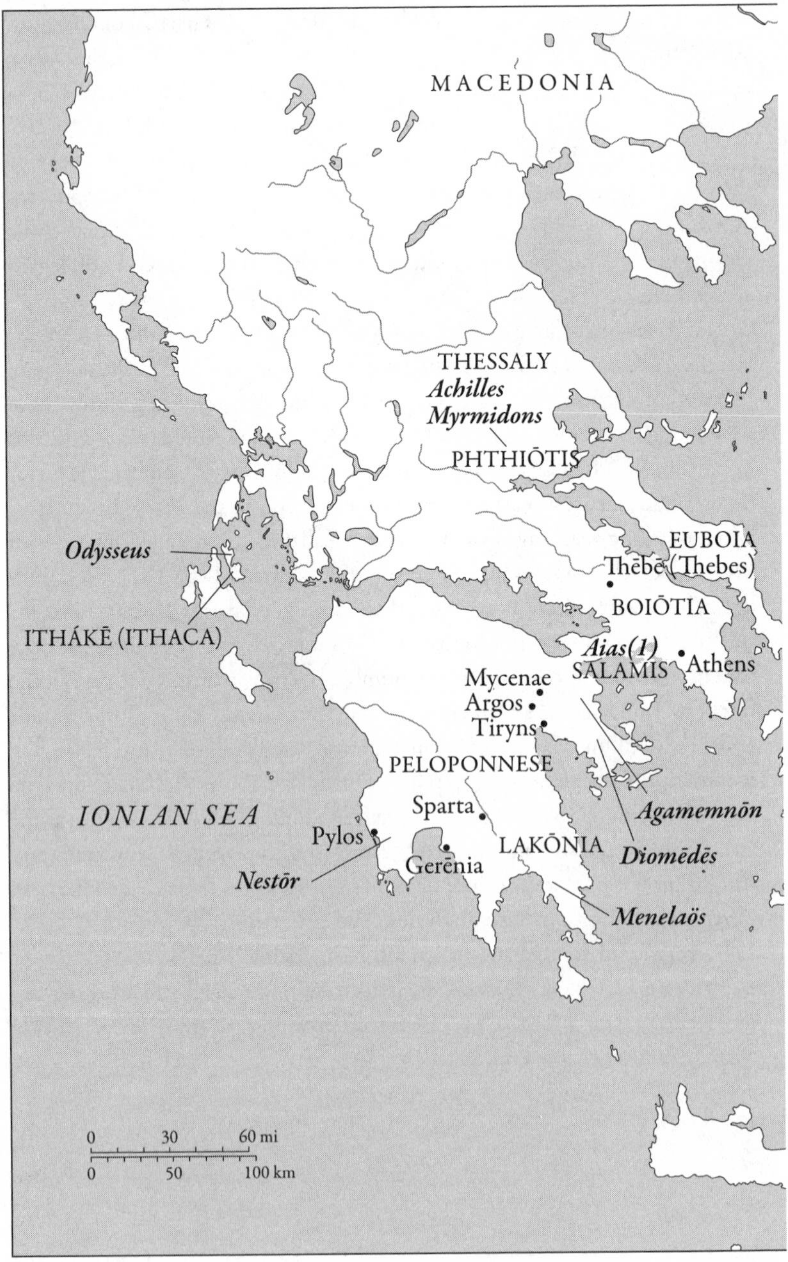

MACEDONIA
THESSALY
Achilles
Myrmidons
PHTHIŌTIS
EUBOIA
Thēbē (Thebes)
BOIŌTIA
Odysseus
ITHÁKĒ (ITHACA)
Aias(1)
SALAMIS
Athens
Mycenae
Argos
Tiryns
PELOPONNESE
Sparta
Pylos
Gerēnia
LAKŌNIA
Agamemnōn
Diomēdēs
Menelaös
Nestōr
IONIAN SEA
0 30 60 mi
0 50 100 km

THRACE
HELLESPONT
LEMNOS
Hektōr
Troy
Priam
TROAD
Aineias
Mt. Ida
N
LESBOS
AEGEAN SEA
CHIOS
LYDIA
SAMOS
IONIA
DELOS
Miletos
Glaukos
Sarpēdōn
LYCIA
RHODES
CRETAN SEA
Idomeneus
Knossos
CRETE

Abbreviations

Ael.	Claudius Aelianus (c. 170–c. 230 C.E.), a Roman freedman from Praeneste, writer (in Greek) of miscellanies.
NA	Ael., *On the Nature of Animals.*
Apollod.	Apollodorus of Athens, grammarian (c. 180–c. 120 C.E.). Certainly not the author of the *Bibliothēkē* (library), a manual of mythology attributed to him by a (probably) near-contemporary forger.
Epit.	*Epitome* to Apollod., *Bibliothēkē.*
arg.	*argumentum*, i.e., argument (in the sense of précis or synopsis).
Athen.	Athenaeus of Naukratis in Egypt (fl. c. 200 C.E.), author of the *Deipnosophistae*, or *Learned Banqueters*, his sole surviving work, a fifteen-book account of a symposium, mostly notable for its excerpts from classical works now otherwise lost.
BA	*Barrington Atlas of the Greek and Roman World.* Edited by R. J. A. Talbot. Princeton, NJ, 2000.
Diod. Sic.	Diodorus Siculus, of Agyrium in Sicily (c. 100–c. 30 B.C.E.), universal historian, author of a *Bibliothēkē* (library).
fr.	fragment.
Hdt.	Herodotus, of Halicarnassus and Thurii (c. 485–c. 420), historian of the Persian Wars
Hes.	Hesiod, epic/didactic poet (fl. c. 700 B.C.E.).
Cat.	Hes., *Catalogue of Women.*
Th.	Hes., *Theogony,*
WD	Hes., *Works and Days.*
HHAphr.	*Homeric Hymn to Aphrodite.*
HE	*The Homer Encyclopedia.* Edited by M. Finkelberg. 3 vols. Oxford (Wiley-Blackwell), 2011.
Il.	Homer, *Iliad.*
JHS	*Journal of Hellenic Studies.*

OCD[3]	*The Oxford Classical Dictionary.* 3rd ed. rev. Edited by S. Hornblower and A. Spawforth. Oxford, 2003.
OCD[4]	*The Oxford Classical Dictionary*. 4th ed. Edited by S. Hornblower, A. Spawforth, and E. Eidinow. Oxford, 2012.
Od.	Homer, *Odyssey*
Pliny	Pliny the Elder, Gaius Plinius Secundus (23/4–79 C.E.), equestrian procurator and literary scholar.
HN	Pliny, *Historia Naturalis*, a thirty-seven-book encyclopedic *Natural History*.
Thuc.	Thucydides of Athens (c. 460–c. 395 B.C.E.), author of an (unfinished) history of the Peloponnesian War.

Introduction

APPROACHING THE PROBLEM

From both the literary and the sociohistorical viewpoints, the situation of anyone embarking on Homer for the first time—and in many ways this applies as much to the classical student as to anyone else—is a unique one. To begin with, in the sense that we normally consider a written work, there is no anterior background: we are at the beginning. To make matters worse, our ignorance concerning both work and author is abysmal.

We do not know for certain who Homer was, or where he lived, or when he wrote. We cannot be absolutely confident that the same man (if it was a man) wrote both the *Iliad* and the *Odyssey*, or even that "wrote" is a correct description of the method of composition involved. Indeed, there is much doubt still as to whether we can talk in terms of a single poet at all, rather than of a traditional sequence of bards fashioning an oral *poème vivant*, a living poem subject to constant modification; though (to complicate matters still further) there is the likelihood (West 2011) of a master poet having used a mass of centuries-old oral lays as material from which to create the masterpieces we possess today. Even the time at which the texts we know were actually written down, and what stage of composition they represent, are equally uncertain. This uncertainty extends to the subject matter. We can no more state for a fact whether a Trojan War actually ever took place, let alone whether it bore any relation to the conflict described in the *Iliad*, than we can form a confident picture of "Homer". All we have, as T. S. Eliot said in a different poetic context, are "hints and guesses, hints followed by guesses."

The plot of the *Iliad* is a good place to begin, since at least we know a reasonable amount about the early myth (itself an ambiguous term) concerning the origin and events of the Trojan War. The first striking fact for any newcomer to the scene is how little of the myth actually takes place within the *Iliad* itself, which covers less than two months—fifty-one days, to be precise—of a war that lasted ten long years, and of which the antecedents looked back almost as far, just as the consequences stretched out a good decade into the future. All that the narrative of the *Iliad* covers are the events precipitated, in the ninth year of the war, by a quarrel between Agamemnōn, commander in chief of the invading Achaian forces, and Achilles, his most brilliant warrior. A Trojan priest of Apollo, Chrysēs, comes to their camp offering ransom for his daughter Chryseïs, currently a prisoner allotted as booty to Agamemnōn. At first Agamemnōn brusquely—and against general feeling—rejects his offer. Chrysēs prays to Apollo, who visits the Achaian camp with a devastating plague. The Achaian priest Kalchas explains the plague, correctly, as a direct result of Agamemnōn's rejection of Chrysēs' offer. Faced with this, Agamemnōn agrees to return Chryseïs, but insists on being given a replacement by the Achaians: honor and status are involved. A contemptuous speech by Achilles sharpens Agamemnōn's resolve: he threatens to take Achilles' own captive woman, Briseïs, in lieu of the one he is giving up, and in due course does so.

This provokes the almost superhuman wrath (*mēnis*) in Achilles that leads him to withdraw himself and his troops from the war effort, with alarming results for the Achaians. His rage persists, defying all efforts to change his mind (including an offer by Agamemnōn to return Briseïs with additional placatory gifts) until the death in battle, at the hands of the Trojan Hektōr, of Achilles' dear comrade Patroklos, who has borrowed Achilles' own armor for the purpose. This finally brings Achilles back into action, with the sole aim of killing Hektōr—which he duly does, and then savagely maltreats his victim's corpse. Outraged, the gods on Olympos, led by Zeus, compel Achilles to accept ransom from Hektōr's father, the aged king Priam, and to return his body for burial. The sight of Priam stirs unexpected feelings of compassion in Achilles; the *Iliad* ends with Hektōr's funeral rites.

This epic tragedy forms a small part only of a general narrative that was, clearly, familiar in detail to all who heard or, later, read it: casual, and unexplained, references to what follows occur at intervals throughout the text of the *Iliad* that we have today, showing that knowledge of the basic plot line was taken as a given from a very early period during the oral transmission of lays concerning the Trojan War. That plot line, in brief, is as follows.

It begins with the Judgment of Paris, an ahistorical legendary scenario if ever there was one. At the marriage of the Thessalian warrior Pēleus to the sea-nymph Thetis, attended by gods as well as mortals, Eris (Strife personified) mischievously makes trouble between three powerful goddesses, Hērē, Athēnē, and Aphroditē, by provoking them[1] to quarrel over which of the three has the best claim to beauty. Zeus (who has long coveted Thetis, but is marrying her off to a mortal because of a prophecy that she'll give birth to a man greater than his father) has Hermēs send the contentious trio to Mt.

1. By throwing down before them the famous golden Apple of Discord, inscribed "To the Fairest".

Ida, where Paris Aléxandros—son of King Priam of Troy, but exposed at birth because of a prophecy that he would bring disaster on his city, and brought up by a shepherd family—is tending his flocks. He is to settle their quarrel, and duly does so. Hērē promises him kingship, Athēnē will ensure that he becomes a great warrior, Aphrodītē guarantees his conquest of the world's most beautiful woman. (Why, apart from pure egotism, goddesses should not only accept the verdict of an admittedly good-looking shepherd boy, but offer him bribes for it, is never made entirely clear.) Inevitably, his vote goes to Aphrodītē. By so doing, he makes enemies of two great goddesses. He also, in the long run, provides a *casus belli* for the Trojan War (as Zeus has planned all along, with a view to shrinking the world's excessively large population through slaughter), since when he meets, and falls for, the world's most beautiful woman, Helen, she is already married to King Menelaös of Sparta.

Years pass. Paris Aléxandros is recognized and restored as a prince of Troy. As such, he makes a state visit to the Spartan ménage of Helen and Menelaös, and, aided by Aphrodītē (who has not forgotten her promise), not only bedazzles and sails off with an all-too-willing Helen while Menelaös's guest, but also compounds his alienation of marital affection by removing a sizable haul of family property in addition to the lady, though her nine-year-old daughter Hermionē, a potential embarrassment on the honeymoon, is left behind. They have a following wind, a calm sea, and reach Troy in three days: clearly Aphrodītē, like Artemis, can control the weather for the benefit of her favorites. (An alternative version has a spiteful Hērē, who clearly hasn't forgotten or forgiven the Judgment, hit them with a storm that takes them to Sidon, which Paris Aléxandros duly captures en route to Troy.)

When embassies fail to have Menelaös's wife, and her property, returned, his brother Agamemnōn, "lord of men" (*anax andrōn*), assembles a huge expeditionary force from the various Mycenean kingdoms of Hellas—Argos, Pylos, Tiryns, Orchomenos, and Ithákē among them, in addition to Menelaös's Sparta and Agamemnōn's own stronghold of Mykēnai (Mycenae)—to recover Helen by force, and sack and destroy Troy into the bargain. (These warriors are known in the *Iliad* not as Hellenes, but, more locally, as Achaians, or Danaäns, or Argives.) An omen is interpreted to mean that the war will last ten years. As though to hint that the length of this campaign will be in large part caused by inefficiency, a first expedition fizzles out embarrassingly after the Achaians make landfall at Teuthrania, mistake it for Troy, sack it, and, on discovering their error, sail back home. When assembled a second time, at the port of Aulis, the fleet is initially held up by contrary winds due (as Kalchas the seer declares) to irritation by the divine huntress Artemis at Agamemnōn, who after shooting a stag boasts that he's an even better hunter than Artemis herself. For expiation of this lèse-majesté, says Kalchas, and to get a favorable wind, Agamemnōn must sacrifice his daughter Iphigeneia. Agamemnōn duly sends for her, under the attractive pretense that she is to marry the Thessalian warlord Achilles—none other than the son of Pēleus and Thetis, who has indeed grown up to be greater than his father: Zeus was well out of that one—and duly sacrifices her, thus making a deadly enemy of Klytaimnēstra his wife. But Artemis's amour propre is placated, and the fleet gets its fair wind for the voyage to Troy.

Since Troy defies all efforts to take it by siege, the Achaians spend literally years raiding the surrounding countryside and reducing lesser cities—what Barry Strauss well describes as "a counterstrategy of slow strangulation" (87). This kind of warfare yields both subsistence to the besiegers and booty for the leading warriors. It is in the ninth year, after the sack of (Cilician) Thēbē (Thebes), that Chryseïs is awarded, in the share-out of the spoils, to Agamemnōn, and the narrative of the *Iliad* begins. It closes with Hektōr's bones collected in a golden box and buried; a great mound is raised, and a funeral feast held. Then the truce expires, and the war goes on.

The Trojans now gain a valuable new ally in the person of the Amazon warrior Penthesilea, a Thracian and daughter of Arēs, who inflicts great slaughter until slain by Achilles. The malcontent Achaian Thersītēs (earlier whipped by Odysseus for an insulting harangue against Agamemnōn [2.211–77]) now jeers at Achilles for supposedly having fallen in love with her, and Achilles, enraged, kills him. This homicide makes it necessary for Achilles to remove himself temporarily to Lesbos, where he sacrifices to Artemis, Apollo, and Lētō, and is purified of blood-guilt by Odysseus. A second new ally then appears to help the Trojans: Memnōn, son of Eōs, the Dawn, leading a force of Aithiōpians from the East, and wearing armor made for him, like that of Achilles, by the smith-god Hēphaistos (who clearly has no hesitation about arming both sides if the client is distinguished enough). Thetis reports on Memnōn to Achilles: in the ensuing battle Memnōn kills Antilochos, but is himself killed by Achilles. His mother Eōs, however, obtains the gift of resurrection and immortality for him from Zeus. Achilles leads a successful charge against the Trojans that would have taken the Achaians into the city and captured it had not Paris Aléxandros, with Apollo's aid, shot him dead at the Skaian Gates, thus fulfilling Hektōr's dying prophecy.

There follows a huge struggle for Achilles' body: finally Aias (better known in his Latinized form as Ajax) manages to heft it up and carry it back to the ships, while Odysseus covers his back and fights off the Trojans. Antilochos is buried; Thetis, her sea nymphs, and the Muses all come to mourn publicly for Achilles. Thetis indeed snatches her son from the pyre and transports him magically to Leukē ("White Island") on the Black Sea. Nevertheless the Achaians build him a great burial mound and hold funeral games in his honor, at which Achilles' arms, the prize for the greatest hero, are competed for by Aias and Odysseus, and awarded (through the intervention of Athēnē on behalf of her favorite) to the latter, thus causing a bitter quarrel that finally leads to Aias's suicide. The Trojan Helenos, captured by Odysseus, prophesies that the taking of Troy will depend on the bringing from Lēmnos of Philoktētēs, an Achaian left there with a malodorous suppurating snakebite years before. Diomēdēs fetches him, and he is healed by the physician Machaōn, after which he fights Paris Aléxandros in single combat and kills him. Menelaös, the cuckolded husband, outrages the corpse, but the Trojans carry it off and give it burial. Helen, in Trojan eyes now a widow, marries Hektōr's brother Deïphobos.[2] Achilles' son Neoptolemos is fetched from Skyros by Odysseus, who presents him with his father's famous arms and armor. The boy is also visited by Achilles' ghost: if to encourage his youthful martial ardor, with remarkable success.

Like father, like son: Neoptolemos goes on a killing spree, his victims including Agēnōr and the newly arrived Eurypylos, son of Tēlephos (who first himself slays Machaōn). But the Trojans, though now closely besieged, are stubbornly holding out. An impatient Athēnē has the idea of introducing an attack force into Troy hidden in the famous Wooden Horse (which the Trojans themselves will be tempted to bring into the city) and instructs Epeios (previously only known as a hulking brawny boxer at Patroklos's funeral games [23.665–99]) in the making of it. Meanwhile a second item in Helenos's prophecy is that Troy cannot be taken until the Palladion, a special sacred image of Athēnē kept in the city, is found and removed. Odysseus and Diomēdēs, disguised as beggars, make their way in via a handy sewer, find the image, and duly carry it off—perhaps, as one source suggests, with the connivance of Helen. Newly remarried she may be, but she's a professional survivor: this is not the only instance of her last-minute dithering between Trojans and Achaians. A commando force is concealed in the Horse; the main body

2. Strauss (167) points out that this may well have been a "levirate marriage": that is, one in which, in order to maintain a family alliance and guarantee the widow a male protector, "a brother is required to marry the widow of his deceased brother". Although unknown in Iron Age Greece, the practice was common in the Near East: we have Hebrew, Hittite, and Ugarit evidence for it. By suggesting that the poet is familiar with such alien mores, introducing this foreign custom would also increase the likelihood that the narrative has a historical core.

of the Achaians, after burning their huts and encampment, sail away (but only as far as the nearby island of Tenedos). The Trojans, with stunning credulity, not only think that, after ten long years, their attackers have given up, and that they themselves have won the war, but also—as the result of discussion: at least some of them are suspicious—vote to bring the Horse into the city as a thank-offering to the gods, and even demolish part of their city wall in order to do so. Then they hold a great feast and retire for the night.

The occupants of the Horse emerge, and send a fire signal to Tenedos: the fleet returns, the Achaians pour into Troy, and the slaughter and rapine begin. Neoptolemos kills Priam at the altar of Zeus, hurls Hektōr's baby son Astyanax down from the battlements (another prophecy fulfilled), and claims the Trojan hero's wife Andromachē as his prize. Menelaös finds Helen with Deïphobos, whom he kills, but decides to save Helen when she hopefully bares her breasts to him. Aias son of Oïleus tears Kassandrē from the protection of Athēnē's altar still clutching the goddess's image, and rapes her (this blasphemous act, at least, provokes hostility in his fellow Achaians, who threaten to stone him). The Achaians, after sacking the city, burn it. Neoptolemos cuts the throat of Polyxeinē, another of Priam's daughters, over the tomb of Achilles at the request of his ghost. The spoils are divided, the Achaians sail for home, and Athēnē, still outraged by the desecration of her altar, is left planning to destroy them on the high seas. The scene is set for the various Returns (*Nostoi*) of the Achaian heroes, of which by far the most famous is that of Odysseus, recounted at length in the *Odyssey*: it takes him a good ten years—as long as the war he has just fought—to get back to Ithákē.

THE MYTH EXAMINED

The genesis and narrative of the Trojan War as a whole are contained in the so-called Epic Cycle, a group of slightly later (seventh–sixth centuries B.C.E.) poems, surviving only in short fragments and late (fifth century C.E.) plot outlines.[3] *The Cypria* (in eleven books, variously attributed to Stasinos of Cyprus or Hegesias of Salamis) covers the origins of the war (including the Judgment of Paris), the setting up of the Achaian expedition (including the sacrifice of Iphigeneia at Aulis), and the campaign itself up to the beginning of the *Iliad*. In direct continuation after the *Iliad* comes the *Aithiopis*, in five books, attributed to Arktīnos of Mīlētos, which ends with the death and funeral games of Achilles. This is followed by the *Little Iliad*, in four

3. These fragments are now easily accessible in a well-edited new Loeb volume, (Biblio. s.v. West 2003 [A]), from the consultation of which, together with West 2011 and 2013, anyone interested in the genesis of Greek epic poetry will derive considerable benefit.

books, attributed to Leschēs of Mytilēnē, during which Philoktētēs arrives from Lēmnos and Achilles' son Neoptolemos from Skyros, and the Trojans fatally haul the Wooden Horse (100 × 50 ft., with moving tail, knees, and eyes!) inside their walls. Finally (for our purposes) comes the *Sack of Ilion*, in two books, also by Arktīnos, which describes the deaths of Priam and Astyanax, the burning of Troy, and the departure for home of the Achaians, with Athēnē planning revenge upon them.

There are several points of great interest apparent here. It seems clear that the poems of the Epic Cycle were specifically designed to complete the Trojan War sequence both before and after the *Iliad*, which would presuppose a body of myth that preceded not only the Cycle but also the *Iliad* itself. That assumption is confirmed both by widespread iconographic evidence, mostly on early illustrated vases, and by various brief allusive references in the texts of the *Iliad* and the *Odyssey*, for example, to the Judgment of Paris, the Wooden Horse, and (almost certainly) the sacrifice of Iphigeneia. Further, the comparative length in books of the works that compose the Epic Cycle, and the periods in years covered by each, when set against the *Iliad*—an average of much less than half the number of books, dealing with an enormously greater total time-span—make it very clear that, in striking contrast to Homer, their authors were exclusively occupied with filling in the gaps in a traditional narrative. This is confirmed by Aristotle, who emphasizes in his *Poetics* (1459ab) that a true epic poem should embody, as does the *Iliad*, a unified action, with a beginning, a middle, and an end, and not, like a work of history, simply cover an extended period of time, which is clearly what the poems of the Epic Cycle do (Aristotle points out, in furtherance of his argument, how many more plots for tragedies poems such as the *Cypria* or the *Little Iliad* yield than do the *Iliad* or the *Odyssey*). Lastly, the respective value placed by the ancient world on the poems of Homer and those of the Epic Cycle is made clear by their relevant degree of survival. The Epic Cycle, except for summaries and a few short quotations, is lost. The *Iliad* and the *Odyssey*, despite their uncertain genesis, have reached us by way of about the best Greek manuscript tradition in existence.

Thus what we have to deal with is, on the face of it, a unique phenomenon. There is no mention, anywhere, of any other poem from this early period in Archaic Greece, lost or surviving, on the vast scale of the two Homeric epics,[4]

4. Creative size seems characteristic of the post-Mycenaean centuries, as though artists of every sort felt somehow emboldened by new horizons, and had fresh confidence in their technical ability to design on an unprecedentedly large scale. The great Geometric Dipylon vases began the trend (cf. Whitman chs. 5 and 11); then came Homeric epic; last of all, in the fifth century, it was the turn of prose, with the structured *Histories* of Herodotos, roughly as long as *Iliad* and *Odyssey* combined.

the *Iliad* in particular, much less one that at the time enjoyed their equally huge cachet. Modern critics join those of antiquity in praising the *Iliad*'s unparalleled subtlety, depth, overall structure, emotional force, and universal appeal. Two and a half millennia later that appeal has lost none of its pristine force—something we need constantly to bear in mind when probing the poem's genesis. Since it is generally agreed that, in order to produce a poem of the *Iliad*'s unparalleled length (twenty-four books, a total of 15,692 lines) that is also, as critics from Aristotle on have shown, beautifully and subtly constructed,[5] the availability of writing is an absolute necessity, it seems safe enough to date the composition of the poem as we know it to a period after the introduction of an adapted Phoenician/Semitic alphabet to Greece in the late ninth or early eighth century B.C.E. Just how long after remains uncertain and much debated. However, we need to balance this conclusion against the equally certain fact that the main body of the Trojan War myth clearly long preceded the composition of the *Iliad* in its present form, and that the casual references the *Iliad* contains to various key events (e.g., the Judgment of Paris) thus presuppose audiences, then and still earlier, that were comfortably familiar with the myth in its entirety.

But this, of course, takes us back beyond the watershed of the written word, into the final years of a centuries-old tradition of oral poetry, with its bardic singers of tales, its improvised *variatio* of narrative, its formulaic phrases and mnemonics, its emphasis, not only on gods and monsters, but on the great deeds of warriors long dead, its enskyment of heroic fame, *kléos* in Greek—the only claim that evanescent individuals could make to any kind of immortality. How far the tradition went back we can glimpse from the inscribed clay tablets that gave us the Assyrian/Sumerian epic of Gilgamesh, prince of Uruk (modern Iraq) in the mid-third millennium (ca. 2600 B.C.E.).[6] As is well known, the *Iliad*, too, contains ample evidence of this long-standing oral tradition. Formulaic titles, epithets, and repetitive phrases abound. Dawn is always rosy-fingered, and Achilles swift-footed. Before a

5. One nice example of this: in book 1, an old father comes seeking the return of his (living, female) child, and is rebuffed; in book 24, likewise, an old father comes seeking the return of his (male, dead) child, and his request is honored. Such balance is not uncommon and suggests a brilliant creative mind at work on the oral material, rather than a many-handed collective bardic evolution.

6. Some peoples (e.g., the Assyrians and Egyptians) had sophisticated writing long before the Greeks did. That Gilgamesh was the actual, documented, fifth king of Uruk in his dynasty is worth recalling when we are considering the historicity of the Trojan War and its characters: like Achilles, he was said to be the son of a goddess and a mortal father; he fought Humbaba, a Grendel-like monster, and made a magical journey to seek immortality and eternal youth at the world's end.

feast the heroes regularly stretch out their hands to the good things set before them, and only move on to other activities when they have satisfied their desire for food and drink. This formulaic phraseology is not as all-pervasive as has sometimes been alleged, but it is very much there, and sometimes can hint at even earlier phenomena that have been lost, but leave a ghost-like presence behind. For instance, the metre of Greek poetry depends on fixed vowel quantities, long or short, with a short vowel immediately preceding two consonants being scanned long (on all this see the section below on *Translation and the Homeric Hexameter*). For long it was a puzzle why certain passages in the Homeric epics seemingly didn't scan right, until the great eighteenth-century scholar Richard Bentley pointed out that in each case a word was involved, such as Agamemnōn's title of *anax*, that had, long before Homer's day, started with a subsequently lost consonant, the digamma, roughly equivalent to initial w-, so that *anax* had originally been the metrically acceptable *wanax*, a point triumphantly confirmed by the decipherment of the Mycenaean Linear B tablets as early Greek.

Thus in one sense the *Iliad* does not stand, unprecedented, at the beginning of European literature as we know it, but comes at the very end (with the appearance in Greece of alphabetic writing) of an age-old oral tradition, of which it displays the unmistakable influence throughout. But this, of course, raises further problems, none of which have as yet been definitively settled, and perhaps never can be. In particular, does the text as we have it today represent the collective effort, over the long haul, of innumerable anonymous professional bards (known in antiquity as rhapsodes), progressively shaping and refining the myth of the Trojan War; or do we have here the work of a brilliant master poet, cashing in on the huge advantage of the recent advent of alphabetical writing in the Greek world, to correlate traditional lays on a scale never before attempted? And in either case, how far, in the age of writing, may that written text, as first conceived, have been edited, modified, or interpolated before reaching its final form? Certainty, I repeat, is impossible. All I or anyone else can do is to lay out what seems the likeliest case on the evidence available, and what follows represents my own considered view of the case (I find the notion of a master poet highly persuasive). This is not the place for scholarly argument: for those who wish to pursue the enigma further the titles listed in my bibliography offer a useful starting-point.

It is worth noting, to begin with, that no commentator on Homer in antiquity, from Herodotus to Aristotle and beyond, has the slightest doubt that an individual called Homer existed, yet at the same time they make it abundantly clear that they know little or nothing about him. When all allowances have been made for the Greek literary convention that posited one early originator for practically every creation or custom, it still seems to me extremely probable that the basic reason for this certainty had everything to do then, as it still does today, with the unique quality of the two great epics themselves. To create such works, it was very reasonably assumed, required a genius quite out of the ordinary, and that meant one supremely creative individual (a few critics, in antiquity as later, the so-called *chōrizontes*, lengthened the odds on genius by arguing that the *Iliad* and *Odyssey* had different authors: some scholars, most notably West, still do).

In any case, for scale, dramatic intensity, and sheer overall brilliance, from the very beginning the *Iliad* and the *Odyssey* stood alone and unrivalled. Had they, as is sometimes argued, reached that point by a kind of oral evolution and crystallization (an argument, it's worth noting, advanced more often by analytical scholars than by creative artists),[7] it is curious that not one other epic in the Cycle—not the *Titanomachy*, not the *Cypria*, not, perhaps most strikingly, the *Thebaïd*—was ever mentioned in the same breath as Homer's two epics, or sufficiently highly prized even to survive as they have done. Nor indeed, as Aristotle noted (see above), did the epics of the Cycle have an overriding dramatic theme; rather, they were spread-out historical narratives that recorded a sequence of events, often over many years, instead of focusing on one theme in depth. While both Homer and the Cycle clearly drew on the oral tradition throughout—to what extent we shall see in the next section—the end product, in Homer's case, was something that had never been attempted before, and, it could be argued, was never to be equaled again. The reason for this, it is often (and I think correctly) alleged, is the unique opportunity presented by the second half of the eighth century B.C.E., those transitional years that witnessed the rapid spread of the new Greek alphabet, at a time when the age-old oral tradition of poetry, to which the text of the *Iliad* as we have it bears eloquent witness, had not yet lost its peculiar force.

Herodotus perhaps overestimated (though not by all that much) when he claimed (2.53) that Homer lived some four hundred years before his own

7. Most notably by the eighteenth-century savant Friedrich Augustus Wolf (see Biblio. s.v.), who claimed that the Homeric epics were not the work of one man but a congeries of folk ballads and folk literature, a patchwork of rhapsodes' lays (eighteen of them in the *Iliad*, according to Karl Lachmann in the *Abhandlungen* of the Berlin Academy, 1837 and 1841). Wolf argued that discrepancies of fact precluded single authorship (had he ever looked at *Don Quixote*?); he believed that alphabetic writing did not exist at the time of the *Iliad*'s composition, and that oral composition on so large a scale was impossible. Time has refuted his beliefs, but his influence on Homeric studies was enormous and long-lasting.

time: the same distance, that is, as between Shakespeare's age and today. Such a date would place him ca. 840 B.C.E. What we know of the diffusion of alphabetic writing in Greece suggests that this is at least half a century too early. But I envisage this mysterious individual at some time after 800—perhaps single-handed, perhaps in collaboration with one of the new scribes—applying himself to the vast and variegated body of traditional oral narrative myth concerning the Trojan War, and seeing its untapped potential for an examination, in depth and at length, of the whole human condition: not only its tragic aspects—Aeschylus the tragedian knew what he was talking about when he claimed (Athen. 8.347e) that his plays were merely "slices from the great banquet of Homer"—but its comic or domestic moments, its political and religious contrariness, its passions, hopes, fears, and fleeting pleasures, all it meant to be mortal. I like to think that Homer may have been at some point a hostage (the meaning of *homēros*), and that the author of the *Homeric Hymn to Pythian Apollo* (169–73) may have had good reason to identify "the sweetest of singers" as "a blind man who lives on rocky Chios"; but these are personal fancies and I wouldn't go to the barricades for them.

PRESERVING THE PAST: HISTORY AND THE EPIC TRADITION

In ways the world presented by the *Iliad* and the Epic Cycle is one that we know today. We can visit the sites of Mykēnai (Mycenae), Pylos, and other Bronze Age kingdoms mentioned by Homer. There have been recent queries concerning the whereabouts of Odysseus's Ithákē, but we take it for granted by now that Turkish Hisarlik is almost certainly Homeric Ilion/Troy. The events of the *Iliad* are thus played out on a stage that still exists. This in itself must, perhaps unconsciously, predispose us to accept a tradition that has, especially over the past two centuries, occasioned as much argumentative dissension as is associated with any other work of literature known to me. Though the idea of the Trojan War as entirely a work of inventive imagination is far less widespread than it once was, the degree, and nature, of its historicity remains a highly divisive question. As before, all I can do here is to set out the evidence and present my own opinion. The scholarship is seemingly endless, with no firm and irrefutable conclusions yet discernible.

One clear fact does stand out: to the early critics of antiquity, from Herodotus through Thucydides to Aristotle, the Trojan War, however much Homer might have dramatized his version of it, was an unquestionable historical actuality. So were its participants. When Alexander the Great, at the start of his invasion of Asia, visited, and laid wreaths on, the tombs of Achilles, Aias, and

Protesilaös (the first Greek ashore in the Trojan campaign, and the first casualty), he was not simply cashing in on dubious tourist attractions: he saw no reason not to accept what he was shown as the real thing. As late as the mid-third century B.C.E. we even find a chronological list, the Marmor Parium, which notes events from 1581/0 to 355/4, moving seamlessly and without distinction from "a dispute at Athens between Arēs and Poseidōn", dated 1532/1, to Marathon, Sokratēs, and Sparta's defeat by Thēbē (Thebes) at Leuktra in 371/0. There has been a modern tendency, especially in the late nineteenth century, to attribute a talent for inventive fantasy to Homer (and ancient authors). This is not only anachronistic but badly misunderstands the Homeric zeitgeist, which deemed memorializing the famous deeds of great men (*klea andrōn)* to be an essential (if almost insurmountably difficult) task, whether accomplished by family tradition, genealogies, annalistic memory, or bardic poems. This ineradicable yearning for *kléos aphthiton*, undying fame, not only for oneself but also for others, is, indeed, one of the most fundamental, and persistent, characteristics peculiar to humankind. Yet satisfying it had always been a risky and inefficient business. Until the arrival of alphabetic writing in Greece, oral memory had been the sole guarantee that the past would not be lost; it was only with writing that Herodotus (for example) could take the next step and not only preserve great deeds from oblivion but ask the question that Homer, too, had faced: Why did they fight each other? There was little room in this world, or indeed for long after, for creative minds inventing their own facts: the real ones were all too hard to obtain, let alone keep. It is no accident that we know only of one dramatist in Greece, Agathōn, in a single play, the *Anthos*, who created his own plot and characters *ex nihilo*; or that the novel was by a long way the latest literary form to appear in Greece, where it never got far beyond the fairy-tale romance.

What are envisaged here—and what a gifted poet, with access to the new alphabetic writing, would, at some point after 800 B.C.E., have heard, memorized, and probably have had transcribed—are a number of traditional oral lays dating back to various indeterminate points, some far back in the Bronze Age, some later, that had gone through at least five centuries of oral transmission, including an illiterate dark age for several hundred years following on the destruction of Mycenaean culture. This is exactly the scenario for which the text of the *Iliad* as we have it offers ample evidence throughout. In looking at this evidence, we need to remember—as Carol Thomas and Craig Conant usefully remind us—that "with the drastic lowering of material culture following the Mycenaean collapse, many of the old references would have become at first irrelevant, then anachronistic, and finally incomprehensible" (59). Fluid oral editing would in the course of time replace many key

Bronze Age allusions in all areas with those familiar to Dark Age and, later, early Archaic Age audiences. What survived, as modern scholars have come to recognize, is a confusing and seemingly random amalgam of the cultures of successive ages, including a fair sampling of those crudely persistent archaic beliefs and practices (especially in the area of religion, where they tend to be preserved as sacrosanct eternal truths) that so embarrass a society in the process of acquiring middle-class gentility, and elicit a mixture of silent suppression, euphemism, allegory, and direct censorship. The *Iliad* offers quite a few of these, and very interesting they are. Luckily for us, the process of moral repudiation was only just beginning when the poem took its final form, and Homer proved so popular at all levels that direct opposition was replaced by a flourishing industry in ever more fantastic allegorization.

Unlike the self-confident rationalists of the nineteenth century, we at least know today, thanks chiefly to archaeology and linguistics, that Homer's world of Achaians and Trojans was not a mere literary fantasy, but a real Bronze Age historical actuality. From the Linear B records at Pylos, Mykēnai, Knossos and elsewhere we catch a glimpse of a palace bureaucracy at work: professional scribes dealing with the nuts and bolts of a profitable mercantile economy while peasants worked for starvation wages and the unlettered aristocracy pursued military glory on the excuse of defending the civilian population.[8] The actual collapse of the Mycenaean kingdoms ca. 1200 B.C.E. would gain an additional explanation were it true that their warlords were all absent fighting a war against Wilusa (the Hittite name for the place the Greeks called Ilion, or Troy). We can see the flow of anachronistic elements in Homer—spears that are the wrong length and shields of the wrong type for the period to which they are assigned; the lump of pig iron given as a prize at Patroklos's funeral games (*Il.* 23.826–35), which, it's said, will last five years for plowshares—which might have been awarded in Homer's own day, but not centuries earlier—as the natural additions made by rhapsodes to bring their tales into line with what a changing audience knew or expected. This kind of thing, worrying perhaps for those seeking Bronze Age authenticity throughout, is exactly what we should expect centuries of oral

8. Surprisingly, some scholars have taken the administrative system revealed by the Linear B tablets as being socially incompatible with the Homeric world of stronghold-based military fiefdoms, and therefore a proof of the latter's unreality. In fact, of course, the world they reveal is exactly parallel to that of mediaeval feudalism, where, similarly, unlettered knights ruled, serfs toiled, and a clerical bureaucracy took care of business. These social distinctions survived: for a well-born warmonger to dirty his hands with trade long remained a class-based taboo in classical Greece.

tradition to accumulate, and no more bothersome than Shakespeare's attribution of clocks to ancient Romans, or the way Quattrocento painters (and others) costume all their ancient figures in contemporary dress.

Thus though modern research has confirmed the existence in the Bronze Age of a world in which Homeric society might have existed, and of long-forgotten warfare around the area of Troy—even of a historical figure, Alaksandu of Wilusa, who may well be identifiable with [Paris] Aléxandros of (W)Ilion[9]—we, not surprisingly considering its genesis, have no more reason than did those nineteenth-century rationalists for connecting the specific conflict described in the *Iliad* with any war or battle revealed in, say, the Hittite royal correspondence with the rulers of Ahhiya or Ahhiyawa, a major power now identified, again with a fair degree of certainty, as Achaia, and located in mainland Greece. As we might expect, the rhapsodes looked back to a real world, an actual society, and sought to preserve the *kléos*, the fame and glory, of these Achaian (or Argive, or Danaän) dynastic warlords who led it. But unless by rare accident, we are no more likely today than those nineteenth-century rationalists were to glean historical facts from what emerged from some five centuries of oral transmission and was then used by Homer and committed to writing.[10].

Nevertheless, the text of the *Iliad* that has come down to us is a wonderful compendium of cultural evidence from all periods of its evolution. Like flies embalmed in amber, details illustrative of past beliefs and practices abound: the transitional period between the collapse of the Bronze Age kingdoms around 1200 and the emergence of early city-state (*polis*) society after the appearance of the new Greek alphabet is especially rewarding. The evidence goes back long before the putative date of the Trojan War: things like Odysseus's boar-tusk helmet and the great, tower-like shield of Aias were obsolete by the fifteenth century B.C.E. Moreover, frescoes datable to ca. 1700 B.C.E. that have been excavated on Thera (Santorini), and were preserved, like Pompeii, by a gigantic volcanic eruption that buried them, could, eerily, be illustrations for the two cities in the *Iliad*, one at war, the other peaceful (18.490–540), depicted on the shield made by Hēphaistos for Achilles. Conversely, a good deal of the military equipment and fighting technique in the *Iliad*

9. The first Trojan victim, killed by Achilles, is Kyknos (listed in the *Cypria:* for his supposed prior invulnerability; see Gantz 594). As Strauss (65) points out, his name bears an interesting resemblance to that of a king of Wilusa before Alaksandu, Kukkunni.

10. At *Il.* 16.702–3, for instance, Patroklos is able to scale the angle of Troy's battlements, and excavation has revealed at least one point at which the tilt of the batter wall and the space between the stones would have made this feasible.

belongs to Homer's own day rather than to the Bronze Age, and the use of chariots in battle has largely been forgotten (in Homer they are mostly used to transport their owners to and from the battlefield). But one aspect of Homeric usage is notably accurate: emphatically throughout, weapons are not iron but bronze, and most often simply named by the noun (e.g., 3.292, "the pitiless bronze"), without any cutting or stabbing referent (e.g., knife, spearhead).

More interesting still are the social implications detectable in the text. There are a number of words and phrases indicative of a period before physical actuality was extrapolated into generalized abstractions: *thymos*, *psyche* and *kēr* notable amongst them. Normally the equivalent, respectively, of "spirit", "soul", and "fate", these terms still carry for Homer the physical connotations of "vapor", "breath", and "death-agent".[11] The regular phrase "winged words", which has occasioned much literary debate about its metaphorical significance, is in fact simply another instance of this prehistoric habit of mind: speech was thought of as physical matter, projected through the mouth.[12] Another formulaic phrase, "what's this talk that's escaped the barrier of your teeth" (e.g., at 4.350), makes this very clear.

At the other end of the scale, the social upheavals engendered during the poverty-stricken centuries immediately after the general collapse of the aristocratic Mycenaean dynasties similarly left their unmistakable transitional imprint on the oral epic handed down to Homer. The rabble-rouser Thersītēs (2.211–77) is the most obvious example of radical hostility to what survives of the ancien régime and its status-based leadership; but he is far from an isolated phenomenon. At the conclusion of Book 9 both Odysseus and Diomēdēs express angry irritation at Achilles' obstinate pursuit of his personal code of honor to the immediate detriment of a war which, fought the old-fashioned way, has already dragged on for over nine years. Book 10 (whether a late insertion or not) shows the two of them giving a nocturnal demonstration of how to win that war, by ruthlessly abandoning not only the traditional formalities of military engagement, but also any scruples about honor.[13] During their night raid they capture a Trojan spy, scare him

11. The locus classicus for discussion of this phenomenon is Onians.
12. In his famous travel book *Mani* Patrick Leigh Fermor demonstrates a remarkable affinity for this kind of sensory impression: "I often have the impression, listening to a Greek argument, that I can actually see the words spin from their mouths . . . the perverse triple loop of Xi, the twin concavity of Omega, the bisected almond of Theta, Phi like a circle transfixed by a spear, Psi's curly trident and Gamma's two-pronged fork . . ." (Leigh Fermor 336).
13. Strauss (139–40) similarly points out how the Trojans, too, could have improved their chances by taking to guerilla warfare, and how such a move was hampered by Hektōr likewise being "addicted to a heroic illusion of a decisive victory."

into telling all he knows, and then kill him, despite his offer of ransom. They then, acting on his information, descend on the newly arrived Thracians, murder their king Rhēsos and his chief officers in their sleep, and return to camp with Rhēsos's famous white horses. Ironically, it has been during Achilles' speech finally rejecting the appeal for his return to the fighting that he admits (9.312–45) that he, too, is beginning to have doubts about the efficacy of the whole code of military honor on which he was brought up. Yet in many ways that code survives, most notably as outlined by Sarpēdōn and Glaukos (12.310–28). On the battlefield (6.215–36), Glaukos and Diomēdēs find they are bound by ties of guest-friendship, and they not only renounce fighting each other, but exchange armor; Hektōr and Aias, after a formal dual, similarly exchange gifts (7.287–314).

Breeding and ancestry still count for a very great deal, and the archer is still despised in comparison to the hand-to-hand warrior. But the most remarkable testimony—and undoubtedly the most disconcerting for anyone coming to Homer for the first time—has to be that concerning religious life and the gods.[14] The deities in the *Iliad* have nothing moral about them (as later Greek critics from Xenophanes through Plato to Longinus were the first to complain). They behave, in fact, like members of a large, unruly, and privileged patriarchal family, distinguished from their mortal opposite numbers only in the special powers given them by their immortality. They quarrel, intrigue, are spiteful, bear grudges against one another, and are deeply involved, for the lowest of motives, and seldom on the same side, with the human participants in the Trojan War, even going so far, on occasion, as to participate in the fighting. Since they can ignore, and at times contravene, the forces of nature, their wounds are instantly healable, while their influence on the outcome of the conflict can be huge. Patroklos (16.786–806) and Hektōr (22.273–305) are both fatally weakened, in the first instance, by the malign attentions of a god, which make them easy prey to an attacker. The to-and-fro ebb and surge of battle is regularly determined by Zeus, who can be, and is, influenced one way or the other by both sides' divine backers, but in the last resort has his own plan, as we have seen, for the entire war (to reduce excess population by encouraging general slaughter). The only curb on all this, itself uncertain, is the fixed pattern of an individual's fate, and even here Zeus several times at least claims to consider overriding what's fated, omnipotence and predestination in uneasy conflict.

14. At the most basic level, in the *Iliad* Trojans and Achaians apparently not only speak the same language (in fact, Trojans probably spoke Luwian), but share the same pantheon of divinities: students I taught sometimes looked at the war in the *Iliad* as a conflict akin to the American Civil War of 1860–65.

Nothing more clearly reveals the survival through oral tradition, into Homer's own day and beyond, of an age-old, bleakly realistic concept of divinity. While highly anthropomorphized—the world of the Olympians comes across in the *Iliad* as a kind of unpredictable, and thus terrifying, parallel universe—these gods are dangerous powers, unknowable, not to be crossed, and amoral in their attitudes. By the sixth century B.C.E., precisely because of Homer's huge popularity and influence, they already aroused strong social objections, as we have seen. The gods' traditional mean pettiness of motive, so integral to the original tale of Troy, clearly bothered Homer himself. There is something splendid about the idea of a war to recover an adulterous queen; but behind this lurk Zeus's plan to start such a war in order to reduce population, and the cases of spiteful divine resentment induced, variously, in Hērē and Athēnē by the Judgment of Paris, and in Poseidōn by the cheating habits of Laomedōn,[15] all of which—the Judgment in particular—are barely mentioned in the *Iliad*, where evolutionary censorship is already evident.[16] Early Greek myth abounded in human sacrifice, but—with the notable exception of twelve Trojan youths sacrificed at Patroklos's funeral (23.175–76)—the *Iliad* avoids direct mention of the practice: even the ritual killing of Iphigeneia at Aulis, a crucial element in the narrative of the Trojan War, gets only one dubious hint, at 1.106–8, when Agamemnōn upbraids Kalchas the seer (who had pronounced the sacrifice necessary) for always being a prophet of doom. There is also the matter of poisoned arrows, habitually used in early myth, presumably in fact and obviously in an earlier version of 4.148–219: what else, originally, would have led Agamemnōn to fear that a mere glancing hit from Pandaros's arrow might kill his brother Menelaös? Why else should Machaön the healer have sucked blood from the scrape? As for Zeus's hesitancy about challenging fate (e.g., over the death of his mortal son Sarpēdōn, at 16.431–57), this too was in tune with the times: divine omnipotence versus predestination was yet another emergent theological problem that was to be argued for centuries.

For modern readers perhaps the most awkward thing about the Olympian pantheon in the *Iliad* is their uncertain transitional status—like some of the poem's archaic terminology—between the physical and the metaphorical. Olympos is both a very real Greek mountain and the celestial home of the gods, but I very much doubt whether in Homer's day anyone would have expected to find the latter at the top of the former. Similarly with encounters between gods and mortals: oral tradition reveals a past

15. Apollo throughout the *Iliad* is aggressively pro-Trojan, without any reason given.
16. On what follows the locus classicus is G. Murray 129–32.

when this was clearly a commonplace,[17] but by Homer's day such meetings seem, at best, like externalizations of inner impulses (cf. Athēnē, invisible, curbing Achilles' urge to kill Agamemnōn, 1.188–222), and at their awkward worst, when the gods—and goddesses—join in the fighting (e.g., 21.382–518), grotesquely comic. Yet here, too, there are terrifying moments, none worse than the way that Apollo in his invincible, and invisible, power disables Patroklos, slamming him from behind with the flat of one hand, leaving him a stunned and helpless victim, to be finished off by Euphorbos and Hektōr (16.786–92). This is the world that Shakespeare's Lear knew: "As flies to wanton boys, are we to the gods; they kill us for their sport."

TRANSLATION AND THE HOMERIC HEXAMETER

It is over half a century now since Richmond Lattimore first published his deservedly famous, and ground-breaking, translation of the *Iliad*.[18] What made his version truly different from its innumerable predecessors was his determination to get as close as possible, in every respect—metre, rhythm, formulaic phrases, style, and vocabulary, as well as the rapidity, plainness of thought, directness of expression and nobility of concept emphasized by Matthew Arnold in his lectures *On Translating Homer*—to the original Homeric Greek. The stimulus for such an English *Iliad* was, of course, the vast expansion of American university education in the humanities, largely fostered by the GI Bill in the years immediately following World War II; and what it sought to do was to give a totally Greekless readership the closest possible idea of what Homer had been about, metrically, linguistically, and in literary terms. My own version, a generation later, has the same objectives in view, with another one added: the determination, when dealing with a poem so oral in its essence, that what I have written should be naturally declaimable.

At first sight what Lattimore was attempting did not seem innovative: ever since the Renaissance there had been an ongoing battle between modernist and Hellenizing translators, with the modernists generally winning.

17. In his remarkable (and unprovable) exercise in speculation, *The Origins of Consciousness in the Breakdown of the Bicameral Mind* (Boston, 1977), Julian Jaynes pinpoints Mesopotamia in the third millennium B.C.E. as the point at which communication between gods and mortals via the right hemisphere of the brain began to break down. It was a slow process: Sappho, the seventh century lyric poet from Lesbos, for one, still seems to communicate freely and comfortably with Aphroditē.

18. Some of what follows here has been adapted from my review-article "Homer Now", published in *The New Republic* 243, no. 10 (June 28, 2012): 36–41, and is used by kind permission.

The essential modernist principle was famously expressed by Dryden, who declared of his version, in relation to the original author's work, that "my own is of a piece with his, and that *if he were living, and an Englishman*, they are such as he would probably have written" (emphasis mine).[19] This formula at once licensed any Anglicization, however inappropriate. It might have been thought that the Hellenizers, whose aim was the preservation of the original characteristics of the Greek, would suit a Greekless audience better; the trouble was that they, like the modernists, assumed, sometimes unconsciously, *an audience that could still read the original Greek*, and thus would be capable of making informed comparisons between text and translation. What Lattimore saw, very clearly, was that communicating the ultra-foreign essence, at every level, of Homer to minds that were virtually tabula rasa where any but English poetry was concerned called for a quite new fidelity—rhythmical and rhetorical no less than idiomatic—to the alien original, together with a comparable avoidance of all those comfortingly familiar, yet wildly misleading, fallbacks (blank verse being the most obvious, and the most misleading) that had served translators so well in the past.

Of all the essential features in this new type of translation—retention of formulaic phrases, syntactical empathy, avoidance of factitious pseudo-similarity to familiar English landmarks—the most difficult by far to achieve has always been an acceptable equivalent to Homer's metrical line, the epic hexameter. At the heart of the matter lies a fundamental difference between Greek and English poetics. In Greek (and Latin) verse, all vowels have a fixed quantity, either long or short. Short quantities can be lengthened by position, that is, by being placed before two or more consonants, which gives a poet more scope; but every metre is determined by an arrangement of vowel quantities. The power of a line is determined by the contrapuntal play of natural stress (*ictus*) against this rigid metrical pattern. In English, on the contrary, vowels have no fixed given length (though diphthongs and naturally long or duplicated vowels—think "chain", "groin", "fame", "teeth", "dice", "home", "dune"—to some extent can be made to follow the classical rule), and in the last resort are stressed solely by the natural syllabic emphases given to any sentence. In the strict sense, English doesn't have metres at all.

In Homer's case the situation is made still more difficult by the fact that the prevalent unit of emphasis ("foot") in the epic hexameter is the dactyl (– ∪ ∪), one long syllable followed by two shorts, dah-didi. This six-foot line can be set out as follows:—∪ ∪ |—∪ ∪ |—|| ∪ ∪ | – || ∪ ∪ |—∪ ∪ |—∪. Any

19. Preface on translation prefixed to the *Second Miscellany* (1685), reprinted in *The Works of John Dryden*, ed. G. Saintsbury (Edinburgh, 1885), 12: 281–82.

dactyl (i.e., any of the first five feet, though a resolved fifth foot is rare) is resolvable into one long, dah-dah, forming a spondee (——). The sixth foot is an abbreviated (catalectic) dactyl, shorn of its last syllable (– ∪). It too can be a spondee (——). The hexameter has a natural mid-break, against the metre, most commonly in the third or fourth foot, as marked (||). To illustrate this line in English, here is a Victorian rendering of *Iliad* 1.44, by C. S. Calverley: "Dark was the | soul of the | god || as he | moved from the | heights of O|lympos." Calverley, a good classicist, knew very well that dactylo-spondaic rhythm runs flat contrary to natural English rhythm, which is essentially iambic (∪—) or, in lighter moods, anapestic (∪∪—), and forms the building blocks of the blank verse line, employed by Milton in *Paradise Lost*, and by the vast majority of would-be translators of Homer, even though that about halves the speed of the hexameter, and has totally alien associations to it (translators like Pope compounded this error by choosing the tightly rhymed heroic couplet, since rhyming was unknown to Homer).

Iambs naturally climb uphill, while dactyls are on the gallop: listen to the onomatopoeia Homer works into a line (*Od.* 11.598) describing the rock of Sisyphos obstinately rolling and bouncing down to the plain again: *Autis epeita pedonde kulindeto lâas anaidēs*.

The combination of alien rhythm and absence of stress/metre counterpoint has always made any sustained attempt at an English stress hexameter a lost cause, not least because the English stress pattern tends both to avoid spondaic resolved feet and to coincide exactly with the metrical schema. Calverley, who understood the problem better than most, sensibly gave up when less than halfway through Book 1 of the *Iliad*. Others persisted. H. B. Cotterill's *Odyssey* is typical, its flat dactylic rhythms boringly soporific (*Od.* 6.85–89):

> Now when at last they arrived at the beautiful stream of the river
> Here the perennial basins they found where water abundant
> Welled up brightly enough for the cleansing of dirtiest raiment.
> So their mules they unloosened from under the yoke of the wagon,
> Letting them wander at will on the bank of the eddying river.

The problem was a daunting one, and compounded by the fact that most translators, who couldn't care less about the needs of a Greekless general audience, never saw it as a problem at all.

What is still by far the best solution, though by no means a perfect one, was hit on by C. Day Lewis in 1940, when translating Vergil's *Georgics*, and later developed in his version of the *Aeneid* (1952). By a real stroke of luck, this translation was commissioned for broadcasting by the BBC, which meant that it was, precisely, aimed at a nonclassical general public that would, in the first instance, hear rather than read it. It therefore had perforce to be, like its original, *declaimable*, a quality sadly to seek in most previous versions, but fundamental to all ancient epic. This meant, among other things, capturing something of Vergil's verbal structures and linear rhetoric, which, in turn, demanded a line-by-line adherence to the original text. Thus two crucial necessities were imposed on Day Lewis from the start, and they in turn made him face the dilemma of the English hexameter, one problem of which had always, allegedly, been that it was unmanageably long.[20] What Day Lewis evolved was a variable 6/5 stress line, ranging from 12 to 17 syllables, and (though he did not claim this) largely dactylo-spondaic in its emphases.

The result made for far less boring rhythms, and even for a certain verbal springiness. Amusingly, Day Lewis's declared intention in varying the line's length had been to remove the need, in translation, to either pad or omit, as occasion required:[21] what he created was in fact the nearest thing to a truly contrapuntal stress hexameter we're ever likely to achieve. Lattimore, who had clearly seen the potential of such a line in Day Lewis's Georgics, used it for his *Iliad* (1951), and I explored its potential further in my version of Apollonius Rhodius's *Argonautika* (1997). While taking advantage of its variable length while translating the *Iliad*—as indeed of English natural rhythms, which allowed, very often, for a short syllable before an initial dactyl (which a strict hexameter wouldn't), quietly converting it to ∪ ∪—that is, an anapest—I was surprised by how often, in fact, the line wrote itself either as a true hexameter or with one syllable short (catalectic) in the final foot:

> The assembly then broke up. The troops now scattered, each man
> off to his own swift ship, their minds on the evening meal
> and the joy of a full night's sleep. But Achilles wept and wept,
> thinking of his dear comrade, so that sleep the all-subduing
> got no hold on him: he kept tossing this way and that,
> missing Patroklos—his manhood, his splendid strength,
> all he'd been through with him, the hardships he'd suffered,
> facing men in battle and the waves of the cruel sea. (24.1–8)

Controlling the hexameter is, in fact, the key to producing a version of Homer that gives one's nonclassical audience some sense of the *Iliad* as a whole poem, and I'm lucky in having had a lifetime of preliminary practice before I finally tackled it.

---

20. In fact it was not as long as the clumsy (and rhymed) "fourteener" employed to translate the *Iliad* (1598–1611) by the Elizabethan scholar George Chapman, who has always had a good press from literary critics.
21. See his remarks in *The Aeneid of Virgil* (Garden City, NY, 1953), 8–9.

LAST THOUGHTS

This translation, then, aims to introduce Homer's *Iliad*, as far as possible without familiar distracting comparisons or personal additions, to an audience that in essence knows nothing about the poem, its antecedents, or the circumstances of its creation. As far as possible I have done nothing to remove those features—not so many as might be supposed—that are often alleged to militate against modern acceptance. The leading characters, and other entities, all retain their repetitive personal epithets. A reader or listener very soon acclimatizes to these, and comes to appreciate the subtly ironic way in which they are often employed. The formulaic oral phraseology governing familiar activities like eating and drinking is no odder than the *da capo* repetition of a dominant theme in, say, a string quartet:[22] and Homer's own subtle sentence-structure and linear rhetoric are at least as effective as the way translators have chopped and changed his language to make it sound more comfortingly like words written by an English poet.

It is true that sometimes—very seldom, in fact—a point can be reached where, through false associations, close adherence to an idiomatic preference risks sounding ridiculous rather than simply strange or alien,[23] and in such cases I have modified the original, generally with an explanatory note. But for the most part, these men and women created long millennia ago (not to mention their heavily anthropomorphized deities) combine a wholly alien background and ethos with all-too-familiar habits that are endearing or alarming according to circumstance: filial and marital devotion, status-conscious pride and arrogance, ancient long-windedness, the confusion of honor and narcissism, the traumatic effects of overexposure to military combat, obstinacy and recklessness, passion and despair. It is the universalism captured by this extraordinary epic poem that gives it its unparalleled staying power. If its gods offer a disconcerting parallel universe, its extraordinary range of similes continually remind us, in their emphasis on the natural world and an agricultural community about its peaceful business in that

22. Indeed, a similar argument, and comparison, could be made in justification of yet another translation of the *Iliad:* would anyone ever raise serious objections to one more interpretation of J. S. Bach's six unaccompanied suites for cello?

23. A nice instance is the Homeric use (paralleled in Latin) of the human head as a summation, personal no less than physical, of the individual: most famous from the Underworld in the *Odyssey* as the "strengthless heads of the dead" (e.g., at 10.521). At 8.281 Agamemnōn greets Teukros, literally, as "Teukros, dear head": other translators have changed this to "dear heart", and, with some misgivings, so do I. On the other hand at 11.55, Zeus sends down bloody rain as "a sign of all the brave heads he'd soon dispatch to Hādēs", and here I've kept the original: the grey area between alien and ridiculous is exceedingly narrow.

world, of the exorbitant price that its aristocracy forces that community to pay in its pursuit of retribution and, even more insidiously because so often unprovoked, of everlasting fame.

As Richard Martin points out, in a penetrating discussion in his Introduction to Lattimore's *Iliad*, this is a work that, above all, provokes questions with uncertain answers:

> Is the *Iliad* a celebration of heroism or an interrogation of its basic—potentially flawed—assumptions? Whom should we emulate, if anyone, in this somber depiction of men and women under extreme conditions? Is it an elegy for a lost golden age, when people lived more out-sized and exciting lives? Or is it a warning about the catastrophes such lives engender? Is it a poem meant to shore up the ideological underpinnings of a fading aristocracy of self-centered warlords? Or does it capture the first glimmerings of a communal consciousness of the type that emerged in increasingly democratic (or at least nonelite) institutions within the city-state?[24]

For me, the poem's greatness is evident in the fact that it is at one and the same time all of these things, and not only because it is the product of a culture in rapid transition between the oral and the written, between historical myth and history, between the memory of the old Mycenaean aristocratic warrior-kings (whose proud and enigmatic gold funeral masks still survive) and the emerging soldier-farmers of the city-state and the hoplite phalanx. The *Iliad*'s extraordinary humanity can contain them all, virtues and vices alike. We understand what instincts drive the heroic Achilles, but Thersītēs the radical demagogue gets his moment, too. That is why, as Martin reminds us, our "experience of the *Iliad* also becomes one of self-exploration and self-definition." In our less ambitious way we are like Aeschylus, feeding at Homer's great banquet, each generation finding what best answers to its needs.

One last word. It will be noticed that I have made virtually no attempt to dictate the literary terms in which anyone new to the *Iliad* should seek to appreciate it as a poem. This is partly because, just as no two historians can fully agree on the poem's genesis, so no two critics are in complete concordance when delineating its literary qualities. But first and foremost, it is because a lifetime devoted to teaching of one sort or another has shown me that initial impressions are crucial, and that if these are imposed externally, they can never be shaken off. First-time readers of the *Iliad* should be

24. Lattimore 52–53.

allowed to establish their own personal impression of it before listening to the competing chorus of professionals, who are all too ready to shape their opinions for them. My bibliography offers a way into this noisy marketplace. Take my advice and don't consult the market until you've familiarized yourself with the great poem itself, preferably on more than one reading.

Book 1

Wrath, goddess, sing of Achilles Pēleus' son's
calamitous wrath, which hit the Achaians with countless ills—
many the valiant souls it saw off down to Hādēs,
souls of heroes, their selves[1] left as carrion for dogs
and all birds of prey, and the plan of Zeus was fulfilled[2]—
from the first moment those two men parted in fury,
Atreus's son, king of men, and the godlike Achilles.

Which of the gods was it brought them into contention?
Lētō's and Zeus's son:[3] for he, enraged by the king,
spread a foul plague through the army, and men were dying,
all because Chrysēs his priest had been dishonored
by Atreus' son. Chrysēs came to the Achaians' swift ships
to win his daughter's release, bringing ransom past counting,
in his hands the laurel wreaths of the deadly archer Apollo
on a golden staff, and made his plea to all the Achaians,
but first to the two sons of Atreus, the host's field marshals:

"Atreus' sons, and you other well-greaved Achaeans,
may the gods who have their homes on Olympos grant you
to sack Priam's city, and win a safe homecoming!
But release my dear daughter, accept the ransom I offer,
show respect for Zeus's son, Apollo, the deadly archer."

Then all the other Achaians spoke up in agreement—
to respect the priest, to accept his splendid ransom.
Yet Atreus's son Agamemnōn's angry heart remained untouched.

---

1. The word "selves" (Greek αὐτούς, *autous*) strikingly emphasizes the epic's intense preference for this mortal physical existence over any vague insubstantial afterlife. The physical body is the real them. This is what Achilles has in mind when he famously says in Hādēs (*Od.* 11.88–91) that he'd rather be a hireling and alive than king of the dead.
2. Here, probably, Zeus's agreement to the prayer of Thetis (see 1.503–30) to recompense her son Achilles for Agamemnōn's insulting treatment of him (the main subject of book 1) by giving the advantage in the war to the Trojans until such time as the Achaians should make him adequate amends.
3. Lētō's and Zeus's son: Apollo.

Brusquely he turned him away with words of harsh dismissal:
"Don't let me find you still here, old man, by the hollow ships,
either loitering now or making your way back later,
lest your staff and the god's wreath afford you no protection!
Her I shall not release—no, sooner will old age reach her
in our house, in Argos, far away from her native country,
working to and fro at the loom and sharing my bed. Now go—
and do not provoke me, if you want to depart in safety."

So he spoke: the old man was scared and obeyed his words.
Silent along the shore of the thunderous sea he went;
but once well away, long and deeply the old man prayed
to Apollo his lord, the child of fair-haired Lētō:
"Hear me, you of the silver bow, protector of Chrysē
and holy Killa, who rule with might over Tenedos—
Smintheus,[4] if ever for you I roofed a pleasing precinct,
if ever I burned for you the fat-rich thighbones
of bulls or goats, now grant me this my desire:
use your arrows to make the Danaäns pay for my tears."

Thus he spoke in prayer, and Phoibos Apollo heard him.
Down from the peaks of Olympos he hastened, enraged at heart,
carrying on his shoulders his bow and lidded quiver,
arrows rattling loud on his shoulders as in his rage
he strode on his way: he came as nightfall comes.
Away from the ships he sat, and let fly an arrow:
fearful the twang of his silver bow. To begin with
it was the mules he aimed at, and the swift dogs; but later
he made the troops the targets of his sharp shafts
and struck: day in, day out the clustering corpse fires flared.

Nine days throughout the army the god's shafts sped: on the tenth
Achilles summoned the troops to the place of assembly,
for white-armed Hērē, the goddess, had put this in his mind
since she pitied the Danaäns as she saw them dying.
So when they had gathered and were all assembled together,
swift-footed Achilles stood up and spoke among them:
"Son of Atreus, I think we shall now be driven into retreat

---

4. Smintheus: an uncertain epithet, but most probably "mouse-god", as protector against rodents (for which there is evidence): the uncertainty is largely due to Hellenistic scholars who thought this something "inappropriate" to the dignity of epic poetry.

and forced back home, even should we escape with our lives,
if indeed war and plague together are to crush the Achaians!
Come, then, let us find and question some priest or diviner,
or even a reader of dreams, since a dream too is from Zeus,
who might explain to us Phoibos Apollo's deep anger—
Is it a missed vow that riles him? Were some oxen not sacrificed?—
Maybe, catching the savor of lambs and unblemished goats,
he'll be willing to give us relief, call off this onslaught."

This said, he sat down, and there next stood up among them
Kalchas, Thestōr's son, of the seers by far the finest:
he knew events present and future as well as from the past,
and had brought the Achaians' fleet safe to landfall by Ilion
through the diviner's art he had from Phoibos Apollo.
He, with friendly intent, now spoke before the assembly:
"Ah, Achilles, dear to Zeus, you bid me explain the reason
for the wrath of my lord Apollo, the deadly archer.
Then tell you I shall. But you must agree, and swear,
to be my willing protector with word and with hand,
since I think I shall anger a man who holds powerful rule
over the Argives, to whom the Achaians owe allegiance.
For a king has the upper hand when enraged by a commoner,
since though he may swallow his wrath that day, yet he still
nurses resentment thereafter, in his heart of hearts,
until he fulfils it. Tell me then: will you protect me?"
Then swift-footed Achilles spoke to him thus in answer:
"Have no fear, reveal any oracle that you know of,
for—by Apollo dear to Zeus, to whom you, Kalchas,
pray when you make plain his oracles to the Danaäns—
no man, while I still live and have sight upon this earth,
shall lay heavy hands on you beside the hollow ships,
of all the Danaäns, not even if it's Agamemnōn you mean,
who claims to be far the noblest of all the Achaians."

At this the blameless diviner was emboldened, and spoke out:
"It's for no missed vow or rich sacrifice that he faults us,
but because of the priest whom Agamemnōn dishonored,
refusing to free his daughter, to accept ransom for her: hence
those griefs that the deadly archer's inflicted, and will inflict:
No way will he free the Danaäns from this loathsome havoc
until we give back to her father the quick-eyed girl, unbought,

unransomed, and take to Chrysē a rich holy sacrifice:
this is the only way we might appease and persuade him."

This said, he sat down again, and there stood up among them
Atreus's heroic son, wide-ruling Agamemnōn,
bitterly troubled, his black heart brimming over
with rage, while his eyes had the semblance of blazing fire.
Kalchas he first addressed, with a look of hatred:
"Prophet of doom, not once have you told me anything pleasing—
what's always dear to your heart is to prophesy disaster:
nothing good have you ever foretold or brought to pass![5]
Now here you come peddling your claims to the Danaän assembly,
alleging the deadly archer has laid these griefs upon them
because I was unwilling to accept a bounteous ransom
for this girl, Chrysēs' daughter, since I'd rather keep her
with me at home. Indeed, I prefer her to Klytaimnēstra,
my wedded wife, whose equal she is in all ways,
being as good-looking, as tall, as clever, as accomplished.
Yet even so I'll return her, if that should be best:
I want to have my troops safe, not facing destruction!
But you must find me a prize, at once, so I'm not
the only Argive left prizeless. That would not be seemly—
for you see this, all of you, that my prize is going elsewhere."

Then to him replied swift-footed godlike Achilles:
"Most glorious son of Atreus, of all men the most covetous,
how can the great-hearted Achaians produce you a prize?
We know of no common stock of goods in store—
what we took when we sacked the cities has been shared out,
and to recall it now from the men would be most improper.
You must give up this girl to the god, and we, the Achaians,
will repay you threefold and fourfold, if Zeus ever grants
that we storm and sack the strong-walled citadel of Troy."

5. Some have seen here a veiled reference to Kalchas's announcement at Aulis that in order to procure a favorable sailing wind to Troy, the wrath of Artemis at Agamemnōn for some slight against her could only be purged by the human sacrifice of Agamemnōn's daughter Iphigeneia—which was duly carried out. The wind then changed, and the fleet sailed. Homer makes no direct mention of the incident, and it was argued in antiquity, improbably, that he did not know the tradition. See also n. 4 to 9.287.

Answering him then lord Agamemnōn declared:
"Fine warrior you may be, godlike Achilles, but don't
play tricks on me: you'll not outwit or persuade me.
Do you plan to keep your own prize, but leave me sitting here
without one, since you tell me to give the girl back again?
Either I get a new prize from the great-hearted Achaians—
chosen to satisfy me, something of equal value—
or, if they give me nothing, I shall come in person and take
your prize, or Aias's, or carry off that of Odysseus,
and he'll have cause for resentment, the man I come to!
These matters, though, we can deal with at a later time.
For now, let us haul down a black ship to the bright sea,
and assemble a crew of oarsmen, place oxen on board
for sacrifice, together with Chrysēs' fair-cheeked daughter
herself; and let one man, a counsellor, go as captain—
Aias, or Idomeneus, or noble Odysseus,
Or you, son of Pēleus, of all men the most fearsome,
to make sacrifice for the appeasement of the deadly archer."

Eyeing him angrily, swift-footed Achilles declared:
"You clotheshorse for shamelessness, mind obsessed with profit,
how could any Achaian be prompt to obey your orders
to march to war or with might face men in battle?
I did not come here on account of Troy's spearmen: why
should I fight them? In no way have they ever wronged me.
Never have they driven off my cattle or my horses;
Never in rich-soiled Phthiē, the nurse of heroes, did they
lay waste the harvest, since great distance lies between us—
shadowy mountains and echoing sea. But you,
you shameless hulk, we accompanied here for your pleasure,
to win honor for Menelaös and for you, you dog-face,
from the Trojans. But none of these things you heed or
care for—
and now you even threaten to rob me of the prize
to get which I suffered much, and the Achaians' sons gave it me.
Never do I rate a prize to match yours when the Achaians
lay waste some populous citadel of the Trojans, though mine
are the hands that bear the brunt of furious battle;
and when the time comes for sharing, then your prize
is by far the greater, while I, with some smaller thing

for my share, trudge back to the ships, still combat-weary.
But now I'm returning to Phthiē: that's better by far,
going home with my curved vessels. I'm not minded
to stay here without honor, amassing you wealth and plenty."

Then the lord of men, Agamemnōn, made answer to him:
"Run away, if your heart so bids you. Far be it from me
to beg you to stay here for my sake. With me are many others
who will treat me with honor—Zeus the Counsellor above all.
Most hateful you are to me of Zeus's royal nurslings:
quarrels are what you love most, and wars and battles.
That great strength of yours, I'd guess, was some god's gift.
Take off homeward now with your ships and your comrades,
lord it over the Myrmidons—for you I care nothing,
I take no heed of your anger. And this is my threat to you:
Since Chryseïs is taken from me by Phoibos Apollo,
her, with a ship of my own and my own companions,
I shall send back—but the fair-cheeked Briseïs, your prize,
I'll come to your hut myself, and take, that you may know well
how much stronger I am than you—and that others may fear
to address me as an equal, to confront me face to face."

So he spoke, and pain seized Pēleus's son, the heart
in his shaggy breast was divided, torn this way and that:
should he draw the sharp sword from beside his thigh,
break up the crowd, and kill the son of Atreus,
or swallow his bitter gall, restrain his passion?
While he still was debating this in mind and spirit,
his great sword half-drawn from its scabbard, Athēnē came down
from the heavens, dispatched by the white-armed goddess Hērē,
who loved and cared for them both alike in her heart.
Standing behind him, she grasped Pēleus's son's fair hair—
appearing to him alone: of the others no one saw her—
and Achilles turned round in amazement, instantly recognized
Pallas Athēnē, the terrible radiance of her eyes,
and uttering winged words, he thus addressed her:
"Why have you come this time, child of Zeus the aegis-bearer?
To witness the arrogant gall of Atreus's son Agamemnōn?
For this I will tell you, and I think it will come about:
Through his insolent conduct he may well soon lose his life."

To him then spoke in answer the goddess, grey-eyed Athēnē:
"I have come here to check your rage—if you'll listen to me—
down from high heaven, sent by the goddess, white-armed Hērē,
who loves and cares for you both alike in her heart.
Come now, leave off your strife, take your hand from your sword:
abuse him with words alone regarding what will happen,
for thus I declare, and it will certainly come about:
one day three times as many fine gifts will be offered you
on account of this insult. So restrain yourself, and obey us."

Then in answer to her swift-footed Achilles declared:
"Needs must, goddess, respect the words of you both,
however angry at heart one may be. It is better so—
and those who comply with the gods are listened to in return."
With that, on the silver hilt he set his heavy hand,
thrust the great sword back in its scabbard, nor disregarded
Athēnē's words; but she had already left for Olympos,
home of Zeus of the aegis, to rejoin the other gods.

So Pēleus's son once again with words of strong contempt
addressed the son of Atreus, his anger not yet ended:
"You wine-sodden wretch, dog-faced, deer-hearted, not once
have you dared to arm yourself for battle with your troops,
or joined in an ambush with the Achaian chieftains!
Oh no, such things spell death to you. Better by far
to range here through the broad camp of the Achaians
and take back the gifts of whoever speaks out against you!
A king that feeds off his commons, who rules mere nonentities!
Otherwise, son of Atreus, this new outrage would be your last.
This, though, I will tell you, and swear a great oath besides:
By this staff—which never again will put out leaves or shoots
since the day it first left its tree stump in the mountains,
nor will it flourish afresh, since the bronze has stripped it
of leaves and bark, and now those sons of the Achaians
who render judgments, who safeguard the ordinances of Zeus,
carry it in their hands—this will be my great oath for you:
One day the need for Achilles will hit the Achaians' sons,
every man jack of them—then, for all your grief, you'll not
be able to help them, when many at the hands of Hector,
killer of men, fall dying; you'll eat out the heart within you,
incensed that you failed to honor the best of the Achaians."

So spoke the son of Pēleus, then dashed to the ground the staff
studded with golden nails, and himself sat down.
Across from him Atreus's son still raged. Then Nestōr,
smooth phrasemaker, arose, the Pylians' lucid spokesman,
a man from whose tongue the speech flowed sweeter than honey.
In his lifetime already two generations of mortals
had passed away—those raised with him—and their offspring,
in sacred Pylos, and now he was king over the third.
He, with friendly intent, now spoke before the assembly:
"Ah me, great grief indeed now besets the land of Achaia!
Priam would surely rejoice, and the sons of Priam,
and all the rest of the Trojans would be happy at heart
if they learned about this quarrel between the pair of you,
who in counsel surpass all the Danaäns, and in fighting.
Now listen to me. You both are younger than I am,
there was a time when I consorted with far better men
than you—and they never wrote me off as a lightweight!
Such men have I not seen since, nor shall see again
as Peirithoös, or Dryas, the shepherd of his people,
or Kaineus or Exadios, or godlike Polyphēmos,
or Thēseus, Aigeus's son, an equal of the immortals.
Strongest were these of all men nurtured by earth;
strongest themselves, and fought against the strongest,
the mountain-laired beast-men,[6] and fearsomely they destroyed them.
I joined these men's company when I'd come from Pylos,
a long trek from a distant land; it was they who invited me.
Single-handed I fought, but against such men as these
no mortal of those on earth today could do battle.
They listened to my advice, were persuaded by my words.
So do you both be persuaded: persuasion is better.
You, great man though you are, do not take away his girl,
but let her be, as the prize the Achaians' sons first gave him.
And *you*, son of Pēleus, do not seek to challenge a king
by main force, since it is no ordinary honor
that's the lot of a sceptered king, to whom Zeus gives the glory.

---

6. The mountain-laired beast-men: the Centaurs, traditionally located on the wooded slopes of Mt. Pēlion: they were most famously in conflict with the Lapiths of Thessaly (Nestōr's father Nēleus was Thessalian by origin), who drove them out, after killing many, when they got drunk at the wedding of King Peirithoös and tried to rape his bride, Hippodameia.

Strong though you are, with a goddess for your mother,
yet this man is the greater, since he rules more subjects.
Son of Atreus, control your rage. I do beseech you,
check your anger against Achilles, who is a great
bulwark for all the Achaians against war's disasters."

Then in answer to him spoke the lord Agamemnōn:
"Yes, all that you say, old sir, is right and proper.
But this man has it in mind to be above all others,
He wants to dominate all, be lord over all, give orders
to all—yet there's one man, I think, will not obey him.
If the gods who live forever have made him a spearman,
is that now an excuse for his insults to run wild—?"

Cutting in on his words then, noble Achilles responded:
"I'd surely be called a coward and a worthless fellow
if over every matter I yield to you, do as you say!
Tell others to act thus, but don't give me such orders,
for I think I'm no longer minded to obey you.
One other thing I will tell you, and do you lay it to heart:
I shan't fight with my hands for the girl, no, neither
against you nor anyone else: you gave her, you'll take her.
But of everything else that is mine by my swift black ship
not one piece shall you carry off against my pleasure!
Go on, then, try it, so that these men here too may learn
how quickly your black blood will gush out round my spear point."

So the two, after exchanging their fighting words, arose
and broke up the assembly by the ships of the Achaians.
Pēleus's son made his way to the huts and his well-trimmed vessels
with Patroklos, son of Menoitios, and his other companions;
but Atreus's son now had a swift ship hauled down to the sea,
chose a score of men to row it, loaded oxen for the god,
brought out the fair-cheeked Chryseïs and put her aboard,
and as captain there went with them resourceful Odysseus.

So these embarked and sailed out over the seaways.
But Atreus's son ordered his people to purify themselves,
and they did so, cast into the sea the filth of their defilement,
then offered up to Apollo their perfect sacrifices
of bulls and goats by the shore of the unharvested sea,
and the savor went up to heaven, circling around the smoke.

Thus throughout the camp they were busy; yet Agamemnōn
did not give up the strife with which he first threatened Achilles,
but gave orders to Talthybios and Eurybatēs,
the two who were his heralds and busy henchmen:
"Both of you go to the hut of Pēleus's son Achilles,
take by the hand the fair-cheeked Briseïs, bring her back here.
If he won't give her up, I shall come in person to get her,
with a large force: and that will be the worse for him."

So saying, he sent them off, with these harsh orders: the two
reluctantly went by the shore of the unharvested sea,
and came to the Myrmidons' ships and huts. They found
Achilles sitting beside his hut and his black ship,
and at the sight of those two he was not best pleased.
They, quaking with terror and in awe of the king,
stood there, not questioning him, not saying a word,
but he understood in his heart, and thus addressed them:
"Greetings, you heralds, messengers of Zeus and of mankind!
Come closer: for me it's not you who are guilty, but Agamemnōn,
who's sent you both here on account of the girl Briseïs.
Very well, then. Patroklos, go fetch the girl out, hand her over
to these two to take away. And let them be witnesses
before the blessed gods and before all mortal men—
yes, and before that ruthless king—if ever hereafter
there shall be need of me, to ward off shameful havoc
from the host at large! How he seethes in his destructive mind,
with no idea how to look at once both before and after,
to ensure that the Achaians might fight safely beside their ships."

So he spoke, and Patroklos obeyed his dear companion.
From their hut he brought the fair-cheeked Briseïs, gave her
to them to take. The two went back to the Achaians'
ships, and the woman went with them, unwillingly. But Achilles,
weeping, moved off apart from his comrades, sat down
on the shore of the grey salt sea, eyes fixed on the boundless deep,
and appealed to his dear mother, arms outstretched:
"Mother, since you bore me, though for a short life only,
some honor, for sure, the Olympian should have guaranteed me—
Zeus, who thunders on high; but now not the slightest regard
has he shown me—and Atreus's son, wide-ruling Agamemnōn,
has done me dishonor, himself took my prize, and keeps it."

So he spoke, shedding tears, and the lady his mother heard him
as she sat in the depths of the sea beside the Old Man, her father.
Swiftly she rose up, like a mist, through the grey sea-brine,
came and sat down in front of him as he wept,
and stroking him with her hand, addressed him by name, and said:
"Child, why are you crying? What grief has possessed your heart?
Speak out, let us both know, don't hide it away in your mind."

Then, with a heavy sigh, swift-footed Achilles answered:
"You know. Why must I tell you this, when you're all-knowing?
We marched out to Thēbē, Eëtiōn's sacred city,
sacked it, brought everything back here. The sons of the Achaians
divided the spoils quite fairly among themselves,
to the son of Atreus allotting Chrysēs' fair-cheeked daughter.
But Chrysēs himself, the priest of Apollo, deadly archer,
came to the swift ships of the bronze-corseleted Achaians,
to win his daughter's release, bearing ransom past counting,
a golden staff in his hands, wreathed with the deadly archer
Apollo's laurels, made his plea to all the Achaians,
but first to the two sons of Atreus, the host's field marshals.
Then all the other Achaians spoke up in agreement:
they should respect the priest, and accept the splendid ransom.
Yet Atreus's son Agamemnōn's angry heart remained untouched.
Brusquely he turned him away, with words of harsh dismissal.
Angered, the old man went back, but Apollo had listened
to the prayer he made, for his priest was most dear to him;
so he let fly against the Argives his deadly shafts. Their men
were now dying one after the other, as the god's arrows ranged
throughout the Achaians' wide camp. But to us the seer,
well aware of the truth, made clear the deadly archer's message.
I was the first, at once, to urge the god's appeasement,
but then bitter anger flared in Atreus's son: he stood up
and quickly uttered a threat, which is now accomplished:
for the sharp-eyed Achaians are sending this girl aboard
a swift ship to Chrysē, along with gifts for the lord Apollo,
while heralds have led away the other girl from my hut,
Briseus's daughter, my present from the Achaians' sons.
But you, if you can, now come to the aid of your son,
go on up to Olympos, petition Zeus, if ever
you've gratified his heart by either word or deed!

For surely I've often heard you in the halls of my father,
boasting—that Kronos's son, lord of black thunderclouds,
was saved from shameful ruin, you said, by you alone
among the immortals, when those other Olympians wanted
to put him in fetters—Hērē, Poseidōn, and Pallas Athēnē.
But you came, goddess, and rescued him from his bonds,
quickly calling to high Olympos the hundred-handed one,
whom the gods name Briareus—but mortals of every sort
Aigaiōn—for he in strength is mightier than his father.[7]
By the son of Kronos he sat down, exulting in his glory,
and the blessed gods, terrified, laid aside their fetters.
Remind him now of these matters, sit by him, clasp his knees,
in case he may be minded to assist the Trojans, drive back
the Achaians past the ships' sterns and along the seashore,
with slaughter, that they may all get joy of the king they have,
and Atreus's son, wide-ruling Agamemnōn, may know
his delusion in failing to honor the best of the Achaians."

Then Thetis answered him, shedding tears: "Ah, my child,
Why, after so ill-starred a birth, did I ever rear you?
I wish it had been your lot to sit by your ships, ungrieving,
tearless, since your life will be brief, of no real length;
but now you are both short-lived and the wretchedest mortal
of all—to a cruel fate I bore you in our halls!
Still to bring this complaint of yours before Zeus, happy thunderer,
I'll go myself to snowbound Olympos. He might just listen.
You, though, sit tight by your swift-sailing ships, rage on
against the Achaians—but yourself abstain from battle.
Zeus yesterday went to Ocean, to visit the blameless[8]
Aithiōpians, for a feast: all the other gods left with him.
In twelve days he'll come back to Olympos, and then
I shall go to the house of Zeus, with its brazen floor,
and clasp his knees; and I think I shall persuade him."

---

7. Briareus was the son of Ouranos (Heaven) and Gaia (Earth): Hes. *Theog.* 147–49: the *bri-* phoneme linguistically suggests "strength". Kirk 1: 94 reminds us that Briareus "existed before men were created, and his name was therefore assigned by primeval gods." The parenthetic punctuation is that of West. Hērē, Poseidōn, and Athēnē are the three main pro-Achaian deities in the *Iliad*, but this act of rebellion is otherwise unknown.
8. The Aithiōpians were thought of as a mysterious race at the known world's periphery (Homer's world was a flat disc, with Ocean its great circumambient river). As Pulleyn says, "The gods like to visit far-away places as a diversion" (228).

This said, she took herself off, and left him there,
enraged at heart on account of the fine-clad woman
they'd taken from him by force, against his will. Meanwhile
Odysseus made landfall at Chrysē, conveying the oxen
for a holy sacrifice. When they entered the deep harbor
they furled the sail and stowed it away in the black ship.
The mast they let down by the forestays, lowered it into the crutch
smartly, then plied their oars to the roadstead anchorage,
cast out the anchor stones, hitched up the stern cables,
and themselves stepped out onto the seashore, disembarked
the sacrificial oxen for Apollo, the deadly archer;
and from the seagoing ship Chryseïs too stepped forth.
Then resourceful Odysseus escorted her to the altar, put her
in the arms of her dear father, and thus addressed him:
"Chrysēs, I am sent here by the lord of men, Agamemnōn,
to bring you your daughter, and offer to Phoibos a holy
sacrifice for the Danaäns, to placate the Lord
who has lately laid on the Argives much grief and lamentation."

So saying, he delivered her into his arms, and Chrysēs
gladly received his dear child. Now quickly and in good order
they set up the god's holy sacrifice around his well-built altar,
washed their hands, took up the barley groats, and before them
Chrysēs now prayed aloud, with arms uplifted:
"Hear me, you of the silver bow, protector of Chrysē
and sacred Killa, who rule in might over Tenedos!
There was a time when I prayed, and you duly listened,
honored my prayer, and wrought havoc on the troops of the Achaians,
so fulfil for me also one new wish, here and now:
take off, without delay, this vile plague from the Danaäns."

So he spoke in prayer, and Phoibos Apollo heard him.

When they had prayed, and scattered the barley groats, first
pulling back the victims' heads, they slaughtered and flayed them,
cut out the thighs, wrapped them up in a double layer
of fat, and placed above them cuts of raw meat. The old man
burned these over split billets, with fire-bright wine
drizzled them, while beside him young men held five-pronged forks.
When the thighs were well broiled and they'd tasted the innards, next
they chopped up the rest, threaded the bits on skewers,

grilled them with care, then drew them all off. But when
they were through with their work, and the meal had been got ready,
they feasted, and no one's heart lacked a fair share in the feasting.
But when they had satisfied their desire for food and drink,
the young men topped up the mixing bowls with liquor
and served it to all, the first drops in their cups for a libation.
The whole day through with song these young Achaians sought
to appease the god, chanting their lovely paean,
that hymned the deadly archer, whose heart rejoiced as he listened.

But when the sun went down and darkness came on,
they settled themselves and slept by the ships' stern cables;
and when early Dawn appeared, the rosy-fingered,
they put out to sea toward the wide camp of the Achaians,
and Apollo the deadly archer sent them a following wind,
and they raised the mast and spread wide the white sail.
The sail bellied out in the wind, and a surging bow wave
sang loud round the vessel's cutwater as she ran.
On she sped, slicing herself a sea-lane through the billows;
but when they arrived at the wide camp of the Achaians,
the black ship they hauled far up the beach, set her high
on the sands, planted the long props against her hull,[9]
and themselves dispersed to their various huts and vessels.

So he sat on, still raging, beside his swift-moving ships,
Pēleus's heaven-sprung son, swift-footed Achilles. Never
did he show up now in assembly, where men attain renown,
never went to the fighting, but let his dear heart waste away,
withdrawn there, though he longed for the war cry and for combat.

But when the twelfth dawn from that day broke, then back
to Olympos the gods who are forever returned,
all together, with Zeus at their head; and Thetis did not
forget her son's entreaties, but rose from the sea's waves
in the early morning, went up through the vast sky to Olympos.
Kronos's loud-thundering son she found apart from the rest,
perched on the topmost peak of many-ridged Olympos.
She sat down before him, with her left hand embraced his knees,
while with her right she touched him beneath the chin,

9. These props were posts or stakes driven into the sand and resting against the sides of the hull to hold the vessel upright.

and in supplication addressed him as Lord Zeus, Kronos's son:
"Zeus, Father, if ever before among the immortals I helped you
by word or deed, then grant me now this wish!
Honor my son, who beyond all other men is fated
to a brief life; for now that lord of men, Agamemnōn,
has done him dishonor, himself took his prize, and keeps it.
Zeus,—Olympian, counselor!—you must show him honor:
give the edge to the Trojans, at least until the Achaians
acknowledge my son's rights, make him honorable amends."

So she spoke; but no word came from Zeus the cloud-gatherer.
Long in silence he sat. Yet Thetis, just as she'd embraced
his knees, now clung to him, asked him a second time:
"Promise me this without fail, and nod in confirmation,
or else say no—you've nothing to fear!—and show me
how far I'm the one least honored among all the gods."

Then, deeply troubled, cloud-gatherer Zeus addressed her:
"This is a nasty business—you'll bring me into conflict
with Hērē, make her provoke me with reproachful words.
As it is, she constantly nags me before the immortal gods,
says that I give my support to the Trojans in the fighting.
You go back home now, lest Hērē notice you; I
shall figure a way to get this matter accomplished.
See now, I'll nod my head to make you believe me,
since among the immortals this from me is the strongest
pledge: no promise of mine can be revoked, mislead,
or remain unfulfilled, once I nod in assent to it."

With that the son of Kronos nodded his dark brows,
and the locks of ambrosial hair swung rippling from the Lord's
immortal head: he made great Olympos tremble.

These two, planning done, now parted: she leapt down
into the salty deep from gleaming Olympos, while Zeus
went to his dwelling. All the gods rose together
from their chairs in respect for the Father, not one of them dared
to stay seated on his arrival: all stood up to greet him.
So he sat down there on his throne. But Hērē was well aware,
when she saw him, that Thetis, the silver-footed, the Old
Man of the Sea's daughter, had been with him, plotting mischief.
At once with mocking words she addressed Zeus, son of Kronos:

"Which of the gods, you trickster, has been with you, plotting
mischief?
Always it's your pleasure to leave me out of things,
make decisions you've worked on in secret. You've never really
wanted to let me share what's going on in your mind."

Then to her the father of gods and men replied:
"'Hērē, do not expect to get to know all my thoughts—
they'd be difficult for you, even though you are my wife.
What is fitting for you to hear there is no one, either
of gods or mortals, who will learn it before you. But
such plans as I aim to devise without the other gods' knowledge
are matters you never must ask me about, or query."

Then to him the ox-eyed lady Hērē responded:
"Most dread son of Kronos, what's this that you're telling me?
In the past, to a fault, I've not questioned or pestered you—
you work out at your ease anything that you've a mind to.
But now I very much fear you've been won over by Thetis,
the silver-footed, the daughter of the Old Man of the Sea,
for at first light she sat down before you, and clasped your knees,
and I think you nodded to her as true token that you'd honor
Achilles, and kill many men by the ships of the Achaians."

Then in answer to her Zeus the cloud-gatherer said:
"Madam, you're full of fancies: I can keep nothing from you.
Yet you won't achieve anything this way, save to find yourself
further still from my heart—which will be the worse for you.
If this business is thus, then it must be to my liking.
So sit down, keep quiet, and be obedient to my orders,
for all the gods on Olympos will avail you nothing
when I come close and lay invincible hands upon you."

So he spoke, and fear seized the ox-eyed lady Hērē:
she sat in silence, wrestling her inner heart to submission,
and throughout Zeus's house the gods of heaven were troubled.
Among them Hēphaistos, famed craftsman, was first to speak,
hoping to calm his dear mother, white-armed Hērē:
"A nasty business we'll have here, something not to be borne
if you two are to quarrel like this for the sake of mortals,
and bring brawling among the gods—there'll be no pleasure
in the splendid feast, since bad feeling's uppermost.

And I would advise my mother (though she knows this herself)
to make up to our dear father Zeus, so that our father may not
fall out with her again, and thus upset our feasting.
Suppose the Olympian, lord of the lightning, were minded
to toss us out of our seats? He's by far the strongest.
So, engage him with soft, fair words; then straight away
the Olympian's sure to show himself gracious to us."

So saying he sprang up, and put a two-handled goblet
in his dear mother's hand, and thus addressed her:
"Be patient, my mother, endure, despite your sorrow,
lest, dear as you are to me, I get to see you beaten
before my eyes, and then I'll be unable to help you
for all my grief: the Olympian's a difficult opponent.
Once before, that other time when I was minded to aid you,
he hurled me, seized by the foot, down from the gods' threshold.
All day long I plummeted, till as the sun was setting
I fell upon Lēmnos, and little the life left in me,
but the Sintian folk cared for me directly after my fall."

So he spoke, and the goddess, white-armed Hērē, smiled,
and smiling received the cup in one hand from her son.
Then, going from left to right, for all the other gods
he poured out sweet nectar, drawn from the mixing bowl,
and unquenchable laughter arose among the blessed gods
as they watched Hēphaistos hobbling around the palace.

Then the whole day long until the sun went down
they feasted, and no one's heart lacked a fair share of the feasting,
nor of the exquisite lyre that Apollo handled, nor of
the Muses who sang, sweet-voiced, responding one to another.

But when the bright light of the sun sank, then they all went
to lie down and sleep, every one in his own dwelling,
where for each of them a house had been built, with cunning skill,
by far-famed Hēphaistos, lame of both legs; and Zeus
the Olympian, lord of lightning, went to his own bed,
where he always had found repose when sweet sleep overtook him.
There he went up and slept, with gold-throned Hērē beside him.

Book 2

All others, both gods, and mortals, chariot marshals,
slept the night through, but on Zeus sweet sleep could get no hold,
for in his mind he was pondering how he might do honor
to Achilles, and slay many beside the Achaians' ships.
And to him, as he thought, this looked to be the best plan:
to send Atreus's son Agamemnōn a destructive Dream.
He spoke to the Dream, addressed it in winged words:
"Go now, destructive Dream, to the swift ships of the Achaians,
and when you reach the hut of Atreus's son Agamemnōn
repeat to him exactly the message that I now give you.
Bid him to arm the long-haired Achaians for battle
as quickly as may be, for now he may take the broad-streeted city
of the Trojans, since no longer are the immortals who dwell
on Olympos at odds, now Hērē has forced them to agreement
by her pleading, and troubles will be the Trojans' lot."

So he spoke: the Dream went, on hearing his charge,
and quickly came to the swift ships of the Achaians.
To Atreus's son Agamemnōn it went, and came upon him
asleep in his hut, and about him divine slumber was shed.
It stood there above his head in the likeness of Nēleus's son
Nestōr, whom Agamemnōn honored above all elders.
So in his likeness the god-sent Dream addressed him:
"You sleep, son of Atreus the warlike, breaker of horses!
Night-long sleep is not fitting for a man that's a counselor,
to whom troops are entrusted, who's burdened with many cares.
But now listen well: I bring word to you from Zeus,
who though far distant greatly cares for and pities you.
He bids you arm the long-haired Achaians for battle
with all speed, for now you may take the broad-streeted city
of the Trojans, since no longer are the immortals who dwell
on Olympos at odds, now Hērē has forced them to agreement
by her pleading, and trouble will be the Trojans' lot
at Zeus's hands. Keep this in your heart, don't permit
forgetfulness to seize you when honey-sweet sleep lets you go."

Thus it spoke and departed, leaving him there
to reflect in his heart on things not destined to be fulfilled.
For he thought he would take Priam's city on that very day,
the fool, and did not know the deeds that Zeus was planning,
that he was yet to afflict with much anguish and suffering
both Trojans and Danaäns through the grind of battle.
He woke, the divine voice still in the air around him,
sat upright, shrugged into his comfortable tunic—
elegant, newly made—flung a great cloak over it,
tied under his smooth-skinned feet his elegant sandals,
and slung from his shoulders his silver-studded sword.
Then he took his ancestral scepter, forever imperishable,
and with it strode by the ships of the bronze-corseleted Achaians.

The goddess Dawn drew near to high Olympos, bringing
her announcement of light to Zeus and the other immortals;
and the king commanded his clear-voiced heralds to call
to assembly, by proclamation, the long-haired Achaians.
They so proclaimed, and promptly the troops then gathered.

But first he held a council of the great-hearted elders
by the ship of Nestōr, the king of Pylian ancestry.
Having convened them, he outlined his crafty plan:
"Listen, my friends. As I slept a heaven-sent Dream approached me
through the ambrosial night; and most it resembled noble
Nestōr, in shape and stature and appearance.
It stood there above my head and spoke these words to me:
'You sleep, son of Atreus the warlike, breaker of horses!
Night-long sleep is not fitting for a man that's a counselor,
to whom troops are entrusted, who's burdened with many cares.
But now listen well: I bring word to you from Zeus,
who though far distant greatly cares for and pities you.
He bids you arm the long-haired Achaians for battle
with all speed, for now you may take the broad-streeted city
of the Trojans, since no longer are the immortals who dwell
on Olympos at odds, now Hērē has forced them to agreement
by her pleading, and trouble will be the Trojans' lot
at Zeus's hands. Keep this in your heart.' So speaking
it flew away and was gone, and sweet sleep released me.
Let's see, then, if we can arm the Achaians' sons for battle!
But first I shall test with them words, this being the custom,

even urge them to take flight in their many-benched vessels,
while you, some here, some there, with words restrain them."

So saying, he sat down, and there then stood up among them
Nestōr, who reigned as king in sandy Pylos.
He, with friendly intent, now spoke before the assembly:
"My friends, leaders and rulers of the Argives,
had it been any other Achaian who informed us of this dream
we'd call it a lie and have nothing to do with it—But
he saw it who claims to be far the best of the Achaians!
So come, let us seek some way to arm the Achaians' sons."

This said, he led the way out of the council.
The other sceptered kings, obeying the people's shepherd,
rose to their feet, as the people came hurrying in to assembly.
Just as close-packed swarms of bees keep on emerging
from some hollow rock, one new group after another,
and hover like clustering grapes above the springtime blossoms,
or fly off in masses, some this way and some that,
so from the ships and huts in their great numbers
along the wide seashore the troops from every homeland
marched in throngs to the assembly. With them flared Rumor,
urging them on, Zeus's messenger. Thus they gathered.
The assembly was all confusion, the earth groaned under
these men as they sat, there was uproar. Nine heralds tried
to restrain them with shouted orders, to make them stop
their noise and attend to the princes, Zeus's nurslings.
With great effort the people were settled, kept in place,
their shouting silenced. Then the lord Agamemnōn
rose, holding the scepter Hēphaistos had toiled to make:
Hēphaistos gave it to Lord Zeus, the son of Kronos,
from Zeus it passed to the courier slayer of Argos,[1]
Lord Hermēs gave it to Pelops, driver of horses; Pelops
in turn bestowed it on Atreus, shepherd of his people,
Atreus, dying, bequeathed it to Thyestēs, rich in flocks,
and Thyestēs in turn left it to Agamemnōn to carry,
as lord over many islands and the whole of Argos.

---

1. An ancient, and obscure, title of Hermēs. Some scholiasts believed that the reference is to a monstrous dog called Argos, full of eyes, that Hērē set to watch Io, Zeus's latest love, after he metamorphosed her into a cow to escape Hērē's maleficent attentions. Zeus allegedly enlisted Hermēs' help to get rid of the dog.

Leaning on this scepter he now addressed the Argives:
"My friends, Danaän heroes, comrades in arms of Arēs,
Great Zeus, Kronos's son, has snared me in a crushing delusion,
harsh god that he is. Once he promised, and bowed his head in assent,
that I should sack strong-walled Ilion before returning home.
Now he's turned to a vile deception, orders me back
in dishonor to Argos, after the loss of so many men.
Such things, I suppose, give pleasure to Zeus in his mightiness,
who has brought down the high towers of many a city,
and will bring down still more, for his power is the greatest.
A shameful thing it is, and for future men to learn, how
in vain it was that so strong, so vast an Achaian army
waged a war to no purpose—though they were fighting
against fewer men—and still with no end in sight!
For if we were so minded, Achaians and Trojans both,
to swear a solemn truce, and to both be counted,
the Trojans numbering all those with city households,
and we Achaians being sorted in groups of ten,
with each group choosing a Trojan to pour our wine,
then many a group would lack for a wine pourer.
So far, I say, do the sons of the Achaians outnumber
those Trojans who dwell in the city. But there are allies
from many cities, spear-wielding warriors, who
thwart me, will not allow me, for all my wanting it,
to take and sack Ilion's populous city. By now
nine years of great Zeus have come and gone, by now
our ships' timbers are rotted, their rigging all gone slack,
while at home our wives and young children may be still
sitting there in our halls and awaiting us. Yet the work
for which we came here remains entirely unaccomplished.
So come, then, let us all agree to do as I say:
pull out with our ships, return to our own native land,
since now we shall never capture Troy of the wide streets."

So he spoke, and roused the spirit in the breasts of all
that throng, none of whom had heard what was said in council.
The assembly was stirred into motion like the long sea rollers
of the Ikarian deep, which winds from the east or south
roil up, rushing on them from the clouds of Zeus, the Father.
As when the west wind's onset flurries the deep-standing

grain with its rough blast, and all the corn-ears bend,
so all the assembly was shifted, and with loud hullabaloo
men raced to the ships, and from under their feet the dust
lifted and hung in the air. They shouted one to another
to lay hold of the ships, drag them down to the bright sea,
started clearing the slipways, voices soaring skyward
in their longing for home, knocked props away from the hulls.

Then for the Argives a homecoming beyond their destiny
would have come about, had not Hērē thus addressed Athēnē:
"Good heavens, unwearying daughter of Zeus of the aegis,
is it thus to their native land the Argives will take flight
homeward, across the broad back of the sea,
leaving—a trophy for Priam and every Trojan to boast of—
Argive Helen, for whom so many of the Achaians
perished in Troy, far distant from their own fatherland?
Go, now, through the ranks of the bronze-corseleted Achaians,
with your gentle words restrain each individual:
don't let them haul their trim vessels seaward!"

So she spoke,
and the goddess, grey-eyed Athēnē, did not demur,
but went her way, swooping down from the peaks of Olympos,
and speedily reached the swift ships of the Achaians.
There she found Odysseus, Zeus's equal in counsel,
standing idle, not setting a hand to his black and well-benched
vessel, since grief had possessed his heart and spirit.
Standing close beside him grey-eyed Athēnē said:
"Zeus-sprung son of Laertēs, resourceful Odysseus,
is it thus to your native land that you'll take flight homeward,
tumbling aboard your many-benched vessels? Would you
leave, as a trophy for Priam and every Trojan to boast of,
Argive Helen, for whom so many of the Achaians
perished in Troy, far distant from their own fatherland?
Go, now, through the Achaians' ranks, hold back no longer,
with your gentle words restrain each individual,
don't let them haul their trim vessels seaward!"

So she spoke.
He knew from her speech that her voice was that of a goddess,
and left at a run, throwing off his cloak, to be picked up

by the herald Eurybatēs, from Ithákē, his attendant.
He himself went straight to Atreus's son Agamemnōn,
who gave him his family's scepter, forever imperishable;
with this he strode by the ships of the bronze-corseleted Achaians.

Any prince or eminent man whom he encountered,
he'd stand at his side, try with gentle words to restrain him:
"My good sir, it's not proper to browbeat you like a coward!
Just sit yourself down, get your people seated too.
As yet you've no clear knowledge of what Atreus's son intends:
Now he's just making trial, but he'll hit the Achaians' sons
soon, and hard. Did we not all hear what he said in council?
May he not in his wrath do hurt to the sons of the Achaians!
Proud is the spirit of kings, Zeus's nurslings: their honor
derives from Zeus, and Zeus the Counselor loves them."

But each commoner that he saw, and discovered shouting,
him he'd thrash with his staff, and assail with words as well:
"You, fellow, sit quiet, attend to the words of others,
better men than yourself! Unwarlike, strengthless,
you're of no account either in battle or in counsel.
No way can we all be kings here, we Achaians:
no good thing is the lordship of many; let there be one lord,
one king, to whom Kronos's son, that devious schemer,
gives scepter and right of judgment, to deliberate for his people."

So, acting the lord, he controlled the troops. They hurried
back from the ships and huts to the place of assembly,
with a noise as when a wave of the loud-resounding sea
thunders upon a great beach, and the deep re-echoes.

The rest had settled, were quiet; one man only,
Thersītēs, a blabbermouth, kept scolding on: he had
a great store of words in his mind, but all disordered,
random, out of true sequence, to wrangle with the kings—
anything that he figured might set the Argives laughing.
Of all who'd come under Troy's citadel, he was the ugliest—
bandy-legged, lame in one foot, both shoulders hunched,
drawn in over his chest; above them his head
came to a peak, and sparse the hair growing on it.
Hated he was above all by Achilles and Odysseus,
stock targets for his haranguing; but at noble Agamemnōn

he now directed his shrill abuse. With him the Achaians
were fearsomely angry, indignant and resentful,
yet still, at the top of his voice, he kept scolding Agamemnōn:
"Son of Atreus, what's your complaint now, what is it you lack?
Your huts are crammed with bronze items, there are women galore
in your huts, real choice ones, given you by the Achaians
first off, whenever we get to capture a citadel!
Or do you still itch for more gold, to be fetched you from Ilion
by some horse-breaking Trojan as ransom for his son—
whom I, or another Achaian, may have captured and brought in?
Or is it some young woman for you to lie with in love,
and keep apart for yourself? It isn't right for one
who's their leader to bring harm to the Achaians' sons!
Weaklings! Cowardly creatures! You women, not men, of Achaia,
let's go back home in our ships, and leave this fellow
here in Troy to gorge on his prizes: let him discover
whether we'll bother to help him, or not—this man who's
subjected Achilles, a far better man than he is,
to dishonor, himself has taken his prize, and keeps it.
Yet there's no gall in Achilles' heart, he's easy-going.
Otherwise, son of Atreus, this insult would be your last."

Thus, railing at Agamemnōn, the shepherd of the people,
Thersītēs. But quickly there came up noble Odysseus,
stood by him, eyed him darkly, reproved him with harsh words:
"Thersītēs, wild babbler, sharp stump speaker you may be,
but shut up! Don't try, on your own, to challenge princes,
for I think there exists no more worthless mortal than you
among all who came below Ilion with the sons of Atreus.
Quit mouthing the names of the kings, leave off your ranting,
the insults you cast at them, watching your chance to pull out!
We still don't know for certain how these matters will be:
shall we, the Achaians' sons, get a good or a bad homecoming?
Yet here you sit, reviling Agamemnōn, son of Atreus,
the people's shepherd, because so much was given to him
by the Danaän heroes: your speech is all jeering mockery.
But this I will tell you straight, and it shall come to pass:
should I find you once more playing the fool, as you are now,
then may Odysseus's head no longer rest on his shoulders,

no longer may I be called Tēlemachos's father,
if I don't seize you and strip off all your clothing,
your cloak and your tunic, that cover your naked shame,
and send you off, howling, back to the swift ships,
whipped out of the assembly with demeaning blows."
So saying, with the scepter he struck Thersītēs' back
and shoulders: he doubled up, the tears gushed from him,
and a bloody welt rose on his back from the golden
scepter. Then down he sat, in pain and terrified,
with a helpless expression, wiping away the tears.
Sorry for him or not, the troops still found him comic,
and one, with a laugh, would turn to his neighbor and say:
"I tell you, Odysseus may have done countless good things—
a master of sound advice, of deployment in battle—but
this is the best deed by far he's performed among the Argives,
to make this slanderous word-slinger cease from his ranting!
Never again will Thersītēs' headstrong spirit impel him
to inveigh in insulting language against the princes."

So spoke the common folk. Then Odysseus, city-sacker,
stood up holding the scepter, while beside him grey-eyed Athēnē
in the form of a herald ordered the people to keep silent,
so that all the Achaians' sons, both front and rearmost ranks,
could hear his words and take cognizance of his counsel.
He, with friendly intent, now spoke before the assembly:
"Son of Atreus! Indeed now, my lord, the Achaians are minded
to name you the most blameworthy among all mortal men,
nor will they fulfil the promise they once gave you
on their way here from Argos, excellent pasture for horses—
that not till walled Ilion fell would you sail away;
for as though they were little children or widowed women
they wail loudly, one to another, about returning home.
It's true that it's hard, this sad longing to be gone;
for anyone parted even one month from his wife with
his many-benched ship feels distress, when wintry gales
and tumultuous seas hold him back. But for us this is
the ninth of the circling years that have seen us still
soldiering on here. I don't blame the Achaians
for fretting beside their curved ships, but, even so,

it's shameful to stay so long and go home empty-handed.
Endure, my friends, hold firm a while longer, until we learn
whether Kalchas is, or is not, a truthful prophet.
There's a moment we well recall, and you can, every one of you,
except those caught by the death-spirits, bear witness to it,
when—it seems only yesterday—at Aulis the Achaian
fleet was assembling, trouble for Priam and his Trojans.
We on the sacred altars set up around a spring
were offering unblemished sacrifices to the immortals
under a lovely plane tree from which the bright water flowed.
Then appeared a great sign: a serpent, backed blood-red,
horrific, sent into the light by the Olympian himself,
slid out from under the altar and made for the plane tree.
There huddled a sparrow's fledglings, babes new-hatched,
on the topmost branch, and cowering under its leaves—
eight, and the mother that hatched them made the ninth.
Then the serpent devoured them, all piteously cheeping,
while the mother fluttered around, bewailing her little ones,
till the snake, coiling, seized her wing as she shrilled in sorrow.
But when it had polished the lot off, mother and all,
the god behind its appearance made it a clear portent:
the son of devious Kronos turned it to stone, and we
stood there, amazed at what had happened. So when
this dread prodigy interrupted our sacrifice to the gods
Kalchas at once declared to us, in prophetic mode:
'Why have you fallen silent, you long-haired Achaians?
This great portent's been shown to us by Zeus in his wisdom:
late, and late in fulfillment, but its fame will never perish!
As this serpent devoured the sparrow's brood, and their mother
with them—all eight, and she that hatched them made nine—
so we for that sum of years shall wage war there,
but in the tenth we shall take the wide-streeted city.'
Such were his words, and now all this is being accomplished!
So come, stand firm all of you, you well-greaved Achaians,
here, till the day that we capture Priam's great citadel."

So he spoke: the Argives gave a great shout, and round them
the ships echoed deafeningly to the Achaians' cheering
as they applauded the speech of godlike Odysseus.
Then the Gerēnian horseman Nestōr spoke out among them:

"Oh really! You're like children when you hold assembly,
mere infants, unacquainted with the business of warfare!
What's to become of our covenants, our sworn oaths?
Shall we toss in the fire all men's counsels and stratagems,
those neat libations, those handshakes in which we placed our trust?
We keep on wrangling with words, yet we can find
no remedy, for all the lengthy time we've been here.
Son of Atreus, you must, as before, maintain unshaken purpose,
be the Argives' leader throughout our fierce engagements!
Leave those others to perish, the one or two Achaians
plotting apart from the rest—but their work will come to
nothing—
to make their way back to Argos, even before we know
if that promise by Zeus of the aegis is a falsehood or not.
For I tell you, he nodded approval, did Kronos's mighty son,
on that day when in their swift-travelling vessels the Argives
set forth, to the Trojans bearing slaughter and destruction:
he struck lightning on our right, showed us signs of his favor.
So let no man be over-hasty to set out homeward until
he has lain with the wife of some Trojan, and got requital
for all our effort and misery in the matter of Helen.
But if anyone is terribly minded to set out homeward,
let him so much as touch his black well-benched vessel,
and the rest will watch his encounter with his death and destiny!
Now, my lord, plan well yourself—and obey another:
not to be tossed aside will be the advice I give you.
Order your troops by their clans and by brotherhoods, Agamemnōn:
Thus brotherhood will bring aid to brotherhood, clan to clan.
If you act thus, and the Achaians do as you command,
then you'll know which of them, leaders and men, are cowards,
and which the brave, since they'll be fighting by themselves,
and whether it's heaven's will that you fail to reduce the city,
or because of your own troops' lack of warlike skill and valor."

To him now spoke in answer the lord Agamemnōn:
"Once more, old sir, you surpass the sons of the Achaians
in debate—Zeus the Father, Athēnē, Apollo! I wish
I'd ten such counselors from among the Achaians! Then
quickly indeed would King Priam's city totter and fall,
taken and sacked by our hands. But the son of Kronos,

Zeus who bears the aegis,[2], has rather brought me sorrows,
tossing me into insoluble quarrels and disputes.
For I and Achilles fought each other over a girl,
exchanging violent words, and my anger it was began it.
But if ever we reach agreement, from then no longer
shall the Trojans' doom be postponed, not for a moment!
Now off with you, get your meal, and then prepare for battle:
let each man sharpen his spear, have his shield in good order;
let each man provide good feed for his swift-footed horses;
let each man look to his chariot, ready himself to fight,
so that all day long we may be matched in hateful warfare.
For there'll be no respite, no, not for a moment,
Till night comes on and parts the warriors' mingled fury.
Sweat-sodden about his chest will stretch the strap of each man's
protective shield, the hand that grips his spear will weary;
sweat-sodden the horse as it strains at his polished chariot.
But any man I observe away from the fighting, who's minded
to hang back by the curved ships—he'll no longer be able
to rely on eluding the dogs and the birds of prey."

So he spoke, and the Argives gave a great shout, like a wave
stirred by a southern gale, crashing into some lofty headland,
a jutting rock face ever assailed by breakers,
that come at it from all quarters, driven by every wind.
Up they got, and scattered hurriedly to the ships,
built fires by their shelters, and set about their dinner;
and each man sacrificed to one of the immortal gods,
praying for escape from death and the grind of battle.
But the lord of men, Agamemnōn now sacrificed an ox—
a fat one, five years old—to Kronos's almighty son,
and summoned the leading elders of all the Achaians:
Nestōr, first of all, and noble Idomeneus,
then, both the Aiases and the son of Tydeus,
and, sixth, Odysseus, Zeus's equal in counsel.
Menelaös, great at the war cry, chose to come with them,

2. The aegis is a divine appurtenance variously likened to a shield, wrap, or apron. It seems to vary with the bearer, which suggests that there may have been more than one: e.g., in Zeus's hands it is a shield, made for him by Hēphaistos; but for Athēnē it is some sort of a wrap, with the Gorgon's head woven into it. In the *Iliad* it is variously described as fringed, tasseled, golden, gleaming, and immortal. Its function is both to protect its wearer and to cause terror in the viewer, mostly on the battlefield.

for he knew in his heart how hard-pressed his brother was.
They stood there around the ox, and held up the barley groats,
and in prayer the lord Agamemnōn spoke among them:
"Zeus, most glorious, greatest, lord of the storm clouds,
heaven-dweller—let not the sun go down, or darkness
come upon us until I have levelled Priam's palace,
left it blackened with smoke, filled its gates with devouring fire,
and slashed open Hektōr's tunic about his chest,
ripped up by the bronze; and may many of his companions
fall prone in the dust around him, teeth grinding into earth."

So he spoke. But not yet did Kronos's son grant him this;
the sacrifice he accepted, but laid yet more grim toil upon him.

When they had prayed, and scattered the barley groats, first
pulling back the victims' heads, they slaughtered and flayed them,
cut out the thighs, wrapped them up in a double layer
of fat, and placed over them cuts of raw meat. These then
they burned on split billets, stripped of all their leaves,
while the innards they spitted and roasted in Hēphaistos's flames.
But when the thighs were well broiled and they'd tasted the innards,
then they chopped up the rest, threaded the bits on skewers,
grilled them with care, then drew them all off, and once
they were through with their work, and the meal had been got ready,
they feasted, and no one's heart lacked a fair share in the feasting.
But when they had satisfied their desire for food and drink,
first to address them was the Gerēnian horseman Nestōr:
"Most glorious son of Atreus, lord of men, Agamemnōn,
let us waste no more time on discussion, nor any longer
postpone the action the god himself puts in our hands!
Come now, let the heralds of the bronze-clad Achaians
gather the troops ship by ship and make proclamation,
while we all go in a body through the Achaians' broad camp,
the quicker to stir up their sharp-edged martial spirit."

So he spoke. Agamemnōn, lord of men, did not ignore him:
at once he ordered the clear-voiced heralds to summon
the long-haired Achaians to battle by proclamation.
They so proclaimed, and the men assembled quickly.
Those around Atreus's son, the princes, Zeus's nurslings,
hastened to marshal the ranks. Grey-eyed Athēnē joined them,

wearing the precious aegis, ageless, immortal,
with a hundred dangling tassels, all of pure gold, and each
finely woven, and worth the price of a hundred oxen.
Thus adorned she flashed swiftly through the Achaian host,
urging them onward: in each man's heart she stirred strength
for ceaseless warfare and fighting, so that to them
war at once became sweeter than any thought of returning
in their hollow ships to the dear land of their fathers.

As annihilating fire burns up a boundless forest
on some mountain summit, and the glare can be seen far off,
so, as they marched, from their marvelous bronze gear
the burnished radiance gleamed up through the air to heaven;
and just as the many species of winged creatures—
wild geese, or cranes, or swans with their long necks—
on the Asian meadowland beside Kaÿstrios's streams
fly hither and thither exulting in their wings' strength,
then settle clamorously, and the meadowland resounds,
just so from the ships and huts their many nations
poured forth to Skamandros's plain, and beneath the tread
of men and horses the earth re-echoed, a fearsome sound,
and they halted and stood, in Skamandros's flowery meadow,
thousands strong, like leaves and blossoms in their season.
Like the multitudinous clusters of teeming flies
that swarm round the shepherd's steading in the springtime
when milk comes flooding the buckets, in such numbers
they stood on the plain, the long-haired Achaians, against
the Trojans, eager, determined, bent on their destruction.
And as goatherds easily sort out their wide-scattered herds
of goats when they've mingled for pasturage, so now the Achaians
were positioned, some here, some there, to join in battle
by their leaders, among them the lord Agamemnōn,
in eyes and head like Zeus who delights in the thunderbolt,
like Arēs in girth, and with the chest of Poseidōn.
As one steer in a herd of cattle stands out, far above them all—
the bull, distinguished among the cows assembled round it—
such a one on that day Zeus rendered Atreus's son,
preeminent among many, of heroes the foremost.

Tell me now, Muses, who have your dwellings on Olympos—
for you are present, and goddesses, and know all things, whereas

we mortals have only hearsay, know nothing for certain—
who were the leaders and princes of the Danaäns?
As for the common throng, I could not report or name them,
not even were ten tongues mine, all in ten mouths,
an unbreakable voice, and a brazen heart within me,
had I not the Olympian Muses, daughters of Zeus of the aegis,
to remind me of all those who came below Ilion. Now
I'll list the ships' commanders and all their squadrons.

Pēneleōs and Lēïtos were leaders of the Boiōtians,
with Arkesilaos and Prothoēnōr and Klonios,
those who dwelt in Hyria and rocky Aulis,
in Schoinos and Skōlos and many-spurred Eteōnos,
in Thespeia, Graia, Mykalessos with its broad dancing floor;
those who dwelt around Harma and Eilesion and Erythrai,
those who held Eleōn[3] and Hylē and Peteōn,
Ôkalea and Medeōn, the well-wrought citadel,
Kōpai, Eutrēsis, dove-haunted Thisbē; those
who dwelt in Korōneia and grassy Haliartos,
who held Plataia and who dwelt in Glisas; those
who held lower Thēbē, the well-wrought citadel, and
sacred Onchēstos, the bright grove of Poseidon;
those who held grape-rich Arnē, and Mideia,
sacrosanct Nīsa, and borderland Anthēdōn.
Of these there came fifty ships, and aboard each one
a hundred and twenty young men of the Boiōtians.

Those who lived in Asplēdōn and Minyan Orchomenos,
them Askalaphos led and Ialmenos, sons of Arēs,
whom Astyochē bore, in the house of Azeïos's son
Aktōr—a bashful virgin, she went up into her chamber
to mighty Arēs, who lay there with her in secret.
With these were mustered thirty hollow vessels.

The Phōkians were led by Schedios and Epistrophos,
offspring of Iphitos, great-hearted Naubolos's son.
These were the ones who held Kyparissos and rocky Pythō,
sacrosanct Krīsa and Daulis and Panopeus,

3. It is interesting, and significant, that Eleōn (like some other places listed in the Catalogue) was completely unknown until the reading of the Linear B tablets, indicating that at least part of the Catalogue dated back to Mycenaean times.

who dwelt around Anemōreia and Hyampolis,
who lived beside Kēphisos, that noble river,
and held Lilaia by the springs of Kēphisos.
Along with these there followed forty black vessels.
Carefully they ordered the ranks of the Phōkians, set them
on the left wing, ready for battle, beside the Boiōtians.

Oïleus's swift son was leader of the Lokrians: Aias,
Aias the lesser, not huge like Aias Telamōn's son,
but smaller by far. Slight of build, he wore a linen corselet,
yet with the spear outclassed all Hellenes and Achaians.
These men dwelt in Kynos, Opoeis, Kalliaros,
Bēssa and Skarphē and beautiful Augeiai,
Tarphē, and Thronion by Boagrios's streams.
Along with Aias there followed forty black ships, belonging
to the Lokrians who dwell across from sacred Euboia.

Next, those who held Euboia, the fierce-breathing Abantes:
Chalkis and Eretria and grape-rich Histiaia,
seaside Kērinthos and Dion's steep citadel, and
those who held Kárystos, those who dwelt in Styra,
whose leader was Elephēnōr, companion of Arēs,
Chalkōdōn's son, the great-hearted Abantes' commander.
With him the Abantes came, all runners, back hair long,
spearmen hot with their out-thrust ash-wood lances
to rip through the corselets that covered their enemies' chests.
Along with him there followed forty black vessels.

Then there were those who held Athens, the well-built citadel,
land of great-hearted Erechtheus, whom once Zeus's daughter
Athēnē reared—the grain-giving plough-land bore him—
and established in Athens, in her own rich shrine;
and there with bulls and rams Athenian young men
continue to seek his favor through the circling years;
of these Menestheus was leader, the son of Peteōs.
No other man on earth was as yet his equal
at marshalling chariots and shield-bearing warriors:
Nestōr alone could match him, for he was the elder.
Along with him there followed fifty black vessels.

Aias from Salamis led twelve ships, and as leader
stationed them where the ranks of the Athenians stood.

Those who held Argos and high-walled Tiryns and
Hermionē and Asinē, lying on the deep gulf, with
Troizēn and Eïonai and vine-clad Epídauros, and
Aigina and Masēs, home to the young men of the Achaians:
these Diomēdēs commanded, he of the great war cry,
and Sthenelos, the dear son of wide-renowned Kapaneus,
and with them as third came Euryalos, a godlike mortal,
of king Mēkisteus the son, and grandson of Talaös—
but Diomēdēs of the great war cry was lord over them all.
Along with them there followed eighty black vessels.

Those who held Mykēnai, that well-wrought citadel.
and wealthy Korinthos, and well-wrought Kleōnai,
and dwelt in Orneai and lovely Araithyréa,
and Sikyōn, over which Adrēstos first was king;
those who held Hyperēsía, steep Gonoessa, and
Pellēnē, who dwelt around Aígion and all
the length of Aigialos, and around broad Helikē: commander
of their hundred vessels was lord Agamemnōn, son
of Atreus, and with him came the most troops by far, and the best,
and among them he himself stood, armed in his gleaming bronze,
exulting, preeminent among all the heroes, since
he was the greatest, and brought by far the largest force.

And those who held hollow ravine-scored Lakedaimōn,
Pharis and Sparta and dove-haunted Messē, those
who dwelt in Bryseiai and lovely Augeiai, who held
Amyklai and Helos, the coastal fortress, and Laäs,
and dwelt around Oitylos: they were commanded by
his brother, Menelaös, of the great war cry, who brought
sixty vessels. These were stationed apart, and he
moved among them in person, confident in his purpose,
urging his men to battle, since above all his spirit longed
to be revenged for the struggles and groans over Helen.

And those who dwelt in Pylos and lovely Arēnē,
and Thryon, the ford of Alpheios, and well-built Aipy,
who occupied Kyparisseïs and Amphigeneia,
Pteleos, Helos, and Dōrion—where the Muses encountered
Thamyris the Thracian, and put an end to his singing,
on his way from Oichalia, from the house of Eurytos

the Oichalian, for his boast that he'd win, even if the Muses
themselves were to sing against him, the daughters of Zeus
of the aegis; but they in their fury maimed him, deprived him
of his marvelous singing, made him forget his skill with the lyre—:
of these the Gerēnian horseman, Nestōr, was leader,
and with him were mustered ninety hollow vessels.

Those who possessed Arkadía, below Kyllēnē's steep mountain,
by the tomb of Aipytos, where combatants are close fighters;
those who dwelt in Pheneos and flock-rich Orchomenos,
in Rhipē and Stratiē and wind-scoured Enispē,
those whose homes were Tegea and lovely Mantineia,
who held Stymphalos and dwelt in Parrhasía: these
were commanded by Ankaios's son, the lord Agapēnōr,
with sixty ships, and aboard each ship came many
Arkadian warriors, well skilled in warfare's business.
For Agamemnōn himself, son of Atreus, lord of men,
had given them well-benched ships in which to traverse
the wine-faced deep, seafaring being no concern of theirs.

For those who lived in Bouprasion and noble Ēlis—
all that Hyrminē and Myrsinos way out on the frontier
and the Ōlenian rock and Alēsion enclose between them—
there were four leaders, and each of these accompanied
by ten swift ships, with many Epeians aboard them. Of these
some were led by Amphimachos and Thalpios, sons, one of
Kteatos, the other of Eurytos, both blood-kin to Aktōr; others
by Amarynkeus's son, the mighty Diōrēs, while
the fourth group was led by godlike Polyxeinos, son
of royal Agasthenēs, whose father was Augeias.

Those from Doulichion and the sacred Echinean
islands, who live facing Ēlis, across the salt water,
were led by Megēs, a man the equal of Arēs, Phyleus's son.
His sire, Zeus's nursling, Phyleus the horseman, long ago
moved away to Doulichion after quarrelling with his father.
Along with Megēs there followed forty black vessels.

Odysseus led the high-spirited Kephallēnians,
who held Ithákē and Nēriton with its rippling leafage,
and dwelt in Krokyleia and rugged Aigilips, with
those who held Zákynthos, those who lived around Samē,

and those who held the mainland and the facing coastline:
of them Odysseus was leader, Zeus's equal in counsel.
With him there followed twelve ships, vermilion-prowed.

The Aitōlians were led by Thoas, Andraimōn's son:
the inhabitants of Pleurōn, Ōlenos and Pylēnē,
Chalkis by the seashore and rock-strewn Kalydōn;
for great-hearted Oineus's sons were no longer living,
nor he himself; dead, too, was fair-haired Meleagros,
so on Thoas the absolute rule of Aitōlians had devolved.
Accompanying him there followed forty black vessels.

Of the Krētans Idomeneus, famed spearman, was the leader:
of those who held Knossos and Gortyn with its high battlements,
Lyktos, Mīlētos, and chalk-bright Lykastos,
Phaistos and Rhytion, well-populated cities; and others
scattered through Krētē of the hundred cities.
Of these, then, Idomeneus, famed spearman, was the leader,
with Mēriones, a match for the man-slaying War God himself.
Accompanying them there followed eighty black vessels.

Tlēpolemos, son of Hēraklēs, a man both brave and tall,
from Rhodos brought nine ships of the lordly Rhodians,
who occupied Rhodos in three separate settlements:
Lindos, Ialysos, and chalk-bright Kameiros.
Of these, then, Tlēpolemos, famed spearman, was the leader,
whom Astyocheia bore to that mighty force Hēraklēs. Her
he brought out of Ephyrē from the Sellēïs river, after
sacking many a city of warriors, Zeus's nurslings.
But Tlēpolemos, when a grown man in their well-built home,
soon afterwards killed his father's maternal uncle,
already an elderly man—Likymnios, scion of Arēs.
At once he fitted out ships, raised a large body of men,
and fled across the sea, since he'd already been threatened
by other sons and grandsons of the mighty force Hēraklēs.
He came to Rhodos, a wanderer, suffering hardship, and there
his people, settled in three tribal divisions, were favored
by Zeus, whose rule is over both gods and mortals;
the son of Kronos showered marvelous wealth upon them.

Nireus too from Symē brought three trim vessels:
Nireus, Aglaïa's son by the lord Charōpos,

Nireus, the handsomest man who came under Ilion
of all other Danaäns after Pēleus's blameless son—
but a weakling, and only a few troops accompanied him.

Those who held Nisyros, Karpathos and Kasos
and Kōs, Eurypylos' city, and the Kalydnian islands,
had as commanders Pheidippos and Antiphos,
the two sons of king Thessalos, whose father was Hēraklēs.
Along with them there were mustered thirty hollow vessels.

Now, too, all those who lived in Pelasgian Argos,
who were settled in Alos and Alopē, whose homes were in Trachis,
who occupied Phthiē and Hellas, the land of fair women,
and were known as Myrmidons, Hellēnes, and Achaians—
of the fifty ships of these men Achilles was the commander.
But to warfare's grievous clamor they gave no thought,
having no one to deploy them into the battle-line,
for the swift-footed noble Achilles lay idle by the ships,
enraged on account of Briseïs, the girl with lovely hair,
whom he'd taken from Lyrnessos after much hard work—
destroying Lyrnessos and the walls of Thēbē,[4]
laying low Mynēs and Epistrophos, spear-battlers both,
sons of King Evēnos, Selēpos's son. And now
grieving for her he lay there—but would rise up soon enough.

Those who held Phylakē and flowery Pyrasos,
Dēmētēr's precinct, and Itōn, mother of flocks,
and seaside Antrōn and turf-bedded Pteleos: of them
warlike Prōtesilāos was the commander
while he still lived; but by then black earth already held him.
His wife, cheeks torn in grief, was left there in Phylakē
with a half-built house, for a Dardanian slew him
as he leapt from his ship, the very first of the Achaians.
Yet his men did not go leaderless, though they missed their leader,
being mustered by Podarkēs, offshoot of Arēs—son
of Iphiklos, grandson of Phylakos rich in flocks,
full brother to Prōtesilāos, he of the great heart,
but younger-born; the elder was the more warlike,
heroic Prōtesilāos, the warrior. Still, his people

4. This is Thēbē (Thebes) in Asia Minor, to be distinguished from Boiōtian Thēbē and Thēbē in Egypt: see Glossary.

did not lack a leader, though missing their good captain.
Along with him there followed forty black vessels.

Those who dwelt in Pherai beside Lake Boibēïs,
and in Boibē and Glaphyrai and well-built Iolkos: they
were led, with eleven ships, by Admētos's dear son
Eumēlos, born to Admētos of that paragon among women,
Alkēstis, the most beautiful of the daughters of Pelias.

Those who dwelt in Mēthōne and Thaumakia,
who held Meliboia and rugged Olizōn,
were commanded by Philoktētēs, an experienced archer,
with their seven ships, in each of which were embarked
fifty rowers, well skilled at hard fighting with the bow.
But he himself lay on an island, racked by violent pains:
sacred Lēmnos, where the Achaians' sons had left him
afflicted with a bad wound from a vicious water-serpent.
There he lay in his agony; but soon the Argives beside
their ships would have King Philoktētēs very much in mind.
Yet his men did not go leaderless, though they missed their leader,
being mustered by Medōn, Oïleus's bastard son,
whom Rhēnē bore to Oïleus, sacker of cities.

Those who occupied Trikka and crag-bound Ithōmē,
and Oichalia, city of Eurytos the Oichalian,
had as their leaders Asklēpios's two sons,
skilled healers both, Podaleirios and Macháōn.
Along with them there were mustered thirty hollow vessels.

Those who held Ormenios and the spring of Hypereia,
those who held Asterion and the white peaks of Titános
were led by Eurypylos, Euaimōn's splendid son.
Along with them there followed forty black ships.

Those who held Argissa and were domiciled in Gyrtōnē,
Orthē, and Ēlōnē, and Oloössōn the white city,
were led by that staunch fighter Polypoitēs, son
of Peirithöos—whom immortal Zeus begot—being
conceived to Peirithöos by renowned Hippodameia
that day he got his revenge on the shaggy Centaurs, drove them
out of Pēlion, sent them packing as far as the Aithikēs—
not alone: there went with him Leonteus, scion of Arēs,

son of bold-hearted Korōnos, Kaineus's son.
Along with them there followed forty black vessels.

Gouneus from Kyphos brought two and twenty vessels;
with him there came the Eniēnes and the battle-tough Peraiboians
who made their homes in the region of hard-wintered Dōdōna,
and worked the land around the beautiful Titaressos,
whose sweet-flowing waters join those of the Pēneios,
yet do not mingle with Pēneios's silvery eddies, but flow
over and separate from them, as though they were olive oil,
for this is a branch of Styx, the terrible oath-river.

The Magnēsians were led by Prothoös son of Teuthrēdōn.
Around the Pēneios and Pēlion's rippling woodlands
they made their homes: swift Prothoös was their commander.
Along with them there followed forty black vessels.

These were the Danaäns' leaders and princes. But who
was outstanding among them? Who, now tell me, Muse,
among all those men, and their horses, that served with Atreus's sons?

Of horses, the best by far were the mares of Phērēs' grandson,
those that Eumēlos drove, bird-swift in their running,
same coats, same age, even-backed as though ruled to a plumb-line.
Bred in Pēreia they were, by silver-bowed Apollo,
both mares, both bearing within them the fearfulness of battle.
Of men, the best was Aias, Telamōn's son—that is,
while Achilles still nursed his wrath, who was far the strongest,
he, and the horses that carried Pēleus's splendid son.
But now by the curved seafaring ships he lay, consumed
by fury against Agamemnōn, shepherd of the people,
Atreus's son; while along the seashore his followers
amused themselves with casting the discus and javelin,
and archery, while their horses, each by his owner's chariot,
stood cropping marsh-parsley and clover, while
the chariots themselves, well-covered, were stored away
in their masters' huts, and the men, missing their warlike leader,
wandered about in the camp, and did no fighting.

The army advanced as though the whole world was on fire,
and the earth groaned under them, as under Zeus with his angry
thunderbolts, when he hammers the land around Typhoios,

among the Arimoi, where men say is Typhoios's bed.
So under their marching feet the earth groaned out aloud
as quickly they made their advance across the plain.

To the Trojans wind-footed swift Iris came as a messenger
from Zeus of the aegis, bearing a grievous message.
They were met in assembly at the gates of Priam,
all of them gathered together, young men and elders.
Standing close, swift-footed Iris now addressed them,
making her voice like that of Priam's son Polītēs,
who sat as the Trojans' lookout, trusting his speed of foot,
on top of the burial mound of aged Aisyētēs,
watching for when the Achaians should set out from their ships.
As him, then, swift-footed Iris now addressed Priam:
"Old sir, as ever, unending talk is your pleasure,
just as in peacetime: but now unceasing war has arisen.
Many battles of warriors have I taken part in,
But never yet have I seen so vast or strong an army—
overwhelming, like leaves of the forest or grains of sand—
as this now crossing the plain to attack our city.
Hektōr, to you above all I give this command for action:
Numerous here are the allies spread out in Priam's great city,
men from many lands, all speaking different tongues.
So let each man give the signal to those he commands,
marshal his own citizens, then lead them forth."

So she spoke,
and Hektōr did not mistake the goddess's voice,
but at once broke up the assembly, and they rushed to arms.
All the gates were flung open, and the troops poured through them,
on foot and mounted both, and a mighty hubbub arose.

Set in front of the city there is a steep mound,
far out in the plain, with a clear space all around it.
This men know as Batieia, that is, Bramble Hill, whereas
the immortals call it the grave-mound of Myrīnē the dancer.
There, now, the Trojans and their allies marshaled their forces.

The Trojans were led by great bright-helmeted Hektōr,
Priam's son, and with him by far the most and the best
troops were deployed, all eager to battle it out with the spear.

The Dardanians were led by Anchīsēs' valiant son
Aineias, conceived to Anchīsēs by shining Aphroditē
among the spurs of Ida, a goddess lying with a mortal.
He was not alone: with him came Antēnōr's two sons,
Archelochos and Akamas, well trained in all fighting skills.

Those who dwelt in Zeleia, below the lowest spur of Ida,
wealthy men, who drink the dark water of the Aisēpos,
Trojans, had as their leader Lykaōn's splendid son,
Pandaros, gifted with bowmanship by Apollo himself.

Those who held Adrēsteia and the district of Apaisos,
who held Pityeia and Tēreia's steep mountain, were led
by Adrēstos and Amphios, he of the linen corselet, the sons
of Merōps of Perkōtē, who outstripped all other men
in seercraft, and tried to prevent his sons from going
off to murderous warfare. But the two of them would not obey him,
for the spirits of black death were urging them onward.

Those who lived in the region of Perkōtē and Praktion,
who held Sēstos and Abydos and noble Arisbē, were led
by Asios, son of Hyrtakos, a leader of men:
Asios, son of Hyrtakos, who was brought from Arisbē
by his tall sorrel horses, from the Sellēïs river.
Hippothoös led the tribes of fierce Pelasgian spearmen,
who had their homes in rich-soiled Lárisa: they
were led by Hippothoös and Pylaios, scion of Arēs,
two sons of Pelasgian Lēthos, Teutamos's son.

The Thracians were led by Akamas and the hero Peiroös—
all those the strong-flowing stream of Hellespont encloses.

Euphēmos was the leader of the Kikonian spearmen,
the son of Troizēnos, Zeus's nursling, Keas's son.

Pyraichmēs led the Paiōnians with their back-bent bows
from far away out of Amydōn, from the broad stream of Axios,
whose waters are the loveliest flowing on this earth.

The Paphlagōnians were led by stout-hearted Pylaimenēs
from the land of the Enetoi, home to a breed of wild mules.
These held Kytōros and dwelt around Sēsamos, in

their famous homes beside the Parthenios river,
in Krōmna, Aigialos, and lofty Erythinoi.

The Halizōnians had Odios and Epistrophos as their leaders,
from far-distant Alybē, where is the birth of silver.

The Mysians were led by Chromis and the bird-seer Ennomos,
who despite his seercraft could not stop the black death-spirit,
but died at the hands of Aiakos's swift-foot grandson[5]
in the river, along with the other Trojans he cut down there.

The Phrygians' leaders were Phorkys and godlike Askanios
from distant Askania, eager to join the press of battle.

The Maiōnians were commanded by Mesthlēs and Antiphos,
Talaimenēs' two sons, whom the Gygaian lake-nymph bore,
and they led the Maiōnians whose homeland was under Tmōlos.

Nastēs commanded the Karians, men of barbarous speech,
who held Mīlētos, Mount Phthirēs with its dense woodlands,
Maiandros's streams, and Mykalē's rocky heights.
They had Amphimachos and Nastēs as their leaders,
Nastēs and Amphimachos, Nomiōn's splendid sons.
Amphimachos went off to war decked out in gold like a girl,
the young fool: that could not save him from a miserable end.
He died at the hands of the swift-foot grandson of Aiakos
in the river, and smart Achilles carried off the gold.

Sarpēdōn and noble Glaukos led the Lycians
from far-distant Lycia, from the eddying Xanthos river.

5. Achilles.

Book 3

When both sides had been marshalled, with their leaders,
the Trojans advanced with clamor and loud cries, like birds,
like the clamor of cranes that goes up high to heaven
when they're escaping winter storms and endless rain,
and, calling, fly towards the streams of Ocean,
to Pygmy warriors bringing death and destruction
down through the air, an offer of grim conflict.
But the Achaians came on in silence, breathing fury,
all determined to stand firm, each one by another.

As when on a mountaintop the south wind sheds thick mist,
no friend to the shepherds, but for a robber better than night,
and a man can see no further than he throws a stone,
just so from under their feet a thick dust cloud went up
as they marched on, making good speed across the plain.
When the two sides had come together, within close range,
out from the Trojans Aléxandros, divinely handsome, pranced,
a leopard skin on his shoulders, with a curved bow and a sword,
clutching a couple of javelins tipped with bronze,
and challenged the best of the Argives, any of them,
to meet him face to face, in fearsome combat.
Now when war-minded Menelaös first caught sight of him
emerging out of the crowd with his lengthy strides,
then, as a lion rejoices at finding, when ravenous,
some hefty carcass—an antlered stag or a wild goat—
and eat it he must, despite being set upon by swift
hunting dogs and tough youngsters, so Menelaös
delighted at seeing Aléxandros, divinely handsome,
with his own eyes, and, hot for revenge on the wrongdoer,
promptly sprang, fully armed, from his chariot to the ground.

But when Aléxandros, divinely handsome, saw him
show up in the front ranks, he was panic-stricken at heart,
and shrank back among his countrymen, evading fate;
and just as a man at the sight of a snake retreats
in some mountain glen, and trembling seizes his limbs,

and he backs away once more, and green pallor drains his cheeks,
so into the crowd of lordly Trojans Aléxandros,
divinely handsome, in fear of Atreus's son, now shrank back.

But Hektōr, seeing him, rebuked him with shaming words:
"Wretched Paris, so handsome, so mad for women, seducer,
I wish you had never been born or had died unmarried!
Yes, that I'd prefer: far better than being left with you
as this object of other men's ridicule and contempt.
Oh, they'll snigger aloud, indeed, will the long-haired Achaians,
and say, here's a leading man who gets to be champion
on good looks alone, without strength or courage in his heart.
Were you such a one when in your seafaring vessels
you sailed the deep, with the trusty comrades you'd mustered,
consorted with foreigners, brought back a beautiful woman
from a far-off land, the child of warrior spearmen,
a great grief to your father, your city, your whole nation:
a delight to our enemies, to yourself a cause of shame?
So will you not, then, confront the warlike Menelaös,
find out the kind of man whose lusty bedmate you've taken?
No help for you from the lyre, or the gifts of Aphrodītē,
or your hair or your good looks, when you're laid low in the dust.
The Trojans are arrant cowards: otherwise by now
you'd be wearing a shower of stones for all your evil deeds."

To him then Aléxandros, divinely handsome, replied:
"Hektōr, since you rebuke me justly, nor more than is proper—
always your heart is like the unwearying axe blade
struck through a beam by some craftsman who uses his skill
to shape a ship's timber, and it adds force to his own effort:
just so is the heart in your breast unshakable—do not
bring up against me the sweet gifts of golden Aphrodītē.
Not to be cast aside are the gods' illustrious gifts,
of whatever sort—even if no man would choose them.
But now, if you want me to play the warrior, to join battle,
then make the other Trojans sit down, and all the Achaians,
and set me there in the middle with warlike Menelaös
to battle it out for Helen and the sum of her possessions.
Whichever one of us wins, and proves himself the stronger,
let him claim the goods and the woman, and go off home with them.
You others must swear solemn oaths of friendship, and then

you can live on in rich-soiled Troy, while they sail home
to horse-pasturing Argos and Achaia's lovely women."

So he spoke, and Hektōr, delighted by his proposal,
went into the middle ground, held back the Trojans' ranks,
grasping his spear in the middle, and they all sat down.
Not so the long-haired Achaians, who chose him as their target,
aiming arrows at him, and showering him with stones,
till there came a loud shout from the lord of men, Agamemnōn:
"Argives, hold off! Don't shoot, you young Achaians!
He's trying to tell us something, is bright-helmeted Hektōr."

So he spoke: they held back from fighting, and all fell silent
readily, while Hektōr, between the armies, addressed them:
"Hear from me, you Trojans and you well-greaved Achaians,
the words of Aléxandros, over whom this strife has arisen.
What he asks is that all the Achaians and the rest of the Trojans
lay aside their fine arms and armor on the bountiful earth,
while he himself, in the middle, and warlike Menelaös
battle it out alone for Helen and all her possessions.
Whichever one wins, and proves himself the stronger,
let him claim the goods and the woman, and go off home with them,
and let the rest of us swear solemn oaths of friendship."

So he spoke: all fell hushed and silent. Menelaös
then spoke up among them, he of the great war cry:
"Hear me too now, since it's my heart that this agony
hurts worst. High time, I hold, for both sides to disengage,
Argives and Trojans: you've suffered troubles galore
on account of my quarrel since Aléxandros began it.
Whichever one of us two has death fixed as his destiny,
let him die; but you others should be parted without delay.
Fetch here two lambs, one white, and the other black,
for Earth and Sun, while for Zeus we provide a third.
And bring Priam the mighty hither, to swear an oath
in person—his sons being arrogant and faithless—
lest overstepping the mark someone void oaths that were sworn
by Zeus. Younger men's ideas are forever flighty,
but whatever an old man's involved in, he'll always look
forward and back as well, ensure what's best for both sides."

So he spoke, and both Achaians and Trojans were joyful,
hoping now for an end to warfare's wretchedness.
They held back their horses in line, stepped down from their chariots,
took off arms and armor, laid them out on the ground,
each close to the next man's, with little space between them.
Hektōr now dispatched two heralds to the city
to bring the lambs at once and to summon Priam.
Talthybios meanwhile lord Agamemnōn sent
back to the hollow ships, with orders to fetch a lamb
nor did he fail in obedience to noble Agamemnōn.

Now Iris went as a messenger to white-armed Helen
in the form of her husband's sister, the wife of Antēnōr's son,
her whom Antēnōr's son, the lordly Helikaōn,
had married: Laodikē, the fairest of Priam's daughters.
Helen she found in her quarters, weaving a great web,
double-sized, purple, including the many struggles
between horse-taming Trojans and bronze-corseleted Achaians
endured on her account at the hands of Arēs.
Standing close, swift-footed Iris thus addressed her:
"Come with me, dear sister, to see the wondrous conduct
of the horse-taming Trojans and bronze-corseleted Achaians!
They who before were waging, one side against the another,
grievous war in the plain, hearts bent on deadly battle,
now are sitting in silence, their conflict abandoned,
leaning on their shields, their lances planted beside them;
for Aléxandros now and the warlike Menelaös
with their long spears are about to battle it out over you,
and you'll be named the dear wife of whichever one's the victor."

With these words, the goddess put sweet yearning in Helen's
heart for her former husband, for her city and for her parents.
At once she put on a veil of white linen, and hurried
out of her private chamber, shedding round tears:
not alone, for two maidservants went along with her,
Aithrē, daughter of Pittheus, and ox-eyed Klyménē,
and quickly they then came to where the Skaian Gates were.

Now Priam and his companions—Pánthoös, Thymoitēs,
Lampos and Klytios, Hiketáōn, scion of Arēs,
Oukalegōn and Antēnōr, astute men both,

the community's elders—sat there above the Skaian Gates,
too old now for fighting, but still most valiant
talkers, like cicadas, that in the woodland,
aloft in trees, emit their fine sawing utterance:
such were the Trojans' leaders, perched on the ramparts.
When they saw Helen there on the ramparts, approaching,
softly they spoke winged words to one another:
"The Trojans and well-greaved Achaians cannot be blamed
for enduring woes so long over such a woman:
terribly like the deathless goddesses she is to look at.
Yet even so, being such, let her sail away, not linger
here to bring grief to us, and our children after us."
So they spoke. But Priam called out, summoning Helen:
"Come over here, dear child, and sit beside me,
to catch sight of your former husband, your friends and kinsmen—
in my eyes you're not to blame, I rather blame the gods
who stirred up against me this wretched Achaian war—
and to put a name for me to that huge warrior down there,
that Achaian leader, of such stature and so strong:
others there may be taller still by a head, and yet
so fine a man have I never set eyes on, nor one
so majestic in bearing—he looks to be of royal blood."

Then Helen, glorious among women, replied in these words:
"I revere you, my husband's dear father, I stand in awe of you!
A sorry death should have been my choice when I came here
following your son, abandoning marriage and family,
my growing daughter, my sweet loving girl companions.
But that's not how things turned out, and I'm worn with weeping.
Still, I'll answer the question you put to me: that man
is the son of Atreus, wide-ruling Agamemnōn,
a noble king, a strong spearman, and, formerly, brother-in-law
to me, the bitch—if all this really happened."
So she spoke, and the old man marveled, and said:
"Ah, happy son of Atreus, fortune's child, blest by the gods!
How many Achaian youths have been made subject to you!
Time was when I traveled to vine-rich Phrygia, where I viewed
Phrygian troops in great numbers, with their spirited horses,
the men of Otreus and of Mygdōn the godlike, at that time
encamped along the banks of the Sangarios river.

For I too, being their ally, was then numbered among them
that day when the Amazons came, a match for men—
yet not even they were as many as these sharp-eyed Achaians."

Next the old man's eye picked out Odysseus, and, pointing,
"Tell me, dear child," he asked, "about *that* one too—who is he?
By a head he's shorter than Agamemnōn, son of Atreus,
but looks broader in the chest and across the shoulders.
His gear he's left on the nurturing earth, but he himself
goes striding through the ranks like a ram. Yes, yes indeed,
it's a ram of which he reminds me, a thick-fleeced bellwether
prowling through a great flock of white sheep."

Then Helen,
scion of Zeus, made him the following answer:
"That man is the son of Laertēs, resourceful Odysseus,
who was reared in the land of Itháкē, a rugged dominion,
and knows all manner of wiles and sharp devices."
Then sagacious Antēnōr in turn addressed her:

"Lady,
what you just said is indeed the truth. He came here
once before, on a mission, did the noble Odysseus,
concerning yourself, along with warlike Menelaös:
it was I who entertained and welcomed them in my halls,
and took heed of the stature of both, and of their sharp devices.
Now when they joined the Trojans in assembly, and stood up,
broad-shouldered Menelaös was taller; but with both seated,
then Odysseus it was who looked the more majestic.
And when they began to weave their words and devices,
Menelaös certainly spoke with nimble fluency,
in few words, but with clarity, being no blabbermouth,
nor given to off-the-mark rambling, though he was the
younger.
But whenever resourceful Odysseus got up to speak,
he'd stand there looking down, eyes fixed on the ground,
not moving that staff of his either forward or back,
but clutching it, rooted firm, like some ignorant fellow—
you'd think him just a curmudgeon, the merest simpleton.
But when he let out that great voice from his chest—
the words resembling some driving wintry snowstorm—

then there was no living man that could match Odysseus,
and we no longer bothered to question his appearance."

Thirdly, looking at Aias, the old man asked: "Now who
is *that* Achaian out there, so sturdy and tall, outstripping
the other Argives in height by his head and broad shoulders?"

Then long-robed Helen, glorious among women, replied:
"That great giant is Aias, the Achaians' bulwark, and there
beyond him, among the Krētans, Idomeneus stands,
godlike, the Krētan captains all gathered round him.
Often he was the guest of warlike Menelaös
in our house, whenever he came across from Krētē.
All the others, too, I see now, every sharp-eyed Achaian—
I know them all well, could tell you all their names—
two only I cannot see, two high commanders,
Kastōr the horse breaker, Polydeukēs the skilled boxer,
brothers of mine, all born of the same mother.
Either they didn't come with them from lovely Lakedaimōn,
or, if they did make the trip in their seagoing vessels,
they're not willing now to join these men in combat
through fear of all the shame and reproaches leveled at me."

So she spoke; but them the nurturing earth already
held under in Lakedaimōn, their dear native land.

Now heralds brought through the city the gods' oath-offerings:
two lambs, with heartwarming wine, fruit of the tilled soil,
in a goatskin bag, while the herald Idaios carried
a shining wine bowl, together with golden goblets.
Standing by the old man, he called on him, saying: "Up now,
son of Laomedōn! You are summoned by the leaders
of the horse-breaking Trojans and the bronze-corseleted Achaians
to come down into the plain and swear a solemn pact.
For Menelaös the warlike and Aléxandros are to do battle
with long spears over the woman; and whichever of them wins,
to him will go both the woman and all her possessions.
The rest must swear solemn oaths of friendship, and then
we can live on in rich-soiled Troy, while they sail home
to horse-pasturing Argos and Achaia's lovely women."

So he spoke. The old man shivered, but ordered his comrades
to yoke the horses, and they quickly obeyed him.
Then Priam mounted and gathered the reins, and Antēnōr
mounted the elegant chariot by his side, and together
they drove the swift horses out through the Skaian gates to the plain.

When they arrived among the Trojans and the Achaians,
they left the horses, stepped down on the nurturing earth,
and took their place amid them, between Trojans and Achaians.
Then at once there sprang up Agamemnōn, lord of men,
and resourceful Odysseus, while the noble heralds brought in
the victims for the gods' oaths, poured wine in the mixing bowl,
and water over the hands of the kings. Then Atreus's son
drew out with his hand the knife he always had by him,
hanging beside his sword's great sheath, and with it
cut hairs from the heads of the lambs. These hairs the heralds
gave out to the Trojan and the Achaian nobles. For them
Atreus's son now prayed aloud, both arms upraised:
"Zeus, Father, ruling from Ida, most glorious, greatest,
and you, Sun, the all-seeing, all-hearing, and you
rivers and earth, and you in the underworld who take
vengeance on men deceased who have sworn false oaths—
be you our witnesses, watch over these solemn pledges!
If Aléxandros should happen to kill Menelaös, then
let him have and keep Helen, with all her possessions,
while we sail away in our seafaring vessels. But should it
befall that fair-haired Menelaös kill Aléxandros, then
the Trojans must give back Helen and all her possessions,
and pay to the Argives such recompense as is fitting
and will stay in the minds of men in time hereafter.
But if Priam and Priam's sons should not prove willing
to pay recompense to us when Aléxandros is fallen,
then will I still fight on for such retribution,
remaining here until I reach an end of warfare."

So saying, he cut the lambs' throats with the pitiless bronze,
and dropped them on the ground, still gasping, their life's breath
ebbing away, now the bronze had taken their strength.
Then drawing wine from the bowl they poured it into the cups,
and made their prayers to the gods who live for ever,
and such words would one of them, Achaian or Trojan, utter:

"Zeus, greatest, most glorious, and you other immortal gods,
whichever side first does violence to these oaths we swear,
may their brains be spilled on the ground as is this wine,
theirs and their children's, may their wives be had by others."

So they spoke, but not yet would Kronos's son grant their prayers.
Then the scion of Dardanos, Priam, addressed them in these words:
"Now hear me, all you Trojans, all you well-greaved Achaians!
For my part, I'm going back now to windy Ilion—
no way could I bring myself to watch my own dear son
battling it out hand to hand with warlike Menelaös.
But Zeus, I suppose, must know, and the other deathless gods,
for which of these two the doom of death is decreed."

So he, the godlike mortal, put the lambs in his chariot,
climbed aboard himself, and gathered the reins,
and Antēnōr boarded the elegant chariot beside him,
and the two set off back into Ilion together.

Now Hektōr, Priam's son, and noble Achilles
first measured out an arena, and next took lots,
put them in a bronze helmet, and shook them to decide
which of the two should first let fly his spear of bronze.
Then the troops prayed together, lifting their hands to the gods,
and words such as these would some Achaian or Trojan utter:
"Zeus, Father, ruling from Ida, most glorious, greatest,
whichever one it was laid these burdens on both sides,
grant that he perish and enter the house of Hādēs;
but for us let there be friendship and binding oaths."

So they spoke. Great Hektōr, bright-helmeted, shook the lots,
face turned away: out jumped the lot of Paris.
The troops now sat down in rows, each grouped where for each
his high-stepping horses waited beside his inlaid armor.[1]
And now noble Aléxandros, fair-haired Helen's husband,
moved to put on round his shoulders his own fine armor.

---

1. This line has not occasioned as much comment as it should. Clearly, the audience is the whole army, not just the aristocratic warriors. Equally clearly, the ordinary ranks did not have horses, chariots, and expensive armor. What seems likely is that each company sat close to their captain's chariot, using it as a marker for location.

The greaves first of all he fastened about his shins—
finely made, and fitted with silver ankle pieces.
Next, to cover his chest, he put on the corselet
of his brother Lykaōn, refitted for his personal use.
About his shoulders he slung the silver-studded sword
of bronze; then came the shield, both large and sturdy,
and on his valiant head he set his well-wrought helmet
with its horsehair crest's plumes nodding terribly above him,
and took a stout spear, well fitted to his grasp,
while warlike Menelaōs likewise donned his battle gear.

So when they were armed, each on his side of the throng,
they advanced to the mid-space between Trojans and Achaians,
eyeing one another fiercely. Those watching were amazed,
both Trojans, breakers of horses, and well-greaved Achaians,
as they came to close quarters in the marked-out arena,
brandishing their spears, each one full of rage at the other.
Aléxandros first let fly his far-shadowing spear and struck
Atreus's son's shield, well-balanced on every side;
but the bronze spear did not break through, its point was turned
in the shield's thickness. At him now charged, spear ready,
Atreus's son Menelaös, with this prayer to Zeus the Father:
"Zeus, Lord, grant me revenge on this man who did me wrong—
the noble Aléxandros! Crush him beneath my hands,
so that any man, even of those born long hereafter,
may shrink from wronging the host who offers him friendship."

He spoke, then poised his far-shadowing spear and threw it
and struck Priam's son's shield, well-balanced on every side.
Right through the shining shield drove the heavy spear,
and through the richly worked corselet it made its way:
straight on, close in by his ribs the spear ripped through his tunic,
but he leaned to one side and escaped the black death-spirit.
Then the son of Atreus, drawing his silver-studded sword,
reached up high and struck down at the helmet's boss; but on it
the sword broke in three or four pieces, escaped from his hand,
so that Atreus's son cried out, eyes raised to heaven:
"Zeus, Father, no other god is more malicious than you!
I thought I would get my revenge for Aléxandros's wrongdoing;
instead my sword broke in my hands, while my spear
flew from my grasp in vain—I failed to hit him."

With that,
he sprang, grabbed Paris's crested helmet, jerked him round,
and was hauling him off towards the well-greaved Achaians,
choking on the sewn strap round his soft throat that was fixed
tightly under his chin to hold the helmet steady.
And he'd have dragged Paris away, won glory past measure,
had not Aphrodītē, Zeus's sharp-eyed daughter, noticed,
and snapped the strap—from the hide of a slaughtered bull!—
so that the empty helmet came away in his strong hand.
Among the well-greaved Achaians the hero then whirled
and tossed it, to be retrieved by his trusty companions,
while he leapt back, in a raging passion to kill
with his bronze spear. But Aphrodītē wafted Paris away,
easily, as a god can, veiled him in a dense mist,
set him down in his own fragrant bedchamber, then herself
went off to summon Helen. Her she encountered
on the high rampart, and round her a throng of Trojan ladies.
She caught hold of Helen's scented robe, and tugged it,
speaking to her in the likeness of an aged woman,
a wool dresser, who, when Helen still lived in Lakedaimōn,
worked up fine wool for her, and was one she dearly loved.
It was in her semblance that Aphrodītē addressed her:
"Come, now: Aléxandros is calling for you to go home!
He's there, in his bedchamber, on that inlaid bed, resplendent—
so handsome, such fine clothes—you wouldn't think
he'd just come from fighting a man, but was off to a dance,
or had just finished dancing, and was sitting there—"

So she spoke
and quickened the heart of Helen in her bosom.
On recognizing the goddess—her elegant neck,
her ravishing breasts and bright-gleaming eyes—although
amazed, Helen now spoke out, addressed her as herself:
"Strange goddess, why are you set on deceiving me like this?
Will you drive me still further afield, to some teeming city—
in Phrygia maybe, or in charming Maiōnia—
where some new mortal man may have caught your fancy,
just because Menelaös has beaten godlike Aléxandros,
and is minded to take hateful me back home again?
Is that why you've come here now, heart brimming with guile?

You go, then, sit at his side, renounce the paths of the gods,
and nevermore let your feet return you to Olympos,
but always just worry about him, take care of *him*,
till he makes you his wedded wife—or maybe his slave girl!
I'm not going back there—it would be too shameful—
to lie in that man's bed: all the women of Troy thereafter
would blame me for it. I have measureless sorrows at heart."

To her then in wrath bright Aphrodītē made answer:
"Don't provoke me, you stubborn woman, lest I abandon you
in my rage, come to hate you as terribly as I now love you,
and work you grim trouble, caught in the middle between
Trojans and Danaäns: a nasty end you'd have then."

So she spoke, and Helen, Zeus's scion, shivered in fear,
and went, veiling her face behind her shining mantle, silent,
unseen by the Trojan ladies, the goddess leading.
When they came to Aléxandros's richly elegant abode,
the handmaidens quickly turned back to their tasks, while she,
queen among women, went up to her high-roofed chamber.
Aphrodītē, that laughter-lover, now fetched a chair for her—
she, a goddess!—and set it in front of Aléxandros.
Then Helen, scion of Zeus the aegis-bearer, sat down
and with eyes averted, thus reproved her husband:
"So you're back from the fight. I'd rather you had died there,
beaten by the strong man who at one time was my husband.
Time was when you vaunted yourself against warlike Menelaös—
you were the better man, with stronger hands, truer spear!
Well, off with you then, go challenge warlike Menelaös
to duel with you once more! But no, I must now require you
to stop this, and not to face the fair-haired Menelaös
man to man, or do battle with him, or risk a fight,
fool that you are, lest you fall a quick prey to his spear."

Then Paris in these words made answer to her:
"Woman, don't chide my heart with such harsh reproofs.
This time Menelaös had Athēnē's help, and beat me,
but another time I shall win: there are gods on our side too.
But now come, let's to bed, and enjoy some lovemaking,
for never has passion so enveloped my senses—not even
when I first snatched you away from lovely Lakedaimōn,

and sailed off, taking you, on our seagoing vessels,
and on the island of Kranaë bedded you lovingly—
as now I want you, and sweet desire takes possession of me."

This said, he led the way bedwards. His wife went with him.

So those two lay down together on the inlaid bedstead,
But Atreus's son like a wild beast raged through the ranks,
hoping to catch a glimpse of Aléxandros the godlike;
but no one, whether Trojan or one of the far-famed allies,
could point out Aléxandros to warlike Menelaös—
nor, had he been seen, would they have kept him hidden
out of love, for all of them hated him like black death.
Then there spoke up among them the lord of men, Agamemnōn:
"Hear me, Trojans, Dardanians, allies! Victory, plainly,
must go to Menelaös, the warlike! Do you now, therefore,
surrender Helen, together with all her possessions,
and deliver to us such recompense as is fitting,
and will stay in the minds of men in time hereafter."

So spoke Atreus's son, and all the Achaians applauded.

Book 4

The gods, seated by Zeus, were gathered together
on the golden floor, and among them the lady Hēbē
was pouring them nectar, and they with their golden cups
pledged one another while gazing out at the Trojans' city.
Now the son of Kronos was minded to irritate Hērē
with taunting remarks, and said, speaking deviously:
"Two goddesses, no less, Menelaös has as his helpers—
Hērē of Argos and Athēnē the Defender.
But they sit here at a distance, getting enjoyment only
as onlookers, whereas Aphrodītē, lover of laughter,
stands by *her* man, protects him from the death spirits—
indeed, just lately she saved him when he thought he'd die!
Still, the victory must go to warlike Menelaös,
so we should be figuring out how these matters shall be:
are we once more to stir up vile warfare and grim fighting,
or rather to bring about friendship between the two sides?
If this last choice should turn out welcome and pleasant to all,
then might King Priam's city remain inhabited,
and Menelaös go home, taking Argive Helen with him."

So he spoke, but Athēnē and Hērē muttered against him,
sitting side by side, planning trouble for the Trojans.
Athēnē kept quiet now, said nothing openly,
though angry with Zeus her father, gripped by wild resentment;
but Hērē's breast could not contain her fury. She said:
"Most dread son of Kronos, what's this you're telling us?
How can you mean to void and nullify all my labor—
the sweat that I sweated in toil, the exhaustion of my horses
as I gathered the troops, bringing trouble to Priam and his sons?
Do this, but we'll not all endorse it: we, the other gods!"

Deeply angered, to her cloud-gatherer Zeus made answer:
"Are you mad? What great harm have Priam and Priam's sons
ever done you, to make you rage endlessly
for Ilion, that well-built citadel, to be destroyed?
Only if you were to penetrate their gates and lofty ramparts,

and devour Priam raw, him and all his sons, together
with every other Trojan, would you finally glut your anger!
Act as you like, but don't let this quarrel in future
become a great cause of dissension between us two.
One other thing I will tell you, and you take it to heart:
Whenever I, too, am minded to bring down a city,
and choose one in which the men are your special favorites,
do nothing to thwart my anger, but let me be,
now I'm willing to yield to you—though with unwilling heart,
since of all cities beneath the sun and starry heavens
in which men bred on earth maintain their dwellings,
sacred Ilion has ever been most honored in my heart,
and Priam, lord of the fine ash spear, and Priam's people.
For never yet has my altar lacked its share of the feasting,
neither libations nor savor, the honor that's due to us."

To him then spoke in answer the ox-eyed lady Hērē:
"Three cities there are that I love far above all others:
Argos and Sparta and wide-streeted Mykēnai:
Lay these waste whenever your heart is stirred against them!
I'm not standing as their defender, I don't grudge them to you.
For suppose I was reluctant, didn't want them destroyed,
My reluctance would be useless, since you're far the stronger.
Yet my toil also must not be made of no account:
I too am a god, of the same descent as yourself,
sired as the first of his daughters by devious Kronos—
on two counts, since I'm the oldest, and because I'm known
as your consort, while you rule over all the immortals.
But on this let us both yield, each one to the other,
I to you, you to me: then the rest of the immortal
gods will follow our lead. So, act now, order Athēnē
to enter the fearful conflict between Trojans and Achaians
and try to arrange that the Trojans are first, and in defiance
of their sworn oaths, to do harm to the arrogant Achaians."

So she spoke, and the Father of men and gods did not
refuse her, but straight away spoke winged words to Athēnē:
"Go quickly down to the hosts of the Trojans and Achaians,
and try to arrange that the Trojans are first, and in defiance
of their sworn oaths, to do harm to the arrogant Achaians."

So saying he urged on Athēnē—already eager to go—
and down she darted from the heights of Olympos.
As the son of devious Kronos dispatches a meteor
to be a portent for sailors or a widespread encampment
of troops—a bright one, and a trail of sparks flies from it—
like that as she swooped to earth was Pallas Athēnē.
She landed between the lines, amazing those who saw her,
both Trojan horse breakers and well-greaved Achaians,
and thus would a man exclaim, turning to his neighbor:
"Surely once more evil warfare and the dread noise of battle
will return—unless now friendship's being set between the two sides
by Zeus, long since the dispenser of warfare to mortals."

Such was the talk among Achaians and Trojans. But she
came down into the thick of the Trojans in the likeness
of a man, Laodokos, Antēnōr's son, a strong spearman,
looking for godlike Pandaros, hoping to find him—
and find him she did, the son of Lykaōn, noble, mighty,
standing there, and around him the mighty ranks of shield-bearing
troops that had followed with him from the streams of Aisēpos.
Then, standing close, she addressed him with winged words:
"Will you do now what I ask you, skilled son of Lykaōn?
Would you dare to let fly a swift shaft at Menelaös?
Among all the Trojans you'd reap great gratitude and renown,
and of them most in the eyes of the prince Aléxandros.
From him you, above all others, would get the richest gifts
if he were to see Menelaös, Atreus's warlike scion,
felled by your arrow, and laid on the grievous funeral pyre!
So come now, shoot that arrow at glorious Menelaös,
and vow to Apollo, the wolf-born, the famous archer,
a splendid rich offering consisting of first-born lambs
when you get back to sacred Zeleia, your city."

So Athēnē spoke,
and thus persuaded the wits of this witless man. At once
he took out his polished bow, made from the horns
of a wild goat he'd once shot beneath the breastbone,
watching from cover as it trotted out from the rocks,
then hit in the chest: it fell back among the boulders.
The horns on its head had grown to sixteen palms in length,
and these a craftsman in horn had worked and fitted together,

smoothing them well overall, and added a golden tip.
This bow he now grounded firmly, bent it and strung it,
his worthy companions sheltering him with their shields
in case the Achaians' warlike sons might try to rush him
before Menelaös, Atreus's warlike son, was hit.
Now he opened his quiver's lid, took out an arrow,
brand-new, winged, a vehicle for dark anguish.
Quickly he settled this bitter shaft to the bowstring,
made his vow to Apollo, the wolf-born, the famous archer,
of a splendid rich offering of first-born lambs
when he got back home to his city of sacred Zeleia,
then drew, clutching notched arrow and ox's sinew together,
brought the string back to his nipple, to the bow the iron arrowhead.
And when he'd drawn the great bow into a curve,
it twanged, the bowstring sang loud, the sharp arrow leapt,
eager to speed its way through the throng.

Yet even now,
Menelaös, the blessed gods, the immortals, did not forget you.
First among them was Zeus's daughter, the spoil bringer,[1]
who stood before you, diverted the piercing missile,
swept it just clear of your flesh—just as a mother
will swat flies away from her child that's bedded in sweet sleep—
and turned it, herself, to where the golden buckles
of the baldric were fastened, and the corselet was folded double.
Into the fitted baldric the bitter arrow struck,
right through the baldric's decorations it was driven,
right through the finely wrought corselet it forced its way,
and the kilted guard he wore to shield his flesh, a defense
against missiles, his chief protection—through that too it sped.
The arrow scraped skin and flesh as it passed, and at once
dark blood trickled down from the wound it made.

As when
some woman—perhaps a Maiōnian or a Karian—
stains ivory with purple, to make a cheek piece for horses,
and it lies in a storeroom, and many the riders who long

1. This is Athēnē: the epithet "spoil bringer" (ἀγελείη, *ageleiē*) is (like so many Homeric epithets) of dubious meaning: most often interpreted as the bringer, driver, or carrier of spoil, it was also sometimes thought to mean "war leader."

to flaunt it, but there it lies, a prince's pleasure—
his horse's adornment and its driver's source of pride—
just so, Menelaös, were your shapely thighs stained with blood:
they, and your shins, and the fine ankles beneath them.

He shuddered then, did the lord of men, Agamemnōn,
when he saw the dark blood trickling down from the wound;
and Menelaös himself, the warlike, likewise shuddered.[2]
But when he saw that the barbs and their binding were still
clear of the flesh, the spirit within his breast recovered.
With a deep groan, the lord Agamemnōn spoke among his comrades,
Menelaös's hand in his, and they groaned in sympathy:
"Dear brother, it was for your death, then, that I swore this oath,
sending you out, alone, before the Achaians, to battle
the Trojans, since they have now shot you, and trampled down
the oaths they swore. Yet an oath's not in vain—the lambs' blood,
the unmixed libations, the handclasps in which we put our trust.
Though the Olympian may not bring instant retribution,
bring it in time he will. Men pay heavily for their atonement—
with their own heads, through their wives, or through their children.
For this I know full well, in my heart and in my mind:
A day will come when sacred Ilion will perish,
with Priam, lord of the fine ash spear, and Priam's people;
and Zeus, high-throned son of Kronos, the sky dweller,
will, in fury at such deceit, shake his black-cloud aegis
over them all. These matters will not fail of fulfillment.
But dreadful sorrow for you will be mine, Menelaös my brother,
if you die now, and fulfil your lifetime's destiny;
and a contemptible creature I'd be, back in thirsty Argos,
for at once the Achaians' minds will turn to their native land,
and we'd be leaving the Trojans and Priam a cause for boasting
in Argive Helen! The plowland will rot your bones
as you lie here in Troy, your mission unaccomplished,
and one of the arrogant Trojans will thus declare,
as he capers upon the grave mound of glorious Menelaös:

2. It has long been wondered why both Menelaös and Agamemnōn should have been so alarmed by what was clearly a very superficial wound. Gilbert Murray was almost certainly right when he argued years ago in *The Rise of the Greek Epic* (129–30) that the passage looked back to an era when poisoned arrows were a commonplace (cf. line 218, where Machaōn sucks blood from the wound), being banned, by general agreement, from warfare only later (like lethal gas after World War I).

'So may Agamemnōn's anger always find fulfillment,
as now all in vain he has brought here his host of Achaians,
and gone back home to his own dear native country
with empty ships, and left brave Menelaös behind.'
Thus someone will speak: that day let the wide earth gape for me."

But fair-haired Menelaös spoke encouragingly to him:
"Take heart—and do not frighten the Achaian rank and file!
Not in any fatal spot did the sharp shaft lodge: before that
my gleaming baldric stopped it, and under that the leather
apron and kilted guard that the coppersmiths armored for me."

In answer to him then spoke the lord Agamemnōn:
"Indeed may it be so, dear brother, dear Menelaös!
A physician will handle your wound, will spread upon it
medicinal herbs to relieve you of your dark pains."

That said,
he then addressed Talthybios, the sacred herald:
"Talthybios, go with all speed, summon Machâōn here,
the mortal son of Asklēpios, peerless healer,
to see to Menelaös, Atreus's warlike son,
whom someone has shot and hit—an expert archer,
some Trojan or Lycian: glory for him, for us sorrow."

So he spoke: the herald heard, and did not disregard him,
but went straight off through the well-greaved Achaians' ranks,
looking out for the hero Machâōn. He found him standing
at ease, all around him the strong ranks of shield-bearing troops
who had accompanied him all the way from horse-pasturing Trikka.
So he approached, and addressed him with winged words:
"Up with you, son of Asklēpios! Lord Agamemnōn needs you
to attend to Menelaös, the warlike son of Atreus,
whom someone has shot and hit—an expert archer,
some Trojan or Lycian: glory for him, for us sorrow."

So he spoke, and stirred up the spirit in Machâōn's breast,
and they set off through the wide camp of the Achaian troops.
When they arrived at the place where fair-haired Menelaös
lay wounded, with all the chieftains in a circle around him,
Machâōn, the godlike mortal, came in among them,
and at once pulled out the arrow through the fitted belt, so that,

as it was drawn through, its sharp barbs broke off backwards.
Then he undid the gleaming baldric, and beneath it the leather
apron and kilted guard that the coppersmiths had armored,
and when he saw the wound that the bitter arrow had made,
he sucked out the blood, with skill applied the healing herbs
that Cheirōn had once given to his father in friendship.

While they were busy around Menelaös of the great war cry,
the ranks of the shield-bearing Trojans began to advance,
so they armed themselves once more, minds reverting to battle.

Then you would not have seen illustrious Agamemnōn
asleep, or shrinking in fear, or unwilling to join battle,
but most eager for the conflict that brings men honor.
His horses he left behind, with his bronze-inlaid chariot,
and these fierce-breathed steeds were held back by his charioteer,
Eurymedōn, son of Peiraios's son Ptolemaios,
with strict instructions to have them on hand for whenever
fatigue might assail his limbs while marshalling so many.
Out there on foot he worked his way through the ranks:
those of the fleet-horsed Danaäns that he saw as hot for the fray
he'd approach, and give them words of rousing encouragement:
"Argives, never relax that fighting spirit of yours!
Zeus, the Father, will lend no support to liars—
Those who first did violence in defiance of their oaths,
surely their tender flesh will be eaten by vultures—yes,
and we shall carry off their dear wives and little children
in our vessels, as soon as we've captured their citadel."

But any he saw holding back from hateful warfare,
these he would strongly reprove with indignant words:
"You contemptible arrow-brave Argives, have you no shame?
Standing there in a dumbstruck daze, like a bunch of fawns,
exhausted after scampering over some lengthy plain,
that stop, stock-still, with no spark of courage left in them!
That's you, stuck in a stupor, away from the fighting—
maybe you're waiting until the Trojans reach your fine-sterned
vessels, hauled up here on the shore of the grey sea?
Or is it to see if Kronos's son will stretch his arm over you?"

So, acting the lord, he ranged through the army's ranks,
and came, as he went through the mass of troops, to the Krētans.

They were arming for battle around doughty Idomeneus,
and Idomeneus stood in the forefront, brave as a wild boar,
while Mērionēs rallied the rearguard companies.
Seeing them, Agamemnōn, the lord of men, rejoiced,
and at once greeted Idomeneus with winning words:
"Idomeneus, you I do honor above all the swift-horsed Danaäns,
whether it be in warfare or any other business,
or indeed at the feast, when the elders' fire-bright wine
is mixed in the bowl by the chief men of the Argives.
For though all the other long-haired Achaians drink
their allotted portion, your cup stands always full,
just as mine does, to drink whenever the spirit moves you.
Now rouse up for battle, like the man you claim you once were!'

To him then Idomeneus, the Krētans' leader, replied:
"Son of Atreus, to you I shall be a trusty comrade
just as I promised and swore, from the very beginning.
But now urge on all the other long-haired Achaians,
so we can join battle the soonest! The Trojans are forsworn,
and for them hereafter there shall be death and sorrow:
by breaking their oath they were the first offenders."

So he spoke, and Atreus's son moved on, gladdened at heart,
and came to the two named Aias as he strode through the throng:
they were arming, and backed by a cloud of troops. As when
from his lookout point a goatherd perceives a cloud
approaching across the deep, blown by the west wind,
and to him, being at a distance, it looks blacker than pitch
as it passes over the deep, bringing a mighty tempest,
and he shrinks at the sight of it, and drives his flock to a cave—
just so, beside both Aiases, the dark and serried ranks
of vigorous youths, Zeus's nurslings, were on the march
into deadly battle, all bristling with shields and spears.
Seeing them, the lord Agamemnōn rejoiced in his heart.
and he then addressed them, speaking with winged words:
"You two Aiases, leaders of bronze-corseleted Achaians,
to you—out of place to urge you—I give no orders: you
yourselves are exhorting your men to battle fiercely!
If only—by Zeus the Father, by Athēnē and Apollo!—
such a spirit might be engendered in every man's heart,

then would King Priam's city soon totter to its fall,
stormed and sacked at our hands."

That said, he left them there
and went on his way in search of others; and next
he came upon Nestōr, the Pylians' lucid spokesman,
arraying his comrades and urging them on to battle,
those led by tall Pelagōn and Alastōr and Chromios,
and lord Haimōn, and Bias, the shepherd of his people.
The mounted fighters he set in front, with their horses and chariots,
and behind them, in large numbers, the valiant foot soldiers,
to be a strong wall of battle. The cowards he drove to the middle,
so that all, even though unwilling, would be forced to fight.
He first briefed the mounted fighters, giving them orders
to rein in their horses and not get entangled with the masses:
"And let no man, trusting in his horsemanship and valor,
be eager to fight with the Trojans alone, in front of the rest—
but don't retreat either: that way you'll be less effective!
When a man in his chariot comes within range of an enemy's, then
let him lunge with his spear, for that's the best way by far—
it's how men in the olden days would storm cities and ramparts,
holding this purpose and spirit within their hearts."

So thus
the old man urged them on, from his knowledge of wars long past;
and at the sight he rejoiced, did the lord Agamemnōn,
and addressed him as follows, uttering winged words:
"Old sir, if only, like the heart in your breast, so might
your knees still serve you, your strength remain unimpaired!
But age, ineluctable, weighs on you: how I wish some other
warrior had your years, and you were among the youths!"

Nestōr, Gerēnian horseman, to him made answer:
"Son of Atreus, I too most heartily wish I still had
the strength that was mine the day I slew noble Ereuthaliōn!
But no way do the gods grant mortals all things at once—
Then I was young, but now old age is my companion.
Even so, I shall go round the mounted fighters, instruct them
with words of counsel: that is an old man's right.
The wielding of spears belongs to a later generation,
men younger than me, men with confidence in their strength."

So he spoke, and Atreus's son moved on, gladdened at heart,
and found Peteos's son Menestheus, whipper of horses,
standing there, and around him the Athenians, war-cry masters,
and close by there stood resourceful Odysseus, and with him
the ranks of the Kephallēnians—no weaklings they—
were waiting: not yet had their forces heard the war cry,
since only now were the ranks of Achaians and horse-breaking
  Trojans
stirring themselves to action. So they stood there, idle,
till some other Achaian body should move forward,
make a charge at the Trojans, get the battle started.
Seeing these drew a rebuke from the lord of men, Agamemnōn,
so that he spoke out, addressed them with winged words:
"You there, son of King Peteos, Zeus's nursling,
and you, the master deceiver, mind set on crafty profit!
Why do you hang back nervously, waiting upon others?
You two should be out up front there with the foremost troops,
ready to play your part in the fiery conflict! You're
always the first to hear my call to the feasting
when we Achaians make ready a dinner for the elders:
then you're happy enough to eat roast meat, and swill
honey-sweet wine by the cupful, as long as you wish—but now
you'd cheerfully stand by and watch, were there ten Achaian
companies battling before you with the pitiless bronze."

With a dark glance resourceful Odysseus answered: "Son
of Atreus, what's this talk that's escaped the barrier of your teeth?
How can you say that we hold back from fighting whenever
we Achaians make bitter war on the horse-breaker Trojans?
You'll see—if you care to, if you have the slightest interest—
Tēlemachos's dear father engaged with the front-line fighters
of these same horse-breaker Trojans. Your words are empty wind."

To this the lord Agamemnōn answered, smiling at him
as he took in his indignation, unsaying the words he'd uttered:
"Son of Laertēs, scion of Zeus, resourceful Odysseus!
Mine was no heavy rebuke, nor am I giving you orders:
Full well I know that the spirit within your breast
harbors friendly thoughts: you think the same way that I do.
Come then, we'll make things right later, if any wrong word
has been uttered—and may the gods reduce all this to nothing!"

So saying, he left them there, and went in search of others,
and came upon Tydeus's son, bold-hearted Diomēdēs,
standing there by his horses and dovetailed chariots,
with Sthenelos, son of Kapaneus, at his side. The sight of him
once more drew a scolding from the lord of men, Agamemnōn,
so that he spoke out, addressed him with winged words:
"Now then, you son of Tydeus, that fierce horse breaker,
why are you skulking down here, one eye on the battlefront?
It wasn't Tydeus's way to shrink back thus: no, rather
he'd be far in front of his comrades, embattled with the foe!
So they tell it who saw him in action: myself, I neither
met him nor saw him; still, they say he excelled all others.
Now once—as guest, not as enemy—he visited Mykēnai
with godlike Polyneikēs, recruiting troops. At that time
they were campaigning against the sacred walls of Thēbē,
and urgently begged to be given some first-class allies.
Our people were ready to help them, had agreed to the request,
but Zeus changed their hearts with a show of ill-omened signs.
So they left, and when they'd got some distance on their way
they came to the reed-thick Asōpos with its grassy banks,
and from there the Achaians sent Tydeus ahead with a message.
So he set off, and found a large group of Kadmeians
banqueting in the house of that mighty force Eteoklēs.
Now, stranger though he was there, Tydeus the charioteer
had no fear at being alone in this crowd of Kadmeians,
whom he challenged to trials of strength, and easily beat
every man jack of them, such a help was Athēnē to him.
But these Kadmeian horse whippers then got furious,
and on his way back they ambushed him in strength—
fifty young fighting men, and a couple to lead them:
Haimōn's son Maiōn, a man like the immortals,
and Autophonos's son, the war veteran Polyphontēs.
But on these too Tydeus let loose an unseemly fate:
he slew the lot, spared one only to go back home again—
Maiōn, in obedience to the gods' signs. Such a man
was Aitōlian Tydeus. Yet the son he sired could not
match him in battle, though a better maker of speeches."

So he spoke, and not one word did mighty Diomēdēs
say in reply, from respect for his honored king's rebuke.

But the son of renowned Kapaneus made this reply:
"Son of Atreus, don't lie when you know how to tell the truth!
We two do call ourselves far better men than our fathers,
seeing we captured the stronghold of seven-gated Thēbē
when we'd brought a lesser force against their stronger ramparts,
trusting in the gods' omens and the support of Zeus—although
it was through their own reckless folly that they perished.
So, never rank our fathers as equal in honor to us."

But to him, with an angry glance, mighty Diomēdēs said:
"Friend, sit down, be silent, and listen to what I tell you:
I do not fault Agamemnōn, the shepherd of the people,
for urging the well-greaved Achaians into battle, since great
honor will come to him should it happen that the Achaians
slaughter the Trojans, and take sacred Ilion—but
great grief, should it be the Achaians who are slaughtered.
So come, let us two also reclaim our fighting spirit!"
With that he sprang, armed and armored, from his chariot to
    the ground.
Fearful the clash of bronze on the king's chest as he moved:
Even the stoutest heart would have quailed in terror at it.

As when on an echoing shoreline the waves of the sea
crash down one after the other, driven on by the west wind—
first cresting out in deep water, but then they break
on the beach with a thunderous roar, and around the headlands
surge, arch, and peak, spew out the frothing brine:
so then, one after the other, the Danäan companies moved
unendingly into battle. Each leader issued the order
to his own troops; the rest marched on in silence. You'd think
the vast numbers following had no voice in their breasts—
so speechless they were, so scared of their captains—while on them
glinted the fine-wrought armor in which they marched.
But the Trojans—like countless ewes in a rich man's steading
that stand and wait to be eased of their white milk, and keep up
a ceaseless bleat as they hear the cries of their lambs—
so the Trojans' clamor went up through their massed forces,
for they had no speech in common, no single language,
but a mixture of tongues, men drafted from many regions.
They were spurred on by Arēs, their foes by grey-eyed Athēnē,

and Terror and Panic, and Strife—so incessantly eager,
the sister and comrade of man-slaying Arēs: at first
she rears her crest only a little, but very soon
her head is set in the heavens while she walks the earth.
She it now was that spread evil contention in their midst
as she passed through the massed ranks, increasing men's
agony.

When they had come to one place, and were met together,
buckler slammed against buckler, spears thrust, the bronze-
clad rage
of warriors pressed the attack, their bossed shields ground
hard each upon the other, and a mighty hubbub went up.
There were groans and triumphant shouts, from warriors killing
or being killed, while the earth ran wet with blood.
As when in winter two mountain torrents discharge
a massive body of water down from their mighty springs
to where the two streambeds meet in some hollow ravine,
and far off in the mountains the herdsman hears their thunder:
so from those met in battle came shouts of triumph and anguish.

Antilochos was the first to take down an armored Trojan,
a seasoned front-line fighter, Thalysios's son Echepōlos:
his first shot struck the boss of his horsehair-crested helmet
and stuck in his forehead: right through into the bone
the bronze spear point pierced. Darkness shrouded his eyes,
and he crashed like a tower amid the grind of battle.
When he fell, the lord Elephēnōr caught hold of his feet—
Chalkōdōn's son, who led the high-spirited Abantes—
and was dragging him out from the missiles, all too eager
to strip off his armor. This effort lasted an instant only,
for as he was lugging the corpse high-spirited Agēnōr
saw him stoop, and where his ribs were exposed beyond the shield
struck home with a bronze-tipped spear, and loosened his limbs.
So the vital breath left him, and a hard-fought tussle took place
between Achaians and Trojans over his corpse: like wolves
they sprang one at another, and fighter battered fighter.

There Telamōnian Aias felled Anthēmiōn's young son,
a bachelor in his prime, Simoeisios, whom his mother
bore on her way down from Ida, by the banks of the Simoeis,

having gone up there with her parents to see to their flocks.
Hence his name, Simoeisios; yet he never repaid
his parents the cost of his rearing—too brief his life span,
eclipsed by a spear thrust he took from high-spirited Aias.
Striding out in front, he was hit in the chest, above the right
nipple: clean through his shoulder the bronze spear drove,
and he slumped to the ground in the dust, like a black poplar
that's grown in the bottom land of a great marsh meadow:
smooth, except for the branches sprouting from its top,
which a wheelwright has felled with his axe of gleaming iron
to bend into a wheel rim for an elegant chariot,
and it lies there drying out by the riverbank. Such was
the slaying of Anthemios's son Simoeisios by Aias,
scion of Zeus. At whom, then, bright-corseleted Antiphos,
Priam's son, aimed through the throng with his knife-sharp spear,
and missed; but struck Leukos, Odysseus's trusty comrade,
full in the groin, as he was dragging away the corpse:
he collapsed on it, and the body slipped from his grasp.
This killing left Odysseus wrathful at heart, and through
the front ranks he strode, in a helmet of gleaming bronze,
coming up close, and stood there, took aim with his bright spear,
glancing quickly around. The Trojans all shrank back
as he threw; not in vain was his missile cast, but struck
a bastard son of Priam's, Dēmokóōn, who'd come over
from Abydos, leaving behind his stable of racing mares.
Him Odysseus, enraged on account of his comrade, speared
full on the temple: clean through to the other temple drove
the sharp bronze point. Darkness blacked out his eyes,
he fell with a thud, and his armor rattled upon him.
Then the front-line fighters gave ground, with illustrious Hector;
the Argives raised a loud cheer, dragged off the bodies,
and advanced still further forward. Apollo, furious
as he looked down from Olympos, cried out to the Trojans:
"Stir yourselves, horse-breaker Trojans, don't yield the battle
to these Argives—their flesh is not made of stone or iron
to resist the flesh-severing bronze when they take a hit:
no indeed, nor yet has Achilles, sweet-haired Thetis's son,
joined battle, but off by the ships is nursing his heartsick wrath."

So, from the citadel, the terrible god. The Achaians
were urged on by Zeus's daughter, illustrious Trītogéneia,[3]
ranging through the ranks, on the watch for men giving ground.
Fate there now ensnared Amarynkeus's son Diōrēs:
by a jagged rock he was struck, on his right shin near the ankle,
and the man who threw it was a leader of Thracians,
Peirōs, Imbrasos's son, who had come to Troy from Ainos.
Both tendons, and leg bones too, the pitiless stone
utterly crushed: he collapsed on his back in the dust,
both hands reaching forward to his own dear comrades
as he gasped out his life. Then the stone thrower ran up,
Peirōs, and speared him beside the navel. Out on the ground
all his guts splashed, and darkness shrouded his eyes.

But as Peirōs withdrew he was speared by Aitōlian Thoas
in the chest, over one nipple, and the bronze jammed in his lung.
Forward at him ran Thoas, tugged out from his torso
the weighty spear, then drew his keen-edged sword,
and thrust it in Peirōs's mid-belly, robbed him of life,
but failed to strip off his armor, for around him gathered
his comrades, topknotted Thracians, grasping their long spears;
and they, huge though he was, both strong and noble,
thrust Thoas back from them: he staggered, gave ground.
The two lay stretched in the dust beside each other, both
leaders, one of the Thracians, the other of the Epeians
in their bronze corselets; and many more died around them.

From now a late entrant could no more make light of the work—
one who'd still taken no hit, was uncut by the sharp bronze—
as he turned through the thick of it, even were Pallas Athēnē
leading him by the hand, warding off the rush of missiles;
for too many Achaians and Trojans on that day
lay one by the other, stretched out face down in the dust.

3. A traditional epithet of Athēnē (also at 8.39, 22.183), but its meaning remains uncertain—and the explanations given in antiquity suggest that Hellenistic scholars were no wiser than we are. Modern philology suggests that *trīto-* (with lengthened iota), i.e. "third" is meant, so that Athēnē was Zeus's "third-born", or genuine, daughter; but this too remains unconvincing. As with so many Homeric epithets, we simply have to admit that the original meaning was lost very early.

Book 5

NOW on Tydeus's son Diomēdēs Pallas Athēnē bestowed
power and courage, that he might be clearly preeminent
among all the Argives, and gather illustrious renown.[1]
From his helmet and shield she made blaze an unwearying flame,
like that star of the harvest season that shines out most intensely
after dipping in Ocean's stream: of such a nature
was the light that she made to gleam from his head and shoulders,
and she thrust him into the center, where the struggle was greatest.

There was a Trojan, one Darēs, both wealthy and virtuous,
a priest of Hēphaistos; and this man had two sons,
Phēgeus and Idaios, well skilled in all kinds of fighting.
These now broke out from the line and went against Diomēdēs—
they mounted in their chariot, while he advanced on foot.
When they got close enough, each of them to the other,
Phēgeus was the first to hurl his far-shadowing spear,
at Tydeus's son, but the point flew over his left shoulder
and missed him. Then Tydeus's son in turn attacked with the bronze.
Not in vain from his hand did the missile fly, but struck
Phēgeus full in mid-breast, threw him clear of his horses.
Then from the fine-crafted chariot Idaios sprang down,
but dared not make a stand over his slain brother,
nor would he himself have escaped the black death spirit
without the aid of Hēphaistos, who saved him, hid him in darkness,
to ensure that aged Darēs was not wholly undone by grief.
But his horses the son of high-spirited Tydeus drove off,
and gave to his comrades to lead to the hollow ships,
and when the high-spirited Trojans saw Darēs' two sons—
one in flight, the other lying slain beside his chariot—
the spirits of all were dismayed. But grey-eyed Athēnē

1. What follows is a remarkable killing spree by Diomēdēs, a sustained sequence of successful assaults only halted by divine intervention. Such spotlighted one-man performances by Iliadic heroes (e.g., Agamemnōn, bk. 11; Hektōr, bk. 15; Patroklos, bk. 16; Achilles bks. 19–22) are a formal feature of Homeric epic, known as *aristeiai*, or "displays of excellence" (see Glossary).

grasped fierce Arēs' hand, and thus addressed him: "Arēs,
Arēs, ruin of mortals, blood-guilty, city-stormer,
should we not now leave both Trojans and Achaians
to battle it out, let our father Zeus apportion
the glory, while we two withdraw, avoid Zeus's anger?"

So saying, she led fierce Arēs away from the fighting,
sat him down beside the Skamandros river. Meanwhile
the Danäans routed the Trojans: each one of their leaders
killed him a man. First of all the lord of men, Agamemnōn,
knocked the Halizōnēs' leader, tall Odios, off his chariot
just as he turned to flee, drove the spear into his back
between the shoulders, and right through to his chest.
He fell with a thud, and his armor rattled upon him.

Idomeneus slew Phaistos, the son of Maiōnian
Bōros, who had come there from rich-soiled Tarnē.
Idomeneus, famous spearman, ran him through with his long
lance, in the right shoulder, just as he was mounting;
he slumped from his chariot, and loathsome darkness took him.

Him Idomeneus's henchmen stripped of his armor; and now
Skamandrios, Strophios's son, well trained in the chase,
Meneläos, son of Atreus, took down with his sharpened spear,
fine hunter though he was, one whom Artemis herself
taught to shoot all wild things that the mountain woodlands
   nourish.
Yet of no avail to him now was Artemis the archer,
nor the skilled bowmanship in which he once excelled,
but Atreus's son Meneläos, that famous spearman,
plunged, as he fled before him, a spear into his back
between the shoulder blades, drove it through to his chest.
He slumped down face first, and his armor rattled upon him.

Mēriones brought down Phereklos, son of Tektōn,
and Harmōn's grandson, whose hands were skilled to fashion
all kinds of intricate work: he was dear to Pallas Athēnē.
He it was built for Aléxandros those trim ships
that started the trouble, became a curse to all Trojans—
and to himself, who knew nothing of the gods' planned ordinances.
When Mēriones in his pursuit caught up with Phereklos
he speared him in the right buttock, and the spear point

pierced right through to the bladder beneath the bone:
he screamed and fell to his knees, and death enfolded him.

Megēs now killed Pēdaios, Antēnōr's son—
a bastard, but noble Theanō reared him devotedly,
like her own children, out of affection for her husband.
But Phyleus's son, famed spearman, rushing forward,
stabbed into his neck tendon with a sharp spear: clean through
his teeth the bronze went, and severed his tongue at the root.
He collapsed in the dust, teeth clamped on the cold bronze.

Eurypylos, son of Euaimōn, took down high-spirited
Dolopiōn's son, the noble Hypsēnōr, who'd been made
priest of Skamandros: the people revered him like a god.
In pursuit of him went Eurypylos, Euaimōn's splendid son,
as he fled, and, still running, closed in, raised his sword,
slashed at one shoulder, cut off the weighty arm,
that dropped, still spurting blood, onto the ground; his eyes
were closed by blood-red death and all-mastering fate.

Thus they were laboring in the grind of battle;
but as for Tydeus's son, you could not tell which side
he was fighting on—was he with the Trojans or the Achaians?—
so wildly he ranged the plain, like some swollen winter torrent
that, rushing onward, sweeps away dikes unable,
however close-packed, to hold back its raging progress,
nor can its sudden coming be stopped by the flourishing vineyard's
walls, when a Zeus-sent rainstorm augments its waters,
and many good man-made works collapse before it. Just so
before Tydeus's son's advance the massed Trojan battalions
were routed, not standing to face him, despite their numbers.

When Lykaōn's fine son Pandaros caught sight of him storming
across the plain, and driving those battalions before him, at once
against Tydeus's son he bent his curved bow, aimed true,
and hit him in the right shoulder as he pressed on forward,
on the plate of his corselet: clean through winged the bitter shaft,
piercing the flesh, and the corselet was blood-bespattered. Then
over him loud exulted Lykaōn's fine son: "Rouse up now,
all you high-spirited Trojans, you spurrers of horses! The best
warrior of the Achaians is hit, and he won't, I assure you,

long survive my strong missile, if it's true it was Lord Apollo,
Zeus's son, who encouraged me to come here from Lycia."

Boastful words; but the swift shaft did not fell Diomēdēs.
He gave ground, went back, stood there in front of his chariot
and horses: called out to Kapaneus's son Sthenelos: "Quick now,
good son of Kapaneus, get down from the chariot, come
and pull this bitter shaft out from my shoulder."

So he spoke,
and Sthenelos instantly leapt down onto the ground
from the driver's place, stood by him, drew the swift arrow out
through his shoulder. Blood spurted from the soft folds of his tunic.
Then Diomēdēs, good at the war cry, made this prayer:
"Hear me, unwearying child of Zeus of the aegis!
If ever with kindly heart you stood beside my father
in the madness of battle, now befriend me too, Athēnē!
Let me take down this man, let him come within my spear cast,
whose shot caught me unawares, who now boasts over me, who
swears that not for much longer shall I look on the sun's bright light."

So he spoke in prayer, and Pallas Athēnē heard him.
She made his limbs buoyant, his legs and the arms above them,
and standing close by his side spoke to him winged words:
"Take heart now, Diomēdēs, for your battle against the Trojans,
for in your breast I have set your father's dauntless fury—
such as he had, he, the horseman, Tydeus the shield wielder;[2]
and the mist that was over your eyes I have taken away
to let you clearly distinguish a god from a mortal. So now
if some god comes here to make trial of you, no way
are you to meet in battle any one of the other immortals
save Aphrodītē alone, Zeus's daughter. But if she enters
the fighting, her you may wound with your keen-edged bronze."

This said,
grey-eyed Athēnē departed. Then Tydeus's son went back
and plunged headlong into the ranks of the foremost fighters.
Though before he'd been hot in his heart to battle Trojans, now
a fury three times as great possessed him, like that of a lion

2. "Shield wielder" (σακέσπαλος, *sakéspalos*) is an interesting epithet: Tydeus did not merely carry a shield, he used it—a mark of his savage fierceness—as an aggressive weapon.

that a shepherd out in the country, guarding his fleecy sheep,
has wounded, but not killed, as it leapt the sheepfold's wall,
arousing its rage, so that he now abandons his defense
and retreats to the steading's shelter, leaving his terrified flock
without protection—the sheep in huddled heaps,
while the lion in its fury springs out from the high sheepfold—
so strong Diomēdēs raged as he mingled with the Trojans.

Astynoös now he slew, and Hypeirōn, his people's shepherd,
the one hit above the nipple with a cast of his bronze-tipped spear,
the other with his great sword on the collarbone by the shoulder
he struck, slicing off the shoulder from neck and back. Leaving these
he went off in pursuit of Abas and Polyīdos,
both sons of a dream interpreter, the aged Eurydamas. Though
the old man read no dreams against their homecoming, still
strong Diomēdēs slew them, and stripped them of their armor.
Next he went after Xanthos and Thoōn, Phainōps's twin sons,
his latest-born: he himself was worn out by bitter old age
and sired no other son to leave heir to his possessions.
Diomēdēs dispatched them both, destroyed their vital spirit,
left for their father mourning and bitter sorrow,
since they never came home alive from the fighting for him
to welcome them back: distant kinsmen divided his property.

Next he took on two sons of Dardanos's scion Priam,
both in one chariot, Echemmōn and Chromios.
Just as a lion springs in among cattle, breaks the neck
of a calf or cow, as they graze in their woodland pasture,
so did Tydeus's son force the pair of them, all unwilling,
out of their chariot, then stripped the armor from them,
and gave his comrades their horses to drive off to the ships.

Aineias watched him wreak havoc among the warriors' ranks,
and set off through the fighting and the chaos of flying spears
looking for godlike Pandaros, to see if he might find him;
and he came on Lykaōn's son, the strong, the illustrious,
and confronted him, and addressed him in these words:
"Pandaros, where now are your bow and your flighted arrows?
Where's your famous skill, in which no man here is your rival,
nor can any in Lycia boast that they're your better?
So come, flight a shaft at this man—but first supplicate Zeus—

whoever he is, whose huge prowess has done such endless harm
to the Trojans, unstringing the knees of so many warlike fighters—
unless this be some god with a grudge against Trojans over
a sacrifice: a god's wrath sits heavily on us mortals."

In answer to him then spoke Lykaōn's splendid son:
"Aineias, counselor to the bronze-corseleted Achaians,
I find him in all respects like the warlike son of Tydeus.
By his shield I recognize him, by his helmet's visor,
by the look of his horses—yet he might, I'm not sure, be a god!
If he's the man I say, though, the warlike son of Tydeus,
not without some god's aid can he rage thus: an immortal
must be standing close by him, shoulders hidden in mist,
who turned aside my swift shaft, the moment it reached him—
for just now I let fly a shaft at him, pierced his right shoulder
clean through the plate of his corselet, so that I told myself
I'd dispatch him straight to Hādēs. Yet nevertheless
I failed to destroy him: some god must be resentful.
Nor have I at hand either horses or a chariot to mount in,
though in Lykaōn's stables there are, I think, eleven—
fine ones, just carpentered, newly made, with canvas
covers spread over them, and by each its two-horse team
stands munching its fodder of white barley and spelt.
Indeed, I got strong advice from Lykaōn, the old spearman,
at my departure, while still in our well-built house:
he wanted me to go mounted, with chariot and horses,
and be to the Trojans a leader in their fierce engagements.
But I ignored his counsel—far better had I listened!—
and spared the horses, for fear they might lack fodder
amid the crush of troops, they that were used to eating
their fill, and left them, and journeyed on foot to Ilion,
trusting my bow. But that, it seems, was to be of no use—
already I've sent shafts winging at two of their leading men,
the sons of Tydeus and Atreus, hit them both squarely,
drew blood from each one, yet only roused them more.
Ill-fated I was, then, when I took my curved bow from its peg
that day on which I first set off to lovely Ilion
with my Trojans, doing a service to illustrious Hektōr.
But if I survive to go home, once more see with my own eyes
my fatherland, and my wife, and my great high-roofed house,

then may some stranger at once strike the head from my shoulders
if I don't break this bow with my hands and cast it away
into a blazing fire: it's served me no better than wind."

To him then Aineias, leader of Trojans, made answer:
"Don't talk in that way. Things will not get any better
until we two together, with chariot and horses,
go out against this man, and make trial of him in arms.
Come now, get into my chariot, see for yourself
the breed of these horses of Trōs,[3] well trained to charge
swiftly over the plain, in pursuit or retreat! This pair
will bring us back safe to the city, if yet once more
to Tydeus's son Diomēdēs Zeus grants the glory.
So come now, you take the whip and the bright-polished
reins, and I'll dismount to join in the fighting—or else
you face this man's charge, while I look after the horses."

In answer to him then spoke Lykaōn's splendid son:
"Aineias, you yourself should keep the reins and the horses.
Better with a known driver will they pull your curved chariot
if we are forced to retreat before the son of Tydeus.
I fear they might take fright and stampede, might well refuse to
carry us out of the fighting, without your voice to rule them,
and high-spirited Tydeus's son would then assail us,
and kill us both, and drive off your whole-hoofed horses.
So you yourself should control your chariot and your horses,
while I meet this man's assault with my keen-edged spear."

After conversing thus they mounted the inlaid chariot,
and eagerly urged their swift steeds against the son of Tydeus.
Now Sthenelos saw them, Kapaneus's splendid son,
and at once to the son of Tydeus addressed winged words:
"Diomēdēs, Tydeus's son, so dear to my heart, I see
two powerful warriors set on doing battle with you,
men of unmeasured strength: one, a well-skilled archer,
Pandaros, also claims to be the son of Lykaōn;
the other, Aineias, claims he was sired by blameless

3. Trōs, who started this breed of divine (and divinely speedy) horses, was the great-great-grandfather of Aineias: the original pair was given to him by Zeus in compensation for the abduction of his son Ganymēdēs. Aineias' father Anchīsēs "later managed to breed from their stock by stealth" (265–72 below; cf. 318–24, 8.105–8, and Kirk, 2: 83).

Anchīsēs, and also that his mother is Aphroditē!
So let's pull back in our chariot—and don't, I beg you,
rage on this way in the forefront, lest you maybe lose your life."

To him with a fierce glance strong Diomēdēs made answer:
"No arguments for retreat! You won't change my mind. It's not
a family tradition of mine to shrink from combat or
to crouch down and hide: my fury remains firm set.
I don't want to mount that chariot. Just as I am I'll go on
and face them: Pallas Athēnē will not let me be afraid.
And as for those two, their swift horses won't carry them both
safely away from us, even should one of them escape.
And another thing I will tell you, and you take it to heart:
If Athēnē of many counsels should grant me the renown
of killing them both, then you must tether these swift horses
in place here, lash their reins firmly onto the chariot rail,
and yourself set your mind to seizing Aineias's horses
and driving them from the Trojans to the well-greaved Achaians;
for they're from that stock which far-seeing Zeus gave Trōs
as amends for his son Ganymēdēs, being the finest
of all horses anywhere under sunlight or daybreak. This
was the breed from which that lord of men, Anchīsēs,
stole, by putting his mares to them, without Laomedōn's
knowledge, and from these mares six foals were born to him
in his stables: four he kept, to be nurtured at his mangers;
the last two he gave to Aineias as harbingers of rout,
so—capture this pair, and we'd win ourselves high renown."

Such was their conversation, the one to the other.
Meanwhile the two approached, driving their swift horses,
and the first of them to speak was Lykaōn's splendid son:
"Stout-hearted warlike son of illustrious Tydeus, indeed
my swift shaft failed to dispatch you, my bitter arrow; but now
I'll make trial of you with my spear, and hope to hit you."

So saying, he swung and let fly his far-shadowing spear,
and hit Diomēdēs' shield: clean through it drove
the bronze spear point in its flight, came near the corselet,
and a great shout went up from Lykaōn's splendid son:
"You're hit in the midriff, right through! I'm pretty certain
you won't survive long now! You've given me great glory!"

To him then, still unperturbed, strong Diomēdēs made answer:
"You didn't hit me, you missed. Still, I fancy the two of you
won't rest until one or the other has fallen, and glutted
Arēs the oxhide-shield warrior with his fill of blood."

So saying he let fly, and Athēnē guided his missile
close by one eye to the nose, and it sheared through the white teeth.
The man's tongue was cut off at its root by the stubborn bronze,
and the spear point came out below, from the back of his jaw.
He fell from his chariot, and his armor rattled upon him,
gleaming and polished bright; and the swift-footed horses
shied away in terror. There his spirit and strength were undone.

But Aineias sprang down with his shield and his long spear,
afraid that somehow the corpse might be dragged off by the Achaians.
Lion-like he bestrode him, trusting in his strength,
holding before him his spear and his nicely balanced shield,
hot to kill any fighter who might come to confront him,
and roaring defiance. But Tydeus's son hefted a rock
in his hands—a great feat, that would take two mortals and more,
such as men are today; yet, alone, he easily wielded it,
struck Aineias's hip, where the thighbone turns
in its socket—what's commonly known as the cup—
and crushed this cup, as well as severing both tendons.
The rock's rough edge tore off the skin. Then the warrior sank
to his knees and remained thus, leaning on one strong hand
thrust to the ground, while black night shrouded his vision.

Now indeed Aineias, that lord of men, would have perished,
if not for the quick sharp eye of Zeus's daughter Aphrodītē,
his mother, on whom Anchīsēs sired him when out herding
his oxen: about her dear son she flung her white arms,
and before him spread a bright fold of her robe to hide him
and act as a wall against missiles, lest some swift-horsed Danaän
might let fly bronze at his body and rob him of life.

So she brought her dear son safely out from the conflict.
Nor did the son of Kapaneus forget the instructions
given him by Diomēdēs, good at the war cry:
he tethered his own whole-hoofed horses well away
from the turmoil, lashing their reins tight to the chariot rail,
and made straight for the fine-maned horses of Aineias,

drove them off from the Trojans to the well-greaved Achaians,
and turned them over there to Deïpylos, his dear comrade—
whom he honored above all of his age: their minds were as one—
to drive to the hollow ships. That done, the hero mounted
his chariot, picked up the gleaming reins, and at once
in search of Tydeus's son urged on his strong-hoofed horses
with furious zest. But the latter had taken his pitiless bronze
in pursuit of Kypris, aware what a weakling goddess she was—
not the kind who lords it in a battle of warriors,
no Athēnē she, for sure, no Enyo, sacker of cities![4]
Now, when he overtook her in his chase through the crowded ranks,
he sprang at her, did high-spirited Tydeus's son, and lunged,
and sliced into the flesh of her hand with his keen-edged bronze—
that delicate hand! The spear drove straight into her flesh—
clean through the fragrant robe toiled on by the Graces themselves—
at the base of her palm: out flowed the goddess's blood, immortal
ichōr, such as flows in the veins of the blessed gods,
for they neither eat bread nor drink fire-bright wine, and so
are bloodless, and come thus to be called immortals.
She screamed aloud, and let her son fall, but Phoibos
Apollo gathered him up in his arms and kept him safe
in a dark cloud, lest one of the swift-horsed Danaäns
might flight bronze into his breast and rob him of life.
But over her Diomēdēs, good at the war cry, shouted:
"Back off, daughter of Zeus! Give up fighting and warfare!
Does it not suffice you to mislead weakling women?
If you meddle with battle again, I tell you, you'll shudder
at its very name, even if you only hear it from others."

So he spoke, but she went off distraught, in a sorry state,
and was met by wind-footed Iris, who led her from the turmoil,
bent double with pain, her lovely flesh now darkened.
Then, away on the left of the battlefield, she found fierce Arēs,
sitting, his spear left leaning against a cloud, with his swift
horses. She fell on her knees before her beloved brother,
and begged him with many prayers for his gold-bridled horses:

---

4. Kypris, i.e., "she of Cyprus", was a common epithet of Aphrodītē, though in the *Iliad* it occurs only here (five times) in bk. 5, and "does not participate in a formulaic system" (*HE* 2: 450). Enyo was a minor war goddess: her name is limited to Diomēdēs' *aristeia*. Arēs (whom she attends at 592) has the linked epithet Enyalios.

"Dear brother, come to my rescue, give me your horses!
I need to go to Olympos, the abode of the immortals—
I have a most painful wound, that this mortal person dealt me:
Tydeus's son, who'd fight now even with Zeus our father."

So she spoke, and Arēs gave her his gold-frontleted horses,
and she climbed aboard the chariot distraught at heart,
and Iris mounted beside her, grasped the reins in her hands,
and whipped up the horses. They, nothing loath, took flight,
and quickly arrived at the gods' abode, steep Olympos.
There wind-footed swift Iris made the horses stop,
unyoked them from the chariot, fed them ambrosial fodder.
But glorious Aphrodītē collapsed in the lap of Diōnē,[5]
her mother, who clasped her daughter in her arms,
soothingly stroked her, and addressed her with these words:
"Which of the gods in heaven, dear child, has done this to you,
without reason, as though you were openly misbehaving?"

To her then sweetly-smiling Aphrodītē made reply:
"It was Tydeus's son wounded me, high-spirited Diomēdēs,
because I was taking my dear son away from the fighting—
Aineias, by far the dearest of all men to me: for now
the grim fighting's no longer between Trojans and Achaians—
these Danaäns are fighting even with the immortals."

To her then the glorious goddess Diōnē made reply:
"Bear up, my child, and endure, despite what you're suffering;
for many of us suffer likewise—we, the Olympos-dwellers—
at the hands of men, and bring harsh grief on one another.
Thus Arēs suffered,[6] when Ōtos and powerful Ephialtēs,
the sons of Alōeus, bound him in prisoning fetters,
and there in a brazen jar he lay chained for thirteen months.
Then indeed would Arēs, that glutton for war, have perished,
had not their stepmother, beautiful Ēëriboia,
told all to Hermēs, who rescued Arēs by stealth—

5. Diōnē (the *di-* may simply indicate "goddess") was of uncertain parentage; and there is a better-known myth (Hes. *Th.* 188–93) reporting Aphrodītē's birth from the foam generated by Ouranos's severed genitals. Perhaps a Homeric desire here to keep clear of the latter?

6. Ōtos and Ephialtēs, sons of Poseidōn, were among the Giants (nine fathoms tall when nine years old) who piled Ossa on Olympos (*Od.* 11.305–20). Their assault on Arēs was in revenge for his killing Adonis, whose safeguarding had been their responsibility.

in a sorry state now, worn out by his harsh bonds.
Thus Hērē suffered, when Hēraklēs, Amphitryōn's strong son,
shot her in the right breast with a three-barbed arrow;
then she too was seized by unquenchable agony.
Huge Hādēs was another one hurt by a bitter arrow,
when this same man, son of Zeus the aegis-bearer,
among the dead shot him in Pylos, gave him over to pain.
So he went to the house of Zeus and high Olympos
grieving at heart, transfixed with pain: for the arrow
had pierced his powerful shoulder, affected his heart.
But Paiëōn,[7] by applying painkilling herbs and ointments
healed him: no mortal he, not made for death.
Brutal and violent man, who did vile acts without thinking,
who with his archery troubled the gods that hold Olympos!
Now against you the goddess, grey-eyed Athēnē, has set
this man: fool that he is, Tydeus's son's mind does not grasp
the fact that there's no long life for a man who fights the gods—
that Papa won't come back for his children to greet or cling round
his knees: no return from the wars and the bitter grind of battle.
So now let Tydeus's son, mighty warrior though he be,
take care lest someone better than you should fight him,
and indeed lest Aigialeia, Adrēstos's watchful daughter,
should rouse her household from sleep with her agonized wailing
for her wedded husband, the finest warrior of the Achaians—
she, the strong-hearted wife of Diomēdēs the horse breaker."

So saying, with both hands she wiped the wrist clean of ichōr:
Aphrodītē's arm was made whole, her sharp pains were allayed.
But as they both looked on, Athēnē and Hērē
kept needling Zeus son of Kronos with sarcastic comments,
the first to speak being the grey-eyed goddess Athēnē:
"Zeus, father, will you be angry with me for what I tell you?
It would seem that our Kypris has been urging some Achaian
lady to go with the Trojans, whom now she madly adores,

7. About Ēëriboia nothing certain was known even in antiquity. Amphitryōn's strong son is Hēraklēs. The shooting of Hādēs at Pylos is recorded only here and was much discussed by baffled Hellenistic scholars (Kirk, 2: 102, cf. Ganz 70). Paiëōn was a god of healing, mentioned on a Linear B tablet from Knossos, who much later came to be identified with Apollo.

and while caressing whichever well-dressed Achaian she chose,
scratched her delicate hand on the lady's golden brooch."

So she spoke; but he smiled, did the father of gods and men,
and spoke thus, calling her over, to golden Aphrodītē:
"Not for you, my child, is the business of warfare: you
should rather be concerned with the charming works of marriage,
and leave all these other things to swift Arēs and Athēnē."

But while they were talking like this, each one to the other,
Diomēdēs of the great war cry sprang at Aineias,
well aware that he was protected by Apollo himself:
yet not even the great god awed him, he was still urgent
to kill Aineias, and strip his splendid armor from him.
Three times he lunged at Aineias, mad-keen to cut him down;
three times his gleaming shield was slammed back by Apollo.
But when for the fourth time he charged, like some divine being,
then in a terrible voice Apollo the archer shouted:
"Think well, son of Tydeus! Withdraw, do not presume
to think like the gods, since in no manner is the race
of immortals akin to that of earthbound men."

Such his words: Tydeus's son gave ground a little, backwards,
to keep clear of the wrath of Apollo the archer, who then
took Aineias out of the turmoil, set him down far away
in sacred Pergamon, where his own shrine had been founded:
there Lētō together with bow-hunter Artemis
healed him in the great sanctuary, shed splendor on him,
while a phantom was fashioned by silver-bowed Apollo,
a clone of Aineias himself, with his kind of armor,
and round that phantom both Trojans and resplendent Achaians
hacked at the ox-hide shields protecting each other's chests,
the round shields and the fringed leather bucklers. Then indeed
to fierce Arēs there spoke Phoibos Apollo: "Arēs,
Arēs ruin of mortals, blood-guilty, city-stormer,
won't you now intervene, drag this man out of the fighting—
Tydeus's son, who at present would even fight Zeus the Father?
First he tackled Kypris, wounded her hand at the wrist,
then he came charging at me like some superhuman creature."
So he spoke, and set himself down on Pergamon's heights,
while killer Arēs entered the Trojans' ranks, spurred them on,

in the likeness of Akamas, quick-footed Thracian leader,
calling on Priam's sons, Zeus's nurslings, to take action:
"You sons of Priam, a king well favored by Zeus,
how long will you let your people be slaughtered by the Achaians?
Will it be till the fighting is round our strong-built gates?
That man is down whom we honored as much as noble Hektōr—
Aineias, great-hearted Anchīsēs' son. So come now,
let's rescue our noble comrade from the tumult of battle."

With these words he aroused each man's urgency and spirit,
while Sarpēdōn severely rebuked illustrious Hektōr:
"Hektōr, that rage you once had—where has it vanished to?
Did you think you'd hold this city without troops or allies?
Just you alone, with your brothers and your sisters' husbands?
Not a single one of these now can I see or recognize—
No, they're cowering back like dogs set around a lion,
And the fighting's left to us, who are only your allies!
Such an ally am I, and I came here from far away—
far distant is Lycia, by the eddying Xanthos river,
where I left my dear wife and my infant son, and many
possessions, things that the needy all eye with longing.
Yet even so I urge on the Lycians, am fired up myself
to engage hand to hand, though there's nothing here of the sort
that the Achaians might want to drive or carry off—
whereas you just stand around, don't even command
your men to be steadfast, and fight to protect their wives!
Take care you're not snared in the seine of a catch-all net
and end as the prey and spoil of enemy warriors,
who'll soon lay waste your city and its flourishing people!
All this should be your concern, both night and day,
with entreaties to the commanders of your far-famed allies
to stand firm: that's how you'll avoid such stern rebukes."

So spoke Sarpēdōn, and his words stung Hektōr's spirit.
At once he sprang to the ground, in his armor, from his chariot,
brandishing two sharp spears, ranged widely through the ranks,
urging them on to fight, stirred up the clash of battle.
So they rallied, stood firm, facing up to the Achaians,
and the Argives closed ranks at their coming, did not falter.
As the wind blows chaff across the sacred threshing-floors
when men are winnowing, when golden-haired Dēmētēr

amid gusts of wind works hard to separate grain from chaff,
and the heaps of chaff slowly whiten, so now the Achaians
became white with the flying dust kicked up amongst them
to the brazen sky by the horses' hooves, as battle was joined
once more, and the charioteers came wheeling around.
They bore their hands' fury straight onward, while fierce Arēs
shrouded the battle in darkness to help the Trojans, ranged
across the whole field, thus fulfilling the injunctions
of gold-sworded Phoibos Apollo, who commanded him
to arouse the Trojans' spirits, seeing that Pallas Athēnē
had gone away, since it was she was supporting the Danaäns.
Now Apollo himself sent Aineias forth from the wealthy
sanctuary, put great strength in the breast of the people's shepherd.
So Aineias was back there among his companions, who rejoiced
to see him rejoin them alive, unhurt and sound of limb,
and full of high courage. But they questioned him not at all,
being concerned with that other work, which he of the silver bow
and Arēs, ruin of mortals, and ever-fierce Strife were rousing.

Meanwhile both Aiases and Odysseus and Diomēdēs
were urging the Danaäns on to battle; but they themselves
had no fear of the Trojans' violence or of their onsets,
but stood there steadfast, like clouds that the son of Kronos
on a windless day sets down on mountain summits—
quite still, while the rage of the north wind sleeps, and the other
furious winds, that scatter the shadowy clouds
with the force of their screaming gales: in such a way
did the Danaäns face the Trojans: steadfast, unyielding,
while Atreus's son ranged through the ranks with many
a call to his troops: "My friends, be men now, make brave your hearts,
feel shame before one another in this violent combat—
of those who feel shame more survive than lose their lives,
while runaways get no glory, win no battles."

With that he threw his spear swiftly, hit a prime fighter,
Deïkoön, a comrade of high-spirited Aineias,
Pergasos's son, whom the Trojans honored like Priam's own
offspring, since he was quick to fight in the front ranks.
His shield was hit by the spear that lord Agamemnōn cast,
and failed to stop it: the bronze point drove clean through,

pierced his baldric, and entered the lower part of his belly.
He fell with a thud, and his armor rattled upon him.

Then in return Aineias killed two Danaän prime fighters,
sons both of Dioklēs, Krēthōn and Orsilochos,
whose father dwelt in Phērē, a well-built settlement,
a man of rich livelihood—his lineage that of the river
Alpheios, whose broad stream flows through Pylian country—
who sired Orsilochos to be lord over many men.
Now Orsilochos in turn sired high-spirited Dioklēs,
and to Dioklēs were born these two sons, being twins,
Krēthōn and Orsilochos, fine all-round warriors both.
When these two reached manhood they went on the black ships
to horse-rich Troy with the Argives, seeking indemnity
for Atreus's sons, Agamemnōn and Menelaös; but
themselves it was that the fate of death now obliterated.
They resembled a pair of lions, high mountain dwellers,
reared by their mother as cubs in some deep woodland thicket:
the pair of them, snatching cattle and fattened sheep, wreak havoc
on the steadings of shepherds, till finally they themselves
fall victim to men's hands, are slain with the sharp bronze.
Just so these two, overcome by the hands of Aineias,
crashed headlong, like a couple of tall felled fir trees.

Now
their falling stirred pity in Menelaös the warlike:
through the front ranks he strode, armored in gleaming bronze,
spear poised and ready—with Arēs inflaming his rage,
so that he might be destroyed at the hands of Aineias.
But Nestōr's high-spirited son Antilochos saw him: through
the front ranks he strode, concerned for the people's shepherd,
lest he suffer some hurt, and lose them all they'd toiled for.
Both men had their arms raised, each with his keen-edged spear
aimed at the other, both in a fury to do battle:
but Antilochos then took his place beside the people's shepherd,
and Aineias did not stand firm, swift warrior though he was,
when he saw those two side by side, and holding the line:
who then, after dragging the corpses to the Achaians' ranks,
left them—ill-fated pair—in the hands of their companions,
and themselves turned back to join the front-line fighters.

There they took down Pylaimenēs, a match for Arēs,
lord of the high-spirited Paphlagōnian shield men:
him the son of Atreus, famed spearman Menelaös,
ran through as he stood there, going in at the collarbone,
while Antilochos caught Mydōn, his henchman and charioteer,
Atymnios's noble son, as he wheeled his whole-hoofed horses,
with a flung rock, square on the elbow: from his hands the reins,
white with ivory inlay, fell, and were dragged in the dust.
Antilochos sprang at him, drove his sword-point through
Mydōn's temple: gasping, he slumped from the fine chariot
headlong into the dust on head and shoulders, held up
firm for a moment—he'd hit a deep sand-drift—but then
his horses downed him, trampled him into the dust,
as Antilochos whipped and drove them back to his own lines.

Hektōr glimpsed them across the lines, ran at them,
whooping aloud, and the ranks of the Trojans followed after
in full strength: Arēs led them, and Enyo, queenly goddess:
she brought with her the reckless tumult of battle,
while Arēs, fists brandishing an enormous spear,
ranged now in front of Hektōr, now behind him.

Seeing Arēs, Diomēdēs of the great war cry shuddered.
As when a man stops, helpless, on his way across a great plain,
confronted by a swift river flowing down to the sea,
and seeing it in foaming spate starts sharply backwards,
so now Tydeus's son gave ground, and called to his troops:
"Friends, we were always in great awe of noble Hektōr—
as a spearman, as a brave warrior, even though there was
always one of the gods at his side, keeping ruin from him:
so now accompanying him is Arēs, clad in a mortal
warrior's form! Keep facing the Trojans, but give ground
steadily. Do not strive to match the gods in battle."

While he spoke, the Trojans drew ever closer to them.
Then Hektōr killed two men well skilled in warfare,
a pair in one chariot, Anchialos and Menesthēs,
and their fall stirred great Aias, Telamōn's son, to pity:
he stepped up close, stood, and hurled his bright bronze spear
and hit Amphios, son of Selagos, who had his dwelling
in Paisos, a man of much wealth, of broad acres; yet destiny

drove him to come as an ally to Priam and his sons.
He was hit through the belt by Telamōn's son Aias,
who into his nether belly plunged the far-shadowing spear.
He fell with a thud, and illustrious Aias ran up
to strip off his armor. The Trojans now showered him
with their sharp and gleaming spears: many lodged in his shield.
He set his heel on the corpse, drew out the bronze
spear, yet was not able to work the man's splendid arms
free from his shoulders, so beset he was by missiles,
and he feared the strong ring-defense of these proud Trojans
facing him, spears in their hands, so many, so brave,
and despite his height, and strength, and manly valor
they thrust him away from them: he staggered and backed off.

So these were laboring in the hard-fought conflict.
Now Tlēpolemos, Hēraklēs' son, a big strong fellow,
was urged against godlike Sarpēdōn by all-mastering destiny;
and when in their advance they were close one to the other—
the son and the grandson of Zeus the cloud-gatherer—
then Tlēpolemos was the first of the two to speak. He said:
"Sarpēdōn, the Lycians' counselor, what necessity
brings you to skulk here, you, a fellow unskilled in battle?
They lie who claim you're the offspring of Zeus the aegis-bearer:
truth is, you fall very far short of those real men
who were sired by Zeus in the days of our ancestors.
Of a different breed, they say, was that mighty force Hēraklēs
—my father, large-spirited, with the heart of a lion,
who once came here on account of Laomedōn's mares[8]
with only six ships and a handful of followers,
yet sacked the city of Ilion, widowed its streets.
But yours is a coward's heart, and your people are perishing.
No help of any sort, I think, to the Trojans
will be your coming from Lycia, be you never so strong:
vanquished, rather, by me you'll pass the gates of Hādēs."

To him Sarpēdōn, the Lycian leader, responded:
"Tlēpolemos, that man did indeed destroy sacred Ilion,

---

8. The semi-divine horses mentioned at 222 (see n. 3). Hēraklēs rescued Laomedōn's daughter Hēsionē from a sea monster; Laomedōn had promised him some of the horses as a reward, but reneged on his promise, after which Hēraklēs sacked Troy.

through the senselessness of one person, lordly Laomedōn,
who rewarded his good work with the harshest of insults,
and refused him the mares for which he had come so far.
But for you, here, I tell you, the black death-spirit will bring
your end at my hands: laid low by my spear you'll give
glory to me, and your soul to horse-proud Hādēs."

So spoke Sarpēdōn. Tlēpolemos lifted his ash spear,
and both men's long lances sped from their hands at the same
instant. Sarpēdōn's struck home square on the neck,
clean through which its lethal point now penetrated,
Tlēpolemos's sight was shrouded by the murky gloom of night;
while his own long spear struck home on Sarpēdōn's left thigh,
and the zestful point drove in forcefully, scraping the bone,
but Sarpēdōn's father Zeus still warded off death from him.

Then his noble comrades began to carry godlike Sarpēdōn
out of the fighting, weighed down by the length of the spear
that dragged behind; yet no one had noticed it, let alone thought
of pulling the ash spear out of his thigh, to let him walk,
so busy they were, such toil they had in his protection.

On the other side, the Achaians, well-greaved, began carrying
Tlēpolemos out of the fighting. This noble Odysseus noticed—
he of the steadfast spirit—and his heart was hot for action.
Now he debated his choice, what he thought, how he felt:
Was he to further pursue the son of loud-thundering Zeus?
Or should he set out to kill many more of the Lycians?
But since it was not fated that great-hearted Odysseus
should lay this strong son of Zeus low with the keen-edged bronze,
Athēnē now turned his mind toward the Lycians in general.
So he went on to take down Koiranos, Alastōr, Chromios,
Alkandros, Halios, Noēmōn, and Prytanis:
and more Lycians still would great-hearted Odysseus have slain
had not great bright-helmeted Hektōr taken sharp notice.
Through the front ranks he strode, in his helmet of gleaming bronze,
bringing fear to the Danaäns. But there was joy at his coming
for Zeus's son Sarpēdōn, who addressed him piteously:
"Son of Priam, don't let me lie here, as prey for the Danaäns,
but come to my aid! Then, afterwards, let life leave me
if it's in your city—seemingly I was not destined

to make the journey back to my own, my native land,
and gladden the heart of my wife, and my infant son."

So he spoke: bright-helmeted Hektōr made him no answer,
but hurried past, eager as quickly as might be
to drive back the Argives, to take the lives of many.
Then the noble companions of godlike Sarpēdōn set him down
under the splendid oak, sacred to Zeus of the aegis,
and out through his thigh the ash spear was thrust by his dear
comrade, strong Pelagōn. The breath of life
left him, and over his eyes a mist was shed. But he got
his breath back again, and the blustering north wind's
gusts now restored the life he'd so painfully gasped out.

The Argives, hard-pressed by Arēs and bronze-clad Hektōr,
though they did not turn and flee to their black ships, yet
could not hold firm in the battle line, kept backing off,
now that they'd noticed Arēs among the Trojans.

So who
was the first, who the last that got to be slaughtered by
Hektōr, the son of Priam, and brazen Arēs?
Godlike Teuthras, and, next, Orestēs, driver of horses,
Trēchos, Aitōlian spearman, Oinomäos,
Helenos, Oinōps's son, bright-kilted Oresbios
who dwelt in Hylē—a man much occupied with wealth—
close by the Kephisian lake, and near him lived other
Boiōtians, all of them owners of rich and fertile acres.

But when the goddess, white-armed Hērē, saw them
busily killing off Argives in violent combat, then
straight away she addressed Athēnē with winged words:
"Well now, unwearying child of Zeus of the aegis,
vain indeed was the promise we made to Menelaös,
that he'd sack strong-walled Ilion before returning home,
if we allow baneful Arēs to rage on in this fashion!
So, let us two likewise put our minds to daring valor."

Thus she spoke; the grey-eyed goddess Athēnē did not
disregard her. Off she went to harness the gold-bridled horses—
she, Hērē, high goddess, daughter of great Kronos!—
while Hēbē quickly, at the chariot's sides, set the curved

and eight-spoked wheels round the iron axle. Of these
the outer rim is of gold, imperishable: laid on it
are tires of fitted bronze, a marvel to look upon,
with hubs of silver, revolving on either side,
while the body is tightly woven with straps of gold
and silver, and there are two rails that run around it.
From it stood out the silver pole, and on its end
she bound fast the yoke, and to it fastened the harness,
both of fine gold, while Hērē brought under the yoke
the swift-footed horses, impatient for strife and the war cry.

But Athēnē, the daughter of Zeus the aegis-bearer,
let fall on her father's floor the soft embroidered robe
that she herself had made, worked with her own hands,
and, donning the tunic of Zeus the cloud-gatherer,
armed herself in all grim warfare's accoutrements.
Over her shoulders she spread the tasseled aegis—
a fearful thing, crowned all around with Panic,
and Strife is on it, and Prowess, and heart-chilling Pursuit;
there too is the Gorgon head of the fearful monster,
fearful and terrible, portent of Zeus the aegis-bearer.
She set on her head the helmet, double-bossed, quadruple-plated,
all golden, its inlay showing the troops of a hundred cities.
Into the fiery chariot then she stepped, grasped her spear—
weighty, huge, thick—with which she quells the ranks of men,
the heroes who've angered this child of a mighty sire.
Now Hērē gave a quick flick of her whip to the horses;
of themselves the sky's gates groaned open, guarded by
the Seasons, to whom are entrusted the firmament and Olympos,
whether to lift off the thick clouds, or impose them.
Straight through those gates they drove their goad-spurred horses,
and found the son of Kronos apart from the other gods,
ensconced on the topmost peak of many-ridged Olympos.
Then the goddess, white-armed Hērē, halted the horses,
and to most high Zeus, son of Kronos, put this question:
"Zeus, father, are you not wroth at these violent deeds of Arēs—
that he's destroyed so many—and such fine—Achaian troops,
pointlessly, out of due order, to my grief, while Kypris
and silver-bowed Apollo, at their ease, rejoice at having
let loose this madman who knows nothing of decent conduct?

Zeus, father, will you hold it against me if I give Arēs
a painful beating, and chase him away from the battlefield?"

Then in reply to her words Zeus the cloud-gatherer said:
"Yes, go to it, rouse up against him Athēnē the spoil-bringer:
she's especially used to inflicting harsh pain upon him."

So he spoke, and the goddess, white-armed Hērē, did not
ignore him. She whipped up her horses, and they, not unwilling,
winged their way between earth and starry heaven. As far
as a man's gaze reaches into the hazy distance
while he sits on a lookout point, staring over the wine-hued deep,
such the span that the gods' neighing horses leap at one bound.
But when they came to Troy and its two flowing rivers,
where Simoeis and Skamandros merge their streams,
then the goddess, white-armed Hērē, halted her horses,
unharnessed them from the chariot, hid them in thick mist,
while Simoeis made ambrosia spring up for their grazing.

Now the two queens strutted off like a brace of wild pigeons,
eager to come to the aid of the Argive warriors;
and when they reached the place where the most and the bravest
stood ranged round the mighty person of Diomēdēs,
the horse breaker, like lions that rend and eat raw flesh,
or wild pigs, boars, whose strength is far from trifling,
then white-armed Hērē, the goddess, stopped and shouted,
in the likeness of great-hearted Stentōr, the brazen-voiced,
whose shout matched in volume that of fifty other men:
"Shame, Argives! Cowardly creatures, good only to look at!
So long as noble Achilles took part in the fighting, then
the Trojans would not even venture beyond the Dardanian gates,
so scared they were of that massive spear of his. But now
they fight far away from the city, out by the hollow ships.'

So saying she aroused the passion and spirit of every man,
while to Tydeus's son now sped the goddess, grey-eyed Athēnē,
and found the king close beside his horses and chariot,
cooling the wound that the arrow of Pandaros dealt him;
for the sweat was giving him trouble under the broad strap
of his round shield. He was troubled, his arm had wearied
from lifting the strap and wiping the dark blood clots away.
Laying hold of his horses' yoke the goddess declared:

"Not much indeed like himself was the son that Tydeus begot—
Tydeus was short of stature, but what a great fighter!
Even that time when I wouldn't let him do battle
or parade his courage—when, no other Achaians with him,
he came to Thēbē as a messenger, to its great crowd
of Kadmeians. I told him to feast in their halls, relax,
but he with his fierce spirit, the same as always,
challenged the young Kadmeians, beat them at everything
easily—such a supporter I was on his behalf!
Now beside you too I stand as a guardian,
ready and eager to bid you battle the Trojans—
yet either fatigue from much fighting has entered your limbs,
or maybe you're in the grip of craven fear—if so,
you're no true offspring of Tydeus, Oineus's warrior son."

Then in response to her words strong Diomēdēs declared:
"I know you, goddess, daughter of Zeus of the aegis:
so I'll answer you readily, tell the truth, hide nothing.
No craven fear grips me, no shrinking from action. But I
still remember the charges that you yourself laid on me:
you would not permit me to battle, at close quarters,
the rest of the blessed gods; but should Zeus's daughter Aphrodītē
enter the fighting, her I should wound with the sharp bronze.
That is why I have pulled back myself, and have ordered all the rest
of the Argives to regroup here, being well aware
that it's Arēs who lords it at present over the battlefield."

Then in answer to him spoke the goddess, grey-eyed Athēnē:
"Diomēdēs, Tydeus's son, so dear to my heart, you need not
fear Arēs because of that, nor any one of the other
immortals—such a supporter I am on your behalf!
So come, straight off at Arēs drive your whole-hoofed horses—
Get up close, hit him, don't be in awe of frantic Arēs,
this raving madman, a sick piece of work, a two-faced
liar, who just now promised, when talking with me and Hērē,
to fight the Trojans, yes, and give aid to the Argives—
but now consorts with the Trojans, his promises forgotten."

So saying, she seized Sthenelos, pulled him backwards,
dumped him out of the chariot. Nimbly he jumped aside,
while she now mounted and stood beside noble Diomēdēs,

a goddess hot for the fray. Loud creaked the oaken axle
under its load: it bore a great man, and a terrible goddess.
Pallas Athēnē then grasped the whip and the reins,
and instantly straight at Arēs she drove the whole-hoofed horses.
He was busy stripping the armor from huge Periphas, by far
the best man among the Aitōlians, Ochlēsios's splendid son.
Him bloodstained Arēs was stripping; but Athēnē put on
the cap of Hādēs,[9] to stop mighty Arēs from seeing her.

But when Arēs, ruin of mortals, saw noble Diomēdēs,
he left giant Periphas lying there, on the same spot
where he'd first cut him down and robbed him of his life,
and made straight for Diomēdēs, the horse breaker, and then
when, in their advance, they were near the one to the other,
Arēs lunged out over the yoke and the horses' reins
with his bronze spear, hungry to snatch the life out of him; but
it was caught by the hand of the goddess, grey-eyed Athēnē,
who jerked it up over the chariot, to miss its target. Next,
Diomēdēs of the good war cry thrust out hard
with his bronze spear, and Pallas Athēnē drove it
into Arēs' lower belly, where the kilt guarded him.
Here he hit, here he wounded him, ripping his fine flesh,
and tore the spear out again. Then brazen Arēs bellowed
as loud as the war cry of nine thousand—no, ten thousand—
fighting troops, as they clash in his, Arēs', strife.
Now Achaians and Trojans were seized by fear and trembling,
so loudly bellowed Arēs, he of warfare insatiate.

Like a black tornado that's formed out of the clouds
after a heat-spell, when a blustering wind arises,
so to Tydeus's son Diomēdēs did brazen Arēs
look, as he rose through the clouds to the wide heaven.
Swiftly he came to the gods' seat, to steep Olympos,
sat down by Zeus son of Kronos, anguished at heart,
showed him the immortal blood still flowing from his wound,
and tearfully thus addressed him with winged words:

9. The sole mention by Homer of this cap of invisibility, a very old, widespread piece of folklore evidently linked to the popular etymology of Hādēs, "the unseen one" (Kirk, 2: 147). "[I]t is of course not necessary to suppose that the poet conceives Athena as literally putting on a cap," Leaf solemnly informs us; this was just "the traditional—almost proverbial—way of saying that she makes herself invisible to Ares" (1: 194).

"Zeus, father, are you not angered at seeing these violent deeds?
We gods must always endure the most cruel suffering
through each others' ill will when we ally with mortals!
We're all at war with you, for you bore this mad accursed
daughter of yours, her mind always set on lawless acts!
Look, all the other gods who are on Olympos
are obedient to you, each one of us is your subject;
yet her you oppose in no way, neither by word nor deed,
but give her her head, since the little horror's your child.
So now Tydeus's son, the arrogant Diomēdēs,
she's incited to vent his fury against the immortal gods.
First he tackled Kypris, wounded her hand at the wrist,
then he came charging at me like some superhuman creature.
But my quick feet let me escape—otherwise long since
I'd have been lying there in agony among the gruesome corpses,
alive still, yet made strengthless by his bronze's strokes."
To him with a fierce glance spoke Zeus the cloud-gatherer:
"Don't sit here by me and whine, you two-faced trimmer!
Of all the gods on Olympos, I find you the most hateful—
quarrels are what you love most, and wars and battles.
You've got all your mother's spirit, ungovernable, unyielding—
Hērē! It's all *I* can do to make her heed my orders,
so it's by her promptings, I'd guess, that you're in this trouble.
Still, I can't bear to let you endure pain any longer—
you're my offspring, it was to me your mother bore you.
Had it been any other god who sired such a little horror,
you'd long since have found yourself down lower than the Titans."

So saying, he commanded Paiëōn to make Arēs whole,
and over his wound Paiëōn spread pain-killing medicines
and healed him: for he was not made of mortal stuff. As when
an infusion of fig juice quickly thickens white milk
that was liquid before, and it curdles as a man stirs it,
so swiftly now did he heal impetuous Arēs, and Hēbē
gave him a bath, and dressed him in elegant garments,
and he sat there by Zeus son of Kronos, exulting in his glory.

Then those two—Hērē of Argos and Athēnē the Defender—
went back to great Zeus's palace, after thus making Arēs,
ruin of mortals, give up his slaughter of warriors.

Book 6

The grim strife of Achaians and Trojans was left then to itself:
now this way, now that, the battle kept shifting across the plain,
as each side aimed at the other their bronze-tipped spears,
between the Simoeis river and the waters of Xanthos.

Aias, Telamōn's son, the Achaians' bulwark, was first
to break through the Trojans' ranks, bringing hope to his comrades;
for he laid low the foremost fighter among the Thracians,
Eussōros's son Akamas, a big strong fellow—threw first,
caught the boss of Akamas's helmet with its horsehair crest:
the bronze spear-point stuck in his forehead, entered
the cranium, and darkness enveloped both his eyes.

Diomēdēs, good at the war cry, now slew Axylos,
Teuthras's son, whose home was in well-built Arisbē:
a person of wealth and substance, hospitable too,
for his house stood on the high road, was open to everyone.
Yet of these not one was there to save him from wretched death,
by facing the foe before him: Diomēdēs cut off both
him and his henchman Kalēsias, at that time
his charioteer; together they entered the underworld.

Euryalos slaughtered Drēsos and Opheltios, then went
after Aisēpos and Pēdasos, whom on a time a nymph,
a naiad, Abarbarea, bore to blameless Boukoliōn.
Boukoliōn was the offspring of noble Laomedōn,
his first-born, though his mother bore him in secrecy.
Tending his flocks he was when he lay with the nymph,
who conceived and delivered twin sons. It was of these
that Mēkisteus's son undid the power and the resplendent
limbs, and stripped off the armor from their shoulders.

Astyalos fell to the staunch fighter Polypoitēs;
Odysseus it was finished off Pidytēs of Perkōtē
with his bronze spear, while Teukros killed noble Aretaōn.
Antilochos, Nestōr's son, with his shining spear laid low
Ablēros; Agamemnōn, lord of men, slew Elatos

who dwelt in steep Pēdasos by the banks of wide-flowing
Satnioeis. The hero Lēïtos caught Phylakos
as he fled him; Eurypylos slaughtered Melanthios.

But Menelaös, good at the war cry, now took Adrēstos
alive, for his two horses, stampeding across the plain,
were snagged by a tamarisk branch, broke loose from the curved
chariot at the pole's end, themselves made off for
the city, to which all the rest were bolting, panic-stricken;
but he himself was thrown from his chariot, over the wheel,
headlong into the dust, on his face. Then stood over him
Atreus's son Menelaös, with his far-shadowing spear,
and Adrēstos clutched his knees and besought him, saying:
"Take me alive, son of Atreus, accept a fitting ransom!
Much treasure's laid up in the house of my rich father—
bronze, gold, and iron worked with much toil: from these
my father would gladly pay you ransom past counting
should he learn I am still alive by the Achaians' ships."

These words moved the spirit in Menelaös's breast:
indeed, he was on the point of having his henchman take
Adrēstos to the Achaians' swift ships, but Agamemnōn
ran up to confront him, crying out in rebuke:
"Menelaös, dear brother, what makes you care so much
for these people? Did you get the best treatment in your home
from Trojans? Not one of them should escape sheer doom
at our hands, no, not even the child whose mother still
carries him in her belly: let the people of Ilion
all perish together, unmourned, eradicated!"

Thus
the hero altered the mind-set of his brother, since what
he urged had been destined. Menelaös with one hand
thrust the hero Adrēstos away from him. Lord Agamemnōn
stabbed him hard in the side. He collapsed. The son of Atreus,
one heel on his chest, tore out the ash-wood spear.

Now Nestōr with a great shout cried out to the Argives:
"My friends, you Danaän warriors, henchmen of Arēs,
let no man now in his thirst for plunder hang back
far in the rear, to let him bring most back to the ships:

no, let us rather kill foemen: that way you'll have leisure
to strip the armor from corpses scattered across the plain."

With these words he aroused each man's fury and spirit:
then would the warlike Achaians have once more driven the Trojans,
overcome by their craven spirit, back up into Ilion
had there not come forward to speak to Aineias and Hektōr
Helenos, Priam's son, far the best of the diviners:
"Aineias and Hektōr, on you, above all other Trojans
and Lycians, lies the weight of battle: you are the best
in every venture, both for fighting and counsel.
Stand firm, then, and rally your troops before the gates,
visit all ranks, before they run off and tumble
into their women's arms, a delight to their enemies!
Then, when you two have aroused all ranks to action,
we'll make our stand here, face the Danaäns in battle,
worn out though we are, since necessity forces us.
Hektōr, you should go into the city, carry back word to
your mother and mine: she's to assemble the older women
at the temple of grey-eyed Athēnē on the acropolis,
and when she's unlocked the doors of that sacred domain,
let her choose the robe that she deems the finest and largest
of those in her hall, the one that's most precious to her,
and spread it over the knees of fair-haired Athēnē, vow
to sacrifice in her shrine a dozen yearling heifers
that have never felt the goad, in the hope that she may pity
our town, and the Trojans' wives and infant children,
and hold back from sacred Ilion Tydeus's son,
that brutal spearman, that powerful source of rout,
who has, I declare, proved the strongest of all the Achaians.
Not even Achilles so scared us, the leader of men,
who they say was born of a goddess; this madman rages
over the mark, there's none can match him for violence."

So he spoke, and Hektōr did not disregard his brother,
but leapt to the ground from the chariot in his battle gear,
brandishing two sharp spears, and ranged widely through the ranks,
urging them on to fight, stirred up the clash of battle.
So they regrouped, stood firm, facing up to the Achaians,
and the Argives now gave ground, left off their killing,

thinking that some immortal from starry heaven
had come down to aid the Trojans, the way they'd rallied.

Now Hektōr with a great shout cried out to the Trojans:
"High-spirited Trojans, and you, our far-famed allies,
be men, my friends, bear in mind your fighting spirit
while I make my way to Ilion, exhort our elderly
counsellors and our wives to offer their prayers
to the immortals, to promise them ample sacrifice."

After so saying, bright-helmeted Hektōr departed,
the rim of black hide that ran round the outer edge
of his bossed shield knocking on both neck and ankles.

Now Glaukos son of Hippolochos and the son of Tydeus
met between the two armies, impatient to fight; and when
they came close, advancing the one against the other,
Diomēdēs, good at the war cry, was the first to speak:
"Who are you, good sir, of all mortal men there are?
Never yet have I seen you in battle that brings men honor
before, yet now you've advanced far ahead of the rest
in daring, since you stand up to my far-shadowing spear.
Unhappy are those whose sons confront my strength!
But if you are some immortal come down from heaven,
then I will not myself do battle with the heavenly gods;
for not even the son of Dryas, mighty Lykourgos,
lived long after striving against the gods in heaven—
that time he harried the nurses of frenzied Dionysos
headlong down from Mount Nysa, and they all together
threw down their ritual wands, assailed by the ox-goad
of Lykourgos the killer, while Dionysos took flight,
plunged under the sea waves in terror, was received,
panicking at the man's shouts, in the bosom of Thetis.
The gods, the easy livers, now took against Lykourgos,
and Kronos's son made him blind; nor did he survive
much longer, since all the deathless gods hated him.
So I would not choose to fight these blessed divinities!
But if you are a mortal, who eats what the earth yields, then
come close, that you may the sooner enter destruction's bounds."

The illustrious son of Hippolochos answered him:
"Great-spirited son of Tydeus, why question my lineage?

As the generation of leaves, so is that of mankind:
some leaves the wind scatters earthwards, but the fertile
woodland grows others as spring returns in season.
So with men: one generation grows, while another dies.
But if you insist on knowing this too, the true facts
of my ancestry—something familiar to many—there is
a city, Ephyrē, back in horse-pasturing Argos,
where Sisyphos dwelt, the most crafty of all mankind,
Sisyphos, Aiolos's son; the son he begot was Glaukos,
and Glaukos in turn begot the blameless Bellerophōn.
On him the gods bestowed both good looks and seductive
manliness, but against him Proitos plotted evil,
drove him out of the realm, since he was far stronger,
though Zeus had made him subject to Proitos's scepter.
Now Proitos's wife was mad for him, queenly Anteia,
yearned to lie with him secretly, yet could never
overcome the high-minded refusals of steadfast Bellerophōn.
So she made up a false story that she told to King Proitos:
"Either die yourself, Proitos, or else kill Bellerophōn,
who attempted to lie with me in love against my will."
So she spoke, and the king was angered by what he heard.
Kill Bellerophōn he would not: his conscience shrank from that.
But he sent him to Lycia, and gave him fatal tokens,
many murderous signs incised in a folded tablet,
to be shown to his father-in-law, and secure his death.[1]
So to Lycia he went, with the gods' faultless protection,
and when he reached Lycia and the Xanthos river,
the king of broad Lycia readily paid him honor:
nine days he entertained him, sacrificed nine oxen,
but when rosy-fingered Dawn appeared on the tenth day,
then he questioned his guest, asked to see whatever
message he'd brought him from his son-in-law, Proitōs.
Now after he got his son-in-law's wicked message,

1. This is the only clear reference to writing in Homer. Whether the poet thought of the "murderous signs" as Hittite hieroglyphs, Linear B symbols, or the new alphabet is quite uncertain. Kirk inclines to the alphabet on the basis of the "folded tablet" (Kirk 2: 181). West argues that Homer "composed the *Iliad* with the aid of writing and over a long period" (West 2011, 10–11). Powell denies that the "signs" are anything more than "marks" and claims that Homer, though aware of writing, "does not use or understand it" (*HE* 3.943–44). The debate continues.

first he ordered Bellerophōn to kill the invincible
Chimaira, a beast of divine, not earthly lineage,
a lion in front, a serpent behind, a goat in the mid-part,
fearsomely breathing forth the fury of blazing fire.
Her Bellerophōn slew, fulfilling the gods' portents;
next he battled the far-famed Solymoi, calling this
the toughest engagement of warriors in which he'd ever fought;
thirdly, he slaughtered the Amazons, women well-matched
against men.
Then, as he was returning, the king wove another smart trick:
choosing from all broad Lycia the very best troops
he set up an ambush. But none of these men came back home,
for every last one was slain by blameless Bellerophōn.
Then, when the king recognized him as a god's strong scion,
he kept him there, offered him his own daughter, gave him
half of all his royal entitlements; and the Lycians
measured him out an estate, the best land there was,
fine acres of orchard and plowland for him to possess.
His consort bore three children to warlike Bellerophōn:
Isandros, Hippolochos, and Laodameia.
With Laodameia Zeus the counselor lay in love,
and she bore him godlike Sarpēdōn, he of the bronze helm.
But finally even Bellerophōn, hated by all the gods,
became a solitary wanderer on the Aleian plain,
eating his heart out, avoiding the trodden paths of men.
Isandros his son was killed by Arēs, that glutton for war,
on a campaign against the far-famed Solymoi;
and his daughter golden-reined Artemis slew in anger.
Hippolochos, though, begot me: I declare myself his son.
He sent me to Troy, and repeatedly urged upon me
always to be the best, preeminent over others,
nor ever to shame the line of my ancestors,
by far the finest in Ephyrē and in all broad Lycia.
This is the bloodstock, the lineage I'm proud to claim as mine."

So he spoke: Diomēdēs, good at the war cry, rejoiced,
planted his spear-point deep in the nurturing earth,
and in friendly terms addressed the shepherd of the people:
"Then you are my family's guest-friend, from way back!
For noble Oineus once did entertain blameless

Bellerophōn in his halls, kept him there for twenty days,
and the two gave each other the fine gifts of guest-friendship—
from Oineus a baldric gleaming with scarlet, and from
Bellerophōn a gold cup, two-handled, the same one
I left back at home when I travelled here! But Tydeus
I don't remember, being still a little child when
he departed, that time the Achaian force perished at Thēbē.
That makes me your friend and host in the Argive heartland,
and you mine in Lycia, when I visit that country. Therefore
let us, even in the close fighting, avoid each other's spears,
seeing I have many, both Trojans and far-famed allies,
to kill—anyone a god grants me, or I can run down, while you
have Achaians in plenty to cut down—if you can catch them!
Now let's exchange armor, so that these men too may know
we declare ourselves to be guest-friends from ancestral times."

After thus speaking they sprang down from their chariots,
clasped one another's hands, gave pledges of friendship;
but Zeus son of Kronos robbed Glaukos of his senses,
for the armor he exchanged with Tydeus's son Diomēdēs
was gold for bronze, one hundred oxen's worth for nine.

When Hektōr reached the Skaian gates and the oak tree,
there ran out and gathered round him the Trojans'
    wives and daughters,
enquiring about their sons and brothers, their neighbors
or husbands; each one of them in turn he urged
to pray to the gods, for mourning was to be the lot of many.

But when he came to Priam's resplendent palace,
with its polished stone colonnades—and in it there were
fifty bedchambers, also of polished stone,
set close each to the next; and in them there all the sons
of Priam slept, by the side of their wedded wives,
while opposite in the courtyard were his daughters'
dozen roofed bedchambers, also of polished stone,
set close each to the next; and there the sons-in-law
of Priam slept, by the side of their wedded wives—
there his bountiful mother came out to meet him,
bringing with her Laodikē, her most beautiful daughter,
and she clasped him by the hand, and thus addressed him:

"Why have you left the rough fighting to come here, my child?
These accursed Achaians' sons must be pressing you hard
in the struggle around our city: did your spirit drive you here
to pray with raised hands to Zeus from the topmost ramparts?
Wait here, let me bring you honey-sweet wine, to pour
a libation to Zeus the Father and the other immortals
first—then enjoy it yourself, if you feel like drinking.
When a man is worn out—just as you are worn out from fighting
to save your fellows—wine greatly augments his strength."

Then great bright-helmeted Hektōr answered her:
"Bring me no mind-soothing wine, my lady mother, lest
you unstring my limbs, and I forget my strength and courage;
besides, with unwashed hands I dare not pour out libations
of fire-bright wine to Zeus; no prayers to the lord of storm clouds,
Kronos's son, by a man who's smeared with blood and filth!
But you should go to the shrine of Athēnē, the spoil-bringer,
bearing burnt offerings, when you've assembled the older women;
and choose the robe that you deem the finest and largest
of those in your hall, the one that's most precious to you,
and spread it over the knees of fair-haired Athēnē, vow
to sacrifice in her shrine a dozen yearling heifers
that have never felt the goad, in the hope that she may pity
our town, and the Trojans' wives and infant children,
and hold back from sacred Ilion Tydeus's son,
that brutal spearman, that powerful source of rout!
So, off with you to the shrine of Athēnē, the spoil-bringer,
and I'll go in search of Paris, require his presence, see if
I can make him listen to me! Ah, how I wish that the earth
would gape where he stands! The Olympian reared him to be
a bane to the Trojans, to great-hearted Priam and Priam's sons.
Should I see him going down to the house of Hādēs, then
I'd say that my mind had forgotten its wretched grief."

So he spoke. She went into the palace, summoned her handmaids,
sent them out through the city to collect the older women.
She herself went down to the fragrant storeroom where
her robes were kept, the fine work of Sidonian women,
whom Aléxandros himself, divinely handsome,
had fetched back from Sidon, sailing the wide seas—
that voyage on which he brought high-born Helen home.

From these robes Hekabē picked her gift to bring to Athēnē—
the finest for its embroidery, and the largest,
that shone like a star, and lay beneath all the others.
Then she set out, accompanied by a crowd of older women.

When they reached Athēnē's temple, high on the citadel,
the doors were opened for them by fair-cheeked Theanō,
Kissēs' daughter, and wife of Antēnōr the horse breaker,
since the Trojans had made her Athēnē's priestess. Then
they all, with ecstatic cries, raised up their hands to Athēnē,
while fair-cheeked Theanō took the robe and laid it
across the knees of Athēnē, the fine-tressed goddess,
and invoked in prayer great Zeus's daughter: "Lady
Athēnē, our city's protector, queen among goddesses,
now break Diomēdēs' spear, now grant that he himself
fall prone in front of the Skaian Gates, and at once
we'll sacrifice in your shrine a dozen yearling heifers
that have never felt the goad, in the hope that you may pity
our town, and the Trojans' wives and infant children."
So she prayed; but Pallas Athēnē shook her head in denial.

Such were these women's prayers to great Zeus's daughter;
but Hektōr had made his way to the house of Aléxandros,
the fine house that he himself had built with the very best
craftsmen then to be found in rich-soiled Troy: they'd made him
a bedchamber, main hall, and courtyard close beside
the houses of Priam and Hektōr, high on the citadel.
There Hektōr, dear to Zeus, entered, grasping a spear
eleven cubits long: its bronze point in front of him
gleamed bright; round the shaft there ran a golden ferrule.
He found the man in his chamber, cleaning his splendid armor,
his shield and corselet, and handling his back-bent bow,
while Argive Helen sat there among her serving women,
assigning to each her rare and delicate handiwork.
Hektōr took one look, and rebuked him with shaming words:
"Wretched fellow, it isn't decent for you to sit and sulk!
Your people are fighting and dying outside the citadel
and its sheer walls: it's you who set the din of battle
as a flaming noose round this township. You'd be quick yourself
to attack those you saw holding back from loathsome warfare!
So up with you, or too soon deadly fire will scorch the city!"

To him then Aléxandros, divinely handsome, replied:
You rebuke me justly, Hektōr, not more than is proper;
so let me too tell you something: listen, and mark my words.
Not so much out of rage or vexation at the Trojans
did I come and sit here: I wished to surrender to my sorrow.
But now my wife, working on me with gentle words,
has been urging me back to the fighting, and I myself feel
that this would be better. Victory shifts from man to man.
So just wait while I put on my battle gear, or else
go, and I'll follow: I'm sure I can overtake you."

So he spoke, but bright-helmeted Hektōr answered not one word,
and him now Helen addressed with words of conciliation:
"My brother-in-law, I'm a bitch, a horrible mischief-maker!
How I wish that on the same day my mother first bore me
a grim blast of the storm wind had carried me off
to some mountaintop, or else to some wave of the thunderous sea
where the wave would have swept me away before any of this
could happen! But no, since the gods ordained these troubles,
then I wish I'd been bedfellow to a better man, who could feel
the righteous wrath of his fellows, their manifold insults.
But his mind is not stable now, nor will ever be hereafter:
for this, too, I foresee, he will reap his just reward.
So come in now, my brother-in-law, relax in this chair,
since it's you above all whose mind is beset with troubles
because of me, the bitch, and Aléxandros's blind folly:
on us Zeus has settled a wretched fate: now and forever
to be subjects of song for listeners as yet unborn."

Then great bright-helmeted Hektōr answered "Don't try
to make me sit, Helen: though you love me, you'll not persuade me.
My spirit's already spurring me on to bring help to
the Trojans, who greatly long for me in my absence.
So, you rouse up *him* there, let him stir himself to action,
soon enough to catch up with me while I'm still in the city:
for I'm going first to my own house, in order to visit
my household, my dear wife, my infant son—who knows
if I'll ever come safely home to them again,
or whether the gods will destroy me at the hands of the Achaians?"

That said, bright-helmeted Hektōr went on his way,
and quickly came to his well-built house, but did not
find white-armed Andromachē there at home: she'd gone,
taking her child, together with one fine-robed attendant,
to stand high up on the ramparts, wailing and shedding tears.
So Hektōr, on not finding his blameless wife inside,
went and stood at the threshold, and spoke with her handmaidens:
"Come now, you handmaidens, answer me truly—where
did white-armed Andromachē go when she left the house?
To visit one of my sisters, or a brother's wife? Or was it
to Athēnē's shrine, where the other fair-tressed Trojan
women have gone to propitiate the awe-inspiring goddess?"

In reply to his question a busy housekeeper said:
"Hektōr, since you urgently need a truthful answer,
she's not gone to one of your sisters, nor to any brother's wife;
nor to Athēnē's shrine, where the other fair-tressed Trojan
women have gone to propitiate the awe-inspiring goddess,
but up onto Troy's great rampart, since she'd heard
the Trojans were weary, the Achaians in great strength.
So she hurried off to the wall, as fast as she could,
like a crazy woman, along with a nurse to hold the child."

So spoke the woman, the housekeeper. Hektōr hurried back
from his house, the way he'd come, down the well-paved streets.
When he'd traversed the great city and reached the Skaian Gates,
through which he'd have to pass to return to the plain,
there his bountiful wife came running to meet him,
Andromachē, the daughter of great-hearted Ēëtiōn—
Ēëtiōn, whose home lay under wooded Plakos,
in Thēbē below Plakos, lord of the Cilician people,
whose daughter was the wife of bronze-clad Hektōr.
She it was who now met him, and with her the servant
clutching to her breast the tender child, still a baby,
Hektōr's beloved son, like some beautiful star,
whom he called Skamandrios, but all others Astyanax,
the city's king, since Hektōr alone guarded Ilion.
Now he smiled as he looked at the child, saying not a word,
but Andromachē came up beside him, still shedding tears,
and clasping his hand in hers addressed him in these words:

"Crazed man, your might will destroy you: you show no pity
for your infant son, or for me, luckless woman, who'll soon
become your widow; too soon will all the Achaians
set upon you and kill you! More profitable for me,
bereft of you, would it be to sink into the earth: no other
consolation I'll have, once you've met your destiny:
nothing but grief. I've no father, no lady mother:
my father was slain by noble Achilles, when
he sacked that teeming city of the Cilician people,
high-gated Thēbē: yes, he cut down Ēëtiōn, though
he would not strip him—he shrank back from that as shameful—
but cremated him there in his fine inlaid armor, heaped
a funeral mound over him, and round it mountain nymphs,
daughters of Zeus of the aegis, planted elm trees.
And of my seven brothers that were in our halls
each one on the same day entered the realm of Hādēs,
for all were slaughtered by noble swift-footed Achilles
as they tended their white sheep and their shambling oxen.
My mother, who was queen below wooded Plakos,
he brought back here, along with the rest of the plunder,
and freed her again in return for ransom past counting;
but in her father's halls archer Artemis struck her down.
Hektōr, you are my father, my lady mother,
my brother too, as well as my young strong husband—
I beg you, show some compassion, stay here on the wall,
don't make your son an orphan, your wife a widow!
Station your troops by the fig tree, where the city's most open
to scaling, where the ramparts are vulnerable to assault—
Three times has a picked force come there to make the attempt,
led by both Aiases, and by famous Idomeneus,
with the sons of Atreus and Tydeus's valiant offspring:
someone, perhaps, well skilled in soothsaying told them,
or else it's their own spirit that drives them, urges them on."

Then great bright-helmeted Hektōr answered her: "Wife,
all this is my concern too, but I'd be deeply ashamed
before the Trojan men and deep-robed Trojan women
if like a coward I hang back, far from the fighting. No,
my spirit won't let me, I've trained myself to excel
always, to battle among the foremost Trojans, striving

to win great glory both for my father and for myself.
For this I know well, in my heart and in my mind:
A day will come when sacred Ilion will perish,
with Priam, lord of the fine ash spear, and Priam's people.
Yet it's not the Trojans' coming miseries that so concern me—
not what Hekabē will endure, or our sovereign Priam,
or my brothers, so many, so valiant, who all may end up
trodden into the dust by their hate-filled enemies—no,
it's your grief I think of, when some bronze-corseleted Achaian
will lead you away, weeping, your day of freedom gone,
to work the loom, maybe in Argos, for some other mistress,
or fetch water back from the spring—Messeïs or Hypereia—
resentful, unwilling, but burdened by harsh necessity.
And someone may say, when he sees you shedding tears:
'Why, this is the wife of Hektōr, the very best warrior
of all the horse-breaker Trojans, when they fought around Ilion!'
That's what they'll say, and for you there'll come still further
    sorrow,
widowed of such a man who could spare you the day of enslavement!
But may the heaped-up earth obliterate my corpse
before I hear your cries, see them dragging you away."

So saying, illustrious Hektōr reached out to his son,
but the child shrank back, screaming, into his fine-sashed
nurse's bosom, distraught at the sight of his dear papa,
terrified by the bronze, and the horsehair crest
he glimpsed nodding scarily from the helmet's top. At this
his dear father and lady mother both burst out laughing,
and at once illustrious Hektōr took off the helmet
and laid it, bright-gleaming, on the ground, and then
kissed his beloved son, and rocked him in his arms,
and uttered a prayer to Zeus and the rest of the gods:
"Zeus and you other gods, grant that this my child
may also become, like me, renowned among the Trojans,
my equal in strength, and rule with might over Ilion; so
one day may someone claim 'He's far better than his father'
as back he comes from the wars, bearing the bloodied gear
of the foe he has killed, and may his mother's heart rejoice."

So saying, he placed in the arms of his beloved wife
his son, and she took him to her sweet-scented bosom,

laughing and crying. At the sight her husband felt pity,
caressed her with his hand, and spoke these words to her:
"My sad wife, don't grieve at heart for me overmuch:
no man shall send me to Hādēs before my fated day—
though that day, I must tell you, no man has ever escaped,
be he coward or hero, when once he's born to this world!
Go back to the house now, attend to your proper tasks,
the loom and the distaff, give your handmaids their orders,
set them to work. But warfare shall be the business of men:
all those—and myself above all—who are native to Ilion."

So speaking, illustrious Hektōr picked up his helmet
with its horsehair crest, and his dear wife went off homeward,
often turning to look back, and shedding big tears. But then
quickly she reached home, the well-built house of Hektōr,
killer of men. Inside she found her many handmaidens,
and now she stirred them all to sad lamentation: so while
Hektōr still lived, in his own house they mourned him,
for they thought he would never again come back from the war
alive, or escape the rage and hands of the Achaians.

Nor did Paris stay long there in his own lofty house, but when
he'd put on his splendid armor, inlaid with bronze,
he hurried out through the city, trusting his nimble feet.
As when some stalled horse, grain-fed at the manger, snaps
his halter and gallops, hooves clattering, over the plain,
off to bathe in the flow of his favorite river, proudly
holding his head high, while about his shoulders
his mane streams loose, and he trusts in his splendid strength
while his knees carry him swiftly to the haunts and pastures
of mares, so Priam's son Paris went striding down from lofty
Pergamos,[2] gleaming bright in his armor like the sun,
laughing aloud as his swift feet carried him on, and quickly
he overtook noble Hektōr, his brother, just as he was
turning back from the place where he'd conversed with his wife.
First to speak was Aléxandros, the godlike: "My brother,
I fear I'm holding you up, when you want to be moving,
by my lateness: I didn't come at the time you told me to."

2. Not to be confused with the Mysian city of Pergamon; Pergamos was the highest quarter of Troy, its acropolis, where Apollo's temple stood (5.446).

In answer to him bright-helmeted Hektōr said:
"Look, no one in his right mind would choose to disparage
your work in battle: your courage is not in question.
But you choose to hang back, not to fight, and it pains me to
the quick of my heart when I hear those shaming comments about you
from the Trojans, who face much harsh combat on your behalf.
Well, let's be off: all this we'll make right later, should Zeus
let us set out one day, for the deathless gods of heaven,
in our halls the wine bowl of freedom, when at last
we've driven the well-greaved Achaians from the land of Troy."

Book 7

So saying, illustrious Hektōr charged out through the gates,
and with him Aléxandros, his brother: in their hearts
both were hungry for battle and combat. Just as a god
will provide eager sailors with a more than welcome
tailwind, when they're weary of thrusting back seawater
with polished pinewood oars, and the labor's loosened their limbs,
so these two now appeared before the eager Trojans.

Then they started in. Paris cut down king Areïthoös's son,
Menesthios, native of Arnē, whom the war-club-wielding
Areïthoös sired on ox-eyed Phylomedousa;
and Hektōr struck Ēïoneus with his sharp-tipped spear
in the neck, under his good bronze helmet, undid his limbs;
and Glaukos son of Hippolochos, the Lycians' leader,
hit Iphinoös with his spear in the hard-fought combat—
Dexios's son—as he leapt up behind his swift mares,
in the shoulder: he fell to the ground, his limbs were loosened.

When the goddess, grey-eyed Athēnē, noticed these two
slaughtering Argives in the hard-fought combat, she
set off, quickly darting down from the heights of Olympos
to sacred Ilion. Apollo hurried across to meet her,
for he'd glimpsed her from Pergamos, and wanted victory
for the Trojans. The two of them met beside the oak tree,
and the first to speak was the son of Zeus, Lord Apollo:
"What's your urgency this time, daughter of mighty Zeus?
Why has your great spirit sent you down from Olympos?
Do you want to give victory, for a change, to the Danaäns?
You've certainly no pity for the Trojans who are dying.
Look, if you'd do as I say, it would make things better by far.
Let's break off the warfare and fighting now, at least
for today—though hereafter they'll battle again, till they witness
Ilion's end, since it's dear to the hearts of you
immortal ladies to see this city at last laid waste."

In answer to him then spoke the goddess, grey-eyed Athēnē:
"Let it be so, archer: it's what I myself had in mind
coming down from Olympos to visit the Trojans and Achaians.
But tell me, how do you plan to stop these men from fighting?"

In answer to her then spoke the son of Zeus, Lord Apollo:
"Let us stir up the mighty passion of Hektōr the horse breaker,
to the end that he may challenge some Danaän to face him,
man against man, in the grimness of single combat. Then
the bronze-greaved Achaians are sure, in their resentment,
to find an individual who'll duel with noble Hektōr."

So he spoke, and the goddess, grey-eyed Athēnē, did not
dissent. Now Helenos, Priam's son, sensed in his heart
the plan that the gods had chosen as they debated,[1]
and he went and stood beside Hektōr, and spoke to him, saying:
"Hektōr, son of Priam, equal of Zeus in counsel,
will you be persuaded by me, since I am your brother?
Tell all the rest, both Achaians and Trojans, to be seated
while you challenge whoever's the best of the Achaians
to fight single-handed against you in fearful conflict, seeing
it's not yet your time to die, to meet your allotted fate:
thus I have heard it said by the gods who live forever."

So he spoke, and Hektōr took great pleasure in his words.
Into the midst he strode, holding back the Trojan ranks
with his spear, grasped in the middle, and they all sat down,
and Agamemnon settled the well-greaved Achaians, while
Athēnē and the lord of the silver bow, Apollo,
perched in the likeness of birds—vultures—high up on
the tall oak of Zeus, the Father and aegis-bearer,
enjoying the sight of the warriors, whose serried ranks
bristled with shields, helmets, spears. Just in the way
the deep sea's ruffled by a cat's-paw breeze each time
the west wind first stirs, and the deep turns black beneath it,
so were the ranks of Achaians and Trojans as they settled
themselves in the plain, and Hektōr, between them both, now
spoke:

---

1. Priam's son Helenos has the power of prophecy (cf. 6.76) and can thus intuit what the gods have decided. His role as seer is not stressed (any more than that of Kassandrē), but as Kirk says, "the Trojans need a prophet, if only to balance Kalkhas" (Kirk 2: 237).

"Hear me out, you Trojans, and you well-greaved Achaians,
while I tell you what the heart in my breast dictates. Our oaths
the high-throned son of Kronos has not let be fulfilled,
but rather has evil in mind for both sides, until either
you capture Troy of the fine ramparts, or else yourselves
are brought low by the side of your own seafaring vessels.
In your ranks are the best men of all the Achaians: from them
let the one whose spirit impels him to fight me now come forth
out of the mass, be your champion, battle noble Hektōr!
So thus I declare, and let Zeus be our witness to it:
If that man cuts me down with the keen-edged bronze,
he can strip off my armor, take it back to the hollow ships,
but must give back my corpse to be carried home, so that Trojans
and Trojans' wives may grant it its proper due of fire.
But if I should slay him, and Apollo lets me triumph,
I shall strip off his armor, take it back to sacred Ilion,
and hang it up there in the shrine of Apollo the archer;
but his corpse I'll surrender at the well-benched vessels,
to let the long-haired Achaians offer him funeral rites,
and raise him a burial mound beside the wide Hellespont.
And one day in the future someone not yet born may say,
as he sails his many-benched vessel over the wine-faced deep,
'This is the burial mound of a warrior long deceased,
slain, fighting valiantly, by illustrious Hektōr.' Thus
someone will speak, and my fame will never perish."

Such were his words, and they all sat quiet, in silence,
ashamed to refuse the challenge, yet scared to accept it.
But at last Menelaös stood up and spoke among them,
with bitter contempt, greatly saddened at heart: "Ah me,
you empty braggarts, you women, not men, of Achaia!
This will be an embarrassing business, deep, deep disgrace,
if no Danaän now steps forward to stand against Hektōr!
But you—may you all become mere earth and water,
sitting here, every one a lifeless clod, without glory!
Against this man I will don arms myself, though it's on high
that the issues of victory rest, with the immortal gods."

This said, he put on his magnificent armor. And now,
Menelaös, the end of your life would have been made manifest
at Hektōr's hands, since he was more powerful by far,

had not the Achaian princes sprung up and caught hold of you,
while Atreus's son himself, wide-ruling Agamemnōn,
clasping your right hand, addressed you in these words:
"You're out of your mind, Menelaös! There's no need
for this madness in you. Hold back, for all your distress,
don't let mere rivalry drive you to fight a better man:
Hektōr, Priam's son, from whom others, too, shrink back—
even Achilles shuddered at meeting this man in battle
that brings men glory, and he is better by far than you.
Go and sit down now in the company of your comrades:
the Achaians will find an antagonist to fight with this man,
and even though he be fearless, and a glutton for battle,
he'll be glad enough, I tell you, to bend knee and rest,
if he escapes deadly warfare and the horrors of combat."

With these words the hero won over his brother's mind,
since what he urged made good sense. Menelaös agreed,
and his attendants, rejoicing, took the armor from his shoulders,
while Nestōr rose to his feet and addressed the Argives:
"What a business! Great grief, for sure, is come upon Achaia.
Loud would be the groans of old Pēleus, driver of horses,
the Myrmidons' noble counselor and spokesman,
who once, in his own house, took pleasure in questioning me,
asking about all the Argives, their birth and lineage.
Were he to hear that they all were now cringing before Hektōr
he'd keep raising his hands in prayer to the immortals
that his spirit might leave his limbs for the house of Hādēs!
How I wish—Zeus, Father, Athēnē, Apollō!—I were
as young as I was when, gathered near swift-flowing Keladōn,
men of Pylos and spear-mad Arkadians fought together
outside the walls of Pheia, around Iardanos's streams.
Ereuthaliōn stood as their champion, a godlike man,
wearing upon his shoulders the armor of the lord Areïthoös:
noble Areïthoös, tagged with the nickname "Clubber"
by warriors—and by their fine-sashed women too—
since his weapon was neither the bow nor the long spear
but a club of iron with which he smashed through the ranks.
Him Lykourgos killed, by trickery, not by might,
in a narrow defile, where his iron club could not save him
from destruction: Lykourgos got his blow in first,

spearing him through the midriff, slammed him down on his back,
stripped him of the armor brazen Arēs had given him.
This gear he then wore himself in war's bruising turmoil;
But when Lykourgos was coming to old age in his halls
he gave it to his dear henchman Ereuthaliōn to wear,
and clad in that armor he challenged all our best warriors;
but they all shuddered in terror, and none dared face him.
My own unflinching spirit set me on in my boldness
to do battle with him, though I was the youngest of them all.
So I fought against him, and Athēnē gave me the glory.
This was the tallest, strongest man that ever I killed—
a sprawling mass, spread-eagled this way and that. How I wish
I were still that young, that my strength were still intact—
then would bright-helmeted Hektōr quickly get his fight!
But you lot, though you're the best the Achaians can muster,
not even so are you minded, much less eager, to face Hektōr."

Thus the old man chastised them. Then nine in all stood up:
by far the first to rise was the lord of men, Agamemnōn,
next came the son of Tydeus, powerful Diomēdēs,
followed by the two Aiases, both clad in daring valor;
after them Idomeneus with Idomeneus's henchman
Mērionēs, a match for Enyalios the killer,
and close behind these Eurypylos, Euaimōn's splendid son.
Next Thoas, Andraimōn's son, stood up, and noble Odysseus:
all these were set on doing battle with noble Hektōr.
Then Nestōr, Gerēnian horseman, spoke among them again:
"Now shake the lots thoroughly, to find out who'll be chosen,
for he'll surely bring good fortune to the well-greaved Achaians
and to his own spirit, should he chance to escape
from deadly warfare and the terrible grind of combat.'
So he spoke: now each man marked his own lot, and they
tossed them into the helmet of Atreus's son Agamemnōn,
while the troops all prayed, arms uplifted to the gods,
and thus would someone say, staring up at the broad sky:
"Zeus, Father, let the lot fall on Aias, on Tydeus's son,
or on the king of gold-rich Mykēnai himself."

So they spoke,
and Nestōr, Gerēnian horseman, shook the helmet,
and out leapt the lot which they themselves had hoped for:

that of Aias. A herald carried it round the crowd
from left to right, displayed it to all the Achaian leaders:
none recognized the lot, each denied it was his. But when,
as the herald went through the crowd, he reached the man
who'd thrown it, marked, into the helmet, illustrious Aias,
then Aias stretched out his hand, and he put the lot in it.
At a glance Aias knew his mark, and rejoiced at heart,
then dropped the lot on the ground beside his foot, exclaiming:
"My friends, this lot is mine, and I rejoice in my heart,
since I'm convinced I shall conquer noble Hektōr.
But come, while I'm putting on my armor for the battle,
you should all pray to Lord Zeus, the son of Kronos,
silently, by yourselves, so the Trojans learn nothing of it—
or out loud, since in any case there is no man we fear,
and none who can put me to flight, his will against mine,
using either force or skill, for I don't think I was born
and raised, on Salamis, completely unskilled myself."

So he spoke, and they prayed to Lord Zeus, the son of Kronos,
and thus would someone say, looking up at the broad sky:
"Zeus, Father, ruling from Ida, most glorious, most great,
grant victory to Aias, let him win a great triumph—
or, if you love Hektōr too, and care for his welfare,
then furnish both men with equal strength and glory."

Such their words, while Aias was arming himself
in gleaming bronze. But when all his gear was attached,
all his body protected, he stepped forth like huge Arēs
when he goes to war among men whom the son of Kronos
has assembled to fight in the rage of heart-devouring strife:
just so sallied forth huge Aias, the bulwark of the Achaians,
with a smile on his grim features, taking lengthy strides
on his feet below, as he brandished his far-shadowing spear.
The Argives indeed rejoiced as they watched him, but a fearful
trembling seized on the limbs of every Trojan—
even Hektōr's own heart beat faster against his rib cage,
yet he had no chance to withdraw, to lose himself in the mass
of his people, since he it was had made the fighting challenge.
So Aias drew near, hefting his tower-like shield of bronze
and sevenfold bull's hide, that Tychios toiled at making:
Tychios, first among hide workers, whose home was in Hylē,

who'd worked Aias's glinting shield with seven layered hides
from well-fed bulls, and on top an eighth, of hammered bronze.
Holding this out from his chest, Aias, Telamōn's son,
marched up close to Hektōr, and addressed him threateningly:
"Hektōr, you're going to learn, very clearly, man to man,
what champions the Danaäns still have amongst them,
even after Achillēs—the lionheart, the rank breaker!
He now beside his curved, deep-voyaging vessels
lies raging at Agamemnōn, the shepherd of the people;
yet we too are such men as can stand and face you—
and we're many! So begin the battle, the warfare!"

To this great Hektōr, the bright-helmeted, made his answer:
"Aias, scion of Zeus, son of Telamōn, lord of your people,
don't try to scare me as though I were some weak child,
or a woman, knowing nothing of the business of warfare!
Not so: I'm well acquainted with combat and killings,
I know how to wield—see, to left, to right—my toughened
oxhide shield: that's real shieldmanship in battle!
I'm skilled at charging into the mêlée of galloping horses,
I can, at close quarters, dance the measure of deadly Arēs;
yet I don't mean to catch such a one as you off guard
by a furtive sighting and cast: I'll throw openly, hope to hit you."
That said, he poised and let fly his far-shadowing spear,
and hit Aias's sturdy shield, with its seven oxhide layers,
on its outermost bronze, that formed the eighth layer on it.
Through six of these folds the tough bronze tore its way,
but was stopped by the seventh hide. Then in response
Aias, scion of Zeus, let fly his far-shadowing spear,
and struck Priam's son on his all-round well-balanced shield:
clean through the gleaming shield pierced the weighty spear,
clean through the subtly worked corselet it forced its way,
and tore a hole in his tunic, close to the rib cage—
but Hektōr leaned off to one side, escaped the black death-spirit.
Both grasped their long spears, pulled them out at the same moment,
and fell on each other like lions that devour raw meat
or wild boars, creatures of no small strength. Priam's son
thrust with his spear, struck the other's shield in the middle,
but the bronze failed to break the surface, its point was bent,
and Aias sprang at him, pierced his shield: the spear point

went clean through, brought his fierce charge to a halt,
tore its way into his neck, and the black blood spurted up.
Yet not even so did bright-helmeted Hektōr yield,
but started back, and hefted in one strong hand
a rock that lay on the plain, black, jagged, huge, and with it
struck Aias's fearsome sevenfold oxhide shield
in the middle, right on the boss, and the bronze re-echoed.
In reply now Aias heaved up an even bigger rock,
whirled and flung it, with measureless force in his throw,
crushed the shield in with this rock that was like a millstone,
and Hektōr's knees gave way, he lay stretched on his back
beaten down under his shield. But Apollo quickly raised him.
Now with their swords they'd have been lunging hand to hand,
had not the heralds, those envoys of Zeus and mortals,
come, one from the Trojans, one from the bronze-clad Achaians:
Talthybios and Idaios, both men of sound understanding.
They held out their staffs between them, and the herald Idaios,
a master of wise advice, made this proclamation:
"Fight no longer, dear sons; abandon your battle!
You both are dear to the heart of Zeus the cloud-gatherer,
both men of the spear: that indeed we have seen for ourselves!
Besides, night is upon us, and it's good to yield to night."

In response to his words then Aias, Telamōn's son, declared:
"Idaios, you must tell Hektōr to give the answer to this,
since it was he who issued the challenge to all our best men.
Let him go first: I am ready to do whatever he says."

Then great bright-helmeted Hektōr spoke as follows:
"Aias, since some god gave you both stature and power,
and good sense too, and with spear you outclass all Achaians,
let us now take a break from fighting, cease our combat—
for today at least: hereafter we'll battle again, until heaven
decides between us, lets one or the other triumph:
besides, night is upon us, and it's good to yield to night.
This way you'll cheer all the Achaians beside their ships,
and most your own kin and comrades, such as you have;
while I, throughout this great city of King Priam's,
shall encourage the men of Troy and their long-robed women
who are bound for the gods' assembly to pray on my behalf.
Come then, let's give one another ennobling gifts,

so that Achaians and Trojans may say amongst themselves:
'Truly these two fought each other in heart-devouring strife,
yet still reached an agreement, parted in friendship.'"

So speaking, he offered Aias a silver-studded sword,
complete with matching scabbard and well-cut baldric,
and Aias gave him a sash, that was dyed bright purple.
So they parted, one to the Achaian host, the other
to the gathering of the Trojans, who rejoiced when they saw
Hektōr alive and whole, and coming towards them—
having got clear of Aias's violence, his irresistible hands—
and escorted him to the city, scarce believing him to be safe.
On the other side now the well-greaved Achaians led off
Aias, agog at his victory, to noble Agamemnōn.

When these arrived at the huts of Atreus's son, for them
the lord of men, Agamemnon, made sacrifice of an ox,
a male, five years old, to Kronos's all-powerful son.
This they then flayed and got ready, butchered the carcass,
cut up the meat with skill, threaded the bits on skewers,
grilled them with care, then drew them all off. But when
they were through with their work, and the meal had been got ready,
they feasted, and no one's heart lacked a fair share in the feasting,
and Aias received in his honor the whole length of the chine
from Atreus's heroic son, wide-ruling Agamemnōn.
But when they had satisfied their desire for food and drink,
for them, first, the old man Nestōr began to weave a plan—
Nestōr, whose counsel had earlier, too, seemed best.
He, with friendly intent now spoke before the assembly:
"Son of Atreus, and you other leaders of all the Achaians:
The dead of the long-haired Achaians now are many,
whose dark blood impetuous Arēs has spilt around
swift-flowing Skamandros: their souls have gone down to Hādēs.
So at dawn you must call a halt to the Achaians' fighting,
and we'll gather up the corpses, wheel them back here
on oxcarts and mulecarts. After that we'll cremate them
a little way off from the ships, so each man may carry home
their bones to their sons—when we're back in our native land.
And round the pyre let us heap up, there in the plain,
one communal burial mound, and quickly build beside it
high walls, a protection for our vessels and ourselves,

and in the walls let us fashion close-fitted gateways,
wide enough to let chariots be driven through them,
and outside, close to these, we should dig a deep ditch
running all round that hold off troops and horses
if ever we're under assault by these overweening Trojans."

So he spoke, and all the princes gave him their assent.
The Trojans too held a meeting, up on Ilion's citadel,
in alarm and disorder, alongside the gates of Priam,
and amongst them wise Antēnōr was the first to speak:
"Listen to me, you Trojans, Dardanians, and allies,
while I say what the heart in my breast is bidding me tell you.
Come, then: Argive Helen, along with her possessions—
let's give her, to take away, back to the sons of Atreus.
Now we're fighting with oaths forsworn, so I have no hope
of anything going our way unless we take this course."

This said, he sat down, and there then stood up amongst them
the noble Aléxandros, fair-haired Helen's husband,
who in reply now addressed him with winged words:
"Antēnōr, the things you are saying no longer please me:
you can think up a different speech, one better than this.
If your public message is meant in all seriousness,
then the gods themselves must surely have addled your wits.
So I will speak out before the Trojans, breakers of horses,
and declare to your face: I refuse. My wife I'll not give back.
But all the possessions I brought from Argos to our home—
all—I'm prepared to return, and add to them from my store."

This said, he sat down, and there then stood up amongst them
Priam, of Dardanos's lineage, a match for the gods in counsel.
He with friendly intent now spoke before the assembly:
"Listen to me, you Trojans, Dardanians, and allies,
while I say what the heart in my breast is bidding me tell you.
For now, take your dinner throughout the city, as usual,
and keep a good lookout, and each of you stay alert;
but at daybreak let Idaios make his way to the hollow ships
to inform Atreus's sons, Agamemnōn and Menelaös,
of the words of Aléxandros, over whom this quarrel began;
and let him add this wise proposal: that they should agree
to a truce from dolorous warfare, until we have burned

our dead: after that we'll fight again, until heaven
decides between us, gives victory to one side or the other."

So he spoke: they listened attentively, and obeyed him.
Their dinner they ate at their posts, throughout the army,
and at daybreak Idaios made his way to the hollow ships.
There he found, in assembly, the Danaäns, henchmen of Arēs,
at the stern end of Agamemnōn's vessel. Standing there
amongst them, the herald, strong of voice, now spoke as follows:
"Son of Atreus, and you other leaders of all the Achaians,
I am ordered by Priam and the rest of our eminent Trojans
to repeat to you—in the hope you may find them agreeable—
the words of Aléxandros, over whom this quarrel began.
The goods that Aléxandros—how I wish he had perished first!—
brought back to Troy in his hollow ships, all these
he's willing to give back, and increase from his own store;
but as for the wedded wife of illustrious Menelaös,
her he will not return, though indeed the Trojans urge it.
This too they bade me propose: that you should agree
to a truce from dolorous warfare, until we have burned
our dead: after that we'll fight again, until heaven
decides between us, gives victory to one side or the other."

So he spoke, and they all became hushed in silence, until
at last Diomēdēs, good at the war cry, addressed them:
"Let no man now accept these goods from Aléxandros,
nor Helen either: it's obvious, even to the witless,
that already destruction's noose is tightening round the Trojans."

So he spoke: the Achaians' sons all roared their approval,
in delight at the words of Diomēdēs the horse breaker.
Then the lord Agamemnōn made this reply to Idaios:
"Idaios, you hear for yourself the Achaians' utterance,
their answer to you: this gives me pleasure as well.
As for the dead, I don't object to your burning them:
You can't dilly-dally with corpses: as soon as they're dead,
you have to quickly give them the comfort of fire. These oaths
let Zeus now witness, Hērē's loud-thundering husband."

So saying, he raised his scepter for all the gods to see,
and Idaios made his way back to sacred Ilion. There
all were met in assembly, Trojans, Dardanians,

gathered together, all waiting upon the return
of Idaios. At last he arrived, and delivered his message,
standing amongst them. Then they quickly made ready
for both tasks, fetching the corpses, and gathering firewood,
while the Argives likewise, setting off from their well-benched ships,
hastened, some for firewood, others to bring in the dead.

The sun's first rays were striking the fields as it rose
from the streams of Ocean—deep-flowing, silent, peaceful—
climbing the sky, as the two sides met one another.
A hard task it was to identify each individual,
but they washed off the clotted gore with water,
shedding warm tears, and hoisted them onto the wagons.
Great Priam forbade all keening, so it was in silence
that they loaded the pyre with corpses, grieving at heart,
and, when they'd burned them, went back to sacred Ilion.
Likewise on the other side the well-greaved Achaians
loaded the pyre with corpses, grieving at heart,
and, when they'd burned them, went back to the hollow ships.

When it was not yet dawn, but a grey half-darkness,
then at the pyre there gathered a chosen troop of Achaians,
and round it they now began raising in the plain
one communal burial mound, and beside it built
high walls, a protection for their vessels and themselves,
in which they then constructed close-fitting gateways,
wide enough to let chariots be driven through them,
while outside, close to these, they dug a deep ditch,
both wide and ample, bristling with sharpened stakes.

Thus they labored on, did the long-haired Achaians;
and the gods, sitting there by Zeus, the lord of lightning,
were amazed at the bronze-clad Achaians' mighty work.
First to speak amongst them was Poseidōn the Earth-Shaker:
"Zeus, Father, is any mortal left on this boundless earth
who'll still tell the immortals his thinking, his intentions?
Don't you see that the long-haired Achaians are at it again—
they've built a wall to defend their ships, and round it
have dug a ditch, yet without fitting sacrifice to us gods!
Its fame will reach out as far as the dawn light spreads,

and men will forget the wall that Phoibos Apollo and I
built, with enormous labor, for the hero Laomedōn."[2]

Greatly troubled, Zeus the cloud-gatherer responded:
"Come, wide-ruling Earth-Shaker, what a thing to have said!
Some other one of the gods might be scared by this idea—
one far feebler than you in both strength and forcefulness.
But *your* fame will surely reach as far the dawn light spreads!
Think now: once they're gone, these long-haired Achaians,
back with their ships to their own dear native land,
you can break up their wall and shred it all into the sea,
and once more cover the whole long shoreline with sand:
so let the Achaians' great wall be leveled, destroyed."
Such was the way they talked, the one to the other.

As the sun went down, the Achaians' work was completed,
and they slew oxen by the huts, and had their dinner,
and ships arrived from Lēmnos, ferrying wine,
a flotilla dispatched by Jason's son Eunēos,
whom Hypsipylē bore to Jason, shepherd of his people;
and for Atreus's sons, Agamemnōn and Menelaös,
Jason's son sent some special wine, a thousand measures.
From this convoy the long-haired Achaians bought their wine,
some in exchange for bronze, others for gleaming iron,
others again for hides, or the cattle themselves, and some
in exchange for war captives. They set up a lavish feast,
and then, all night through, the long-haired Achaians
feasted, as did the Trojans and their allies in the city;
and all night through Zeus the counselor planned them harm,
thundering fearfully, so that pale terror seized them.
They spilt on the ground the wine from their cups: no one dared
to drink more till they'd poured a libation to the almighty
son of Kronos. Then they lay down and took the gift of sleep.

2. Perhaps in punishment for some divine indiscretion (the sources are unclear), Poseidōn and Apollo were obliged to build the walls of Troy for Priam's father, Laomedōn, king of Troy, and take care of his flocks and herds. When Laomedōn refused to pay them for their work, Poseidōn dispatched a sea monster against the Trojans (20.145–48) and Apollo afflicted the city with plague. Further references at 12.3–33 and 21.441–57.

Book 8

As saffron-robed Dawn was spreading over the whole earth,
Zeus, who delights in the thunderbolt, assembled the gods
up on the highest peak of many-ridged Olympos.
He addressed the meeting himself, and the gods all listened.
"Hear me out, all you gods, and all you goddesses,
while I tell you what the heart in my breast commands me.
And let none of you deities—whether male or female—
make an attempt to thwart my scheme, but all alike
assent to it, so I may speedily bring these things to pass!
Any I note as minded to leave the gods, and go off
to bring help to either the Danaäns or the Trojans,
will return to Olympos smitten and in bad shape—
or I'll seize him and cast him down into gloomy Tartaros,
far off, where lies the deepest chasm below the earth,
where the gates are fashioned of iron and the threshold of bronze,
as far beneath Hādēs as the sky is above the earth:
then you'll see by how much I'm the strongest of all gods!
Come on, you gods, just try it, that you all may know the truth—
take a cable of gold, suspend it from the heavens,
and all of you lay hold of it, both gods and goddesses:
you still couldn't drag out of heaven down to earth
Zeus, supreme counselor, however great your effort!
But I, were I minded to pull with a will, could haul it up
along with earth itself, and all the sea besides;
as for the cable, thereafter I'd loop it around a peak of
Olympos, and leave the whole mass to hang in space!
It's by *that* much I outmatch the gods, outmatch mankind."

So he spoke, and they all became very quiet and silent,
shocked by his words, so powerfully had he addressed them.
But at last the goddess, grey-eyed Athēnē, took him up:
"Son of Kronos, our father, supreme among potentates,
we too indeed know well that your strength is ungovernable,
yet even so we feel pity for the Danaän spearmen
who will now fulfill a wretched fate, and perish.

Yet though we'll keep out of the battle, as you order,
we'll offer advice to the Argives, such as may help them,
so that they don't all perish through your fit of anger."
Zeus the cloud-gatherer smiled at her, and replied:
"Cheer up, Trītogéneia, dear child: the things I just said
were not meant seriously, and to you I'm kindly disposed."

That said, to his chariot he harnessed his bronze-shod team,
racers both, with their flowing golden manes,
arrayed himself likewise in gold, took hold of the whip—
well-wrought, of gold—stepped up to the driver's place,
and lashed his steeds into action: they eagerly flew off
midway between the earth and the starry heavens.
To spring-rich Ida he came, the mother of wild beasts,
and Gargaros, site of his precinct and smoking altar.
There the Father of gods and men reined in his horses,
unharnessed them from the chariot, hid them in thick mist,
and sat himself down on the heights, exulting in his splendor,
gazing out at the Trojans' city, the ships of the Achaians.

Now the long-haired Achaians hurriedly took their meal,
separately in their huts: that done, they donned their armor.
The Trojans likewise, on their side, in the city, armed themselves;
though fewer, they too were hot to join the crush of battle
through the harsh need of protecting their wives and children.
Then all the gates were flung open, the troops poured through them,
on foot and mounted both, and a mighty clamor went up.

When they had come to one place, and were met together,
buckler slammed against buckler, spears thrust, the bronze-clad rage
of warriors pressed the attack, their bossed shields ground
hard each upon the other, and a mighty clamor went up.
There were groans and triumphant shouts, from warriors killing
or being killed, and the earth ran wet with their blood.

While it was morning still, and the sacred light brightening,
both sides' shots struck home, and men dropped, hit; but when
the sun reached, and bestrode, the midpoint of the sky,
then Zeus, the father, held up his golden scale
and on it set two dooms of grief-laden death,
for horse-breaker Trojans and bronze-corseleted Achaians.
By the middle he grasped and raised it: the Achaians' fated day

sank, and their fates all settled on the provident earth,
while those of the Trojans were raised to the wide sky.
Zeus himself thundered loudly from Ida, sent a fiery
flash down among the Achaian troops; when they saw it
they were struck with amazement. Pale fear seized them all.

Then neither Idomeneus dared stand fast, nor Agamemnōn,
nor the two Aiases, servants of Arēs both; Gerēnian
Nestōr alone remained, the Achaians' protector, and he
not willingly; his horse was done for, hit by an arrow
from noble Aléxandros, husband of fair-haired Helen,
on the top of its head, where the first hairs of the mane
spring from the skull, its most vulnerable point.
It reared up in agony as the shaft struck into its brain,
and, reeling from the wound, stampeded the yoke horses.
Then, while the old man jumped down and with his sword
was cutting the horse's traces, through the rout there came
Hektōr's swift horses, bringing a daring charioteer—
Hektōr himself. And now the old man would have perished
had not at once Diomēdēs, good at the war cry, noticed,
and with a fearsome shout now urged Odysseus on:
"Son of Laertēs! Scion of Zeus! Resourceful Odysseus!
Where are you off to, back turned, like some coward, with the rest?
Hey, someone may plant a spear in your back as you run!
Stand firm then, let's keep this wild fellow away from the old man!"

So he spoke, but noble Odysseus, the much-enduring,
paid him no heed, hurried on to the Achaians' hollow ships;
and Tydeus's son, though alone, moved up to the front line,
stood there before the horses of the old man, son of Nēleus,
and addressed him, speaking with winged words: "Good old sir,
these young fighters, clearly, are wearing you down:
your strength is not what it was, a harsh old age attends you,
your charioteer's a weakling, your horses are sluggish.
Come now, get into my chariot, see for yourself
the breed of these horses of Trōs—how well they're trained
to course on the plain here, in pursuit or flight—
the ones I took from Aineias, harbingers of rout!
Your team here our squires can attend to, while these we'll drive
straight at the horse-breaker Trojans, so even Hektōr
may know well whether my spear too is raging in my grasp."

Nestōr, Gerēnian horseman, did not ignore his words.
While Nestōr's mares were looked after by the two squires,
powerful Sthenelos and the courtly Eurymedōn,
both warriors climbed aboard Diomēdēs' chariot,
and Nestōr took in his hands the shining reins,
whipped the horses, and quickly they came abreast of Hektōr,
who charged straight at them. Tydeus's son let fly
his spear, and missed him, but hit his charioteer,
Ēniopeus, the son of high-spirited Thēbaios,
in his chest beside the nipple, as he gathered the reins,
and he fell from the chariot, and the galloping horses
swerved aside, and there his life and strength were undone.
Bitter grief for his charioteer now spread over Hektōr's heart,
yet he left him—though sad for his comrade—to lie there,
and looked for another bold driver; not very long
did his pair lack a master, for in short order he found
Iphitos's son, the dashing Archeptolemos, made him mount
up there behind the horses, put the reins into his hands.

Destruction would have followed, actions irreparable,
and they'd have been penned up in Ilion like sheep,
had the Father of gods and men not quickly taken note,
thundered terribly, and let fly a white-hot bolt,
hurling it earthwards in front of Diomēdēs' horses,
so that a terrible flame of burning sulphur shot up,
and the two horses cowered in terror under the chariot.
Then the shining reins slipped out of Nestōr's hands,
and he, terrified at heart, cried out to Diomēdēs:
'Son of Tydeus, turn back your whole-hoofed horses, flee!
Can't you see that the might of Zeus is not behind you?
For now it's him, it's Hektōr, to whom Zeus, son of Kronos,
gives glory today; hereafter, if he so pleases,
he'll grant it to us. But there's no man can thwart his purpose,
however valiant: Zeus is more powerful by far."

Diomēdēs, good at the war cry, answered him thus:
"In all this, indeed, old sir, you have spoken duly;
but there's this bitter concern besets my heart and spirit,
that one day Hektōr will say, speaking among the Trojans,
'Tydeus's son fled before me, all the way to the ships.'
So he'll boast: when he does, let the earth gape wide for me."

Then Nestōr, Gerēnian horseman, answered him thus:
"Ah me, son of doughty Tydeus, what a thing to have said!
Even were Hektōr to call you coward and weakling,
neither Trojans nor Dardanians would be persuaded,
nor all those high-spirited Trojan warriors' wives
whose manly bedfellows you've cast down into the dust."

This said, he wheeled round the whole-hoofed team for flight
back through the rout, while the Trojans and Hektōr raised
a fabulous clamor, showered them with baleful missiles,
and great bright-helmeted Hektōr shouted loudly at him:
"Son of Tydeus, the swift-horsed Danaäns used to honor
you above all, with meat, full cups, a privileged seat;
but now they'll despise you—it seems you're a woman at heart!
On your way, craven dolly! Not through any yielding of mine
will you set foot on our ramparts, or in your vessels carry
our women off: long before that I'll have settled your destiny."

So he spoke, and Tydeus's son was divided in his mind:
should he wheel round his horses, fight Hektōr head-on?
Thrice he debated, uncertain, in his mind and spirit;
and thrice from Ida's mountains Zeus the counselor thundered,
sending the Trojans a sign: victory in the conflict
was changing sides. Hektōr now shouted to the Trojans:
"Trojans! Lycians! Dardanian hand-to-hand fighters!
Be men, my friends! Remember your fighting valor!
Kronos's son, I see, has now chosen me in earnest
for triumph and great glory—but for the Danaäns, woe!
Fools they were, the ones who contrived these ramparts,
flimsy, useless, that won't stop my raging charge—
our horses will jump without effort over the ditch they dug!
But when I get in there, right among their hollow ships,
then you be mindful to have destructive fire at hand,
so I can both burn their ships and kill the Argives themselves,
panic-stricken with all the smoke, there by the ships."

That said, he called out to his horses, addressed them thus:
"'Xanthos, and you, Podargos, Aithōn, and noble Lampos—
now recompense me for all the generous upkeep
that Andromachē, daughter of great-hearted Ēëtiōn,
lavished on you first of any—the honey-sweet wheat,

the wine she mixed you to drink, when your fancy called for it—
even prior to me, who indeed am her strong young husband.
Come on then, look sharp, move smartly, so we can seize
Nestōr's shield, its fame now spread across the heavens—
it's said to be all of gold, both it and its hand grips—
and strip from the shoulders of Diomēdēs the horse breaker
the intricate corselet that Hēphaistos labored to make him.
If we could get these two things, I'd hope to force
the Achaians aboard their swift ships this very night."

So he spoke,
boasting: the lady Hērē waxed indignant at him,
started up on her throne, making high Olympos tremble,
and directly addressed the mighty god Poseidōn:

"Shame on you, wide-ruling Earth-Shaker! Even in
your private heart there's no grief for the Danaäns dying,
though for you to Aigai and Helikē they bring pleasing gifts
in abundance—and once, indeed, you were all for their victory!
For if we chose, all those of us who side with the Danaäns,
to force back the Trojans, curb the will of wide-thundering Zeus,
he'd soon be sitting alone there, in a pet, on Ida."

Deeply troubled, the lordly Earth-Shaker answered her:
"Hērē, rash chatterer, what a thing it is you've said!
I for one wouldn't want all the rest of us fighting against
Zeus, son of Kronos, since he's the mightier by far."

This was how they were speaking, one to the other. By now
all the space, away from the ships, between wall and ditch
was full of horses and shield men, penned in together,
and he who'd penned them all was that equal of swift Arēs,
Hektōr, Priam's son, when Zeus gave him the glory.
And now he'd have burned the trim ships with blazing fire
had the lady Hērē not put it in Agamemnōn's mind
to quickly bestir himself, urge the Achaians into action.
So he set out along the line of their huts and vessels,
clutching his great purple cloak in one solid fist,
and stopped by Odysseus's ship, black and deep-hulled,
that lay halfway along, so a shout could reach either end,
be heard at the huts both of Aias, Telamōn's son,
and those of Achilles: the two who had drawn up their trim ships

furthest away, relying on their prowess, their hands' strength.
Now in a carrying voice he cried out to the Danaäns:
"Shame on you, Argives, base cowards, good only to look at!
What's become of our boasts, when we swore we were the best—
those empty public boasts you would utter on Lēmnos,
as you wolfed down plentiful meat of straight-horned cattle,
and swilled the bowls that were brimming over with wine,
that each man would take on in battle a hundred—no, two hundred!—
Trojans; but now we're not even a fit match for one,
Hektōr, who'll all too soon torch our ships with blazing fire!
Zeus, Father, was there ever a powerful king before this
that you so struck with delusion, so robbed of his great glory?
Yet I never, I tell you, ignored any splendid altar of yours
on my ill-fated journey here in my many-benched vessel,
but stopped at each to burn the fat and thighbones of oxen,
impatient though I was to lay waste strong-walled Troy.
Still, Zeus, this plea at least fulfill on my behalf:
allow us ourselves to escape, get clean away—
don't let the Achaians be thus vanquished by the Trojans."

So he spoke: the Father felt pity for him as he wept,
and nodded assent, that his people should indeed go safe, not perish.
Then he at once sent an eagle, best omen of all winged creatures,
a fawn, born of a swift hind, clutched in its talons.
It dropped the fawn close beside Zeus's splendid altar,
where the Achaians sacrificed to him as sender of all such signs;
and so, when they saw that the bird had come from Zeus,
they attacked the Trojans more fiercely, had ardor for battle.

Then not one of the Danaäns, many though they were,
could claim to have urged his swift steeds ahead of Tydeus's son
across the ditch and into the hand-to-hand combat: he was
the first by far to bring down a leading Trojan warrior,
Phradmōn's son Agelaös, who was turning his horses to flee;
but as he wheeled Diomēdēs rammed a spear in his back
squarely between his shoulders, drove it through to his chest.
He fell from the chariot: his armor rattled upon him.

Close behind came Atreus's sons, Agamemnōn and Menelaös,
and after them the two Aiases, both clad in daring valor,
followed by Idomeneus, along with Idomeneus's henchman

Mērionēs, a match for Enyalios, killer of men,
and close behind these Eurypylos, Euaimōn's splendid son;
and Teukros came as the ninth, stringing his back-bent bow,
hidden behind the shield of Aias, Telamōn's son.
When Aias pulled back his shield, then this hero would
take a quick look round, shoot off an arrow at someone
there in the fray; the man would fall, yield up his life,
and back the archer would dart, like a child to its mother,
to Aias, who'd shelter him behind his gleaming shield.

So, who was the first Trojan that blameless Teukros slew?
Orsilochos first, then Ormenos, and in third place Ophelestēs,
Then Daitōr, Chromios, and godlike Lykophontēs,
Polyaimōn's son Amopaōn, and finally Melanippos—
all these in turn he stretched on the nurturing earth.
The lord of men, Agamemnōn, rejoiced at the sight of him
with his powerful bow sending death into the Trojans' ranks,
and he came and stood close by, and spoke these words to him:
"Teukros, dear heart, son of Telamōn, your people's lord,
keep shooting like this! You may bring a ray of hope to the Danaäns
and to your father Telamōn, who reared you as a child
and cared for you in his home, his bastard though you were:
bring him, however distant, into your glory's sphere!
This too I'll declare to you, and indeed it will come to pass:
If it's granted to me by Zeus of the aegis and Athēnē
to lay waste Ilion's well-built citadel, then
in your hands first, after mine, I'll place the prize of honor—
either a tripod, or else two horses with their chariot,
or a woman who's ready to go up and share your bed."

Then blameless Teukros answered him in these words:
"Most glorious son of Atreus, why urge me on when I
myself am eager already? While there's still strength in me
I'll not stop; ever since we forced them back towards Ilion,
from that time on I've been watching my chance with my bow
to bring down men. Eight long-barbed shafts I've shot off,
and all are fixed in the flesh of lusty spry young fighters:
it's only this mad dog I'm unable to hit." That said,
he let fly one more shaft from his bowstring, aiming straight
at Hektōr, his will dead-set on bringing him down—
but missed again: instead his arrow struck blameless Gorgythiōn,

Priam's fine son, in the chest: the mother who bore him
had come as a bride from Aisymē, the beautiful Kastianeira,
a woman most like to the goddesses in stature.
His head drooped to one side: as a garden poppy sinks
under the load of its seed and the springtime showers,
so bowed his head sideways, weighted down by its helmet.

Teukros now let fly one more shaft from his bowstring,
straight at Hektōr, his will dead-set on bringing him down—
but missed yet again, for Apollo diverted his arrow,
and struck Archeptolemos, Hektōr's dashing charioteer,
as he plunged into the fray—in the chest, beside the nipple.
He fell from the chariot: his swift horses shied away
in terror, and there his spirit and strength were undone.
Bitter grief for his charioteer now spread through Hektōr's heart;
nevertheless he left him—though sad for his comrade—to lie there,
and ordered Kebrionēs, his brother, then close nearby,
to take over the horses' reins: he heard, and did not fail him.
Hektōr at once leapt down from his gleaming chariot,
with a terrible shout, scooped up a rock in one hand,
and charged straight at Teukros, dead-set on bringing him down.
Teukros had drawn from his quiver another bitter arrow,
and laid it against the bowstring, but bright-helmeted Hektōr—
as Teukros drew the string back to his shoulder, where
the collarbone's fixed between neck and chest, a fatal spot—
hit him right there, as he aimed, with his jagged rock,
snapping the bowstring; his hand went numb at the wrist,
he sank on his knees, and stayed thus. The bow dropped from his hand.
But Aias did not fail to notice his brother's collapse:
he ran up, and stood over him, covering him with his shield,
till there reached down beneath it two of his trusty henchmen,
Echios's son Mēkisteus, and the noble Alastōr,
who bore Teukros off, groaning heavily, to the hollow ships.

Then once more the Olympian whipped up fury in the Trojans:
they thrust the Achaians straight back towards the deep ditch,
and Hektōr pressed on with the foremost, exultant in his strength.
As when a hound on the heels of a wild boar or lion
will snap at it from behind, while in swift pursuit,
pouncing on flank or quarter—but watches in case it turns—
so Hektōr harried the long-haired Achaians, again and again

killing the hindmost, and they took to flight in terror.
But when they'd got past the palisade and the ditch
in their flight, with many laid low by Trojan hands,
then they halted and made a stand beside their vessels,
calling to one another, each man with lifted hands
shouting his prayers to all the gods. But Hektōr
kept wheeling his fine-maned horses this way and that,
his eyes like those of the Gorgon, or murderous Arēs.

Seeing and pitying them, the goddess, white-armed Hērē,
at once addressed Athēnē with winged words: "Look now,
daughter of Zeus of the aegis, are we two no longer
to care for these dying Danaäns, even at their last moment?
They're about to fulfill their wretched destiny, finished
by the onslaught of one man, his mad rage unstoppable—
Priam's son Hektōr! Already he's done them so much harm—"

In reply to her the goddess, grey-eyed Athēnē, said:
"How I wish this man might lose both strength and life,
slain by the Argives here, on his own native soil!
It's my father who rages madly in his unwholesome mind,
stubborn, always malicious, thwarter of my desires!
He has no recollection whatever of the many times
I rescued his son[1] when he buckled under Eurystheus's tasks,
and would cry to high heaven, and then from high heaven Zeus
would send me down to help him. Had I only been
sharp-witted enough to figure this business out
when he was dispatched to the realm of Hādēs' gatekeeper,
to bring back from Erebos the hound of loathsome Hādēs,
he'd never have got past those sheer falls of Stygian water!
But now Zeus hates me, and has furthered the plans of Thetis,
who kissed his knees and, taking his chin in her hand,
begged him to honor Achilles, the sacker of cities. And yet
some day he'll once more call me his grey-eyed darling!
But now you get ready for us our whole-hoofed horses,
while I go into the palace of Zeus of the aegis,

1. The son is Hēraklēs, and the reference is to the fetching up from Hādēs of the three-headed dog Kerberos, one of the twelve Labors imposed on him (probably, as Apollodorus records, in expiation for killing his children), and carried out under the direction of his cousin Eurystheus. The river Styx, with its famous falls, was thought to guard one of the Peloponnesian entrances to Hādēs.

and arm myself in my war gear. I want to find out
whether this son of Priam, bright-helmeted Hektōr,
will be glad when we two show up along the battle lines,
or whether a Trojan, too, will glut the dogs and birds
on his fat and flesh, after falling by the Achaians' ships."
So she spoke: the goddess, white-armed Hērē, did not ignore her,
but went off to harness the gold-frontleted horses—
she, Hērē, high goddess, daughter of mighty Kronos!—
while Athēnē, the daughter of Zeus the aegis-bearer,
let fall on her father's floor the soft embroidered robe
that she herself had made, worked with her own hands,
and, donning the tunic of Zeus the cloud-gatherer,
armed herself in all grim warfare's accoutrements.
Into the fiery chariot she then stepped, grasping her spear—
weighty, huge, thick—with which she quells the ranks of men,
those heroes who've angered this child of a mighty sire.
Now Hērē gave a quick flick of her whip to the horses;
of themselves the sky's gates groaned open, kept by the Seasons,
to whom are entrusted the great firmament and Olympos,
whether to lift off the thick clouds, or impose them.
Straight through those gates they drove their goad-spurred horses.

Zeus the Father, seeing them from Ida, exploded in wrath,
and sent golden-winged Iris out to them with a message:
"Up, go now, swift Iris! Turn them back, don't let them
come face to face with me here! We'd do no good by fighting.
For this I say straight out, and it will come to pass:
I'll cripple their swift horses in their harness, I'll hurl
themselves from the chariot, which I'll smash to pieces:
not in ten circling years will they get over the wounds
that my thunderbolts will inflict upon them! That way
Miss Grey-Eyes will learn what it means to fight her father!
With Hērē, though, I'm not so displeased or angry:
she's always been used to frustrating whatever I decree."

So he spoke, and gale-footed Iris took off with his message,
setting out from the mountains of Ida to high Olympos.
Right outside the gates of Olympos the many-clefted
she met the pair, stopped them, and passed on the word from Zeus:
"Where's the hurry, you two? What's put you in such a rage?
Kronos's son won't allow you to give aid to the Argives:

this was his threat, and he'll certainly carry it out—
he'll cripple your swift horses in their harness, he'll hurl
yourselves from the chariot, which he'll smash to pieces;
not in ten circling years will you get over the wounds
that his thunderbolts will inflict upon you! That way,
Miss Grey-Eyes, you'll learn what it means to fight your father!
With Hērē, though, he's not so displeased or angry:
she's always been used to frustrating whatever he decrees.
But you're a real horror, you shameless bitch, if you truly
dare to lift up your prodigious spear against Zeus."

So saying, swift-footed Iris went on her way,
and Hērē addressed Athēnē in the following words:
"Look, child of Zeus of the aegis, I no longer endorse
this scheme for us to fight Zeus on behalf of mortals—
as for them, let one die, and another survive, by chance,
while *he* can judge entirely as he's a mind to
between Trojan and Danaän. That is what's fitting."

She spoke,
and proceeded to wheel her whole-hoofed horses around.
So the Hours unharnessed their fine-maned horses for them,
and tethered them at their ambrosial mangers, and propped
the chariot over against the shining courtyard wall,
while they themselves sat down on golden chairs
among the other gods, both vexed at heart.

Zeus, the Father,
from Ida now drove his strong-wheeled chariot and horses
quickly back to Olympos and entered the gods' assembly,
and the famed Earth-Shaker unyoked his horses for him,
set the chariot on its stand, and spread a cloth over it,
while far-seeing Zeus himself settled down on his golden throne,
and under his feet the whole of great Olympos trembled.
Only Athēnē and Hērē took their seats apart from Zeus,
and neither greeted nor questioned him. Nevertheless
he understood in his heart, and addressed them, saying:
"Why are you vexed in this fashion, Athēnē and Hērē?
Surely you two aren't tired of destroying Trojans in battle
that brings men honor, so great is your grim hatred of them?
But such is my might, so irresistible my hands,

there's no way that all the gods on Olympos could shift me—
and as for you two, trembling seized your illustrious limbs
before you ever glimpsed warfare, and warfare's hurtful deeds.
This I'll tell you straight out, and it would have happened:
not on your chariot, once my thunderbolts had struck you,
would you have come back to Olympos, the immortals' abode."

So he spoke, but Athēnē and Hērē went on muttering against him,
sitting side by side, planning trouble for the Trojans.
Athēnē kept quiet now, expressed nothing openly,
though angry with Zeus her father, gripped by wild resentment;
but Hērē's breast could not contain her fury. She exclaimed:
"Most dread son of Kronos, what's this you're telling us?
As we too know well, your strength is far from trifling—
nevertheless we feel pity for the Danaän spearmen,
who'll fulfill their wretched destiny, and so perish.
Yes, we'll abstain from battle, if you so command us;
but advice we'll still offer the Argives, that will help them,
and ensure that not all of them perish through your anger."

In answer to her cloud-gatherer Zeus declared:
"At dawn tomorrow the yet-mightier son of Kronos—
you can watch if you want to, my ox-eyed lady Hērē—
will be destroying a great mass of Argive spearmen:
for mighty Hektōr will not abstain from battle until
Pēleus's swift-footed is stirred to action by the ships
on that day when they'll be fighting, in the direst straits,
at the ships' sterns, over the body of Patroklos.
For thus it's ordained. As for you, I do not care one jot
for your anger, not even should you go to the nethermost
limits of earth and sea, where Iapetos and Kronos
sit, without joy from Hyperiōn Helios's rays,
or from any breeze, but deep Tartaros surrounds them!
Should you even wander that far, I still care nothing
for your wrath, since nothing more shameless than you exists."

So he spoke, but white-armed Hērē made no answer,
and down into Ocean dipped the sun's bright light,
drawing night's blackness across the grain-giving earth:
against the Trojans' will daylight ebbed, but to the Achaians
most welcome, much prayed for, was dark night's arrival.

Now illustrious Hektōr called an assembly of the Trojans,
led them away from the ships to an open space beside
the eddying river, where the ground was clear of corpses.
Stepping down from their chariots they heard out the speech
that Hektōr, beloved of Zeus, now made, in his hand a spear
eleven cubits in length: before him its bronze point
gleamed bright; round the shaft there ran a golden ferrule.
Leaning on this, he spoke his mind to the Trojans:
"Listen to me, you Trojans, Dardanians, and allies:
I thought, just now, we'd destroy the Achaians with their ships,
and then would make our way back to windy Ilion;
but too soon darkness fell, and that, above all, preserved
the Argives and their vessels out there by the breaking waves.
So for now we must needs yield to the blackness of night,
and make ready our supper. Unyoke your fine-maned horses
from their chariots, and set out fodder before them,
and bring from the city both oxen and fattened sheep,
quickly, provide yourselves with honey-hearted wine
and bread from your homes, and gather plentiful wood,
so that all night long until early-stirring dawn
we can burn many fires, have their flames light up the sky,
in case under cover of night the long-haired Achaians
hurry to make their escape on the broad back of the sea.
Don't let them board ship at ease, without a struggle:
rather make sure that many take home a wound
to nurse there, dealt by an arrow or sharpened spear
while boarding their vessels, so that others may think twice
before launching war's miseries against the Trojans!
And let heralds, men dear to Zeus, now proclaim through the city
that stripling youths and grey-haired elders all must
take station around the city on the god-built ramparts;
and as for the women—our wives, each in her own house,
should kindle a great fire; and let a constant watch be set
lest a raiding force enter the city when our troops are away.
Be it done, great-hearted Trojans, as I now proclaim,
and let this good counsel of mine suffice for the present:
at daybreak I shall have more for you Trojan horse breakers!
In high hope I pray now to Zeus and the other gods
to drive off from here these dogs, brought in by the death-spirits

[whom the death-spirits brought here aboard their pitch-black vessels!].[2]
For this night we shall keep good watch over ourselves.
Tomorrow at dawn, then, fully armed and ready,
let's go to the hollow ships, start some sharp engagements:
I'll find out if Tydeus's son, this mighty Diomēdēs,
will drive me back from the ships to the wall, or whether
I'll cut him down with the bronze, carry off his bloodied spoils.
Tomorrow he'll measure his prowess: will he stand firm
against my spear's onset? Among the foremost, I think,
he'll lie pierced through, and many a comrade round him,
as the sun comes up tomorrow. For myself I wish
I might be immortal and ageless all my days,
and honored as highly as are Athēnē and Apollo,
as surely as now this day will bring trouble to the Argives."

Such was Hektōr's speech, and the Trojans cheered it loudly.
They unharnessed their sweating horses from under the yoke,
and each man tethered his own with straps by his chariot;
and they brought from the city both oxen and fattened sheep
quickly, provided themselves with honey-sweet wine
and bread from their homes, and gathered plentiful wood,
[and offered full rich sacrifices to the immortals, so that]
the wind bore the smell of them skyward, up from the plain,
[savorous, sweet: but the blessed gods did not share it,
nor did they wish to: hateful to them were sacred Ilion,
and Priam, he of the good ash spear, and Priam's people.][3]

So these, planning great endeavors, all night through
stayed there on the battle lines, with many a fire ablaze.
Just as in the heavens about a bright moon the stars
shine clear when the high air is windless, and sharply visible
is each mountain peak, each tall headland and ravine,

2. Line 528 has been rightly suspected as an interpolation.

3. Apart from 549, none of these lines appear here in our medieval MSS; they are quoted in the pseudo-Platonic dialogue *Alcibiades II* (149D) and are, except for 550, a cento of verses put together from different contexts (548: 1.315 = 2.306; 551–52: 24.27–28). Kirk reminds us that not only do the gods not consume part of the sacrifice in the *Iliad*, but that even their appreciation of the meat's aroma has been suppressed; and, further, that the idea that the gods were all hostile to Troy is absurd (Kirk 2: 340).

and down from heaven breaks out the infinite air,
and every star can be seen, and the shepherd is glad at heart:
in such numbers, between the ships and the streams of Xanthos,
gleamed the fires that the Trojans kindled, out there before Ilion.
A thousand fires were alight in the plain, and by each one
fifty men were gathered in the glow of the blazing fire
while their horses, munching away at white barley and spelt,
stood by their chariots awaiting the bright-throned Dawn.

Book 9

So the Trojans kept watch, but the Achaians were possessed
by an awesome panic, the fellow of icy terror:
all their best men were assailed by unendurable grief.
As two winds whip up the deep sea, flush with fish,
winds of the north and west, a gale from Thrace
tearing in suddenly, and at once the dark wave swells
and crests, strewing much seaweed along the water's edge:
just so the Achaians' spirit was shredded in their breasts.

The son of Atreus, heart-stricken with great sorrow,
went to and fro, commanding the clear-voiced heralds
to call every man by name to the place of assembly, but not
to shout names aloud; and himself went to work among the foremost.
So they sat in assembly, much troubled, and Agamemnōn
stood up, shedding tears, like a blackwater spring that pours
down some sheer rock face its dark cascade: just so,
heavily sighing, he addressed the Argives in these words:
"My friends, you leaders and lords of the Argives, Zeus,
great son of Kronos, has snared me in a vile deception—
harsh god, who once promised me, gave his nod to it,
that I'd not return home until I'd sacked strong-walled Ilion;
but now he's thought up this mean trick, commands me to go
back in dishonor to Argos, when I've lost so many men.
This, I suppose, is almighty Zeus's idea of a joke—
he who's brought down the high ramparts of so many cities,
and will bring down still more, since his is the greatest power.
Come, then, let us all agree to do as I declare:
Let us flee in our ships, sail back to our own country,
for now we'll never capture Troy of the wide ways."

Such his words: hushed in silence were all the Achaians' sons.
For a long time, deeply concerned, they said nothing. But at last
Diomēdēs of the great war cry spoke up among them:
"Son of Atreus, with you and your folly I'll first contend—
here, king, as is my right, in assembly, so curb your anger!
My courage, first, you slighted in front of the Danaäns,

calling me weak and unwarlike: with these accusations
the Argives both young and old are familiar. You received
a double-edged gift from the son of Kronos, devious schemer:
with the scepter he granted you honor above all others,
yet courage, the highest power, he did not give you.
Wretched man, do you really suppose the Achaians' sons
to be as weak and unwarlike as you proclaim them?
If your own heart is truly so set on returning home,
then go! The way lies before you, your ships are drawn up
by the sea, all those many that came with you from Mykēnai!
But the other long-haired Achaians will stay on here
until we've sacked Troy. Suppose even these likewise
choose to flee in their ships, sail back to their own country,
yet we two, I and Sthenelos, will fight on till we attain
our object in Ilion, since a god it was brought us here."

So he spoke, and all the Achaians' sons roared approval,
applauding the words of the horse breaker Diomēdēs.
Then next there rose and addressed them Nestōr the horseman:
"Son of Tydeus, in warfare you're strong above all others,
and the wisest man in counsel among those of your age:
of all the Achaians not one man will disparage your words
or dismiss them; yet your speech did not conclude the matter.
Well, you're still young: you could even be my son,
my youngest-born! Even so, there was shrewdness in your advice
to the Argive princes: what you said was fairly stated.
But now I, who can claim to be older than you, will speak out
and go through each point: nor will any man treat my words
lightly—no, not even our lordly Agamemnōn!
Outlaw from clan, hearth, society is the man
who's in love with the chilling horrors of civil conflict.
But let us for now submit ourselves to night's darkness,
and prepare our meal; let the guards man their several stations
along the length of the ditch we dug outside the ramparts.
This is my charge to our younger men. But after that you,
son of Atreus, must take the lead, for you are the most royal.
Set up a feast for the elders: that's proper, not unbecoming.
Your huts are filled with wine that the ships of the Achaians
bring you in daily across the wide sea from Thrace—
all entertainment's your province; you're lord over many.

When many are gathered together you'll follow whoever
offers the best advice; and sore need have the Achaians
of shrewd and close counsel, since enemies near our ships
are lighting numerous watch fires. Who could be pleased at that?
This night will either shatter our army or preserve it."

So he spoke; they listened attentively, carried out his orders.
The sentries hurried forth, dressed in their war gear,
Nestōr's son Thrasymēdēs, his people's shepherd, leading,
and Askalaphos and Ialmenos, sons both of Arēs,
together with Mēriones and Aphareus and Dēïpyros,
and Kreiōn's son, the illustrious Lykomēdēs.
These seven commanded the sentries, and with each
a hundred youths sallied forth, all clutching their long spears.
They went and sat themselves down between ditch and ramparts,
and lit their fires there, and each man prepared his meal.

But Atreus's son led all the Achaian elders together
to his hut, and set before them a feast to warm their hearts.
So they reached out their hands to the good things ready for them;
but when they'd satisfied their desire for food and drink
the first to set about weaving a web of counsel for them
was old Nestōr, whose past advice too had proven the best.
He with friendly intent now spoke before the assembly:
"Most glorious son of Atreus, Agamemnōn, lord of men,
with you I'll begin, with you end, since over many men
is your royal rule, and Zeus to you has entrusted
both scepter and precedent, to make good judgments for them.
So you must, above all others, both speak and listen,
and implement for another whatever his spirit may bid him
declare for our good: yours to finish whatever he begins.
Now I shall speak out as it seems to me to be best.
No other man will conceive a better idea than the one
that I've long had in mind—and which I still hold now—
ever since you, Zeus's scion, went and took that girl,
Briseïs, away from the hut of the furious Achilles—
not something I approved of: for my part I tried hard
to dissuade you; but you were swayed by your proud spirit,
and on a most noble man, whom the very immortals honored,
you heaped dishonor by taking, and keeping, that prize of his.

Yet even now let's consider how we still might make amends,
persuade him with winning gifts and conciliatory words."

To him the lord of men, Agamemnōn, then replied:
"Old sir, there was nothing amiss in your telling of my blindness.
Deluded I was: I admit it. Worth a whole crowd
of common folk is the man whom Zeus cherishes in his heart,
as now he's honored that man and routs the Achaian forces.
But since I was blinded, a slave to my wretched passions,
I'm willing to make amends, to pay boundless compensation.
Let me, before you all, name my splendid gifts:
seven tripods untouched by fire, ten talents of gold,
twenty shining cauldrons, and a dozen horses—
sturdy race winners, whose speed has brought them prizes.
Not landless would be that man, nor lacking in possession
of precious gold, to whom there accrued the amount of wealth
brought to me by my whole-hoofed racehorses' prizes.
I'll give him, too, seven women, skilled in fine handiwork,
from Lesbos, whom—when he took that well-built island
himself—I picked out: they surpassed all women in beauty.
These will I give him, including her whom I took away,
Brīseus's daughter; and, further, I'll swear a great oath
that I never went up to her bed nor lay with her, as is
the custom of humankind, between men and women.
All these things will be given him now; and if hereafter
the gods grant that we take down Priam's great city,
let him go in and load up his ship with gold and bronze
when we, the Achaians, are dividing up the spoils,
and choose for himself a score of Trojan women—
the most beautiful, after Argive Helen herself! And if
we get back to Achaian Argos, rich mother of plowland,
my son-in-law he can be, I'll honor him like my own son,
Orestēs, late-born, reared in the midst of plenty.
Three daughters of mine there are in my fine-built hall—
Chrysothemis, Laodikē, and Iphianassa: of these
let him take whichever he pleases, no bride-price paid,
to Pēleus's house; and I'll offer him richer bride-gifts
than any man ever yet provided with his daughter.
Seven well-established townships I will give him:
Kardamylē, Enopē, and Hirē with its grasslands,

sacred Phērai, together with deep-meadowed Antheia,
lovely Aipeia and Pēdasos of the vineyards—
all of them near the sea, and bordering sandy Pylos,
their inhabitants men who are rich in sheep and cattle,
who'll honor him like a god, shower him with gifts,
and under his sway will fulfill his beneficent ordinances.
All this will I do for him if he'll only give up his wrath!
Let him yield! Look at Hādēs: unbending, implacable—why
of all gods he's the one that mortals hate the worst—
and acknowledge himself as lower than me, who am
of far superior ancestry, so much more royal."

To him then answered Nestōr, Gerēnian horseman:
"Most glorious son of Atreus, Agamemnōn, lord of men,
these gifts cannot be faulted that you now offer Lord Achilles.
Come then, let us choose delegates, send them quickly
to the hut of Achilles, Pēleus's son—no, rather
let those on whom my eye falls undertake this mission:
First and foremost, Phoinix, Zeus's favorite, should be leader,
and next I'd choose great Aias and noble Odysseus,
and of the heralds let Odios and Eurybatēs go with them.
Bring water now for our hands, and order holy silence,
so we can pray to Zeus, son of Kronos, for his compassion."

So he spoke, and they all were pleased with what he said.
At once the heralds poured water over their hands,
and young men filled mixing bowls to the brim with wine,
dripped libations into the cups, then served it to all,
and when they had poured libations, and drunk all they wanted,
then they set out from the hut of Atreus's son Agamemnōn;
and Nestōr, Gerēnian horseman, kept giving them instructions—
eyeing each one of them, but Odysseus most of all—
as to how they should try persuasion on Pēleus's blameless son.

So the two[1] set off down the shoreline with its thunderous surf,
making many a heartfelt prayer to the earth-holding Earth-Shaker

1. The use of the dual rather than the plural here and elsewhere in this scene indicates *two* characters only. These are clearly Odysseus and Aias. But there is also Phoinix to be considered, as well as a couple of heralds. Several explanations have been offered, of which the most plausible is that we have here the incomplete reshaping (perhaps by Homer himself: West 2011, 13–14) of an earlier version in which only the two acknowledged leaders of the embassy took part.

to easily sway the great mind of Aiakos's grandson.[2]
They made their way to the Myrmidons' huts and ships,
and found him delighting his heart with a clear-toned lyre,
fine and inlaid, with a silver bridge set on it,
that he'd got from the spoils when he laid waste Ēëtiōn's city.[3]
With this he was cheering his heart, and he sang of men's great deeds:
only Patroklos was there, sitting opposite him, silent,
waiting till Aiakos's grandson should finish his singing.
Now the two came forward, led by noble Odysseus,
and stood there before him. Surprised, Achilles sprang up
still clutching the lyre, from the seat on which he'd been sitting,
and so too Patroklos, when he saw these men, stood up.
Then swift-footed Achilles greeted them with these words:
"Welcome! As good friends you've come—surely some urgent need
brings you? Despite my wrath, you're still to me the dearest
of all the Achaians."

So saying, noble Achilles
led them in, and sat them down on purple-draped chairs,
and quickly told Patroklos, still standing at hand there:
"Son of Menoitios, fetch out a larger bowl now,
mix the wine stronger, fill a cup for each one of them,
for these men under my roof are my dearest friends."

So he spoke,
and Patroklos did as his dear companion told him.
He set down a great chopping block in the light of the fire,
and on it laid the backs of a sheep and a fat goat,
and the chine of a grown hog, glistening with lard:

---

2. In Homer, Aiakos, the father of Pēleus, seems to be associated with the latter's kingdom of Phthiē in Thessaly; but a parallel early tradition makes him a native of the island of Aigina, indeed its first human inhabitant. The Myrmidons ("ant people") were allegedly created for Aiakos by Zeus there, but were later relocated to Phthiē.

3. Ēëtiōn was the father of Hektōr's wife, Andromachē: he and his sons were killed by Achilles at the sacking of his city, Cilician Thēbē, and Achilles honored him with a proper funeral (6.417–19). In addition to the lyre, Achilles also had from him a horse, Pēdasos (16.152–54), and the mass of iron that was one of the prizes offered at Patroklos's funeral games (23.826–27). Achilles is the only hero in the *Iliad* who is seen singing or playing an instrument.

Automedōn held them for him, and noble Achilles carved.
He chopped the meat skillfully, spitted it on skewers,
while Menoitios's godlike son stoked the fire to a blaze.
Then, when the fire burned down and the flames died out,
he spread the embers and laid the spits over them,
resting on firedogs, then sprinkled sacred salt on the meat.
When the roasting was done, and the bits set out on platters,
Patroklos brought bread and put it on the table
in handsome baskets, while Achilles shared out the meat.
He himself chose to sit down facing noble Odysseus
against the opposite wall, told his comrade to offer the gods
sacrifice, and Patroklos threw the firstlings in the fire.
So they reached out their hands to the good things ready for them;
but when they'd satisfied their desire for food and drink,
Aias nodded to Phoinix. Noble Odysseus saw this,
and filling his cup with wine he thus toasted Achilles:
"Greetings, Achilles! We've not lacked our fair share of feasting,
both in the hut of Atreus's son Agamemnōn
and now here: there's rich plenty, all that our hearts could want
to dine on. Still, tasty food is not our business now.
It's over-great trouble we're looking at, Zeus's nursling—
we're terrified, it's a toss-up whether we'll save or lose
our well-benched ships—unless you array yourself in your might!
For it's close by our ships and the wall that their camp is now pitched
by the high-spirited Trojans and their far-famed allies;
they've lit a great number of fires there, claim they'll no longer be
held back, but are going to descend upon our black ships,
and Zeus, son of Kronos, shows them good omens—lightning
sent on their right—while Hektōr, exulting in his power,
rampages fearsomely, trusting in Zeus, respecting
neither men nor gods: a strong battle lust has possessed him.
He prays that the bright dawn may come up with all speed,
for he's threatening to lop off the tops of our ships' sternposts
and to burn the ships themselves with devouring fire and slay
the Achaians, panic-stricken because of the smoke, beside them.
This is my deep private dread, that the gods may bring
his threats to pass, and our destiny may be to perish

here, far away in Troy, remote from horse-pasturing Argos.
Up, then, if you're now minded, though late, to rescue the sons
of the Achaians, worn out by the Trojans' noisy onslaught!
Grief will be yours, too, hereafter: there's no cure to be found
for this evil once it's inflicted. Rather, long before that
think how to save the Danaäns from this day of evil!
My friend, your father Pēleus surely laid this charge upon you,
that day he sent you out from Phthiē to Agamemnōn:
'My son, strength is something that Hērē and Athēnē
will give you if they're so minded. You must hold back
the pride in your breast: a friendly approach is better.
Steer clear of strife that breeds trouble: that way the Argives
both young and old will accord you the greater honor.'
That's what he advised: you're forgetful. But even now
stop, let go of your heart-aching wrath! Agamemnōn
offers you worthy gifts if you'll only cease your wrath.
Just hear me out, and I'll catalogue all the gifts
that back in his hut Agamemnōn promised he'd give you:
seven tripods untouched by fire, ten talents of gold,
twenty shining cauldrons, and a dozen horses—
sturdy race winners, whose speed has brought them prizes.
That man would not be landless, not indeed unpossessed
of precious gold, to whom there accrued all the wealth
that Agamemnōn's prize horses have brought him by their speed.
He'll give you, too, seven women, skilled in fine handiwork,
from Lesbos, whom—when he took that well-built island
himself—he picked out: they surpassed all women in beauty.
These he will give you, including her whom he took from you,
Briseus's daughter; and, further, he'll swear a great oath
that he never went up to her bed or lay with her in love,
as is the custom, my lord, between men and women.
All these things will be given you now; and if hereafter
the gods grant that we lay low Priam's great city, then
you can go in and fill your ship's holds with gold and bronze
when we, the Achaians, are dividing up the spoils,
and yourself choose twenty Trojan women—those who are
the most lovely, save only for Argive Helen! And if
we get back to Achaian Argos, rich mother of plowland,
his son-in-law you can be, he'll honor you like his own son,
Orestēs, late-born, reared in the midst of plenty.

Three daughters of his there are in his fine-built hall—Chrysothemis,
Laodikē, and Iphianassa;[4] of these
you can take whichever you please, paying no bride-price,
to Pēleus's house; and he'll offer you richer bride-gifts
than any man ever yet provided with his daughter.
Seven well-established townships he will give you:
Kardamylē, Enopē, and Hirē with its grasslands,
sacred Phērai, together with deep-meadowed Antheia,
lovely Aipeia and Pēdasos of the vineyards—
all of them near the sea, and bordering sandy Pylos,
their inhabitants men who are rich in sheep and cattle,
who'll honor you like a god, shower you with gifts,
and under your sway will fulfill your beneficent ordinances.
All this he will do for you if you'll only cease your wrath!
But if Atreus's son still leaves too much hatred in your heart,
both himself and his gifts, yet pity the rest of the Achaians,
hard pressed throughout their ranks, men who'll hold you in honor
like a god, for you could win great glory in their eyes,
since you might now take down Hektōr, who'd surely make for you
in his murderous fury: he claims no man is his match
among all the Danaäns who came here in their ships."

In answer to him swift-footed Achilles then said:
"Scion of Zeus, Laertēs's son, resourceful Odysseus,
I must choose my words bluntly, say straight out, regardless,
what's on my mind, the way things are going to be,
so you don't all sit coaxing me, in your different ways:
for hateful to me as the gates of Hādēs is that man
who hides one thought in his mind, but speaks another.
So I shall say exactly what I believe to be right.
I'll not, I think, yield to Atreus's son Agamemnōn,
nor to the other Danaäns, since gratitude there was none
for my battling against the enemy without any respite.
Equal the lot of the skulker and the bravest fighter;
courage and cowardice rank the same in honor;

4. The number of Agamemnōn's daughters was disputed in antiquity (no mention here of Electra). If, as seems likely, Iphianassa is a variant form of Iphigeneia (or Iphimēdē), then Homer, here as elsewhere, characteristically makes no mention of that daughter's human sacrifice at Aulis in order to obtain a favorable sailing wind to Troy for the Greek fleet: she is safe at home, and available for marriage (one tradition has Agamemnōn send for her at Aulis ostensibly to marry Achilles).

death comes alike to the idler and to the hardest worker.
No profit to me that I suffered agonies at heart,
constantly risking my life in warfare. Just as a bird
brings back to her unfledged chicks whatever morsel
she can find, yet herself will suffer a heap of troubles,
so I too have kept vigil many a sleepless night,
and spent bloodstained days engaged in battle, fighting
warriors for their women. Twelve cities of men
have I laid waste with my ships; on land as well
I claim eleven more, throughout Troy's rich territory,
and from all I took many splendid items of treasure,
and carried them back, turned them over to Atreus's son,
Agamemnōn: he, waiting back there, beside his swift ships,
took them, shared out a little, kept the bulk for himself.
Some he bestowed as prizes upon leaders and princes:
these gifts still hold good. From me, alone of the Achaians,
he took, and keeps, a heart-warming wife. Let him lie with her
and take his pleasure! But why must the Argives wage war
against the Trojans? Why did Atreus's son gather an army
and bring it here, if not on account of fair-haired Helen?
Do they, then, alone of mankind, have love for their wives,
these sons of Atreus? Don't all decent and sensible men
love their own wives and care for them, just as I loved mine
with all my heart, my spear-captive though she was?
But since he's cheated me, snatched my prize from my hands,
let him not tempt me: too well I know him, he'll not
persuade me! Rather, Odysseus, with you and the other princes
let him figure how to ward off consuming fire from the ships!
Indeed he's done much hard work here during my absence—
even built a wall, and dug out a ditch beside it,
wide and deep, and bristling with stakes—yet not
even so can he hold back the might of Hektōr, killer of men!
So long as I was out there, battling among the Achaians,
Hektōr had no stomach for fighting far out from the wall,
would advance no further than the Skaian Gates and the oak tree—
he met me alone there once, only just survived my attack.
But now, since I have no wish to fight against noble Hektōr,
tomorrow I'll offer sacrifice to Zeus and all other gods,
then haul my ships down to the sea and load them up,
and you'll see—if you want to, if it concerns you at all—

at first light, sailing over the teeming Hellespont,
my flotilla, its rowers all eagerly plying their oars;
and if the renowned Earth-Shaker gives me good sailing,
on the third day I should arrive at rich-soiled Phthiē. I own
much that I left behind when, to my cost, I came here,
and more that I'll take back home with me: gold, red bronze,
women with their fine sashes, grey iron, everything
I got by lot; but my prize—that, he who gave it me
has outrageously taken back, he, the lord Agamemnōn,
the son of Atreus! To him declare all, just as I charge you,
openly, so that other Achaians may be incensed
if perhaps, ever clad in shamelessness, he's hoping
to cheat one more Danaän yet! But he wouldn't dare,
shameless dog though he is, to look me straight in the face.
I will have no part in his counsels or his actions,
so much has he cheated and failed me. Never again
let him beguile me with words: once is enough! Let him coast
at his ease to perdition: Zeus the counsellor's stolen his wits.
Hateful to me are his gifts, him I rate at a split chip's worth!
Not if he offered me ten, no, twenty times as much
as his total possessions, and from somewhere threw in more,
or all the wealth that comes in to Orchomenos, or Egyptian
Thēbē, where private houses are chockablock with treasure,
that has a hundred gates, from each of which go forth
two hundred warriors with their horses and chariots—
not even were his gifts as countless as sand or dust,
no, not even then would Agamemnōn change my heart,
until he'd paid the full price for all my bitter shaming!
Nor would I marry a daughter of Atreus's son Agamemnōn,
not even if her beauty outshone golden Aphroditē's
and her handiwork was a match for grey-eyed Athēnē's. No,
not even so would I wed her! Let him choose another Achaian,
one who suits him better, who's more kingly! For if
the gods indeed preserve me, and I get home safely,
then Pēleus himself will seek out a wife for me.
There are many Achaian women in Hellas and Phthiē,
daughters of leading men, their citadels' guardians,
and of these whichever I want I shall make my own dear wife.
Often enough back home my manly heart would urge me
to take on a wedded wife, a suitable bedmate,

get the joy of those treasures old Pēleus had made his own.
For me, to be alive has nothing to match it, not all
the fabled wealth of Ilion—once a flourishing city
in peacetime, before the coming of the Achaians' sons;
not even all that's stored beyond the marble threshold
of the archer, Phoibos Apollo, in rocky Pythō![5]
Cattle and fat sheep can be lifted by raiders;
tripods and chestnut bloodstock are winnable; but to bring
a man's life back neither raiding nor victories suffice
once it has fled beyond the barrier of his teeth.
My mother, silver-footed Thetis the goddess, tells me
that two contrary spirits go with me until the end that's death.
If I stay here, and fight around the Trojans' city
I'll lose my homecoming, but gain imperishable renown.
On the other hand, if I return to my own dear country
my fine renown will have perished, but my life will long endure,
and the end of death will not find me any time soon.
To the rest of you I would offer this piece of advice:
Hoist sail, return home. You will never attain your goal
of taking steep Ilion. Wide-thundering Zeus has strongly
reached out his hand to protect it: its people are made bold.
Go back now, and report to the leaders of the Achaians
my message in full—free speech is the privilege of you elders—
to make them think up in their minds some better plan:
one that may save both their ships and the troops of the Achaians
beside their hollow ships, since their present purpose cannot
be implemented because of my implacable anger.
But let Phoinix remain behind, and sleep here with us,
so he can come with me by ship to our own dear country
tomorrow—if he so wishes: I won't force him to go."

So he spoke, and they all became quiet and silent, amazed
by what he had said, so forcibly did he refuse them.
But at last there spoke up among them Phoinix, the old horseman,
in a flood of tears, much concerned for the Achaians' ships:

5. Pythō was the ancient name for Delphi, the site of the Delphic Oracle, where fabulous votive offerings were amassed over the centuries. Homer has one explicit reference only to the Oracle itself (at *Od.* 8.79–82). But the allusion here implies success and wealth; and since the oracle got going no earlier than the eighth century B.C.E., we have a putative date for at least this passage, and text, of the *Iliad* (unless we assume a mere interpolation) of c. 750 B.C.E., which fits well with other calculations.

"If you truly mean to go home, bright-famed Achilles,
and you're not minded at all to keep off consuming fire
from the swift ships, since rage has possessed your spirit,
how then, dear child, could I stay here alone, without you?
He had me go with you, did the old horseman Pēleus,
the day that he sent you from Phthiē to Agamemnōn,
just a child, with no knowledge yet of warfare's common business,
or of the assemblies where men achieve distinction.
That was why he sent me, to teach you all these matters,
to be both a speaker of words and a man of action.
So I would never choose, dear child, to be left behind
without you, not even should a god himself undertake
to scrape off my years and make me a vigorous youth again,
as I was when I first left Hellas, that land of fair women,
running from strife with my father, Ormenos's son Amyntōr,
who was angry with me because of his fair-haired concubine,
whom he was in love with, disregarding his wife,
my mother—who kept imploring me, clutching my knees,
to sleep with his concubine first, make her loathe the old man.
I obeyed her and did it. But my father soon found out,
heaped curses on me, invoked the dread Furies to ensure
that he never held on his knees any son sired by me;
and the gods indeed in due course fulfilled his curses—
Zeus of the underworld and fearsome Persephonē.
[I conceived a plan to kill him with the keen-edged bronze,
but then an immortal curbed my fury with the reminder
of how people would talk, of how much men would censure me,
so I shouldn't be labeled a patricide among the Achaians.][6]
But the heart in my breast could no longer bear the thought
of daily life in a house where my father was thus angered—
though indeed my fellows and cousins rallied round me,
pleading with me to stay on there in his halls,
and many fat sheep and sleek and shambling cattle
they slaughtered, and many a hog, bulked up with lard,

6. Lines 458–61 are not in the MS tradition or the scholia. Plutarch (*Mor.* 26) guessed, wrongly, that they were expunged by Aristarchos out of shock at Phoinix having considered killing his father. Were they, as some believe, interpolated in a post-Aristarchan branch of the MS tradition? Or are they an improvisation by "Homer" to help motivate Phoinix's flight (see Hainsworth 123)? The lines are convincingly Homeric, not only in language but also in style.

was stretched out by them to be singed in Hēphaistos's flame,
and wine in plenty was swilled from the old man's jars.
For nine whole nights they kept vigilant watch around me,
relieving each other in relays. The fires were never let die—
there was one by the portico of the well-walled courtyard,
and one at the entrance, outside the door of my room.
But when the tenth dark night arrived for me, then
I burst through my room's close-fitted door, got out,
vaulted easily over the courtyard wall, unnoticed
by the men on guard and the household's women servants.
Then I fled far away, through the broad realm of Hellas,
and came to rich-soiled Phthiē, mother of flocks,
to the lord Pēleus, and he most readily welcomed me,
and loved me just as a father would love his only son,
his last-born child, the heir to rich possessions.
He made me wealthy, too, gave me rule over many,
and I lived in Phthiē's borderland, the Dolōpians' lord.
And what you are, I made you, godlike Achilles,
loving you from my heart, for you'd go with no one else
either to a feast, or to meals in your hall at home
until I'd picked you up and settled you on my knees,
and fed you the first cut of meat, put the wine to your lips.
There were many times that you'd wet the front of my tunic,
sputtering out the wine in your bothersome childishness.
I've put up with plenty for you, had a lot of hard work,
never forgetting the gods would not grant me a son of my own.
So, godlike Achilles, it was you that I treated as my son
so that one day you could ward off unseemly ruin from me.
Achilles, please master this great passion of yours! Don't nurse
a pitiless heart. Why, the gods themselves can be moved,
whose dignity, honor, and power are far greater than ours,
and whom, with sacrifices and propitiatory prayers,
libations and piquant aromas, humankind wins over,
imploring them, when anyone steps out of line, does wrong.
There are, too, Prayers of Repentance, great Zeus's daughters,
lame and wrinkled, these—eyes furtive, sidelong glances—
their task to keep close on the heels of Blind Delusion;
but Blind Delusion is strong and swift-footed, so she by far
outstrips them all, goes ahead of them over the whole earth,
harming mortals; the healing Prayers follow on behind her.

One who reveres these daughters of Zeus when they approach him
they unstintingly help, pay attention to his prayers;
but should a man deny and persistently reject them
then they go and petition Zeus, the son of Kronos,
for Blind Delusion to hunt him, so he's hurt, suffers retribution.
Achilles, you too must ensure that the daughters of Zeus
are met with such honor as bends other good men's minds.
If you hadn't been offered gifts now, with more to come later,
by Atreus's son, if he were still in a furious temper with you,
I wouldn't be telling you now to cast aside your wrath
and come to the aid of the Argives, great though their need is.
But he offers you much at once, and has promised more later,
and the men he's sent to plead with you he picked from the best
of all the Achaians: men whom you hold as dearest
among the Argives! Don't make a futility of their words,
their visit! Earlier, true, your anger could not be questioned.
Such tales from old times we've heard, famous deeds of heroic fighters,
of how then too such furious rage would come upon them;
but they could be turned by gifts, talked round with words.
There's this affair I recall—from long ago, not recent—
the way it was, and I'll tell you: we're all friends here.
The Kourētes and the Aitōlians, tough warriors, were fighting
over the city of Kalydōn, and killing one another,
the Aitōlians in defense of beautiful Kalydōn,
the Kourētes eager to storm and ravage it in battle.
For golden-throned Artemis had sent them bad trouble,
piqued that she hadn't been offered first-fruits by Oineus
from his fertile orchard. The other gods savored rich offerings,
but for great Zeus's daughter alone he did nothing, whether
he'd forgotten, or hadn't thought to: a most grave omission.
Irate, she, Zeus's offspring, the archer goddess,
sent a wild boar out against him, savage, white-tusked,
that did plenty of damage, trampling Oineus's orchard,
uprooting and tossing about a whole lot of big fruit trees,
roots, apple blossom, and all. This boar was killed
by Oineus's son, Meleagros, only after he'd assembled,
from many cities, a number of huntsmen, along with
their hounds: it called for more than a few men to overcome
such a huge brute, that already had been the death of many.
The goddess whipped up a great outcry, angry shouting

over the dead boar's head and bristling hide, between
Kourētes and prickly Aitōlians. Now so long as
Meleagros, that keen warrior, was in the battle,
all that time the Kourētes got nowhere, could not even
hold firm ground outside the wall, despite their numbers.
But when wrath possessed Meleagros—wrath that distorts
the good sense in the breasts of even careful thinkers—
he then, irate at heart with Althaiē, his own mother,
was lying with his wedded wife, the lovely Kleopatra—
child of neat-ankled Marpessa, Evēnos's daughter,
and Idas, mightiest then among warriors on this earth,
who took up his bow to fight against lord Phoibos
Apollo, all for the sake of the neat-ankled maiden. So
Kleopatra was known at home by her father and lady mother
as Halcyonē, because Marpessa had suffered the fate
of the sorrowful halcyon bird, ever weeping because
Phoibos Apollo the archer had snatched her child away.
—By her Meleagros lay now, brooding over his bitter rage,
rage induced by his mother's curses. She to the gods
made endless prayers, aggrieved by her brother's killing,
kept beating the nurturing earth with her hands as she now
called upon Hādēs, along with fearsome Persephonē—
sitting crouched forward, breast soaked with tears—to bring
death to her son. The Fury that walks in darkness,
with the implacable heart, heard her from Erebos:
soon from around the gates there came an uproar, the sound
of men battering at the ramparts. The Aitōlian elders
besought him—sending the best of the gods' priests—
to come out and help them, promised a great reward:
at the richest point on the plain of beautiful Kalydōn,
they told him, he could make his own splendid estate,
fifty acres, the half of it land for vines, the rest
cleared plowland, all to be marked off from the plain.
Urgently did the old horseman Oineus entreat him,
standing there at his high-roofed chamber's threshold,
shaking its bolted doors, while supplicating his son;
urgently, too, did his sisters and his lady mother implore him
to act—he refused them the more—as did his comrades,
those who were closest and dearest to him of all,
yet not even so could they move the heart in his breast,

till his room was being fiercely battered, while the Kourētes
were mounting the ramparts and setting fire to the great city.
It was only now that his fine-sashed bedfellow, weeping,
pleaded with Meleagros, reminding him of all
the griefs that befall a people when their city is captured—
the menfolk slaughtered, the city destroyed by fire,
their children and deep-sashed wives led captive by strangers.
His heart was stirred then, hearing about these horrors:
he got up to go, put on his bright body-armor.
Thus he saved the Aitōlians from their day of evil,
after yielding to his own heart. They never paid him
the many fine gifts he'd been promised; he rescued them anyhow.
So please, don't harbor such thoughts, don't let some maleficent
spirit turn you that way! Indeed, it would be too hard
to save ships already on fire. Come now, while gifts are still
there to be had—the Achaians will honor you like a god.
But if giftless you enter this murderous war, you will not
enjoy the same honor, ward off war's perils though you may."

In answer to him then spoke swift-footed Achilles:
"Phoinix, old sir, Zeus's nursling, of this honor I have no need.
Enough that I have been honored by Zeus's ordinance,
that will still guard me here among the curved ships, for so long
as there's breath in my body, and my knees have power.
And another thing I'll tell you, and you take it to heart:
Don't confuse my mind with lamentation and sorrow
trying to please Atreus's son, that hero. Support him in nothing,
lest my love for you be turned to hatred. Much better
if you take my side in vexing the man who vexes me!
So share my kingdom, enjoy the half of my honor!
These men will take back my message: do you remain,
take your rest on a soft bed; and tomorrow at daybreak
we'll make our decision: whether to go back home or stay."

With that he silently nodded an eyebrow to Patroklos,
to spread a thick bed for Phoinix, a hint to the others
to leave the hut soon, go back; and among them Aias,
Telamōn's godlike son, now spoke up, saying:
"Son of Laertēs, scion of Zeus, resourceful Odysseus,
let us be off: as I see it, the object of our coming
won't be achieved on this visit. We must quickly report

his reply—though by no means a welcome one—to the Danaäns,
who may well now be sitting awaiting it. But Achilles
has turned his breast's great-hearted spirit to savage fury,
stubborn man, nor does he in his ruthlessness show regard
for the affection that we, his comrades, here by the ships
have shown him above all others. A man accepts recompense
even from his brother's or his own son's murderer—
while the killer pays a steep price, and then stays in his home town,
and the kinsman's emotional passion is duly tempered
by the blood-price he has received. But obdurate and malign
is the spirit the gods have put in your breast, and all because
of just one girl! Yet now we're ready to give you seven,
the best there are, and much else besides! Be gracious,
respect your own house—we're guests under your roof
representing the Danaän people, and we want to remain
your closest and dearest friends, of all the Achaians."

In answer to him swift-footed Achilles then said:
"Aias, scion of Zeus, son of Telamōn, lord of your people,
all that you say seems in line with my own thinking;
but my heart swells with rage whenever I remember
this one fact: the vile treatment I got among the Argives
from Atreus's son, as though I were some unhonored refugee.
So you can go now, and announce my message: I shall not
consider taking part in the bloody business of battle
till the son of Priam the prudent, noble Hektōr,
reaches the huts and ships of the Myrmidons, as he
slaughters the Argives, and burns their vessels with fire!
But around my own hut and my black ship I rather think
Hektōr, though eager for battle, will find himself held up."

So he spoke. They each took a two-handled cup and poured
a libation; Odysseus then led them back down the line of ships.
Patroklos instructed his companions and the handmaids
to make a thick bed for Phoinix as quickly as might be,
and they obeyed, spread the bed just as he ordered,
with fleeces, a rug, and sheets of the softest linen.
There the old man lay down, and awaited the bright dawn.
But Achilles slept in his well-built hut's back room,
and with him a woman whom he had brought from Lesbos,
the daughter of Phorbas, fair-cheeked Diomēdē.

Patroklos lay down on the other side, and likewise with him
was Iphis of the fine sashes, whom noble Achilles gave him
after he took steep Skyros, Enyeus's citadel.

Now when the others arrived at the huts of Atreus's son
they were pledged in golden cups by the sons of the Achaians,
who stood up, on this side and that, to greet and question them,
and the lord of men, Agamemnōn, was the first to ask:
"Come, tell me, storied Odysseus, great glory of the Achaians,
is he willing to fight off consuming fire from the ships,
or did he refuse, does wrath still own his great-hearted spirit?"

In answer to him much-enduring noble Odysseus declared:
"Most glorious son of Atreus, Agamemnōn lord of men,
that man will not quench his wrath, is rather filled
yet further with fury, rejects both you and your gifts:
you personally he tells to take counsel among the Argives
as to how you might save the ships and the Achaian army;
he himself now threatens he will, at daybreak tomorrow,
haul down to the sea his trim and well-benched vessels.
He would, he said, also advise all those remaining
to sail back home, since they would never attain the goal
of taking steep Ilion: wide-thundering Zeus has strongly
reached out his hand to protect it, its people are made bold.
That's what he said: these men who came with us can confirm it—
Aias and the two heralds, both men of good sense. But Phoinix,
the old man, is bedded down there, on Achilles' invitation,
so he can go with the ships to his own dear country
tomorrow, if he so wishes: Achilles won't force him to go."

So he spoke. They all became quiet and silent, amazed
by what he had said: very forcibly had he addressed them.
Long were they kept silent by their grief, these Achaians' sons,
but at last there spoke among them Diomēdēs, of the great war cry:
"Most glorious son of Atreus, Agamemnōn, lord of men,
I wish you had not gone begging to Pēleus's blameless son,
with that offer of countless gifts. The man's arrogant anyhow,
and now you've spurred him on to acts of yet greater arrogance.
For sure, we can let him be now: he's free to take off
or stay here; hereafter he'll join the fight whenever
the heart in his breast's so minded, or some god so stirs him.

So come now, let's all agree to do as I tell you!
You should go off to bed now, when you've pleasured your hearts
with food and wine, our courage and our strength;
but at the first appearance of fair rosy-fingered Dawn,
quickly in front of the ships array both troops and horses,
and urge them on, and yourself join the battle amongst the foremost."

So he spoke, and all the princes assented, marveling
at these words of Diomēdēs, the horse breaker. Then they poured
a libation, after which each man went off to his hut
and lay down to rest there and got the good gift of sleep.

Book 10

Hard by their ships all the other Achaian leaders
slept the night through, overcome by gentle slumber;
but on Atreus's son Agamemnōn, the shepherd of his people,
sweet sleep got no hold, as he thrashed over much in his heart.
Just as fair-haired Hērē's husband flashes his lightning
when preparing a fearful rainstorm, or ungodly hail,
or driving snow, when snowflakes blanket the plowland—
or somewhere yawns the great mouth of piercing war,
so often, within his breast, Agamemnōn would groan aloud,
from the depths of his heart, and his inner reason trembled.
Indeed, when he gazed out towards the Trojan plain,
he marveled at all the fires that now burned before Ilion,
at the sound of flutes and pipes, at the clamor of men;
but when he looked at the ships, and the Achaian forces,
many hairs he tore from his head by the very roots
while appealing to Zeus on high; loud groaned his mighty heart.
And this, to his mind, now seemed to be the best plan:
to go first of all to Nestōr, the son of Nēleus,
to see if with him he might fashion some sure device
that would serve to ward off disaster from all the Danaäns.
So up he got, shrugged a tunic on over his chest,
strapped on a pair of fine sandals under his shining feet,
wrapped himself round in the tawny hide of a lion—
huge, swarthy—that reached his ankles, and picked out a spear.

Tremors likewise beset Menelaös, nor on his eyelids
had sleep settled either, out of fear that some harm might
befall
the Argives, who for his sake had crossed the wide waters,
and had made their way to Troy, minds set on daring warfare.
First he draped his broad shoulders with the skin of a spotted
leopard; next he picked out and set on his head
a helmet of bronze, grasped a spear in his brawny fist,
then set off to rouse his brother (who held great sway
over the Argives, was honored by his people like a god),

and found him, setting his fine armor about his shoulders,
by his ship's stern. His brother's arrival pleased him.
Menelaös, of the good war cry, was the first to speak:
"'Why are you arming thus, brother? To urge some comrade
to go and spy on the Trojans? I very much fear
that no one will undertake this duty on your behalf:
setting off out there alone to keep watch on the enemy
through the ambrosial night—that calls for special courage."

Then in answer to him lord Agamemnōn declared:
"Both you and I need a plan, Menelaös, Zeus's nursling—
a cunning plan, one that will rescue and protect
the Argives and their ships, now Zeus has abandoned us,
his mind rather favoring Hektōr's sacrifices:
for I myself never saw—nor heard from another—how
one man in one day could create such fearful havoc
as Hektōr, Zeus's favorite, wrought on the Achaians' sons
alone, though himself the son of neither god nor goddess.
Long, long will the Argives be troubled, I tell you, by the deeds
he's already achieved, such damage they did the Achaians!
But off with you now, bring here Idomeneus and Aias—
run quickly by the ships—while I'll go to noble Nestōr,
and urge him to rouse himself up, find out if he's willing
to inspect the guards on duty, issue them orders.
He's the man they'd obey most readily, since his son's
the guard commander—he, and Idomeneus's comrade
Mērionēs: to them we especially gave this duty."

To him then Menelaös, good at the war cry, replied:
"What do you mean by this order? Are you telling me I should
stay there with them and wait until you arrive,
or hurry back here, once I've told them your requirements?"

To him then Agamemnōn, lord of men, replied:
"Stay there, in case we fail to meet each other
as we go: there are many paths running right through the camp.
And wherever you go, call out, tell the troops to stay awake;
address each man, cite his lineage and his father's name,
treating all with respect. And don't put on airs, but rather
let's join the hard work ourselves, for this, it would seem,
is the burden of evil that Zeus laid on us at our birth."

So saying, he sent off his brother, having briefed him well,
and himself went in search of Nestōr, his people's shepherd.
Him he found by his hut and his black ship, lying on
his soft bed, and beside him, laid out, his well-wrought gear:
his shield, his two spears, his gleaming helmet, and
at his side the bright-polished belt with which the old man
would gird himself when arming for murderous battle
at the head of his troops, since he never deferred to grim old age.
He raised himself on one elbow, lifted up his head,
and addressing the son of Atreus, questioned him thus:
"Who is this, walking alone by the ships, through the camp,
in the dark of the night, when other mortals are sleeping?
Is it one of your mules you're looking for? Or some comrade? Speak!
Don't sneak up on me silently! What are you after?"

To him then answered the lord of men, Agamemnōn:
"Ah, Nestōr, son of Nēleus, great glory of the Achaians,
you should know Atreus's son Agamemnōn, whom beyond all others
Zeus has set amid endless troubles, as long as the breath
still remains in my body, while my knees can still respond!
I am driven to wander thus, since on my eyes sweet sleep
will not settle: the war, and the Achaians' woes, obsess me.
I fear terribly for the Danaäns, my mind refuses
to stay quiet, I'm distraught, my heart leaps pounding
out of my breast, my bright limbs tremble beneath me.
But if you too want action—since sleep won't visit you either—
we could both go check on the sentries, make an inspection,
just in case, worn out by toil, exhausted and drowsy,
they've fallen asleep, their guard duties all forgotten.
Enemy troops are encamped close by, and for all
we know they may well mean to fight us, even at night.'

To him then answered Nestōr, Gerēnian horseman:
"Most glorious son of Atreus, Agamemnōn, lord of men,
surely not all his plans for Hektōr will Zeus of the counsels
fulfill: not all, I'd guess, he now hopes for. No, I think
he'll have troubles redoubled to cope with, should Achilles
chance to turn his spirit away from destructive wrath!
I'll gladly come with you—but let's also rouse some others:
that famed spearman, the son of Tydeus, and Odysseus,

together with swift Aias, and Phyleus's valiant son—
and someone should also go summon, as well as these,
Aias the godlike and lordly Idomeneus,
since their ships lie furthest off, not close at hand.
But—dear man though he is, and well-liked—I have to reproach
Menelaös: it may make you angry, but I can't hide my feelings!
He's sleeping, has left the difficult work to you alone,
when he should have been working hard on all our leaders,
imploring them, now unbearable need is upon us."

To him then answered the lord of men, Agamemnōn:
"Old sir, at another time I'd agree you should blame him,
since he does leave much undone, is unwilling to shoulder work—
not because of inertness or indifference of mind, but since
he's always looking to me, awaiting my lead.
But this time he woke before I did, and came to find me,
and I sent him off to summon those about whom you ask.
Now let's be going: we'll find them in front of the gates,
with the guards. That's where I told them to assemble."

To him responded Nestōr, the Gerēnian horseman:
"Then not one man of the Argives will either contradict
or ignore him, whenever he exhorts them or gives them orders."

This said, he shrugged on a tunic over his chest,
strapped a pair of fine sandals under his shining feet,
flung round him a purple cloak, held fast with a buckle,
of double-weave broadcloth, the napped wool thick upon it,
picked up a mighty spear, tipped with sharp bronze, and then
set out down the line of the bronze-clad Achaians' ships.
Odysseus it was, Zeus's equal in counsel, whom
the Gerēnian horseman Nestōr first aroused from his sleep,
calling to him. At once the shout rippled round his senses,
and out he came from his hut, and spoke to them, saying:
"Why are you wandering round the camp, alone, by the ships,
in the ambrosial night? What's your great urgency?"

To him responded Nestōr, the Gerēnian horseman:
"Son of Laertēs, scion of Zeus, resourceful Odysseus,
do not be angry! Great grief has overwhelmed the Achaians:
so come, there's one more to wake, a man well suited
to offer advice on whether to run for it or fight."

So he spoke, and resourceful Odysseus went back to his hut,
shouldered an inlaid shield, and accompanied them. They now
went looking for Tydeus's son Diomēdēs, and came upon him
outside his hut with his battle gear. Round him his comrades
were sleeping, shields under their heads. Their spears stood upright,
rammed in on their butt-spikes, bronze gleaming bright and far
like Zeus the Father's lightning. The hero himself
was asleep too: spread beneath him was the hide of a field ox,
and under his head a rolled-up bright-colored blanket.
So Nestōr, Gerēnian horseman, went over and woke him
with a kick of his foot, aroused him, chided him to his face:
"Wake up, son of Tydeus! Will you slumber all night through?
Don't you see that the Trojans are now encamped on the rise
of the plain, right by the ships, hardly any distance from us?"

So he spoke. Diomēdēs suddenly started up from sleep,
found utterance, addressed him then with winged words:
"What a tough old bird you are! Do you never stop working?
Are there no other, younger, sons of the Achaians
who could rouse up each one of the princes, bustling around
throughout the camp? Old man, you're impossible!"

To him responded Nestōr, the Gerēnian horseman:
"Ah yes, friend, all that you say is fairly spoken:
well-mannered sons I have, I have men under me,
many men, any of whom could be sent to summon people;
but a very great need has overwhelmed the Achaians,
and now, indeed, matters stand on the razor's edge:
vile destruction for the Achaians, all of them—or survival.
So go now, wake up swift Aias, and Phyleus's son,
if you feel sorry for me—you being the younger man."

So he spoke. Diomēdēs flung a lion-skin about his shoulders—
huge, tawny, reaching his ankles—grasped his spear,
went off, got these two men up, brought them back with him.

When they met with the sentries at their assembly point,
the guard commanders, they found, were far from asleep:
rather sitting awake and vigilant, their arms beside them.
Just as dogs keep stressful watch on the flocks in a steading
when they hear some fierce wild beast come down from the hills
through the timber, and there's a loud clamor of men and dogs

going after it, and their sleep is all lost: so too for these
sweet sleep from their eyelids perished, as they kept
vigilant through this bad night, eyes fixed on the plain
to catch any sound of a Trojan advance. At the sight of them
the old man rejoiced, and gave them encouragement:
[and spoke out then, addressed them with winged words.][1]
"Keep watch as you're doing, dear children; don't let sleep
overtake any one of you, make a sport of us to our foes."

That said, he hurried across the ditch, and was followed
by those Argive princes who'd been summoned to the council,
and Mērionēs and Nestōr's fine son went with them,
since the princes themselves had asked them to contribute.
So they crossed the dug ditch and settled themselves down
in an open space where the ground was seen to be clear
of the corpses of the fallen, the point at which mighty Hektōr
had turned back from killing Argives, when night embraced him.
There they sat down, and debated one with another,
and the first to speak was Nestōr, the Gerēnian horseman:
"My friends, is there really no man who'd trust his own daring
spirit enough to venture among the great-hearted
Trojans, in case he might catch some enemy straggler,
or perhaps overhear some rumor among the Trojans,
or what they're planning between themselves—do they mean
to remain out here by the ships, or will they withdraw
back to the city, now they've defeated the Achaians?
All this he might learn, and make his way back to us
unscathed—and great, under high heaven, would be
his renown among all men, with a noble gift besides;
for of all our leaders, who lord it over their ships,
every one will make him a gift of a black ewe
with a suckling lamb—there's no comparable possession,
and he'll always have a place at our feasts and banquets."

So he spoke, and they all became quiet and silent. Then
amongst them there spoke Diomēdēs of the great war cry:
"Nestōr, my own heart and proud spirit urge me on
to enter the camp of these hostile men close by,

1. A number of MSS omit this verse as an interpolation inserted merely to provide a specific verb of speaking.

these Trojans: but if some other man were to follow
with me, there'd be greater comfort and greater confidence.
When two go together, one reasons ahead of the other
what's for the best; alone, he may figure the odds,
but his mind has a shorter range, his judgment is slighter."

So he spoke, and many were eager to join Diomedēs:
Eager were both Aiases, henchmen of Arēs; eager
was Mērionēs; very eager was Nestōr's son; eager too
Menelaös the son of Atreus, the far-famed spearman;
eager was steadfast Odysseus to enter among the throng
of the Trojans, since ever daring was the spirit in his breast.
Then there spoke among them the lord of men, Agamemnōn:
"Diomēdēs son of Tydeus, delight of my heart,
choose whichever man you prefer as your companion,
the best one of those here present, since many are eager.
And don't, through unspoken respect, leave the better man
unchosen, and take the worse, with an eye to his ancestry—
however much more kingly he may happen to be."

So he spoke, alarmed on behalf of fair-haired Menelaös.
But Diomēdēs of the great war cry once more responded:
'If you honestly want me to choose my own companion,
how then could I fail to call on godlike Odysseus,
whose heart and gallant spirit are ready and willing
for all manner of ventures—and Pallas Athēnē loves him!
If this man goes with me, we two might come back unscathed
from a blazing fire, such his unmatched quick-wittedness!"

To him then replied much-enduring noble Odysseus:
"Son of Tydeus, don't over-praise me—or fault me, either:
you're telling the Argives what they know well already.
Let's be off now: night's nearly over, dawn is near,
the stars have advanced in their courses, more than two-thirds
of the night is gone; the third watch is all that's left us."

So they both spoke, and put on their fearsome gear.
To Tydeus's son that staunch fighter Thrasymēdēs
gave a two-edged sword—his own had been left by his ship—
and a shield; on his head he settled a helmet of bull's hide,
lacking both boss and crest, the kind that's known
as a skullcap: the favored guard for the heads of lusty youths.

Mērionēs gave Odysseus a bow and a quiver,
a sword too; and on his head he settled a helmet
made out of leather: inside it many laces were tightly stretched,
while on the outside a boar's white gleaming tusks
were patterned this way and that, packed close together
with consummate skill; it was lined with felt inside. This cap,
long ago, from Ormenos's son Amyntōr in Eleōn
Autolykos stole, breaking into his solid house, and gave it
to Kytheran Amphidamas to take to Skandeia,
but Amphidamas gave it to Molos as a guest-gift, and he
gave it to Mērionēs, his own son, to wear; and now
it was set on Odysseus's head and fitted it closely.[2]

So when the two had put on their fearsome gear,
they set out, leaving all the leading men there behind them;
and for them, on the right, a heron was sent, close beside
their path, by Pallas Athēnē. Though they could not see it
through the dark of the night, they still heard its sharp cry,
and Odysseus, glad at the omen, now prayed to Athēnē:
"Hear me, child of Zeus of the aegis, you who always
stand by me in all my ventures—nor am I forgotten
when I move into action—now above all, Athēnē,
favor me, let us enjoy a heroic return to the ships
after carrying out some great feat to trouble the Trojans."

Then Diomēdēs of the great war cry prayed in his turn:
"Hear me now too, child of Zeus, unwearying one!
Accompany me as you once did my father, noble Tydeus,
to Thēbē, when he went there as the Achaians' envoy: them—
the bronze-corseleted Achaians—he left beside the Asōpos
while he carried a friendly message to the Kadmeians
in Thēbē; but while returning he did some fearsome deeds
with you, bright goddess: you were ready to stand at his side.
So now stand willingly by me too, and protect me,
and to you I'll sacrifice in return a yearling heifer,

2. It was "common epic practice to identify an object by its history," Hainsworth observes (180–81): cf. Agamemnōn's scepter (2.101–8) and Megēs' corselet (15.529–34). The convention of the guest-gift tended to keep valuable objects circulating in the heroic world. The boar's tusk helmet (one example survives) was a genuine early Bronze Age item, which later fell out of use.

broad-browed, unbroken, that no man's yet brought under
the yoke: I'll offer her up to you, horns sheathed in gold."

Such were their prayers, and Pallas Athēnē heard them;
and when they'd finished praying to great Zeus's daughter,
they set off like two lions through the black night, amidst
the carnage and corpses, through the war gear, the black blood.

Nor were the proud Trojans left to sleep undisturbed
by Hektōr; he summoned the best of them in a body,
all those that were leaders and overlords of the Trojans,
and when he had them assembled he outlined a smart plan:
"Who'll take on a task for me, and carry it out
for a big reward, his recompense guaranteed?
I'll present a chariot and a pair of high-necked horses—
the best there are around the ships of the Achaians—
to anyone who'll dare—and win himself glory, too—
to steal up to those swift-sailing ships, and find out for us
if said swift ships are still being guarded as in the past,
or if, after taking a drubbing from us, these people
are planning amongst themselves to pull out, and don't now care
to keep watch all night, worn out by all their toil."

So he spoke, and they all became quiet and silent. Now
among the Trojans there was one Dolōn, a son of Eumēdēs
the sacred herald, a man of much gold, much bronze,
and ugly to look at, but nevertheless a swift runner,
the only son of the family, among five sisters.
He it was who now addressed the Trojans and Hektōr:
"Hektōr, my heart and my proud spirit urge me
to steal up to those swift-sailing ships, find out about them.
But come, raise your scepter before me, swear me an oath
that you'll truly give me these horses, this bronze-inlaid
chariot, that now carry Pēleus's peerless son!
And for you I'll be no idle scout, nor fail your expectations,
since I'll make straight for the camp, until I reach
Agamemnōn's ship, where I guess the leaders will be
deciding in council whether to pull out, or fight."

So he spoke: Hektōr held up the scepter and swore to him:
"Let Zeus himself, Hērē's loud-thundering spouse, bear witness

that no other Trojan man shall mount behind those horses,
but you, I declare, will have the joy of them for ever."

So he spoke, and swore: a vain oath, but it heartened Dolōn.
At once he slung over his shoulders his back-bent bow,
and above that draped the skin of a grey wolf,
donned a marten-skin cap, and took a sharp javelin,
and moved off towards the ships from the camp, but was never
to return from the ships, or bring back word to Hektōr.
So when he left behind him the throng of men and horses
he pressed eagerly on his way, but was noticed approaching
by Odysseus, scion of Zeus, who then spoke to Diomēdēs:
"Here's some man, Diomēdēs, coming out from the camp—
I don't know whether he's planning to spy on our ships,
or means to rob one of these battlefield corpses. We should
first let him get a little ahead of us on the plain,
and then we can make a quick rush and pounce upon him;
but if he's quick on his feet, and outruns us both, then keep
herding him with your spear towards the ships, well away
from the camp—don't let him somehow escape to the city!'

That said, they both left the path, lay down among
the cadavers, and in his folly Dolōn ran quickly past them.
When he'd gone as far beyond them as the range of a mule
plowing—and they're far preferable to oxen
for drawing the jointed plow through deep and fallow ground—
then they both went after him. He, on hearing their footsteps,
stopped, hoping that they were comrades come from Troy
to turn him back, that Hektōr had ordered his withdrawal.
But when they were distant a spear's throw, or even less,
he knew them for enemy warriors, moved his swift limbs
into precipitous flight. They at once set off after him.
As when two keen-fanged hounds, well-practiced hunters,
sprint close in on the heels of a doe or hare
through some wooded tract, and it runs screaming from them,
so now did Tydeus's son and Odysseus the city-sacker
in their close relentless pursuit cut him off from his people.
But when he was on the point of coming among the sentries
as he fled toward the ships, then Athēnē put force
into Tydeus's son, so that no bronze-corseleted Achaian
might boast of being first to hit Dolōn, leaving Tydeus's son behind.

Rushing on him with his spear strong Diomēdēs cried:
"Stop, or my spear will nail you! Then, believe you me,
you'd not long escape sheer destruction at my hands."

With that he let fly his spear, but deliberately missed: above
Dolōn's right shoulder passed the polished spear's keen point,
and stuck fast in the ground. He froze, stood there terrified,
stammering. In his mouth the teeth began to chatter,
he turned pale with fright. Panting, the two came up
and caught hold of his arms. He burst into tears and cried:
"Take me alive! I can ransom myself! Back home there's stored
bronze, gold, and iron worked with much toil: from these
my father would gladly pay you ransom past counting
should he learn I am still alive by the Achaians' ships."

Then in answer to him resourceful Odysseus said:
"Take heart, remove the idea of death from your mind!
Now come, tell me this, and give me a true account:
Where are you off to, alone, from your camp, towards the ships,
in the dark night, when other mortals are sleeping?
Would it be to strip the gear from one of these dead men?
Did Hektōr send you out to discover what was afoot
by the hollow ships? Or was it some impulse of your own?"

To him then Dolōn replied, legs trembling beneath him:
"My mind was seduced by all Hektōr's deceptive tricks—
the whole-hoofed horses of Pēleus's lordly son
he promised me, along with his bronze-inlaid chariot,
and told me to make my way through the swift dark night,
steal up to the enemy troops, and find out whether
the swift ships are still being guarded as in the past,
or if, after taking a drubbing from us, these people
are planning amongst themselves to pull out, and don't care
to keep watch all night, worn down by all their toil."

Then, smiling at him, resourceful Odysseus replied:
"To great rewards indeed did your heart aspire—the horses
of the warrior grandson of Aiakos! But they're a hard challenge
for mortals to master or drive, excepting only
Achilles—and he was born of an immortal mother.
But come now, tell me this, and give me a true account:
Where, just before coming here, did you leave Hektōr,

his people's shepherd? Where's his battle gear, where his horses?
How are the Trojans' watches arranged? Where do they sleep?
And what are they planning among themselves? Do they intend
to remain out here by the ships, or will they withdraw
back to the city, now that they've defeated the Achaians?"

Then Dolōn son of Eumēdēs answered him thus:
"Very well, I'll give you a true account of these things.
Hektōr, together with all his advisers, is holding
a council beside the tomb of Ilos the godlike,
well away from the din. But as for the sentries, hero,
you ask about, no special guard watches over the camp.
By every Trojan watch fire there are those who must
stay awake themselves, and order one another
to keep the watch; but the allies, fetched in from many countries,
are all asleep—they leave guard duty to the Trojans,
seeing that their own wives and children are nowhere near."

In answer to him resourceful Odysseus now asked:
"Where are they now? Do they sleep by the Trojan horse breakers,
or somewhere apart? Tell me clearly, I need to know."
Then Dolōn son of Eumēdēs answered him thus:
"Yes, I'll give you a true account of these things also.
Down by the sea lie the Karians, the bent-bowed Paiōnians,
the Leleges, the Kaukōnes, and the noble Pelasgians;
the Lycians and proud Mysians occupy a site towards Thymbrē,
with the Phrygian chariot fighters and Maiōnian horse marshals.
But why do you question me about all these matters?
If you're so hot to get in among the Trojan forces,
here, off apart, just arrived, beyond the rest, are the Thracians,
and with them Rhēsos, their king, son of Eïoneus.
His horses are the finest and largest that ever I saw:
They're whiter than snow, and run as fast as the winds.
His chariot's skillfully inlaid with gold and silver, and gold's
the huge battle gear he arrived in, a marvel to look at—
such armor this as should never even be worn
by us mere mortals, but only by the immortal gods!
And now either take me with you to the swift-travelling ships,
or truss me up firmly and leave me here while you go
and make trial of my information, find out whether or not
what I've told you is accurate."

Then with a stern glance
Powerful Diomēdēs addressed him in these words: "Dolōn,
"I tell you, nurse no thoughts of escape in your heart,
though you've told us useful facts since you came into our hands.
For if we release you for ransom, or let you go free now,
you'll make your way back later to the Achaians' swift ships,
either, again, as a spy, or fight in the open against us;
but if, overcome by my hands, you give up your life,
never again will you make any trouble to the Argives."

At that, Dolōn tried to touch his chin with one stout hand
and implore him, but Diomēdēs came at him with his sword
and hit his neck squarely, slashing through both sinews,
and while he still spoke his head fell in the dust.
Then they took the marten-skin cap from his head, along with
the wolf's pelt, the back-bent bow, and the long spear,
and these things to Athēnē the spoil-driver noble Odysseus
lifted high in his hand and prayed, addressing her thus:
"Hail, goddess! These are for you. On you, first of all, we'll call,
of all the immortals up on Olympos! Now help us once more,
guide us towards the Thracians' horses and sleeping quarters."

So he spoke, and raised high the spoils, and hung them up
on a tamarisk bush, and made a conspicuous marker
beside them, bundling up reeds and leafy tamarisk branches,
so as not to miss the spot coming back through the swift black night.
Then they both went on, through the war gear, the black blood,
and quickly arrived at the Thracian warriors' post.
These they found sleeping, exhausted, with their fine battle gear
neatly piled on the ground beside them, all in order,
in three rows, and by each man was his yoke of horses.
Rhēsos slept in their midst, and close to him his swift horses
were hitched by their reins to the top of the chariot rail.
Odysseus saw him first, pointed him out to Diomēdēs:
"That's the man, Diomēdēs, and those are his horses—
as Dolōn described to us, he whom we just slew!
Come on, then: use your great strength, don't stand around
idly, not using your weapons! Untether the horses—
or else I'll see to the horses, you kill the men."

He spoke: into Diomēdēs grey-eyed Athēnē breathed force.
To and fro he went killing, and hideous groans went up from
those struck by his sword: the ground grew red with blood.
Just as a lion comes upon unshepherded flocks,
sheep or goats, and with grim intent springs at them,
so at these Thracian warriors went the son of Tydeus
till he'd slain a dozen. But resourceful Odysseus,
each time that Tydeus's son squared up and used his sword,
came from behind and, catching the corpse by one foot,
dragged it aside, concerned that the fine-maned horses
should have easy passage through, and not take fright
from treading upon dead men, being as yet unused to them.
When the son of Tydeus came to the Thracian king,
this was the thirteenth man that he robbed of honey-sweet life,
gasping, because a bad dream stood over his head that night:
the grandson of Oineus, brought there by Athēnē's wiles.[3]
Now steadfast Odysseus untethered the whole-hoofed horses,
used their reins to tie them together, drove them out of the camp,
whipping them with his bow, because he hadn't remembered
to grab himself the bright whip from the inlaid chariot.
Now he whistled, giving a signal to noble Diomēdēs,
who, still back there, was debating the most outrageous action
he could perform: take the chariot, with its inlaid war gear?
Haul it out by its pole? Or heft it and carry it? Or
should he rather take the lives of still more Thracians?
While he was debating all this in his mind, Athēnē came up,
stood close, and spoke thus to noble Diomēdēs:
"Think about your return now, great-hearted son of Tydeus,
to the hollow ships, lest maybe in headlong flight you come there,
if it chance that some other god should awaken the Trojans."

So she spoke, and he knew it for the voice of a goddess,
and quickly mounted. Odysseus slashed the horses with his bow,
and they flew on their way towards the Achaians' swift ships.

But no blind watch was that kept by silver-bowed Apollo:
he sighted Athēnē attending to Tydeus's son: enraged
against her he went down into the great mass of the Trojans,

3. Oineus's grandson, of course, was Diomēdēs himself: thus the bad dream became a horrific reality.

and woke one of the Thracians' counselors, Hippokoōn,
a noble cousin of Rhēsos. He started up from sleep,
and when he saw the bare space where their swift steeds had been,
and men gasping their last amid that bloody shambles,
then he groaned aloud, and called his dear comrade by name,
and the Trojans, clamoring loudly, in boundless confusion,
came crowding round, to stare at all the horrific deeds
done by those men before they returned to the hollow ships.

But when they got back to where they'd killed off Hektōr's spy,
then Odysseus, dear to Zeus, reined in the swift horses,
while Tydeus's son jumped down, seized the bloodstained spoils
to place in Odysseus's hands, and then remounted.
He whipped the horses, and they, nothing loath, sped on
[to the hollow ships, where their hearts desired to be.][4]
First to catch the sound of their hoofbeats was Nestōr. He exclaimed:
"My friends, leaders and rulers of the Argives,
am I mistaken, or right? My heart bids me speak!
The hoofbeats of galloping horses beat on my ears!
How I hope that this is Odysseus and powerful Diomēdēs
back from among the Trojans, driving whole-hoofed steeds—
yet I dreadfully fear in my heart that they've suffered some hurt,
these valiant Argives, caught in turmoil with the Trojans."

The words were not out of his mouth when the two arrived,
and stepped down onto the ground, while the rest, rejoicing,
greeted them with handshakes and words of welcome.
Nestōr, Gerēnian horseman, was the first to question them:
"Come, tell me, storied Odysseus, great glory of the Achaians,
how you two took these horses—by confronting the mass
of the Trojan army? Or did you encounter some god
who gave them you? They're amazing, like the rays of the sun!
I've long been fighting Trojans—and I can assure you
I don't hang back by the ships, old warrior though I am—
but never yet have I seen, or imagined, such horses! So,
I do think it must be a god that met you, gave you them,
since both of you are loved by Zeus the cloud-gatherer,
and the daughter of Zeus of the aegis, grey-eyed Athēnē."

4. Some MSS omit this formulaic line as being an interpolation here: why should Rhēsos's Thracian horses long to be among the Greek ships?

In answer to him resourceful Odysseus now declared:
"Nestōr, Nēleus's son, great glory of the Achaians,
easily could a god, if he wanted, have given us even
better horses than these, since gods are far mightier than us.
No, these horses, old sir, about which you're enquiring,
are Thracian, new arrivals; brave Diomēdēs slew
their king, with his comrades—twelve in all, and those the best!
The thirteenth man was a scout we caught near the ships,
who'd been sent out as an observer to spy on our camp
by Hektōr and the rest of the noble Trojans."

That said,
across the ditch he then drove the whole-hoofed horses,
laughing, and happily with him went the other Achaians.
When they came to the strong-built hut of Tydeus's son,
the horses they tethered by their fine-cut leather reins
at the same manger where Diomēdēs' own swift-footed
horses stood, munching away at honey-sweet grain; and on
the stern of his ship Odysseus set Dolōn's bloodstained spoils,
to be prepared as a sacred offering to Athēnē.
Then they plunged in the sea, wiped off the abundant sweat
that had gathered upon their shins and necks and thighs;
and when the waves of the sea had washed away all that sweat
from their skin, and their hearts were refreshed, then they went
and climbed into polished bathtubs and bathed themselves.
Having bathed, they massaged their bodies with oil, and then
sat down to a meal and from the full mixing bowl
drew honey-sweet wine to make their offering to Athēnē.

Book 11

Now Dawn from her bed at the side of noble Tithōnos
rose up, to bring light to immortals and humankind;
and to the Achaians' swift ships Zeus now sent out Strife—
that baneful spirit—cradling a portent of war in her hands.[1]
She stopped by Odysseus's ship, black and deep-hulled,
that lay halfway along, so a shout could reach either end,
could be heard at the huts both of Aias, Telamōn's son,
and those of Achilles—the two who had drawn up their trim ships
furthest away, relying on their prowess, their hands' strength.
The goddess stood there and uttered a loud and terrible cry,
shrilly, infusing great strength into every Achaian's
heart, to engage in unceasing warfare and battle;
so that to them, at once, war now became much sweeter
than going back in their hollow ships to their own dear country.

Atreus's son roared his command to the Argives to gird themselves,
and himself amongst them now donned the gleaming bronze.
His greaves first he fastened on about his shins—
finely made, and fitted with silver ankle-pieces.
Next, to cover his chest, he put on his corselet,
the one he'd received as a guest-gift from Kinyras, who had
heard the great news on Cyprus, that the Achaians
were about to make the voyage to Troy in their ships,
and so sent him this present, to seek favor with the king.
On it were ten bands of darkest cobalt enamel,
along with twelve of gold and twenty of tin,
and dark cobalt serpents writhing up towards the neck,
three on each side, like the rainbows that Kronos's son
sets in the clouds, as a portent for humankind.
Then about his shoulders he settled his sword, and on it
the studs gleamed golden, while the scabbard that held it
was made of silver, and fitted with golden chains.

1. "[W]hat Eris [Strife] held in her hands it is impossible to say and perhaps was never precisely conceived.... Like her war-shout it is the more awesome for being vague," as Hainsworth says (214).

Next he hefted his fine shield—all-protective, richly inlaid,
battle-hungry: around it ran ten bands of bronze,
and on it were set twenty bosses fashioned of tin,
gleaming white, and a single central one of dark cobalt,
encircling the Gorgon, with her menacing features,
glaring horribly, flanked by Terror and Panic;
from the shield hung a silvered baldric, and upon it
writhed a dark cobalt serpent, that had three heads
turned in different directions, yet growing from one neck.
Then he put on his leather helmet, double-bossed, quadruple-plated,
with its horsehair crest nodding terribly above it,
and picked out two strong spears, each tipped with bronze,
and sharp: the gleam of the bronze shone from him to high heaven,
and Athēnē and Hērē sent the thunder pealing
in salute to the king of great and golden Mykēnai.

And now to his own charioteer each man gave orders
to hold his horses in place, in good order, there by the ditch,
while they themselves, on foot, arrayed in their battle gear,
charged. An unquenchable clamor filled the early morning
as they got in line by the ditch ahead of their charioteers,
who advanced a little behind them. This fearsome uproar
was stirred up amongst them by Kronos's son: from the heights
of the airy sky he sent down raindrops dripping with blood,
a sign of all the brave heads he'd soon dispatch to Hādēs.

The Trojans on their side, on the rise of the plain,
were drawn up around great Hektōr and peerless Poulydamas,
and Aineias, who was honored like a god by the Trojan people,
and Antēnōr's three sons, Polybos and noble Agēnōr
and youthful Akamas, in appearance like the immortals.
Hektōr among the foremost bore his well-balanced shield:
like the baleful star that from among the clouds emerges,
a bright point, soon lost again behind those shadowy clouds,
so Hektōr kept appearing, now out among the foremost,
now in the rear, giving orders. Clad all in bronze,
he shone like the lightnings of Zeus, the aegis-bearer.

So they, like rows of reapers confronting one another
who drive their line ahead through a wealthy man's field
of wheat or barley, and the swathes fall thick and fast,

so Trojans and Achaians both came charging forward,
cutting down men: neither side gave a thought to fatal flight,
but stayed head to head in the struggle, attacked like wolves,
and Strife, that great misery-maker, watched in delight.
Alone of the gods she was there among them as they struggled;
the other gods were not present, but sitting apart, uninvolved,
in their own halls—where, for each one of them,
along the folds of Olympos, a fine house had been set up—
all blaming the lord of the storm clouds, Kronos's son,
because he was minded now to give glory to the Trojans.
But the Father paid them no heed: he'd moved away,
and was sitting apart from the others, exultant in his glory,
staring out at the Trojans' city, the ships of the Achaians,
the glinting of bronze, the killed and those killing them.

While it was morning still, with the sacred light brightening,
both sides' shots struck home, and men dropped, hit;
but at the hour when a woodcutter gets out his meal,
in some mountain glen, when hands and arms are weary
from felling tall trees, and exhaustion quells his spirit,
and a longing for tasty food invades his mind, then it was
that the Danaäns by their valor broke through the battle line,
cheering their comrades along the ranks. Here Agamemnōn
was first to charge: he took out Biēnōr, shepherd of men,
and, next, his comrade Oïleus, whipper of horses,
who'd sprung down from his chariot to confront him,
and, charging, was hit in the forehead by Agamemnōn's
sharp spear: his bronze-laden headpiece failed to block it,
through metal and bone it drove, mashing up as it went
all the brain inside. It stopped his charge stone-dead.
Agamemnōn, king of men, left these two prostrate there,
bare torsos white, when he'd stripped them, tunics and all,
and pressed on then to slaughter Isos and Antiphos
two sons of Priam, one bastard, the other from wedlock,
both in one chariot: of whom the bastard was driver,
while famed Antiphos stood beside him. These two Achilles,
among the foothills of Ida, once trussed up with pliant willow
after catching them herding their sheep, let them go for a ransom.
But now the son of Atreus, wide-ruling Agamemnōn,
speared Isos in the chest, up over the nipple,

slashed Antiphos close by his ear, knocked him off the chariot;
then, hastening to strip both of their fine gear, recognized
who they were: he'd already seen them, by the swift ships,
when fleet-footed Achilles brought them in from Ida.
As a lion that catches a speedy hind's young fawns
easily crunches them up, when it gets its strong teeth on them,
after breaking into their den, rips out their tender hearts,
and their mother, even though near, remains unable
to protect them, since over her too come fearful tremors,
and quickly she runs away through dense thickets and woodland,
sweating in haste to avoid the mighty beast's attack—
so not one of the Trojans was able to ward off death
from these two, being themselves in flight before the Argives.

Next for him were Peisandros and steadfast Hippolochos,
the sons of shrewd Antimachos, who'd been the firmest—
since he'd taken Paris's gold, splendid presents—in refusing
to let them give Helen back to fair-haired Menelaös.
It was his two sons that the lord Agamemnōn now captured,
in the same chariot, both trying to manage their swift horses,
for the shining reins had slipped from their hands, and the team
was bolting; but Atreus's son went against them like a lion,
and they from the chariot now begged him: "Take us alive,
son of Atreus! You'll get a worthy ransom for us!
There are treasures in plenty stored up in Antimachos's house—
bronze, gold, and iron worked with much toil: from these
our father would gladly pay you ransom past counting
should he learn we are still alive by the Achaians' ships."

So these two, weeping, addressed themselves to the king
with honeyed words, but no honey was in the reply they heard:
"If you indeed are the sons of that same shrewd Antimachos,
who, in the Trojans' assembly, recommended that Menelaös—
who'd come there on an embassy with godlike Odysseus—
should be killed on the spot, not let go back to the Achaians,
then you'll pay the price now for your father's vile behavior."

That said, he forced Peisandros out of his chariot
with a spear-thrust to the chest: thrown, he lay prostrate.
Hippolochos sprang down, and him he killed on the ground,
severed both arms with his sword, slashed through his neck,

sent his torso off through the ranks like a roller. These two
he left now, and where the disorderly rout was thickest,
there he charged in, and with him other well-greaved Achaians.
Footmen were killing those footmen forced into flight
and horsemen horsemen: beneath them there rose from the plain
the dust stirred up by their horses' thundering hooves
as they dealt death with the bronze. And the lord Agamemnōn,
ever killing, followed the rout, urging on the Argives:
and as when devouring fire falls upon unthinned woodland,
and a roiling wind spreads it everywhere, and thickets
are consumed down to their roots by its blazing onslaught,
so before Atreus's son Agamemnōn went down the proud heads
of fleeing Trojans, and many the proud-necked horses
that rattled their empty chariots across the battlefield,
lacking their peerless drivers, who lay there on the ground,
far more attractive by now to vultures than to their wives.

Zeus was drawing Hektōr away from the missiles, the dust,
the blood, the confused uproar, and the slaughter of men;
and Atreus's son followed, loudly urging the Danaäns on.
Past the burial mound of old Ilos, Dardanos's son,
across the mid-plain, by the wild fig tree they panted,
pressing on to the city, with Atreus's son at their heels,
in full cry, his invincible hands besmeared with bloody filth.
But when they reached the Skaian Gates and the oak tree,
there the Trojans halted, stood waiting for one another.
Some were out in the plain still, stampeding like cattle
that a lion has routed, coming on them at dead of night—
all except one cow, and for her sheer destruction is manifest:
when she's caught, first he breaks her neck with his powerful
fangs, then gulps down her blood, along with all her innards.
Just so did the lord Agamemnōn, Atreus's son, press hard
on the routed Trojans, kept killing the hindmost as they fled.
Many were thrust from their chariots, prone or supine,
by Atreus's son's hands, as he raged all around him with his spear.
But when he'd near got in beneath the city and its towering
ramparts, then it was that the Father of men and gods
seated himself on the peaks of spring-rich Ida,
coming down from the heavens, a thunderbolt in his hands,
and sent off golden-winged Iris to deliver a message:

"Go now, swift Iris, convey this charge to Hektōr:
so long as he sees Agamemnōn, the people's shepherd, ranging
among the front-line fighters, cutting down the ranks of men,
he's to hold back himself, while urging the rest of his troops
to battle the enemy in the grinding conflict. But when,
either spear-struck or shot with an arrow, Agamemnōn
takes to his chariot, then I shall guarantee to Hektōr
the strength to go on killing till he reaches the well-benched ships,
and the sun goes down, and sacred darkness comes on."

So he spoke: wind-footed swift Iris did not ignore him,
but went down from the heights of Ida to sacred Ilion,
and found wise Priam's son, illustrious Hektōr,
standing behind his horses in his dovetailed chariot.
Swift-footed Iris came up beside him and said:
"Hektōr, son of Priam, Zeus's equal in counsel,
Zeus the Father has sent me to give you this message:
So long as you see Agamemnōn, the people's shepherd, ranging
among the front-line fighters, cutting down the ranks of men,
you're to hold back yourself, but should urge the rest of your troops
to battle the enemy in the grinding conflict. But when,
either spear-struck or shot with an arrow, Agamemnōn
takes to his chariot, then Zeus will guarantee you
the strength to go on killing till you reach the well-benched ships,
and the sun goes down, and sacred darkness comes on."

That said, swift-footed Iris went on her way, and Hektōr
leapt to the ground from the chariot in his battle-gear,
brandishing two sharp spears, and ranged widely through the ranks,
urging them on to fight, stirred up the clash of battle.
So they rallied, stood firm, confronting the Achaians,
and the Argives opposite them now strengthened their ranks,
and the battle was set. They stood face to face. Agamemnōn
was the first to charge, mind set on fighting ahead of them all.

Tell me now, Muses, you who have your homes on Olympos,
who was it first came forward to stand against Agamemnōn,
of the Trojans themselves, or of their far-famed allies?
Iphidamas son of Antēnōr, a valiant man and tall,
who was brought up in rich-soiled Thrace, the mother of flocks:
Kissēs reared him at home while he was still a small child—

his mother's father, who sired the fair-cheeked Theanō.
But when he reached the milestone of glorious youth,
Kissēs, to keep him there, gave him his daughter; yet
from the bridal chamber he went seeking glory from the Achaians,
with twelve curved ships that accompanied him. Now these
trim vessels he later abandoned at Perkōtē,
and himself continued, on foot, his journey to Ilion.
He now came out to face Agamemnōn son of Atreus.
When they'd advanced to within close range of one another,
Atreus's son threw and missed, his spear going wide,
but Iphidamas hit on his baldric below the corselet, put
all his weight into the thrust, trusting his strong hand,
yet failed to pierce the bright baldric: far short of that
his spear-point struck against silver, was bent like lead.
Then seizing it in one hand wide-ruling Agamemnōn
dragged it toward him, mad as a lion, and wrenched it
out of Iphidamas's grasp, slashed his neck with his sword,
unstrung his limbs. So he fell, and slept the sleep of bronze,
wretched youth, helping his countrymen, far from his wife,
the bride that he'd had no joy of, much though he'd paid for her:
a hundred oxen he first gave, then promised a thousand
goats and sheep from the countless flocks herded for him.
But now Atreus's son Agamemnōn stripped his body
and went back among the Achaians with his fine battle gear.

When Koön—distinguished warrior, Antēnōr's eldest son—
caught sight of him, huge overpowering grief
blinded his eyes for the sake of his fallen brother.
Up on one side he came, with his spear, unseen by noble
Agamemnōn, and pierced his mid-arm below the elbow.
The point of the bright spear went clean through his arm,
and at that the lord of men, Agamemnōn, shuddered;
yet not even so did he break off from battle and warfare,
but sprang upon Koön, wind-toughened spear[2] in hand.
Now Koön had seized Iphidamas, his brother, his father's son,
by one foot, was dragging him off, and appealing to all the bravest;
but then, as he dragged him, right under his bossed shield

2. The epithet "wind-toughened" (ἀνεμοτρεφής, *anemotrephēs*) puzzled ancient scholars: the consensus was that trees buffeted by the winds yielded tougher timber, and irrespective of the truth of the assumption, this seems the likeliest explanation.

Agamemnōn thrust his bronze spear tip, unstrung his limbs,
stepped close, and cut off his head, right over Iphidamas.
So there both Antēnōr's sons met their destined fate at the hands
of the king, Atreus's son, and went down to the house of Hādēs.

Agamemnōn continued to range up and down the Trojan ranks
with spear and sword and great stones,[3] just as long as the blood
still flowed warm from his wound; but from the moment
the wound started drying up, and the flow of blood ceased,
sharp pains began to weaken the powers of Atreus's son;
just as a keen dart targets any woman in labor—the piercing
pains sent by the Eileithyai, spirits of hard childbirth,
Hērē's daughters, who have bitter birth-pangs in their keeping—
so sharp pains began to weaken the powers of Atreus's son.
Now he climbed up into his chariot, ordered his driver
to make for the hollow ships, since his heart was heavy-laden;
and in a carrying voice he called out to the Danaäns:
"My friends, leaders and rulers of the Argives,
it's up to you now to keep far from our seagoing vessels
the grievous business of fighting, since Zeus the counselor will not
allow me to war all day long against the Trojans."

So he spoke, and his driver whipped the fine-maned horses
towards the hollow ships, and they, nothing loath, sped off:
foam spattered their chests, dust coated their underbellies
as they bore the afflicted king away from the fighting.

When Hektōr became aware of Agamemnōn's withdrawal
he called out in a carrying voice to the Trojans and Lycians:
"Trojans! Lycians! You Dardanian front-line fighters!
Be men now, my friends! Remember your fighting spirit!
Their best man has gone, and to me great glory is granted
by Zeus, son of Kronos: now drive your whole-hoofed horses
straight for these Danaän battlers, win yourselves still greater glory!"

By his words he stirred up each man's force and spirit.
The way that a hunter sets his white-fanged bloodhounds

---

3. Lines 265–89 are found in a late third-century B.C.E. papyrus (see Hainsworth 254ff.). Comparison with the standard text shows at least nine extra lines (mostly undecipherable) and some very dubious readings, which, as Hainsworth says, offer "striking testimony to the deterioration of Homer's text in the hands of Hellenistic booksellers" and "show the difficulty, and the necessity, of the work of the Alexandrian scholars."

in pursuit of a wild boar or lion, just so against the Achaians
did Priam's son Hektōr, a match for Arēs, killer of mortals,
urge on the great-spirited Trojans, and himself advanced,
with high resolve, amongst the very foremost fighters,
and flung himself into the conflict like some high-gusting storm
that swoops down to roil the deep sea's violet waters.

Who then was the first, and who the last, to be slaughtered
by Priam's son Hektōr, when Zeus now granted him glory?
Asaios first, and then Autonoös and Opitēs,
and Dolops, Klytios's son, Opheltios, Agelaös,
Aisymnos, and Ôros, and steadfast Hipponoös—these
were the Danaän leaders he took down, and then he assailed
the mass of troops. As when the west wind rolls back the clouds
brought by the cleansing south wind, hits them with a deep squall,
wave rolls upon swollen wave, and aloft the spindrift
is dispersed by the force of the veering wind, so high
was the head-count of soldiers now laid low by Hektōr.

Then there would have been havoc, and actions irreparable,
and the fleeing Achaians would have fallen, aboard their ships,
had not Odysseus called out to Tydeus's son Diomēdēs:
"Tydeus's son, what's made us forget our fighting spirit?
Come here, stand by me! Shame indeed it will be
if bright-helmeted Hektōr gets to capture our vessels."

Answering him, strong Diomēdēs declared:
"Indeed I'll remain and stand firm, but all too brief
our satisfaction will be, since Zeus the cloud-gatherer
surely wants a win for the Trojans rather than for us."

With that he thrust Thymbraios clean out of his chariot,
spearing him through his left nipple, while Odysseus
took down Molíōn, the prince's godlike henchman.
These then they left, after finishing them as fighters,
and both went creating havoc among the ranks: as when
two fierce wild boars turn against a pack of hunting dogs,
so they turned, attacked, killed Trojans; and the Achaians
were glad of a breathing space in their flight from noble Hektōr.

A chariot they caught next, with two warriors in it—the sons
of Merōps of Perkōtē, who outstripped all other men

in seercraft, and tried to prevent his sons from going
off to murderous warfare.[4] But they flatly refused
to obey him: black death's spirits were driving them on.
So now Tydeus's son, the famed spearman Diomēdēs,
deprived them of breath and life, took away their fine battle gear,
while Hippodamos and Hypeirochos fell to Odysseus.

Then for them Kronos's son stretched the battle taut and even[5]
as he looked down from Ida; and they kept killing one another.
The son of Tydeus wounded Agastrophos with his spear,
Paiōn's warrior son, on the hip joint: his horses weren't at hand
for him to escape—he, blindly deluded, had left them
to be held, some way off, by his henchman, while he on foot
charged through the front-line fighters till he lost his life.
But Hektōr soon glimpsed them across the lines, ran at them,
whooping aloud, and the ranks of the Trojans followed.
At the sight of him Diomēdēs of the great war cry shuddered,
but at once exclaimed to Odysseus, standing beside him:
"Here's calamity rolling in on us, it's mighty Hektōr!
Come on, let's make a stand, hang firm here, drive him back!"

With that he poised and let fly his far-shadowing spear,
and his cast did not miss, struck home high on Hektōr's head,
caught the top of his helmet; but the bronze was stood off by bronze,
failed to reach his fine flesh, was stopped by the triple layers
of the eyeholed helmet that Phoibos Apollo gave him.
Hektōr backed off a great distance, merged with the throng,
fell to his knees and stayed so, one strong hand propped
on the ground, and dark night now enveloped his eyes.
But while Tydeus's son was going after the cast of his spear,
far beyond the front-line fighters, where it had hit the ground,
Hektōr came to again, and reboarded his chariot,
drove into the mass of troops, escaped the black death-spirit.

4. "Seers and priests are popular as fathers of the slain, their disregarded warnings . . . being a ready source of pathos," Hainsworth says (262). See, e.g., 5.148–51, 13. 663–72.

5. There is a clear echo here of the image of Zeus's heavenly scales, used to favor one side or the other: see 8.69–75 and 22.209–14. The weighing was most commonly connected with wool (cf. 12.433–35), regularly checked in households by the housekeeper (*tamiē*); Zeus in this connection is referred to as the male equivalent (*tamias*), generally translated as "steward". The metaphor borrows the most popular social practice for fair adjudication to express an act of completely arbitrary divine authoritarianism. See Onians 408–10.

But strong Diomēdēs with his spear pursued him, shouting:
"Once more, dog, you've dodged death, though close indeed
that evil came to you! But once more Phoibos Apollo
saved you, to whom it must be you pray before entering
the clash of spears—and for sure, when I meet you later,
if there's any god who's *my* helper, I'll finish you off!
Meanwhile I'll go after the others, see whom I can catch."

With that he started to strip the famed spearman, Paiōn's son.
But Aléxandros, the husband of fair-haired Helen,
drew his bow upon Tydeus's son, the shepherd of the people—
leaning against the column set up on the mound men raised
for Ilos, Dardanos's son, a folk-elder in former times—
as he was pulling off the shining corselet from sturdy
Agastrophos's chest, and the shield from off his shoulders,
and his weighty helmet. Paris drew back his arm from the bow
and shot. Not in vain did the arrow fly from his hand,
but hit Diomēdēs' right foot, on the flat part: the shaft went through,
stuck fast in the ground. Then, with loud laughter, Paris
sprang out from his hiding place and shouted boastfully:
"You're hit! Not in vain did my shaft fly! Oh, how I wish
I'd caught your nether belly, and taken your life away!
Then would the Trojans have had some relief from their troubles,
who now tremble before you like bleating sheep with a lion."

To him, quite unafraid, strong Diomēdēs replied:
"Bowman, foul-mouthed curser, pretty-locks, ogler of virgins!—
If you'd only make trial of me face to face, wearing armor,
then your bow and your showers of arrows would not protect you;
and even now your boast is just to have scratched my foot!
I don't care—it could well have been a daft child or a woman
that shot me, so blunt the shafts of a weakling, a nobody!
Very different indeed, if it only grazes its target,
is the sharp spear sped by *my* hand: it brings a man instant death,
and the cheeks of his widow are torn in grief and mourning,
and his children are orphaned, while he reddens the earth
with his blood, and rots, more vultures than women round him."

So he spoke, and Odysseus, famous spearman, came up
and stood over him while he sat there and pulled out the sharp
shaft from his foot, and a flash of agony lanced his flesh.

Diomēdēs then boarded his chariot, ordered his driver
to make for the hollow ships, since his heart was heavy-laden.

Odysseus, famous spearman, was now alone: not one
of the Argives remained with him, since fear had gripped them all,
and deeply stirred he addressed his own proud spirit:
"Ah, what's to become of me? A black mark if I run for it,
scared off by their numbers—and yet much worse if I'm taken,
alone, now the rest of the Danaäns have been put to flight
by Kronos's son. Yet why does my heart debate these things?
For this I know well: a coward may walk away from battle,
but a first-class fighter is under an obligation
to hold his ground, whether striking another, or stricken."

While he pondered these matters in his mind and spirit,
the ranks of shield-bearing Trojans advanced, surrounding him
on all sides—yet setting up disaster for themselves.
And just as round a boar, dogs and strapping young hunters
close eagerly in as he bursts from some deep thicket,
sharpening the white tusks set in his curving jaws,[6]
and come at him from all around, and the sound of grinding
fangs is heard, but they stand firm, alarming though he is—
so now around Odysseus, beloved of Zeus, the Trojans
pressed close. But he first wounded peerless Deïopeitēs
from above, in the shoulder, springing at him with sharp spear,
then cut down Thoōn and Ennomos; after them
Chersidamas, who'd just jumped down from his chariot,
he speared in the navel, striking under his embossed shield,
and he fell in the dust, one bent hand clawing the ground.
These he left, and then speared Charōps, Hippasos's son,
full brother of wealthy Sōkos; and Sōkos now,
a godlike man, came up to protect him, and stood
close in front of Odysseus, and addressed him, saying:
"Ah, storied Odysseus, ever hungry for tricks and trouble!
Today you'll either boast over both sons of Hippasos,
having slain two such men, and stripped off their battle gear,
or else, struck by my spear, you'll lose your life."
So saying,

6. See Leaf, 1: 366–67: "The ancient legend was that the boar prepared for battle by whetting his teeth upon smooth rocks."

he thrust with piercing force at Odysseus's well-balanced shield:
through the bright shield his heavy spear went, and through
the richly wrought corselet it drove its path, and severed
all the flesh from the ribs; yet Pallas Athēnē did not
let it tear in as far as the vitals. Odysseus sensed
that the shaft had failed to get through to a fatal spot,
so he backed off, and then had this to say to Sōkos:
"Ah, wretch, surely now sheer destruction's on your heels!
You may have stopped me fighting against the Trojans,
but I tell you, death and the black death-spirit will find you,
here and today: laid low by my spear you'll give
glory to me, and your soul to horse-proud Hādēs."

At that Sōkos turned away, preparing to run for it,
but as he was in mid-turn Odysseus planted his spear
squarely between his shoulders, drove it through to his chest.
He fell with a thud, and over him noble Odysseus exulted:
"Ah, Sōkos, son of shrewd Hippasos, breaker of horses,
the end of death overtook you, you couldn't escape it!
Wretched man, your father and lady mother will never
close your eyes in death now: the flesh-eating birds of prey
will tear them out raw, wings beating madly around you—
but I, should I die, will get burial from the noble Achaians."

So saying, he pulled fierce Sōkos's heavy spear
from his flesh and his embossed shield; and when it was out
the blood came spurting, sickened him to his heart.
But when the great-hearted Trojans saw Odysseus's blood,
they called through the crush to each other, and all went at him.
So he now drew back, and cried out to his comrades:
thrice he shouted, as loud as any man's head could compass,
and thrice Menelaös the war-lover heard him shout,
and at once said to Aias, who was standing near him:
"Aias, Zeus's scion, son of Telamōn, lord of men,
the cry that came to my ears was from steadfast Odysseus—
sounding as though he was being overpowered, alone,
cut off by the Trojans in the raging conflict!
Let's get to him through the turmoil: relief's our best answer.
I fear he may come to harm, left alone among the Trojans,
tough though he is, and the Danaäns may suffer a great loss."

That said, he led on: Aias, mortal but godlike, followed.
They found Odysseus, beloved of Zeus, surrounded
by Trojan attackers, like tawny mountain jackals
round an antlered stag that's wounded, that some man has hit
with a shot off his bowstring. The stag has escaped from him,
running swiftly, so long as it has warm blood, responsive knees;
but when in the end the swift arrow overcomes it,
then the flesh-eating jackals rend it, high in the mountains,
in a shadowy glen. But some spirit directs against them
a ravening lion: the jackals scatter, it scoffs their prey.
So now round shrewd Odysseus, that man of many wiles,
pressed a crowd of valiant Trojans; but the hero,
charging out with his spear, fended off the pitiless day.
Then Aias moved in, hefting up his tower-like shield,
and stood at his side. The Trojans scattered, this way and that,
and Menelaös the war-lover led Odysseus out of the crush,
held by one hand, till his henchman drove up with their chariot.
But Aias charged the Trojans, taking down Doryklos,
a bastard son of Priam, then wounded Pandokos,
and went on to wound Lysandros, Pylartēs, and Pyrasos.
As when a flooded river pours down into the plain
in winter spate from the mountains, lashed on by the rains of Zeus,
and masses of dried-out driftwood, both oak and pine,
come with it, and it discharges much silt into the sea—
so now, in disruptive pursuit across the plain, illustrious
Aias charged, slaying both horses and men. But Hektōr
knew nothing of this, was fighting on the battle's far left flank,
by the banks of the river Skamandros, where men's heads
were dropping thickest, and an unquenchable clamor
was going up around great Nestōr and warlike Idomeneus.
Among these Hektōr joined battle, was doing grim work
with spear and skilled horsemanship, breaking young fighters' ranks.
Yet no way would the noble Achaians have faltered in their course
had not Aléxandros, the husband of fair-haired Helen,
cut short the great deeds of Machaōn, his people's shepherd,
shooting him in the right shoulder with a three-barbed arrow.
Then, breathing rage, the Achaians were alarmed on his behalf,
lest the tide of battle should turn, and he be captured,
and at once Idomeneus spoke to noble Nestōr, saying:
"Ah, Nestōr, son of Nēleus, great glory of the Achaians,

be quick, get aboard your chariot, have Machaōn mount
beside you, and drive your whole-hoofed steeds to the ships,
with all speed, for a healer's worth many ordinary men,
being skilled at cutting out arrows and applying soothing herbs."

So he spoke, and Nestōr, Gerēnian horsemen, did not
ignore him, but quickly boarded his chariot, with Machaōn
beside him, the son of Asklēpios, peerless healer.
He whipped the horses, and they, nothing loath, flew on
to the hollow ships, where their own hearts yearned to be.

Now Kebrionēs saw the Trojans being routed in disorder
as he stood at Hektōr's side, and spoke to him, saying:
"Hektōr, while you and I are engaged with the Danaäns here,
at the furthest edge of this wretched battle, the rest
of the Trojans are fleeing in disorder, themselves and their horses,
driven by Aias, Telamōn's son—I know him well
by that wide shield slung from his shoulders! We too should take
our horses and chariot there, where the conflict is worst,
where foot and horse both, competing in dread strife,
are killing each other, and raising an unquenchable clamor."

So saying, he lashed the fine-maned horses with his
whistling whip, and they, in reaction to the stroke,
speedily bore the swift chariot among Trojans and Achaians,
trampling corpses and shields: all the axle beneath
was spattered with blood, and the rails round the chariot,
flecked with the flying drops from the horses' hooves
and the rims of the wheels. Now Hektōr was straining to leap in
and shatter the mass of troops; appalling the turmoil
he wrought on the Danaäns, little rest did he give his spear,
but ranged to and fro down the ranks of the other fighters
with spear and sword and great stones, yet always avoided
engaging in combat with Aias, the son of Telamōn
[since Zeus was indignant with him when he battled a better man].[7]

Zeus the Father, seated aloft, now stirred terror in Aias:
dazed, his seven-layered oxhide shield slung behind him,

7. Line 543 (referred to by both Aristotle and Plutarch) is absent from all medieval MSS and would seem to have been inserted very early in order to satisfy those who were curious as to why the leading attacker, Hektōr, avoided the leading defender, Aias, in defiance of traditional epic etiquette (Hainsworth 282).

he stared nervously at the crowd, like a wild beast, and backed off,
often turning around, moving step by slow step. Just as
a tawny lion's driven off from their oxen's steading
by country folk with their dogs, who won't allow him
to get in and seize the fattest steer, who are vigilant
the whole night through—yet he, so desperate for meat,
keeps coming, but gets nowhere, has to face a shower
of hunting spears flung by strong hands, and blazing firebrands
before which, for all his eagerness, he shrinks back,
and at dawn goes on his way, his spirit sorry:
so Aias, before the Trojans, sorry at heart, gave ground
against his will, much afraid for the ships of the Achaians.
As an ass, passing a wheat field, breaks loose from boys—
a stubborn beast, on which many cudgels have been broken—
and goes in, and scoffs the ripe grain, and the boys flail at him
with cudgels, but their strength's only that of children,
and they can barely remove him, even when he's stuffed himself—
so now was great Aias, the son of Telamōn, dogged
by the arrogant Trojans and their allies from many countries,
all thrusting with spears at the center of that great shield of his.
Now Aias would be mindful once more of his fighting valor,
wheel round and face them, and stand off the advance
of the horse-breaking Trojans; and now he would turn and retreat.
But he halted them all in their march against the swift ships,
one man embattled, alone, between Trojans and Achaians,
making his stand. Spears came at him from powerful arms:
some in their forward flight stuck fast in his great shield,
and many fell short, never reached his white flesh, yet still
yearned, though fixed in the ground, to glut themselves on flesh.

When Euaimōn's splendid son Eurypylos observed him
being hard-pressed by showers of missiles, he came up
and stood at his side, and cast his own gleaming spear,
and hit Phausios's son Apisaön, shepherd of the people,
in the liver, under his midriff, and at once unstrung his knees.
Eurypylos sprang on him, to strip the gear from his shoulders,
but the moment godlike Aléxandros perceived him
stripping the gear from Apisaön, straightway he drew
his bow at Eurypylos, hit his right thigh with an arrow,
and the arrow's shaft broke off, and his thigh went heavy.

He withdrew to his comrades' company, dodging fate,
and in a carrying voice called out to the Danaäns:
"Friends! Argive leaders and rulers! Stop! Turn back!
Make a stand! Fight off the pitiless day of doom
from Aias, a target for spears now! I hardly think
he can survive this rough conflict alone—so stand firm,
face the enemy, gather around great Aias, Telamōn's son!"

So spoke the wounded Eurypylos: they came and stood
close beside him, shields lined up against their shoulders,
spears couched; and Aias came on, facing them,
and turned, and stood, when he reached his comrades' ranks.

These, then, were battling on in the likeness of blazing fire;
but the mares of Nēleus, sweating, bore Nestōr from the battle,
taking with him Machaōn, the shepherd of the people.
Now he was observed by noble swift-footed Achilles
as he stood on the afterdeck of his deep-hulled vessel,
watching the burdensome struggle and unhappy rout;
and at once he spoke to Patroklos, his companion,
calling to him from the ship; and he heard, and came out
as battle-minded as Arēs: so began his undoing.
He it was, Menoitios's noble son, who spoke first:
"Why did you call me, Achilles? What is it you need?"
In answer to him swift-footed Achilles then said:
"Noble son of Menoitios, delight of my heart,
now, I think, the Achaians will come crowding round my knees,
entreating me, now that need past bearing's come upon them!
But go now, Patroklos, dear to Zeus, and ask Nestōr
who this wounded man is that he's bringing from the battle?
Certainly from behind he looked much like Machaōn,
Asklēpios's son, but I didn't see the man's eyes—
the horses sped too fast by me, galloping onward."

So he spoke, and Patroklos obeyed his dear companion,
and ran off down the line of the Achaians' huts and ships.

When those others arrived at the hut of Nēleus's son,
they themselves dismounted onto the bounteous earth,
while old Nestōr's henchman Eurymedōn unyoked his horses
from the chariot. They dried off the sweat on their tunics
standing to face the breeze from the seashore, then they went

into the hut, and sat down on chairs, and for them
lovely-tressed Hekamēdē mixed a posset—old Nestōr
had taken her from Tenedos when Achilles sacked it,
great-hearted Arsinoös's daughter, whom the Achaians
chose for him, since he always gave them the best advice.
First she brought out a table and set it before them,
a fine one, well polished, its feet enameled in cobalt,
and set on it a bronze basket, with an onion as relish
for their drink, and pale honey, and sacred barley-meal,
with an exquisite cup, that old Nestōr had brought from home,
studded with golden rivets. Its handles were ears,
four in number; round each a pair of golden
doves were feeding: it rested upon a double base.
Others needed to strain to hoist this cup from the table
when full, yet Nestōr, the old man, raised it without effort.
In it, for them, this woman resembling the immortals
now mixed a posset, grating goat's cheese on Pramnian wine
with a bronze grater, and sprinkled white barley meal over it,
and when she'd prepared this brew, desired them to try it.
So when both had drunk, and allayed their parching thirst,
they then began chatting, took pleasure in conversation.
Patroklos, godlike mortal, appeared now, stood at the door,
and the old man, seeing him, sprang up from his polished chair,
took his hand, led him in, invited him to be seated.
But Patroklos, for his part, demurred, and thus addressed him:
"I can't stay, old sir, Zeus's nursling: you won't persuade me.
Demanding respect, quick to censure is he who sent me
to learn who this man is you've brought back wounded. But I
know him myself, can see he's Machaōn, the people's shepherd.
So I'll go back as messenger, bring this word to Achilles.
Well do you know, old sir, Zeus's nursling, just what kind
of fearsome fellow he is—quick to blame even the blameless."

In answer to him then Nestōr, Gerēnian horseman, said:
"Why is Achilles so sorry for the sons of the Achaians,
all those wounded by missiles? He knows nothing at all
of the grief that's arisen in camp, now our best warriors
are laid up aboard their ships, either shot or speared:
shot is the son of Tydeus, mighty Diomēdēs,
speared are Odysseus, famed spearman, and Agamemnōn,

shot, too, is Eurypylos, with an arrow through his thigh,
as well as this man whom I just brought back from the fighting,
struck by a shaft from the bowstring. Yet Achilles,
brave though he is, neither pities nor cares for the Danaäns—
Is he waiting until our swift ships there by the sea,
in despite of the Argives, are ablaze with devouring fire,
and we ourselves, one by one, are killed? For my strength
is not what it once was, when my limbs were supple.
I wish I were that young now, with all my strength
as unimpaired as when we and the Eleans quarreled
about cattle-rustling, that time I killed Itymoneus—
Hypeirochos's excellent son, who had his home in Ēlis—
when driving off beasts in reprisal. While defending his oxen
among the foremost, he was hit by a spear from my hand,
and fell, and the country folk round him fled in terror.
So a vast amount of booty we herded out of the plain:
fifty droves of oxen, as many flocks of sheep,
no fewer herds of swine and wide-ranging goats,
while of chestnut horses we took one hundred and fifty,
all mares, and many with suckling foals. All these
we drove at night to Pylos, city of Nēleus, brought them
inside the walls, and Nēleus rejoiced at heart that so much
had come my way while going to war for the first time.
And at daybreak heralds made their loud-voiced proclamation
that all who were owed a debt in noble Ēlis should now
come forward, and the Pylians' leaders gathered together
and divided the spoil: the Epeians had debts to many,
since we in Pylos were few, and weakened by violence,
after Hēraklēs' mighty force had done us outrage
in the years before, and all our best men had been killed.
We sons of peerless Nēleus were twelve in number,
of whom I alone was left: all the rest had perished:
Made arrogant by this, the bronze-corseleted Epeians
devised in contempt outrageous acts against us.
Now old Nēleus had chosen of oxen a drove, and of sheep
a great flock, three hundred in all, and their shepherds too,
he being owed a sizable debt in noble Ēlis—
four racehorses, prizewinners, along with their chariot.
They had gone to the games, were due to enter a race
for a tripod, but Augeias, king of men, kept them there,

and sent back their driver lamenting for his lost horses.
The old man, infuriated by things both said and done,
helped himself to a huge amount, gave the people the rest
to divide, so that none should miss out on a fair share.

"So we were settling all this, and around the city
making sacrifice to the gods; on the third day the Epeians
came, in great numbers, they and their whole-hoofed horses
all together, and with them, armed, Molos's two descendants,[8]
still youths, with as yet no knowledge of fighting valor.
There's a city, Thryoessa, a steep site on a hilltop,
remote, by the Alpheios, on the marches of sandy Pylos,
and this they laid under siege, mad keen to destroy it.
But when they'd scoured all the countryside, Athēnē came to us,
by night, rushing down from Olympos, with the message
to arm ourselves. Nothing loath was the force she raised in Pylos,
but zealously eager to fight. However, Nēleus refused
to let me arm myself, and hid away my horses,
because, he said, as yet I knew nothing about war's business.
But even so I stood out among our horsemen,
on foot though I was, since thus Athēnē shaped the conflict.
There's a river, the Minyēios, that flows out into the sea
near Arēnē, where we waited for bright Dawn—we, the horsemen
of the Pylians—while the foot soldiers' companies
came flowing in. From there, quickly arming ourselves,
we made our way at noon to Alpheios's sacred stream.
There we made fine offerings to all-powerful Zeus,
and a bull to Alpheios, a bull also to Poseidōn,
but to grey-eyed Athēnē a cow from the herd; and then
we took our supper by companies throughout the camp,
and lay down to sleep, each man in his battle gear,
by the flowing river. Meanwhile the great-spirited Epeians
had the city under siege, were mad keen to destroy it;
but before that could be, they were faced with war's mighty action,
for when the sun rose radiant over the earth, then we
joined battle, making our prayers to Zeus and Athēnē.
At the outset of combat between the Pylians and Achaians

8. The Epeian twins Kteatos and Eurytos were officially sons of Aktōr, in fact of Poseidōn (751); here and at 750 they are, unusually, identified by descent from their maternal grandfather Molos, a member of the Aiōlian royal house.

I was the first to kill my man, get his whole-hoofed horses—
Moulios the spearman, Augeias's son-in-law,
wed to his eldest daughter, the fair-haired Agamēdē,
who knew every medical herb that the wide earth nourishes.
Him, as he charged me, I stopped with my bronze-tipped spear,
and he fell in the dust. I boarded his chariot,
took my place with the foremost fighters. The bold Epeians
scattered and fled when they saw that the man had fallen
who was their horsemen's leader and a first-class warrior.
I descended upon them then like a dark whirlwind:
fifty chariots I took, in each of which a couple
of warriors bit the dust, laid low by my spear.
And I'd have killed Aktōr's sons, Molos's two descendants,
had not their true father, the wide-ruling Earth-Shaker,
wrapped them in heavy mist, and saved them from the battle.
So there Zeus granted great power to the men of Pylos,
for we kept up our pursuit across the far-flung plain,
killing the men and collecting their splendid armor,
driving our horses as far as Bouprasion's rich wheat fields
and the Olēnian rock and the district where stands the hill
of Alēsion: there Athēnē turned back our troops,
and I slew my last man, and left him, and the Achaians
brought their swift horses from Bouprasion back to Pylos,
and all extolled Zeus among gods, and, among men, Nestōr.

"Such was I—if truly I ever was—among men. But Achilles
alone will have joy of his valor: and I suspect he'll weep
bitterly when it's too late, when our men have perished!
Dear boy, thus indeed it was that Menoitios charged you
that day he sent you out from Phthiē to Agamemnōn—
we were both in the house there, I and noble Odysseus,
and heard it all, just as he told you, every word of it.
We'd made our way to the well-built home of Pēleus
while recruiting an army through richly fertile Achaia,
and there in the house we found the hero Menoitios,
and you, and Achilles with you. Old Pēleus, the horse-driver,
was burning a bull's fat thighs for Zeus the thunderer
in his enclosed courtyard, and holding a golden cup
to pour the fire-bright wine on the flaming sacrifice.
You two were watching the ox meat. We came and stood

in the doorway. Achilles leapt to his feet, amazed,
clasped our hands, led us in, invited us to be seated,
set rich fare before us, a fitting welcome for strangers.
But when we'd assuaged our desire for food and drink,
I was the first to speak, urged you to follow with us:
you both agreed, and your fathers both offered much advice.
Old Pēleus gave this instruction to his son Achilles,
always to be the best, preeminent over others;
but you got this exhortation from Menoitios, Aktōr's son:
'My child, in birth Achilles is higher than you are,
but you are the older, though in strength he far outstrips you.
It's your job to speak wisely to him, to give him shrewd advice,
to guide him; and he'll obey you, to his profit.' Thus
did the old man instruct you, but you're forgetful. Yet even
now you could talk this way to warlike Achilles, perhaps
get his consent. Who knows? With some god's aid you might
touch his heart, bring him round: a comrade's persuasion's useful.
But if in his mind there's some prophecy he's evading—
some word from Zeus that his lady mother told him—
at least let him send you out, and the rest of the Myrmidon
force with you: maybe you'll prove a light to the Danaäns!
He should give you his splendid armor to wear into battle:
then the Trojans may take you for him, back off
from the fighting, and thus the Achaians' warlike sons,
worn out now, may relax: too brief is battle's respite.
You—fresh, not tired—should easily drive men exhausted
by battle back to the city, away from the ships and huts."

So speaking, he stirred the spirit in the breast of Patroklos, who
now ran back past the ships to Achilles, Aiakos's grandson.
But when in his running Patroklos reached the ships
of godlike Odysseus—site of assemblies and the tribunal,
where they'd also built their altars to serve the gods—
there it was he encountered Eurypylos, scion of Zeus,
Euaimōn's son, with the arrow-wound in his thigh,
limping away from the fighting. The sweat was running down
from his shoulders and head, and out of his grievous wound
the black blood oozed, yet his mind was still unimpaired.
At the sight of him Menoitios's valiant son felt pity,
groaned aloud, and addressed him with winged words:

"Ah, wretched men, you Danaän leaders and rulers,
thus it was, then, you were destined, far from friends and homeland,
with your white fat to glut the scurrying dogs of Troy!
But tell me this, Eurypylos, you hero, Zeus's nursling—
is there some way for the Achaians to hold back great Hektōr,
or must they now perish, vanquished by his spear?"

Then the wounded Eurypylos made him this answer:
"Patroklos, Zeus's scion, no longer will the Achaians
have any defense: they'll die beside their black ships.
For indeed all those who before were the best fighters
are laid up aboard their vessels, spear-struck or shot with arrows
at the hands of the Trojans, whose strength grows ever greater.
But take care of me now, lead me back to my black ship,
cut the arrow out of my thigh, wash the black blood from the wound
with water that's warm, spread it with soothing herbals,
those good ones that, they say, you learnt from Achilles,
whom Cheirōn taught, the most just of the Centaurs.
For of the healers we have, Podaleirios and Machaōn,
the one, I think, lies wounded here in the huts,
himself in need of a peerless healer; the other
is out on the plain, awaiting the Trojans' sharp assault."

Then the valiant son of Menoitios made him this answer:
"How can such things be? Lord Eurypylos, what shall we do?
I'm on my way with a message to warlike Achilles
from Gerēnian Nestōr, protector of the Achaians.
But I'll not, even so, abandon you in your distress."

With that, one arm round the waist of the people's shepherd,
he led him off to his hut. His henchman saw them, spread oxhides.
Patroklos made him lie down, with a knife cut out of his thigh
the sharp arrow,[9] washed the black blood from the wound
with water that was warm, then applied a bitter root
after crushing it up in his hands, a painkiller, that allayed
all his pangs: the wound began drying, the blood ceased to flow.

9. Thus partially avoiding the agony that Diomēdēs had suffered (396–98) by simply pulling an arrow out of his wound against the barbs.

Book 12

So there, back at the huts, Menoitios's valiant son
was tending the wounded Eurypylos; but meanwhile Argives
and Trojans were in a massed battle, nor was the Danaäns'
trench to save them much longer, or the broad wall above it:
the wall they'd made for their ships, and dug the encircling ditch
—but without any proper grand sacrifices to the gods—
to keep their swift ships and a mass of plunder safe
inside its circuit. But since it was built without the approval
of the immortal gods, not long did it stay unbreached.
While Hektōr still lived and Achilles nursed his wrath
and King Priam's city remained unsacked, so long
did the great wall of the Achaians also hold firm;
but when all the best of the Trojans had lost their lives,
many Argives too, some dead, some still surviving,
and Priam's city was sacked in the tenth year, and the Argives
had gone back in their ships to their own dear fatherland,
then it was that Poseidon and Apollo hatched their scheme
to level the wall, threw at it the force of all the rivers
flowing out from the mountains of Ida to the sea:
Rhēsos and Heptaporos, Karēsos and Rhodius,
Granikos, Aisēpos, bright Skamandros, and Simoeis—
where there fell in the dust many helmets and oxhide shields,
along with a whole generation of half-divine warriors—
the mouths of all these streams Apollo brought together,
and for nine days sent this torrent against the wall, while Zeus
brought rain without cease, to more quickly plunge the wall in
the sea.
The Earth-Shaker meanwhile, trident in hand, himself
was the leader: he used the waves to trash all those foundations
of logs and stones the Achaians had labored to set in place,
made smooth the shore beside the Hellespont's strong current,
and, the wall once leveled, decked the great beach once more
with sand; then turned the rivers all back to flow
in the channels where earlier they'd poured their rapid streams.

Thus were Poseidon and Apollo to act in time to come;
but at the moment battle and war's din blazed all about
the well-built wall, and the beams of its towers resounded
as they took hits, while the Argives, beaten down by Zeus's lash,
and held back by their hollow ships, were kept from action
through their terror of Hektōr, the mighty deviser of rout,
and he, as before, was battling like a whirlwind.
As when, surrounded by dogs and hunters, a wild
boar or lion turns at bay, exulting in his strength,
while the men form a solid line, and make their stand
against him, and they assail him with hunting-spears
thick and fast, yet even so his indomitable spirit
neither quails nor panics, although his courage can kill him;
he keeps turning from side to side, making trial of the men's line,
and wherever he charges, there the ranks give way—
so Hektōr went through the mass exhorting his comrades,
urged them on to get over the ditch. But his own horses,
fleet though they were, did not dare, stopped dead at the edge
neighing loudly: the ditch terrified them by its width,
easy neither to jump at one bound nor to drive across,
for round its whole circuit the banks on both sides stood
overhanging, and up at the top it was planted with sharpened
stakes all its length, driven in there by the Achaians' sons—
large stakes, set close together, a defense against enemy fighters.
No horse drawing even a well-wheeled chariot could
surmount it with ease, but foot soldiers were hot to try it.
It was now that Poulydamas came to bold Hektōr, saying:
"Hektōr, and you other leaders of the Trojans and allies,
trying to drive our horses over the ditch is senseless—
crossing it's really hard, what with those sharp stakes
set upright in it, so close to the wall of the Achaians!
Nor is there any way that charioteers can dismount
and fight there: space is cramped, I think we'd get hurt.
If in his fury against the Achaians high-thundering Zeus
intends to wipe them out utterly, really means to aid the Trojans,
then for sure, I'd want this to happen immediately—
the Achaians perishing here, far from Argos, forgotten.
But if they turn and attack us, drive us back from the ships,
and we get tangled up in the ditch they've dug, I think

not one of us then would get back to the city, even
to bring the news, once the Achaians had rallied their forces.
Let's all go with my proposal: we should have our henchmen
hold the horses in check, by the ditch, while we ourselves,
on foot, armed in our battle gear, all in one mass,
advance behind Hektōr. Then the Achaians will not face us,
if it's true that death's noose is already fastened on them."

So spoke Poulydamas: his shrewd words gave Hektōr comfort.
At once he sprang, armed, from his chariot to the ground,
nor did the other Trojans stay gathered behind their horses,
but all, when they saw noble Hektōr, themselves dismounted,
and each man instructed his personal charioteer
to rein back his horses, hold the line there by the ditch,
while they regrouped, drew themselves up, and, formed
into five companies, followed behind their leaders.

Some went along with Hektōr and peerless Poulydamas—
the biggest group and the best, those most determined
to break through the wall and fight by the hollow ships.
With these two went Kebrionēs as a third, for by his chariot
Hektōr had posted a less-seasoned replacement.
The second group Paris led, with Alkathoös and Agēnōr,
and the third was commanded by Helenos and godlike Deïphobos,
both Priam's sons: third with them went heroic Asios—
Asios, Hyrtakos's son, brought to Troy from Arisbē
by his team of big chestnut horses, from the Sellēïs river.
Of the fourth group the leader was Anchīsēs' valiant son,
Aineias, and with him went the two sons of Antēnōr,
Akamas and Archelochos, well trained in all fighting skills.
The far-famed allies were led by Sarpēdōn, who had chosen
as his fellow commanders Glaukos and warlike Asteropaios,
since they seemed to him clearly the best, beyond all others,
after himself: but he was first over all. So they
lined up, protecting each other with their oxhide shields,
and made straight for the Danaäns, eagerly, sure they would not
be stood off longer, that now they'd assail them at their black ships.

Then the rest of the Trojans and their far-famed allies
acted on the advice of sagacious Poulydamas;
but Asios, Hyrtakos's son, that leader of men, refused

to abandon his horses along with their driver, his henchman,
and set out to drive with them against the swift ships—
fool that he was, not destined to escape the foul death-spirits,
or, exulting in horses and chariot, to ever return
from the ships, ever get back safely to windy Ilion,
since too soon his accursed fate was to enfold him
through the spear of Idomeneus, Deukaliōn's noble son:
for he charged at the ships' left wing, which was where the Achaians
were coming back from the plain with their horses and chariots.
There it was he drove his own chariot and team: at the entrance
he found that the gates weren't shut or the crossbar in place,
but men were keeping them open, hoping to rescue any
comrades of theirs in flight to the ships from the fighting.
Straight for this point he drove, and after him followed
his troops, yelling loudly, convinced the Achaians would not
hold them back any longer, but would fall by their black ships—
fools that they were: they found at the gates two first-class fighters,
both high-spirited sons of Lapith spearmen, one
the son of Peirithoös, powerful Polypoitēs,
the other Leonteus, a match for Arēs the killer.
These two stood there in front of the lofty gateway
like high-crested oaks in the mountains, that day by day
stand up to wind and rainstorms, solidly set
on their thick and lengthy roots: this was how they both,
trusting the mighty strength of their hands, stood up
to great Asios's onslaught, did not flee in panic
as the Trojans made straight for the well-built wall, their oxhide
shields held high, with loud war cries, gathered around
Lord Asios, and Iamenos, Orestēs and Adamas
son of Asios, and Thoön and Oinomäos. For a while
the Lapiths, from inside the wall, had been urging on
the well-greaved Achaians to fight in defense of the ships;
but when they perceived these Trojans charging the wall,
and the noisy confusion and flight of the Danaäns, then
they both rushed out and fought in front of the gates,
like a pair of wild boars that up in the mountains
face the rabble of men and dogs closing in, make sorties
from the flank, tearing through the undergrowth around them,
ripping it up by the roots, and the sound of their gnashing
tusks is loud, till a spear strikes home and robs them of life:

such was the clash of bright bronze on the chests of these two
taking hits man to man: most valiantly they fought,
trusting the troops above them, and their own might.
Those high up were showering stones from the well-built towers
in defense of themselves, and their huts, and their swift ships:
thick as snowflakes the stones came plummeting earthward,
flakes that a strong gale, driving the shadowy clouds,
pours down thick and fast on the richly nurturing earth.
Like them flew the missiles from these men's hands, both Achaians
and Trojans alike, and helmets and bossed shields rang
jarringly, when battered by great quern-like stones.
Then Asios, Hyrtakos's son, groaned, slapping both his thighs
in frustrated fury, and cried aloud: "Zeus, Father,
it seems you too are a wholehearted lover of lies!
I never really imagined that these Achaian heroes
would be able to hold off our strength, our powerful hands—
but like a swarm of fine-waisted wasps or bees
that build a nest on some rocky track and refuse
to abandon their hollow home and stay in place
and fight off, for their offspring's sake, the men on their trail,
so these men will not, though there's only the two of them,
fall back from the gates while they're killing, or until they are
killed."

So he spoke, but his words did not move the mind of Zeus:
for to Hektōr it was his heart longed to give the glory.

But others were battling it out around the other gates,
and hard it would be for me, like a god, to tell the whole tale,
for all around the stone wall there arose devouring fire,
since the Argives, though distressed, were forced to defend
their ships; and the gods, too, were cast down in spirit—
all those who were the supporters of the embattled Danaäns.
Now the Lapiths launched themselves into warfare's combat,
and the son of Peirithoös, powerful Polypoitēs,
speared Damasos through his helmet's cheekpiece of bronze:
the bronze helmet failed to deflect the spear point: it drove
clean through metal and bone, mashing up as it went
all the brains inside. It stopped his charge stone-dead.
Polypoitēs next dispatched both Pylōn and Ormenos,
while Leonteus, the son of Antimachos, scion of Arēs,

speared Hippomachos, striking him through his baldric;
then, drawing from its scabbard his keen-edged sword
he charged through the press and cut down, hand to hand,
Antiphatēs first, who slumped to the ground, on his back,
then Menōn, Orestēs, Iamenos—all of them he brought down,
in quick succession, onto the richly nurturing earth.

While they were stripping these of their shining armor,
Poulydamas and Hektōr and the young men following them—
the biggest group and the best, those most determined
to break through the wall and set the ships on fire—
were still hesitant, stood uncertain beside the ditch.
They'd been eager to cross it—but then there was this omen,
a high-flying eagle, skirting the army on the left,
clutching a huge blood-red serpent in its talons,
alive still and struggling: no way had it given up the fight,
but reared back and struck at its captor, on the breast,
close to the neck, and the eagle dropped it to the ground,
agonized by the pain, in the midst of the troops, and then
itself, with a scream, winged off on the wind's blast,
while the Trojans shuddered at seeing the writhing serpent
lying there in their midst, a portent from Zeus of the aegis.
Poulydamas now came up and addressed bold Hektōr:
"Hektōr, you always manage to chide me in assembly,
however good my advice. It would not, of course, be proper
for a commoner to gainsay you, either in council
or in war, but rather always to enhance your authority—
despite that, I'll now tell you what seems to me our best course.
Let's not go on to fight the Danaäns for their ships,
since here is the end I foresee, if it's true that this omen
came for the Trojans, so eager to cross the ditch—
a high-flying eagle, skirting the army on the left,
a huge blood-red serpent clutched in his talons, still
alive: yet he let it drop before he reached his dear home,
and never managed to get it there, or let his young have it—
so we, even if we break through the Achaians' gates and wall
by our great strength, and the Achaians yield the ground,
shall come back from the ships by the same path in disarray,
leaving many a Trojan behind, slain by the Achaians
with the bronze, in defense of their ships. This is the way

a seer would interpret this matter, one with clear knowledge
of omens at heart, a man to whom the people listened."

Scowling darkly, bright-helmeted Hektōr then said:
"Poulydamas, what you're proposing no longer pleases me—
you know how to think up a better speech than that!
But if you're really making this suggestion in earnest,
then indeed the gods themselves must have killed your common sense!
You're telling me to forget loud-thundering Zeus's
own plan, that he promised me, sealed with his assenting nod?
Yet you want me to pay attention to long-winged birds of prey,
creatures I neither bother with nor have regard for,
whether they're flying right, towards dawn and the rising sun,
or left, in the direction of night and darkness! Rather
let us submit ourselves to the purposes of great Zeus,
the ruler over all, both mortals and immortals.
One omen is best, to fight in defense of your country!
Why should you be afraid of warfare and conflict? Even
were the rest of us to be slain, to the very last man,
at the ships of the Argives, there's no fear of your dying,
since your heart is not a staunch fighter's, is not battle-minded.
Even so, if you yourself shrink from combat, or persuade
some other man with your arguments, turn him against the war,
you'll lose your life at that moment, felled by my spear."

This said, he led the way, and the rest came after him,
with a deafening clamor, and Zeus the thunderer
whipped up from the mountains of Ida a gale-force wind
that blew dust straight at the ships, confused the Achaians' minds
while granting great glory to the Trojans and to Hektōr.
So, trusting in his portents and their own strength,
they went about breaching the great wall of the Achaians.
They wrenched out the towers' footings, tore down the breastwork,
pried loose the jutting timbers that the Achaians had first
embedded in the ground as the towers' buttresses,
and hoped, by dragging these out from the Achaians' wall
to breach it. Yet not even so would the Danaäns give ground,
but stuffed the gaps in the breastwork with their oxhide shields,
hurling missiles from there at the foemen now nearing the wall.

Both Aiases kept ranging to and fro between the towers,
barking out orders, arousing the Achaians' strength and fury.
One man they'd upbraid gently, another with harsh words—
anyone they perceived giving up the fight altogether:
"Friends, Argives, fighters prominent, middling, or
of lesser account—in no way are all men equal
in warfare—there's work here for all of you: this
I reckon you know yourselves. Let no one turn back
to the ships now he's heard these words of encouragement,
but press forward, give heart to each other—it may yet be
that Olympian Zeus, lord of the lightning, will grant us
to stand off this assault, drive our enemies back to the city."

So the two cheered them on, roused the Achaians to battle.
Just as snowflakes fall thickly on a winter day
when Zeus the counselor stirs himself to produce
a snowstorm, displaying these arrows of his to mankind,
and, stilling the winds, will strew flakes until he's covered
the lofty mountain peaks and the headlands' summits,
the clovered plains and the fertile plowlands of men,
and over the grey sea's harbors and beaches the snow descends,
but the waves beat against it, repel it: everything else
wears its mantle, when Zeus's snowstorm comes thickly down—
just so from both sides the stones flew thick and fast,
some at the Trojans, some from the Trojans at the Achaians,
hurled back and forth: the whole wall thudded and clattered.

Yet not even then would illustrious Hektōr and the Trojans
have breached the wall's gates and long door bolt, had not Zeus
the counselor stirred up Sarpēdōn, his own son,
against the Argives, like a lion against sleek cattle.
Straightway he held out before him his well-balanced shield,
a fine one, of hammered bronze, that the bronze smith had
beaten out, and inside it had stitched oxhides, thickly layered,
with golden hasps deployed all round its circumference.
This he held before him, and brandished his two spears,
and set out like some mountain-bred lion that for a long while
has been without meat, and his bold spirit drives him on
to attack the flocks, even to enter the close-built farmstead:
for though there he encounters the herdsmen, who

with dogs and spears are setting a guard around the sheep,
yet he won't be forced from the steading till he's made his attempt,
but either he then springs in and snatches his prey,
or is hit, while attacking, by a spear from some quick hand.
In such wise did his spirit urge godlike Sarpēdōn on
to make a rush at the wall, and break down its breastwork.
At once he spoke to Glaukos, the son of Hippolochos:
"Glaukos, why is it that we two are honored so highly,
get the best places at table, choice meat, cups always full,
back in Lycia? Why do all men there look on us like gods?
We have that vast estate too, by the banks of the Xanthos—
fine acres of orchard and good wheat-bearing plowland.

"That's why we must take our stand among the front-line Lycians,
and face up with them to the searing heat of battle,
so that Lycia's corseleted soldiers may say this of us:
'Not short of renown, then, are Lycia's overlords,
these kings of ours: they may banquet on fattened sheep,
and drink the best honey-sweet wine, but there's also great
valor in them—they're out there with Lycia's foremost fighters.'
Ah, my friend, if the two of us could escape from this war,
and be both immortal and ageless for all eternity,
then neither would I myself be among the foremost fighters
nor would I send you out into battle that wins men honor;
but now—since come what may the death-spirits around us
are myriad, something no mortal can flee or avoid—
let's go on, to win ourselves glory, or yield it to others."

So he spoke. Glaukos neither ignored nor disobeyed him,
and both marched straight forward, leading the Lycian horde.
At sight of them Menestheus, son of Peteos, shivered:
it was his tower they were making for, bringing destruction.
He looked out down the line of Achaian battlements,
in the hope he'd find one of the leaders, to fend off disaster
from him and his comrades, and saw the two Aiases, both
gluttons for war, standing there, with Teukros beside them,
just come from his hut. Yet no way could he make himself heard
by shouting, so great was the din: the sound rose up to heaven
of blows struck on shields and horsehair-crested helmets,
or battering at the gates, all now shut, with the enemy outside
up against them, striving to breach them, force their way in.

At once he dispatched to Aias the herald Thoōtēs:
"Go, noble Thoōtēs, run, summon Aias back here—
both of them, rather: that would be by far the best,
for very soon here sheer destruction will be wrought,
so hard do the Lycian leaders assail us, who've for long
been fearsome opponents in these fierce engagements!
But if for them there too hard fighting has arisen,
then at least let one of the Aiases, Telamōn's valiant son,
come over here, and bring Teukros, that skilled archer, with him."
So he spoke. The herald heard, and did not ignore him,
but ran off along the wall of the bronze-corseleted Achaians,
and went up to the two Aiases, and quickly said:
"You Aiases, leaders of the bronze-corseleted Achaians,
the dear son of Peteōs, Zeus's nursling, is insistent
that you go to him, if only briefly, to face war's toil—
both of you, for choice, since that would be far the best,
since very soon there sheer destruction will be wrought,
so hard's the attack by the Lycian leaders, who've long
been our fearsome opponents in the raging conflicts!
But if here for you too a crisis in the fighting has arisen,
then at least let one Aias, Telamōn's valiant son,
come, and bring Teukros, that skilled archer, with him."

So he spoke. Great Aias, Telamōn's son, took notice,
and promptly addressed winged words to the son of Oïleus:
"Aias, you stay here, with powerful Lykomēdēs,
and urge on the Danaäns to fight with all their strength,
but I shall go over there, meet the enemy head-on,
and quickly come back, after I've rescued the defenders."

So saying, Aias the son of Telamōn departed,
and with him Teukros, his brother, son of the same father,
and Pandiōn, who was carrying Teukros's curved bow.
When they arrived at the tower of great-hearted Menestheus,
moving inside the wall, they found men sorely pressed,
for all the mighty leaders and rulers of the Lycians
were assailing the breastworks like a black tornado,
and they clashed head-on in battle, and loud clamor arose.

Aias the son of Telamōn was the first to kill his man,
Sarpēdōn's comrade, great-spirited Epiklēs—

with a great jagged rock he hit him, that was lying inside
the wall, by the breastwork, at the top of a heap. No man—
such as mortals today are, even those in the prime of youth—
could shift it using both hands; but Aias hefted it high
and flung it, smashing the plated helmet, crushing in
the whole mass of his skull. Like a diver Epiklēs plunged
off the high tower: the breath of life fled from his bones.
Now Teukros hit Glaukos, Hippolochos's mighty son,
as he charged, with an arrow shot from the high wall—
caught sight of his bared arm, put him out of the fight.
Glaukos sprang down from the wall, but discreetly, so no Achaian
would see he'd been hit, and boast loudly over him.
Grief possessed Sarpēdōn over Glaukos's departure
the moment he noticed it; yet he did not neglect the fighting,
but with a thrust of his spear pierced Alkmaiōn, Thestōr's son,
and pulled the spear out again. Alkmaiōn followed the spear,
fell headlong, his bronze-inlaid armor rattling about him.
Sarpēdōn seized the breastwork in his powerful hands
and pulled. The whole length of it came free, and the wall
was laid bare from above: he opened a path for many.

But Aias and Teukros now assailed him at once: the latter
with an arrow to the bright baldric that held his protective shield
in place over his torso; but Zeus warded off from his son
the death-spirits, to stop him being killed at the ships' sterns.
Aias sprang at him, thrust at his shield: the spear point
failed to go through, but nevertheless stopped his charge.
He backed off a bit from the breastwork, yet did not withdraw
completely, for his heart was still set on winning glory.
So, turning around, he called out to the godlike Lycians:
"Hey, Lycians, why thus abandon your fighting valor?
It's hard for me, strong though I am, to breach this wall
single-handed, and open up a path to the ships—so come,
join in the attack! The more men, the better the work gets done!"

So he spoke, and they, abashed by the king's rebuke,
pressed on harder around their lord and counselor,
while the Argives against them now reinforced their ranks
inside the wall. A huge task confronted them both.
Neither were the strong Lycians able to breach the Danaäns'
wall, and open up a path to the ships, nor yet

could the Danaän spearmen ever thrust the Lycians
back from the wall, once they'd got up close to it;
like two men in a dispute over boundary stones, who hold
measuring rods in their hands, on some common plowland,
each contending for his fair share of a narrow patch,
so did the breastworks keep these men apart, while above them
they hacked at the oxhide shields protecting each others' chests,
the round shields and the fringed leather bucklers. Many now
suffered flesh wounds from thrusts of the pitiless bronze, both when
any one of the fighters turned round, exposing his back,
while others were speared clean through the shield itself,
and all down the line breastworks and towers were splashed
with men's blood from both sides, Achaian and Trojan alike.
Not even so could they bring about panic among the Achaians,
who held out—just as an honest woman, a wool-worker,
holds her scales, raises the weight and the wool in either pan,
till they balance, to earn a paltry sum for her children:
so these men's embattled conflict was stretched out, taut and equal,
until Zeus granted the greater glory to Hektōr,
Priam's son, the first to leap down inside the Achaians' wall.
Now, in a carrying voice, he called out to the Trojans:
"Up with you, horse-breaker Trojans! Breach the Argives' wall!
Fling your devouring fire in among their vessels!"

So he spoke, urging them on: they all gave ear,
charged straight at the wall in a mass, then clambered up
on the footings, sharp spears in their hands, while Hektōr
snatched up and carried a rock that he found lying
before the gates: broad-based, but at its top sharp-pointed.
Not without effort could two ordinary men
have heaved it from ground to wagon—the best there were,
such as mortals today are—yet he easily lifted it
on his own, since the son of Kronos, that devious schemer,
lightened it for him. As when a shepherd easily carries
a ram's fleece in one hand, its weight a small burden for him,
so Hektōr hefted the rock and made straight for the beams
that framed the close-set and strongly jointed gates—
tall double gates, backed inside with a pair of cross-bars
made fast with a single bolt. Up he came, stood close,
put his whole weight into his throw, hit the gates in the middle—

legs spread well apart, so the shot would not lack force—
and smashed them out of their sockets. The rock fell inside
by its own weight. The gates groaned on either side:
the cross-bars failed to hold, the doors were cracked wide open
by the rock's force. Illustrious Hektōr leapt through,
his face like swift nightfall. He shone in the terrible
bronze that he wore on his body, he carried a couple
of spears in his hands. None meeting him could have stopped him,
none but the gods, once he'd leapt past the gates, and his eyes
were ablaze with fire as he whirled about in the crowd
and called on the Trojans to climb the wall. They responded
to his appeal: at once some scaled the wall, while others
streamed in by the well-made gates. The Danaäns fled in panic
among their hollow ships, and a ceaseless clamor arose.

Book 13

Zeus, when he'd brought the Trojans and Hektōr to the ships,
abandoned them there, to endure toil and suffering
without respite, but himself turned his bright eyes away,
gazing far off at the lands of the Thracian horsemen,
of the Mysian close-quarter fighters, of the noble milk-drinking
Hippomolgoi, and of the Abioi, the most righteous of mankind;
but to Troy he longer turned his bright eyes at all,
never expecting that any of the immortals would
go to the help of either the Danaäns or the Trojans.

But it was no blind watch that the lordly Earth-Shaker kept:
no indeed, for he sat marveling at the war and its conflicts,
high on the topmost peak of wooded Samothrakē.
From there he had a clear view of the whole of Ida;
clear too were Priam's city and the Achaians' ships.
Fresh up from the sea he sat there, full of pity for the Achaians'
rout by the Trojans, and in a furious temper with Zeus.

Down he now started at once from the rocky mountain,
striding on with brisk footsteps: the high range and the woodlands
shook under the tread of Poseidōn's immortal feet.
Three strides he took; with the fourth he reached his goal,
Aigai, where lies his famed palace, built in the depths
of the water, golden and gleaming, forever imperishable.
Arrived there, he yoked to the chariot his bronze-hoofed horses,
his swift-flying pair, with their flowing manes of gold,
and clad himself in gold, and flourished his whip—
of gold too, finely made—and, mounting his chariot,
drove out over the waves. Beneath him sea-beasts gamboled
all around, up from the deep—well they knew their lord—
and in joy the sea parted before him. His steeds flew on
so lightly, the axle of bronze beneath was never wetted,
and nimbly bore him across to the ships of the Achaians.

There's a certain wide cavern out there, down in deep water,
midway between Tenedos and rugged Imbros. Here

Poseidōn, the Earth-Shaker, reined in his horses,
unyoked them from the chariot, tossed them ambrosial fodder
to eat, and around their hooves fastened golden hobbles
they could neither break nor slip off, to make sure they waited
till their lord returned: then he went to the Achaians' camp.

The Trojans, all in one mass, like a flame or a gale blast,
were pressing hotly on behind Hektōr, the son of Priam,
shouting and yelling together, confident that they'd capture
the Achaians' ships, and massacre all the best men there.
But Poseidōn, the Earth-Shaker, the Earth-Encircler,
came up from the salty deep to encourage the Argives,
in Kalchas's bodily form, with his untiring voice.
First he addressed the two Aiases, both eager for action:
"You two now between you can save the Achaian forces,
if your minds are set on your prowess, not on chilling rout!
Nowhere else do I fear the invincible hands of those
Trojans who, in a body, have swarmed up our great wall:
the well-greaved Achaians will hold them all at bay.
No, it's here I'm really afraid we may meet disaster—
here, where that madman, flame-like, is leading them on:
yes, Hektōr, who boasts he's a son of almighty Zeus!
May some god put the strong will in the hearts of you both
to make a firm stand yourselves, bid others do the same:
that way, for all his onslaught, you still might force him back
from the swift ships, even though the Olympian's backing him."

With that the Earth-Shaker and Earth-Encircler tapped
both men with his staff, filled them with strength and courage,
and made their limbs light, both their legs and their arms above.
Then, just as a swift-flying hawk will take to the air,
lifting off from some sheer and inaccessible rock face,
to hunt down another bird, in pursuit across the plain—
such was the flight of Poseidōn the Earth-Shaker from them.
It was Oïleus's son, swift Aias, who recognized him first,
and straightway declared to Aias, Telamōn's son:
"Aias, that was one of the gods who dwell on Olympos,
in the seer's likeness, urging us to fight by the ships!
That was not really Kalchas the prophet, the diviner—
the form of his feet and legs from behind as he went
I easily knew: though gods, they're still recognizable—

and my heart in the breast of me is made that much more eager
to plunge with zest into warfare and battle: my own
feet under and hands above are impatient to go!"[1]

Aias, Telamōn's son, then made him this answer:
"So too with me: my invincible hands are urgent
to grasp the spear, my power's aroused, I'm borne forward
by both feet beneath me: I'm ready, even alone, to do battle
with Priam's son Hektōr, hot to fight though he always is."
Such were their words to each other, while rejoicing over
the lust for battle the god had put in their hearts.
Meanwhile the Earth-Encircler aroused those Achaians behind them,
now refreshing their spirits beside the swift ships,
their limbs undone by grievous fatigue, while anguish
swelled and possessed their spirits as they observed
the Trojans in countless numbers swarm up the great wall:
looking at them they shed tears, never once supposing
that they could escape calamity. But the Earth-Shaker,
easily passing among them, strengthened their ranks
by his exhortations. He first approached Teukros and Lēïtos,
then Thoas, Dēïpyros, the heroic Pēneleōs,
Mēriones and Antilochos, lords of the battle cry:
These he urged on now, addressed them with winged words:

"Shame on you, Argives, young warriors! It was in your prowess
as fighters I trusted to keep our ships in safety—
but if you're about to shrink from warfare's grievous business,
the day's indeed come for us to be beaten by the Trojans!
Alas, this is a great wonder that my eyes now behold,
a terrible sight, something I never thought could happen:
the Trojans attacking our ships—the same men who before
resembled timorous hinds, that in the woodlands
become the prey of jackals, of wolves and leopards,
wandering cravenly, no fighting spirit in them:
just so, until now the Trojans refused to stand and face
the Achaians' hands, their power, not even briefly.
But now, far from the city, they're engaged by the hollow ships

1. We're not told what was special, and recognizable, about gods' nether extremities, or how Aias knew them. This has seemingly not bothered commentators, ancient or modern, as much as it might.

because of our leader's weakness and our troops' lack of discipline—
being at loggerheads with him, they have no will to fight
for the swift-faring ships, but are getting killed among them.
Yet even if it's the truth that the person at fault
is Atreus's heroic son, wide-ruling Agamemnōn,
because he dishonored the swift-foot son of Pēleus,
that's no reason for us to stay aloof from the fighting!
Let's mend this rift quickly—good men's hearts can be healed—
but it's no good thing that you're still shy of warlike valor—
you, the elite troops, the army's finest! I'd have
no quarrel with any man that hung back from the fighting
who was a worthless fellow, but with you lot I'm furious!
Gentlemen, this abstention of yours will soon
make matters a good deal worse, and each one of you should
take shame—and men's censure—to heart, for the struggle
now unfolding is crucial. Strong Hektōr, of the great war cry,
is fighting beside our ships, has smashed our gates and their bar!"

Thus the Earth-Encircler's commands urged on the Achaians,
and about the two Aiases the ranks assembled, in strength,
such as Arēs himself would not fault if he came among them,
or Athēnē, the host-rallier; for these were the pick of the best
that now awaited the Trojans and noble Hektōr,
spears in serried rows, bucklers pressed against bucklers,
shields overlapping, helmets by helmets, men packed so tight
the horsehair crests on the gleaming boss of their helmets
nudged as they bent their heads, so close were the ranks,
and the spears, brandished in bold hands, intermingled,
a woven lattice. Their minds were unswervingly set on battle.

The mass of the Trojans now charged, with Hektōr at their head,
driving straight on, like a boulder that rolls down a rock face,
when some winter torrent has shifted it off the hilltop,
its huge flood undermining the ruthless stone's embedment,
and up it bounces, in flight, and the woods echo beneath it
as it plunges straight on down, until it reaches
the level plain, and there it stops rolling, for all its hurry—
so, for a while, Hektōr threatened to break right through to the sea
easily, by way of the Achaians' ships and huts,
on his killing spree; but when he came to those close-packed ranks
he stopped, brought up short. The Achaians' sons stood against him,

jabbing at him with their swords and double-edged spears,
and drove him back: he gave ground, badly shaken,
and in a carrying voice called out to the Trojans:
"Trojans! Lycians! You Dardanian front-line fighters!
Stand by me! Not for long shall the Achaians hold me back,
though they've closed their ranks like a wall. No, I rather think
they'll give ground before my spear, if indeed I was urged on
by the highest of gods, Hērē's own loud-thundering lord."
So saying Hektōr stirred up each warrior's force and spirit.
Deïphobos, Priam's son, strode out amongst them,
set on greatness, holding his balanced shield before him,
[advancing light-footedly, under cover of his shield],[2]
and Mērionēs took aim at him with his gleaming spear,
and threw, and did not miss, but struck the balanced shield
of oxhide, yet could not pierce it: far short of that,
the long spear snapped at its head socket, and Deïphobos
held his oxhide shield away from him, inwardly scared
by the spear of Mērionēs, the skilled warrior. But that hero
backed off to the mass of his comrades, deeply angered
both by missing a victory and at breaking his spear,
and set out back to the huts and ships of the Achaians
to fetch another long spear that he'd left in his hut.

But the rest fought on, and an unquenchable clamor went up,
and Teukros, Telamōn's son, was the first to slay his man:
Imbrios, spearman, the son of horse-rich Mentōr,
who lived in Pēdaion before the Achaians' sons appeared,
and married Mēdesikastē, a bastard daughter of Priam.
But when the Danaäns came, in their well-rounded ships,
to Ilion he returned, won renown among the Trojans,
and lived with Priam, who honored him like one of his own sons.
Him it was Telamōn's son now struck beneath one ear
with his long spear, then withdrew it: like an ash tree he fell
that on the peak of a mountain in clear view all around
is cut down by the bronze and scatters its tender leaves
abroad on the ground: so he fell, his bronze-inlaid armor
rattling upon him, and Teukros, eager to strip his gear,
rushed up. As he ran, Hektōr flung a gleaming spear at him

2. Probably—but not certainly—an interpolation or alternative line to 157.

but he, watching carefully, avoided the bronze missile—
a near miss—and it hit Amphimachos in the chest,
Kteatos's son, Aktōr's grandson,[3] returning to the battle.
He fell with a thud, and his armor rattled upon him.
Now Hektōr moved quickly to rip from Amphimachos's head—
that great-hearted man—the helmet enclosing his temples;
and Aias lunged out with his gleaming spear at Hektōr
as he came on, never reaching his flesh—his whole body
was clad in fearsome bronze—just striking his shield's boss,
and thrusting him back with huge force. So Hektōr gave ground,
backwards, from the two corpses. The Achaians dragged them off.
Amphimachos was taken by Stichios and noble Menestheus,
Athenian leaders, back to the mass of the Achaians,
and Imbrios by the two Aiases, full of fighting valor.
Like two lions that have snatched a goat from sharp-toothed hounds,
and carry it off through thickly growing brushwood,
high up off the ground, held tight in their jaws, so these
two commanders called Aias hefted Imbrios aloft,
and stripped off his battle gear. Out of rage for Amphimachos
Oïleus's son cut Imbrios's head from his tender neck,
swung his arm, and threw the head off into the crowd,
like a ball, and it fell in the dust right at Hektōr's feet.

Poseidōn was now very deeply angered at heart
since his own grandson had fallen in the ruthless struggle;
and he made his way past the huts and ships of the Achaians
urging the Danaäns on, but planning harm for the Trojans.
There he encountered Idomeneus, famed spearman,
come from tending a comrade just in from the fighting,
cut in the ham of his knee by the keen-edged bronze:
his comrades had carried him back. Idomeneus, having left orders
for the healers, was going to his hut, still eager to join in
the battle. To him now spoke the lordly Earth-Shaker,
likening his voice to that of Thoas, Andraimōn's son,
who in the whole of Pleurōn and rugged Kalydōn
ruled the Aitōlians, being honored by his people like a god:

3. Aktōr was only nominally Kteatos's father: his real sire was Poseidōn, which is why the god is deeply angered at the death of Amphimachos, who thus was indeed his grandson (206–7).

"Idomeneus, Krētan counselor, where now are the threats
that the sons of the Achaians once made against the Trojans?"

To him then Idomeneus, leader of Krētans, replied:
"Ah, Thoas, so far as I know, there's no one man to blame now—
we're all of us skilled, these days, in warfare's business.
No man here's been gripped by spiritless terror; none,
yielding to hesitancy, has shirked grim war. This must,
I suppose, be what pleases the almighty son of Kronos:
that here, far from Argos and nameless, the Achaians should
perish.
But Thoas, you were one who always stood strong in battle,
and prompt to urge on others you noticed hanging back—
so don't give up now, but call upon every man!"

In answer to him Poseidōn the Earth-Shaker then said:
"Idomeneus, may that man never get back home
from Troy, but stay here and become the sport of dogs,
who on this day chooses to shirk the fighting! So then,
fetch your battle gear, come with me: we have to work together
to advance our goal. Though two only, we might still help.
When the weakest men unite, their valor's augmented—
But we two know how to fight even against the best."

So saying, he went back, a god to the struggle of mortals,
and Idomeneus, on reaching his well-built hut,
put on his fine battle gear, picked out two spears,
and set forth, like branched lightning that the son of Kronos
grasps in his hand and flourishes from bright Olympos,
displaying a sign to mortals, and its clear rays dazzle:
so gleamed the bronze around his torso as he ran.
Mēriones, his good henchman, met him a short distance
from the hut, being on his way to collect another spear
of bronze, and mighty Idomeneus now addressed him:
"Mēriones, Molos's son, swift-footed, dearest of comrades—
what brings you here, away from the war and the conflict?
Are you wounded, perhaps? Is an arrowhead giving you trouble?
Or have you brought me a message? Myself, I'm not minded
to sit here, back in my hut; what I want now is to fight."

Then sagacious Mēriones made him this answer:
"Idomeneus, counselor to the bronze-corsleted Krētans,

I'm on my way to get me a spear, if there's still one left
in the hut, since the one I had before, I shattered
when I let fly at the shield of haughty Deïphobos."

To him then Idomeneus, leader of Krētans, replied:
"If it's spears you want, be it one or twenty, you'll find them
lined up there in my hut, against the bright inner wall—
Trojan spears, that I take from men I've killed—I don't
care to stand well away when I fight my opponents,
and so I've a store of spears, and shields with bosses,
and helmets, and bright-glinting corselets."

Then to him
sagacious Mēriones declared in answer:
"In my hut too, and in my black ship, there are many
spoils from the Trojans, but not handy for me to fetch.
Neither have I, I can tell you, forgotten my prowess:
among the foremost in battle, where glory is won,
is where I take my place when war's conflicts arise.
Though some other bronze-armored Achaians are perhaps
unaware of my fighting record, you, I think, know it well."

To him then Idomeneus, leader of Krētans, replied:
"I know how brave you are: what need to tell me?
If the best of us were being chosen beside the hollow ships
for an ambush—a task where men's bravery shows most clearly,
and one in which courage and cowardice both are revealed:
for the coward's complexion will always keep changing hue,
his inner thoughts never are calm, won't let him sit still,
he shifts from ham to ham, puts his weight on either foot,
and his heart goes thump thump in his breast as he thinks
about the death-spirits, and his teeth begin to chatter;
but the brave man's complexion's unchanging, nor is he overly
scared when he first takes his place in a warriors' ambush,
but prays for a speedy entry to the grievous conflict—
not even then would your power, your strong hands come in
question!
For if you were shot, or struck, in the course of the struggle,
not on the nape of your neck would the blow fall, or your back,
but rather would make its mark on your chest or nether belly
as you pressed on among the foremost to grapple the foe

like a lover! But come, let's not loiter here, chattering
as though we were children: that's to invite a rebuke.
Off with you to the hut now, pick up that hefty spear."

So he spoke, and Mērionēs, swift Arēs' equal,
speedily fetched from the hut a new bronze spear,
and followed Idomeneus, his mind firmly set on battle.
Just as Arēs the killer goes about looking for war,
with his dear son Panic Rout, the mighty and fearless,
who sends even the sturdiest warrior fleeing in terror,
and they arm themselves and go from Thrace to the Ephyroi
or the great-hearted Phlegyes, yet never listen
to both sides, but just hand out glory to one or the other—
so Mērionēs and Idomeneus, leaders of men,
went out to the war, both armored in gleaming bronze.
It was Mērionēs who first addressed his companion:
"Son of Deukaliōn, where do you want to join the main body?
At the far right wing of the army, or in the middle?
Or out on the left—since I figure there's nowhere else
that the long-haired Achaians will fall so short in the struggle."

To him then Idomeneus, leader of Krētans, replied:
"At the ships in the center there are others to mount a defense:
the two Aiases, and Teukros, who's the best among the Achaians
in bowmanship—no slouch, either, at hand-to-hand combat!
These will give Priam's son Hektōr his fill of warfare,
however avid he is for it, never mind his mighty strength!
A hard climb he'll have, with all his fighting passion,
to vanquish the strength of their irresistible hands
and set fire to the fleet—unless the son of Kronos himself
should hurl a blazing torch there, in among the swift ships!
But great Aias, son of Telamōn, would yield to no mere man,
any person who's mortal, who eats Dēmētēr's grain,
who can be broken apart by the bronze or by great rocks:
not even to Achilles, the rank-breaker, would he submit
in a stand-up fight—though at running Achilles has no rivals.
So, yes, on to the army's left, and we'll know soon enough
whether we'll win ourselves glory or yield it to others."

So he spoke, and Mērionēs, the equal of swift Arēs,
led on, until they reached the troops where he'd commanded.

When the Trojans saw Idomeneus, of flame-like prowess,
and with him his henchman in his fine-wrought armor,
they passed the word down the line and all went at him,
and a general struggle took place around the vessels' sterns.
The way that whining gales can generate wind-gusts galore
on a day when the dust lies thickest along the roads,
and all together stir up an enormous dust cloud,
just so their battle was joined, and they were urgent at heart
in the throng to cut down each other with the keen-edged bronze.

The battle that's death to mortals bristled with lengthy
spears, that they used to rip flesh with, and eyes were blinded
by the bronze radiance from those burnished helmets
and newly buffed corselets and brightly shining shields
as they clashed in their masses. Hardhearted would that man be
who, seeing this scene, experienced joy, not grief.

Opposed in purpose, Kronos's two mighty sons
were fashioning miserable troubles for these warrior heroes:
Zeus sought victory for Hektōr and the Trojans,
to honor swift-footed Achilles; yet no way did he
want the Achaian army wiped out before Ilion,
wished only to honor Thetis and her stronghearted son.
But Poseidōn had joined the Argives, was urging them on—
risen secretly from the grey sea—deeply distressed
at their rout by the Trojans, and in a furious temper with Zeus.
Nevertheless, though they shared the same ancestry and father,
Zeus was the elder brother, had more knowledge,
and so Poseidōn avoided providing open support,
but kept stirring up Argive troops, while disguised as a man.
So these two drew tight the cords of strong strife and common war
over both sides, to and fro, made a knot that could be neither
untied nor broken, but would unstring the knees of many.

Now, despite his grey hairs, Idomeneus rallied the Danaäns,
and charging among the Trojans, turned them to flight,
for he cut down Othryoneus, from Kabēsos, a guest in Troy
lately arrived, brought there by report of the war,
who'd asked to marry the fairest of Priam's daughters,
Kassandrē: offered no bride-price, but made a grandiose promise,
that he'd force the Achaians' sons, against their will, from Troy;

and the aged Priam assented, bent his head in agreement
to give him the girl; he trusted the promise, went to war.
But Idomeneus aimed at him with his gleaming spear
as he high-stepped forward: threw, and struck home. His bronze
corselet failed to protect him, the spear lodged in his mid-belly.
He fell with a thud, and Idomeneus boasted over him, saying:
"Othryoneus, I must compliment you above all mankind,
if it's true that you're going to accomplish all that you promised
to Dardanos's scion Priam! He promised you his daughter,
and we too would make the same promise, and fulfill it—
would give you the son of Atreus's loveliest daughter,
bring her here from Argos for you to wed, if you'd join us
in sacking the populous city of Ilion! So, come along,
here by the seafaring ships we'll work out our agreement
over the marriage—and no, we're not fussy about the bride-price."

So saying, the hero Idomeneus dragged Othryoneus out
through the crush of battle, but Asios came to the rescue,
on foot, ahead of his horses—their breath kept right on his shoulders
by the charioteer, his henchman—eager to take a shot at
Idomeneus, but he threw first, hit Asios with his spear
in the throat, under the chin, driving the bronze right through;
and he fell as falls an oak or white poplar, or a lofty
pine tree that up in the mountains shipwrights fell
with their newly sharpened axes to serve as a ship timber:
so there in front of his horses and chariot Asios lay
stretched out, screaming, hands clutching the bloody dust,
while his charioteer, scared out of the wits that he had before,
dared not wheel his team round, and so escape
the hands of the enemy. Steadfast Antilochos took
aim, hit him squarely. The corselet of bronze that he wore
failed to protect him, the spear lodged in his mid-belly,
and gasping for breath he slumped from his well-built chariot,
while his horses Antilochos, great-hearted Nestōr's son,
drove off, away from the Trojans to the well-greaved Achaians.

Now Deïphobos came right up close to Idomeneus,
grieving for Asios, took a shot with his gleaming spear,
but Idomeneus, on the lookout, ducked the bronze-pointed shaft,
took cover behind the well-balanced shield he bore,
fashioned from circles of oxhide and glinting bronze,

and well-equipped with two cross-bars. Beneath this shield
he crouched, and the bronze spear flew over and past him,
harshly scraping the shield's rim. Yet not in vain
had Deïphobos launched it from his brawny hand:
Hippasos's son Hypsēnōr, shepherd of men, it struck
in the liver below his midriff, and at once unstrung his knees;
and Deïphobos shouted aloud, vaunted terribly over him:
"Not unavenged does Asios lie now: no, I declare,
though he's going to the house of Hādēs, mighty gate-guardian,
he'll rejoice at heart, since I've furnished him with an escort!"

So he spoke: and grief stirred the Argives at his boasting,
but roused most passion in warlike Antilochos's heart:
yet despite his sorrow he wasn't unmindful of his comrade,
but ran up and stood over him, protecting him with his shield,
while two other trusty comrades—Echios's son Mēkisteus
and noble Alastōr—stooped and lifted him up,
and carried him, groaning deeply, back to the hollow ships.

Idomeneus never slackened his raging attack, kept up
his drive either to shroud some Trojan in black night,
or to fall himself, while keeping disaster from the Achaians.
Next, the dear son of Aisyētēs, Zeus's nursling,
the hero Alkathoös—son-in-law to Anchīsēs,
having married his eldest daughter, Hippodameia,
whom her father and lady mother cherished in their house
since she excelled all other girls of her age
in beauty and wit and fine handiwork, this being why
the man she wed was the best in all broad Troy—
him, by Idomeneus's hand, Poseidōn laid low,
holding his bright eyes spellbound, shackled his glorious limbs,
so he could neither flee backwards nor dodge aside,
but stood, like a pillar or some high leafy tree,
motionless, while he was run through in mid-chest
by the hero Idomeneus's spear. It tore clean through the bronze
corselet, that hitherto had kept death from his flesh,
but now rasped harshly around the rending spear.
He fell with a thud, the spear lodged firm in his heart,
which, beating still, sent vibration out to the spear's
butt-end; then at last mighty Arēs stopped its force.
Idomeneus shouted aloud, vaunted terribly over him:

"Deïphobos, now perhaps we can call it fair recompense—
the way you boast—three killed in exchange for one?
Crazed man, now stand up against me yourself, and learn
how I'm descended from Zeus, I who have voyaged here:
first Zeus begot Mīnōs to be Krētē's guardian; then
Mīnōs in turn sired a son, the peerless Deukaliōn,
and Deukaliōn fathered me, to be lord over many warriors
in spacious Krētē; and now the ships have brought me to Troy
to make trouble for you, and your father, and the Trojans generally."

So he spoke. Deïphobos pondered, mind uncertain:
should he seek out a comrade from the great-hearted Trojans,
withdrawing to do so, or make trial of Idomeneus on his own?
And to him, on reflection, this seemed the better course:
to go and look for Aineias. He found him standing idle
on the far side of the action, still resentful of noble Priam,
who would accord him no honor, good warrior though he was.[4]
Deïphobos now came up and addressed him with winged words:
"Aineias, the Trojans' counselor, there is sore need for you
to rescue your brother-in-law—if the loss of kin can move you!
Come with me and rescue Alkathoös, who, long years ago,
as your sister's husband, kept you as a child in his house:
he's been killed by Idomeneus, the famous spearman."[5]

So he spoke, and aroused the spirit in the breast of Aineias,
who charged straight at Idomeneus, mind set on battle.
Idomeneus was not seized by panic, like some youngster,
but waited, as when a boar in the mountains, trusting his strength,
awaits the huge pack of men that's coming against him
at a lonely spot: he pricks up the bristles along his back,
his eyes blaze with fire, he whets his tusks, makes ready
to fight off, zestfully, attacks from both dogs and hunters—
so Idomeneus, famous spearman, awaiting Aineias's charge,
did not back off, but rather called out to his comrades,
looking round at Askalaphos, Dēïpyros, and Aphareus,
Mērionēs and Antilochos, lords of the battle cry,

---

4. There was a traditional rivalry between Priam's and Anchīsēs' branches of the royal house of Troy for the kingship: see also 20.178–86, 302–6; Janko 106; A. T. Murray 2: 37n1.
5. This may sound a rather odd appeal, until we recall that, both in Homer's day and later, giving a corpse proper burial rites, at home, was essential to ensure that the dead man's spirit was not condemned to wander in limbo. See Vermeule, 11–12.

to whom he addressed now winged words of exhortation:

"Come help me, friends! I'm alone, and terribly afraid
of swift-footed Aineias, now advancing to attack me—
very strong he is, very good at killing men in battle,
and he's in the flower of youth, when a man's strength is greatest.
Were we in our present mood, but of a like age,
then straightway either he or I would win a great victory."

So he spoke, and they all, with a single end in mind,
came and stood round him, shields settled on their shoulders.
On the other side Aineias called out to his own comrades,
looking round at Deïphobos, Paris, and the noble Agēnōr,
leaders with him of the Trojans. Arrayed in their rear
there followed a mass of troops: as sheep will trail a ram
to water from feeding place, and the shepherd's glad at heart—
so the heart in Aineias's breast rejoiced at the sight
of these massed troops that were following on behind him.
So over Alkathoös they went at it hand to hand
with their long spears: the bronze girding their chests
rang loudly with thrusts made to and fro in the turmoil
one at another. Two men, fighters skilled above the rest,
Idomeneus and Aineias, both equals of Arēs, hungered
to cut up each other's flesh with the pitiless bronze:
Aineias had the first shot, let fly at Idomeneus,
who, watching carefully, avoided the bronze spear,
and Aineias's shaft ended quivering, stuck point first
deep in the ground, flung in vain from his sturdy hand.
But Idomeneus hit Oinomäos square in the mid-belly,
broke the plate of his corslet, so that his guts spilled out
through the bronze: in the dust he fell, hand clawing the earth,
and Idomeneus from his corpse pulled the far-shadowing
spear, yet could not also strip the splendid battle gear
from off his shoulders, so hard-pressed he was by missiles;
for his leg joints no longer were steady when he ran,
wouldn't let him retrieve his own spear, or dodge another's.
So in close combat he stood off his pitiless death-day,
but his feet could no longer hurry him out of the fighting,
and as, step by step, he backed off, Deïphobos—who'd long nursed
an undying grudge against him—let fly his gleaming spear
but missed him once more, and instead hit Askalaphos,

Enyalios's son: through his shoulder the mighty spear
drove: in the dust he fell, hand clawing the earth.
(As yet mighty loud-voiced Arēs knew nothing about
the fall of his son[6] in the relentless grind of battle;
he sat on the heights of Olympos, beneath the golden clouds,
kept there by the will of Zeus, like all the other
immortal gods, well away from the war and the fighting.)

Now over Askalaphos they battled hand to hand.
Deïphobos tore loose from the corpse his gleaming
helmet, but Mērionēs, swift Arēs' equal,
sprang at him, jabbed his arm with his spear. From his hand
the visored headpiece fell, clanged as it hit the ground,
and Mērionēs, like a vulture, pounced once more,
pulled out his mighty spear from Deïphobos's arm,
then backed off to rejoin his companions, while Polītēs,
Deïphobos's brother, one arm around his waist,
led him out of warfare's grim clamor, till he reached
the swift horses awaiting him, out back behind the fighting,
that stood there along with their driver and their inlaid chariot.
These bore him away to the city, groaning deeply, in great pain,
the blood still dripping down from his newly wounded arm.

But the rest fought on, and a clamor unquenchable went up.
Aineias now went for Aphareus, Kalētōr's son,
as he turned to face him, drove a sharp spear into his throat;
and his head lolled to one side, and his shield fell on him,
his helmet too; death, the life-queller, was shed about him.
Then Antilochos, seizing his chance, as Thoön turned away
pounced and stabbed him, completely severed the vein
that runs the length of the back till it reaches the neck:[7]
this he severed completely, and Thoön slumped down
on his back in the dust, stretching out both hands to his comrades.
Antilochos crouched, started stripping the gear off his shoulders,
but kept an eye out, for the Trojans were all around him,
taking shots at his broad bright shield; yet they could not get through

6. Though Arēs and Enyalios were originally different war gods, their identities tended, as here, to merge: the second becomes no more than a mere epithet attached to the first at 17.211 below.

7. There is in fact no such vein, but the idea of it was widespread in antiquity, supposedly either running close to the spine, or, sometimes, in the spinal column itself.

to mar with their pitiless bronze Antilochos's soft flesh,
since Poseidōn, the Earth-Shaker, protected Nestōr's son
too closely, even amid a shower of missiles—
for Antilochos never lacked enemies. He kept turning about
amongst them, nor was his spear ever still, but always
poised, brandished, while he debated in his mind
whether to throw from a distance or close in hand to hand.
His sighting for shots down the ranks was not lost on Adamas,
Asios's son, who struck his shield with the pitiless bronze,
squarely, up close. But his spear point was robbed of its force
by dark-maned Poseidōn, who grudged it his favorite's life:
half the spear, like a charred stake, stayed stuck fast
in Antilochos's shield; the other half lay on the ground,
and Adamas backed away to his comrades, avoiding fate.
But Mēriones followed after him, speared him midway
between navel and genitals, the place where a battle-wound
inflicts on wretched mortals the sharpest pain of all.
Here he thrust in his spear, and Adamas, flung forward,
convulsed on the spike, like an ox that herdsmen in the mountains
have bound with ropes and are dragging off against its will:
so he, when hit, convulsed for a little, but not for long,
till the hero Mēriones came up and tore the spear
out of his flesh, and darkness shrouded his eyes.

Then Helenos at close quarters hit Dēïpyros on the temple
with a great Thracian sword, and ripped off his helmet.
Torn from his head it dropped groundwards, and an Achaian
scooped it up as it rolled among the fighters' feet,
and night's darkness fell on Dēïpyros, shrouding his eyes.

This grieved Atreus's son Menelaös, of the fine war cry:
out he strode, with loud threats for heroic prince Helenos,
and waving his sharp spear. But Helenos drew his bow,
and they both let fly together, the one with his sharp spear,
the other with an arrow sped from the bowstring.
Priam's son hit Menelaös in the chest with his arrow,
on the plate of his corselet, and off it the bitter arrow glanced.
Just as off a broad shovel on a big threshing-floor
the dark-hued beans or chickpeas fly through the air
before the shrill storm blast and the sweep of the winnower,
in such wise from the corselet of glorious Menelaös

the bitter arrow glanced off, and flew wide of the mark.
But Atreus's son Menelaös, of the fine war cry, threw
and hit Helenos in the hand that held his well-polished bow.
Through his hand into the bow the bronze spear was driven;
he backed off to rejoin his comrades, avoiding fate,
hand inert at his side, the ash spear dragging behind it,
and great-hearted Agēnōr drew the spear from his hand,
and closed the wound with a length of twisted wool,
a sling, that his henchman, the people's shepherd, kept for him.

Next Peisandros went straight for glorious Menelaös;
but an ill fate was leading him to the end that's death,
to be brought down by you, Menelaös, in the grim conflict.
When in their advance they'd drawn close, the one to the other,
the son of Atreus missed, his spear flew wide,
and Peisandros hit on the shield of glorious Menelaös,
yet could not manage to drive the bronze clean through,
for the broad shield stopped it, his spear broke off at the socket.
Even so he was cheerful at heart, looked for a victory,
but Atreus's son drew his silver-studded sword,
and sprang at Peisandros, who, from behind his shield,
brought out a fine bronze axe on a haft of olive wood,
long and well-polished. Each attacked at the same moment:
Peisandros caught Menelaös on his helmet's central strip,
at the top, by the horsehair crest; but Menelaös hit him
as he came, in the forehead above the bridge of his nose.
Bone crunched, both bloody eyeballs fell in the dust at his feet,
he crumpled and fell. Menelaös set one foot on his breast,
stripped off his armor, and boasted over him: "This
is how you'll all leave the ships of the swift-colted Danaäns,
you arrogant Trojans, never sated with war's dread clamor,
who have no lack of other shaming or wrongful acts
that you've done against me, foul dogs, no fear in your hearts
of the harsh wrath of thundering Zeus, guest-friendship's lord,
who in time to come will lay your high city low:
for my wedded wife it was, and a load of my possessions,
that you wantonly sailed away with, after being entertained
in her home—and now, again, among our seafaring ships
you're minded to fling fatal fire, to kill Achaian heroes!
But you'll be stopped short, however hot you are for fighting!

Zeus, Father, they claim that in wisdom you beat all others,
both men and gods—yet all these things happen through you,
such as now, when you're favoring the arrogant wrongdoers,
these Trojans, whose power's forever outrageous, who cannot
ever glut their urge for the clamor of common warfare.
All things attain their satiety: sleep and love,
sweet song and the blameless dance—these are the things
of which any man would, most happily, get his fill
rather than war; but these Trojans are insatiate of battle."

So saying, having stripped from its flesh the bloodied armor,
and given it to his comrades, Menelaös the blameless
himself went back again, mixed with the front-line fighters.
Then there sprang out against him king Pylaimenēs' son,
Harpaliōn: he'd come with his father to Troy to join
the fighting, but never returned to the land of his birth. He now
came close, scored a clear hit on the son of Atreus's shield,
yet could not manage to drive the bronze clean through,
and backed off to rejoin his comrades, avoiding fate,
glancing all round, lest someone should wound him with the bronze.
But as he went, Mērionēs let fly a bronze-tipped arrow
that hit him on the right buttock. The shaft passed through
along the line of the bladder, under the bone. He sank,
sat where he was, and in the arms of his comrades
breathed out his life, and like a worm lay stretched
there on the ground: his dark blood ran, soaked the earth.
The great-hearted Paphlagōnians attended to him,
lifted him into a chariot, bore him to sacred Ilion,
lamenting; and with them went his father, shedding tears—
but no blood-price was ever paid for his dead son.

His killing left Paris incensed beyond measure, since he—
out of so many Paphlagōnians—had at one time been his host.
Angered on his behalf, Paris flighted a bronze-tipped arrow.
There was a man named Euchēnōr, the seer Polyïdos's son,
rich, a fine warrior, who made his home in Korinthos.
He'd shipped out well aware of his baneful death-spirit,
since often told by his father, the virtuous Polyïdos,
that he'd either perish at home of some fatal disease,
or else be slain by the Trojans among the Achaians' ships.

This way he avoided both a heavy Achaian fine[8]
and the loathsome disease, suffered no grief at heart.
Him Paris hit under the ear and jaw: swiftly the breath
of life fled from his limbs, and hateful darkness claimed him.

So these fought on in the likeness of blazing fire:
But Hektōr, so dear to Zeus, had not heard, was quite unaware
that out to the left of the ships his men were being slaughtered
by the Argives: soon great glory would have been the Achaians' lot,
such a force was the Earth-Shaker, Earth-Enfolder
now urging the Argives on, and himself also aiding them.
Where Hektōr had first made his charge at gates and wall,
breaking the serried ranks of the Danaän shield men,
around the ships of Aias and Prōtesilaös,
drawn up along the shore of the grey sea, where beyond them
the wall was built lowest—it was here that those warriors
fighting with chariots and horses now showed the strongest.
Here troops from Boiōtia, robe-trailing Ionians,
men of Lokris and Phthiē, illustrious Epeians,
strove hard to repel the attack on the ships, yet could not
fend off from themselves noble Hektōr, so like a flame,
not even the picked Athenians—whose leader was
Peteōs's son Menestheus, accompanied by men
such as Stichios, Pheidas, strong Bias; while the Epeians
were led by Phyleus's son Megēs, by Amphíōn, Drakios,
and Medōn and staunch Podarkēs headed the Phthians—
one of these, Medōn, a bastard of godlike Oïleus
and brother to Aias, nevertheless lived far away
from his native land, in Phylakē, after killing a man, a kinsman
of his stepmother Eriōpis, wife to Oïleus. The other,
Podarkēs, was Iphiklos's son and grandson of Phylakos.
These, in their armor, headed the great-hearted Phthians,
who, with the Boiōtians, were fighting to save the ships.
Now Aias, Oïleus's swift son, would no more stand apart
from Aias the son of Telamōn, not for one instant,

8. Apparently a payment required to purchase exemption from military service: see 23.296–99, where Echépōlos bribes Agamemnōn with a mare in order to continue the uninterrupted enjoyment of his wealth at home. Buying or bribing your way out of going to war has a long and widespread history: in neither case here, interestingly, does the narrator indicate overt disapproval.

but as in a fallow field two wine-hued oxen
both strain with one accord at the jointed plow,
while round the base of their horns sweat breaks, and trickles,
and only the polished yoke keeps the two apart
as they force on down the furrow, plow to the field's edge:
just so did both Aiases stand, together, side by side,
and after Telamōn's son there followed a mass of valiant
soldiers, his comrades, relieving him of his shield
whenever sweat and exhaustion took over his limbs.
But the Lokrians did not follow with Oïleus's great-hearted son,
for their hearts were not in close-quarter fighting, seeing
they'd arrived with neither bronze horsehair-crested helmets,
nor trimly rounded shields, nor ash-wood spears;
it was trusting their bows, their slings of braided sheep's wool
that they'd followed him here, to Ilion, and using these,
shooting thick and fast, that they'd tried to break the Trojans' ranks.
So the ones with their fine-wrought war gear, out in front,
fought against the Trojans and bronze-armored Hektōr,
while the others, behind, kept shooting from cover: the Trojans
lost their taste for the fight, upset by this shower of arrows.

In sad disarray, then, thrust back from the ships and the huts,
would the Trojans have retreated to windy Ilion, had not
Poulydamas gone to bold Hektōr, and, standing beside him, said:
"Hektōr, there's no way to persuade you through argument!
In your god-given knowledge of warfare you have no rival,
but that makes you also want to outshine others in counsel.
Never will you be able to master all things yourself:
on one man heaven bestows expertise in warfare,
on another in dancing, or in singing and playing the lyre,
while in yet another man's breast far-seeing Zeus implants
a clever mind, from which many people get benefit,
and many he saves, but he knows it most clearly himself.
Anyway I will declare what seems to me to be best:
All round you now there blazes a ring of warfare,
and the great-hearted Trojans, now they've surmounted the wall,
are some of them standing by with their gear, while others
fight on, few against many, scattered among the ships.
I say pull back now, summon here all the leaders,
then let's debate every single suggestion—should we

make our assault on the many-benched ships, if maybe
some god is willing us victory, or rather retreat
unscathed from those ships hereafter? For my own part,
I fear the Achaians may pay back yesterday's debt,
since beside the ships there lingers a war-obsessed man
who will not, I think, much longer hold off from battle."

So spoke Poulydamas: his shrewd advice pleased Hektōr,
who at once sprang, fully armed, from his chariot to the ground,
and then addressed him, speaking in winged words:
"Poulydamas, while you're assembling all the leaders here
I shall go up to the front, take a close look at the fighting,
and come straight back, when I've given them my full orders."

So he spoke, and at once set off, like some snowclad mountain,[9]
shouting, and sped through the ranks of the Trojans and their allies,
who all rallied to Pánthoös's son, hospitable Poulydamas,
when they heard the voice of Hektōr. But he meanwhile
went in search of Deïphobos, and the mighty prince Helenos,
and Adamas son of Asios, and Asios, Hyrtakos's son,
ranging among the front-line fighters in his quest.
But he found them no longer unscathed or disaster-free:
some lay dead by the sterns of the Achaian ships,
who'd lost their lives at the hands of the Argives; others
were inside the wall, all wounded, either shot or cut up. However,
there was one he soon found, to the left of the tearful battle:
the godlike Aléxandros, husband of fair-haired Helen,
cheering his comrades on and urging them to fight,
and he went and stood close and addressed him in shaming words:
"Wretched Paris, so handsome, so mad for women, seducer,
where is Deïphobos, tell me? or the mighty prince Helenos?
Or Adamas son of Asios, or Asios, Hyrtakos's son?
Yes, and Othryoneus? Now the whole of steep Ilion's
on the brink of disaster, now sheer destruction's certain—"

Then Aléxandros the godlike made him this response:
"Hektōr, since your mind-set is to blame the blameless,

9. It is hard not to be brought up short by this image. We are here being asked to consider not only Hektōr's hugeness, but also his speed (and perhaps the dazzle of his armor). Despite scholarly support, the metaphor remains disconcerting. Mountains neither move (at any speed) nor do they shout. Yes, Homer sometimes nods.

at other times indeed I may have thought of withdrawing
from battle, but not now: I wasn't born wholly a weakling.
From the moment you roused your comrades to fight beside
the ships,
we've been engaged here nonstop against the Danaäns!
As for the comrades you're asking after, they're dead—
all but two: Deïphobos and the mighty prince Helenos,
and they've both left the field, both with arm wounds inflicted
by long spears, though Kronos's son saved them from death.
So now lead on, wherever your heart and spirit tell you,
and we'll follow you gladly, nor do I think you'll find us
in any way lacking in valor, while we still have strength:
but beyond their strength none can fight, however eager."

With these words the hero persuaded his brother's mind,
and they went where the uproar of battle was most intense,
all around Kebrionēs and the peerless Poulydamas,
Phalkēs and Orthaios and godlike Polyphētēs,
Palmys, Askanios, and Morys, Hippotiōn's son,
who'd arrived from rich-soiled Askania as reliefs
the morning before, and now Zeus stirred their fighting spirit.
They came on as strong as the blast of threatening winds
that beneath the thunder of Zeus, the Father, scours the plain,
its wondrous clamor confused with the sea's roar, and in the mix
wave after boiling wave of the thunderous ocean,
arching high, foam-flecked, some ahead, others behind—
so the Trojans, in order, some ahead, others behind,
gleaming in bronze, now followed behind their leaders.
Hektōr was their commander—a match for Arēs the killer,
this son of Priam; before him he bore his balanced shield,
with its close-packed hides, on which abundant bronze
was layered, and, set round his temples, his shining helmet bobbed
as this way and that he strode, making trial of the ranks,
finding out if they'd shrink before him as he came on under his shield;
but no way could he daunt the spirit in the Achaians' breasts,
and Aias challenged him first, advancing with long-legged strides:
"Hey, crazy, come closer! Why are you uselessly trying
to scare the Argives? We're no beginners in warfare—
it was through the vile scourge of Zeus that we Achaians were beaten!
In your heart, at a guess, you're expecting to despoil

our ships, but we too have strong hands to defend them!
Before that day, indeed, this populous city of yours
may well be taken, laid waste beneath our hands—
and as for yourself, I declare that day near when you
will pray, in flight, to Zeus the Father and other immortals
to make your fine-maned horses swifter than falcons
as they carry you citywards, raising dust-clouds over the plain!"

As he spoke thus, a bird flew across on the right,
a high-soaring eagle: the Achaian troops raised a cheer,
made bold by the omen. But illustrious Hektōr replied:
"Aias, you bumbling speaker, you braggart, what mere stuff
your words are! I wish I were the son of Zeus of the aegis
all my days, and it was the lady Hērē who bore me,
and I was honored as are Athēnē and Apollo,
as surely as this day is bringing disaster to the Argives,
every last one, and amongst them you too will die, if you dare
await my long spear, that will tear your lily-white skin,
and you'll glut the Trojans' dogs, and their birds of prey
with your fat and flesh, after you fall beside the Achaians' ships!"

So saying, he led on, and they followed on after him
with a deafening clamor, and the troops behind them cheered.
The Argives facing them shouted in answer, did not forget
their valor, stood firm as the Trojan leaders advanced:
both sides' clamor went up the high sky to Zeus's glory.

Book 14

Nestōr was drinking, but still picked up the sounds of battle,
and so addressed winged words to the son of Asklēpios:
"Consider, noble Machaōn, how this business will turn out:
the clamor of lusty young fighters around the ships is louder!
Now you just sit where you are, and drink your fire-bright wine
till fair-tressed Hekamēdē heats you a warm bath
and washes you clean of all that dried blood! I myself
am off to a vantage point to see what's going on."

So saying, he took the well-made shield of his son,
Thrasymēdēs the horse breaker, that was lying there in the hut,
all gleaming with bronze—his own shield his son had taken—
and selected a solid spear, tipped with keen-edged bronze.
Standing outside the hut, he at once saw a wretched scene:
his own side in disarray, with the enemy, the high-hearted
Trojans, in hot pursuit, and the Achaians' wall torn down.
As when the vast deep darkens up with a silent comber,
vaguely foretelling the shrill winds' rapid courses—
the waves don't roll forward towards one side or the other
until some decisive gale comes down from Zeus—
just so the old man meditated, pondering in his mind
this way and that: join the swift-colted Danaäns' throng?
or seek Atreus's son Agamemnōn, shepherd of the people?
and as he debated, this struck him as being the better way:
to go after Atreus's son. But meanwhile the rest fought on,
killing each other; the tireless bronze sheathing their bodies
clanged as they thrust with their swords and twin-edged spears.

Now Nestōr encountered those kings, Zeus's nurslings, who'd been
maimed by the bronze, as they made their way back from the ships:
the son of Tydeus, Odysseus, and Atreus's son Agamemnōn.
Far distant from the fighting the ships of these were drawn up
on the shore of the grey sea: they'd been the first to be dragged
up to the plain, and the wall was built well beyond their sterns.
For wide though the beach was, there was no way that it could
contain all the ships, and the army was short of camp space.

So they hauled up the ships row by row, and filled the entire
shore the two headlands enclosed.[1] So these kings were going,
together, to witness the uproar and the fighting,
each leaning on his spear; and sorrow afflicted the spirit
in the breasts of them all. It was thus that the old man, Nestōr,
met them, alarming the hearts in the breasts of these Achaians,
and the lord Agamemnōn now addressed him, saying:
"Ah, Nestōr, son of Nēleus, great glory of the Achaians,
why have you left the murderous conflict to come here?
I fear mighty Hektōr's fulfilling the promise he made me—
those threats that he issued when speaking before the Trojans—
that he wouldn't go back to Ilion from our ships
until he'd set fire to the ships and killed their defenders too:
such were his words, and now all this is being accomplished!
Curse it, it must be that the other well-greaved Achaians
are storing a grudge against me, as is Achillēs,
and don't mean to make a fight of it by the sterns of our vessels!"

Then Nestōr, Gerēnian horseman, answered him as follows:
"Yes, indeed, these things have happened, are on us: not even
high-thundering Zeus himself could have ordered them differently.
The wall indeed is down that we put our trust in
to be an unbreakable bulwark for our vessels and ourselves,
while those at the swift ships fight on ceaselessly, without end:
you could no longer tell, even by watching closely,
from which side the Achaians are being driven in flight,
so mingled their deaths, as the battle cry rises to heaven.
We need to consider how this business will turn out—
Is there any plan can affect it? But I'm against our joining
the battle: a wounded man is in no position to fight."

Then once more spoke in response the king of men, Agamemnōn:
"Nestōr, since they are fighting now by the sterns of the ships,
and neither the wall we built, nor the ditch, has helped us at all—
though the Danaäns labored hard at them, hoped in their hearts

1. This agrees well with the geography. The two headlands, of Rhoiteion in the east and Sigeion in the west, are "some two and a half miles apart as the crow flies" (Hainsworth 154). The beach was not large enough for the whole fleet, so the ships were drawn up "in rows in a curve round the entire shore". A logistics expert might calculate how far the available space is compatible with the traditional number of Homeric galleys (Casson 43–48).

that they'd be an unbreakable bulwark for the ships and
themselves—
this, I think, must be the pleasure of all-powerful Zeus,
that we Achaians should perish here, namelessly, far from Argos.
I knew it when he was prompt in support of the Danaäns,
and I know it now, when he honors our foes as he would
the blessed gods, and has shackled our strength and hands.
So, let us now all agree to the action that I propose:
all the vessels drawn up in the first line, close to the sea,
we should haul down into the bright brine, set them afloat,
and moor them with anchor stones, until the coming
of immortal night—if even then these Trojans take a break
from the fighting! Later we could relaunch the whole fleet.
There's no blame in fleeing disaster, even at night:
Escape by flight is better than getting caught."

Angrily eyeing him, resourceful Odysseus responded:
"Son of Atreus, what words have escaped the barrier of your teeth!
Accursed man, you should be in command of some other
miserable ragtag army, not lord over us, to whom Zeus
has given the task, from youth to old age, of winding
the skein of grim war, till we perish, every last man!
Are you really so eager to leave the Trojans' spacious city,
for which we've endured so much hardship? Be silent,
in case some other Achaian hears this statement
that you've just made, words no man should ever utter,
let alone one who knows in his mind what's proper to say,
who's a sceptered king, to whom as many owe their allegiance
as the number of Argives over whom you have lordship!
I wholly despise your thinking, in what you just said,
for telling us, when warfare and combat are in progress,
to relaunch our well-benched vessels, so that the Trojans,
with the upper hand already, may win yet more of their hopes,
while we suffer sheer destruction! The Achaians won't pursue
this war any further once our vessels are seaborne;
they'll be looking elsewhere, disengaging from the conflict,
and it's then your advice will destroy us, commander in chief!"

To him then the king of men, Agamemnōn, made his answer:
"Ah, Odysseus, you've pierced my heart with this reproof of yours,
it's so harsh! I would never tell the sons of the Achaians

to haul our benched vessels seaward against their will!
I wish there was someone to offer us better advice than mine,
either young man or old: this is what I'd really welcome."

Among them now spoke Diomēdēs, good at the war cry:
"Such a man is close by: we'll not need to seek him long—
that is, if you'll listen, if you're not, each one of you, angry
because in years I'm the youngest among you. Even so,
I too can boast of my lineage, have an excellent father,
Tydeus, whom now in Thēbē the heaped earth covers.
For to Portheus were born three peerless sons, who had
their home in Pleurōn and mountainous Kalydōn:
Melas and Agrios, and, third, the horseman Oineus,
my father's father, who in valor outshone them all.
He stayed there; my father wandered, settled in Argos—
such, I suppose, was the will of Zeus and the other gods.[2]
He married one of Adrēstos's daughters, dwelt in a house
rich in possessions, owned abundant wheat-bearing
plowland, with numerous orchards round about,
and plentiful flocks, besides excelling every Achaian
as a spearman. All this you'll have heard, and know the truth of it.
So you can't say that by descent I'm a coward or weakling,
and therefore scorn any good advice I give you!
Come then, let's to the battle, though wounded: go we must.
Ourselves we'll hold back from the conflict, out of the range
of missiles, lest one of us suffer a wound upon his wound;
but the others we'll urge into combat, those who till now,
nursing their mood, have held back, stayed out of the fighting."

So he spoke. They willingly heard him out, and obeyed:
set forth and went, Agamemnōn, the king of men, leading them.

No blind watch did the far-famed Earth-Shaker keep,
but accompanied them in the likeness of an old man,
and grasped the right hand of Atreus's son Agamemnōn
and spoke to him, uttering winged words: "Son of Atreus,
now, I fancy, Achilles' baneful heart must be rejoicing

2. Diomēdēs here tactfully skates over a piece of murderous family feuding: his father Tydeus, traditionally not only short but short-tempered, in fact fled Aitōlia after killing a relative, probably an uncle. "[N]obody [in Homer] 'wanders' save perforce and 'by the gods' will', a euphemism for 'by necessity,'" Hainsworth remarks (164).

in his breast as he watches this slaughter and pursuit
of the Achaians, since there's no sense in him, not a scrap—
so may he perish, so may some god undo him!
But with you the blessed gods are in no way angered:
even yet the leaders and rulers of the Trojans
may raise dust clouds on the wide plain, and you'll see them
fleeing back to the city from the ships and huts."

So saying, he bellowed aloud as he charged across the plain:
as loud was the shout that nine—no, ten—thousand men
utter in wartime as they engage in Arēs' strife—
so great was the cry that the lord, the Earth-Shaker, sent forth
from his chest, putting great strength in every last Achaian's
heart to engage in warfare and battle without cease.

Hērē the golden-throned now observed him from where
she stood on a peak of Olympos: she recognized him at once
as he bustled about in the battle that wins men glory,
her own and her husband's brother; and she rejoiced at heart.
Zeus too she observed, ensconced on the topmost peak
of spring-rich Ida; and hateful he was to her heart.
So the ox-eyed lady Hērē now took thought as to how
she could best delude the mind of Zeus of the aegis,
and this to her way of thinking seemed the best plan:
to beautify herself nicely, then make her way to Ida,
and see if he might desire to embrace her body
in love, and she might then shed a warm and peaceful
sleep on his eyelids and his sharp and devious mind.
So she went to the private chamber that her dear son
Hēphaistos had built her, fitting strong doors to the door frame,
with a secret key, to be opened by no other god.
In there she went, and shut the shining doors.
First with ambrosia she cleaned off the whole of her lovely
body; then she gave it a massage it with olive oil,
specially perfumed for her ambrosial robe,[3]
and which, merely shaken in Zeus's bronze-built abode,
would spread its aroma out to both earth and heaven.
With this she anointed her sweet flesh, then combed out
her hair, and with her hands plaited the shining tresses,

3. Text uncertain: here I follow Hainsworth 174–75.

fine and ambrosial,[4] from her immortal head;
put on an ambrosial robe, that Athēnē had skilfully
made for her, and adorned with many embroideries:
this with golden brooches she pinned at the breast,
and round her waist tied a sash with a hundred tassels,
and in her pierced ears put earrings, embellished with triple
mulberry clusters, that shone in an alluring fashion.
Over all this Hērē, bright among goddesses, spread
a fine glistening veil, as white as the very sun,
and under her gleaming feet bound her beautiful sandals.
Now, having decked out her body with every adornment,
she emerged from her chamber, and called to her Aphrodītē,
away from the other gods, and had this to say to her:
"Will you listen now, dear child, to what I shall ask you,
or refuse me, out of vexation at heart, because
I give support to the Danaäns, you to the Trojans?"

Then answered her Aphrodītē, daughter of Zeus:
"Hērē, elder goddess, daughter of mighty Kronos,
tell me what you've in mind—my heart says I should do it
if do it I can and it's something that can be done."

To her the lady Hērē, deception in mind, replied:
"Give me now love and passion, those things with which
you vanquish all men, both mortals and the immortal:
for I'm going to visit the ends of the bounteous earth,
and Ocean, who gave gods their being, and Tethys my mother,
who brought me up well and cared for me in their home
after taking me over from Rhea when Zeus, the far-seeing,
thrust Kronos down under the earth and the unharvested[5] sea.
Them I am going to visit, to resolve their unsettled quarrel:

4. The epithet "ambrosial" (ἀμβρόσιος, *ambrosios*) has been variously identified as meaning "immortal", "beautiful", and "fragrant" or "sweet-scented", while "ambrosia" (ἀμβροσίη, *ambrosiē*), as a noun, can signify either the food of the gods (and divine horses, 5.777), an unguent (presumably scented), a cleaning agent (either as cosmetic, or for corpses), or even immortality. In the circumstances I have chosen to keep the original term, and let its original associations speak for themselves.

5. "Unharvested" (ἀτρύγετος, *atrygetos,* formed from *a-* privative and τρύγη, grain crop or vintage) was the scholiasts' convincing interpretation of this formulaic epithet, accepted by scholars until comparatively recently, when linguists decided that it meant either "restless" or "murmuring", thus (on highly speculative grounds) changing a striking and original epithet into a mere cliché. I have preferred to stick with the scholiasts.

for too long they've held aloof each from the other
in love and the marriage bed, since anger's filled their hearts.
If I could talk those two over, bring their hearts back
to bed, to be reunited in love together, then I'd
forever known be as their friend, one worth their respect."

To her then replied laughter-loving Aphrodītē:
"It's not possible, nor is it seemly, that I should deny
this request from you, who sleep in almighty Zeus's embrace."

With that she undid from her bosom the embroidered breast band,
intricately worked, with all kinds of allurement set in it—
therein were love, and desire, and dalliance: beguilement
that steals away the sharp wits of even sensible people.
She put this in Hērē's hands, and addressed her, saying:
"Here, take this breast band, lay it up in your bosom,
intricately worked, and in it all kinds of things set: you'll not,
I tell you, return with your heart's wish unaccomplished."

So she spoke, and Hērē, the ox-eyed lady, smiled,
and with that smile laid the breast band up in her bosom.

The daughter of Zeus, Aphrodītē, now went to her house;
but Hērē darted down, leaving the heights of Olympos,[6]
traversed Pieria and lovely Emathia, flew over
the snowclad mountains of the horse-herding Thracians—
their topmost peaks, her feet never catching the ground;
from Athos she moved on over the wave-swept deep,
and came to Lēmnos, the city of godlike Thoas.
Here she encountered Sleep, the brother of Death,
whom she took by the hand, and addressed in the following words:
"Sleep, you lord over all gods and all mankind,
if you ever listened to words of mine, so now once more
obey me—I'll be in your debt for all my days!
Make drowsy for me Zeus's bright eyes beneath his brows
the moment I'm through with lying beside him in love,
and gifts I'll give you—a fine throne that'll last for ever,

6. The goddess's flight plan, followed on a map, looks somewhat roundabout until one realizes that, as Graziosi 2011 (432) points out, "she avoids open water, just as real-life sailors did." Greek sailors in particular steered from island to island, unlike the Phoenicians of the Eastern Mediterranean, who in that vast expanse had to learn true navigation the hard way, by the stars or dead reckoning.

of gold, too, skillfully made for me by my own son,
Hēphaistos, lame of both legs, and he'll add a footstool to it,
on which you can rest your sleek feet while you sit and feast."

In answer to her soothing Sleep had this to say:
"Hērē, elder goddess, daughter of mighty Kronos,
some other one of the gods that live on for ever
I might easily lull to sleep—yes, even the streams of the river
Ocean, that established genesis of them all;
but to Zeus, son of Kronos, I'd never come too close,
nor would I lull him to sleep, unless he so ordered me;
for once in the past another such order of yours
taught me a lesson, the day when that arrogant son of Zeus
sailed from Ilion, after he'd sacked the Trojans' city.[7]
Then indeed I beguiled the mind of Zeus of the aegis,
swirling gently about him, while for his son you plotted
trouble, stirred over the deep a gale of dangerous winds,
and sent him out of his way to well-populated Kōs,
far from his kin. Zeus woke, was enraged, strong-armed
the other gods in his palace, sought me especially, would have
hurled me from heaven into the deep, to be lost for ever,
had Night not saved me, who lays low both gods and men.
To her I came in my flight, and Zeus, though enraged, held off me,
to avoid displeasing swift Night, whom he revered. And now
you're telling me to perform this other task! Out of the question."

Then the ox-eyed lady Hērē once more addressed him:
"Sleep, why are you brooding over all these things in your heart?
Do you think far-seeing Zeus would help the Trojans,
be enraged for them as he was for his own son Hēraklēs?
Look, I'll make you a present of one of the younger Graces
to take in wedlock, and to be known as your wife—
Pasithēē, whom you've yearned for your whole life."

So she spoke,
and Sleep, delighted, replied to her in these words:

7. Sleep is recalling another incident, when he got in trouble with Zeus for performing a very similar service for Hērē to that which she is now soliciting. This earlier request had to do with the aftermath of a previous sacking of Troy by 'that arrogant son of Zeus', i.e. Hēraklēs (cf. 15.18–30 for Zeus's version of the same episode, and 19.106–34 for Hērē's rooted dislike of Hēraklēs), after which Zeus was lulled to sleep while Hērē disposed of Hēraklēs to the island of Kōs.

"Come, then, swear to me by Styx's sacrosanct waters,
with one hand laying hold of the nurturing earth, and the other
the glistening main, that between us two they may all
bear witness, all the gods that are below with Kronos,
that you will make me a present of one of the younger Graces,
Pasithēē, whom I've longed for my whole life."

So he spoke,
and the goddess, white-armed Hērē, did not ignore him,
but swore as he wanted, invoked by name all the gods
that dwell under Tartaros, and are known as Titans.
When she'd sworn the oath, accomplished it fully, they both
went on their way, left the townships of Lēmnos and Imbros,
shrouded in mist, and swiftly followed their chosen path.
To spring-rich Ida they came, the mother of wild creatures,
and Lekton, where first they left the sea, and together
went on over land, and the treetops rippled beneath their feet.
There Sleep stopped, before the eyes of Zeus perceived him,
and climbed a very tall fir tree, the highest then on Ida,
reaching up through the mist to the clear air above.
Here he sat, well hidden by the fir tree's crowding branches,
like that sharp-voiced bird in the mountains, called by the gods
Chalkis, but mortal men refer to it as Kymindis.[8]

But Hērē pressed on swiftly, came to Gargaros, the topmost
peak of high Ida; and Zeus the cloud-gatherer saw her.
The moment he did so, passion eclipsed his reasoned thinking,
such as he'd felt the first time they went to bed
and made love together, unseen by their own dear parents.[9]
Now he stood before her, and addressed her in these words:
"Hērē, with what in mind are you come here, down from Olympos?
Your horses are not here, nor your chariot to ride in."

To him, with deception in mind, the lady Hērē replied:
"I'm going to visit the ends of the bounteous earth,
and Ocean, who gave gods their being, and Tethys my mother,

8. The *kymindis* was in fact some kind of Ionian owl: most probably the eagle owl (*Strix bubo*), but possibly either the hawk owl (*Strix uralensis*) or the long-eared owl (*Asio otus*). See Janko 196–97.

9. A gentle indirect reminder by Homer that this was no ordinary teenage experiment. That they shared the same parents meant, of course, that they were brother and sister: the coupling was incestuous.

who brought me up well and cared for me in their halls.
Them am I going to visit, to resolve their unsettled quarrel:
for too long now they've held aloof each from the other
in love and the marriage bed, since anger has filled their hearts.
As for my horses, they're waiting in spring-rich Ida's
foothills, to carry me over dry land and the watery deep.
But now it's because of you I've come here, down from Olympos,
since you might be annoyed with me later, if I departed,
without saying a word, for the home of deep-flowing Ocean."

In answer to her then Zeus the cloud-gatherer said:
"Hērē, you can go there at some later time: let us both
now take our pleasure in bed, since never before
has so strong a passion for goddess or mortal woman
encompassed my body and mastered the spirit in my breast—
not when I was making love with the wife of Ixiōn,
who bore me Peirithoös, the gods' own equal in counsel,[10]
nor when I had neat-ankled Danaë, Akrisios's daughter,
who gave birth to Perseus, most prestigious of warriors,
nor when I loved the daughter of far-famed Phoinix,
who bore me both Mīnōs and godlike Rhadamanthys,
nor when it was Semelē, or Alkmēnē in Thēbē—
she it was that bore Hēraklēs, my stouthearted son,
while Semelē bore Dionysos, the delight of mortals—
nor when it was Dēmētēr, that fair-tressed queen,
nor glorious Lētō, no, nor even yourself, as now
I'm enamoured of you, and possessed by sweet desire."

To him, with deception in mind, the lady Hērē replied:
'Most dread son of Kronos, what's this that you're telling me?
Is what you want to go to bed now and make love
here on the peaks of Ida, where everything's in plain view?
How would it be if a god, one of those who live for ever,
should see us in bed, and tell tales when he got back among

10. Aristophanes and Aristarchos both athetized 317–18; Plato (*Rep.* 390c) did not have these lines. I suspect prurience here. There is no reason to doubt their genuineness: the whole episode is full of such embarrassing oddities. Zeus sounds like an adulterer; and as a Homeric audience would well have known, not only did Ixion—in one tradition a son of Zeus—try to rape Hērē (? tit for tat?), but both he and Peirithoös, also Zeus's offspring, by Ixion's wife Dia (Gantz 278, 718), were (Janko 203, with a string of lurid examples) "notorious rapists" (like father, like son?).

all the other gods? Then, I tell you, I'd not be able to go
from bed here back to your house: I'd feel too ashamed.
But if that's what you want, if it's your heart's desire,
you have a bedchamber that your dear son Hēphaistos
built for you, fitting solid doors into the door frame:
let's go there and lie down, since bed is now your pleasure."[11]

In answer to her then Zeus the cloud-gatherer said:
"Hērē, you need not fear that either god or mortal
may see us, with such a cloud I shall wrap you about,
of gold, through which not even Hēlios could discern us,
whose vision is unsurpassed for keenness of perception."

With that the son of Kronos clasped his wife in his arms,
and beneath them the noble earth made fresh grass spring up,
and dewy trefoil and crocus and hyacinth, soft and thick,
that cushioned them from the ground. On these they lay,
and were wrapped about in a cloud, lovely and golden,
and from it drops of glistening dew rained down.

So the Father slumbered in peace, on the summit of Gargaros,
by sleep and love-making vanquished, his wife in his embrace.
But soothing Sleep ran off to the ships of the Achaians
with a message for the Earth-Shaker and Earth-Enfolder,
and standing beside him addressed him in winged words:
"Readily now, Poseidōn, you can succor the Danaäns
and grant them glory, if but for a little, as long as Zeus
remains asleep—since on him I've shed soft oblivion,
when Hērē beguiled him, made him lie with her in love."

So saying, he went on his way to the famous tribes of men,
but Poseidōn was stirred yet further to rescue the Danaäns.
At once, dashing up to the front ranks, he called out loudly:
"Argives! Must we again cede the victory to Hektōr,
Priam's son, allow him to take the ships, to win glory?
This he says, thus he boasts it will be, on account of Achilles
staying back by the hollow ships, enraged at heart.

11. There is more than ladylike modesty involved here. As a scholiast points out (Hainsworth 205), had Zeus acceded to his sister-wife's request, he would not only have been lured well away from Troy, but would have also risked imprisonment in her private room, since (166–68) it had been fitted by Hēphaistos with a secret key, so that only she could open or shut its door.

But we'll not miss his presence too much so long as the rest of us
rouse ourselves now and lend support to one another!
Come then, let's all of us do what I suggest:
Let's find the biggest and best shields in the army,
cover our heads with gleaming helmets, and take
in our hands the longest lances, and so arrayed
go forth! I shall be the leader, nor do I anticipate
that Priam's son Hektōr, however eager, will face us!
And any tough warrior, a small shield on his shoulder,
should now exchange that for a lesser man's bigger one."[12]

So he spoke: they heard him out readily, and obeyed,
and the kings themselves, though wounded, joined the array:
Tydeus's son, and Odysseus, Agamemnōn, son of Atreus,
and going throughout the ranks they made an exchange of armor:
good fighters donned the good gear, gave the less good to lesser men.
Then, when they'd sheathed their bodies in gleaming bronze,
they set out, under the leadership of Poseidōn the Earth-Shaker,
in his strong hand a fearsome sword, long and keen-edged,
like the lightning, with which it's forbidden that men should meddle
in grim war: sheer terror holds warriors back from it.
On the other side illustrious Hektōr arrayed the Trojans:
now indeed war's most terrible strife was stretched out taut
by dark-maned Poseidōn and illustrious Hektōr,
bringing aid the one to the Trojans, the other to the Argives,
and the sea surged up towards the huts and the ships
of the Argives, and with a great shout the sides engaged.
No wave rolling in on the shore, driven up from the deep
by the North Wind's fierce blast, thunders so mightily,
no blazing fire in the mountains roars so loud
when it leaps from a glen to burn up the forest, no wind
howls so fiercely among the high crests of the oaks,
even the gale that's the noisiest in its fury—as then
was the roar of Achaians and Trojans, raising a fearsome
clamor in their assault, one side against the other.

12. Suspension of disbelief (as commentators on this passage have noted from antiquity to the present day) can go only so far. Presumably Poseidōn plans to drop his old-man disguise and lead the charge as himself. But not even Homeric military convention extends to everyone hurrying back to the huts during a Trojan attack to get a bigger shield, a bronze (rather than leather) helmet, or a longer lance.

At Aias illustrious Hektōr first let fly his spear,
when Aias was turned full towards him; he did not miss,
but hit him where the two baldrics crossed on his breast—
the one of his shield, the other of his silver-studded sword—
and they guarded his delicate flesh. Now Hektōr was enraged
at the swift shaft having been flighted in vain from his hand,
and drew back to the ranks of his comrades, avoiding fate.
But as he backed off, great Aias, Telamōn's son, picked up
a large rock—of which there were many, props of the swift ships,
that rolled under the feet of the combatants as they fought—
and flung it, hitting Hektōr high on his chest, near the neck,
over his shield rim: the blow spun him round like a whipped top.
As when an oak struck by Zeus, the Father, is laid low,
uprooted, and from it there drifts the mephitic reek
of brimstone, and courage drains from the man who witnesses it
standing nearby, so fearsome is great Zeus's thunderbolt—
thus instantly fell mighty Hektōr to the ground in the dust,
and the spear dropped from his hand, but his shield fell with him
and his helmet, while round him his inlaid bronze gear rattled.
Then, shouting loudly, the Achaians' sons ran up,
hoping to drag him off, and letting fly their spears
thick and fast; yet none of them managed to stab or shoot
the people's shepherd—before that, the best men surrounded
him:
Aineias, Poulydamas, and the noble Agēnōr,
the Lycians' leader Sarpēdōn, the peerless Glaukos;
of the rest no man failed to heed him, they all held out
their round shields before him. His comrades lifted him up
and carried him out of the conflict, till he reached the swift horses
that were waiting for him out back, at the rear of the fighting,
along with their driver and his richly wrought chariot.
These bore him off to the city, heavily groaning.
But when they came to the ford of the swift-flowing river,
eddying Xanthos, whom immortal Zeus begot,
they lifted him from his chariot to the ground, poured water
on him, and he revived, opened his eyes, looked up,
and, kneeling, vomited up dark blood, but then
sank back on the ground, and both his eyes were shrouded
in black night: the missile still overwhelmed his spirit.

When the Argives saw that Hektōr had quit the field
they pressed the Trojans still harder, their minds on battle.
Then, out and away the first, swift Aias, Oïleus's son,
sprang at Satnios, wounded him with his keen-edged spear—
Satnios, sired on a blameless nymph, a Naiad,
by Ēnōps while he was herding near the Satnioeis river.
Him Oïleus's son, famed spearman, met at close quarters,
and stabbed in the flank: he fell on his back, and around him
Trojans and Danaäns contested the grind of battle.
Poulydamas, son of Pánthoös, spear-wielder, now appeared
to his rescue, and hit Prothoēnōr on the right shoulder—
Areïlykos's son, and the heavy spear drove its way through
his shoulder: he fell in the dust, clawed the earth with his hand,
and Poulydamas shouted loudly, in vehement exultation:
"Ah, once again, not in vain, I think, a spear's
leapt from the strong hand of Pánthoös's doughty son!
Some Argive has got it stuck in his flesh, and I think he'll
go down to the house of Hādēs leaning on it as a staff."

So he spoke, and his exulting brought grief to the Argives,
and most of all stirred the fiery heart of Aias,
Telamōn's son, who was nearest the man when he fell.
Quickly he let fly at Poulydamas his bright spear
as he backed off: Poulydamas escaped the black death-spirit,
jumping aside; but the spear struck Antēnōr's son,
Archelochos, since the gods intended that he should perish.
It caught him where head and neck meet, at the highest
joint of the spine, and sheared clean through both tendons:
head, mouth, and nose got to the ground much quicker
than his thighs and knees as he fell. Then Aias in his turn
called out in a loud voice to blameless Poulydamas:
"Think about it, Poulydamas, and tell me truly:
Isn't this man fit to die in return for Prothoēnōr?
No mean fellow I find him, nor one of mean ancestry,
but a brother perhaps of Antēnōr, breaker of horses,
or a son: in appearance they're much alike."

Thus he spoke,
well aware of the truth; and grief struck the Trojans' hearts.
Then Akamas, standing over his brother, speared Boiōtian

Promachos as he was dragging the body away by the feet,
and shouted aloud at him, in vehement exultation:
"You Argive arrow-fanciers, with your never-ending threats!
There will be toil and sorrow, oh, yes, but it won't be only
for us: a day will come when you too will be killed this way!
Just ponder on how your Promachos sleeps, laid low
by my spear—to make sure that the blood-price for my brother
does not go for long unpaid, which is why any man will pray
that a kinsman be left in his halls, a protector against ruin."

So he spoke, and his exulting brought grief to the Argives,
and most of all touched Pēneleōs's fiery heart:
at Akamas he charged, who did not await the attack
of the lordly Pēneleōs, and instead he hit Ilioneus,
the son of flock-rich Phorbas, he whom Hermēs loved
best of all the Trojans, and endowed with much wealth;
and Ilioneus was the sole son his mother bore to Phorbas.
Him then he struck beneath the brow, at the eye's base,
drove the eyeball out of its socket: the spear went clean through
his eye and the neck's tendons. Arms outstretched, he sank,
and then Pēneleōs, drawing his keen-edged sword,
slashed through his mid-neck, striking off to the ground
helmet and head together; and still the heavy spear
stuck firm in the eye-socket. He held it aloft, displayed it
like a poppy head to the Trojans, and spoke exultingly:
"Trojans, tell the dear father and mother of the lordly
Ilioneus, from me, to begin mourning in their halls;
for the wife of Alegēnōr's son Promachos will never
welcome back her dear husband with joy when we youthful
Achaians return with our ships out of the land of Troy."

So he spoke: trembling seized the limbs of them all: each man
glanced around, for some way that he might escape sheer ruin.

Tell me now, you Muses who have abodes on Olympos,
who was the first Achaian to bear off the bloodstained spoils
of a slain foe, once the battle was turned by the famed Earth-Shaker?
Aias, Telamōn's son, was the first, who wounded Hyrtios,
Gyrtios's son, the leader of the stout-hearted Mysians;
Antilochos stripped off the gear of Phalkēs and Mermeros,
Hippotiōn and Morys were cut down by Mēriones,

and Teukros dispatched Prothoōn and Periphētēs;
Atreus's son stabbed Hyperēnōr, shepherd of the people,
in the flank, and the bronze, shearing through, spilled out
his innards, and his soul now burst through the open wound,
fled away fast, and darkness shrouded his eyes.
But Aias, the swift son of Oïleus, laid low the most men,
for there was no one to match him in the pursuit on foot
of fugitive fighters when Zeus had stirred them to flight.

Book 15

But when the Trojans had recrossed both stakes and ditch
in their retreat, and many had fallen by Danaän hands,
they came to a halt by their chariots, and remained there,
pale with fear, panic-stricken; and meanwhile Zeus awoke
on that topmost peak of Ida, beside Hērē the golden-throned.
He sprang to his feet, and stood, and saw Trojans and Achaians—
the first in rout, and behind them, driving them on,
the Argives, and there among them the lord Poseidōn.
Hektōr too he saw, stretched out on the plain, his comrades
sitting around him, his breathing painful, his mind dazed,
vomiting blood: it was no weakling Achaian who'd hit him.
At this sight the Father of gods and men felt pity,
glared furiously at Hērē, and thus addressed her:
"There's no stopping you, Hērē! It's your vile deceitful plotting
that's put Hektōr out of the fighting and routed his troops!
Well, maybe once more you'll be the first to reap the rewards
of your own dangerous scheming, and I'll give you a whipping!
Don't you remember that time when you were strung up aloft,
and I weighted your feet with two anvils, and fastened about
your wrists
an unbreakable golden chain? In the upper air amid clouds
you hung, and the gods throughout high Olympos raged,
but stood there, unable to free you: any I caught
I'd toss down from the threshold, already half-dead by the time
they reached the earth. Yet not even so was my heart
relieved of incessant pain over godlike Hēraklēs,
whom you—along with the North Wind, whose gales you'd bought—
sent on the unharvested deep, with evil intent, and then
carried away to Kōs, that well-populated island.
Him I rescued from there, and brought back once more
to horse-pasturing Argos, after his many travails.
Need I once more remind you of this to stop your deceptions,
make you see if the bed love you had with me when you came
from the gods, and deceived me with, gives you any protection?"

So he spoke, and the ox-eyed lady Hērē shivered,
and, speaking in winged words, replied to him thus:
"To this let Earth now bear witness, and the broad skies above,
and Styx's cascading water—which is the greatest,
most terrible oath for the blessed gods themselves—
and your own sacred head, and the bed that we two share
in wedded love—an oath that I'd never swear to falsely:
not by my wish is Poseidōn, the Earth-Shaker, bringing
grief to the Trojans and Hektōr, and aiding their enemies.
It's his own heart dictates his actions, after seeing
the Achaians in rout by their ships, and taking pity on them.
But truly, even him I'd advise to go wherever
you, my lord of the dark cloud, might lead the way."

So she spoke, and the Father of men and gods smiled,
and in response with winged words now addressed her:
"If ever hereafter, my ox-eyed lady Hērē,
were our thoughts to agree, when sitting among the immortals,
then would Poseidōn, however contrary his own wishes,
at once change direction, follow your heart and mine!
But if you're speaking honestly, and mean what you say,
go now to the gods assembled, and summon hither
both Iris and Apollo, the far-famed archer. She is
to visit the troops of the bronze-corseleted Achaians,
and carry a message from me to the lord Poseidōn:
that he must abandon warfare and go back home.
Phoibos Apollo's to go to Hektōr and urge him to fight,
once more breathe power into him, make him forget
the pains now afflicting his senses, and drive the Achaians
back once more, fill them with craven panic
so that they're routed, and fall among the benched ships
of Achilles, Pēleus's son, who'll send out into battle
his comrade Patroklos: but him will illustrious Hektōr slay
with the spear before Ilion, though first Patroklos will kill
many other young men, including my noble son Sarpēdōn.
Then, in his wrath for Patroklos, noble Achilles will slaughter
Hektōr. Then I'll set up a countercharge from the ships—
continuous, unremitting—until, through the counseling
of Athēnē, the Achaians capture steep Ilion.
But till then I'm neither abating my anger, nor will I

let any other immortal there give aid to the Danaäns
until Pēleus's son's desire is wholly fulfilled
as I promised him at the beginning, with my nod of assent,
that day when the goddess Thetis clasped my knees, and begged me
to honor the sacker of cities, Achilles."

So he spoke,
and Hērē, white-armed goddess, did not disobey him,
but went from the mountains of Ida to lofty Olympos.
Like a man who's travelled to many countries, who
hurries about, reflects, "How I wish I was here, or there",
whose sharp mind speeds its way through a mass of desires,
so rapidly in her eagerness flew the lady Hērē,
and came to lofty Olympos, where she found the immortal
gods assembled in Zeus's house. On seeing her
they all stood up, and lifted their cups in welcome.
The rest she ignored, but accepted the cup from fair-cheeked
Themis, for she was the first to run up and greet her,
speaking with winged words, and saying: "Hērē,
why have you come here? You look quite distraught—
Kronos's son, your own husband, must have scared you badly."

Then the white-armed goddess Hērē answered her thus:
"Themis, goddess, don't ask me—you yourself know
how arrogant and unbending his temper is! Rather set out
for the gods in his halls the fairly apportioned feast,
and then, together with all the immortals, you'll hear
Zeus announce all the vile acts he's planning: in no way,
I tell you, will this please the hearts of all, either mortals
or gods—if indeed even now any feast with a cheerful mind."

After making this speech the lady Hērē sat down,
and throughout Zeus's hall the gods were troubled. She smiled
with her lips, but above the dark brows her forehead revealed
no comfort: it was in anger she now spoke among them all:
"Fools we are, who so witlessly rage against Zeus,
or are even hot to confront him, thwart his intentions
by argument or force! He sits apart, quite indifferent,
not caring at all, for he says that among the immortal gods
for power and strength he's beyond all doubt the best.
So each of you must put up with whatever ills he sends you—

as now already, I think, grief's been fashioned for Arēs,
since his son's perished in the fighting—no man he loves more—
Askalaphos, whom strong Arēs claims as his own."

So she spoke.
Both muscular thighs Arēs struck with his flattened palms,
and, lamenting aloud, then made this declaration:
"You can't blame me now, you who have homes on Olympos,
if I seek the Achaians' ships to avenge my son's killing,
though it may be my fate to be struck by the bolt of Zeus,
and to lie among other corpses in the blood and the dust."

So he spoke, and commanded Terror and Rout to yoke
his horses, while he himself put on his gleaming armor.
Then would yet greater, less endurable resentment
and anger have been engendered between the immortals
and Zeus, had not Athēnē, in great fear for all the gods,
hurried out through the doorway, leaving the chair she sat on:
she took Arēs' shield from his shoulders, the helmet from his head,
the bronze spear from his brawny hand, and set it down,
and lit into reckless Arēs with words of rebuke: "You're mad,
out of your senses, done for! Your ears listen, but uselessly,
your understanding and sense of shame have perished!
Didn't you hear what the goddess, white-armed Hērē, told us—
she who indeed has come straight here from Olympian Zeus?
Or do you intend to get your quota of suffering,
and be forced back, in great distress, to Olympos,
to sow for the rest of us the seeds of great misfortune?
Zeus will very soon leave the Achaians and the high-spirited
Trojans, will come to Olympos and throw us into confusion,
laying hands on all alike, the innocent with the guilty.
So I'm telling you now to forego your wrath for your son,
since in times past there's many a stronger, more dexterous fighter
has been killed—and will be hereafter: it's a difficult business
to safeguard the line and the offspring of every last mortal."

So saying, she made reckless Arēs return to his seat.
But Hērē summoned Apollo to come outside the hall,
and Iris too, the messenger of the immortal gods,
and addressed them both, speaking in winged words:
"Zeus orders the two of you to come with all speed to Ida,

and when you've come, and looked on the face of Zeus,
then to do whatsoever he may urge and command you."

So saying, the lady Hērē returned inside, and sat
down on her chair, while the two went quickly on their way.
To spring-rich Ida they came, mother of wild beasts,
and found Kronos's far-seeing son perched on the topmost peak
of Gargaros, wreathed about with a fragrant cloud.
They approached, and stood before Zeus the cloud-gatherer.
At the sight of them he felt no wrath in his heart,
since they'd quickly obeyed the instructions of his dear wife.
To Iris first of the two he then addressed winged words:
"Go now, swift Iris, report to the lord Poseidōn
all that I tell you; you're not to be a false messenger!
My command is, he shall cease from warfare and battle,
and seek the gods' company, or go down to the shining sea.
But if he ignores my words, or fails to obey them,
let him ponder this well in his mind and in his heart:
Will he, strong though he is, have the will to confront
my coming? I declare that I far surpass him in might,
am, too, the elder by birth—yet his heart does not hesitate
to rank himself equal to me, whom all others dread."

So he spoke,
and wind-footed swift Iris did not disregard him,
but went down from the mountains of Ida to sacred Ilion;
as when from the clouds snowflakes or frozen hail
pelt down, impelled by the north wind's blast, that's born
in the clear heavens, so swiftly did urgent Iris fly,
and stood by the far-famed Earth-Shaker, and addressed him:
"A message for you, O dark-maned Earth-Encircler,
I'm here to deliver, from Zeus who bears the aegis.
His command is that you must cease from warfare and battle,
and seek the gods' company, or go down to the shining sea.
But if you ignore his words, or fail to obey them, then
he threatens to come here in person, and to confront you
in man-to-man combat; and you should stay clear of his hands,
he says, since he far surpasses you in might,
is, too, the elder by birth—yet your heart does not hesitate
to rank yourself equal to him, whom all others dread."
Then to her,

much troubled, the far-famed Earth-Shaker responded:
"Look now, great though he is, he's speaking arrogantly
if he means to restrain me, his equal in honor, by force,
against my will! Three brothers were born to Rhea by Kronos:
Zeus and I, the third being Hādēs, lord of the dead.
All was divided three ways: each of us got his domain—
I was allotted the grey sea to dwell in forever when
the lots were shaken, while Hādēs obtained the murky darkness,
and Zeus won the wide airy firmament and the clouds;
but the earth and lofty Olympos remain common to us all.
So I will in no way walk as Zeus is minded—let him,
powerful though he is, stay at ease in his own third portion,
nor try to scare me with toughness, as though I were some
mere weakling: better for him to threaten with violent words
his own sons and daughters, those he sired himself,
who'll be obliged to obey him, whatever his commands."

Then wind-footed swift Iris answered him: "Is this
really the message, O dark-maned Earth-Encircler,
that I'm to take back to Zeus—so forceful, so unyielding?
Or will you concede a little? Good men's minds can be changed—
and you know how the Furies always side with the elder-born."

Poseidōn the Earth-Shaker now answered her once more:
"Iris, goddess, your message you delivered correctly:
an excellent thing it is when the messenger knows what's right!
But there's this bitter resentment comes over heart and soul
whenever a person's minded to upbraid in angry terms
one of like station, to whom fate's allotted an equal share.
Still, for now, despite my indignation, I'll yield—
but another thing I'll tell you, and I make this threat in my rage:
if, in despite of me—and Athēnē the spoil-bringer,
and Hērē, and Hermēs, and Lord Hēphaistos—he spares
steep Ilion, and proves unwilling to lay it waste,
or to concede to the Argives their great victory, then
let him know this: that between us will be bitterness without cure."

So saying, the Earth-Shaker left the Achaian forces,
and plunged in the sea. The Achaian heroes missed him.
Then Zeus the cloud-gatherer thus addressed Apollo:
"Go now, dear Phoibos, in search of bronze-clad Hektōr:

already the Earth-Encircler and Earth-Shaker
has gone down into the shining sea, avoiding
our unbridled wrath; others too must have learned of our fight,
those gods who are in the lower world with Kronos.[1]
But this way was far better, both for me and for him,
that though earlier angered he still should yield to my hands,
since not without sweat would this business have been settled.
So do you now take in your hands the tasseled aegis,
shake it at these Achaian heroes, put them to flight!
For yourself, long-distance archer, let illustrious Hektōr
be your concern: stir up great rage in him, until
the Achaians, routed, flee to their ships and the Hellespont.
But from then on I myself will devise, in deed and word,
how the Achaians once more shall have respite from the toil of war."

So he spoke, and Apollo did not disregard his father,
but went down from the mountains of Ida like a falcon—
that swift dove-killer, of all winged creatures the swiftest.
He found the son of wise Priam, noble Hektōr,
no longer flat on his back, but sitting: he'd come round,
recognized the comrades around him; his gasping and sweating
had stopped, ever since the will of Zeus of the aegis
revived him. Apollo, far-worker, standing close, now said:
"Hektōr, son of Priam, why, quite apart from the rest,
are you sitting here, barely alive? Are you in some trouble?"

Bright-helmeted Hektōr asked faintly: "Which of the gods
are you, noble sir, who thus question me face to face?
Have you not heard how, at the ships' sterns of the Achaians,
as I was killing his comrades, Aias of the fine war cry
hit my chest with a great rock, cut short my fighting valor?
Truly, I thought that day I'd be looking upon the dead
in the house of Hādēs, after gasping my dear life out."

Lord Apollo the far-worker then addressed him again:
"Take heart now: such is the helper that the son of Kronos
has sent from Ida to stand by you and protect you—
Phoibos Apollo of the golden sword! As in the past

---

1. The "lower world" is Tartaros, "as far beneath Hādēs as the sky is above the earth" (8.13–16), used as a kind of dumping ground and prison for defeated or rebellious gods and primeval monsters; the gods referred to here are the Titans (8.479–81).

I'm here to guard both you and your steep citadel!
So come now, urge all your many charioteers
to drive their swift horses on against the hollow ships,
and I shall go forward, make the whole way smooth
for the horses—and I'll turn the Achaian heroes to flight."

So saying, he breathed great strength into the people's shepherd.
Just as a stabled horse, that's fed well at its manger,
will snap its halter and charge, hooves clattering, over the plain—
since it likes to bathe in the nearest fast-flowing river—
proudly, head held high, its full mane streaming out
over its shoulders, as, confident in its splendor,
it plies its nimble limbs towards the haunts and pastures of mares:
so Hektōr worked feet and knees fast, while urging on
his charioteers, now that he'd heard the voice of the god.
As when an antlered stag or a wild goat
is pursued by country folk along with their dogs,
but is saved by some high rock face or shady thicket—
the hunters are out of luck, they weren't fated to catch it,
—and then a great bearded lion appears in their path,
roused by their shouting, turns all back, even the eager:
so, for a while, the Danaäns kept up the chase in a body,
jabbing away with their swords and double-edged spears;
but when they saw Hektōr going to and fro in the ranks
of the Trojans they panicked, their courage sank to their boots.

Then there spoke up among them Thoas, Andraimōn's son,
far the best of the Aitōlians, well skilled with the javelin,
a good hand-to-hand fighter too, while few Achaians
outdid him at public speaking, when young warriors debated.
He now with friendly intent spoke before the assembly:
"Something truly amazing I'm now witnessing—the way
he's recovered, has somehow eluded the death-spirits—yes,
Hektōr! Every man jack of us had high hopes he'd died
at the hands of Aias, Telamōn's son, but once more
some god or other has rescued him, kept him alive—
Hektōr, who's unstrung the knees of so many Danaäns,
as I fear will happen again now, since it can't be without
loud-thundering Zeus that he stands as so ardent a champion!
Come then, let's all of us do what I suggest:
let's order the rank-and-file to return to the ships,

but we—all those who claim we're the cream of the army—
let's stand and face him, see if we can thrust him back first,
with leveled spears: I think, despite his determination,
he'll be scared at heart to venture into the Danaäns' ranks."

So he spoke: they heard him out readily, and obeyed.
Those who were comrades of Aias and the lord Idomeneus
and Teukros and Mēriones and Megēs, Arēs' equal,
summoned the finest warriors and prepared for battle,
lined up to face the Trojans and Hektōr: meanwhile
the common troops went back to the ships of the Achaians.

Now the Trojans advanced in a body, led by Hektōr,
taking long strides, while in front of him Phoibos Apollo,
shoulders enveloped in cloud, bore the fearsome aegis—
terrible, shaggy-fringed, gleaming: the smith Hēphaistos
gave it to Zeus to carry, to cause panic in mortals:
this Apollo had in his hands as he headed the attack.

The Argives in close order awaited them, and a piercing
clamor arose from both sides, while arrows leapt
from the bowstring, and many spears, hurled by bold hands,
lodged, some of them, in the flesh of battle-swift youths,
though many, before they could reach a white body, stood fixed
in the earth midway, still yearning to glut themselves with flesh.
Now so long as Phoibos Apollo kept the aegis still in his hands,
the missiles from both sides struck home, and men kept falling;
but when, looking straight at the swift-horse Danaäns,
he shook it, and gave a great shout, he cast a spell
on the hearts in their breasts: they forgot their fighting valor.
Just as a herd of cattle or a great flock of sheep can be
stampeded in black night's darkness by a couple of wild beasts
that come on them suddenly, when no herdsman's nearby,
so the Achaians were routed, their courage lost; for Apollo
loosed panic on them, gave the glory to Hektōr and the Trojans.

Then man slew man once the conflict was broken open:
Hektōr brought down Arkesilaös and Stichios,
the first a leader among the bronze-corseleted Boiōtians,
the second a trusty companion of great-hearted Menestheus,
while Aineias finished off Medōn and Iasos. One of these,
Medōn, was the bastard son of godlike Oïleus

and Aias's half-brother; but the place where he dwelt
was in Phylakē, far from his homeland, since he'd killed a kinsman
of Eriōpis, his stepmother, whom Oïleus married;
Iasos was a commander of the Athēnians, known
as Sphēlos's son, and the grandson of Boukolos. Mēkisteus
was taken down by Poulydamas, while Polītēs slew Echios
in the battle's forefront, and noble Agēnōr laid Klonios low,
and Paris stabbed Deïochos as he fled with the front-line fighters,
from behind, in the lower shoulder, and drove the bronze clean
through.

While they were stripping the gear from these men, the Achaians,
tripped up by the stakes, caught in the ditch they'd dug,
fled this way and that, were forced inside their own wall,
and Hektōr called out to the Trojans, in a carrying voice:
"Press on to the ships, and forget the bloodstained spoils!
Any man I see going elsewhere, not making for the ships,
I'll do to death on the spot: he'll not get his due share
of fire as a corpse from his kinsmen or kinswomen:
no, rather will dogs tear his flesh here, outside our city!"

So he spoke, brought the whip down hard, lashed on his horses,
calling out to the Trojans along the ranks; and they all,
cheering, together with him drove their horses onward,
raising a fearsome clamor. Ahead of them Phoibos Apollo
easily kicked down the banks of the deep ditch,
heaping them into the middle, creating a causeway
both long and wide, as far as a spear will fly
when a man's making trial of his strength. Along this now
they streamed, still in formation, with Apollo in front
holding the awesome aegis, breaking down the Achaians' wall
with no trouble. In the way that a child at the seaside
first builds—as children will—sandcastles, but as part
of the game, with feet and hands will then knock them down again,
so you, lord Phoibos, destroyed all the long hard work
of the Argives, and also panicked them into flight.

So these made a halt by the ships, and held their ground,
calling out one to another; then lifting up their hands
to all the gods, prayed aloud, and most fervently of all
Gerēnian Nestōr, protector of the Achaians,

prayed, stretching out his hands to the starry heavens:
"Zeus, Father, if ever any of us, back in wheat-rich Argos,
burned fat thigh-pieces of sheep or cattle, and prayed
for a safe return, and you promised, and nodded in consent,
remember that now, Olympian! Stand off our pitiless day—
don't let the Achaians be thus worsted by the Trojans!"

So he spoke in prayer: Zeus the counselor thundered loudly
on hearing the prayer of the old man, Nēleus's son.

But the Trojans, on hearing the thunder of Zeus of the aegis,
pressed the Argives still harder in their relish for battle,
and as a great wave of the wide-roaming sea bears down
over a ship's bulwarks, when winds at full gale force
are driving it on—this really swells big breakers—
so the Trojans, with loud shouts, kept coming beyond the wall,
driving their horses on, joined the fight at the ships' sterns
with two-edged spears, in close combat: they fought from their
chariots,
and their foes, who'd climbed to the decks of their black ships,
wielded long naval pikes that lay there for sea battles,
jointed in sections, their ends all tipped with bronze.

Now Patroklos, so long as the Achaians and the Trojans
were fighting for the wall, away from the swift ships,
remained sitting back in the hut of kindly Eurypylos,
cheering him up with chat while on his grievous wound
he spread powerful applications to ease the black agony.
But when he perceived the Trojans rushing the wall,
and the Danaäns crying out in their panicked flight,
then he groaned aloud, struck both thighs with the flat
of his hands, and then, lamenting, uttered these words:
"Eurypylos, there's no way, despite your need for me,
that I can remain here: a great conflict's under way!
Your attendant can entertain you—but I myself
am going in all haste to Achilles, to urge him into battle.
Who knows? With divine assistance I may yet arouse
his spirit by argument: a friend has persuasive power."

So saying, he hurried away. The Achaians stood firm,
awaiting the Trojans' assault, yet proved unable
to thrust them back from the ships, though they were fewer,

while the Trojans never managed to break the Danaäns' ranks,
and so get through in among the huts and the vessels.
As the chalked string marks off a straight line on a ship's timber
in the hands of a skilled carpenter, who's familiar with all
aspects of his high craft through Athēnē's promptings—
so tautly and evenly was their conflict stretched between them.
Some were fighting by one ship, some beside another,
but Hektōr charged straight at famous Aias. They both
were battling for possession of the same ship, but were unable,
the one to dislodge the other and set the ship on fire,
or the other to force him back, since a god had brought him there.
Then illustrious Aias speared Kalētōr in the chest—
Klytios's son, who was bringing fire to burn up the ship,
and he fell with a thud, and the torch dropped from his hand.
But when Hektōr took in the fact that it was his cousin
who was down in the dust, out in front of the black ship,
then he called to the Trojans and Lycians, in a carrying voice:
"Trojans and Lycians! You Dardanian hand-to-hand fighters!
Don't back off one step from the fighting on this narrow front,
but rescue the son of Klytios, don't let the Achaians
strip a fallen man of his armor in this battle for the ships!"

So saying, he let fly his gleaming spear at Aias:
him he missed, but Lykophrōn, Mastōr's son,
Aias's henchman from Kythēra, who lived with him now,
after killing a man in sacred Kythēra—him he struck
on the head, just over the ear, with the keen-edged bronze
as he stood beside Aias: he slumped from the stern of the ship
on his back in the dust, and his limbs were unstrung, and Aias
shivered, and said to his brother: "Teukros, dear heart,
a most loyal comrade of ours has been killed, yes, the son
of Mastōr, that guest from Kythēra whom we honored
like our own parents during his stay in our halls—
great-hearted Hektōr has slain him! Where, now, are your shafts
of swift death, where's the bow that Phoibos Apollo gave you?"

So he spoke: Teukros heard, ran up and stood beside him,
grasping the back-bent bow and the quiver that held
his arrows, and quickly let fly at the Trojans. His first
shaft struck Kleitos—the splendid son of Peisēnōr,
comrade to Poulydamas, Pánthoös's noble son—

who, reins in hand, was occupied with his horses,
driving them where the most troops were in headlong flight,
to oblige the Trojans and Hektōr. But a disaster soon
caught him that none, though wanting to, could prevent:
for into the back of his neck flew the grief-laden arrow,
and he fell from the driver's seat, while his horses shied aside,
rattling the empty chariot. Lord Poulydamas, quickly
observing this, was the first to come up and stop the horses:
these he gave to Astynoös, Protiaōn's son,
with firm orders to keep them in check, and close, and watch him,
while he himself went back to rejoin the front-line fighters.

Teukros lined up another shaft against bronze-clad Hektōr,
that would have cut short his fighting by the Achaians' ships
had he hit him as he fought valiantly, would have taken his
    life away;
but he failed to escape the notice of sharp-minded Zeus,
who, guarding Hektōr, robbed Teukros of his glory,
snapping the well-twisted string of his matchless bow
as he drew it, so that the shaft with its weight of bronze
flew wide of its target, and the bow dropped from his hand.
Then Teukros shivered, and thus addressed his brother:
"Look, our battle plan's being ruined by some maleficent
spirit, which struck the bow from my hand and broke
the fresh-twisted bowstring I gave it this morning, to stand
the force of shafts leaping out from it, thick and fast!"

Then great Aias, Telamōn's son, made him this answer:
"So, brother, leave your bow and your showering arrows
to lie where they are: some god with a grudge against the Achaians
has disabled them. Take a lance, put a shield on your shoulder,
join the fight with the Trojans, urge on our other troops!
Don't let them capture our benched ships without a struggle
even though they've outfought us: let's put our minds to battle!"

So he spoke. Teukros stowed away his bow in the hut,
and over his shoulders slung a fourfold shield,
and on his strong head settled a well-made helmet
with horsehair crest, its plume nodding terribly above it,
and picked out a solid spear, tipped with sharpened bronze,
and went on his way, at the double, to stand with Aias.

When Hektōr saw that Teukros's shafts were made useless
He called out to Trojans and Lycians in a carrying voice:
"Trojans and Lycians! You Dardanian hand-to-hand fighters!
Be men, my friends! Remember your fighting valor
here by the hollow ships, for I've seen, with my own eyes,
one of their best men's weapons rendered harmless by Zeus!
Easily recognized is the aid Zeus gives to men,
both by those on whom he bestows the greater glory
and those whom he diminishes, has no mind to assist,
as now he's reducing the Argives' strength, and supporting us.
So close ranks, and fight by the ships; and if any man,
whether shot or speared, meets his death and destiny,
let him die! No dishonor if it's in defense of one's country
that he dies: his wife will be safe, and his children after him,
and his house and land intact if it be that the Achaians
sail away with their ships to their own dear fatherland."

So saying he stirred the strength and spirit of every man.
On the other side Aias too called out to his comrades:
"For shame, Argives! Now it's certain: we must perish, unless
we can save ourselves by removing this danger from the ships!
Do you think, if bright-helmeted Hektōr captures our ships,
you'll each of you then walk home to your native country?
Can't you hear the way that Hektōr's firing up all his troops
in his consuming passion to set the ships ablaze?
It's not to a dance he's inviting them, but to battle!
For us there's no better counsel or purpose than this,
to grapple with them, in furious hand-to-hand combat—
better, once and for all, either to perish or survive
than to be worn out in this grim and hopeless conflict
beside the ships, by men inferior to ourselves."

So saying, he encouraged each man's strength and spirit.
Then Hektōr slew Schedios, Perimēdēs's son,
a leader of Phokians, and Aias took down Laodamas,
an infantry captain, Antēnōr's handsome son,
while Poulydamas killed a Kyllēnian, Ōtos, the comrade
of Phyleus's son, the great-hearted Epeians' leader.
Megēs, on seeing this, sprang at Poulydamas, who
ducked away from the blow. Megēs missed him—Apollo would not
let Pánthoös's son be vanquished among the front-line fighters—

but instead hit Khroismos full in the chest with his spear.
He fell with a thud: Megēs started stripping the gear
from his shoulders, but Dolops, a highly skilled spearman,
attacked him,
Lampos's most warlike son, and Laomedōn's grandson,
a man well acquainted with fighting valor, who now
thrust his spear squarely into the shield of Phyleus's son,
coming at him from close quarters. But the thick and plated
corselet he wore protected him, that Phyleus long ago
brought back out of Ephyrē, by the Sellēïs river,
a gift from a guest-friend—Euphētēs, lord of men—
to wear in battle, a defense against enemies: this
was what now kept destruction from the flesh of his son.
Megēs took aim at Dolops's bronze horsehair-plumed
helmet with his sharp spear, hit its topmost plate,
broke off its horsehair crest, so that the whole piece,
freshly dyed scarlet, fell to the dusty ground.
As Megēs, holding his ground, fought Dolops, still hoping to win,
Menelaös the warlike came over to help him, stood
with his spear, unseen, broadside on: threw, from behind,
and pierced Dolops's shoulder. The point tore through his chest,
driving onward: he collapsed on his face. They both rushed forward,
eager to strip the bronze armor off his shoulders.
But Hektōr called out to his kinsmen, one and all: the first
to get the rough edge of his tongue was Hiketaōn's son,
strong Melanippos. Till lately, the foe still far off, he'd stayed
to pasture his shambling cattle back at Perkōtē,
but when the Danaäns came with their curved ships, then
he went back to Ilion, won distinction among the Trojans,
and lived with Priam, who treated him like his own son. Him now
Hektōr upbraided in these words: "Are we to give up
like this, Melanippos? Does your dear heart feel nothing
for your slain cousin? Do you not see the way
they're busily taking possession of Dolops's battle gear?
So come on with me: no longer can we fight the Argives
from a distance—either we must slaughter them now, or else
root and branch they'll vanquish steep Ilion, slaughter her people."

That said, he led on: Melanippos, mortal but godlike, followed,
while Telamōn's son, great Aias, urged on the Argives:

"My friends, be men now, let shame into your hearts,
feel shame before one another in this violent combat—
of those who feel shame more survive than lose their lives,
while runaways get no glory, win no battles."

So he spoke. They themselves were hot to stand off the foe,
and laid up his words in their hearts, fenced the ships about
with a hedge of bronze. While Zeus roused the Trojans against them,
Menelaös, of the fine war cry, encouraged Antilochos:
"No other Achaian, Antilochos, is younger than you,
or a swifter runner, or as valiant in battle—
could you not spring out in front, hit a Trojan fighter?"

So saying, he backed off himself, but stirred up Antilochos,
who emerged from the front-line troops, took aim with his
bright spear,
glancing quickly around. The Trojans all shrank back
as he threw; not in vain was his missile cast, but struck
Hiketaōn's son, overconfident Melanippos,
in the torso, by one nipple, as he came to the battle line,
and he fell with a thud, and darkness shrouded his eyes,
and Antilochos leapt upon him, like a hunting dog
pinning down a wounded fawn, that some hunter aims at
and hits as it darts from its den, and unstrings its limbs:
even so on you, Melanippos, did warlike Antilochos leap
to strip you of your armor. But he failed to escape the notice
of noble Hektōr, who ran through the fighting to confront him.
Antilochos didn't stay put, nimble fighter though he was,
but fled like a wild beast that's done something really bad—
such as kill a dog or a herdsman guarding his cattle—
and makes its escape before a mass pursuit gets started:
so fled the son of Nestōr, while the Trojans and Hektōr
noisily showered their pain-laden missiles at him—
but he turned and stood at bay when he reached his comrades.

The Trojans still, like lions that devour raw flesh, kept up
their assault on the ships, obeying the behests of Zeus,
who constantly stirred up great fury in them, but beguiled
the Argives' hearts, stole their glory, spurred on their opponents,
since to Hektōr, Priam's son, it was that his heart longed
to give the glory, to let him cast fire, consuming

and weariless, on the curved ships, and thus finally to fulfill
the exorbitant prayer of Thetis. What Zeus the counselor
was waiting for was to see the flare of a burning ship,
since at that point he'd arrange a repulse of the Trojans
from the ships, and thus to the Danaäns now grant glory.
With this end in mind, he urged Priam's son Hektōr on
against the hollow ships—he being eager enough already,
as enraged as Arēs the spear-wielder, or like a deadly fire
raging up in the mountains, in a deep wood's thickets.
Foam gathered round his mouth, and his eyes blazed bright
under his shaggy brows, and about his temples
fearsomely quivered the helmet of this embattled man,
of Hektōr, for from high heaven came as his helper—
alone though he was among many—Zeus himself,
to grant him honor and glory, since he was fated to be
short-lived, for already his day of doom at the hands
of Pēleus's violent son was being hastened by Pallas Athēnē.
And now his aim was to break the ranks by assault,
wherever he saw the most troops and the finest armor:
yet not even so could he break them, enraged though he was,
for they stood firm, set like a high wall, or a rocky
headland, huge and sheer, that faces the grey sea,
holding its own against the screaming gales' swift tracks
and the swollen breakers that belch forth their might against it.
Just so the Danaäns stood off the Trojans, were not routed.
But Hektōr, agleam like bright fire, now assailed their ranks,
fell upon them, as when a wave falls on a swift ship
beneath the clouds, fierce, wind-driven, and the entire
vessel is hidden in foam, and the gale's wild blast
comes roaring against the sail, and the mariners quake
in terror, being borne along on the very edge of death—
so too the Achaians' courage was shredded in their breasts,
for Hektōr assailed them like a killer lion that's found
cows grazing the bottomland beside an extensive marsh—
lots of them, watched by a herdsman who as yet has no idea
how to fight a wild beast off from a sleek heifer's carcass:
he always either keeps pace with the leading cows, or with those
in the rear; but it's in the middle the lion now pounces
to devour a heifer: the rest stampede in panic. Just so
the Achaians were now stampeded by Hektōr and Zeus the Father:

all of them, even though Hektōr slew only Periphētēs
from Mykēnai, dear son of Kopreus, who'd served as a messenger
from the lord Eurystheus to that mighty force Hēraklēs:
by him, a far meaner father, was sired a son who proved
better in all kinds of excellence—speed of foot, warfare,
brains: in all these he ranked with Mykēnai's leading men.
This it was now that increased the glory he gave Hektōr,
for as he turned back, he tripped over his own shield's rim,
one that reached to his feet, a defense against javelins:
on this he stumbled, fell backwards, and about his temples
loud clanged the helmet as he went down. Now Hektōr
was quick to note this, ran swiftly up beside him,
planted a spear in his chest, and—so close to his own comrades—
slew him. Though sad for their comrade, these could not
rescue him, being themselves too scared of noble Hektōr.

They came in among the ships, and the beam-ends of those
vessels first drawn up confined them; but their enemies still
followed: the Argives were forced to make a further retreat
from the outermost ships, but held a line by their huts
all in a body, not scattering through the camp
for very shame and fear. They kept calling to one another,
and above all Gerēnian Nestōr, the Achaians' guardian,
begged each man, imploring him in his parents' name:
"My friends, be men now, let shame into your hearts
before other men; and remember, each one of you,
your children and wives, your possessions and your parents
whether for you they're living or dead! On behalf
of them, far distant now, I who am here beseech you
to make a strong stand, not to turn back in craven flight!"

So saying, he stirred up each man's strength and spirit.
From their eyes Athēnē removed the heavenly cloud of mist,
and clear light shone down on them on either side,
on that of the ships, and that of levelling warfare. Thus all
could see Hektōr, good at the war cry, and his comrades—
both those holding back in the rear, not committed to battle,
and all who were fighting the good fight beside the swift ships.

No longer did it suffice the courageous heart of Aias
to stand back where the other Achaians' sons had withdrawn to:

he went with great strides from deck to deck of the ships,
in his hands a huge pike that was intended for sea battles,
jointed in sections, and twenty-two cubits long.
As a man who's an expert rider of horses harnesses four
out of many together, and drives them at a smart clip
from the plain towards a great city, using the public highway,
with everyone marveling at him, both men and women,
while he, quite safely, and controlling all his movements,
will leap from horse to horse as they gallop on—
so Aias kept ranging from deck to deck of the various
ships with long strides, and his voice went up to heaven
as, fearsomely shouting, he kept exhorting the Danaäns
to safeguard their ships and huts. Nor did Hektōr hold back
among the common mass of the well-corseleted Trojans,
but as a tawny eagle will swoop down on a covey
of winged fowl feeding beside the bank of a river—
geese or cranes, or long-necked swans—so Hektōr
made straight for a dark-prowed ship, charging right at it,
while Zeus from behind thrust him forward with one mighty hand,
cheering on both Hektōr himself and the troops that went with him.
So once more bitter fighting took place beside the ships:
you'd have thought they were facing each other now in battle
fresh and unwearied, so determinedly did they fight,
and as they fought, these were their thoughts: the Achaians feared
they would never escape from danger, but would perish;
and as for the Trojans, the heart in each man's breast
hoped to fire the ships and to kill the Achaian heroes.
Such were their thoughts as they stood confronting one another.
Now Hektōr caught hold of the stern of a fine seafaring ship,
swift to traverse salt water, that had carried Prōtesilaös
to Troy, but never returned him to his own dear fatherland.
It was all around his ship that Achaians and Trojans
were engaged in hand-to-hand slaughter, nor did they now
await volleys of arrows and javelins, but came right in,
squared off at close quarters, the same thought in every mind,
and battled it out with sharp axes and hatchets, large swords
and double-edged spears; many fine sword blades there were,
hilts bound with black cord, that found their way to the ground,
some dropped from the hands, some fallen from shoulder baldrics
of men as they fought, and the black earth ran with blood.

Hektōr, the ship's stern once grasped, would not let go of it,
kept his hands on the sternpost as he called out to the Trojans:
"Bring fire here, and you all as one man raise the war cry,
for Zeus has now granted us a day worth all the rest,
to take the ships that came here against the gods' will
and have brought us much trouble, through the cowardice of
old men
who, when I was ready to fight by the ships' sterns
held me back, and restrained my troops. Though it may have been
far-seeing Zeus who at that time addled our wits,
now it's he who's urging us on—indeed, commanding us!"

So he spoke, and they redoubled their onslaughts on the Argives.
Now Aias, hard pressed by missiles, stood firm no longer
but backed off a little, thinking he well might die,
along the seven-foot cross-bench, and left the trim ship's deck,
and stood there, watching warily, using a spear to thrust back,
away from the ships, any Trojan who came with a flaming torch,
and kept urging the Danaäns on, in his terrifying voice:
"Friends! Danaän heroes! You henchmen of Arēs!
Be men, my friends! Call up your fighting courage!
Do we suppose we have other helpers at our backs?
Or some stronger wall, to ward off disaster from our troops?
No way—and there's no close city, well fortified with towers,
where we could find allies, turn back this assault together!
Here we're stuck, here, on the well-armored Trojans' terrain,
our backs to the sea, far away from our native country:
In our own hands lies our salvation, not in respite from battle!"

So saying, Aias, enraged, made fierce play with his keen-edged spear:
any Trojan who now came charging against the hollow ships
with a blazing torch, in answer to Hektōr's exhortations,
Aias would wait for, and wound with that same long spear,
and a dozen men he laid low in close combat beside the ships.

Book 16

While these fought on around the well-benched vessel,
Patroklos came and stood by Achilles, the people's shepherd,
shedding warm tears, like a spring of black-sourced water
that sends its dark stream coursing down some deserted rock face.
At the sight of him swift-footed noble Achilles felt pity,
and addressed himself to him, speaking with winged words:
"Why are you weeping, Patroklos, like a girl, a small child
who runs to her mother's side and begs to be picked up,
clutching at her dress, delays her when she's busy,
looks up at her tearfully, till she gives in and carries her?
That's what you're like, Patroklos, shedding those big round tears!
Have you got some news for the Myrmidons, or for me myself,
or a message from Phthiē that you alone know about?
Menoitios, Aktōr's son, still lives, they say, and Pēleus
Aiakos's son, is alive there, among the Myrmidons—
for those two indeed we'd grieve sorely if they were dead!
Or is your lament for the Argives, the way they're being slaughtered
by the hollow ships, on account of their own presumption?
Speak up, don't keep it a secret—we both should know it."

Then, horseman Patroklos, sighing heavily, you replied:
"Ah, Achilles, Pēleus's son, far the mightiest of the Achaians,
do not be angry! Such trouble has come upon the Achaians—
for all those who were once the very best of our warriors
are laid up aboard their ships, either shot or speared:
shot is the son of Tydeus, mighty Diomēdēs,
speared are Odysseus, famed spearman, and Agamemnōn,
shot, too, is Eurypylos, with an arrow through his thigh.
Healers well-skilled in medicaments are now busy about them,
treating their wounds. But Achilles, you are so stubborn!
Never may such wrath master me, as that which you cherish
in your lethal valiance! How will men not yet born
profit by you, if you don't keep vile ruin from the Argives?
Pitiless man, your father was not Pēleus the horseman,
nor was Thetis your mother: no, the grey sea bore you,

and the towering rocks, for your mind is unchangeable!
But if in your thoughts it's some prophecy you're evading,
—some word from Zeus passed on by your lady mother—
at least send me out now, and the rest of the Myrmidon
force with me, and maybe I'll prove a light to the Danaäns—
and give me your armor, to wear on my own shoulders,
so the Trojans may take me for you, back off from the fighting,
let the Achaians' warlike sons, who are now exhausted,
catch their breath: too brief is the breathing space from battle.
We're fresh, not tired—we should easily drive men exhausted
by battle back to the city, away from the ships and huts."

Such his entreaty, the great fool: but as fate decreed,
his own ghastly death and destruction it was for which he prayed.

To him swift-footed Achilles, deeply troubled, then replied:
"Ah, me, Zeus-born Patroklos, what's this that you've said?
I'm not bothered by any prophecy that I know of,
nor has my lady mother told me of any word
from Zeus; but there's bitter grief invades both heart and spirit
when a man decides to rob somebody who's his equal
and take back his prize, just because he has the greater power!
Bitter grief this to me, for I was wounded in my pride.
That girl the Achaians' sons had given me as an award,
whom I won with my spear after sacking a well-walled city—
her now has the lord Agamemnōn, yes, Atreus's son, snatched back
from my arms, as though I were some unhonored refugee!
Still, all this we'll let go as past and done with: no way
was it in my heart to be wrathful for ever, although
I did declare I'd not put an end to my anger until
the sounds of war and the fighting arrived at my own ships.
So do you, then, array my famed armor on your shoulders,
and lead out the war-loving Myrmidons into battle,
if indeed the dark cloud that's the Trojans has surrounded
the ships by main force, and the seashore with a thin
strip of land is all that's left in the hands of the Argives,
and the Trojans' whole city has come out in force against them,
boldly, since they don't see the light glinting off my helmet
up close—soon enough they'd be routed, choking the creeks
with their corpses, if only the lord Agamemnōn had been minded
to treat me well, whereas now they're fighting around the camp!

For not in the hands of Diomēdēs, Tydeus's son,
is the spear now raging to hold off disaster from the Danaäns,
nor as yet have I heard the voice of Atreus's son bellowing
out of his loathsome head; no, it's man-killing Hektōr's
I hear echoing round me, exhorting the Trojans, while they
with their war whoops fill all the plain, as they trounce the Achaians.
Yet even so, Patroklos, to keep disaster from the ships
have at them mightily, lest with their blazing torches
they fire the ships and deprive us of our longed-for return!
Now: follow well the instructions I shall put in your mind,
so you'll win me great honor and glory from all
the Danaäns, and they'll deliver that beautiful girl
back to me, along with more splendid gifts besides.
When you've driven them from the ships, come right back here!
Should Hērē's loud-thundering husband let you achieve glory,
don't be too eager to go battling on without me
against the war-loving Trojans: you'd diminish my honor.
Nor should you become so exultant in warfare and fighting
that, while you're killing Trojans, you press on towards Ilion,
lest one of the gods eternal descends from Olympos
and pitches in: Apollo the archer loves them dearly.
Turn back as soon as you've set the light of deliverance
among the ships; leave the others to battle it out on the plain.
How much I wish—Zeus, Father, Athēnē, and Apollo!—
that not one out of all the Trojans might escape death,
nor a single Argive, but that only we two should not perish,
and together, alone, should loosen Troy's sacred diadem![1]

Such was their conversation, each to the other. Meanwhile
Aias no longer held firm, being hard-pressed by missiles,
overcome by the will of Zeus, and the noble Trojans
all letting fly at him: terribly rang the gleaming
helmet about his temples as it was struck: the well-wrought
cheekpieces took endless hits, his left shoulder grew weary
as he held up his bright shield. Yet they remained unable
to knock it away from him, despite their many missiles.
He kept gasping painfully, the sweat poured down in rivers

1. "[T]he breaching of the citadel's ring of walls is compared to a captive woman's headdress being torn off," Janko explains (329). The word here translated metaphorically as "diadem" (κρήδεμνον, *krēdemnon*), originally meant something like a mantilla or formal veil.

from all his limbs, he never was given the least chance
to catch his breath: on all sides trouble was piled on trouble.

Tell me now, you Muses, whose homes are on Olympos,
how fire first came to be flung on the Achaians' ships!

Hektōr confronted Aias and struck his ash-wood spear
with his own great sword, near the socket below the tip,
and sheared the tip clean away, so that Aias, Telamōn's son,
was left with a mere lopped shaft, while far from him
the bronze spearhead clanged as it fell to the ground, and Aias
recognized, with a shudder, in his peerless heart
the work of the gods, saw all his battle plans had been wrecked
by loud-thundering Zeus, who wanted victory for the Trojans.
He backed off from the missiles; the Trojans flung weariless fire
on the swift ship: at once unquenchable flames broke out,
and the whole stern was set ablaze. But now Achilles
struck both hands upon his thighs, and called out to Patroklos:
"Up with you now, Zeus-born Patroklos, master horseman!
I clearly see by the ships the rush of devouring fire!
Don't let them take the ships, leave us no way of escape!
Arm yourself quickly, I'll muster the men."

So he spoke,
and Patroklos accoutered himself in the gleaming bronze.
The greaves first he fastened on about his shins—
finely made, and fitted with silver ankle-pieces.
Next, to cover his chest, he put on the corselet,
fine-wrought and starry, of Aiakos's swift-footed grandson.
About his shoulders he slung the silver-studded sword
of bronze, and next grasped the shield, both huge and sturdy.
Then he set on his noble head the well-made helmet,
with its horsehair crest nodding terribly above it,
and picked out two strong spears, well fitted to his grasp;
but of Aiakos's peerless scion the spear alone he left—
massive and strong, that no other Achaian fighter
could wield, but only Achilles had the strength to wield it,
the Pēlian spear of ash wood, that Cheirōn had given his father,
felled on Pēlion's heights, to be the death of heroes.
The horses he ordered Automedōn to harness quickly—
the man whom he honored highest after Achilles the rank-breaker,

and held as most trustworthy to await his battle orders.
For him now Automedōn yoked up the swift horses—
Xanthos and Balios, fleet as the gale's blast,
that the storm mare Podargē conceived to the west wind
as she browsed in the meadows beside the stream of Ocean—
while in the side traces he harnessed unmatchable Pēdasos,
the horse that Achilles bore off when he took Ēëtiōn's city,
and which, though mortal, kept pace with those immortal coursers.

Meanwhile Achilles went to and fro through the huts,
getting the Myrmidons armed in their battle gear: like wolves
that devour raw flesh, boundless fury in their hearts,
and have killed a great antlered stag up in the mountains,
and tear at the corpse, their jaws all reddened with blood,
and then go off in a pack to some black-water spring
to lap with their narrow tongues at its dark flow's surface,
belching up blood from the killing, while in their breasts
the spirit is dauntless, and their bellies are glutted—so
did the Myrmidons' leaders and chieftains quickly assemble
around the noble henchman of Aiakos's swift-foot grandson,
while there in the midst of them stood warlike Achilles,
urging on both horses and shield-bearing warriors.

Fifty were the swift ships that Achilles, beloved of Zeus,
had brought to Troy as commander, and in each one
fifty men, his companions, sat at the thole-pins:
five in whom he had trust he'd made captains, to issue orders,
while he himself was the high commander over them all.
The first squadron's captain, Menesthios, he of the bright corselet,
was the son of Spercheios, Zeus's rain-fed river,
whom Pēleus's daughter, the beautiful Polydōra, bore,
to unwearying Spercheios, a woman laid by a god,
though in name she conceived him by Bōros, Periērēs' son,
who openly wed her, and paid a bride-price past reckoning.
Of the second squadron the captain was warlike Eudōros,
born, though out of wedlock, to a fine dancer, Polymēlē,
daughter of Phylas: it was the strong Argos-slayer
who fell in love when he saw her among the maiden singers
dancing for Artemis, she of the loud chase, the golden arrows.
No waiting: Hermēs the healer went up into her room,
lay with her secretly: she bore him a splendid son,

Eudōros, outstanding as both swift runner and warrior.
  But when finally Eileithyia, goddess of childbirth, brought him
out to the light, and he saw the sun's rays for the first time,
Echeklos, Aktōr's son, a man of might and power,
took him home, having paid a bride-price past reckoning,
and old Phylas brought him up well, and cherished him dearly,
giving him all the love he'd have given a son of his own.
The captain of the third squadron was warlike Peisandros,
Maimalos's son, unrivalled among all the Myrmidons
in spear-fighting, second only to the comrade of Pēleus's son.
The fourth squadron was led by Phoinix the old horseman,
and the fifth by Alkimedōn, Laerkēs' peerless son.
Then when Achilles had mustered them all in good order,
them and their captains, he spoke very harshly to them:
  "Let none of you Myrmidons be unmindful of those threats
with which beside the swift ships you menaced the Trojans
throughout the time of my wrath, each one of you blaming me:
'Stubborn Achilles,' you cried, 'did your mother rear you on gall?
Pitiless man, who hold back your comrades by the ships
against their will! Let's go home, then, with our seafaring vessels,
since this loathsome bile has so invaded your spirit!'
With such charges you'd often assail me when you all met; but now
a great work of war confronts you, what you once longed for,
so let each of you with a bold heart go battle the Trojans!"

So saying he roused the passion and spirit of every man,
and their ranks drew closer together when they heard their king.
As a man with close-fitting stones erects the wall
of a tall house, builds to defy the fury of the winds—
so closely pressed were their helmets and bossed shields,
bucklers, helmets, and men packed so tight together
that the horsehair crests on their helmets' gleaming bosses
nudged as they bent their heads, so close were the ranks,
while, out in front of them all, two armed warriors stood—
Automedōn and Patroklos, each with the same intent:
to do battle before the Myrmidons. But meanwhile Achilles
went into his hut, and lifted the lid of a chest—
fine, intricately wrought, that silver-footed Thetis
had stowed on his ship to go with him, filled it with tunics
and cloaks to keep out the wind chill, and thick woolen rugs.

In it Achilles kept a fine-crafted cup, from which
no other man could drink the fire-bright wine,
and he poured libations from it to no god but Zeus the Father.
This cup he took from the chest, first cleansed it with sulphur,
then rinsed it off in fresh-flowing streams of water,
washed his own hands, and drew the fire-bright wine.
Now he stood in the forecourt and prayed, poured out the wine
gazing skyward, not unseen by Zeus who delights in thunder:
"Zeus, king, Pelasgian, Dōdōnean, distant-dweller,
ruler in wintry Dōdōna—where round you live the Selloi,
with unwashed feet, your interpreters, who sleep on the ground—
just as before you heard my message when I prayed,
and honored me by smiting the forces of the Achaians,
so once again for me now accomplish my desire!
I myself shall remain here, where the ships are drawn up,
but my comrade I'm sending out, with a body of Myrmidons,
to do battle: far-seeing Zeus, send out glory with him,
make strong the heart in his breast, that Hektōr too may know
whether my henchman's skilled in the business of warfare
when he's alone, or whether his hands irresistibly rage
only when I myself also enter the grind of battle.
And after he's freed our vessels from the fight and its clamor,
then unscathed let him come back to me at the swift ships
with all my battle gear and my front-rank comrades."

So he spoke in prayer, and Zeus the counselor heard him.
One wish the Father granted, but refused him the other:
that Patroklos from their ships should drive off warfare and
    combat
he granted, but a safe return from battle he denied him.

His libation made, after praying to Zeus the Father
Achilles returned to his hut, put away the cup in its chest,
then went back outside the hut, and stood there, still determined
to watch the fearsome conflict between Trojans and Achaians.

Now those armed and ready with great-hearted Patroklos
marched on, till with high resolve they assailed the Trojans.
All at once they came charging out like a swarm of wasps
by the roadside that boys have a way of provoking to fury,
constantly teasing them in their nests along the highway,

as children will, creating a widespread nuisance,
so that if some traveller passing by should happen
to annoy them by accident, they with aggressive spirit
all come buzzing out in defense of their offspring—
like them in heart and spirit the Myrmidons now
streamed forth from the ships, and an endless clamor arose,
and Patroklos called in a carrying voice to his comrades:
"Myrmidons, comrades of Pēleus's son Achilles,
be men, my friends, bear in mind your fighting spirit,
win honor for Pēleus's son, far the best of the Argives
by the ships, he and his henchmen, all of them front-line fighters—
that Atreus's son, wide-ruling Agamemnōn, may know his blind
delusion in failing to honor the best of the Achaians!"

So saying he stirred the strength and spirit of every man,
and they fell in a pack on the Trojans, while all around them
the ships echoed dauntingly to the Achaians' war cries,
and when the Trojans saw Menoitios's valiant son,
himself and his henchman, both agleam in their armor,
their hearts quaked, and all their ranks were shaken: they thought
the swift-footed son of Pēleus, there by the ships,
had foregone his wrath and turned instead to alliance,
and each man looked for some way to escape sheer ruin.

Patroklos was the first to let fly his gleaming spear,
right into the midst, where most troops were huddled together,
by the stern of the ship of great-hearted Prōtesilaös,
and he hit Pyraichmēs, who'd brought his Paiōnian horsemen
from Amydōn, close by the wide-flowing Axios river.
Pyraichmēs' right shoulder he hit, and he fell back in the dust,
groaning aloud, and his comrades around him panicked;
for Patroklos by killing their leader, that outstanding fighter,
spread terror throughout the ranks of all the Paiōnians.
Back from the ships he drove them and put out the blazing fire,
leaving the ship half-burnt there, while the Trojans retreated
with an astonishing outcry, the Danaäns hot on their heels
among the hollow ships: the outcry was never-ending.
As from the topmost peak of some lofty mountain
a thick cloud is moved away by lightning-gatherer Zeus,
and all the heights are revealed, the towering headlands
and glens, and from on high the infinite air shines clear—

so the Danaäns, when they'd thrust off devouring fire from the ships
got a short breathing space. Yet from warfare there was no respite,
for not yet were the Trojans by the warlike Achaians
driven in headlong rout, away from the black ships,
but still fought back, even when forced to give up ground.

Then, as the conflict spread widely, man slew man
among the leaders: first, Menoitios's valiant son
hit Areïlykos in the thigh with a cast of his sharp-edged spear
just as he turned to run. The bronze was driven clean through,
the spear shattered his thighbone, he sank to the ground
face downward. Menelaös the warrior wounded Thoas
where his shield left his torso exposed and unstrung his limbs;
and Phyleus's son, waiting as Amphiklos made his charge,
got his own blow in first, at the top of the leg, where a man's
muscle is thickest: around the point of his spear
the tendons were sliced apart, darkness shrouded his eyes.
One son of Nestōr, Antilochos, with his sharp spear wounded
Atymnios, drove the bronze point clean through his flank,
and he slumped at his feet. Then Maris from close quarters
faced Antilochos with his spear, enraged for his brother's sake,
standing in front of the corpse, but godlike Thrasymēdēs
moved in before he could strike, and did not miss,
but hit his shoulder: the spear point stripped away
the base of his arm from its muscles, shattered the bone.
He fell with a thud, and darkness shrouded his eyes.
So these two, laid low by two brothers, went on their way
to Erebos—noble comrades, both, of Sarpēdōn,
spearmen sons of Amisōdaros, who reared the monstrous
Chimaira to bring disaster to many a mortal.
Aias the son of Oïleus now went for Kleoboulos
and took him alive, a man who'd tripped in the crush;
then unleashed his strength, struck with his hilted sword
at the man's neck: the whole blade was warmed by his blood,
scarlet death and all-mastering fate overpowered his eyes.
Pēneleōs and Lykōn now ran at each other—they'd both
missed with their spears, had let fly to no purpose,
so now they moved in with their swords: Lykōn aimed a blow
at the helmet's boss with its horsehair crest, but his sword
broke off near the hilt, while Pēnelaōs struck him under

his ear on the neck—the blade sheared in so deep
that only the skin held firm: his head hung, his limbs went slack.
Mēriónēs, striding quickly, now overtook Akamas
as he mounted his chariot, scored a hit on his right shoulder:
he slumped from the chariot, a mist obscured his eyes.
Idomeneus speared Erymas with his pitiless bronze
in the mouth: the bronze point sheared clean through
beneath the brain, split the white bones apart,
shook his teeth loose, while both his eyes were flooded
with blood, and, as he gaped, from his mouth and nostrils
blood spurted, and death's black cloud enshrouded him.

So these Danaän leaders each of them slew his man,
and as wolves attack lambs or kids in their ravening hunger,
picking them off from the flocks, when through their shepherd's
carelessness they're scattered up in the hills, and the wolves,
seeing this, promptly snatch the timorous young ones—
just so did the Danaäns fall on the Trojans, who then
sought refuge in ill-famed flight, forgot their fighting spirit.

Great Aias as always was eager to let fly a spear
at bronze-panoplied Hektōr, who, highly skilled in warfare,
broad shoulders protected by his bull's-hide shield,
kept alert for the whirr of arrows, the thud of spears:
though he recognized that the tide of victory was turning,
even so he remained, did his best to save his loyal comrades.
As from Olympos a cloud comes into the heavens
from the bright upper air, when Zeus deploys a tempest,
so from the ships came the sound of cheers and panic
as the Trojans, disordered, recrossed the ditch. Now Hektōr
was carried out, with his gear, by his fast horses,
left the Trojan troops behind, to be stopped, frustrated,
by the Greek-dug ditch, in which many swift horses broke
their pole at the end, abandoned their masters' chariots.
Patroklos, hot in pursuit, called urgently on the Danaäns,
planning ills for the Trojans, who, shouting and panic-stricken,
choked all the ways, broken-ranked, while high in the air
a dust storm formed under the clouds, and the whole-hoofed horses
strained hard back to the city from the ships and huts.
Wherever Patroklos saw men huddled the thickest,
there he drove, shouting: beneath his axles new victims

kept slumping down from their chariots, that then overturned;
and right over the trench his swift horses—those immortal
steeds that the gods gave to Pēleus, glorious gifts—
pressed eagerly forward; his heart now urged him against Hektōr,
hot to attack; but Hektōr's own swift horses saved him.
As under a storm cloud the whole black earth's weighed down
at harvest time, when rainfall from Zeus is torrential,
as he, enraged, takes punitive measures against those men
who in the assembly enforce their crook-backed judgments
and drive justice out, indifferent to the scrutiny of the gods;
and all their swollen rivers are overflooded, and many
a hillside's scored deeply by the plunging torrents
that roar headlong down from the mountains into the dark sea,
and men's tilled fields are ruined—so loud and grieving
was the neighing of those Trojan mares as they sped on their way.

When Patroklos had cut off the front ranks from their retreat
he herded them back to the ships, would not let them go on
to the city, much though they longed to, but in between
the ships, the high wall, and the river he ranged amongst them
killing, exacting requital for the deaths of many.
Here he hit Pronoös first with his gleaming spear,
in the chest, left exposed by the shield, and unstrung his limbs:
he fell with a thud. Next Patroklos charged at Thestōr,
Ēnops's son, who crouched there in his polished chariot,
out of his mind with terror, while from his hands
the reins slipped away. Patroklos closed in with his spear,
rammed the right side of his jaw, drove the spear through
his teeth,
dragged him over the chariot's rim, like a man who, perched
on a jutting rock, reels in a sacred fish from the deep
on his line and bright bronze hook: just so from the chariot
on his bright spear he hauled in the gaping Pronoös,
dumped him face downwards. He dropped, and life fled from him.
Next Erylaös, charging at him, he hit with a rock
square on the head, which split completely in two
inside his heavy helmet: he collapsed on the ground
face foremost, and death, the spirit-queller, embraced him.
Amphoteros next, Erymas and Epaltēs, Tlēpolemos son
of Damastōr, then Echios, Pyris, and Ipheus,

as well as Euippos, and Argeas's son Polymēlos—
all these in turn he laid low on the nurturing earth.

When Sarpēdōn saw his comrades of the unbelted tunics
being felled at the hands of Menoitios's son Patroklos,
he cried out, addressing his words to the godlike Lycians:
"Shame on you, Lycians! Where are you fleeing? Be keen now!
I myself shall confront this fellow, so I may learn
just who he is that's unmatched here, who's inflicted such hurt
on the Trojans, who's unstrung so many fine men's limbs!"

So saying, he sprang, armed, from his chariot to the ground,
and Patroklos on the other side, seeing him, sprang down too;
and as two vultures, with hooked beaks and crooked talons,
fight, screaming loudly, up on some lofty rock,
so these two, shouting, charged the one at the other.
When he saw them, the son of Kronos, that devious schemer,
felt pity, and said to Hērē, his sister and wife:
"Woe is me, that it's fate for Sarpēdōn, my best-loved mortal,
to be laid low by Patroklos, the son of Menoitios!
My heart is divided two ways as I debate the matter—
Shall I snatch him up while he lives still, and then set him down,
far from this grievous warfare, in Lycia's rich terrain,
or shall I let him be vanquished by Patroklos, Menoitios's son?"

Then the ox-eyed lady Hērē replied to him, saying:
"Most dread son of Kronos, what's this that you're telling me?
Here's a man, a mortal, his fate long since determined:
Are you minded to free such a one from sorrowful death?
Then do it; but we other gods will not all approve.
One other thing I will tell you, and you should take it to heart:
If you send back Sarpēdōn alive to his own abode,
think of this: that hereafter some other god may be minded
to send his own dear son away from the grind of battle—
for fighting round Priam's great city there now are many
sons of immortals, in whom you'll cause serious resentment.
But if he's so dear to you, and you're grieved at heart,
then let him be vanquished in the grind of battle
at the hands of Patroklos, the son of Menoitios;
and when the soul and life have departed from his body,
send Death and soothing Sleep to convey him away

till they reach the land of broad Lycia, and there
his brothers and kinsfolk will give him due funeral rites
with burial mound and gravestone, a dead man's entitlement."

So she spoke. At this the father of gods and men
did not ignore her, but showered bloody raindrops on the earth
in honor of his dear son, whom Patroklos was very soon
to kill off in rich-soiled Troy, far away from his own country.

Now when, advancing, they finally joined battle,
then it was that Patroklos hit illustrious Thrasymēlos,
the valiant henchman of the lord Sarpēdōn;
him he speared in the nether belly, unstrung his limbs.
Sarpēdōn, letting fly next with his gleaming spear,
missed the man himself, but speared the horse Pēdasos
in its right shoulder: it screamed, gasped out its spirit,
dropped neighing into the dust, and the breath of life fled from it.
The other two pulled apart, the yoke creaked, and the reins
were tangled, now that the trace horse lay there in the dust.
But for this the famed spearman Automedōn found an answer:
unsheathing the long sword from beside his sturdy thigh
he jumped down and cut free the trace horse, wasted no time,
and the other two were thus righted, strained at the reins,
while the two fighters got back together in heart-devouring strife.

Then once more Sarpēdōn missed with his gleaming spear,
and over Patroklos's left shoulder the spear point flew,
not hitting him, and Patroklos in turn made play
with the bronze, and not vainly did the shaft fly from his hand,
but struck at the point where the lungs enclose the solid heart,[2]
and Sarpēdōn fell like an oak tree or a white poplar,
or a tall pine that up in the mountains shipwrights fell
with their newly sharpened axes to serve as a ship timber:
so there in front of his horses and chariot he lay
stretched out, bellowing, hands clutching the bloody dust.
As a lion that comes on a herd will slaughter a bull,
tawny, great-hearted, in among the shambling cattle,

2. Onians (26–27) is, as usual, valuable here. The φρένες (*phrenes*) are originally the lungs, not (as often, and nonsensically, supposed) the midriff or diaphragm. "Solid" or "dense" is Onians's interpretation of ἁδινόν (*hadinon*), recognized by Janko as giving "an anatomically correct description" (379). See also n. 3 to 504.

and it perishes, bellowing still, in the jaws of the lion,
so now, laid low by Patroklos, the Lycian spearmen's leader,
dying, still struggled, and called his comrade by name:
"Dear Glaukos, warrior among men, today there's urgent need
for you to be both spearman and dauntless warrior too—
if you're ready, let violent warfare be your choice!
First, you must urge on the Lycians' warrior leaders—
checking them all—to fight for Sarpēdōn's body,
then join them, and battle in my defense with the bronze:
For even in time to come I'll be a reproach and a cause
of disgrace to you all your days, unendingly, should the Achaians
strip my gear from my fallen body by the drawn-up ships!
Now hold the line bravely, and urge on all our troops!"

As he spoke thus death's conclusion enshrouded him,
his eyes and his nostrils. Patroklos set one foot on his chest,
and tugged the spear from his flesh. The lungs followed with it.
Sarpēdōn's soul and the spear point he drew out together,[3]
as the Myrmidons reined in the snorting horses that now,
freed from their masters' chariot, wanted only to escape.

Terrible grief seized Glaukos as he heard Sarpēdon's voice,
and his heart was wrung, since he'd not been able to help him.
With one hand he gripped and pressed his arm, for the wound
vexed him, that Teukros had dealt him with an arrow—
in support of his own comrades—as Glaukos charged the high wall.
Now he addressed in prayer Apollo, the deadly archer:
"Hear me, lord, you who may be in Lycia's rich terrain
or perhaps here in Troy: wherever you are, you're able
to listen to men in trouble, just as trouble's come on me now,
for I have this serious wound, and my arm's shot through
with sharp cutting pains, nor can the flow of blood
be stanched, and my shoulder's a dead weight because of it.
I can't hold my spear in place, or join the battle against
our enemies, while our best fighter has perished—Sarpēdōn,
son of Zeus, who won't even save his own flesh and blood!
But do you, lord, now at least heal this serious wound of mine,

3. Since θυμός (*thymos*), which came to be equated with "soul" or "spirit", originally meant "breath", as the physical sign of life (Onians 44–53), it is tempting to see a neat zeugma here: "the soul is imagined as breath which escapes through the wound," as Janko (381) does.

lull my pains to sleep, and give me the strength
to exhort my Lycian comrades to keep up the fight,
and myself to join the battle for Sarpēdōn's body."

So he spoke in prayer, and Phoibos Apollo heard him.
The pains the god stopped at once, dried up the black blood
that flowed from his hurtful wound, put strength in his heart.
Glaukos knew what had happened, rejoiced in silence
that the great god had listened, and answered his prayer so soon.
First he urged on the Lycians' warrior leaders,
checking them all, to fight for Sarpēdōn's body;
then he made his way, taking long strides, to the Trojans,
to Poulydamas, Pánthoös's son, and noble Agēnōr,
and sought out Aineias and the bronze-panoplied Hektōr,
whom he now went up to, and addressed with winged words:
"Hektōr, it's plain you've completely forgotten your allies,
who on your account, far distant from friends and country
are wasting their lives away—yet you will not help them!
Sarpēdōn lies dead now, the Lycian spearmen's leader,
whose judgments and strength were Lycia's protection:
him brazen Arēs has vanquished through Patroklos's spear!
My friends, stand beside him now, think shame to hold back,
lest he be stripped of his arms and his corpse maltreated
by the Myrmidons, angered at all the Danaän deaths,
those whom we killed with our spears at the swift ships."

So he spoke,
and the Trojans were possessed from head to foot by grief,
uncontrollable, unendurable, for Sarpēdōn had been
their city's prop, though a foreigner, since numerous troops
came with him, and he himself was a champion warrior.
They made straight for the Danaäns, fiercely, their leader Hektōr
enraged for Sarpēdōn's sake. The Achaians were urged on
by the shaggy heart[4] of Patroklos, Menoitios's son.
First he addressed both Aiases, already hot for the fray:
"You two needs must be keen to defend yourselves, as brave
as you were in time past among fighters, or even braver!

4. Onians (28–29) reminds us that the epithet "bushy, shaggy" (λάσιος, *lasios*) is most appropriate for the heart itself, with "the multitudinous branching veins and arteries growing immediately out of it, like bushes, many through the lungs."

The man who first got beyond the wall of the Achaians,
Sarpēdōn, is lying there dead—let's grab him, disfigure his corpse,
strip the battle gear from his shoulders, with the ruthless bronze
dispatch any comrade of his who tries to defend him!"

So he spoke, and they themselves were raging to attack.
Then, when on both sides they'd reinforced their ranks,
Trojans and Lycians, Myrmidons and Achaians,
they clashed in battle over Sarpēdōn's corpse,
with terrible shouts, and their battered armor rang loud,
and Zeus spread deadly darkness over the grinding conflict,
to match the deadly war work centered on his dear son.

At first the Trojans forced the sharp-eyed Achaians back,
for a man by no means the worst of the Myrmidons was stricken—
the son of great-hearted Agaklēs, noble Epeigeus,
who'd formerly ruled as king in well-populated Boudeion,
but at this time, after he'd killed a noble kinsman,
came as a suppliant to Pēleus and silver-footed Thetis,
and they sent him to serve with Achilles, the breaker of ranks,
at Ilion, rich in foals, as a fighter against the Trojans.
Him, as he grabbed at the corpse, illustrious Hektōr
struck, with a rock, on the head, which split completely in two
inside his heavy helmet: he collapsed on the body
face foremost, and death, the spirit-queller, embraced him.
Then over Patroklos came grief for his slaughtered comrade,
and he charged through the front ranks like a speedy hawk
in pursuit of fleeing jackdaws and starlings: even so,
Patroklos, driver of horses, straight for the Lycians
and the Trojans did you charge, in your wrath for your comrade!
Sthenelaös too he struck, dear son of Ithaimenēs,
on the neck with a rock, and tore away the tendons.
Front-line fighters gave ground, illustrious Hektōr with them:
as far as is the flight of a good long hunting spear
thrown by a man making trial of his strength in sport,
or even in war, when hard pressed by murderous foemen,
so far did the Trojans retreat, and the Achaians drove them.
Glaukos, the Lycian spearmen's commander, was the first
to turn around, and he slew high-spirited Bathyklēs,
Chalkōn's dear son, who made his home in Hellas,
and ranked high among Myrmidons for wealth and prosperity.

Him Glaukos struck full on the chest with his spear,
turning suddenly on him when about to be overtaken,
and he fell with a thud, and thick grief now seized the Achaians,
since a good man had fallen, while the Trojans, with loud cheers,
closed and crowded round them. Yet the Achaians did not
forget their fighting spirit, but pitted their strength against them.
Mērionēs next took down a helmeted Trojan fighter,
Laogonos, Onētōr's bold son, a priest of Idaian
Zeus, who was honored by his people like a god.
Him he struck under the jaw and ear: at once the breath
of life fled his limbs, and loathsome darkness seized him.
Aineias then let fly his bronze spear at Mērionēs,
hoping to hit him as he advanced behind his shield;
but Mērionēs was watching, and avoided the bronze spear
by ducking down forward, so that its long shaft
stuck in the ground behind him, its butt end quivering,
and there mighty Arēs took its power away from it.
[And Aineias's shaft ended quivering, point first,
deep in the ground, flung in vain from his sturdy hand.][5]
At this Aineias was angered, and spoke to him, saying:
"Soon enough, Mērionēs, dancer though you are,
my spear would have stopped you for ever, had I but hit you."

Mērionēs, famed spearman, made him this answer:
"Aineias, it's hard for you, however strong you may be,
to quench the strength of every man who confronts you
in his own defense: you too were born a mortal!
Should I aim and hit you squarely with my sharp bronze,
soon enough—strong though you are, with trust in your
hands—
you'd give glory to me, and your soul to horse-proud Hādēs."

So he spoke; but Menoitios's valiant son rebuked him:
"Mērionēs, you're a good man, why carry on like this?
Look, friend, insulting words are not what will make the Trojans
back off from the corpse: that would take killing most of us.
War's outcome rests in our hands, talk's place is the council.
No point in endless words—what we need is to fight."

---

5. Lines 614–15 = 13.504–5: originally they were written in the margin as a parallel, but at some point they were accidentally interpolated into the text.

So saying, he led the way, and the other, mortal but godlike,
followed, and from the armies—like the din made by woodcutters
at work in some mountain clearing, audible far away—
there went up off the wide-wayed earth the thud and clatter
of bronze and oxhide and cleverly fashioned shields
as they thrust at each other with swords and two-edged spears;
and no longer could any man, though he knew him well,
have recognized noble Sarpēdōn, now covered with blood
and dust and missiles, from his head to the soles of his feet.
Men crowded around the corpse the way that flies
in a farmyard buzz round the brimming pails of milk
in springtime, when the milk spurts down into the buckets:
just so they kept crowding around the corpse. Nor did Zeus
ever turn his sharp gaze away from the grind of battle,
but watched them closely, debating a problem in his mind,
uncertain regarding the matter of killing Patroklos—
was illustrious Hektōr right now, in the grind of battle
over godlike Sarpēdōn, to slay him too with the bronze,
and strip the gear off his shoulders, or rather should he, Zeus,
prolong the sheer labor of fighting for yet more men?
And as he debated, this struck him as being the better way:
that the excellent henchman of Pēleus's son Achilles
should once more drive the Trojans and bronze-clad Hektōr
back to the city, and take the breath of life from many.
In Hektōr first he aroused craven panic: Hektōr boarded
his chariot, turned to flight, and called upon the rest
of the Trojans to flee, having seen Zeus's sacred scales in action.
Nor did the brave Lycians stand fast, but panicked to a man
when they saw their king laid low, pierced through the heart,
lying in a heap of corpses, for many had fallen on him
since Kronos's son stretched taut the cords of powerful strife.
They stripped from Sarpēdōn's shoulders the gleaming
armor of bronze, which Menoitios's valiant son now
gave to his comrades, to carry back to the hollow ships.
Then Zeus the cloud-gatherer thus addressed Apollo:
"Go now, dear Phoibos, and wipe the dark clotted blood
from Sarpēdōn—first get him clear of the missiles—then take him
far off, find a river, wash him clean in its flowing waters,
spread ambrosia on him, have him clothed in immortal raiment,
then give him to fast-moving escorts, to carry him away—

Sleep and Death, twin brothers, who'll lose no time,
but speedily set him down in broad Lycia's rich terrain.
There his brother and kinsfolk will give him due funeral rites
with burial mound and gravestone, a dead man's entitlement."

So he spoke, and Apollo did not disregard his father,
but went down from the heights of Ida to the grim battlefield,
and at once raised noble Sarpēdōn, got him clear of the missiles,
took him far off, found a river, washed him clean in its flowing waters,
spread ambrosia on him, had him clothed in immortal raiment,
then gave him to fast-moving escorts, to carry away—
Sleep and Death, twin brothers: they lost no time,
but speedily set him down in broad Lycia's rich terrain.

Patroklos now commanded Automedōn as driver
to keep chasing the Trojans and Lycians—being blindly deluded,
the fool, since had he followed the advice of Pēleus's son
he'd surely have kept well clear of black death's foul spirits!
But the mind of Zeus is always more potent than that of men,
turns even a hero cowardly, steals victory from him—
easily, too, and as easily stirs up a man to fight.
He it was now who put spirit in Patroklos's breast.

So whom
did you slaughter first, and whom last, Patroklos, when
the gods thus summoned you deathward? First of all
was Adrēstos, and then Autonoös, Echeklos, Perimos
son of Megas, Epistōr, followed by Melanippos,
Elasos next, and Moulios, and Pylartēs: these he killed,
and the rest of them then chose flight, every last man of them.

Then the Achaians' sons would have taken high-gated Troy
through Patroklos's hands, so widely he raged with his spear,
had Phoibos Apollo not stood on the well-built ramparts
with death in mind for him, while aiding the Trojans.
Three times Patroklos climbed up the lofty wall's elbow-bend,
and three times Apollo violently beat him back,
thrusting against the bright shield with his immortal hands.
But when for the fourth time he came on like a god,
in a terrible voice Apollo addressed him with winged words:
"Withdraw, Patroklos, scion of Zeus! It's not fated

that the lordly Trojans' city should be laid waste by your spear,
nor by that of Achilles, a far better man than you!"

So he spoke, and Patroklos backed off a healthy distance,
to avoid the wrath of Apollo, the deadly archer.

At the Skaian Gates Hektōr reined in his whole-hoofed horses,
in two minds: should he drive them back to the tumult and fight,
or should he recall his forces, regroup inside the wall?
As he pondered thus, Phoibos Apollo approached him
in the form of a man both vigorous and strong—
Asios, who was uncle to Hektōr the horse-breaker
and Hekabē's brother, but the son of Dymas,
who dwelt in Phrygia near the Sangarios river:
in his likeness now Apollo, the son of Zeus, addressed him:
"Hektōr, why have you quit the fight? You must not!
If I were stronger than you, as much as I'm really weaker,
it'd be to your instant hurt that you'd hold back from the battle!
Come on, now! Set at Patroklos your strong-hoofed horses!
You might kill him, and then win glory from Apollo!"

So he spoke, and went back, a god to the struggle of mortals,
and to warlike Kebrionēs illustrious Hektōr gave
the word to whip on his horses to battle. Meanwhile Apollo
had made his way to the troops, loosed dangerous confusion
on the Argives, thus giving glory to the Trojans and Hektōr.
Other Danaäns Hektōr ignored, made no effort to slay them,
but set his strong-hoofed horses at Patroklos alone;
and Patroklos over against him sprang down from his chariot,
a spear in his left hand, while the other grasped a rock,
jagged and glinting: his hand enclosed it. With all his weight
behind it he threw. The missile did not fall short;
he did not throw in vain, but hit Hektōr's charioteer,
Kebrionēs—a bastard of glorious Priam's, now holding
the reins—in his forehead with the sharp rock: it crushed
both eyebrows together, the bone did not hold firm,
both eyeballs bolted out, dropped to the ground in the dust
right in front of his feet, and he, like a diver, fell
from the well-built chariot. The breath of life left his bones.
Then mockingly you addressed him, horseman Patroklos:
"Oh ho, such a nimble fellow, such an effortless tumbler!

I'm sure if he were out there on the fish-breeding deep
this fellow would catch enough sea squirts to feed a multitude,
diving in from his ship, even when it's bad weather,
so lightly he somersaults now from his chariot on the plain!
It would seem that even the Trojans have their share of acrobats."

So saying, he went after Kebrionēs the hero
with the pounce of a lion that, while ravaging a farmstead,
is hit in the chest, and thus it's its own courage that destroys it:
just so at Kebrionēs, Patroklos, you sprang in your fury,
while on the other side Hektōr jumped down from his chariot,
and they fought over Kebrionēs like a pair of lions
that high up in the mountains over a slain hind—
both ravenous, both determined—battle it out. Just so
for Kebrionēs these two veterans of the war cry,
Patroklos son of Menoitios and illustrious Hektōr,
longed to cut up each other's flesh with the pitiless bronze.
Hektōr seized the corpse by the head, and would not let go,
while Patroklos on the other side clung to a foot, and round them
Trojans and Danaäns contested the grind of battle.
As the east and south winds compete the one with the other
at shaking some deep wood in a mountain clearing—
a wood of beech and ash and smooth-barked cornel,
their long boughs grinding together with an amazing
racket, along with a crackle of snapping branches—
so the Achaians and Trojans now went for one another,
killers all: neither side had deadly rout in mind,
and all round Kebrionēs many sharp-edged spears were planted,
and flighted arrows that had leapt from the bowstring,
and many large rocks that shattered against the shields
of the men fighting over him; but amid the swirling dust
great in his greatness he lay, his horsemanship forgotten.

As long as the sun still straddled the midpoint of the sky,
both sides' shots struck home, and men dropped, hit; but when
the sun declined to the point at which oxen are unyoked,
then it was the Achaians proved stronger, beyond what was destined:
the hero Kebrionēs they pulled out of the range of missiles,
away from the Trojans' war cries, stripped the gear from his shoulders,
and Patroklos with deadly intent now went after the Trojans.
Three times he charged them, the equal of swift Arēs,

shouting terribly: three times he slew nine men.
But when for the fourth time he came on like a god,
then for you, Patroklos, the end of your life showed clear,
for Phoibos confronted you in the grind of battle,
dread god—yet Patroklos missed him coming through the turmoil,
for he was wrapped in a thick mist when they met.
Standing behind him, Apollo slammed his back and broad shoulders
with the flat of one hand. His eyes turned in his head,
from which now Phoibos Apollo struck off the helmet,
and it rolled away, clattering, under the horses' hoofs
crest, visor, and all, its horsehair plumes besmirched
with blood and dust. Never till then had the gods
allowed that crested helmet to be besmirched with dust,
when it guarded the head and fine brow of a godlike man,
Achilles; but now Zeus made a present of it to Hektōr
to wear on his head, though his own doom was very near.
In Patroklos's hands the far-shadowing spear, so huge,
so solid, bronze-tipped, was all broken, and from his shoulders
the fringed shield with its baldric fell to the ground,
and his corselet the son of Zeus, Lord Apollo, now undid.
Delusion clouded his mind, his bright limbs were unstrung,
he stood in a daze, and was struck from behind, at close range,
midway between the shoulders, with a sharp-edged spear,
by Euphorbos, Pánthoös's son, a Dardanian, who excelled
all those of his age as a spearman and horseman, and at running:
twenty men by now he'd dislodged from driving their horses
since he first arrived with his chariot, still a novice at warfare.
He it was first threw his spear at you, horseman Patroklos,
yet did not kill you, but pulled his ash spear from your flesh
and ran back into the ranks, did not stay there to face
Patroklos, even unarmed, in hand-to-hand combat,
while Patroklos too, overcome by the god's blow and the spear,
turned back towards the ranks of his comrades, avoiding fate.

But Hektōr, when he perceived great-hearted Patroklos
backing off, after taking a hit from the sharp-edged bronze,
came up close to him through the ranks, and with his spear
stabbed into his nether belly, driving the bronze clean through:
and he fell with a thud, greatly grieving the troops of the Achaians.
As a lion brings down an unwearying boar in battle

when the two of them up in the mountains battle with high resolve
for a small spring from which both are determined to drink,
and the boar pants hard, but the lion's might prevails—
from Menoitios's valiant son, when he'd killed so many,
Priam's son Hektōr now took the life with his spear,
close up, and, boastfully, over him spoke winged words:
"Patroklos, you imagined you were going to sack our city,
and take the day of freedom from the women of Troy,
and carry them off in your ships to your dear fatherland.
You fool! It was for their protection Hektōr's swift horses
galloped out to battle, and with the spear I myself,
outstanding among warlike Trojans, am here to ward off
the day of doom from them: but you the vultures will eat here,
you wretch! And brave though he is, Achilles couldn't save you—
he stayed behind, but I'm sure he gave you marching orders—
'Don't you come back to me, Patroklos, master horseman,
at the hollow ships, before you've sliced up the tunic of Hektōr,
killer of men, round his chest, left it bloody.' That's how, I fancy,
he spoke to you, thus persuading your mind in its mindlessness."

Then, strength ebbing, you answered him, horseman Patroklos:
"Go on, boast big while you can! You were handed this triumph
by Apollo and Zeus, son of Kronos, who overwhelmed me
easily: they themselves removed the gear from my shoulders.
If twenty men such as you had confronted me, all
would have perished here, quelled by my spear! Oh no, it was
deadly fate and the son of Lētō that slew me, and of mortals
Euphorbos: you're only the third hand in my killing.
And another thing I'll tell you, and you lay it to heart:
You yourself are not for a long life: now already
death's moved in close beside you, your all-mastering fate
to be slain at the hands of Achilles, Aiakos's peerless grandson."

When he'd spoken thus, death's end enshrouded him,
and the soul fled from his limbs, fluttered down to Hādēs
bewailing its fate, youth and manhood all abandoned.
Yet still Hektōr harangued him, dead though he was:
"Patroklos, why do you prophesy sheer destruction for me?
Who knows if perhaps Achilles, fair-haired Thetis's son,
may, struck by my spear, lose his life before that happens?"

So saying, he tugged out his bronze spear from the wound,
with one foot on Patroklos's chest, eased him backward off the spear.
Then he and his spear were gone, pursuing Automedōn,
the godlike henchman of Aiakos's swift-footed grandson,
very zealous to hit him; but him the swift horses carried away,
immortal steeds, that the gods gave to Pēleus, glorious gifts.

Book 17

It did not escape Atreus's son, the warlike Menelaös,
that Patroklos had been brought down in the struggle with the Trojans:
through the front ranks he went, armored in gleaming bronze,
and stood there, straddling his corpse, as over her first-born
calf its mother stands lowing, plaintively, having never
given birth before: so over Patroklos fair-haired Menelaös
stood, holding before him his spear and well-balanced shield,
ready to kill any fighter that came out and confronted him.

Nor was Pánthoös's son, of the good ash spear, indifferent
to the fall of peerless Patroklos; he came and stood
near warlike Menelaös, and thus addressed him:
"Atreus's son Menelaös, Zeus's nursling, leader of armies,
yield ground now, leave the corpse, forego these bloodstained spoils!
No man prior to me of the Trojans or their famed allies
put a spear in Patroklos during the grind of battle,
so you now allow me to win true glory among the Trojans,
or else I'll let fly and hit you, rob you of honey-sweet life."
Deeply stirred, fair-haired Menelaös answered him thus:
"Zeus, Father, such over-proud boasting is most unseemly!
Of neither lion nor leopard is the rage so great,
nor of the deadly wild boar—in whose breast the greatest
fury exults in its strength—as is the arrogant spirit
of Pánthoös's sons, they of the good ash spear! Not even
Hyperēnōr, the mighty one, the tamer of horses,
had any joy of his youth, when he mocked and confronted me,
called me the feeblest warrior among the Danaäns:
not on his own feet, I tell you, did he make his way back home
to gladden his dear wife and his devoted parents!
Just so will I unstring your strength, if you persist
in standing against me: back off, I tell you, into the crowd,
don't try confrontation, get out before you suffer
some hurt: what's done even a fool can recognize."

So he spoke, but did not persuade him: Euphorbos replied:
"Now indeed, Menelaös, Zeus's nursling, you'll pay the price

for the brother of mine you killed: you rant boastfully over him,
his wife you left a widow in her new bridal chamber,
unspeakable grief and sorrow you brought on his parents!
Surely for them in their misery I could be an easing of grief
if I bring them your head and your armor, lay these
in the hands of Pánthoös and of noble Phrontis!
No longer shall this struggle between us go untested
or unfought, whether it end in victory or in flight."

That said, Euphorbos struck Menelaös's well-balanced shield,
but the bronze failed to break through, its point was turned
by the strong shield; then Atreus's son Menelaös
in his turn attacked with the bronze, praying to Zeus the Father,
and as Euphorbos drew back, speared him hard at the base
of his throat, leaning into the thrust, relying on his strong fist;
and clean through his delicate neck the spear point passed.
He fell with a thud, and his armor rattled upon him.
Blood soaked his hair that was such as the Graces have—
those locks wasp-waisted with spirals of gold and silver.[1]
As a man cultivates an olive tree's flourishing slip
in a lonely spot, where spring water wells up in abundance—
a fine, healthy sapling, and breezes from every quarter
make it shiver, and soon it bursts out in white blossom,
but then a sudden gale comes, with abundance of storm winds,
tears it up root and all and lays it out flat on the ground:
in such wise Pánthoös's son, the ashen-speared Euphorbos,
was slain by Atreus's son Menelaös, stripped of his armor.
As some mountain-bred lion, confident in its strength,
from a grazing herd snatches a cow, the best one there—
when he's caught her, he first breaks her neck with his powerful teeth,
then gulps down her blood, along with all her innards,
tearing her flesh, while all round him hunting dogs and herdsmen
make much noise, but from a distance, not being minded
to confront him, for pale fear has them in its grip:
just so the heart in the breast of no Trojan dared

1. "Golden spirals apparently for binding the hair are common in sub-Mycenean and Geometric graves," Edwards 1991 notes (67). The verb ἐσφήκωντο (*esphēkōnto*), here only in Homer, means to be pinched in like a wasp's waist. It has also been suggested that color—golden/yellow bands on black hair—may have contributed to the wasp image.

to come out and confront illustrious Menelaös.
Easily, then, would the famed arms of Euphorbos
have been borne off by Atreus's son, had not Phoibos Apollo
—in a man's likeness, as Mentēs, the Kikōnians' leader—
begrudging this, stirred against him Hektōr, peer of swift Arēs,
whom he addressed as follows, in winged words: "Hektōr,
while you're vainly chasing a quarry you'll never catch,
the horses of Aiakos's warrior grandson—hard
are they for any mortal to master or to drive,
save only Achilles, who had an immortal mother—
meanwhile Menelaös, the warlike son of Atreus,
straddling Patroklos's corpse, has slain the best of the Trojans,
Pánthoös's son Euphorbos, cut short his fighting spirit."

So he spoke, and went back, a god to the struggle of mortals.
Bitter grief now spread round Hektōr's dark spirit: he glanced
along the ranks, and at once perceived both men, the one
stripping off the famed armor, the other one lying there,
blood trickling out of the stab wound. Then Hektōr gave
a sharp cry, strode out through the foremost fighters, armed
in gleaming bronze, like Hēphaistos's unquenchable flame.
Nor did Atreus's son miss that sharp cry: deeply perturbed
he now communed with his own great-hearted spirit:
"Ah, me, if I leave that fine armor behind, and Patroklos too,
who lies here dead in his quest to restore my honor,
any Danaän who sees it, I fear, will blame my action!
But if, single-handed, I take on Hektōr and the Trojans
out of shame, I fear they'll surround me, being many against one—
bright-helmeted Hektōr's bringing every last Trojan here.
Yet why should my heart and I be debating any of this?
When, against heaven's will, a man chooses to fight with a mortal
whom some god honors, at once great trouble rolls over him.
So, no Danaän will be indignant on seeing me retreat
before Hektōr, since he's fighting with a god as his backer.
Yet, if I could only find Aias of the fine war cry, then
we two might turn back and battle it out, even
against divine will, in the hope of rescuing the corpse
for Achilles, Pēleus's son: that would be the best of evils."

Meanwhile, as he was pondering thus in his mind and spirit,
the Trojan ranks advanced, with Hektōr leading them.

Menelaös began to retreat now, abandoning the corpse,
but constantly looking back, like a bearded lion
that dogs and men are chasing away from the cattle pen
with spears and shouting—the bold spirit in his breast
is chilled, and reluctantly he slinks off from the farmstead:
so fair-haired Menelaös moved away from Patroklos.
But on reaching his comrades' division he stood there, looking round,
attempting to find great Aias, Telamōn's son,
and quickly located him, at the far left side of the battle,
encouraging his companions, urging them on to fight,
because of the awesome fear put in them by Phoibos Apollo.
He set off at a run, reached him quickly, addressed him thus:
"Aias my friend, come with me, we must hurry to save
dead Patroklos—at least let's rescue his body for Achilles—
his naked body: his armor bright-helmeted Hektōr holds."

So speaking he roused the spirit of warlike Aias:
through the front-line fighters he strode, Menelaös with him.
Now Hektōr had stripped Patroklos of his famed battle gear,
and was dragging him off to cut his head from his shoulders
with the sharp bronze, and leave his body for Trojan dogs;
but up came Aias, behind his towering shield,
and Hektōr retreated into the body of his comrades,
boarded his chariot, turned the famed armor over
for the Trojans to take to the city, to bring him great glory.
But Aias with his broad shield covered Menoitios's son,
and stood there like a lion protecting its young,
one that hunters meet as it leads these cubs in the forest,
and it bears itself proudly, glorying in its strength,
hooding its eyes with the down-drawn skin of its brow:
just so did Aias bestride the hero Patroklos, while
on the other side Atreus's son, the warlike Menelaös,
stood there, nursing great sorrow within his breast.

And now
Glaukos, son of Hippolochos, the Lycian warriors' leader,
scowling darkly at Hektōr, upbraided him with harsh words:
"Hektōr, so handsome, but sadly wanting in battle—
this fine reputation of yours conceals a girlish coward!
You'd better start thinking now of some way to save your city
and citadel on your own, helped only by native Trojans,

for at least of the Lycians not one man will turn out to fight
the Danaäns over this city, since I now see there's no thanks
for struggling, without respite, forever against the foe!
How would you rescue a lesser fighter, one of the crowd,
you callous brute, when you leave Sarpēdōn—your guest,
your comrade—there for the Argives, to be their prey, their booty?
Often enough he helped you, your city and yourself,
while he lived—yet now you don't dare keep the dogs off him!
So now, if my Lycian troops will obey my orders,
we're going home, and for Troy sheer ruin is like to follow!
If only that dauntless courage was in the Trojans,
unflinching, that comes to men who, for their country's sake,
shoulder the strife and the struggle with their foes,
then soon enough would we drag off Patroklos to Ilion—
and if this man came, dead, to King Priam's great city,
when we'd dragged him out of the battle, then quickly enough
would the Argives surrender Sarpēdōn's fine battle gear
and we'd bring the man himself back into Ilion;
for such a fighter is he whose squire has been slain, the best
of these Argives by their ships—he and his veterans!
But you lacked the courage to stand up, face to face,
against great-hearted Aias, amid enemies' battle cries,
and fight him head on, since he's a better man than you."

Scowling darkly, bright-helmeted Hektōr replied:
"Why, Glaukos, being who you are, have you spoken so arrogantly?
My friend, I once regarded you as the most sensible man
of all those who have their homes in rich-soiled Lycia;
but now what you say makes me doubt your sense entirely—
when you claim that I failed to stand against huge Aias!
I tell you, I don't fear battle or the hoof beats of horses—
but the mind of Zeus of the aegis is always too strong,
he scares even the valiant, deprives men of victory
without effort, and as easily stirs them up to fight.
Come, friend, stand by me, watch my actions, see whether,
as you proclaim, I'm a coward the whole day through,
or whether many a Danaän, however fierce a fighter,
I'll stand off from battling over the dead Patroklos."

So saying, he called out to the Trojans, in a carrying voice:
"Trojans! Lycians! You Dardanian hand-to-hand fighters!

Be men, my friends! Remember your fighting spirit,
until I put on the armor of peerless Achilles, the splendid
gear that I stripped from mighty Patroklos when I slew him!"

Having spoken thus, bright-helmeted Hektōr withdrew
from war's deadly turmoil, ran fast, overtook his comrades
who were not far off yet, hastened on swift feet after
those bearing towards the city the famed armor of Pēleus's son.
Then he halted, away from the grievous conflict, changed
his armor: his own he gave, to be taken to sacred Ilion,
to the Trojans, lovers of warfare, and himself put on
the immortal gear of Achilles, Pēleus's son, that the heavenly
gods gave to his father, and he bequeathed, when old,
to his son; but the son did not grow old in his father's armor.

Now when from far off Zeus the cloud-gatherer saw him
arming himself in the war gear of Pēleus's godlike son,
he shook his head and said, addressing his own heart:
"Ah, wretched man: death has no place in your thoughts,
near though it is to you: you're putting on the immortal
gear of a prince among men, before whom others, too, tremble.
His comrade you've slain, a man as gentle as he was strong,
and improperly stripped the armor from his head and shoulders.
Still, for now I'll allow you great power, in compensation
for the fact that no way are you coming back from battle,
nor will Andromachē get from you the famed arms of Pēleus's son."

So the son of Kronos spoke, and, nodding his dark brows,
made the armor fit Hektōr's body, and there entered him then
fearsome Enyalian Arēs, and his limbs were filled with inner
courage and strength. Then he went in among the far-famed
allies, shouting his war cry, and displayed himself to them all,
agleam in the battle gear of Pēleus's great-hearted son,
urging on every man he approached with his winged words—
Mesthlēs and Glaukos, Medōn, Thersilochos,
Hippothoös, Deisēnōr, and Asteropaios,
Phorkys and Chromios, the bird-augur Ennomos—
these he approached, to these his winged words were addressed:
"Hear me, you countless tribes of allies that dwell around us!
It was not in search of mere numbers, or because I lacked them,
that I brought each one of you here from your cities, but rather

for you to rescue the Trojans' wives and children,
of your own will, for me, from these war-loving Achaians.
It's with this aim that I'm straining my people's resources
for gifts and food to keep strong the spirit in you all!
So let each man make straight for the foe, whether to perish
or come safely through: that's the sweet embrace of warfare.
And whoever drags Patroklos, dead though he is for sure,
back among the horse-breaker Trojans, and Aias yields to him,
half my booty I'll share with him, keep only half
myself: for his glory will be as great as mine."

So he spoke: they charged, full force, straight at the Danaäns,
spears raised, the hearts within them brimming with hope
that they'd drag the corpse away from Aias, Telamōn's son—
the fools, for over that body he robbed many of their life.
Yet now Aias spoke to Menelaös of the fine war cry, saying:
"My friend Menelaös, Zeus's nursling, no longer do I hope
that the two of us will ever come home safe from this war—
it's not so much the corpse of Patroklos that concerns me,
which all too soon will glut the dogs and vultures of Troy:
it's my own head I'm afraid for, lest ill befall it,
and yours as well, for a cloud of war—I mean Hektōr—
now enshrouds everything: it's sheer destruction confronts us.
Still, call to the Danaäns' leaders: someone may hear us."

So he spoke: Menelaös of the fine war cry did not
ignore him, called out to the Danaäns in a carrying voice:
"Friends, leaders and rulers of the Argives, you
who with Atreus's sons, Agamemnōn and Menelaös,
drink at the public cost, who, each of you, issue orders
to your people, who from Zeus have honor and glory!
Hard it is for me to distinguish each individual leader,
so vast the strife of war that's flared up—so let each man
advance unnamed, but with fury in his heart
that Patroklos should end as a plaything for the dogs of Troy."

So he spoke: Oïleus's son, swift Aias, heard him clearly.
He was the first who came to him, at a run, through the fighting,
and after him Idomeneus, and Idomeneus's comrade
Mērionēs, the equal of Enyalios, killer of men.

As for the rest—who, from memory, could reel off all the names
of those who followed, who woke the Achaians' battle spirit?

The Trojans charged in a massed body, Hektōr leading.
As at the outflow of some rain-fed river, giant
waves come roaring against the current, and all around
the coast's headlands re-echo as the salt sea breaks in foam,
with such huge clamor the Trojans came on. But still
the Achaians stood steadfast around Menoitios's son,
united in purpose, fenced with bronze shields: upon them
Kronos's son shed thick mist, hid their gleaming helmets,
since, even before, he'd not hated the son of Menoitios,
the squire of Aiakos's grandson, while he still lived; so now,
hating the thought of his becoming the prey of his Trojan
enemies' dogs, Zeus stirred up his comrades to defend him.

At first, the Trojans thrust back the sharp-eyed Achaians,
who retreated, leaving the corpse. Not a single one of them
did these spirited Trojans spear, though they longed to, but
started dragging the body away. Yet for a short while only
were the Achaians to hold off, being quickly rallied
by Aias, a man who for handsome looks and war craft
surpassed all Danaäns, after Pēleus's peerless son.
Through the front-line fighters he stormed, in prowess resembling
a wild boar, that in hill country easily scatters dogs
and vigorous youths as it charges, swerving, through the glens:
just so lordly Telamōn's son, illustrious Aias,
easily, once in among them, scattered the Trojan ranks
that had closed in over Patroklos, determined above all
to drag him back to their city, and so win glory.

Hippothoös now, Pelasgian Lēthos's illustrious son,
was dragging the corpse by one foot through the grind of battle
with his baldric lashed fast around the ankle's tendons,
delighting the Trojans and Hektōr; but swiftly disaster
struck him, that no one, though desperate to, could ward off:
out from the crowd darted Telamōn's son, closed in,
and hit him, right through his bronze cheek-pieced helmet,
which, horsehair crest and all, split round the spear point,
struck by a heavy spear from a powerful hand: the brains,

all blood-bespattered, shot out from the wound along
the spear's socket, his strength was loosened, his hands let fall
great-hearted Patroklos's foot. It fell to the ground
and lay there. He fell prone, close by it, on the corpse,
far from rich-soiled Lárisa, and never repaid his parents
the cost of his upbringing: brief indeed was his life,
cut off short by the spear of mighty-spirited Aias.
Hektōr let fly in turn at Aias with his gleaming spear,
but Aias, watching him closely, avoided the bronze-tipped
shaft, a near miss; it hit Schedios, great-hearted Iphitos's son,
best by far of the Phokians, who in famous Panopeus
had his dwelling, and reigned as king over many subjects.
Hektōr hit him under the collar-bone, in the mid-part: the bronze
spear point drove right through, emerged at the shoulder's base.
He fell with a thud, and his armor rattled upon him.
Next Aias hit Phorkys—the warlike son of Phainōps,
who was standing over Hippothoös—in the mid-belly,
broke the plate of his corselet, so that his guts spilled out
through the bronze: in the dust he fell, hand clawing the earth.

Then the front-line fighters and illustrious Hektōr gave ground,
and the Argives, cheering loudly, dragged off the corpses—Phorkys,
Hippothoös—and started stripping the gear from their shoulders.

Now would the warlike Achaians have once more driven the Trojans,
undone by their lack of spirit, back up to Ilion,
and the Argives would have won glory—even beyond the measure
approved by Zeus—through their forceful strength; but Apollo
himself roused up Aineias, assuming a herald's likeness—
that of Periphas, Ēpytos's son: in Aineias's aged father's
house he'd grown old as a herald, was on friendly terms with him.
In his likeness now Zeus's son Apollo addressed Aineias:

"Aineias, how, against a god's will, could you all
safeguard steep Ilion? I've seen other men who relied
on their forceful strength, on their bravery, on their common
people, even when their numbers were very few;
but now it's for us Zeus wants victory, not for the Danaäns—
yet nevertheless you're scared witless, refuse to fight!"

So he spoke: Aineias, face to face with him, recognized
Apollo, the deadly archer, and shouted to Hektōr, saying:

"Hektōr, and you other leaders of the Trojans and allies!
This is a shameful business, that by the warlike Achaians
we're being driven back up to Ilion, undone by our lack of spirit!
But one of the gods just approached me, who says that Zeus,
the all-highest counselor, is our backer in this battle!
So let's go straight for the Danaäns, not leave them undisturbed
to carry the corpse of Patroklos back to their ships!"

So he spoke,
then charged far beyond the front-line fighters, and stood there.
The Trojans rallied to him, confronting the Achaians,
and Aineias with his spear now wounded Leiōkritos,
Arisbas's son, Lykomēdēs' worthy comrade;
and Lykomēdēs, fierce warrior, in sorrow for his death
advanced to close quarters, let fly with his gleaming spear,
hit Hippasos's son Apisaōn, a shepherd of men,
in his liver, below the midriff, and at once unstrung his knees—
Apisaōn, who'd come out there from rich-soiled Paiōnia,
and after Asteropaios was Paiōnia's finest fighter.
Asteropaios, fierce warrior, in sorrow for his death
likewise charged forward, eager to challenge the Danaäns,
but no longer could, for their shields now fenced them in
as they encircled Patroklos, spears couched before them,
while Aias ranged round them all, with endless directions—
that none of them should give ground, fall back from the corpse,
or come pushing forward in front of the other Achaians to fight,
but keep close order round the body, battle hand-to-hand.
Such were huge Aias's orders: the earth grew sodden
with dark red blood, and jostling men dropped dead
in mingled heaps, Trojans and their proud allies,
and Danaäns too: though these did not avoid bloodshed,
far fewer of them were falling: they took constant care
in the crush of battle to save one another from death.

So they battled on like fire, and you could not tell
if the sun and the moon were still in their place, intact,
for a dark mist now enshrouded all the bravest who stood
and fought in the struggle around Menoitios's dead son,
while the rest of the Trojans and well-greaved Achaians engaged,
unimpeded, in the clear air, with the sun's keen rays
spread over them, and not one single cloud to be seen

above plain or mountain. These fought with occasional breaks,
avoiding each other's grief-laden missiles, and standing
well apart, whereas those in the center were under duress
from the conflict as well as the darkness, all the bravest worn down
by the pitiless bronze. But two men who'd not yet learned—
Antilochos, Thrasymēdēs, famous fighters both—
of peerless Patroklos's death, and thought he was still
alive, and battling the Trojans there in the foremost ranks,
were now—though alert for their comrades' death or rout—
fighting off at a distance, as Nestōr had told them to do
while urging them into battle, away from the black ships.

All day long the great struggle of their grievous conflict
raged on, and endlessly with the sweat of action
every man's knees and calves, and the feet below them,
and his arms and eyes, were bespattered, as they fought
over the noble squire of Aiakos's swift-footed grandson.
As when a man consigns the hide of a hefty bull
to his people for stretching—one already made supple with fat—
and they take it and all stand round in a circle and stretch it,
so that at once the moisture goes out, while the fat sinks in,
with many hands pulling, and the whole hide's surface is stretched—
so this way and that both sides were tugging the corpse
in a narrow space, and they all were hopeful at heart
that they'd get it away: the Trojans to Ilion, the Achaians
to the hollow ships; and around it a contest arose, so fierce
that neither Arēs, driver of armies, nor yet Athēnē
could have made light of it, however great their rage.

Such was the grim labor of men and horses that Zeus
stretched taut that day over Patroklos. Nor did noble
Achilles yet have any knowledge of Patroklos's death,
for far distant from the swift ships the conflict raged,
beneath the Trojans' ramparts. So he never expected
that Patroklos would die, thought that once he'd reached Troy's gates
he'd come back alive; for it did not enter his mind
that Patroklos would try to sack Troy, with or without him,
having often heard that from his mother, in private talk,
when she brought him news of mighty Zeus's intentions;
while now indeed his mother did not tell him the great disaster,

that his comrade, of all men the dearest to him, had been slain.

The combatants round the corpse, sharp spears in hand,
pressed on without pause, kept up their killing of one another,
and of the bronze-corseleted Achaians thus would one declare:
"Friends, we'd achieve no glory by going back at this point
to the hollow ships: here and now let the black earth gape
for us all—far better indeed that would be for us,
if we must surrender this man to the Trojan horse breakers,
to drag back to their city and so win glory."

Thus likewise
would one of the great-hearted Trojans declare: "My friends,
even though it may prove our destiny to be slaughtered
beside this man, one and all, let no one give up the battle!"

This was how they spoke, arousing each man's passion.
So they fought on, and an iron clatter went up
through the still upper air till it reached the brazen heavens.
But the horses of Aiakos's grandson, now far from the conflict,
were weeping, since first they learned that their charioteer
had been laid low in the dust by Hektōr, killer of men.
Automedōn, valiant son of Diōrēs, again and again
lashed them with blows from his swift whip, many times
tried shifting them with kind words, many times with curses;
yet neither back to the ships by the broad Hellespont
were they willing to go, nor yet to join the Achaians in battle,
but as firm as stands the marker that's set up over
the burial mound of some dead man or woman, so they
stood immovable, still hitched to the exquisite chariot,
heads bowed down to the ground, while the warm tears
flowed from their eyelids earthward as they shed them,
mourning their charioteer, and dust soiled the rich manes
that streamed down from the yoke-pad, both sides of the yoke.
Their mourning was viewed, with compassion, by Kronos's son,
who shook his head while communing with his own heart:
"Wretched pair, why, oh, why, did we give you to King Pēleus,
a mortal, when you yourselves are immortal and ageless?
Was it to bring you sorrows among these wretched humans?
For surely there's nothing more pitiable than man
among all the creature that breathe and creep on this earth!

But never behind you, upon that subtly worked chariot,
will Priam's son Hektōr mount: I shall not let him!
Is it not enough that he has the armor, brags over it?
Into your knees and spirit I'll channel strength,
to bring Automedōn also back safe from the fighting
to the hollow ships, since I'll still bestow glory on the Trojans,
to go on killing until they reach the well-benched ships,
and the sun goes down, and sacred darkness comes on."

So saying, he breathed great power into the horses: they both
shook off the dust from their manes to the ground, and lightly
took their swift chariot in among Trojans and Achaians,
while behind them Automedōn, though grieving for his comrade,
fought on, swooped with his team like a vulture after geese:
easily would he retreat from the Trojans' noisy conflict,
easily make his charge, force a passage through the crowd.
Yet not one man did he bring down during his urgent pursuit,
since no way was he able, alone in that headlong chariot,
both to attack with a spear and rein in his speeding horses.
In the end a comrade of his observed his behavior—
Alkimedōn, son of Laerkēs and Haimōn's grandson,
and getting behind the chariot now spoke to Automedōn:
"Automedōn, which of the gods has put such profitless counsel
into your mind? Who's so robbed you of common sense
that you're fighting among the foremost Trojan troops
alone? Your comrade's dead, and his armor—Achilles' own—
Hektōr himself now wears on his shoulders, flaunts it!"

To him Automedōn, son of Diōrēs, responded:
"Alkimedōn, what other Achaian save you is able
to curb and control the might of these immortal steeds—
except for Patroklos, the gods' own equal in counsel,
while he still lived? But now death and his fate have claimed him.
So you take from me the whip and shining reins,
and I'll dismount from the chariot, join the fighting."
So he spoke. Alkimedōn boarded the rescue-swift chariot,
quickly gathering in his hands both the reins and the whip,
while Automedōn jumped down. Illustrious Hektōr saw them,
and at once said to Aineias, who was standing near by:
"Aineias, counselor of the bronze-corseleted Trojans,
I've just seen the team of Aiakos's swift-footed grandson

showing up in the battle line with incompetent charioteers!
These two horses I'd hope to capture, if you in your heart
are agreeable, since if the two of us went at them
they wouldn't dare to stand firm, to face us in battle."

So he spoke, and Anchīsēs' fine son did not disregard him:
the pair strode forward, shoulders hooded with oxhide—
dried, stiff, with thick bronze hammered upon it—
and with them went both Chromios and the godlike Arētos,
hearts brimming with hopeful expectation that they'd now
kill the two men and drive off their strong-necked horses—
fools that they were, for they wouldn't come back without bloodshed
from Automedōn, who now was praying to Zeus, the Father,
his dark heart within him filled with courage and strength.
Quickly he spoke to Alkimedōn, his trusty comrade:
"Alkimedōn, don't keep the horses any distance from me—
let their breath fall close on my back, for I don't suppose
Hektōr, the son of Priam, will be stayed from his raging might
till he either mounts behind Achilles' fine-maned horses
after killing us both, and routing the rank and file
of the Argives—or else himself is slain in the front line."

So saying, he called out to both Aiases and Menelaös:
"Aiases, leaders of Argives, and you, Menelaös!
Entrust the body to those who are the best men we have,
to stand around it and fend off these crowding assailants—
But we're alive! Come help us, keep the ruthless day from us,
for here, bearing hard down on us in grievous battle
are Aineias and Hektōr, the Trojans' best fighting men!
Still, the outcome of all this lies on the knees of the gods—
I too will let fly my spear: for the rest, let Zeus decide!"

So saying, he poised and threw his far-shadowing spear,
and hit the well-balanced shield of Arētos, that failed
to stop its passage: clean through the bronze it drove,
and pierced through the baldric into the nether belly.
As when a strong young man, wielding a sharpened axe,
lands a blow behind the horns of a country ox, cuts clean
through the tendon, and the ox starts forward, falls,
so Arētos jerked forward, then fell on his back: the spear,
razor-sharp, quivered deep in his innards, unstrung his limbs.

Now Hektōr with his bright spear let fly at Automedōn,
but Automedōn was watching, and avoided the bronze spear
by ducking down forward, so that its long shaft
stuck in the ground behind him, its butt-end quivering,
and there mighty Arēs took its power away from it.
They'd have faced off with their swords then, fought hand to hand,
had the two Aiases not parted them—both hot for battle—
coming out through the ranks in response to their comrade's call,
so that from fear of them both Hektōr and Aineias,
together with godlike Chromios, retreated once more,
leaving Arētos behind, mortally wounded, still
lying there. Automedōn now, the peer of speedy Arēs,
stripped off Arētos's armor and boasted over him, saying:
"Indeed, if only a little, I've eased my heart of its grief
for Menoitios's son, though it was a lesser man that I killed."

So saying, he picked up the bloodstained trappings, put them
in the chariot, climbed aboard it himself, his feet and hands
above them all bloody, like a lion that's devoured a bull.

Once more over Patroklos the grinding battle was stretched,
tear-laden and agonizing: Athēnē stirred the conflict,
coming down from the sky, dispatched by far-seeing Zeus
to urge on the Danaäns, for by now his mind had been changed.
As Zeus from heaven stretches a rainbow's shimmering arc
as a portent for mortals—it may be either of war,
or of some chill winter storm, that stops men from working
outdoors on the land, and distresses their flocks—just so
Athēnē, enshrouding herself in a dark cloud, now ranged through
the Achaian forces, began spurring each man on.
First, with encouraging words she addressed the son
of Atreus, brave Menelaös, since he was near at hand,
assuming the form of Phoinix, and his unwearying voice:
"For you indeed, Menelaös, there will be sure disgrace
and shame, if lordly Achilles' trusty comrade
is torn apart by quick dogs beneath the walls of Troy!
So hold your position firmly, encourage all your men."

Menelaös of the fine war cry made her this answer:
"Phoinix, old daddy, aged sir, if only Athēnē
would give me strength, fend off the oncoming missiles,

then I'd be ready to stand by Patroklos, protect him,
for his death touched my heart to the quick. But Hektōr's
strength is like fire's, he never rests from slaughtering
with the bronze, since it's to him Zeus now grants glory."

So he spoke, and the goddess, grey-eyed Athēnē, rejoiced,
since it was to her, before all other gods, that he'd prayed;
and she put power into his knees and shoulders,
and filled his breast with the aggressiveness of the fly:
however often swatted away from a man's skin, still
it persists in biting him, so sweet it finds human blood.
Such the daring with which she flooded his dark spirit:
he went and stood over Patroklos, let fly his gleaming spear.
Now among the Trojans there was one Podēs, Ēëtiōn's son,
both wealthy and a good fighter, and honored by Hektōr,
above all the people, as his friend and dinner-companion.
Him fair-haired Menelaös struck on the baldric as
he leapt into flight; the bronze made its way clean through.
He fell with a thud, and Atreus's son Menelaös
dragged his corpse from the Trojans into his comrades' ranks.

Then Apollo intervened, gave encouragement to Hektōr,
in the likeness of Phainōps, Asios's son, who of all
his guest-friends was dearest him, whose house was in Abydos.
In his likeness the deadly archer Apollo now addressed him:
"Hektōr, what other Achaian will be afraid of you, now
you've fled before Menelaös, who—at least in the past—
seemed a faint-hearted fighter? Yet single-handed
he's snatched a corpse from the Trojans, and killed your trusty
comrade, a good front-line fighter—Podēs, Ēëtiōn's son."

So he spoke, and a black cloud of grief enshrouded Hektōr,
and he strode through the front-line fighters, clad in gleaming
bronze.
Now, too, the son of Kronos took his aegis—tasseled,
glittering bright—enveloped Ida in clouds,
sent lightning, made a huge thunderclap, shook the aegis,
gave victory to the Trojans, put the Achaians to flight.

First to panic and flee was Boiōtian Pēneleōs,
who, turning to face the enemy, was hit in the upper shoulder,
a glancing blow, yet Poulydamas's spear point nicked

the bone (it was he who'd speared him, at close range).
Lēïtos too, great-hearted Alektryōn's son, was wounded,
in the wrist, at close quarters, by Hektōr, put out of the fight:
he backed off, glancing round, since he no longer hoped,
spear in good hand, to do battle with the Trojans.
As Hektōr chased after Lēïtos, Idomeneus struck
his corselet, upon the chest by the nipple; but the long
spear shaft broke off at the socket, so that the Trojans
raised a loud cheer. Now Hektōr had a shot at Idomeneus,
Deukaliōn's son, as he stood in his chariot—just missed him,
but hit the charioteer and comrade of Mēriones,
Koiranos, who'd accompanied him from well-built Lyktos.
Idomeneus had at first come on foot from the curved ships,
and would have yielded a great triumph to the Trojans
had Koiranos not quickly driven up his swift horses, come
as a light of deliverance to him, warding off his pitiless day,
but died himself at the hands of Hektōr, killer of men,
who hit him below the ear, in under the jawline. The spear
dashed his teeth out by their roots, cut his tongue at the midpoint.
He fell from the chariot, dropped the reins on the ground.
Mēriones bent down, gathered them up in his own hands
from the earth, and addressed Idomeneus:

"Use the whip now
till you get to the swift ships! You yourself can recognize
that the upper hand is no longer with the Achaians."

So he spoke, and Idomeneus lashed the fine-maned horses
back to the hollow ships, for fear had seized his heart.

Nor did great-hearted Aias and Menelaös fail to see
that Zeus was backing the Trojans, turning the tide of battle.
Of these it was Telamōn's son, great Aias, who spoke first:
"What's to be done? By this time even the merest idiot
could figure that Zeus himself, the Father, is for the Trojans:
all their missiles, whoever throws them, coward or hero,
hit their target—Zeus anyway steers them straight—but for us
every man's shot falls uselessly to the ground!
So let's think up a plan, the best way we can contrive
to drag that corpse out of the fray, and as for ourselves,
manage to get back home, a great joy to our comrades,

who must be distressed by the scene here, who don't believe
that the rage and invincible hands of Hektōr, killer of men,
can now be stood off, are sure they'll descend on the black ships!
If only there were some comrade to take a message posthaste
to Pēleus's son, since I don't think he's yet received
the sorrowful news that his own dear comrade is slain.
But such a one I can't see amongst the Achaians,
since they're all shrouded in mist—themselves and their horses!
Zeus, Father, rescue the Achaians' sons from this mist,
make the sky clear, let us see with our eyes; if you mean
to kill us, if that's your pleasure, at least do it in daylight."

So he spoke: the Father pitied him as he wept,
and forthwith scattered the darkness, drove the mist away:
the sun shone on them, the battle was all now in clear view.
Then Aias addressed Menelaös of the fine war cry:
"Take a look, Menelaös, Zeus's nursling, in case you can spot
Antilochos still alive there, great-hearted Nestōr's son,
and send him, as fast as may be, to warlike Achilles
to tell him his dearest comrade by far has been killed."

So he spoke: Menelaös of the fine war cry did not
disregard him, but went on his way like a lion from a steading,
tired of provoking the dogs and men that won't let him
get in and seize the fattest steer, who are vigilant
the whole night through—yet he, so desperate for meat,
keeps coming, but gets nowhere, has to face a shower
of hunting spears flung by strong hands, and blazing firebrands
before which, for all his eagerness, he shrinks back,
and at dawn goes on his way, his spirit crushed—
so from Patroklos went Menelaös, of the fine war cry,
against his will, for he greatly feared that the Achaians
in their disastrous flight might leave him a prey for his foes.
Repeatedly he adjured Mēriones and both Aiases:
"You Aiases, Argive leaders, and, Mēriones, you too—
each one of you should remember the gentleness of Patroklos—
unhappy soul!—for he knew how to be kind to all men
while he still lived: but now death and destiny have claimed him."

This said, fair-haired Menelaös went on his way,
glancing from side to side like an eagle—which, they say,

has the keenest eyesight of all the sky's winged creatures,
and from it, high though it glides, the hare is not hidden
crouching under a leafy bush, but the eagle swoops
straight down, and having caught it, quickly robs it of life.
Thus then, Menelaös, Zeus's nursling, did your glinting eyes
roam everywhere over the company of your many comrades,
in the hope of discovering Nestōr's son still alive there.
Menelaös soon picked him out—at the far left of the battle,
encouraging his comrades and urging them on to fight—
and went over, and said, standing near him: "Come here,
Antilochos, Zeus's nursling: there's news you need to learn,
distressing news, that I wish had never come about!
By now I think you must know, from what you've seen,
that there's some god's who's rolling disaster upon the Danaäns,
that the Trojans are winning. Slain is the best of the Achaians—
Patroklos, leaving the Danaäns with a huge sense of loss:
so you must run, at once, to the Achaians' ships, bring word
to Achilles, let him quickly bring the body back to his ship—
the naked body: his armor bright-helmeted Hektōr holds."

So he spoke: Antilochos heard his words with horror.
For long he was stricken speechless, while both his eyes
were brimming with tears, and his strong young voice was stilled.
Even so he did not ignore the command of Menelaös:
he set off at a run, gave his gear to his peerless companion
Laodokos, who was turning his whole-hoofed team close by.

So Antilochos's feet bore him, weeping, away from the battle
to bring these evil tidings to Pēleus's son Achilles.
Nor, Menelaös, Zeus's nursling, was your spirit minded
to lend help to those hard-pressed Pylian comrades
whom Antilochos, going, had left with a huge sense of loss.
He sent noble Thrasymēdēs to them, but himself, at a run,
went back to the hero Patroklos, stood once more over him.
Going first up to the Aiases, he told them at once:
"That man you mentioned I've sent on to the swift ships,
to go to swift-footed Achilles, who, even now, I don't think
will come out, enraged though he is at noble Hektōr—
there's no way he would fight without armor against the Trojans.
So let's think up a plan, the best way we can contrive

to drag that corpse out of the fray, and as for ourselves,
to stay clear of death and its spirits amid the Trojans' clamor."

Then great Aias, Telamōn's son, responded to him:
"All you've said, renowned Menelaös, is right and proper.
So you and Mēriones go quickly, shoulder the corpse,
carry it out of the struggle: we two behind you
will do battle with the Trojans and noble Hektōr,
one in name as in spirit, we who in times gone by
have stood firm in sharp battles, each supporting the other."

So he spoke: they gathered the corpse in their arms
and with huge effort heaved it up, while behind them the Trojan
troops all cried out when they saw Achaians lifting the body,
and charged straight at them, like hounds that go for a wounded
wild boar, out in front of their young huntsmen: at first
they keep rushing at it, eager to tear it apart,
but when, trusting its strength, it turns at bay amongst them,
they back off, scatter in panic, one this way, one that—
so the Trojans at first kept after them in a body,
stabbing at them with swords and two-edged spears;
but each time the two Aiases turned and made a stand
against them, then would their color change, and none
now dared to come forward and do battle for the corpse.

So these two, hurriedly, bore the body out of the fighting
back to the hollow ships: against them pressed a conflict
as savage as flames that race to reach a populous city,
set it ablaze in an instant, and houses collapse
in the vast fire that's driven, roaring, by the wind's force—
so against these now the uproar of chariots and spearmen
came beating ceaselessly as they struggled on their way;
but like mules that put their strong backs into the effort
and drag from the mountains, down some steep stony track,
a beam or a huge ship timber, their hearts within them
worn down with sweat and exhaustion as they strive onward—
so these two, straining, bore off the corpse, while behind them
the Aiases held back the foe, as a ridge holds off a flood,
a wooded ridge, that by chance lies right across a plain,
and checks the dangerous onset of even the strongest rivers,
turns all their streams back to wander over the plain,

nor can their mighty torrent ever burst through it—
so the two Aiases constantly stood off the assaults;
yet the Trojans kept on coming, two of them above all,
Aineias, son of Anchīsēs, and illustrious Hektōr.
As a cloud of starlings or jackdaws will take wing, and cry
the alarm when they catch sight of a hawk approaching—
the creature that bodes plain murder for all small birds—
so from Aineias and Hektōr fled the Achaians' young warriors,
crying the alarm, forgetful of their fighting spirit. Many
fine pieces of armor were lost now, round and about the ditch,
as the Danaäns fled; but from warfare there was no respite.

Book 18

So these fought on in the likeness of blazing fire;
but swift-footed Antilochos came to Achilles as messenger,
and found him in front of his high-sterned ships, his mind
foreboding what indeed had already been fulfilled.
Deeply vexed, he addressed his own proud spirit: "Ah me,
why yet again are the long-haired Achaians being driven
over the plain, panic-stricken, back to their ships?
May the gods not be fulfilling that grim grief for my heart
spelled out to me once by my mother, when she told me
that the very best of the Myrmidons, while I still lived,
would flee the light of the sun, at the Trojans' hands!
It must be that he's dead, Menoitios's valiant son!
The fool! I told him, when he'd beaten the fierce fire back,
to return to the ships, not match his strength with Hektōr's."

While he was reflecting thus, in his mind and heart,
the son of illustrious Nestōr came into his presence
shedding hot tears, and announced his unhappy message:
"Alas, son of warlike Pēleus, painful indeed
is the news you must hear, of what never should have been—
Patroklos lies dead, and they're fighting over his body,
his naked body: his armor bright-helmeted Hektōr holds."

So he spoke: a black cloud of grief closed over Achilles.
With both hands he gathered up the dark grimy dust,
scattered it over his head, befouled his handsome features,
and on his fragrant tunic the black ash settled.
There stretched in the dust, great in his greatness he lay;
with his own hands he tore and defiled his hair.
Those maidservants won as spoils by Achilles and Patroklos
shrieked aloud in their heartfelt anguish, ran out of doors,
stood around warlike Achilles, all with their hands
beat on their breasts, the limbs of all were weakened.
Antilochos, opposite them, lamented, shedding tears—
and grasped the hands of Achilles, whose heartfelt groans

made Antilochos fear he might cut his throat with his knife.
So terrible was his outcry, his lady mother heard him,
ensconced in the sea's depths, beside the Old Man, her father,
and shrieked in her turn, and the goddesses gathered round her,
all of Nereus's daughters there were in the sea's depths.
Thither came Glaukē and Thaleia, Kymodokē,
Nēsaia, Speiō, and Thoē, and ox-eyed Haliē,
Kymothoē and Aktaia, along with Limnōreia,
Melitē and Iaira, Agauē, Amphithoē,
Dōtō and Prōtō, Dyamenē and Pherousa,
Dexamenē and Amphinomē and Kallianeira,
Dōris and Panopē and far-famed Galateia,
Nēmertēs, Aspeudēs, and Kallianassa.
With these also came Klyménē, Ianeira, and Ianassa,
Maira and Ōreithyia and fair-tressed Amatheia,
and other Nēreïds from elsewhere in the sea's depths;
and with them the bright cave was filled, and all alike
beat their breasts, and their lamentation was led by Thetis:
"Listen, my Nēreïd sisters, that one and all you may hear
and know well the sum of the sorrows within my heart!
Ah, wretch that I am, most miserable in my splendid offspring!
A son indeed I bore, incomparable and mighty,
preeminent among heroes: like a sapling he shot up,
and when, like a tree on an orchard knoll, I'd reared him,
I sent him out to Ilion in the curved ships, to fight
the Trojans; but now I'll never welcome him back
to his home, he'll never return to the house of Pēleus!
Now, even while he still lives and sees the sunlight,
he has sorrow, nor can I be of help by going to him;
but go I will, to see my dear child, and learn what grief
has come upon him while he's still keeping out of the war."

So saying, she left the cave, and the nymphs went with her,
shedding tears: on each side of them the waves of the sea
broke into surf. When they came to rich-soiled Troy they stepped
out onto the beach one by one, where, in serried ranks,
the Myrmidons' ships were drawn up round swift Achilles.
As he groaned heavily, his lady mother went to him,
gave a sharp cry, then cradled the head of her son
in her arms, and, lamenting, addressed him with winged words:

"Why are you weeping, child? What grief has touched your heart?
Tell me, don't hide it! What you wanted has been fulfilled
by Zeus, what you earlier prayed for, hands uplifted—
that all the Achaians' sons should be huddled by their ships,
in desperate need of you, enduring shameful treatment."

To her, sighing deeply, swift-footed Achilles replied:
"Mother, all this indeed the Olympian managed for me,
but what joy have I from it, now my dear comrade is dead—
Patroklos, whom I honored above all other comrades,
as I would my own life? Him I've lost, while his armor
Hektōr stripped when he'd killed him—a marvel to look at,
fine gear, that the gods gave to Pēleus as glorious gifts
the day they delivered you into the bed of a mortal!
Better you'd stayed among the sea's deathless maidens,
and that Pēleus had brought to his home a mortal bride!
But now there's measureless grief awaiting you too,
for the death of your son, whom you'll not welcome home
ever again: my heart won't let me live on, either,
in mankind's company, unless it happens that Hektōr,
struck down by my spear, shall lose his life first, and pay
for the way he despoiled Patroklos, Menoitios's son."

Thetis then answered him, shedding tears: "Oh, my child,
what you say now means that you're doomed to an early death,
since your own fate awaits you very soon after Hektōr's."

Deeply moved, swift-footed Achilles replied:
"Let me die very soon, then! Clearly I wasn't fated to save
my comrade from being killed—far away from his native soil
he perished, in need of me as his protector from harm!
So now, since I'll not return to my own dear fatherland,
nor have been of the slightest help to either Patroklos
or my other comrades—those many destroyed by noble Hektōr—
but sit, a useless burden on earth, here by the ships—
I, who am such as no other bronze-corseleted Achaian
is as a fighter, though others may be better in council—
would that strife might perish among both gods and men,
and bitter resentment, that stirs even sensible men
to fury, and, far sweeter than honey dripping down,
increases in men's breasts like billowing smoke! Thus, lately,

did the lord of men, Agamemnōn, arouse my resentment. Still,
all this, despite our grief, we'll treat as past and done with,
restraining, because we must, the heart in our breast. So now
I shall come out, to run down that dear soul's killer,
Hektōr; my own death I'll accept whenever Zeus
and the other immortal gods decide to bring it on;
for not even the mighty Hēraklēs could escape death,
dearest of all though he was to Zeus the son of Kronos,
but fate overcame him, and Hērē 's grim resentment.
So I too—if indeed there's a like fate's in wait for me—
shall lie when I'm dead. But for now, let me win high renown,
causing many a one of all those deep-bosomed women—
Trojan, Dardanian—to wipe tears from their tender cheeks
with both hands, to keen ceaselessly, to get it into their heads
that I'd held off too long from battle! So do not try,
though you love me, to stop me fighting: you'll not persuade me."

Then the goddess, Thetis the silver-footed, replied:
"Yes, this is certainly true, child: it's no bad thing
to fend off sheer destruction from hard-pressed comrades.
But your fine battle gear's in Trojan hands, your armor
of gleaming bronze: bright-helmeted Hektōr himself
wears it now on his shoulders, flaunts it—but won't, I think,
glory in it for long, since his own killing's very close.
Do not, for now, go into the turmoil of battle
until with your own eyes you see me return here:
I'll be back in the morning at sunrise, bringing with me
fine new armor for you from the lord Hēphaistos."

With that
she turned away from her son, and having left him
approached her marine sisters, and spoke thus among them:
"You now go back down into the sea's wide gulf,
call on the Old Man of the Sea, visit our father's house,
tell him all the news. I myself am off to high Olympos,
to approach Hēphaistos, famed craftsman, and see if he'll agree
to furnish my son with new battle gear, fine and gleaming."

So she spoke: at once they plunged under the sea's waves,
while she, Thetis, the goddess, silver-footed, made her way
to Olympos, to fetch splendid armor for her beloved son.

Her then her feet took to Olympos; but the Achaians,
with deafening outcry, pursued by Hektōr, killer of men,
came in their flight to the ships and the Hellespont.
Nor could these well-greaved Achaians drag Patroklos
out of missile range, corpse though he was, and Achilles' squire,
for now once more Troy's troops and chariots were on him,
and Hektōr, Priam's son, a man of flame-like valor.
Thrice did illustrious Hektōr seize his feet from behind,
bent on dragging him off, and yelling to the Trojans,
while thrice the two Aiases, clothed in courage and daring,
beat him back from the corpse—yet, sure of his own prowess,
he'd now make a charge in the fray, and now stand firm,
shouting aloud; but he backed off not one step.
Just as there's no way country shepherds can drive off
a tawny lion from a carcass when he's starving hungry,
so the two Aiases could not, prime warriors though they were,
scare Priam's son Hektōr away from the corpse. And now
he'd have dragged it off, and garnered ineffable glory,
had not swift Iris, wind-footed, come to Pēleus's son
from Olympos in haste, with a message to arm himself for battle,
sent by Hērē, unknown to Zeus and the other gods.
Now standing beside him she addressed him with winged words:
"Up with you, son of Pēleus, of all men the most fearsome,
and rescue Patroklos, on whose account grim fighting
is going on before the ships: men are slaughtering one another,
some striving to defend the fallen warrior's corpse,
while others, the Trojans, are determined to haul him away
from the fighting to windy Ilion. Of them all, illustrious Hektōr
is most set on dragging him off, for his heart's bidding him
cut the head from that tender neck, stick it up on a sharp stake!
Up, then, lie here no longer: shame should possess your heart
that Patroklos may become sport for the dogs of Troy—
yours the disgrace, if his body should reach us at all disfigured."

Swift-footed noble Achilles responded to her: "Iris,
goddess, which god was it sent you as messenger to me?"

Swift Iris, wind-footed, made him this reply:
"It was Hērē who sent me, Zeus's far-famed bedfellow—
The high-throned son of Kronos knows nothing about it, nor
any other immortal that dwells upon snow-clad Olympos."

In answer to her then swift-footed Achilles said:
"But how can I enter the struggle? They have my armor,
and my mother told me not to arm myself for the fray
until with my own eyes I see her come back here, since
she promised to bring me fine new armor from Hēphaistos.
No other man do I know whose famed battle gear I might use,
except for the shield of Aias, the son of Telamōn—
but he, I think, will be out himself with the front-line fighters,
dealing death with his spear in defense of dead Patroklos."

To him again spoke swift Iris, the wind-footed: "We too
are well aware that the Trojans now have your famous armor!
Go just as you are to the ditch, show yourself to these Trojans,
see if they fear you enough to back off from the fighting!
Let the warlike Achaians' sons, now worn out, catch their breath
for a little: too brief is the breathing space from battle."

This said, swift-footed Iris went on her way,
but Achilles, beloved of Zeus, now stood up, and Athēnē
around his powerful shoulders arranged the tasseled aegis,
and about his head she, bright among goddesses, set
a golden cloud, and from him made blaze a shining flame.
As when smoke rises up to heaven from a city
on some distant island that enemies are besieging,
and all day long men contend in hateful warfare
from the city's walls, and then when the sun goes down
the beacon fires are lit one after another, their flames
blazing high for those dwelling round about to observe,
in the hope that they'll come in their ships, help fix the trouble,
so from Achilles' head the gleam went up to heaven.
From wall to ditch he went, and stood there, but did not mingle
with the Achaians, respecting his mother's wise advice.
There he stood, and shouted—and Athēnē, standing apart,
gave voice too—arousing vast panic among the Trojans.
As clear as the trumpet's note sounds out when a township's
encircled by enemies with destruction on their minds,
so clear was the war cry uttered by Aiakos's grandson: when
the Trojans heard that brazen voice, and knew its author,
the spirits of all were confounded. The fine-maned horses
turned their chariots backwards, sensing trouble ahead;
their charioteers were in panic when they saw the tireless fire

blaze marvelously over the head of Pēleus's great-hearted son—
a fire lit and kept shining by the goddess, grey-eyed Athēnē.
Three great shouts over the ditch did noble Achilles give,
and three times the Trojans and their far-famed allies panicked:
twelve of their finest fighters perished there and then,
among their own spears and chariots.[1] But the Achaians
happily dragged Patroklos out of range of the missiles,
laid him down on a litter. His comrades gathered around him,
weeping: swift-footed Achilles accompanied them,
shedding warm tears, on seeing his loyal comrade
stretched out on the bier, cut about by the sharp bronze:
he'd sent him out, along with his chariot and horses,
to war, but never was he to welcome him back again.

The ox-eyed lady Hērē now forced the unwearying sun
to make its unwilling return to the streams of Ocean: so
the sun set, and the noble Achaians had some respite
from the powerful turmoil and warfare's uncertain outcome.

The Trojans, for their part, when back from the grind of battle,
unyoked the swift horses from their chariots, and gathered
in assembly, before any thought of supper. They stayed
on their feet right through the meeting: not one man dared
to sit down, scared to trembling as they all were
by Achilles' appearance, so very long he'd been gone
from injurious battle. Shrewd Poulydamas spoke first,
Pánthoös's son, who alone looked both forward and back:[2]
Hektōr's comrade he was, and born on the same night,
though the one excelled with words, with a spear the other.
He with friendly intent now spoke before the assembly:
"Think hard on both sides, my friends. For myself, I urge you
to go back now to the city, not to wait for the bright dawn
out on the plain by the ships: we're far from our walls here.

---

1. How are we to assume that these twelve fine warriors died? The question has bedeviled everyone from the earliest Hellenistic scholiasts on. Textual emendation has offered no convincing solutions. Was there such panic that they were crushed in the frantic rout of their own troops? One intriguing suggestion (Jasper Griffin, *Homer on Life and Death*, 1980, 39, cited by Edwards 2011, 173) is that they are supposed to have died of fear at the terrible sound of the great hero's war cry. But I know of no clearly satisfying explanation.
2. This refers not to any prophetic powers, but simply to "the wisdom of experience" (Edwards 2011, 176).

While this man remained wrathful at noble Agamemnōn,
it was an easier business to fight against the Achaians:
I too gladly stayed all night out by the swift ships then
in the hope of seeing them captured, rounded hulls and all;
but now I'm truly afraid of Pēleus's swift-footed son—
his spirit's so headstrong, he won't be willing to stay
here in mid-plain, where both Trojans and Achaians
share the rage of battle between them on disputed ground:
it's for our city he'll be fighting, and for our women!
So, back to the city: this, believe me, is how things will be.
For now night has stilled the swift-footed son of Pēleus,
ambrosial night; but if tomorrow he comes out armed,
and finds us still here, there are those who'll get to know him
too well, and then happy the man who escapes to sacred
Ilion, for many the victims that dogs and vultures will eat—
Trojans! But may such tidings never reach my ears!
Now: if we follow my plan—however reluctantly—
tonight we'll keep our forces in the place of assembly,
while the ramparts, the high gateways, and the tall polished doors
close-fitted in them, well bolted, will safeguard the city.
Tomorrow at dawn, then, armed, armored, and ready,
we'll position ourselves on the ramparts: the worse for him,
if he wants to come up from the ships and fight us for *our* wall!
Back he'll go to the ships, after glutting his high-necked horses
with all his to-and-fro dashing, in vain, beneath the city!
As for getting inside—that he won't, however great his rage,
nor ever sack Troy: before that swift dogs will devour him."

Scowling darkly, bright-helmeted Hektōr responded:
"Poulydamas, what you're proposing no longer pleases me—
telling us to retreat, to stay cooped up in the town!
Haven't you yet had your fill of being stuck inside the ramparts?
Time was when Priam's city was talked of by all mankind,
how rich it was in gold, all its wealth of bronze;
but its homes have now lost their fine treasures, while many
possessions have gone to Phrygia and to lovely Maiōnia,
sold for cash, ever since great Zeus turned his wrath against us.
But now, when the son of devious Kronos has let me
win renown at the ships, blockade the Achaians by the sea,
no longer, you fool, promote such ideas as these in public:

not one Trojan will support you, I'll not allow it!
So come, then, let us all agree to do as I say:
For now, take your dinner throughout the camp, as usual:
and keep a good lookout, every one of you stay alert;
any Trojan who's overmuch concerned for his possessions
should turn them all in for the populace to eat up—
better that they should enjoy them than the Achaians!
Tomorrow at dawn, then, armed, armored, and ready,
let's go to the hollow ships, start some sharp engagements—
and if noble Achilles has really stood up to fight by the ships,
so much, if he's that way minded, the worse for him: I for one
won't avoid him or miserable warfare, but face to face
I'll confront him, and see whether he then triumphs, or I do.
Enyalios is impartial: he kills the would-be killer."

Such was Hektōr's address, and the Trojans cheered him,
the fools, for their wits had been stolen by Pallas Athēnē:
on Hektōr, for his bad counsel, they all heaped praise; but none
praised Poulydamas, though he'd offered them excellent advice.
So throughout the camp they ate dinner; but the Achaians
wailed all night long in their mourning for Patroklos.
Pēleus's son it was led them in their heartfelt lamentation,
laying his murderous hands upon his comrade's breast,
with quick loud sobs. He was like a bearded lion
whose cubs a deer hunter has stolen away from some
dense thicket: later, the lion returns and ranges,
grieving, through many a glen on the hunter's tracks,
hoping to catch him somewhere, possessed by bitter fury.
So, groaning deeply, to the Myrmidons spoke Achilles:
"Ah, me, vain indeed were the words I uttered that day
reassuring the hero Menoitios in our halls—
I said I'd bring his son home to Opoeis wreathed in glory
from the sacking of Ilion, with his fair share of the spoils!
But not all their designs does Zeus fulfil for mortals—
we two are both fated to redden the selfsame earth
here in Troy, since I too shall never come back home
to be welcomed by the old horseman Pēleus in his halls
or by Thetis my mother: the earth will hold me here for ever.
But now, Patroklos, since the earth will claim me later
than you, I'll not bury you till I've brought here Hektōr's

armor and head—he, the killer of your mighty heart;
and in front of your pyre I shall cut the throats of a dozen
noble Trojan youths, so enraged I am at your slaying.
Till then you'll lie as you are alongside my curved ships,
and round you deep-bosomed women, Trojans, Dardanians,
will mourn for you, shedding tears, by day and by night—
women we toiled to win by the force of our long spears,
laying waste the wealthy cities of mortal men."

That said,
noble Achilles now gave the word to his comrades
to set on the fire a great cauldron, so they might quickly
wash Patroklos clean of oozing blood and gore.
They stood in the blaze a vessel for heating bathwater
and filled it, and under it gathered and kindled much firewood:
flames licked round the cauldron's belly, the water warmed.
When the water came to a boil in the shining bronze
then indeed they washed him, and rubbed his body with oil,
filled his wounds with an ointment nine years old, then laid him
out on a bier, wrapped from head to foot in soft linen,
and over that they dressed him in a white robe.
The whole night through then, round swift-footed Achilles,
the Myrmidons wailed in mourning for their Patroklos.

Now Zeus spoke to Hērē, his sister and his wife:
"You've had your way, then, my ox-eyed lady Hērē:
you've aroused swift-footed Achilles! Surely they must be
your very own offspring, all these long-haired Achaians."

The ox-eyed lady Hērē then responded to him:
"Most dread son of Kronos, what is this that you've said?
Even a human, surely, will do things for his fellow-man—
though, being mortal, he doesn't possess all the wisdom
that I do—I who declare I'm the highest of all goddesses,
as the eldest born, and because I'm recognized
as your consort—and you're the king of all the immortals!
How, in my rage, could I not cobble trouble for these Trojans?"

Thus they spoke to each other; but meanwhile Thetis,
the silver-footed, came to the house of Hēphaistos—
imperishable, starry, outstanding among gods' homes,
made of bronze, and built by the little clubfoot himself.

Him she found sweating as he bustled around his bellows,
working fast: he was making tripods, twenty in all,
to stand round the wall of his solidly built dwelling,
and under the base of each he'd fixed golden wheels,
so that of themselves they could enter the divine assembly
and come back again to his house, a marvel to behold.
So far, then, they were finished, but the intricately wrought
ear-handles had not yet been added: these he was fitting,
and hammering in the rivets. As he worked with expert skill,
he was approached by Thetis, the silver-footed goddess.
She was seen by bright-veiled Charis, who now came forward—
lovely Charis, wed by the far-famed lame-of-both-legs god—
and clasped her hand, and addressed her in these words:
"What, long-robed Thetis, brings you now to our house?
Though a dear and respected friend, you've not visited us
before.
Do come in, and let me offer you entertainment."

So saying, the bright goddess led her inside the house,
seated her on a chair, all silver-studded, finely
and intricately worked, with below it a stool for the feet,
and called to Hēphaistos, famed craftsman, in these words:
"Hēphaistos, come out here! Thetis has need of you."

The far-famed lame-of-both-legs god answered her:
"It's an awesome and venerable goddess who's in my house!
She rescued me, when I was hurting, having fallen so far
because of my bitch of a mother, who had her mind set
on hiding me and my lameness. I'd have suffered agonies
had Eurynomē and Thetis not welcomed me warmly—
that Eurynomē who's the daughter of encircling Ocean. The nine
years I was with them I made much intricate metalwork:
brooches, spiral earrings, rosettes and necklaces,
in their hollow cave, and round it the stream of Ocean flowed,
boiling with foam and boundless; nor was anyone else,
whether god or mortal man, aware of my presence:
only Thetis knew, and Eurynomē, they who'd saved me.
Now herself has come to our house, and I have a great need
to repay fair-tressed Thetis fully for having saved my life.
So you set before her our best entertainment for a guest,
while I put away my bellows and all my working tools."

With that, he rose from his anvil, hard-breathing, bulky,
limping: yet under him his stunted legs moved lightly.
His bellows he put well away from the fire, and all
his tools that he worked with he stored in a silver chest.
Then with a sponge he cleaned his face and both his hands,
and his bull neck and shaggy breast, and put on a tunic,
and chose a thick stick, and took himself to the door,
limping; and quickly there moved to support their master
handmaids of gold, in the likeness of young living girls.
There was mind and intelligence in them, they could speak,
they had bodily strength, the immortal gods taught them skills.
Now they bustled around their lord, while he limped across
to where Thetis was, sat down on a shining chair,
took her hand in his, and greeted her with these words:
"What, long-robed Thetis, brings you now to our house?
Though a dear and respected friend, you've not visited us before.
Tell me what's on your mind: my heart bids me fulfill it
if fulfill it I can, and if it's fulfillable."

Thetis then answered him, weeping: "Is there any
goddess today, Hēphaistos, of all those on Olympos,
who's endured so many grievous sorrows in her heart
as the woes that Zeus son of Kronos has given me, far beyond
all others? Of all marine nymphs only me he made wed a mortal—
Pēleus, Aiakos's son: I endured that mortal's bed
greatly against my will. Now he lies in his halls, broken up
by wretched old age; but today there are other woes I endure.
A son indeed he gave me, to bear and to bring up,
preeminent among heroes: like a sapling he shot up,
and when, like a tree on an orchard knoll, I'd reared him,
I sent him out here to Ilion in the curved ships, to fight
the Trojans; but now I'll never welcome him back
to his home, he'll never return to the house of Pēleus!
Now, while he still lives and sees the sunlight
he has sorrow, nor can I be of help by going to him.
That girl given him as a prize by the Achaians' sons
has been snatched back out of his hands by the lord Agamemnōn.
In grief for her he was eating his heart out; then the Trojans
penned the Achaians in by their ships' sterns, would not
let them break out. The Argive elders appealed to him for help,

detailed by name the many rich presents they'd offer:
he himself still refused to keep disaster from them,
but instead arrayed Patroklos in his own armor,
and sent him to fight the war, with many men besides.
The whole day long they struggled around the Skaian Gates,
and that day they'd have sacked the city, had not Apollo,
after much damage done by Menoitios's brave son,
killed him in the front line, giving Hektōr the credit.
This is why I now beg you, clasping your knees, to agree
to make my short-lived son a shield and a helmet,
and a corselet and fine greaves equipped with ankle-pieces;
for the gear he once possessed his trusty comrade lost
when slain by the Trojans, and now he lies heartbroken on the ground."

The far-famed lame-of-both-legs god then answered her: "Don't despair,
and don't let these matters become a burden on your mind!
I just wish that I could conceal him, far away from grievous death,
when his dread fate comes on him, as surely as now
he'll get his fine new armor, such gear that in time to come
all mankind will be thunderstruck at the sight of it."

So saying,
he left her there, and went back to where his bellows were,
turned them to face the fire, gave them their working orders;
and the bellows, twenty all told, blew through their nozzles,
sending out blasts of air from every angle—
at times to support Hēphaistos's quick actions, or again
to do whatever he needed to make his work complete.
Into the fire he now cast solid bronze and tin,
silver and precious gold; next he set a large anvil
to stand on its anvil block, and then grasped in one hand
a weighty hammer, in the other his forging tongs.

First he fashioned a shield, both huge and sturdy, adorned
intricately all over, and around it set a bright rim,
three-layered and glinting, complete with silver baldric.
Five were the layers of the shield itself, and on it
with consummate skill he set a number of decorations.

On it he fashioned the earth, the sea, and the heavens,
the unwearying sun, the moon on its increase to full,

and every constellation with which the heavens are crowned—
the Pleiadēs, the Hyadēs, the majesty of Orīōn,
and the Bear, that's also known to mankind as the Wain,
that revolves in one place, keeping a watchful eye on Orīōn,
and alone never sinks into the baths of Ocean.

On it he also fashioned two cities of humankind,
fine ones: in the first there were marriages and banquets,
with brides being led from their quarters by flaring torchlight
through the city, to the accompaniment of many a wedding song,
and young men awhirl in the dance, while for them the pipes
and lyres played on without stopping, and the women stood
at their doors, admiring spectators. There was a crowd
of citizens drawn to the meeting place: a dispute had arisen
between two men, at loggerheads over the blood-price
of a man who'd been killed: one claimed, in a public speech,
to have paid it all, but the other swore he'd been given nothing,
and both were determined to win the arbitrator's verdict.
People were backing both sides, cheering one or the other,
while heralds held them back, and the elders were sitting
on polished seats of stone in the sacred circle,
the loud-voiced heralds' staffs in their hands: holding these
they would rise to deliver judgment, each in turn;
and there between them were set two talents[3] of gold,
to go to the one who delivered the fairest verdict.

But around the other city there lay two bodies of troops,
agleam in their armor, divided by two competing plans—
should they lay the place waste, or share between both sides
all the wealth that this lovely city contained? However,
the besieged would have none of it, were arming for an ambush.
The ramparts were manned by their dear wives and children,
and along with them such men as were crippled by old age;
but the rest were out after action, led by Arēs and Athēnē—
both of gold, and golden the raiment in which they were clad,
handsome and tall in their armor, as befits gods, and clearly
visible all around: the men below them were smaller.

3. If Ridgeway (cited by Leaf, 2: 253–54) was right, the Homeric talent equaled the price of one ox, which would seem a fair enough recompense in this context (and elsewhere in Homer, e.g., 23.269, 614). We are certainly not dealing here with the later classical talent of roughly 57 ½ lbs weight, which in gold would represent a sizable fortune.

When they reached the spot where they'd chosen to set their ambush,
in a riverbed, with a watering place for flocks and herds,
then they settled down, all of them, armored in gleaming bronze,
and two scouts were posted, some way from the main body,
to watch out for a glimpse of the sheep and well-fed cattle.
These very soon arrived, and with them a pair of herdsmen
playing their pipes, unaware of the trap. Then the ambushers,
when they saw them coming, charged out, and in a trice
cut off the herded cattle, the splendid flocks
of white-fleeced sheep, and slaughtered both the herdsmen.
The besiegers, now hearing loud tumult among the cattle
from the meeting place where they sat, mounted at once behind
their high-stepping horses, set off, and quickly reached them.
Then they halted, and fought there beside the river's banks,
letting fly, each side at the other, with their bronze-tipped spears;
and Strife and Tumult mixed with them, and the baneful Death-Spirit,
seizing one man alive, but wounded, another without a wound,
yet another dragged through the turmoil, dead, by the feet;
and the shift Strife wore round her shoulders was scarlet
with men's blood; like living mortals they engaged and fought,
and each of them dragged off bodies that the others had slain.

On it he also fashioned a broad field of rich plowland,
soft-soiled, thrice-plowed from fallow, with many plowmen
on it, turning their teams, driving them up and down,
and when, at the turning point, they reached the edge of the field,
then a man would come up and hand them a cup of wine,
honey-sweet, and the plowmen would speed to the furrow's end,
eager to reach the turn in the deep soil; and behind them
the field grew black, as though it had really been plowed,
though made of gold: here indeed was marvelous artistry.

On it he also fashioned a royal estate, where farmhands
were reaping, sharp sickles in hand. Of the cut swathes
some were falling in rows, along the line of the furrow,
while others the sheaf-binders were tying with twists of straw.
Three binders stood there ready, while behind them boys
collected the swathes and delivered them, by the armful,
without pause, and all the time the king stood by, in silence,
at the line of the swathes, staff in hand, and happy at heart.
Away under an oak tree were heralds, preparing a feast,

dressing a great ox that they'd sacrificed, while women lavishly
sprinkled white barley upon it for the farmhands' dinner.[4]

On it he also fashioned a vineyard, lush with clusters,
fine and golden; black the bunched grapes, while the vines
were propped up throughout on silver poles. Around it
he set a ditch, done in cobalt enamel, and outside that a fence
made of tin, with one path to the vineyard, on which
the grape pickers went to and fro when harvesting the vines:
and he had girls and boys, all innocently light-hearted,
carrying the honey-sweet fruit in wicker baskets,
while in the midst of them a boy with a clear-toned lyre
made sweet music, and accompanied his own singing—
soft and exquisite—of the Linos Song,[5] while they,
stamping the beat and shouting, danced along after him.

On it he also set a herd of straight-horned cattle:
the cows were fashioned out of gold and tin, and went
eagerly, lowing, on their way from byre to pasture
beside a rushing river, a rippling reed bed.
Of gold were the herdsmen accompanying the cattle—
four of them, together with nine swift-footed dogs.
But among the foremost cattle two fearsome lions
had got hold of a noisy bull, which, bellowing loudly,
was being dragged off, with dogs and youths in hot pursuit.
The lions had ripped up the great bull's hide and were
gobbling its innards and black blood, while the herdsmen
tried, in vain, to scare them, urging on their swift dogs;
but these fought shy of biting the lions: instead
they ran up close, barking, then swerved aside.

---

4. The Greek is ambiguous: was the barley sprinkled as dressing for a general feast or to form a kind of porridge for the workers, while the king and others enjoyed roast meat? At least two modern translations have assumed the latter; but both Leaf (2: 257–58) and Edwards 2011 (224) prefer, rightly I think, the former: Edwards points out that the verb παλύνω (*palynō*) can *only* mean "sprinkle" as opposed to "boil in water", and there is no reason, linguistically or socially, why Homer should not here be describing a general popular feast somewhat like a modern Greek *panēgyri*.
5. Linos was a mythical musician, supposedly the first human divinely endowed with the art of song, but killed out of jealousy by Apollo (Paus. 9.29.3), and mourned by the Muses. The Linos Song, according to Herodotos (2.79) was an eastern dirge; it was popular with singers at feasts and dances (*HE* 2: 478, Edwards 2011, 225), so something more cheerful than a dirge in the modern sense: perhaps autumnal /harvest-related, an ancestor of the John Barleycorn songs?

On it the far-famed lame-of-both-legs god made a pasture
in a charming glen: a large pasture of white-fleeced sheep
along with their sheepfolds and pens and covered shelters.

On it the far-famed lame-of-both-legs god subtly
inlaid a dancing floor like the one in spacious Knossos
that long ago Daidalos fashioned for fair-tressed Ariadnē.
Here were young men, with maidens worth many oxen
in bride-price, dancing, hands on each other's wrists,
the girls robed in fine linen, while the men wore
fine-woven tunics, softly gleaming from worked-in oil,[6]
and the girls had on sweet garlands, the men
their daggers of gold, suspended from silver baldrics.
Now they would dance in a circle, feet well-skilled,
very lightly, as when a potter sits at a wheel that matches
his hands' grasp, and tries it, to see how it will run;
and now they'd approach each other in dancing lines
while a crowd of spectators stood round them, much enjoying
such an elegant dance, [and among them a sacred bard
sang to his lyre,][7] and two tumblers whirled among them,
taking the lead in all their sport and pleasure.

On it he also set the mighty stream of Ocean
to run round the outermost rim of this strongly fashioned shield.

Then, when he'd finished the shield, both large and solid,
he forged him a corselet more bright than the blaze of fire,
and forged him a heavy helmet to fit his temples closely,
a fine piece, cunningly wrought, with a golden crest set on it,
and lastly fashioned him greaves, made out of pliant tin.

The far-famed lame-of-both-legs god, this battle gear all finished,
took it and laid it before Achilles' mother, who then
swooped down like a hawk from the high snows of Olympos,
bringing from Hēphaistos the glinting armor he'd made.

6. C. W. Shelmerdine, *The Perfume Industry of Mycenaean Pylos* (1985), 595–96, cited by Janko 175, assures us, surprisingly, that linen thus treated with oil "becomes, not greasy, but supple and shining, and it remains so after washing."

7. The phrase in brackets was allegedly (Athen. 180c–d) added in antiquity from a similar passage in the *Odyssey* (4.15–19), in all likelihood "to provide the dancers with music" (Edwards 2011, 230); it does not figure in either the MSS or surviving papyri, though some modern editors have included it in the text.

Book 19

Now saffron-robed Dawn rose up from Ocean's streams
to bring light to the immortals and to mortal mankind,
and Thetis arrived at the ships bearing the god's gifts.
She found her beloved son lying clasping Patroklos to him,
and weeping loudly, while round him large numbers of his
comrades
were shedding tears too. The bright goddess came among them,
stood at his side, clasped his hand, and spoke to him, saying:
"My child, this man we must let lie, for all our sorrow,
since from the start it was the gods that willed his death.
Accept rather now, from Hēphaistos, this splendid armor,
fine gear, such as never man yet wore upon his shoulders."

So saying, the goddess set down the pieces of armor
in front of Achilles: each rang clear in its intricate splendor.
Trembling swept through the Myrmidons: no man dared
to look directly at them, but flinched away. As Achilles
viewed them, his wrath swelled further, his eyes glared out
terribly under their lids, like blazing fire, and he
rejoiced as he handled these dazzling gifts from the god.
But when, to his mind, he'd spent enough time admiring
their workmanship, then to his mother he spoke winged words:
"Mother, these arms the god's given me are such as
immortal work should be, what no mortal could accomplish!
Now indeed I shall arm myself. Yet I'm desperately anxious
for the valiant son of Menoitios, lest meanwhile flies
may enter the wounds that the bronze has inflicted on him,
engender worms there, to outrage his body, now that
the life's killed from it—and so all his flesh will rot."

Then the goddess, silver-footed Thetis, replied: "My child,
don't let these things bother your mind! I'll take good care
to fend off from his body those savage tribes, the flies
that feed on the flesh of men lately slain in battle. Suppose
that he lies for a year's full cycle, his flesh will remain
fresh and whole, or even better than now! But first

you must call the Achaian heroes to assembly, and renounce
your rage against Agamemnōn, the people's shepherd:
that done, you can arm yourself for battle, be clad in valor."

So saying, she filled him with dauntless strength, while for
Patroklos she dripped ambrosia and red nectar
through his nostrils, to keep his flesh forever unspoiled.

Along the seashore he went now, did noble Achilles,
shouting scarily loud, to alert the Achaian heroes,
and even those who before had stayed where the ships
were hauled up—the steersmen, those who handled the ships'
steering oars, or the ships' stewards, who served out rations—
all now made their way to the meeting place, since Achilles
had appeared, after long abstention from grievous battle.
Two men, veterans both, came limping in together—
Tydeus's son, steadfast fighter, and noble Odysseus,
both of them leaning on spears, since their wounds still hurt them—
and went and sat down in the front of the assembly.
Last of all there arrived the lord of men, Agamemnōn,
he too nursing a wound: in the grind of battle he'd been
hit by the bronze-tipped spear of Koōn, Antēnōr's son.
Then, when all the Achaians were gathered together,
swift-footed Achilles stood up and addressed them, saying:
"Son of Atreus, was it really the best thing for both of us,
for you, for me, that we two, grief-filled as we were,
should rage on in heart-eating strife because of a girl?
I wish she'd been killed by an arrow from Artemis
that day at the ships when I chose her, after sacking Lyrnessos!
Fewer Achaians then would have bitten the boundless earth
at the enemy's hands, on account of my fierce wrath.
Good news, this, for the Trojans and Hektōr; but the Achaians
will long, I think, remember the strife between you and me!
Still, despite our grief, we'll treat this as past and done with,
restraining, as now we must, the spirit in our breasts.
So now I renounce my wrath: that I should rage on for ever
unrelentingly is not fitting. Come then, waste no time,
urge on the long-haired Achaians into battle,
let me, once again, face these Trojans, make trial of them,
find out if they're still ready to spend a night by the ships—

though I think there are some who'll be happy to rest their knees—
those who escape my spear, and the struggle of battle."

So he spoke, and the well-greaved Achaians all rejoiced,
because Pēleus's great-hearted son had abandoned his wrath.
There then addressed them the lord of men, Agamemnōn,
from the place where he sat, not standing up among them:[1]
"My friends, you Danaän heroes, you henchmen of Arēs!
It's good to hear out a man on his feet, nor is it seemly
to interrupt him—vexation to even a skilled speaker!
Against the clamor of many how can a man either listen
or speak? He's disabled, however clear his voice.
It's to Pēleus's son I'll declare myself, but you other Argives
should pay attention too, and mark my words, all of you.
Many times have the Achaians addressed me in the same terms,
reviling me; yet it's not I who am the one at fault,
but rather Zeus, and Fate, and some night-walking Fury,
who in the assembly cast wild delusion on my mind
that day when, acting alone, I took his prize from Achilles.
But what could I do? It's a god that fulfills all matters:
Zeus's eldest daughter, Delusion, who blinds all mortals—
accursed creature, with delicate feet, for it's never
the ground she touches: she treads on the heads of men,
damaging mortals' minds, has trapped others before me.
Indeed, she once blinded Zeus, though men declare him
the greatest of men and gods both: him even Hērē,
though only a woman, deceived by her crafty wiles
the day when that mighty force Hēraklēs was due to be born,
to Alkmēnē, in Thēbē with its fair crown of walls.
Zeus spoke in boastful tones, among all the gods:
'Listen to me, every god, and all you goddesses,
while I tell you what the heart in my breast now bids me say.
Eileithyia, spirit of birth pangs, today will bring to the light
a man who will rule over all those dwelling about him,
one of that line of men whose ancestry is my own.'
To him, with deception in mind, Lady Hērē then declared:

1. The Greek is ambiguous, and there has been considerable debate as to what exactly Agamemnōn does, and why. I agree with those who argue that he not only stays put, but delivers his speech sitting, using the privilege of a wounded man to emphasize the difference between himself and Achilles, who has for long been safely out of the fighting. See Edwards 2011, 243–44.

'You'll turn out a liar, once more not see your words fulfilled!
Very well, then, Olympian: swear me a strong oath
that he'll truly rule over all those dwelling about him,
he who today drops between the feet of a woman
and is of the line whose blood is also your own.'
So she spoke, but Zeus failed to understand her deception,
and swore a great oath, and thus was greatly deluded.
Now Hērē swooped down from the peaks of high Olympos,
and quickly made her way to Achaian Argos, where,
she knew, was the noble wife of Perseus's son Sthenelos,
then pregnant with a son, and her seventh month had come.
This child Hērē brought out, though its months were incomplete,
while delaying Alkmēnē's delivery, restraining her birth pangs.
Then she herself broke the news to Zeus, the son of Kronos:
'Zeus, Father, lord of the bright thunderbolt, just let me
drop a word in your mind. A great man indeed is born,
who'll be lord of the Argives: Eurystheus, Sthenelos's son,
Perseus's grandson[2]—your line, so not unfit to rule Argos.'
So she spoke, and sharp pain struck him, deep in his mind,
and promptly he seized Delusion by her glossy-tressed head,
infuriated at heart, and swore a powerful oath
that never more to Olympos and the starry heavens
should Delusion come, she who blinds all. So saying,
he flung her down from the starry heavens, whirling
her round with one hand, and soon she reached human soil.
Ever after Zeus groaned at the thought of her, when he saw
his son demeaned by the tasks that Eurystheus set him.[3]
So I too, then, at the time bright-helmeted Hektōr
was busy slaughtering Argives at the sterns of their ships,
could not forget Delusion, by whom I was first blinded.
But since blinded I was, and robbed of good sense by Zeus,
I'm willing to make amends, to give recompense past counting.
So up with you to the battle, rouse the rest of your troops!
Gifts I'm ready to offer you, all that you were promised
by noble Odysseus earlier when he came to your hut!
Or wait a bit, if you'd rather, eager to fight though you are,

2. Thus great-grandson of Zeus (who begot Perseus on Danaë) and cousin to Hēraklēs, son of Zeus and Alkmēnē (though Amphitryōn was his nominal father).
3. These were the famous Twelve Labors, imposed upon Hēraklēs by Eurystheus as a penalty for having in a fit of madness killed his three children by Kreōn's daughter Megara.

and attendants will gather and fetch you these gifts from my ships,
to let you see that I'll give you what will satisfy your heart."

Then in answer to him swift-footed Achilles declared:
"Most glorious son of Atreus, Agamemnōn lord of men,
as regards the gifts, if you want to, present them, as is proper,
or keep them—your choice. But for now, let's turn to battle
right away! We've no business to sit here wasting our time
in idle chatter when there's great work still to be done!
As each of you once again sees Achilles among the foremost,
with his bronze spear spreading death through the ranks of the
Trojans,
let him have that in mind as he battles his own opponent."

In answer to him resourceful Odysseus now said:
"Do not thus, godlike Achilles, brave warrior though you are,
urge the Achaians' sons to go against Ilion fasting
to fight the Trojans, since it's for no short time
that this struggle will last, from when the warriors' ranks
first engage, and the god breathes might into either side.
Rather command the Achaians by their swift ships to consume
both food and wine first, for in them is strength and courage.
No man through the livelong day, till the setting of the sun,
will be able to stand and fight who hasn't eaten:
for though in his heart he may be eager for battle,
yet his limbs unawares grow heavy, hunger and thirst
come on him, while as he moves his knees get weaker—
but the man who's taken his fill of wine and food
can fight with enemy warriors all day long:
the heart in his breast's still steadfast, his limbs don't tire
until everyone's disengaged from the business of fighting.
Come then, dismiss the troops, give the order to make ready
their meal; and as for the gifts, the lord of men, Agamemnōn,
should have them brought to the meeting place, where all
the Achaians can see them, and your heart may be comforted;
and let him stand up and swear an oath before the Argives,
that he never went into that woman's bed nor lay with her—
as is the custom, my lord, between men and women—
and let the heart in your own breast be gracious!
Let him give you a feast in his hut by way of amendment,
a lavish one, that you may lack nothing that's due to you.

And you, son of Atreus, will be more just in future
to others; there's nothing blameworthy in a king,
when he's started the trouble, making amends to any man."

Then the lord of men, Agamemnōn, answered him, saying:
"I'm very glad, son of Laertēs, to have heard your speech:
all you set forth and discussed was properly stated.
This oath I'm ready to swear: my heart bids me do so,
nor will I perjure myself to a deity. But Achilles
should stay here, however eager he may be for battle,
and all the rest of you too, until the gifts are fetched
from my hut, and we pledge ourselves in solemn agreement.
And you yourself I charge with this duty, that you
choose the best young warriors out of all the Achaians
to bring the gifts from my ship, all that earlier we promised
to bestow on Achilles, and also to fetch the women.
And in the Achaians' broad camp let Talthybios right now
prepare a boar, to sacrifice to Zeus and the Sun."

Then swift-footed Achilles made answer to him, saying:
"Most glorious son of Atreus, Agamemnōn lord of men,
better at some other time for you to fix these matters,
when perhaps there's a break in the fighting, when at least
the rage in my breast's less intense. But at this moment
they are lying there, flesh rent open, all those warriors
that Priam's son Hektōr slew when Zeus gave him his glory—
and you two are saying we should eat! If I had my way
I'd tell the Achaians' sons to join battle, here and now,
fasting, unfed, and *then*, when the sun went down,
to prepare their great feast—when we'd wiped out this defilement!
But until that moment, down my own throat at least,
neither food nor drink will pass, now my comrade is dead,
who lies in my hut, flesh rent by the keen-edged bronze,
feet facing the door,[4] while around him our companions
shed tears. So it's not such things that at all concern me now,
but killing, and blood, and the groans of dying men."

Then in answer to him resourceful Odysseus said:
"Ah, Achilles, Pēleus's son, far the greatest of the Achaians,

4. As Leaf reminds us (2: 275) this was an ancient funeral custom, symbolic of imminent departure—"facing the journey", as Vermeule says (12–13).

You are stronger than me, and greater by no small measure
with the spear; but as for wisdom, I'd far surpass you,
since I'm the older man, with much more knowledge—
so let your heart be receptive to what I have to say.
Mankind very soon gets surfeited with its crop of fighting,
the stalks of which the bronze spreads in plenty on the ground;
but the harvest is all too small, since the scales are tipped
by Zeus, who is for mankind the steward of warfare.
No way by denying the belly can Achaians mourn a corpse:
too many, one after another, are endlessly falling
day after day—when would anyone get a respite?
No: what we have to do is to bury our casualties,
harden our hearts, shed tears on that one day only,
and all those of us who survive the loathsome struggle
must be mindful of drink and food, that we may the better
battle it out with our enemies, for ever, unceasingly,
flesh clad in the stubborn bronze. Let no one of our troops
hold off from action while awaiting some other order:
there's one order only: ill betide any man who hangs back
at the ships of the Argives! Let's all advance together,
and raise a sharp battle against these horse-breaking Trojans!"

That said, he took with him far-famed Nestōr's sons,
and Phyleus's son Megēs, and Thoas, and Mērionēs,
and Kreiōn's son Lykomēdēs, and Melanippos,
and they made their way to the hut of Atreus's son Agamemnōn.
The word had been given, and straightway the thing was done:
seven tripods they fetched from the hut, as he'd promised Achilles,
a score of bright cauldrons, a dozen horses; and then
quickly they led out the women, skilled in fine handiwork:
seven there were of these, with fair-cheeked Briseïs the eighth.
Odysseus weighed out gold, ten talents in all, and led off,
while the other Achaian warriors carried the gifts, and set them
down in the midst of the meeting place. Then Agamemnōn rose,
while Talthybios, a man whose voice was like a god's,
stood, with the boar in his hands, beside the people's shepherd.
The son of Atreus now grasped and drew the knife
that always hung at the side of his sword's great scabbard,
cut the first ritual hairs from the boar, and raising his hands
prayed to Zeus, while every Argive sat silent in his place,

as was right and proper, ears alert to the king, who now,
looking up to the broad heavens, made his prayer:
"Let Zeus, first, be my witness, highest and best of gods,
and Earth, and Sun, and the Furies that underground
exact retribution from those men who swear false oaths,
that never did I lay hands on the girl Briseïs, either
to bed her, or with any other intention, and that
she's remained untouched all the time she's been in my huts!
If any of this is sworn falsely, may the gods give me
all the many griefs they inflict on perjurers in their name."

That said, he cut the boar's throat with the pitiless bronze,
and the body Talthybios swung round and hurled into
the grey sea's wide gulf, food for fishes. Then Achilles
stood up and spoke among the battle-minded Argives:
"Zeus, Father, great the delusions with which you visit mankind!
Not otherwise would the son of Atreus have so stirred up
the heart in my breast, nor would he have taken the girl
against my will, so determinedly: it may be that Zeus
was set on bringing death to large numbers of Achaians!
Go eat your meal now, and then let's move to battle."

So he spoke, and broke up this very brief assembly.
The rest all scattered, each man to his own vessel,
while the great-hearted Myrmidons busied themselves with the gifts,
and carried them off to the ship of godlike Achilles.
Some they stowed in the huts, and settled the women there,
while stalwart henchmen drove off the horses to the herd.

But now Briseïs, the image of golden Aphrodītē,
when she saw Patroklos, his flesh all rent by the sharp bronze,
flung herself on him, keening shrilly, her hands
tearing her breasts and tender neck and lovely face;
and amid her weeping this woman, so like a goddess, exclaimed:
"Patroklos, in my misery the man most dear to my heart,
it was living I left you when last I went out from the hut,
and now, great leader, it's dead I return to find you!
Thus in my life does trouble always breed trouble:
the husband bestowed on me by my father and lady mother
I saw rent by the sharp bronze in front of our city,
and the three men who were born to that self-same mother,

my much-loved brothers, all these met their day of death.
Yet you'd not even let me weep when swift Achilles
killed my husband and sacked the city of godlike Mynēs—
you said you'd see me the lawful wedded wife
of godlike Achilles, you'd take me back on your ships to Phthiē,
and hold a marriage feast for me among the Myrmidons. So
I mourn your death without cease: you were always kind to me."

So she spoke, weeping: the women lamented with her,
for Patroklos professedly, but each one for her own sorrows.
Meanwhile the Achaian elders gathered around Achilles,
all imploring him to eat: but he refused them, sobbing:
"I beg you—if any of you, my dearest comrades, will listen—
please, please don't tell me to glut my heart with food
or drink, now this terrible grief has come upon me:
until sundown I shall remain thus, and endure, whatever."

So saying, he sent away all the other princes, except
the two sons of Atreus, who stayed, as did noble Odysseus,
and Nestōr and Idomeneus and Phoinix the old horseman,
to comfort him in his great sorrow, but not one whit
would his heart be comforted till he'd entered war's bloody jaws,
and as he reflected, he heaved a deep sigh, and said:
"Time was when you—so ill-fated, my dearest comrade—
would yourself lay out an enjoyable meal in our hut,
quickly and skillfully, when the Achaians were impatient
to bring grievous warfare against the horse-breaking Trojans.
But now here you lie, flesh rent, and my heart's indifferent
to food and drink, though both are to hand, through yearning
for you: no other worse thing is there that I could suffer,
not even news of the death of my own father,
who now perhaps in Phthiē is shedding heavy round tears
for the loss of a son such as I am, who now in a foreign land,
all because of hateful Helen, am at war with the Trojans;
not even were it my own dear son, now being raised on Skyros—
if indeed it is true that godlike Neoptolemos still lives.
Until now the heart in my breast had cherished the hope
that I alone should die far from horse-grazing Argos,
here at Troy, but that you should return to Phthiē,
and that you'd pick up my son in your swift black ship
from Skyros, and show him everything that was mine—

my possessions, my servants, my splendid high-roofed house,
since by now I suppose that Pēleus must either be at last
dead, or, if barely alive still, bowed down by the inroads
of loathsome old age, and by waiting forever to hear
unhappy tidings of me, that at last I've perished."

So he spoke, weeping: the old men lamented with him,
remembering, each of them, all that he'd left back at home;
and as they mourned, the son of Kronos observed them,
was moved to pity, and quickly spoke winged words to Athēnē:
"My child, you're completely neglecting your favorite mortal!
Do you no longer have the least care in your heart for Achilles?
There he sits, in front of his high-sterned vessels,
in mourning for his dear comrade: the others indeed
have all gone to dinner, but he stays fasting and foodless.
So off with you now, dribble nectar and sweet ambrosia
into his breast, so that hunger may not come on him."

So saying,
he encouraged Athēnē, herself already most eager,
and she, like a shearwater, long-winged and raucous-voiced,
swooped down through the high air from heaven. The Achaians
were promptly arming throughout the camp, while she
into Achillēs' breast dribbled nectar and sweet ambrosia
in order that joyless hunger should not come upon his knees.
Then she herself was gone to the strong abode of her mighty
father, while from their ships the Achaians poured out.
As when, thick and fast, Zeus's snowflakes come floating down,
ice-cold, and driven by the sky-born north wind's blast,
so now, thick and fast, the brightly gleaming helmets
emerged from the ships, and with them the bossed shields,
the well-plated corselets and the ash-wood spears. Their radiance
shone up to heaven, all the earth around was stirred
to laughter by the bright bronze, and a din rose from under
men's tramping feet: in their midst was noble Achilles,
arming himself, teeth grinding, eyes all ablaze
like flames of fire, while into his heart there now entered
unbearable grief. Enraged at the Trojans, he now put on
the god's gifts, that Hēphaistos had labored hard to make him.
The greaves first he fastened on about his shins—
finely worked, and fitted with silver ankle-pieces.

Next, to cover his chest, he put on the corselet.
About his shoulders he slung the silver-studded sword,
of bronze; then came the shield, both huge and sturdy,
from which gleamed afar a brightness like the moon's.
As out at sea the gleam is visible to sailors
of a burning fire, one alight high up in the mountains,
in some lonely farmhouse, but they cannot stop the gale
from driving them over the teeming deep, far distant from
their friends—so a gleam went skyward from Achilles' shield,
so fine, so intricate. Then he lifted the mighty helmet
and set it upon his head: it shone like a star,
this helmet with horsehair crest, and around it there waved
the lovely gold plumes that Hēphaistos had set thick about its crown.
Then noble Achilles tested himself in his armor
to see if it fitted well, if his lithe limbs had free movement,
and it buoyed him like wings, delighting the people's shepherd.
Lastly he drew from its stand his father's spear,
weighty and huge and massive. No other Achaian
could wield it: only Achilles could manage its handling—
that spear of Pēlian ash wood that Cheirōn gave his dear father,
felled on Pēlion's summit, to embody death for heroes.
Alkimos and Automedōn were about the business of yoking
the horses: fitting fine girth straps, thrusting the bits between
their jaws. Now they drew back the reins to the dovetailed
chariot; then grasping the bright whip that fitted his hand
Automedōn sprang aboard, to the driver's place,
and behind him, armed and ready, came Achilles,
agleam in his battle gear like Hyperiōn the bright Sun.
and called out in a terrible voice to his father's horses:
"Xanthos and Balios,[5] famed offspring of Podargē!
Think of some other way to bring your charioteer
back safe to the Danaän camp when we're through with fighting—
don't leave him dead there, as you did Patroklos."

Then
from under the yoke the fleet-footed horse addressed him—
Xanthos: he bent his head sharply, and all his mane
streamed to the ground from the yoke-pad, on both sides of the yoke,

5. I.e., "Bay" and "Dapple"; their dam, Podargē, is "Swiftfoot".

and the goddess, white-armed Hērē, made him articulate:
"Yes, this time we'll bring you back safely, mighty Achilles!
But the day of your death is near, though we shall not
be its cause, but rather a great god and all-mastering Fate:
it was through no slowness or sloth of ours that the Trojans
succeeded in stripping the armor from Patroklos's shoulders:
it was the best of the gods, whom fair-hired Lētō bore,
that slew him among the front-liners, gave Hektōr the glory.
We two could run with the speed of the west wind's blast,
which, they say, is the swiftest of all! But you yourself
are destined to be laid low by a god's might, and a man's."

When he'd said this, the Furies cut off his power of speech.
Then, deeply moved, swift-footed Achilles addressed him:
"Xanthos, why foretell my death? You need not do so.
I know well myself that it's my fate to perish here,
far from my father and mother. But nevertheless
I shan't stop till I've driven the Trojans to their fill of war."
With a shout,
out among the foremost he urged on his whole-hoofed team.

Book 20

So by the curved ships, and around you, Pēleus's son,
never glutted with fighting, the Achaians were arming themselves,
and across from them likewise the Trojans, on the rise of the plain.
Zeus meanwhile ordered Themis to call the gods to assembly
from high, many-clefted Olympos. She went around everywhere,
with the message that they should come in to Zeus's own abode.
Not a single river was absent, save only Ocean,
nor any of all the nymphs that frequent the lovely groves,
the sources of rivers, the grassy meadows. So when
they arrived at the abode of Zeus the cloud-gatherer,
they sat down in the polished stone porticos that Hēphaistos
with cunning expertise had built there for Zeus, the Father.

Thus they gathered in Zeus's house; nor did the Earth-Shaker
ignore the goddess's summons, but came from the sea
to join them, sat in their midst, asked Zeus what his purpose was:
"Why, lord of the bright bolt, have you once more summoned
the gods
to assembly? Are you concerned about the Trojans and Achaians,
since battle and warfare are close to flaring up between them?"

In answer to him then Zeus the cloud-gatherer said:
"You know, Earth-Shaker, what's on my mind, the reason
I summoned you all: they're dying—yes, I'm concerned for them!
Even so, I myself will stay here, in a glen of Olympos,
seated, enjoying the spectacle.[1] As for the rest of you,
take yourselves off now, among the Trojans or the Achaians,
give aid to either side, whichever one you prefer!
Should Achilles, even alone, now fight against the Trojans,
they won't for one moment stop Pēleus's swift-footed son—
why, even before, they shook just at the sight of him,

1. Edwards 2011 (289) well remarks here that Zeus "does not lack sympathy for the human warriors, and it is the gods from whom he (justifiably) expects to get a good deal of amusement . . . his very active sense of humour breaks through when he thinks about the antics some of his relatives will surely get up to now that he has turned them loose."

and now, when his heart's so enraged by his comrade's death
I fear he may override fate, and storm their ramparts too."

So saying, the son of Kronos stirred up unending warfare.
Battlewards now went the gods, but with purposes divided:
Hērē to where the ships were beached, and with her Pallas
Athēnē, Poseidōn the Earth-Encircler, Hermēs
the Helper, who for smart thinking excels all others,
accompanied by Hēphaistos, exultant in his strength,
limping, but under him his stunted legs moved lightly.
To the Trojans went bright-helmeted Arēs, and with him
Phoibos, whose hair is unshorn, and Artemis the archer,
and Lētō and Xanthos[2] and smiling Aphrodītē.

For so long as the gods stayed apart from mortal men
the Achaians kept winning great glory, now that Achilles
had appeared, after lengthy absence from the grievous struggle,
while dread trembling came on the limbs of every Trojan
when, terrified, they caught sight of Pēleus's swift-footed son
agleam in his battle gear, a match for Arēs the killer.
But when the Olympians entered this throng of warriors,
and Strife sprang up, that strong rouser of nations, then Athēnē
cried out aloud: now standing by the ditch dug outside the wall,
and now on the thunderous shore, she gave her long battle cry.
Arēs bellowed as well, on the other side: black as a storm cloud,
now from the topmost ramparts he urged the Trojans on,
and now as he hastened by Simoeis toward Kallikolōnē.[3]

So both sides now did the blessed gods encourage
to clash head-on, and broke out oppressive strife between them.
Fearsomely thundered the Father of men and of gods
from on high, while down below Poseidōn caused the boundless
earth to quake, and the lofty mountain peaks:
all the foothills of spring-rich Ida were shaken, and all
her heights, and the Trojans' city, and the Achaians' ships.
In the underworld fear now gripped Hādēs, lord of the dead:

2. This Xanthos is not Achilles' recently mentioned immortal horse, but rather the local river god, known to the gods as Xanthos but to men as (the) Skamandros (73–74), against whom, or which, he is very soon to have a fearsome and protracted encounter (21.211–382).

3. Kallikolōnē (Καλλικολώνη, "Pleasant Hill"): exact position in relation to the Simoeis river uncertain, but traditionally believed to have been the site of the Judgment of Paris (*HE* 2: 430).

he leapt from his throne in panic and cried out, lest above him
the ground be split open by Poseidōn the Earth-Shaker,
and his own realm be laid bare to both gods and mortals—
dreadful and dank, abhorred even by the gods themselves.
Huge now was the crash when god faced god in strife,
for lined up against the lord Poseidōn there stood
Phoibos Apollo, winged arrows clutched in his hand,
and against Enyalios the grey-eyed goddess Athēnē,
while Hērē was faced by her of the loud chase, the golden arrows—
Artemis, archer herself, the deadly archer's sister.
Arrayed against Lētō was the mighty Helper Hermēs,
and against Hēphaistos the great deep-eddying river
known to the gods as Xanthos, but as Skamandros by mortals.

Thus gods went forth to stand against gods; but Achilles
was hungry to confront, above all, in the general mass,
Priam's son Hektōr: his heart was dead set on glutting
Arēs, that war god with oxhide shield, on Hektōr's blood.
However, it was Aineias whom Apollo, rouser of troops,
sent straight against Pēleus's son, and filled with mighty power.
Making his voice resemble that of Priam's son Lykaōn,
in his likeness Apollo, son of Zeus, now spoke to Aineias:
"Aineias, the Trojans' counsellor, where now are those threats
you once made to the Trojan lords while you were drinking,
that you'd fight, man to man, against Pēleus's son Achilles?"

Then Aineias in answer spoke to him in these words:
"Son of Priam, why urge me on, when I'm not so minded,
to match myself against Pēleus's all too arrogant son?
This would not be the first time I've faced swift-footed Achilles:
once before this he drove me headlong with his spear
from Ida, that time when he'd come out against our cattle,
and sacked both Lyrnessos and Pēdasos—but Zeus saved me,
stirred up my strength, put swiftness into my knees.
Else I'd have surely been slain at the hands of Achilles
and Athēnē, who went before him as his protector, urged him
to kill with his bronze spear both Lelegēs and Trojans.
Look, no mere man can meet Achilles in battle,
since there's always some god beside him, warding off trouble.
Besides this, his spear flies straight, and never rests
till it's gone through some human flesh. But supposing a god

were to stretch warfare's outcome evenly, then he'd not
beat me with ease, though he claimed to be made all of bronze."

To him then replied Zeus's son, the lord Apollo:
"Well, hero, you too can boast to the gods who are forever—
for they say that it was Zeus's daughter Aphrodītē
who bore you, while Achilles is the son of a lesser goddess,
your mother being Zeus's daughter, while his has as her father
the Old Man of the Sea. So, at him, with your unyielding bronze!
Don't let him scare you off with words of scorn or contempt!"

So saying he breathed great strength into the people's shepherd,
who now joined the foremost fighters, armored in gleaming bronze.
Nor did Anchīsēs's son go unnoticed by white-armed Hērē
as he went through the mass of troops to confront the son of Pēleus;
she called the gods together, and addressed them, saying:
"It's you two—Poseidōn, Athēnē—who now have need
to figure out in your minds how these matters are to be.
Aineias here has marched out, armored in gleaming bronze,
to confront Pēleus's son, spurred on by Phoibos Apollo!
So come, let's either turn him back here and now,
or else one of us should likewise stand by Achilles,
and endow him with mighty strength, let his heart lack nothing,
let him know that those who love him are the finest
of the immortals, while it's mere windbags who till now
have fended off warfare and fighting from the Trojans!
We've all come down from Olympos to play our part
in this battle, so that Achilles may suffer no hurt
from the Trojans today, though later he'll suffer whatever
Fate spun for him at his birth, when his mother bore him.
But if Achilles isn't told this, by some god in person,
he'll take fright later on, if a god comes up against him
in battle: gods are terrifying when visible as themselves."

Then Poseidōn the Earth-Shaker answered her, saying:
"Hērē, don't be enraged beyond reason: you've no need to.
Myself, I wouldn't choose to have the gods clash in strife
[us versus the rest, since we're by far the stronger];[4]
so I think we should leave the beaten track for a spot

4. The sense is uncertain: the line may have been adapted from 8.211 at an early date.

to watch from, sit down there, let humans get on with the war.
Yet if Arēs starts up a fight, or Phoibos Apollo,
or they hold Achilles back, won't allow him to fight,
then from us too they'll be hit by the burgeoning strife
of battle: quite soon, I think, they'll pull out from the fighting
and scuttle back to Olympos, to the other gods' gathering,
overwhelmed by the irresistible force of our hands."

With that
the dark-maned deity led the way to where there stood
those heaped-up ramparts named for Hēraklēs the godlike,
the high wall built for him by the Trojans and Pallas Athēnē,
to provide him a refuge in his flight from the sea beast
when it chased him from the seashore onto the plain.[5]
There the other gods and Poseidōn sat themselves down,
wrapping their shoulders about with a dense unbroken cloud,
while the opposing group settled on the brow of Kallikolōnē,
round you, Phoibos the archer, and Arēs, sacker of cities.

So they sat there on opposite sides, still busily planning
their strategies; yet to plunge into grievous warfare
both sides were reluctant, though Zeus on high urged them on.

By now the whole plain was filled with the glinting bronze
of men and horses: the earth resounded beneath their feet
as both sides charged as one. The two best of all these fighters
faced each other, eager to fight, out there in the middle—
Aineias son of Anchīsēs and noble Achilles.
Aineias was first to emerge, with threatening mien,
his weighty helmet's plumes nodding, his warlike shield
held in front of his body: he was wielding a spear of bronze.
Opposing him, Pēleus's son came at him like a lion,
a ravening beast, that men are determined to kill—the whole
neighborhood in a body. At first he goes on his way,

5. Bilked of his reward by Laomedōn for having built him Troy's walls, Poseidōn dispatched an amphibious sea beast to be a general menace in the region. An oracle told Laomedōn to put out his daughter as the monster's prey. He did this, having previously secured Hēraklēs' services to kill the creature by offering him some of his immortal horses. Aided by the defensive wall described here, Hēraklēs did the job, saving Laomedōn's daughter in the process; but Laomedōn, a chiseler to the core, rewarded him with mortal rather than immortal steeds; whereupon Hēraklēs returned with an expeditionary force and sacked Troy. See Gantz 400–401, 442–43.

uncaring; but when some youth, a brisk fighter, throws his spear
and hits him, then he crouches, jaws open, foam gathering
round his teeth: the mighty spirit groans within his heart,
with his tail he lashes his ribs and flanks on either side,
works himself up for the coming fight, and then,
eyes glaring, charges straight ahead in his raging power,
to kill some man, or himself to die among the foremost.
Just so Achilles' own strength and proud heart impelled him
to come out and confront great-hearted Aineias. When they
were close, as the two of them moved one against the other,
the first to speak was swift-footed Achilles: "Aineias,
why have you come so far out, away from the main body,
to make a stand here? Does your spirit urge you to fight me
in the hope of becoming lord, among the Trojan horse breakers,
of Priam's power? But supposing you were to kill me,
not even for that would Priam place his realm in your hands!
He has sons, he's of sound mind, he isn't crazy! Or have
the Trojans marked you out an estate that outstrips all others,
fine both for orchard and plowland, for you to possess
if you slay me? That, I think, you'd find a tough task.
Once in the past, I'd remind you, I put you to flight
with my spear—don't you remember?—when you were alone
and I sent you scampering headlong down Ida's slopes
as you ran from me! Then you fled to Lyrnessos, but I,
with Athēnē and Zeus the Father, assaulted and sacked it,
led its women captive, took their day of freedom from them,
while you were rescued by Zeus and the other gods.
But now, I think, they won't rescue you, as in your heart
you fondly imagine: so go off back, I urge you,
into the common crowd—don't confront me here—before
you suffer some hurt; what's done even fools can recognize."

Then Aineias in his turn now answered him, declaring:
"Son of Pēleus, don't try to frighten me like a child
with mere words, since I too know very well myself
how to frame the language of taunts and unseemly abuse.
We each know the other's lineage, we know his parents,
through hearing the tale of old from mortal tellers—
yet you've never set eyes on my parents, nor I on yours.
They say that you're the offspring of peerless Pēleus,

and your mother is fair-tressed Thetis, the sea goddess;
while I claim I am the son of the great-hearted
Anchīsēs, and that my mother is Aphrodītē.
Of these one pair will be weeping for a beloved son
this very day: for it won't be with mere childish insults
that we two settle our business and return from battle.
Still, if you insist, hear this too, and gain full knowledge
of our ancestry—something many men know already.
Dardanos first was begotten by Zeus the cloud-gatherer,
and founded Dardania, since not yet was sacred Ilion
built in the plain, a city of mortal humankind,
but people then still dwelt on the slopes of spring-rich Ida.
Dardanos sired a son, Erichthonios the king,
who lived to become the richest of mortal men:
three thousand mares he had grazing in the water meadows,
breeders, rejoicing in their newborn foals. Of these
mares out at pasture the north wind became enamored,
and taking the shape of a black-maned stallion, covered them:
twelve foals were conceived and born of this coupling,
and these, when bounding over the grain-rich plowland
skimmed the topmost ears of ripe corn, never crushed them,
and when bounding across the broad back of the sea
skimmed the crests of the grey brine's breakers. Then came Trōs,
whom Erichthonios sired to be king among the Trojans,
and Trōs in his turn fathered three peerless sons—
Ilos, Assarakos, and godlike Ganymēdēs
who was born the best-looking mortal man of them all,
and because of his beauty the gods wafted him aloft
to be Zeus's cup-bearer and dwell among the immortals.
Ilos too sired a son, the peerless Laomedōn,
and Laomedōn in turn sired Tithōnos and Priam,
Lampos and Klytios, and Hiketaōn, scion of Arēs,
while Assarakos begot Kapys, and Kapys Anchīsēs,
and Anchīsēs begot me, and Priam noble Hektōr:
from this blood and lineage, then, I claim descent.
But valor is something that Zeus increases or lessens
in mortals as he is minded, being the mightiest of all.
So come on then, let's stop arguing like children,
standing here in the midst of the grind of battle. Insults
are to hand for us both to cast, the one at the other—

so many, not even a hundred-benched ship could hold them!
The human tongue's voluble, the words on it are many
and of every sort, the range of man's speech is broad
on all sides: any word you speak, you can also hear.
But what need for us to exchange abuse and accusations,
yelling one at the other like a pair of housewives
who work themselves up over some gut-wrenching quarrel
and end in a lengthy slanging match on the public highway
with some true charges, some false—rage makes for lies!
It's not with words that you'll kill my urge to valor,
not until we've fought face to face with the bronze—so come,
let's make trial of each other, now, with our bronze-tipped spears."

With that he cast his great spear at Achilles' fearsomely daunting
shield, and loudly the shield clanged round the spear point.
With one strong hand Pēleus's son was holding the shield
out from him: alarmed, since he thought the far-shadowing spear
of great-hearted Aineias would easily pierce through it—
fool that he was, not knowing, by reason and by instinct,
that it's far from easy for the splendid gifts of the gods
to be vanquished, or made to yield, by mortal warriors!
So now the massive spear of warlike Aineas failed
to break through the shield: the gold, the god's gift, stopped it.
[Through two layers only he forced it; there still were three,
since five in all the lame cripple had welded together,
two of bronze, two inner layers of tin,
and one of gold, where the spear of ash was halted.][6]

Then Achilles in turn let fly his far-shadowing spear,
and hit the nicely balanced shield of Aineias, below
its outermost rim, where the bronze ran at its thinnest,
and thinnest, too, was the oxhide: clean through now passed
the Pēlian spear, and the struck shield rang with the blow.
Aineias, crouching down, held his shield out away from him
in terror: the flung spear passed over his shoulder, stuck

6. These lines have been argued over, bracketed as dubious, or rejected as spurious from antiquity on. The layers as described make "no practical sense either for the purpose or the appearance of the shield" (Edwards 2011, 323): the gold is invisible and being a soft metal would be worse than useless for stopping a spear. Hēphaistos's selection of material [18.474–75] seems to have been borrowed, and the order of metals maintained, to produce "this improbable and impractical artifact."

in the ground, after breaking through both layers
of the sheltering shield.[7] Then he, having dodged the long spear,
stood up, his eyes now showing measureless alarm,
scared on account of the spear's near miss. But Achilles
drew his sharp sword and sprang upon him in fury,
with a terrible shout. Now Aineias hefted a rock in his hands—
a mighty feat, that would take two men and more
such as men are today; but, alone, he easily wielded it,
and would have thrown it to meet Achilles' onslaught, aiming
at his helmet, or else at the shield that kept him from grim death,
and Pēleus's son with his sword, closing in, would have slain
  Aineias,
had not Poseidōn the Earth-Shaker quickly taken notice,
and straightway spoken up among the immortal gods:[8]
"Alas, I feel grief for Aineias, the great-hearted, who too soon
vanquished by Pēleus's son will go down to the realm of Hādēs
after believing the tales of Apollo, the deadly archer—
the fool! And Apollo won't even save him from wretched death!
Why should this guiltless man now suffer calamity
in vain, because of the troubles of others, he who always
gives welcome gifts to the gods who hold the broad heavens?
Come then, let's snatch him away from death ourselves,
for the son of Kronos may well be wrathful, should Achilles
slaughter Aineias here, who's destined to survive
that his race may not perish unseen for lack of seed, the line
of Dardanos, whom Kronos's son loved above all children
who have ever been born to him of mortal women. So now
he's come to look with hatred upon Priam's line: now surely
mighty Aineias will reign as king among the Trojans,
he and his sons, and his sons' sons born in time to come."

To him the ox-eyed lady Hērē replied: "Earth-Shaker,
you must decide yourself concerning Aineias—

---

7. Another physical improbability that suggests that this passage may be the work of an interpolator. How likely is a spear, even when flung by Achilles, not only to have its entire length pierce right through two layers of a shield but, despite the arresting shock, to then *continue its flight?*

8. Still more physical improbability: we are required to think of the two combatants suddenly freeze-framed, as it were, in the middle of their incipient duel, and waiting thus while the gods discuss their case, until Poseidōn comes and magically removes Aineias from the scene.

whether to rescue him, or let him be vanquished,
brave though he is, by Achilles, Pēleus's son.
The two of us have sworn a number of oaths in the presence
of all the immortals, Pallas Athēnē and I,
that we'll never ward off from the Trojans their day of evil—
not even when all Troy is ablaze with devouring fire,
and the Achaians' warlike sons are those who lit the flames."

On hearing her words, Poseidōn the Earth-Shaker
set off through the fighting and the tumult of spears,
and came to where Aineias and far-famed Achilles were.
Swiftly he shed a mist over the eyes of Achilles,
Pēleus's son, then pulled his well-bronzed ash-wood spear
out from the shield of great-hearted Aineias, and set it
at the feet of Achilles; but Aineias himself he picked up,
lifted high off the ground, and flung him: over many ranks
of fighters Aineias soared, and many of horses, thrown
in a great arc by the god's hand, till he landed
at the outermost edge of the violent conflict, where
the Kaukōnians were armed and ready for battle. Then
Poseidōn the Earth-Shaker came up close beside him,
and addressed him with winged words, saying:

"Aineias,
what god is it who's been urging you, in your rash folly,
to measure yourself, face to face, in battle against the arrogant
son of Pēleus, who's stronger than you, and better loved
by the immortals? Withdraw, any time you encounter him,
lest you enter the realm of Hādēs before your fated time!
But after Achilles meets his death and destined end
then take heart and fight among the foremost: no other
warrior of the Achaians will be able to take your life."

So saying, he left him there, when he'd revealed all this,
and at once from Achilles' eyes the marvelous mist
dispersed; and then he at once, staring hard at what he saw,
in amazement addressed his own proud spirit: "See now,
what's this strange thing I behold with my own eyes?
My spear lies here on the ground, yet he at whom I threw it,
determined to kill him, is nowhere to be seen!
Aineias, too, must be dear to the immortal gods, although

I assumed that his boasting was the merest idle bombast.
Ah, let him go: he'll not have the courage to confront me
ever again: he's too happy to have dodged death now!
So, after passing the word to the war-loving Danaäns,
I'll go face the rest of the Trojans, and make trial of them."

With that
he raced down the ranks, exhorting each warrior as he went:
"No longer now hang back from the Trojans, noble Achaians,
rather let man go face man, be raging for the battle!
It's hard for me, strong though I am, to battle against
such a mass of men, to fight them all single-handed:
not even Arēs, immortal god, nor Athēnē, could toil
and engage with the jaws of such a huge grinding conflict!
Nevertheless, as far as I'm able, with hands and feet
and human strength, I promise you, in no way
will I yield the slightest, but press right through their ranks,
and no Trojan, I think, who comes near my spear will be happy."

So he spoke, urging them on, while illustrious Hektōr
cried out to the Trojans, swore he'd go and confront Achilles:
"You great-hearted Trojans, don't be scared of Pēleus's son!
I too with words would battle even the immortals,
though not with the spear, since they're mightier by far.
Nor will Achilles accomplish everything he's promised:
a part he'll fulfill, but a part he'll leave half-finished.
Yet I shall go forth against him, though his hands be like fire—
though his hands be like fire, and his passion like red-hot iron."

So he spoke, urging them on, and the Trojans faced the foe,
spears raised: the two sides' rage mingled, the war cry went up.
Then to Hektōr came Phoibos Apollo, and spoke to him, saying:
"Hektōr, no longer challenge Achilles out front: instead
wait for him with the main body, in the tumult of battle,
lest he spear you, or wound you at close quarters with his sword."

So he spoke, and Hektōr went back into the throng of troops
alarmed, after hearing the speaking voice of the god.

But Achilles went for the Trojans, heart clad in prowess,
yelling his terrible war cry. Iphitiōn first he killed,
Otrynteus's fine son, a commander of many men,

born of a nymph, a Naiad, to Otrynteus, sacker of cities,
under snowcapped Tmōlos, in Hydē's rich countryside.
As he charged, noble Achilles took him out with a spear cast
square in the face: his head was split in two, he fell
with a thud, and over him noble Achilles exulted:
"Lie there, son of Otrynteus, most fearsome of warriors!
Here you met your death, though it was by the Gygaian
lake you were born, on your ancestral estate, beside
fish-rich Hyllos and eddying Hermos."

So he spoke,
vauntingly, but darkness now covered his victim's eyes,
and the wheels of Achaian chariots tore him asunder
in the first grinding onset: over him Dēmoleōn—
a fine battler, the son of Antēnōr—Achilles now speared
in the temple, through the bronze cheek-piece of his helmet:
the bronze helmet was no protection, the flighted spear point
tore into it, split the bone open, and all his brains
were mashed up inside: he died while still attacking.
Hippodamas next, who'd just jumped down from his chariot
and was trying to escape him, Achilles speared in the back.
As he breathed his last he bellowed, the way that a bull
will bellow when it's dragged out by young men at the lord
of Helikē's shrine[9]: the Earth-Shaker loves such things.
So did Hippodamas bellow as the proud spirit fled his bones.
Achilles now with his spear made for godlike Polydōros,
a son of Priam. His father refused to allow him to fight,
since among his children he was the latest-born,
and his favorite as well, and beat everyone at running:
but then, in his childishness, to show how fast he could sprint,
he went tearing down the front line, and lost his life there,
speared square in the back by swift-footed noble Achilles
as he dashed by, where the baldric's golden clasps
were fastened, and the two ends of the corselet overlapped.
Clean through beside the navel went the spear point, and he
sank on his knees with a groan: a dark cloud enshrouded him,
and, collapsing, he grasped his innards in his hands.

9. The "lord of Helikē" was Poseidōn, who had a famous shrine at Helikē on the coast of Achaia.

But when Hektōr perceived his brother Polydōros,
with his innards clutched in his hands, collapsing on the ground,
a mist was shed over his eyes, no longer could he bear
to range over the battlefield, but made straight for Achilles,
like a flame, brandishing his keen-edged spear. When Achilles
saw him, up he sprang, and vauntingly declared:
"Here comes the man who has most deeply vexed my spirit,
since he slew my much-beloved comrade: not for much longer
shall we two avoid each other along the battle lines."

That said, with an angry glance he called to noble Hektōr:
"Come close, that you may the sooner enter destruction's
bounds."

To this, untouched by fear, bright-helmeted Hektōr replied:
"Son of Pēleus, don't try to frighten me like a child
with mere words, since I know perfectly well myself
how to frame the language of taunts and rancorous abuse.
I know, too, you're a great fighter, and that I rank well
below you.
Yet it's true that such matters rest on the knees of the gods—
whether I, though the lesser man, may still rob you of life
when I cast my spear: it's been sharp enough in the past."

With that he swung and let fly his spear, but Athēnē
blew it back, well away from glorious Achilles,
with a light breath only: it returned to noble Hektōr,
fell right at his feet. Then Achilles sprang upon him,
hot for action, determined to cut him down,
with a terrifying shout. But Apollo snatched Hektōr away—
very easily, as a god can, and hid him in dense mist.
Three times did swift-footed noble Achilles rush him
with his bronze spear; three times he only struck thick mist.
But when for the fourth time he charged at him like a god,
after his fearsome war cry he spoke winged words to him:
"Now once more, dog, you've dodged death, though close indeed
that bad thing came to you! But once more Phoibos Apollo
saved you, to whom it must be that you pray before entering
the clash of spears—and for sure, when I meet you later,
if there's any god who's *my* helper, I'll finish you off!
But for now I'll go after the others, see whom I can catch."

So saying, he struck Dryōps full in the neck with his spear,
and Dryōps slumped at his feet. He left him there,
and Philētōr's son Dēmouchos, a big strong fellow,
he hit with his spear on one knee, cut short his advance,
then savaged with his great sword, deprived him of life.
Next Dardanos and Laogonos, two sons of Bias,
he attacked, forcing both from their chariot to the ground,
one speared, the other cut down by his sword, hand to hand.
Then Alastōr's son Trōs—who'd come up to clasp his knees
in the hope that he'd take him prisoner, let him live,
out of pity for one of his age group, rather than kill him:
    the fool,
unaware that there wasn't a chance of ever persuading him,
since this was a man without kindness of mind or heart,
but raging to kill—flung his arms now around Achilles' knees,
tried to beseech him. A sword-stroke found his liver,
the liver protruded, and black blood poured down from it,
filling his tunic's fold. Darkness shrouded his eyes
as he lost hold of life. Achilles then closed in on Moulios,
hit one ear with his spear, and the bronze point drove
clean through to the other ear. Agēnōr's son Echeklos
he slashed square on the head with his hilted sword:
its whole blade was warmed with his blood, and both his eyes
were invaded by scarlet death and all-mastering fate.
Deukaliōn next, at the point where the elbow's tendons
are joined, Achilles pierced through one arm with his bronze
spear point: Deukaliōn faced him, arm weighed down,
seeing his death before him. Achilles' sword severed his neck,
sent both head and helmet flying, while marrow spurted out
from his spine, and the trunk lay spread-eagled on the ground.
Then Achilles went in pursuit of Peirēs' blameless son,
Rhigmos, who'd come from rich-soiled Thrace. Him now
Achilles speared in mid-torso: the bronze stuck in his belly,
and he fell from his chariot. While his driver Areïthoös
was wheeling his horses around, he too was hit, in the back,
by Achilles' sharp spear, and thrown out: the horses panicked.

As devouring fire rages onward through the deep glens
of a dried-out mountainside, and the thick maquis flares up,
and on all sides the blaze is fanned by a roiling wind,

so Achilles, like some demon,[10] raged everywhere with his spear,
hard on the heels of his victims: the earth ran black with blood.
As a man yokes broad-browed bulls for the treading out
of white barley strewn on a strong-based threshing-floor,
and quickly the grain's unhusked by the feet of the bellowing bulls,
so, urged by great-hearted Achilles, his whole-hoofed horses
galloped over the dead and their shields; with blood all the axle
below was splashed, and the rails round his chariot,
with the drops flung up by the wheels and the horses' hooves
as Pēleus's son charged on, his invincible hands
bespattered with flying gore, in his pursuit of glory.

---

10. The Greek word δαίμων (*daimōn*) is nuanced in a bewildering variety of ways. In essence it means a divine or superhuman power, a spirit: sometimes neutral, sometimes aggressive, occasionally kindly; sometimes personal, sometimes vaguely abstract; at times fate, or divinity, or heaven, or a god, or the gods collectively. For some reason the one thing the scholarly tradition shies away from ever translating it as is "demon," the modern version of the word itself, perhaps feeling that this is too tarred with the post-Christian tradition. But a malevolent spirit is clearly at work at 9.600 and 15.468, and Achilles does indeed attack like a demon, in the extended English sense as well, both here and at 21.93, 227; in these cases I have translated accordingly.

Book 21

But when they came to the ford of the swift-flowing River,
eddying Xanthos, whom immortal Zeus engendered,
Achilles now split the rout. Some he pursued across the plain
towards the city, where the Achaians were fleeing in panic
the day before, when faced with illustrious Hektōr's fury—
they'd broken, fled in disorder, and Hērē had spread
a dense mist in front to confuse them—but half the Trojans
were herded into the River, deep-flowing and silver-eddied.
In they splashed in with great outcry: the deep streambed
  resounded,
both riverbanks echoed the tumult as they went swimming
this way and that, still shouting, spun round by the eddies.
As when, with an onrushing fire, clouds of locusts will take wing
in flight towards a river, and the never-wearying blaze
in its sudden onset will scorch them, and they cringe in the water,
so at Achilles' onset the stream of deep-eddying Xanthos
was loud with a mingled confusion of men and horses.

Achilles, scion of Zeus, now left his spear on the bank,
leaning against a tamarisk, and charged in like a demon,
armed only with his sword, horrific deeds in mind.
He turned and struck at random, and ghastly cries went up
from those caught by his sword: the water ran red with blood,
and as, fleeing a huge-mawed dolphin, the other fishes
scurry to fill the bolt-holes of some sheltering harbor,
terrified, since the dolphin devours all it catches—
so these Trojans, caught in the current of the terrible River,
cowered under its banks. When his hands grew weary with killing,
Achilles pulled twelve youths up alive from the water,
to be blood-price for the death of Menoitios's son Patroklos.
He led them ashore, all dazed, like so many fawns,
and bound their hands behind them with the well-cut belts
that they wore to cinch in their soft tunics, and then turned them
over to his companions to take back to the hollow ships.
This done, he sprang back again, his mind hard set on slaughter.

There it was he encountered a son of Dardanian Priam
fleeing from the River: Lykaōn, whom once before he'd caught
and snatched, struggling, out of his father's orchard
during a night raid: he was busy cutting young branches
from a fig tree with the sharp bronze, to make rails for a chariot,
when on him—an unlooked-for disaster—came noble Achilles,
who took him by ship to well-built Lēmnos and sold him
off as a slave: Jason's son had paid the price demanded,
but a guest-friend then ransomed him, for a very large sum—
Ēëtiōn of Imbros, who sent him to noble Arisbē,
from where, slipping off in secret, he reached his ancestral home.
For eleven days he took pleasure among his friends
on arrival from Lēmnos; but on the twelfth some god threw him
back into the hands of Achilles, who this second time
would dispatch him to Hādēs' realm, loath though he was to go.
When noble swift-footed Achilles noticed this man,
unarmed, minus helmet or shield, no spear in his hand—
he'd thrown them all away, being tired and sweaty
as he clambered out of the river, knees weak from exhaustion—
in amazement he then addressed his own proud spirit:
"Ah, me, what's this strange thing I see with my own eyes?
Surely those great-hearted Trojans whom I've slaughtered
will rise once more from the murk of the underworld,
seeing that this fellow is back, after dodging his day of doom,
though sold into sacred Lēmnos; nor has the deep
of the grey sea held him back, that stops many against their will.
Well, now indeed he'll also get a taste of my spear,
so that I'll be able to see, and be sure in my mind,
whether he'll come back likewise from that too, or rather
be stopped by the life-giving earth, that holds down even the strong."

So he reflected, waiting: Lykaōn now approached him,
dazed, eager to clasp his knees, and desperate at heart
to escape an unpleasant end and the black death-spirit.
Then noble Achilles lifted and poised his long spear,
ready to kill: but Lykaōn ducked under it, embraced
Achilles' knees. The spear passed over his back and stuck
in the ground, still longing to glut itself with men's flesh.
Then Lykaōn besought Achilles—one hand clasping his knees,
while the other kept a firm grip on his sharpened spear,

not letting go—and addressed him with winged words:
"By your knees, Achilles, I beg you, respect me, take pity on me!
Zeus's nursling, I'm your suppliant, I deserve your respect,
since you were the first with whom I tasted Dēmētēr's grain[1]
on the day you captured me in our well-planned orchard,
and shipped me far away from father and friends,
to sacred Lēmnos, for the price of a hundred oxen!
To free me by ransom cost three times as much, and this
morning's the twelfth since I returned to Ilion,
after much hardship—and now my fatal destiny's put me
back in your hands: I must be hateful to Zeus the Father
since he's given me to you again! Too short the life my mother
bore me to—Laothoē, old Altēs' daughter—Altēs,
who rules as lord over the war-loving Lelegēs,
from steep Pēdasos, his city on the Satnioeis river.
His daughter Priam married—among many other women—
and of her we two sons were born: now you'll slaughter us both—
one you've already done for among the front-line fighters,
Polydōros the godlike, laid low by your sharp spear;
and now a bad end awaits me too, for I don't imagine
I'll escape your hands: some god it was brought me to you.
And another thing I'll tell you, and you bear it in mind:
I'm not born from the same womb as Hektōr, so don't kill me:
He it was that slew your comrade, so kindly and so strong."

Thus Priam's illustrious son addressed him, with words
of entreaty, but there was no honey in the reply he heard:
"Fool, don't talk ransom to me, don't make speeches!
Before Patroklos encountered the day of his destiny,
till then I was more inclined to spare the lives
of Trojans, and many I captured alive and sold;
but of them now not one shall escape death, whomsoever
before Troy's ramparts a god puts into my hands
of all Trojans—and least of all one of Priam's sons!
So, friend, you too must die: why then lament thus?
Patroklos too is dead, a far better man than you are.

1. I.e., Achilles was the first Greek with whom Lykaōn broke bread after being captured. Richardson (60) quotes a scholiast's explanation of Lykaōn's hopeful argument: "It would be incongruous to offer food, the source of life, to someone, and then take away his life. And he mentions Demeter to evoke religious scruples."

Can't you see what I'm like, how handsome and tall I am?
A fine father sired me, the mother who bore me was a goddess—
Yet over me too hang death and all-mastering destiny:
A day will come when, at dawn, or noon, or evening,
my life too will be forfeit to someone in battle,
by a flighted spear or an arrow shot from the bowstring."

So he spoke, and Lykaōn's knees and heart were unstrung:
he let go the spear, and sat there, both hands outstretched
in supplication. But Achilles drew his sharp sword, and plunged it
in by the neck at the collarbone: the two-edged blade
sank in its full length, and Lykaōn fell prone, lay stretched out
there on the ground. His dark blood gushed, soaked the earth.
Achilles now seized one foot, flung him into the river
as flotsam, and, vaunting, spoke winged words over him:
"Lie there now with the fishes, that'll lick the blood
from your wound, quite indifferent to you; nor will your mother
lay you out on a bier and wail over you: rather will Skamandros
roll you away in its eddies to the wide gulf of the sea,
and fish darting through the waves will surface amid
their black ripples to nibble Lykaōn's white lustrous fat!
So die all, till we reach sacred Ilion's citadel,
with you in full flight, and I in murderous pursuit!
Not even the swift-flowing and silver-eddied River
will protect you, long though you've offered him bull after bull,
and thrown whole-hoofed horses alive still into his eddies:
you'll all suffer the same evil fate, till every one of you
has paid for Patroklos's death, and the loss of those Achaians
whom you slaughtered by the swift ships while I was absent."

So he spoke, and the River grew yet more enraged at heart,
pondering in his mind how to make noble Achilles
stop his war work, how to fend off calamity from the Trojans.
Meanwhile the son of Pēleus, with his far-shadowing spear,
went for Asteropaios, hungry to kill him—the son
of Pēlegōn, who was begotten by wide-flowing Axios
on Periboia, the eldest of Akessamenos's daughters:
with her the deep-eddying River mingled in love. Him now
Achilles charged, as he came up from the water,
holding two spears, making for him, fierce strength put in his heart

by Xanthos, irate on account of the young men slaughtered
by Achilles along the River on his pitiless killing spree.

When they came close, advancing the one against the other,
swift-footed noble Achilles was the first to speak:
"Who are you, from where, that you dare to come out and
face me?
Unhappy are those whose sons confront my strength!"

To him then replied Pēlegōn's illustrious son:
"Great-hearted son of Pēleus, why query my lineage?
I come from rich-soiled Paiōnia, a distant land,
in command of Paiōnian lancers, and this is now
the eleventh day since I arrived here in Ilion. As for
my ancestry, I'm descended from wide-flowing Axios—
Axios, who sends forth the sweetest water on earth,
who begot Pēlegōn, famed for his spear; and he,
they say, was my father. So now, renowned Achilles, let's fight!"

Menacingly he spoke, and noble Achilles raised
his spear of Pēlian ash; but the hero Asteropaios
let fly both spears at once, being double-handed,
and with one spear he struck his opponent's shield, but failed
to break through: the gold layer, a god's gift, held it off;
but the other spear struck Achilles' forearm a grazing blow—
his right one: dark blood gushed, but the spear point passed on,
and stuck in the ground, still hungry to glut itself on flesh.
Then Achilles flung his true-flying ash-wood spear
at Asteropaios, in fierce determination to kill him,
but missed the man and struck the high riverbank,
sank the spear half its length, fixing it in the earth.
Pēleus's son drew the sharp sword from beside his thigh,
and sprang at him, hot to kill. Asteropaios failed
to pull Achilles' spear from the bank in his massive fist:
three times, trying to free it, he made it quiver,
three time he gave up. The fourth time his heart was set on
bending and breaking the ash spear of Aiakos's grandson:
but, before he could do it, Achilles' sword at close quarters
took his life, struck into his belly, beside the navel: his guts
gushed out on the ground, and darkness shrouded his eyes
as he lay there, gasping still, and Achilles jumped on his chest

and stripped off his armor, and shouted exultantly:
"Lie there! It's hard to strive with the sons of mighty Kronos,
even for someone sired by a River! You claim
a wide-flowing River for ancestor, whereas I
declare myself of the lineage of mighty Zeus! The man
who begot me is lord over the numerous Myrmidons—
Pēleus, Aiakos's son; it was Zeus who sired Aiakos.
So, as Zeus is mightier than all seaward-flowing rivers,
Zeus's line likewise outranks a River's ancestry!
You may have a great River beside you—always supposing
it can protect you: but still there's no fighting Kronos's son
Zeus! With him not even the lord Achelōïos contends,
nor the vast might of deep-flowing Ocean, from whom
all rivers derive, and the whole mass of the sea,
and every spring and deep well has its beginning;
no, even he goes in fear of the bolt of mighty Zeus,
and his awesome thunder, whenever it crashes out of the sky."

With that he pulled his bronze spear out from the riverbank,
and left Asteropaios there, when he'd taken his dear life,
sprawled out among the sand shoals, lapped by dark water,
with the eels and fishes all busy about him,
nibbling and tearing the fat surrounding his kidneys.
Achilles moved on to harass the Paiōnians, chariot marshals,
who still lay in scattered confusion alongside the eddying River
after seeing their best warrior in the grind of battle
laid low by the might of Achilles and his sword.
There he took down Thersilochos, Astypylos, and Mydōn,
Mnēsos and Thrasios, Ainios, Ophelestēs—
and yet more Paiōnians would swift Achilles have slain,
had the deep-eddying River, enraged, not now addressed him
in the semblance of a man, voicing speech from a deep eddy:
"Ah, Achilles, beyond all in strength, beyond all men in evil
acts, since the gods themselves are forever your protectors!
If the son of Kronos is letting you kill every Trojan, at least
drive these well away from me, do your vile work on dry land!
My lovely streams are currently all awash with corpses;
I can't get to discharge my waters into the bright sea,
I'm so choked with the dead, while you ruthlessly keep on killing!
Come, now, let me be: I'm dumbfounded, O High Commander."

Then swift-footed Achilles answered him in these words:
"All this, Zeus's nursling Skamandros, shall be done as you request.
But I'll not cease from the slaughter of these arrogant Trojans
till I've cooped them up in their city, and made trial of Hektōr,
man against man, and either he slays me, or I him."

So saying, he charged at the Trojans like a demon,
and then the deep-eddying River said to Apollo: "Look here,
child of Zeus, lord of the silver bow, you've not honored
the wishes of Kronos's son, who strongly required you
to stand firm by the side of the Trojans, and help them until
the late-setting sun goes down, and darkens the rich earth."

So he spoke. Achilles, famed spearman, leapt to midstream
from the high bank. But the River, now rushing onward in turbulent
spate, stirred all his streams, swept up the countless
corpses that cluttered his channel, whom Achilles had killed:
these he, bellowing bull-like, tossed up onto dry land,
while the ones still alive he protected with his sweet streams,
concealing them in his eddies, which were both large and deep.
Fearsomely round Achilles surged his turbulent wave: its crest
crashing onto his shield forced him back, he could no longer
stand firm on his feet, so reached out and grasped an elm,
one full-grown and lofty, but it came away roots and all,
tearing up the whole bank, and with its clustering branches
dropped right across the fine streambed, damming the River himself
by falling its whole length within him. Achilles sprang clear
of his whirling waters, ran swift-foot across the plain
in some alarm. But the great god did not give up,
pursued him, surging black-crested, to stop the actions of noble
Achilles, fend off destruction from the Trojans.
But Pēleus's son leapt back the whole length of a spear cast
with the swoop of a black eagle, the hunting falcon,
that is the strongest and swiftest of all winged creatures:
such was his speed, and the bronze strips on his torso
rattled fearfully. He dodged aside from under the River
and kept running: the River's huge bore roared on behind him.
As a man who digs a channel from a dark-water spring
to the plants in his garden will guide the water's flow,

mattock in hand to clear obstructions from the channel,
and, as the rill flows on, all the pebbles that litter its bed
are swept along with it while it chuckles quickly down
a slope in the channel, even getting ahead of its guide—
just so did the River's bore keep overtaking Achilles,
swift runner though he was: gods are mightier than mortals.
Every time swift-footed noble Achilles attempted
to stand firm and confront the River, to find out if all
the immortals who hold the wide heavens were his pursuers,
the sky-fed River's huge crest would come crashing down
on his shoulders, he'd jump away from it, much wearied
in spirit, while the River's rough spate kept sapping the strength
of his knees beneath him, sucked the earth from under his feet.
Then Pēleus's son cried out, looking up to the wide heavens:
"Zeus, Father, not one god has undertaken to save me,
pitiable as I am, from the River—after this, I could
endure any trouble! Yet none of the Heavenly Ones is as much
to blame as my mother, who beguiled me with lies,
saying that under the walls of the corseleted Trojans
I'd perish, slain by the swift shafts of Apollo!
If only Hektōr had killed me, the best-bred warrior here,
then noble had been the slayer, noble the man he slew—
whereas now it's my wretched fate to perish miserably,
trapped in a great river, like some swineherd's boy
who's swept away by the torrent he tries to cross in winter."[2]

So he spoke; and very quickly Poseidōn and Athēnē
came and stood by him, in the likeness of mortal men,
took him by the hand, and spoke reassuringly to him.
Of them Poseidōn the Earth-Shaker now addressed him, saying:
"Son of Pēleus, don't be too scared, no need for alarm
when you have two such helpers as we are, from the gods,
and with Zeus's approval—Pallas Athēnē and I!
Since it's not your destiny to be overcome by the River
he'll very soon ease off—as you'll see for yourself.

2. It is generally assumed that Achilles would regret not having been killed by another champion warrior, and this thought is certainly present. But both ἀγαθός (*agathos*, "good") and ἄριστος (*aristos*, "best"), the epithets used here, while regularly in Homer denoting excellence in a warrior, also regularly denote nobility of birth. The reference to the swineherd's boy is significant: Achilles would most regret not having died, like a gentleman, in single combat with another such.

Now, if you will listen, we have good advice for you:
Don't let your hands cease from the work of common warfare
until you've cooped up inside Troy's famous ramparts
the whole routed Trojan army; when you've taken Hektōr's life
return to the ships. This much glory we grant you."

So saying, they both went back to the immortals,
but Achilles, greatly encouraged by the gods' behest,
went on over the plain, now swamped with a flood of water,
and much fine armor and weapons of young slain warriors
lay floating there with their corpses: his knees rose high
as he charged, straight against the current. Now the wide-flowing
river could not stop him, such strength he had from Athēnē.
Yet Skamandros did not abate his force, but rather swelled
his wrath against Pēleus's son, brought his waters up to a crest,
raising himself aloft, and shouted to Simoeis:
"Dear brother, to face this man's strength will need both of us
if we're to stop him from sacking King Priam's great city
any time now! The Trojans won't withstand him in battle,
so help me at once, go flood your streams with the flow
from your springs, put all your torrents in spate,
raise a huge wave, stir up a thunderous racket
of driftwood and pebbles! We must halt this wild warrior,
who now has the upper hand, wants to match the gods in action!
For I tell you, neither his violence nor his good looks will save him,
nor his fine armor, which in some flooded pool of mine
will lie, all coated with mud; while the man himself
I'll wrap in sand, pour over him an abundance of shingle.
That way the Achaians will have no idea where to gather
his bones, under such a mass of silt I shall entomb him!
Here will his grave be prepared, and he'll have no need
of a burial mound, when Achaians perform his funeral rites."

With that he rushed at Achilles, turbulent, surging high,
seething with foam and blood and slaughtered corpses.
The dark and heaving wave of the sky-fed River
towered above him, began to take down the son of Pēleus;
then Hērē cried out in a loud voice, being scared for Achilles,
lest the huge deep-eddying River should sweep him away,
and at once called upon Hēphaistos, her own dear son:
"Up with you, my lame child! You are the one, we thought,

best matched in battle with Xanthos, the eddying River—
so bring help at once to Achilles, create widespread fire,
while I quickly stir from the sea a violent gale, its force
fed by the west and the white-cloud southern winds,
that will burn up the Trojans—themselves and their battle gear—
by spreading destructive flames. Along Xanthos's banks now
go set his trees alight, ring him with fire, don't allow him
in any way to dissuade you, with honeyed words or threats,
and don't relax your pressure until the moment
when I call to you: only then should you curb your tireless fire."

So she spoke. Hēphaistos set up a marvelous conflagration:
First on the plain the blaze was kindled, burning the dead,
all the corpses thickly strewn there, slain by Achilles,
and the whole plain was dried up now, the bright water halted.
As when at harvest time the north wind quickly parches
a fresh-watered threshing floor, and he who raked it rejoices,
so now the whole plain was scorched, and the corpses completely
consumed. Then against the River he turned his blazing flames:
the elms caught fire, and the willows and tamarisks,
the celandine burned, the rushes, the galingale—everything
that grew in abundance along the sweet course of the River,
and the eels and fish in the eddies were sorely distressed,
somersaulting this way and that along the sweet streams,
tormented by the fire blast that wily Hēphaistos discharged.
Burned too was the mighty River, who now addressed the god:
"Hēphaistos, no other god can match himself against you,
nor am I minded to fight you, ablaze with fire as you are!
So, stop your assault! The Trojans? Let noble Achilles drive them
out of their city! Why should I help or hinder here?"

Ablaze with flames he spoke, his sweet streams bubbling up:
as a cauldron will boil over when forced by a hot fire,
that's rendering down the lard of a fattened porker,
bubbling up all round, dry firewood stacked beneath it—
so the River's sweet streams blazed, and their water bubbled,
and he stopped, with no will to flow further: the fiery blast
of inventive Hēphaistos had stalled him, and now to Hērē
he addressed an urgent prayer, speaking in winged words:
"Hērē, why is your son giving me and my waters trouble
above all others? I surely am not so much at fault

as all those who have acted as supporters of the Trojans!
Even so, I'll desist, if that's what you want of me—but
let this fellow desist as well! What's more, I'll swear an oath
that I'll never ward off from the Trojans their day of evil,
not even when all Troy is ablaze with devouring fire,
and the Achaians' warlike sons are those who lit the flames!"

When the goddess, white-armed Hērē, heard these words,
she at once addressed Hēphaistos, her dear son:
"Hēphaistos, desist, famed child! It is not seemly
to assail an immortal god thus on behalf of mortals."

So she spoke, and Hēphaistos quenched his astounding blaze,
and the current went rolling back down the River's sweet streams.

When the might of Xanthos was vanquished, both he and Hēphaistos
desisted, held back by Hērē, furious though she was;
but upon the rest of the gods strife descended, both momentous
and agonizing: their spirits were blown in opposite directions,
they engaged with a huge clatter, the wide earth reechoed,
the great firmament trumpeted. Zeus heard it all
from where he sat on Olympos, broke out in delighted
laughter to see the gods all fighting with one another,
standing aloof no longer. First into combat was Arēs,
piercer of shields, who began by assailing Athēnē,
bronze spear in hand, with a stream of insulting words:
"Why once more now, you dog fly, are you setting gods
against gods—as your proud heart bids you, so fierce, so daring?
Don't you recall setting up Diomēdēs, Tydeus' s son,
to wound me? You yourself, in full view, grabbed his spear
and thrust it straight at me, tore open my handsome flesh!
So now I think you'll pay me the price for all you did."

So saying, he hit her full on her tasseled aegis,
that fearsome thing, not subduable even by Zeus's bolts:
there it was bloodstained Arēs struck home with his long spear.
Athēnē started back, and hefted in one strong hand
a rock that lay on the plain, black, jagged, enormous,
set up by men in the past as the boundary mark of a field.
With this she hit furious Arēs on the neck, unstrung his limbs.
Seven furlongs he stretched in his fall, fouled his hair in the dust,
and his armor rattled about him. Pallas Athēnē laughed,

and vauntingly addressed him, speaking in winged words:
"Fool! Have you still not learned how much more warlike than you
I can claim to be, when you pit your strength against mine?
This is how you'll pay the price to the Furies of your mother,
who's planning trouble for you in her anger because
you've left the Achaians, are supporting the arrogant Trojans!"

This said, Athēnē turned her keen gaze from Arēs,
whom then Aphrodītē, Zeus's daughter, caught by the hand
and led away, groaning deeply, still barely catching his breath.

But when white-armed Hērē, the goddess, noticed Aphrodītē,
straight away she addressed Athēnē with winged words:
"Well, now, unwearying child of Zeus of the aegis,
there's that dog fly again, leading Arēs, ruin of mortals,
out through the fighting, away from grim warfare! After her!"

Thus she spoke, and Athēnē was glad to set off in pursuit,
caught up, and struck Aphrodītē a blow on the breast
with her strong fist, unstrung both her knees and her spirit.
So there Aphrodītē and Arēs lay on the nurturing earth,
and Athēnē exulted over them, speaking winged words:
"Let all suffer thus who lend support to the Trojans
when they dare to confront the mail-corseleted Achaians!
May they prove as daring and resolute as Aphrodītē,
who came out to rescue Arēs, and then faced my might—
this way we'd have long since put an end to the war,
by sacking Ilion, that well-founded citadel!"

So she spoke, and the goddess, white-armed Hērē, smiled.
But Poseidōn, the lordly Earth-Shaker, now called out to Apollo:
"Why, Phoibos, are we two standing aloof? That's not seemly
when others have joined in! Too shameful, if without fighting
we went back to Olympos, to Zeus's bronze-floored abode!
You begin: you're the younger, it's not proper for me to,
since I was born before you, and have more wisdom.
You fool, what a witless heart you have! Don't you recall
all the ills that we two, alone of the gods, endured
in Ilion, when we came to serve haughty Laomedōn,
by Zeus's command, for a year, as hired workers,
at a fixed wage, and he was our taskmaster, gave us orders?
I built for the Trojans a wall encircling their city—

both wide and splendid, to make the city unbreachable;
while you, Phoibos, herded their sleek and shambling cattle
among the foothills and woodlands of many-ridged Ida.
But when the year's happy seasons brought round the due time
for payment, then we were defrauded of all our hire
by that monster Laomedōn, who dismissed us with threats,
saying he'd put us in fetters, bound hand and foot,
and sell us both abroad, dispatch us to some far island—
threatened, too, to cut off our ears with the bronze!
So home we both went, infuriated at heart
because of the wages he'd promised, but not delivered—
and now it's *his* people you're helping, you won't work with us
to make sure these arrogant Trojans perish—and miserably,
in utter ruin—they, their children, their honored wives."

Lord Apollo, the deadly archer, made him this answer:
"Earth-Shaker, you would not speak of me as one that's sound
of mind, were I to fight you on behalf of those wretches—
mortals, who, like the leaves, in one season are ablaze
with life, and consuming the harvested fruits of the earth,
in another waste into lifelessness. So let us speedily
desist from our combat, leave them to fight it out on their own."

So saying, he turned back, since he felt embarrassed
at the prospect of coming to blows with his father's brother.
But he got a strong rebuke from his sister, the Lady of Beasts,
Artemis, wild huntress, who addressed him in scathing words:
"Running away, deadly archer? Conceding a total triumph
to Poseidōn? Letting him boast of his effortless victory?
You fool! Then why carry that bow? It's useless as wind!
From now on don't let me hear you, in our father's halls,
boast—as you did a while back before the immortal gods—
that you'd fight in single combat against Poseidōn!"

So she spoke, and Apollo, deadly archer, made no reply.
But Zeus's revered bedmate, losing her temper, now
upbraided the bow huntress in abusive language:
"You shameless bitch, how come you're so hot to make a stand
against me now? I'm a tough one for you to take on,
though you carry that bow: Zeus made you a lion, but against
women—let you kill any one of *them* that you chose to!

Better, I'd think, in the mountains to be hunting beasts of prey
and wild deer, than to battle those stronger than yourself!
Still, if you're bent on war, you'll find out, the hard way,
how much stronger I am, when you match your strength against mine."

This said, with her left hand Hērē gripped Artemis by both wrists,
while her right hand snatched from her shoulders the bow and quiver,
and beat her about the ears with them, a smile on her face,
as Artemis struggled, and her swift shafts were spilled. Then, weeping,
the goddess broke from Hērē's grasp, fled like a dove
that flies, pursued by a hawk, into some hollow rock's cleft,
and escapes, since it's not her destiny to be caught—
so Artemis fled in tears, bow and arrows left where they fell.

To Lētō then spoke Hermēs the guide, the slayer of Argos:
"Lētō, I'll not fight you: it's a disastrous business,
this exchanging of blows with the wives of Zeus the cloud-gatherer!
You can boast all you want among the immortal gods
that you vanquished me forcefully, by dint of your mighty strength."

So he spoke. Lētō picked up her daughter's back-bent bow,
and the arrows that had been scattered amid the swirling dust,
and retreated, taking them with her. But Artemis the maiden
made her way to Zeus's brazen-floored home on Olympos,
where she sat down, weeping, on the knees of her father,
and the ambrosial robe she wore quivered. Then her father,
Kronos's son, hugged her to him, and, laughing quietly, asked:
"Which of the gods in heaven, dear child, has done this to you,
without reason, as though you were openly misbehaving?"

Fine-garlanded Artemis of the loud chase answered him:
"Your wife it was beat me up, father, white-armed Hērē,
because of whom strife and fighting are the lot of the immortals."
Such was their conversation, the one to the other.

Phoibos Apollo now went down into sacred Ilion,
concerned in his mind for the wall of the well-built citadel,
lest the Danaäns sack it that day, before its destined time.
But the other immortal gods made their way to Olympos,
some enraged, some greatly exultant, and took their seats
in the house of the lord of the dark clouds. Now Achilles
was still slaughtering Trojans and their whole-hoofed horses;

and as smoke goes up and reaches the broad heavens
from a burning town, fanned on by the wrath of the gods,
causing hard work for all and suffering for many,
so Achilles brought hard work and suffering to the Trojans.

Old Priam was standing out on the god-built rampart,
and watching huge Achilles, and the way that before him
the Trojans scattered in headlong flight, without resistance.
He groaned, and went down from the ramparts to ground level,
instructing his trusty gatekeepers along the wall:
"Hold the gates wide open until our routed troops
can make their way into the city—Achilles is right
behind them, driving them on, I think disaster's upon us!
So the moment they're inside the wall, still breathing hard,
then slam shut the close-fitting gates, for I greatly fear
that calamitous warrior may rush in beyond the ramparts."

So he spoke: they undid the fastenings, shot back the bars,
and the gates were flung wide, brought deliverance, while Apollo
sprang out to meet the rush, fend off ruin from the Trojans,
who were fleeing straight for the city and its lofty ramparts,
parched with thirst and covered with dust from the plain,
in rout, while Achilles herded them savagely with his spear,
heart ever ruled by madness, ardent to harvest glory.

Then would the Achaians' sons have taken high-gated Troy,
had Phoibos Apollo not stirred up noble Agēnōr,
Antēnōr's son, a warrior of unmatchable power:
in his heart he put boldness, and himself stood by him,
ready to fend off from him the heavy hands of death:[3]
against the oak tree he leaned, enshrouded in thick mist.
When Agēnōr caught sight of Achilles, the sacker of cities,
he stood still, and much his heart brooded on while waiting,
and deeply stirred he addressed his own proud spirit:
"Ah, me! If faced with mighty Achilles I should now
retreat to where all the others are being driven in rout,
even so he'd still catch me and slit my throat as a coward.

---

3. One MS and one ancient commentator read not "hands" (χεῖρας, *cheiras*) here but "[death]-spirits" (κῆρας, *kēras*). Like Leaf and Richardson (99), but unlike Monro and Allen, Lattimore, and some other translators), I prefer χεῖρας. The phrase is striking, and hands are more likely than spirits to carry weight, whether physically or metaphorically.

But suppose I leave these men to be chased and herded
by Pēleus's son Achilles, and run from the wall in a different
direction, towards the Ilian plain, until I reach
the foothills of Ida, and take refuge in their thickets?
Then, when evening came, I'd wash myself in the river,
clean off the sweat, and make my way back to Ilion.
But why is my heart debating such matters with me?
he might spot me taking off from the city towards the plain,
and, being swift-footed, pursue and overtake me.
No chance then of my avoiding death and the death-spirits,
so strong he is, far stronger than all other mortal men.
But suppose that I go to confront him before the city?
His flesh, too, can be pierced by the keen-edged bronze,
and there's only one life in him—men say he's mortal—
however much Zeus son of Kronos endows him with glory."

That said, he crouched awaiting Achilles, and in him
his courageous heart was eager for warfare and battle.
As a leopard will sally forth from the deepest thicket
to confront a hunter, nor does her courage fail her,
nor does she panic on hearing the baying of hounds,
for though the hunter may spear her or shoot her first,
yet she'll still not abandon her prowess, even when spitted
on the spear, till she either grapples with him or is slain—
so the son of lordly Antēnōr, noble Agēnōr,
would not retreat till he had made trial of Achilles,
but holding before him his trimly balanced shield,
and pointing his spear at Achilles, now shouted aloud:
"I'm sure you hoped in your heart, illustrious Achilles,
that on this day you'd sack the proud Trojans' citadel—
you fool! Much sorrow's to come still in the matter of Troy,
since within her we, her warriors, are many and strong,
who, protecting our beloved parents and wives and sons,
stand guard over Ilion. It is you who will meet your end here,
however fearsome and daring a warrior you may be."

With that he let fly the sharp spear from his massive hand,
and did not miss, but hit Achilles' shin under his knee,
and the greave of fresh-wrought tin that was fastened round it
rang fearsomely when struck; but the bronze rebounded
and did not pierce through, for the god's gift held it back.

Then Pēleus's son in his turn went at godlike Agēnōr,
but Apollo did not allow him to gain fresh glory:
he snatched Agēnōr away, enshrouding him in thick mist,
and sent him off quietly to take himself out of the fighting;
but Pēleus's son by a trick was kept well clear of the troops
by the deadly archer—assuming Agēnōr's exact likeness
he stood close in front of Achilles. Achilles rushed after him,
and during the chase across the wheat-rich plain Apollo
nudged him towards the river, deep-eddying Skamandros,
while keeping a little ahead, tricked Achilles into thinking
he was always just on the point of catching up with his quarry.
Meanwhile the rest of the Trojans, a routed mass, were happy
to get to Troy, and the city was overflowing with them.
They no longer dared to wait outside the city ramparts
for one another, to learn which warriors had escaped
and who had died fighting: instead they hurriedly crowded back
into the city, each one whose feet and knees could save him.

Book 22

So these throughout the city, after fleeing like fawns,
were cooling their sweat and drinking and slaking their thirst,
leaning against the fine battlements, while the Achaians advanced
right up to the ramparts, shields resting on their shoulders.[1]
But Hektōr's fatal destiny constrained him to remain
where he was, outside Ilion and the Skaian Gates.

Now to the son of Pēleus Phoibos Apollo spoke:
"Why, son of Pēleus, are you scampering after me when
you're a mortal, while I'm an immortal god? You've still
not recognized me for a god, so ceaselessly do you rage!
Aren't you concerned to deal with the Trojans you've routed—
who crowded into the city while you wandered off out here?
You'll never kill me: it's not in my destiny to die."

Deeply incensed, swift-footed Achilles responded:
"You've fooled me, deadly archer, of all gods the most lethal,
by diverting me here from the wall: else many more men
would have bitten the dust before they ever reached Ilion!
Of great glory now you've robbed me, while these you've saved—
an easy task, with no fear of retribution to come,
though had I the power, I'd certainly be revenged on you."

So saying he took off towards the city with high resolve,
dashing along like some prize-winning chariot horse,
one that easily gallops at full stretch across the plain—
so speedily now did he exert his feet and knees.

The aged Priam was first to set eyes upon Achilles
as he swept on across the plain, agleam like the star
that rises at harvest time, and brightly its rays shine out
among the myriad stars in the darkness of night,

1. Apparently a reference to advancing under the cover of a shield held horizontally over one's shoulders, to protect against missiles from the walls of a besieged city: a practice better known from Rome, where legionaries locked shields together in this way and advanced collectively: a protection known, aptly, as the "tortoiseshell" (*testudo*), which, seen from above, it must indeed have resembled.

and men call it the Dog of Orīōn, the brightest star of all;
yet nevertheless it's a warning of trouble to come,
and brings with it much fever to wretched mankind:
so gleamed the bronze on Achilles' breast as he ran.
Priam now groaned aloud, beat his head with his hands,
lifting them high, and cried out in his distress,
entreating his own son, who was standing outside
the gates, dead set on battling it out with Achilles:
to him the old man spoke pitiably, stretching out his arms:
"Hektōr, dear child, for my sake don't stay there and face
that man, alone, without backup: too soon you'd meet your fate,
laid low by Pēleus's son, since he's by far the stronger,
and pitiless—how I wish he were as dear to the gods
as he is to me! Soon, then, would dogs and vultures devour him
as he lay there, and sore grief would vacate my spirit
over one who's deprived me of many valiant sons
by killing or shipping them off to far distant islands.
Even now two sons of mine, Lykaōn and Polydōros,
I can't see among those Trojans penned up in the city—
sons that Laothoē bore me, that queen among women.
If they're alive, in the enemy camp, then for certain
we'll pay ransom with gold and bronze—there's plenty stored here,
all the gifts that far-famed old Altēs bestowed with his daughter.
But if they're already dead, and down in Hādēs' realm,
then there's grief for myself and for the mother who bore them!
For others the pain will be briefer, so long as you too
don't die now, slain by Achilles! So, my dear child,
come back here, inside the walls! Do that, and you'll save
the Trojans and Trojan women—while denying great glory
to Pēleus's son—and not lose your own dear life. Besides,
pity me, the unhappy one, while I'm still alive—
an ill-fated wretch, whom the Father, Kronos's son, will slay,
in a hard death, when I'm old, after seeing many horrors:
my sons destroyed, my daughters forcibly taken,
their chambers ransacked, and their infant children
dashed to the ground, in warfare's savage conflict,
my sons' wives dragged off as booty by cruel Achaian hands!
Myself last of all my dogs, by my own front doorway,
will tear and eat raw, when some man with the sharp bronze—
stabbing or shooting—has parted the spirit from my limbs:

dogs that I reared at my table, trained to guard my home,
and now, turned wild by the drinking of my blood,
will lie out there in the forecourt. For a young man killed in battle
it's seemly to lie dead, cut about by the sharp bronze:
nothing, even in death, that's visible is repugnant.
But when it's a slaughtered greybeard's grey head and private parts
that dogs are shamefully worrying—that has to be
the most piteous thing that can happen to wretched mortals."

So spoke the old man, and with his hands tore and plucked
the grey hairs from his head, yet could not shift Hektōr's will;
and his mother in turn lamented, shedding tears,
opened her dress with one hand, in the other held out her breast,
as, weeping, she addressed him, speaking with winged words:
"Hektōr, child, show this respect, have pity for me,
if ever I gave you the breast to make you forget your pain!
Think on these things, dear child, fend off this deadly man
from inside our ramparts—don't face him alone out there,
an obstinate champion: if he kills you, I shall never
mourn you laid on a bier, dear sprig that I, myself, bore,
nor will your cherished wife: no, far, far from both of us
beside the ships of the Argives brisk dogs will devour you."

So the two of them, weeping, called upon their dear son,
with heartfelt entreaties, yet could not shift Hektōr's will,
who stood firm while huge Achilles advanced towards him.
As a mountain snake awaits a man beside its hole,
well fed on poisonous herbs,[2] flush with bitter distemper,
glaring terribly as it uncoils itself from its lair,
so Hektōr, his might unquenchable, would not give ground
but stood, bright shield propped against a jutting bastion;
and deeply stirred he addressed his own proud spirit:
"Ah me! If I now retreat within the gates and the ramparts,
Poulydamas will be first to heap reproaches on me,
having urged me to lead the Trojans into the city
during this last cursed night, when noble Achilles took action.
I would not obey him then—much better had I done so!

2. Snakes were apparently believed to derive their poison directly from the food they ate: Ael. *NA* 6.4, cf. Richardson 116. Pliny (*HN* 8.139) claims that they have no venom during hibernation, which, Richardson plausibly suggests, implies the same assumption.

Now, through my reckless folly I've ruined my own people,
and feel shame before the Trojans and their long-robed women,
lest maybe some other fellow, baser than me, may say:
'Hektōr destroyed his people through trust in his own might.'
So they will say; for me far better to meet Achilles
face to face, and return home only should I kill him,
or else myself to die gloriously out in front of the city.
But supposing I lay aside my embossed shield,
and my weighty helmet, prop my spear up against the wall,
and go out alone to meet with peerless Achilles,
guarantee him that Helen, and with her all the possessions,
every last item Aléxandros in his hollow ships
carried off Troywards—which was how this quarrel started—
we'll return to the sons of Atreus to take home, and moreover
will share out with the Achaians all the goods this city contains;
and I then have the Trojan elders swear me an oath
that they'll hide nothing, will divide up all the treasure
that this elegant citadel contains within its walls—
But why is my dear heart debating these matters?
Heaven forbid I approach him as suppliant, he'll not pity
or show me respect, but slaughter me when I'm unweaponed
and out of my armor, as though I were some defenseless woman.
There's no way now, from oak tree or from rock,[3]
to sweet-talk him, oh, like a girl and her young man—
a girl and her young man!—flirting with one another:
better to meet and fight him as soon as I can—
Let's learn to whom the Olympian will grant glory."

Thus he pondered, waiting, while Achilles approached him—
the equal of Enyalios, that bright-helmed warrior!—
above his right shoulder wielding his spear of Pēlian ash,
so fearsome, while all about him the bronze now glinted
like blazing fire or the rays of the rising sun.
As Hektōr looked, trembling seized him, he no longer dared

3. If this was originally a proverbial phrase, its exact meaning has been lost: the scholia (Willcock 242–43) claim it had to do "with old stories about the origins of man." Yet, as Richardson says (120) "to a modern reader the phrase conjures up a pastoral scene", appropriate to the flirtation that follows, and (as so often with Homer) almost unbearably moving because of the grim context in which it is set. Willcock is right: "Hektor's mind reverts to peacetime and the long private conversations of young lovers."

to stand firm: the gates left behind him, he fled in terror,
and Pēleus's son went after him, trusting his fleetness of foot.
As up in the mountains a hawk, the fastest of winged creatures,
swoops effortlessly in pursuit of a timorous dove:
she seeks to escape him, but he, screaming shrilly, and close,
keeps swooping at her, heart driving him on to kill—
so Achilles raged straight after Hektōr, who ran for his life
beneath the wall of the Trojans, knees pumping, going flat out.
Past the lookout post and the windswept fig tree they sped,
away from under the wall, and along the wagon track,
to the two full-flowing springs, where gush up both
the sources that feed the waters of eddying Skamandros.
The one flows with warm water, and from it smoke
goes up as though from a blazing fire, while the other,
even in summer, still flows as chilly as hail,
or freezing snow, or the ice that crystallizes from water.
There, close to these springs, are spacious washing tanks,
fine and stone-built, where the wives and lovely daughters
of the Trojans would formerly wash their glistening garments
in the days of peace, before the Achaians' sons arrived.
Past these they ran, one in flight, the other hot on his heels:
ahead, a fine warrior fleeing, a far better one in speedy
pursuit—and neither for bull's hide nor for sacrificial beast
were these now competing, a footrace's usual prizes:
the two of them were now running for horse-taming Hektōr's life.
As prize-winning whole-hoofed horses gallop lightly around
the turning-points of a racetrack, where some great prize
is displayed—a tripod or woman, to honor a warrior slain—
so these two, quick-footed, thrice circled Priam's city,
with all the gods watching them, amongst whom the first
to express his thoughts was the Father of men and gods:
"Alas, it's indeed a well-loved man that I see now
being chased round the city's walls: my heart is sore grieved
for Hektōr, who's burnt in my honor many thighs of oxen
on the heights of many-ridged Ida, and at other times
on the lofty citadel; but now here's noble Achilles
pursuing him on swift feet round and round Priam's city!
So, gods, consider this matter, give me your opinion—
shall we save him from death, or let him be laid low,
fine man though he is, at the hands of Achilles, Pēleus's son?"

Then the goddess, grey-eyed Athēnē, answered him thus:
"Father, lord of bright bolt and black cloud, what's this you're
saying?
Here's a man, a mortal, his fate long since determined—
Do you mean to reverse that, release him from woeful death?
Well, do it; but know this: we other gods don't all approve."

Replying to her then, Zeus the cloud-gatherer said:
"Cheer up Trītogéneia, dear child: the things I just said
were not meant seriously, and to you I'm kindly disposed.
Act as your mind dictates, hold back no longer."

So saying he urged on Athēnē—already eager to go—
and down she darted from the heights of Olympos.

But swift Achilles kept on in relentless pursuit of Hektōr.
As up in the mountains a dog will go after a hind's fawn,
starting it from its covert, chase it through glens and dells;
and though it may hide for a time, crouching low in a thicket,
that dog will still track it down, running steadily, till it's found—
so Hektōr could not shake off swift-footed Achilles:
whenever he made a rush for the Dardanian gates,
and tried to slip in past the strongly built bastions,
hoping that those on the walls would cover him with their missiles,
each time in anticipation Achilles would head him off, nudge him
back to the plain, while himself pressing on by the city wall.
As in a dream one can't overtake the quarry one's chasing—
the fugitive can't escape, nor his pursuer catch him—
so Achilles could not catch up, nor Hektōr get clear away.
How could Hektōr then have eluded the death-spirits,
had Apollo not come to his aid, for the last, the final time,
standing close, to arouse his strength, put speed in his knees?
To his troops, too, noble Achilles, with a shake of the head,
signaled they shouldn't let fly their bitter shafts at Hektōr—
a good shot might win the glory, leave himself as an also-ran!
But when for the fourth time they came round to the springs,
then Zeus, the Father, held up his golden balance
and on it set two dooms of grief-laden death,
one for Achilles, the other for horse-taming Hektōr.
By the middle he grasped and raised it: Hektōr's fated day
sank, pointing down to Hādēs, and Phoibos Apollo left him.

To Pēleus's son now came the goddess, grey-eyed Athēnē,
stood at his side, and addressed him in winged words:
"Now indeed I'm sure, Achilles, illustrious favorite of Zeus,
we two will bring back to the ships great glory for the Achaians
by killing Hektōr, great glutton for combat though he is!
No longer can he escape us, not even were it to be
that Apollo the deadly archer should suffer humiliation
by groveling on his behalf before Zeus of the aegis!
So stay here, and get your breath back, while I myself go
to Hektōr, and talk him into fighting you man to man."

So spoke Athēnē: he obeyed, and was glad at heart,
and stood there, leaning upon his bronze-barbed ash-wood spear.
Athēnē now left him, and went over to noble Hektōr,
in appearance and speaking voice resembling Deïphobos.
She came up close, and addressed him with winged words, saying:
"Honored brother, swift Achilles is pressing you really hard
with this pursuit on foot all round Priam's city—so come,
let's make a stand, hold fast here and defend ourselves!"

Then great bright-helmeted Hektōr made her this answer:
"Deïphobos, in the past you've been far the dearest to me
of all my brothers, those born to Hekabē and Priam;
and now I'm minded to do you yet greater honor,
since you dared, for my sake, when you saw me, to come out
beyond the ramparts, while all the others are staying inside."

To him then replied the goddess, grey-eyed Athēnē:
"Honored brother, indeed my father and lady mother
begged and implored me in turn, as did my comrades,
to stay back, so greatly do all of them fear Achilles;
but the heart within me was worn down by bitter grief.
Now let's both attack him head-on, let us fight it out
with no sparing of spears, and discover whether Achilles
will kill us both, and carry our bloodstained armor back
to the hollow ships—or rather fall victim to your spear."
Speaking thus, with her cunning Athēnē led him on.

When the warriors came within close range of one another,
the first to speak was great bright-helmeted Hektōr:
"No longer, son of Pēleus, will I run from you, as before,

when thrice around Priam's great city I fled, and never
dared to await your attack! No, this time my heart tells me
I must stand and confront you, whether to slay or be slain.
So come, let's swear oaths by the gods, for they are the best
witnesses and protectors of our agreements:
I'll not mistreat you vilely, should it be that Zeus grant me
the endurance to win, and I deprive you of life;
but when I've stripped off your famous armor, Achilles,
I'll return your corpse to the Achaians—or you likewise mine."

To him, with an angry glance, swift-footed Achilles replied:
"Hektōr, don't, damn you, make me speeches about agreements!
Between lions and men binding oaths do not exist,
nor are wolves and lambs ever like-minded at heart
but ceaselessly plotting trouble, each against the other.
So there's no way for us to be friends, we can't exchange
sworn oaths: no, before that one or the other must fall,
and glut Arēs, the oxhide-shield combatant, with his blood.
So summon up all your valor: you're going to need to be
both spearman and doughty combatant. There's no longer
any escape left for you—very soon will Pallas Athēnē
lay you low through my spear. Now you'll pay the full price
for the loss of my comrades, speared in your wild attack."

With that he poised and let fly his far-shadowing spear,
but illustrious Hektōr, watching carefully, dodged it,
crouching down, and the bronze spear flew over him,
fixed itself in the ground; but Athēnē snatched it up,
gave it back to Achilles, unseen by Hektōr, the people's shepherd,
and Hektōr now exclaimed to the peerless son of Pēleus:
"You missed! And you haven't, it seems, O godlike Achilles,
yet found out my fate from Zeus, despite what you supposed!
Turns out you're just a glib talker, a tricky wordsmith, aiming
to scare me, make me forget all my strength and valor!
Now it won't be my fugitive back that you plant your spear in,
you'll have to aim for my breast as I charge you—if indeed
some god grants you that much! Your turn now to avoid
my bronze spear—may you catch the whole of it in your flesh!
The war would certainty be much easier for the Trojans
once you were dead, for you are their greatest trouble."

With that he poised and let fly his far-shadowing spear,
struck Pēleus's son's shield in the middle, didn't miss it.
Yet the spear bounced back off the shield, left Hektōr enraged
because the swift missile had flown in vain from his hand.
He stood there downcast, and, having no second ash-wood spear,
called out, in a carrying voice, to white-shielded Deïphobos,
demanding a lance; but he was nowhere near at hand.
Then Hektōr knew the truth in his heart, and exclaimed:
"Alas! The gods have indeed now summoned me to my death!
I thought the hero Deïphobos was here by my side,
but he's inside the wall—it's Athēnē who's been here deceiving me!
A vile death now awaits me—no longer distant, but close,
and no escape: this must always have been what Zeus was after,
he and his son, the deadly archer: at one time they
were glad to protect me; but now my fate has caught up with me.
So let me die—not ingloriously, or without a struggle,
but having done some great deed for those unborn to learn of."
So saying, he drew from its scabbard the keen-edged sword
that hung at his side, a huge and solid weapon,
collected himself, and charged, like a high-flying eagle
that swoops down plainward, plummeting through dark clouds
to snatch up in its claws a young lamb or a cowering hare:
so Hektōr charged, his sharp sword flashing high,
and Achilles rushed at him, heart full of wildly raging
strength, with his shield—fine, intricately wrought—
out in front to protect his body, while the bright helmet,
four-plated, nodded above, and, waving all round it,
the lovely gold plumes that Hēphaistos had set thick about its crown.
Like that star that goes among other stars at nightfall,
the star of evening, the loveliest star in the heavens,
was the gleam that shone from the sharp spear that Achilles
brandished in his right hand, planning trouble for noble Hektōr,
studying his sweet flesh to see where it might best yield.
Now all the rest of his body had its bronze battle gear,
the fine armor he'd stripped from Patroklos after his killing,
but one spot showed, where the collarbones held apart
shoulders from neck—the gullet, where life's most quickly ended.
Here, as Hektōr charged, was where noble Achilles speared him:
clean through his tender neck drove the spear point, and yet
the bronze-laden ash-wood spear never severed the windpipe,

so he could still frame words, could make a response
when down in the dust, with Achilles exulting above him:
"Hektōr, you doubtless thought, while stripping Patroklos,
you'd be safe—I was elsewhere, to me you gave not a thought.
You fool! His distant avenger, stronger by far,
was left behind by the hollow ships: that was I, who have now
unstrung your limbs! You the dogs and birds of prey
will tear apart vilely, while he will get burial from the Achaians."

To him bright-helmeted Hektōr faintly replied: "By your life
I implore you, by your knees, by your parents, do not let
the dogs make a meal of me beside the Achaians' ships!
Rather take the bronze and gold, unstinted, that my father
and lady mother will give you, and return my body
to be conveyed to my home, in order that the Trojans
and Trojan wives may give me my share of fire in death."

Then with an angry glance swift-footed Achilles said:
"Don't entreat me, you dog, by my knees or by my parents!
I just wish there was a way for my raging heart to let me
carve your flesh raw and eat it, in return for what you've done,
as surely as there's no man who'll keep the dogs from your head,
not though they bring here and weigh out ten or twenty
times a fair ransom, and promise even more;
not even if they were ordered to pay me your weight in gold
by Priam, Dardanos's son: not even so
will your lady mother lay you, the son she bore, on a bier
and mourn you: no, dogs and birds will eat every last scrap of you."

Then, dying, bright-helmeted Hektōr said to him:
"I know you too well, I foresee my fate: I could never
persuade you. Truly the heart in your breast is of iron.
Think on this, then: it may be I who provoke the gods' wrath
against you, that day when Paris and Phoibos Apollo
kill you, for all your valor, before the Skaian Gates."

When he'd spoken thus, death's end enshrouded him,
and the soul fled from his limbs, fluttered down to Hādēs,
bewailing its fate, youth and manhood all abandoned.
Yet noble Achilles still harangued him, even when dead:
"Lie there, corpse! My own fate I'll accept whenever
Zeus may determine it—he, and the other immortal gods."

With that he tore out his bronze spear from the body,
and laid it aside, and began to strip from Hektōr's shoulders
his bloodstained armor. The other sons of the Achaians
ran up round him, gazed at the build and amazing beauty
of Hektōr—yet not one failed to stab him as he stood there,
and turning, would say to his neighbor as he did so:
"Well, it's a great deal easier to deal with Hektōr now
than when he burned up our vessels with blazing fire."
Thus a man would speak—then step up and stab the corpse.
But swift-footed noble Achilles, after stripping him, stood up
among the Achaians, and then addressed them in winged words:
"My friends, you rulers and leaders of the Argives,
since the gods have granted that we bring this man down
who's done us more harm than all others put together,
come, let's now make trial in arms around the city,
and so more clearly learn what the Trojans have in mind—
will they leave their high citadel now this man is fallen,
or hold out regardless, even though Hektōr is no more?
But why is my heart debating such matters with me?
There lies by the ships a corpse unwept, unburied—
Patroklos! Him I'll never forget, while I'm still
among the living, my limbs still quick and active!
And though men forget the dead in the realm of Hādēs,
yet even there I'll remember my dear comrade.
Come then, you young Achaians, chanting our victory paean
let's go back to the hollow ships, take this fellow with us!
We've achieved great glory: we've slain noble Hektōr, to whom
the Trojans throughout their city prayed as to a god."

With that he devised vile treatment for noble Hektōr:
in both feet behind he pierced holes along the tendons
from heel to ankle, and through them then strung oxhide straps
that he tied to his chariot, leaving the head to be dragged.
Then he mounted, taking the famous battle gear with him,
and whipped up his horses. They, nothing loath, took flight,
and from the dragged body the dust rose up: on either side
its dark hair was spread out, and all in the dust there lay
the head that was once so handsome: now to his foes
Zeus gave Hektōr for outrage on his own native soil.

So all his head was befouled with dust, and his mother
tore at her hair, flung her glimmering veil far from her,
and screamed out loud when she set eyes on her son,
while his father groaned piteously, and the folk around them
set up a great wailing and weeping throughout the city.
This was what it was most like: as though all towering
Ilion, top to bottom, were left smoldering with fire;
and the people could barely restrain the old man, in his frenzy
to break free and rush out through the Dardanian gates:
he kept begging them all as he rolled about in the filth,
calling out names, appealing to each man in turn:
"Hold off, friends! If you care for me, leave me alone,
to make my way out of the city, to the ships of the Achaians,
where I'll plead with that man—so violent, so ungoverned in act—
if he's any respect for my years, any pity for my old age!
He too has a father, a man, surely, much as I am—
Pēleus—who sired him and brought him up to work
disaster upon the Trojans; me above all he's saddened,
so many the flourishing sons of mine he's slaughtered!
Yet for all these I mourn not so much, despite my sorrow,
as for one, grief over whom will consign me to Hādēs' realm—
Hektōr! Ah, how I wish he'd died in my arms, for then
we'd at least have had our fill of wailing and shedding of tears,
the ill-fated mother who bore him, and I, myself."

So he spoke,
weeping: the citizens added their lamentation to his,
and among the Trojan women it was Hekabē led the keening:
"Ah, child, wretched me! How I've suffered! Why live on
now you're dead? For me, by day, by night, you were
my pride and boast through the city, a comfort to all,
both the men and the women of Troy, who would salute you
like a god; for indeed to them you embodied great glory
while you lived—but now death and your destiny have caught you."

So she spoke, weeping. But Hektōr's wife as yet
knew nothing, for no honest messenger had so far arrived
with the news that her husband had stayed on outside the gates.
She was at her loom in a back room of their high house,
weaving a red double cloak, with figured patterns on it.

Now she called out through the house to her neat-tressed handmaids
to set on the fire a great cauldron, make sure that there was
a hot bath for Hektōr when he came home from the fighting—
unaware, in her folly, that far from all baths he'd been
slain, through Achilles' hands, by grey-eyed Pallas Athēnē;
but then she heard screams and wailing from the wall,
and her limbs trembled, the shuttle dropped from her hand,
and once more she spoke among her neat-tressed handmaids:
"Two of you come and attend me, while I see what's happened—
It was my husband's revered mother whose voice I heard, and in
my own breast the heart leaps into my mouth, my knees
are paralyzed: some disaster's at hand for Priam's children!
May my ears never hear such tidings! Yet I'm sore afraid
that noble Achilles may have cut off daring Hektōr
alone, and have driven him from the city out to the plain,
and by now may have put an end to the dangerous courage
that always possessed him—he'd never stay back in the ranks,
but always would charge out ahead, yield to none in his might."

So saying, she rushed through the hall like a crazy woman,
heart beating wildly, accompanied by her handmaids.
But when she reached the crowd of men at the ramparts
she stood on the wall, and looked round, and then perceived him
being dragged in front of the city: the galloping horses
were ruthlessly hauling him off to the Achaians' hollow ships.
Then down came black night on her eyes, enshrouding them,
and she sank backward, gasping out her vital breath,
and far from her head she flung the shining headbands,
the diadem, the hairnet, the plaited clasp, and lastly
the veil that had been a present from golden Aphrodītē,
on the day that bright-helmeted Hektōr led her out as his bride
from Ēëtiōn's house, after bringing bride-gifts past counting;
and round her thronged Hektōr's sisters and his brothers' wives,
who held her between them, in shock to the verge of death.
But when she recovered, and the spirit returned to her breast,
then, between heaving sobs, she cried out before Troy's women:
"Hektōr, how wretched I am! To one fate, then, we were born,
both of us—you here in Troy, in the house of Priam,
and I in Thēbē, down there under wooded Plakos,
im the house of Ēëtiōn, who brought me up from a baby—

luckless father, doomed child! Better he'd never had me!
Now you're going to the realm of Hādēs, deep under the earth,
but me you're abandoning to my hateful grief,
a widow left in your halls! Our son's still an infant,
the child you and I, so unlucky, created: you'll never,
now you're dead, be a help to him, Hektōr, nor he to you,
since even should he survive the Achaians' baleful war
for ever thereafter toil and sorrow will be his lot,
since others will set their boundary stones on his land.
The day an orphan is made cuts him off from his age group:
he goes with head downcast, tears moisten his cheeks.
A needy child, he approaches his father's comrades,
tugs at the cloak of one, the tunic of another.
Some will pity him, briefly. One holds out his cup—
long enough to wet his lips, yet not his palate. Then one
with both parents alive will kick him out of the feast,
punching him up, and reviling him in harsh terms:
'Out of here, quick! You've no father feasting with us.'
Then the child runs back weeping to his widowed mother—
he, Astyanax, who before, on his father's knee,
would eat nothing but marrow and the rich fat of sheep,
and when sleep came on him, and he stopped his childish
play, would sleep in a bed in the arms of his own nurse—
in his own soft cot, his heart replete with good cheer. But now
he may suffer much, being bereft of his dear father,
my Astyanax, 'lord of the city', whom the Trojans speak of thus
since you alone, Hektōr, preserved their gates and their lofty walls.
But now beside the curved ships, and far from your parents,
coiling worms will devour you when the dogs have had their fill
of your nakedness, while your bedclothes lie unused in your halls—
fine, closely woven, well-fashioned by women's hands.
But all these things now I'll burn to ashes in blazing fire—
they're no longer of use to you, you'll never lie on them—
in honor of you, from the Trojans and from the women of Troy."

So she spoke, weeping, and the women lamented with her.

Book 23

So these were mourning throughout the city; but the Achaians,
when they all had made their way back to the ships and the Hellespont,
now scattered, the rest of them, each man to his own vessel:
but Achilles would not permit the Myrmidons to disperse,
and among his war-minded comrades thus he spoke up:
"Myrmidons! Lords of swift horses, most loyal of comrades,
let's not yet unyoke our whole-hoofed steeds from their chariots,
but with horses and chariots let us now drive close
to Patroklos, and mourn him: this is a dead man's privilege.
Then, when we've had our fill of painful lamentation,
We'll unyoke our horses and all take our evening meal together."

So he spoke: they all cried out as one, and Achilles led them:
three times round the corpse they drove their fine-maned steeds,
weeping, while Thetis stirred in them an urge for lamentation.
Damp with tears was the sand, and damp the men's battle gear,
such a maker of rout was he whose loss they mourned.
The son of Pēleus now led them in their heartfelt lamentation,
laying his murderous hands upon his comrade's breast:
"Greetings, Patroklos, even in Hādēs' realm: for now
all I promised you earlier I'm bringing to fulfillment—
that I'd drag Hektōr here, give him raw to the dogs to rend,
and in front of your pyre would cut the throats of a dozen
noble Trojan youths, so enraged I was at your killing."

With that he devised vile treatment for noble Hektōr,
stretching him out face down by Menoitios's son's bier,
there in the dust; each man took off his arms and armor
of gleaming bronze, unyoked his neighing horses. Then they
sat down beside the ship of Aiakos's swift-footed grandson
in their thousands; he gave them a heart-warming funeral feast.
Many sleek oxen now struggled around the iron knife
while being slaughtered, many sheep and bleating goats;
and many a white-tusked hog, bulked up with lard,
was stretched out there to be singed in Hēphaistos's flame,
and around the corpse blood ran thick, by the cupful.

The swift-footed lord, son of Pēleus, was now escorted
to noble Agamemnōn by the Achaians' princes—although
they'd barely convinced him, so incensed he was for his comrade.
But when their procession arrived at Agamemnōn's hut,
they issued instructions at once to the clear-voiced heralds
to set on the fire a great cauldron, hoping they'd persuade
Pēleus's son to wash himself clean of the clotted gore.
But he adamantly refused them, and swore an oath besides:
"No, by Zeus, who's the highest and best of all the gods,
it isn't right that water should come anywhere near my head
till I've burned Patroklos's body, and raised him a burial mound,
and have cut my hair—since never again will such grief
possess my heart, while I'm numbered among the living!
For now, then, feast if we must, though the thought revolts me;
but tomorrow at dawn, Agamemnōn, you lord of men,
have the troops forage for firewood, make ready all that's proper
for the dead man to have when he goes down into darkness:
so the unwearying fire may burn him away, may quickly
remove him from our sight, and the troops return to their work."

So he spoke, and they listened attentively, did as he asked.
Each man quickly made ready his evening meal, and then
they feasted, and no one's heart lacked a fair share in the feasting.
But when they had satisfied their desire for food and drink,
they went, each to his own hut, to get their rest;
but Pēleus's son lay on the shoreline of the thunderous sea,
heavily sighing, with all his Myrmidons around him,
in a clear space, where the combers came crashing on the beach.
But when sleep laid hold of him, soothing the cares of his heart,
sweetly descending—since his bright limbs were exhausted
from harrying Hektōr as far as windy Ilion—then
there came to him the spirit of unhappy Patroklos,
like his live self in all aspects—his stature, his fine eyes,
his voice; and even the clothes he had on were the same.
He stood over Achilles' head and addressed these words to him:
"You sleep, and you've proved forgetful of me, Achilles.
While I lived you didn't neglect me—now I'm dead you do!
Bury me with all speed, let me pass through Hādēs' gates—
The spirits, the shades of the dead, are keeping me out,
won't let me cross the river to mingle with them, so here

I uselessly wander outside Hādēs' wide-gated realm.
And give me your hand, I beseech you, for never again
will I come back from Hādēs, once you give me my share of fire.
Nevermore, as in life, will we sit apart from our comrades
making plans together: the dread death-spirit assigned me
from birth has now opened her jaws to swallow me down!
And for you too your lot is destined, godlike Achilles—
to perish beneath the ramparts of the noble Trojans.
One more thing I'll say, and ask of you, if you'll agree:
Don't have my bones interred apart from yours, Achilles,
but together, the way we were both brought up in your house
after Menoitios brought me, a child still, from Opoeis
to your home, because of that wretched manslaughter business,
the day that I lost my temper and killed Amphidamas's son,
through childish folly, not meaning to, over a game of dice,
and then Pēleus the horseman took me into his own house,
and brought me up caringly, and named me to be your squire.
So have the same vessel enclose our bones together—
golden, two-handled, the one your lady mother gave you."

In answer to him swift-footed Achilles then said:
"Why, dearest comrade, have you come here to me thus?
Why all these detailed instructions? Of course I shall make sure
that everything's done, and exactly as you want it.
Come closer, I beg you: if only for a brief moment
let's embrace, and get our full measure of painful lamentation."

So saying, he reached out to him with his hands, but failed
to clasp him: Patroklos's spirit disappeared like smoke
beneath the earth, crying thinly. Achilles, stunned, sprang up,
clapped both hands together, and said, sadly wondering:
"Well, so there really is something, even in Hādēs' realm—
a spirit, a phantom—though with nothing substantial to it;
for all night long the spirit of poor Patroklos
stood over me, weeping and wailing, making requests for all
he wanted done—looking marvelously like his living self."

So he spoke, and stirred in them all the urge for lamentation,
and Dawn, the rosy-fingered, revealed them weeping still
around the piteous corpse. Now the lord Agamemnōn
sent out mules and men from all the huts in camp

to bring back firewood: they had a fine warrior in charge—
Mērionēs, who was squire to kindly Idomeneus.
Off they went, hands clutching axes for felling timber
and well-braided ropes, with the mules going ahead of them:
back and forth, uphill and down they went, across and aslant—
and when they reached the spurs of spring-rich Ida, at once
they briskly set to, began felling tall leafy oaks
with the keen-edged bronze, and a mighty crash they made
on falling, after which the Achaians split them apart
and hitched them behind the mules. These churned up the earth
with their feet, straining plainwards through the thick undergrowth.
The woodcutters all carried logs, having been so ordered
by Mērionēs, the squire of kindly Idomeneus:
on the shore in a row they stacked them, at the point where Achilles
was planning a great burial mound for Patroklos and himself.

When they'd amassed great piles of timber all around
they sat down in a group and waited. Then Achilles
promptly issued his orders to the war-loving Myrmidons
to gird on their bronze gear, and for each man to yoke his horses
to their chariot. Up they all got, and donned their equipment,
then mounted their chariots, both warriors and drivers.
The chariot teams went ahead; a cloud of infantry followed,
thousands strong: in their midst his comrades bore Patroklos,
his body clothed with the hair they'd cut off and laid upon it.
Behind them noble Achilles in sorrow cradled the head
of the peerless comrade he now was sending to Hādēs' realm.

When they came to the place that Achilles had indicated
they laid down the body, and quickly stacked wood in plenty
for it.
Then swift-footed noble Achilles thought of something else:
standing away from the pyre he cut a lock of his fair hair
that he'd let grow long to offer to the river Spercheios;
and said, deeply troubled, looking out at the wine-faced deep:
"Spercheios, all in vain did my father Pēleus assure you
that when I came back home to my native land, for you
I'd cut off my hair and make a fine sacred offering—
fifty ungelded rams I'd sacrifice on the spot
into your waters, beside your precinct and fragrant altar.
Such the old man's vow, but you failed to fulfill his purpose.

Now, since I'll not be returning, ever, to my own country,
let me give this lock to the hero Patroklos, to take with him."

So saying, in the hands of his dear comrade he placed
the lock, and thus stirred in them all the urge for mourning;
and indeed the sun's light would have set on their sorrow,
had not Achilles at once approached Agamemnōn, saying:
"Son of Atreus—since it's your word that the Achaian troops
will most readily obey—one can have one's fill of wailing.
Dismiss them now from the pyre, bid them ready their meal.
We, to whom the dead man was closest, will take care
of all matters here; but let the commanders stay with us."

On hearing this, the lord of men, Agamemnōn,
at once dispersed the troops among their trim ships;
but the close mourners remained, and stacked the timber,
making a pyre with each side one hundred feet in length,
and upon it, silently grieving, set the dead body.
Then many fattened sheep and sleek shambling oxen
they flayed and dressed by the pyre; and from all these
great-hearted Achilles took fat, and covered the corpse
from head to foot, piled the flayed carcasses round it,
and two-handled jars of honey and oil he set down,
resting against the bier.[1] Then four horses with arching necks
he hastily, sobbing aloud, flung onto the pyre.
Nine dogs there had been that were fed from their master's table:
two of these he tossed on the pyre after cutting their throats;
and twelve noble sons of the high-spirited Trojans
he slew with the bronze: vile actions were in his mind.[2]
Then to the pyre he set fire's iron might, to consume it,
and groaned aloud, and called on his dear comrade by name:
"Greetings, Patroklos, even in the realm of Hādēs!
See, now I'm fulfilling all that I promised you earlier:
twelve noble sons of the high-spirited Trojans—all these,
with you, the flames will devour; but Priam's son
Hektōr I'll not give to fire, but to dogs to feed on."

---

1. These jars are clearly the kind of amphora (or, later, funeral *lēkythos*) with a pointed foot, that was meant to be stuck in the ground, and could not stand unsupported on the logs of the pyre: Leaf, 2: 392; Richardson 189.
2. Thus fulfilling the promise he had earlier made to the dead Patroklos: cf. 18.336–37.

So he spoke, threatening; yet no dogs were getting at Hektōr,
for the daughter of Zeus, Aphrodītē, kept him safe from them
by day and by night, anointed his body with rose-scented
ambrosial oil, so the dragging would not lacerate his flesh,
and Phoibos Apollo upon him projected a dark cloud,
from the heavens down to the plain, enshrouding the whole site
that the dead man occupied, to stop the strength of the sun
from shriveling the flesh that embodied his sinews and his limbs.

But the pyre of the dead Patroklos would not catch fire.
So now swift-footed Achilles had another idea:
standing away from the pyre, he prayed to two of the winds,
the north and west—Boreas, Zephyros—promised fine offerings,
implored them, while pouring libations from a golden goblet,
to come, help set the body quickly ablaze with fire,
by speeding the wood to its kindling. Iris, hearing his prayers,
lost no time, but carried his message on to the winds.
They were all met at the home of blustery Zephyros,
in the midst of a banquet. Iris came running, stopped
on the stone threshold. When they caught sight of her
they all jumped up, and each one wanted her by him.
But she wouldn't sit and join them, explained herself thus:
"I can't stay—I have to go back to the streams of Ocean,
to the land of the Aithiōpians: they're making fine sacrifices
to the immortals, and I am to share in their sacred feast!
But Achilles is praying that Boreas and blustery Zephyros
will come—and promising them fine offerings if they do—
to fan the flames of the pyre on which there lies
Patroklos, for whom the Achaians are all making loud lament."

So she, having thus spoken, went on her way; they rose
with a marvelous clamor, stampeding the clouds before them,
and quickly reached the deep sea, blowing on it: the waves surged up
before that shrill blast. They came to rich-soiled Troy,
and swooped on the pyre: loud roared a wondrous conflagration!
So the whole night through they fanned the flames of the pyre,
blowing shrilly; the whole night through swift Achilles, clutching
a two-handled cup, took wine from a golden bowl
and poured it out on the ground, till the earth was drenched,
calling upon the spirit of the unlucky Patroklos.
As a father mourns for a son while he's burning his bones—

a son just wed, whose death has shocked his unlucky parents—
so Achilles wept for his comrade as he burned his bones,
dragging himself round the pyre, and ceaselessly sobbing.

At the hour that the morning star goes heralding light on earth,
followed by Dawn, saffron-clad, spreading over the deep,
then the funeral pyre died down, and ceased to flame.
Now the winds set out back on their homeward journey,
over the Thracian sea—at their coming it surged and thundered—
and the son of Pēleus withdrew from the smoldering pyre
and lay down, exhausted, and sweet sleep swept over him.
But when Atreus's son and his people all assembled together,
the clamor and noisy tread of their coming awoke him:
He sat up and called out to them, saying: "Son of Atreus,
and you other lords and chieftains of all the Achaians,
first quench the still-smoldering pyre with fire-bright wine,
in each part that the fire's force reached. When that's accomplished,
let us collect the bones of Patroklos, Menoitios's son,
sorting them carefully—they're easy enough to distinguish:
he lay at the heart of the pyre, while the rest had to burn
at its edges, horses and men all mingled together—then
lay them up in a golden bowl, with a double layer
of fat as cover, until I too am vanished to Hādēs.
But you're not to toil at raising a huge grave mound now,
just one that's befitting: though afterwards you Achaians
can make it broader and higher—those of you, that is,
still left among the benched vessels when I myself am gone."

So he spoke, and they heeded Pēleus's swift-footed son.
They quenched the still-smoldering pyre with fire-bright wine
in each part that the fire's force reached, where the ash had settled.
Weeping, they gathered their kindly comrade's white bones
into a golden bowl, with a double layer of fat:
this they laid up in his hut, put a soft cloth to cover it.
They marked out the grave-mound's circle, laid a base of stones
upon it around the pyre, then piled on loose earth,
and, the mound once raised, began leaving; Achilles however
kept them all where they were, made them sit in broad assembly,
fetched out prizes then from his ships: cauldrons and tripods,
horses and mules and sturdy heads of oxen,
and women with elegant sashes, and ingots of grey iron.

First, for swift charioteers he set out splendid prizes:
a woman to take away, one skilled in fine handiwork,
an eared tripod of twenty-two measures—these for the winner;
for the runner-up, he provided a six-year-old mare,
unbroken, and pregnant with a mule foal; for third place
he set out a cauldron as yet untouched by fire,
a fine one, four measures capacity, new, bright, polished;
for the fourth, two talents of gold was the prize allotted,
for the fifth, a two-handled bowl, as yet untouched by fire.
Then he stood up and spoke as follows among the Argives:
"Son of Atreus, and all you other well-greaved Achaians,
here are the prizes awaiting the horsemen in this contest.
If we Achaians were now competing in honor of someone else,
then I'd surely win first prize, and bear it away to my hut;
for you know by how much my horses surpass all others,
being immortal: Poseidōn bestowed them as a present
on Pēleus, my father; and he bequeathed them to me.
But I shall remain here: I, and my whole-hoofed horses.
So great the renown of the charioteer that they've lost—
a kindly man too, who'd frequently work soft oil
into their manes, when he'd washed them with shining water!
Now both of them stand and mourn him: low on the ground
their manes are trailing; they stand still, grieving at heart.
But you others in camp here, get ready—any Achaian
with confidence in his horses and his dovetailed chariot!"

So spoke Pēleus's son, and the horsemen quickly gathered.
The first of all to come forward was Eumēlos, lord of men,
Admētos's dear son, a man highly skilled in horsemanship.
Next there stood up Tydeus's son, the mighty Diomēdēs,
leading beneath the yoke Trōs's horses,[3] that he'd earlier
taken by force from Aineias (himself rescued by Apollo).
Next up was Atreus's son, the fair-haired Menelaös,
scion of Zeus, who yoked a speedy team of horses—
Agamemnōn's mare Aithē, and his own Podargos.
Echepōlos, son of Anchīsēs, gave Agamemnōn the mare
as a bribe, to avoid going with him to windy Ilion,
so he'd get to stay home and enjoy life—since he'd been granted

3. On these horses, see 5.222–23 and note, 263–74, 319–27; on the rescue of Aineias, 5.344–46, 443–50.

vast riches by Zeus—in broad Sikyon, where his home was.
This mare Menelaös now yoked: she was straining to race.
Antilochos was the fourth to ready his fine-maned horses—
the splendid son of Nestōr, that high-spirited king,
and grandson of Nēleus: Pylos-bred were the swift-foot steeds
that drew his chariot. His father stood there beside him,
with well-meant advice for a son who knew plenty himself:
"Antilochos, young though you are, you've been befriended
by Zeus and Poseidōn, who've taught you every aspect
of horsemanship—no great need, then, for me to instruct you—
you know just how to wheel your horses round the turn mark!
But since yours are the slowest, I think you'll have some trouble.
Still, their horses may be swifter, but your competitors can't
match you in clever planning, so it's up to you, dear boy—
get your mind round every kind of cunning contrivance,
don't let those prizes slip away out of your grasp!
Shrewdness serves woodcutters better than mere brute force;
it's through shrewdness a steersman, out on the wine-faced deep,
can control a swift ship when it's battered by gale-force winds;
shrewdness is what lets one driver edge out another.
Some are content to rely on their horses and chariot,
will carelessly take turns wide on this side and that,
let their team swerve over the track, not keep them in hand;
but the man who knows every trick, though driving worse horses,
will keep his eye on the turn, hug it close;—he never forgets,
from the start, to maintain taut control of his oxhide reins,
but steadily holds them in hand, one eye on the team ahead.
Now I'll tell you about a clear marker: you cannot miss it.
There's the dried wooden stump of a tree, about six feet high—
of oak or pine: it doesn't rot in the rain—
with two white stones set against it, on either side,
at the track's turning point, with smooth driving all round it.
A memorial, maybe, of some mortal long since dead,
or perhaps set up as a race mark by men in olden times—
and now swift-footed Achilles has made it his turning post.
Steer tight round this, driving horses and chariot close,
and yourself, at the taut leather rail, lean a touch to the left
of your team, while you also cheer on your offside horse,
give it the goad, let the rein run loose in your hand!
But have the nearside horse run close to the turning post—

so close, that the crafted wheel's hub seems to graze its surface
yet doesn't in fact touch the stone: do that, and you risk
having your horses maimed and your chariot wrecked!
A delight for your competitors that would be, but for you
a disaster. So, my dear boy, use your wits, be on your guard;
for if at the turning post you get ahead of the others,
there's no one who'll catch or pass you in a final spurt,
not even were he to chase you driving noble Arīōn,
Adrēstos's swift horse, divinely sired, or the team
of Laomedōn, fine thoroughbreds brought up in these parts."

With that, Nestōr, Nēleus's son, sat down again in his place,
having instructed his son how to master every last detail.

Mēriones was the fifth to ready his fine-maned horses.
Then they mounted their chariots, threw in their lots.[4]
Achilles shook them: out flew the lot of Nestōr's son
Antilochos. Lord Eumēlos drew the place next to him,
followed by Atreus's son, famed spearman Menelaös.
The next starting place fell by lot to Mēriones;
last place went to Tydeus's son, far the best of them all.
So they lined up, and Achilles showed them the turning post
far off on the level plain: he set an observer by it,
the godlike Phoinix, his father's old deputy,
to umpire the race, give a true report of its outcome.

Then they all at once raised their whips above their horses,
started them with the reins, drove them on with urgent commands,
and they swiftly advanced across the plain, at full gallop,
moving away from the ships; and from under their breasts
the dust, kicked up, rose high, like a cloud or a whirlwind,
and with the blast of the wind their manes streamed out.
At times the wheels would run smoothly over the nurturing earth,
but at times were bumped into the air, while their drivers, standing,
held on, and each man's heart beat fast with excitement
as they all strove to win, and kept urging their horses on,
and the horses flew forward, raising the dust on the plain.

4. Lots are drawn to determine the starting position in the lineup: presumably the luckiest competitor in the draw would, like Antilochos, choose the "inmost place on the left, giving an advantage at the turn" (Richardson 213). For the practice of shaking the lots out of a helmet, see 7.175–83.

But when the swift teams were completing the final stretch,
back towards the grey sea, then each one's true quality
became clear, as the horses were stretched to the limit. The racing
mares of Pherēs' grandson, Eumēlos, moved into the lead,
and, next, Diomēdēs' stallions, the horses of Trōs,
were not far behind—indeed, so close upon their heels
that they seemed on the point of mounting Eumēlos's chariot,
and with their breath his back and his broad shoulders
grew warm, so close they bent their heads as they sped;
and now Tydeus's son would have passed or dead-heated him,
had he not stirred up resentment in Phoibos Apollo,
who struck the shining whip clean out of his hand.
Then from his eyes there started tears of fury
as he saw Eumēlos's mares going still faster than before,
while his own pair were handicapped, running without a goad.
But the trick played on Tydeus's son by Apollo had not escaped
Athēnē: quickly she chased after the shepherd of men,
returned his whip to him, put power into his horses;
then in her fury she went for the son of Admētos: his team's
yoke was smashed by the goddess: the mares both bolted
off-track, and the yoke pole slipped to the ground. Eumēlos
was flung headlong out of the chariot, by the wheel,
stripping skin from his elbows and mouth and nose, and leaving
his forehead above the eyebrows all bruised, while both his eyes
were brimming with tears, and his strong young voice was stilled.
Tydeus's son then swerved his whole-hoofed horses round him,
and led the field, far ahead of the rest—for Athēnē
had put strength in his horses, bestowed on him great glory—
with Atreus's son, fair-haired Menelaös, the next behind him.

Antilochos now called out to his father's horses:
"You two, get moving as well! Put your full strength into it!
I'm not asking you to compete with those up front there—
Tydeus's warlike son's horses, those to which Athēnē
has just given strength, and on him bestowed great glory—
no, overtake Atreus's son's team, don't be left behind!
So, *move it!* Unless you both want to be put to shame
by Aithē, and her a mare? You champions, why so slow?
For I'll tell you this, and it will certainly be fulfilled:

No care will you get from Nestōr, the people's shepherd—
rather he'll kill you at once with the keen-edged bronze—
if through your lack of spirit all we win is a lesser prize!
So get in pursuit, gallop after them at full stretch,
and what I'll contrive and work to achieve is this:
we'll pass them where the track narrows—I'll not miss it!"

So he spoke; and they, terrified by their master's reproof,
quickened their pace for a little. Then, almost at once,
steadfast Antilochos sighted the narrow point where the road
ran hollow: a gully had formed, where winter floods, collecting,
had torn away part of the track, deepened the whole stretch—
and here steered Menelaös, to avoid teams jostling abreast.
But Antilochos now took his own whole-hoofed pair off-track,
and began to overtake him, driving close in, side by side,
and Atreus's son, in alarm, shouted out to Antilochos:
"This is crazy driving, Antilochos! Rein in your horses!
Here the track's narrow: it'll soon be wider for passing—
This way you'll run into my chariot, wreck us both!"

So he spoke; but Antilochos pressed on still more fiercely,
urging his team with the goad, as though not hearing. About
as far as the range of a discus swung from the shoulder,
that a young man throws when making trial of his strength,
so far they ran thus—but then the mares of Atreus's son
dropped back, as he decided he'd race them hard no longer,
to avoid their whole-hoofed horses colliding on the track
and upsetting the well-strapped chariots, and themselves
being thrown out in the dust, through their great lust to win.
Then fair-haired Menelaös cried out in stern reproof:
"Antiochos, no other mortal's more malignant than you!
Keep on, then—we Achaians were mistaken to think you wise!
Even so, you won't get the prize without a challenge on oath."[5]

So he spoke, and then called out to his horses, saying:
"Don't hold back, don't stop now, through grief at heart! Their feet

5. Menelaös indeed has it in mind to challenge Antilochos to take an oath that he has not cheated by using an improper trick to secure the victory, and in fact does so at 581–85. Antilochos (with good reason) prefers to yield gracefully, youth respecting age, rather than to take an oath that would in fact involve him in perjury.

and laboring knees will tire out long before yours do—
old nags, age deprives them of their youthful vigor."

So he spoke; and they, terrified by their master's reproof,
quickened their pace, and soon came up close behind the others.

Now the Argives were sitting assembled, watching out
for the horses as they flew onward, raising the dust on the plain;
and Idomeneus, Krētan chieftain, perched away from the crowd,
high up on a lookout point, was the first to glimpse them.
When he heard a man's distant voice urging his horses on
he recognized that, and spotted a horse way out ahead,
all chestnut in color, except for its forehead, and there
it had a round white blaze resembling the full moon.
Up he stood, and addressed the Argives in these words:
"My friends, rulers and leaders of the Argives,
am I the only one who can actually see these horses,
or can you see them too? Other horses now seem to leading,
and a different driver's in sight! The mares that were in front
on the first stretch, must have tripped up at some point:
I certainly saw them reach the turning post in the lead,
but now I can nowhere discern them, although my eyes
have searched for them everywhere, all over the Trojan plain.
Did the driver perhaps drop his reins, was he unable
to hold his course well round the post? Did he fail on the turn?
He must, I fear, have been thrown there, his chariot wrecked,
and his mares, in a wild frenzy, must have bolted from the track.
But stand up and look for yourselves—I myself cannot
recognize
anything clearly; to me, the man looks as though he is
an Aitōlian by birth, a ruler among the Argives—
Tydeus the horse-breaker's son, the mighty Diomēdēs."

Oïleus's son, swift Aias, now shamefully rebuked him:
"Idomeneus, always the big-mouth! Those high-stepping mares
are still a long way off, racing over the broad plain!
You're nowhere near the youngest among the Argives,
nor are the eyes in your head by far the sharpest,
yet your big mouth's forever yapping! You've no right
to be such a blabbermouth—others here are better than you!

The same mares are in the lead now as were before—
those of Eumēlos, and he's the driver, holding the reins."

Growing angry at him, the Krētan leader retorted:
"Aias, peerless at insults, dim-witted, in all other ways
you lag far behind the Argives: your mind is so rigid!
Come on then, let's wager a tripod or a cauldron,
and both accept Atreus's son Agamemnōn as the judge
of which horses are in the lead: you'll learn that when you pay!"

So he spoke; and swift Aias, Oïleus's son, at once
jumped up, in a fury, to answer him with hard words;
and their quarrel would certainly have gone still further,
had not Achilles himself stood up and made this speech:
"No more of these angry insults to and fro between you,
Aias, Idomeneus! This is bad talk, most improper—
You'd reprimand anyone else who behaved that way!
Sit down now in the assembly, both of you, keep a watch
for the horses—they're going flat out to win, they'll be here
any moment now! Then you'll know, each one of you,
which Argives' horses are lagging, and which are in the lead."

While he was speaking, Tydeus's son drove up at speed,
plying his whip from the shoulder; and his horses,
high-stepping, came lightly skimming down the track,
while the raised dust kept blowing against their charioteer,
and the chariot itself, decorated with gold and with tin,
ran behind the swift-footed team, and barely a trace
of the wheel rims' passage was left behind in the powdery
dust as the pair sped onward. Then at last he pulled up
in the midst of the place of assembly, the sweat still coursing
down from his horses' necks and chests to the ground.
To the ground he too sprang from his gleaming chariot,
and propped his whipstock against the yoke. Nor did sturdy
Sthenelos waste any time, but briskly claimed the prize—
the woman, the eared tripod—which he gave to his high-hearted
comrades to carry off, and himself unyoked the horses.

Next to bring in his team was Antilochos, Nēleus's grandson,
having outstripped Menelaös not by speed, but by cunning guile.
Yet even so Menelaös had his own pair right behind him—

as near as a horse to the wheel, a horse that draws its master
over the plain, straining hard at his chariot, with the outermost
hairs of its tail just brushing the wheel's rim, since it runs
very close in front, and there's only the narrowest space
between horse and wheel as it gallops over the wide plain—
by so little was Menelaös behind peerless Antilochos
now—though at first it had been as far as a discus throw—
having quickly caught up with him, since Agamemnōn's mare,
fine-maned Aithē, kept finding and using yet greater power;
and if the course for the two of them had been much longer,
then he'd have passed him, and not left the outcome in dispute.
Mēriones, Idomeneus's excellent henchman, came in
a spear's flight behind illustrious Menelaös,
for his fine-maned horses were the tardiest of them all,
and he himself the least skillful at racing a chariot.
The son of Admētos arrived long after the rest,
dragging his splendid chariot, driving his team before him.
At the sight of him swift-footed noble Achilles felt pity,
and stood up among the Argives, and spoke winged words to
them:
"Driving his whole-hoofed horses now comes in, last of all,
by far the best man: so let's give him a prize, as is proper—
for second place: the first let Tydeus's son carry off."

So he spoke, and they all approved his proposal; and now,
with the Achaians' backing, he'd have given Eumēlos the mare,
had Nestōr's high-spirited son, Antilochos, in response
not risen to lodge an appeal with Pēleus's son Achilles:
"Achilles, you'll anger me deeply if you persist
with this proposal: you'll be robbing me of my prize
through dwelling on his misfortune—horses and chariot wrecked,
and him too, for all his skill. But if he had made a prayer
to the immortals, he wouldn't have ended last in the race!
Look, if you feel sorry for him, if he's so dear to you,
back in your hut there's gold in abundance, there's bronze,
and sheep too, and handmaids, as well as whole-hoofed horses!
Choose from among these later, and give him a better prize—
or right now, if you want some applause from the Achaians—
but the mare I will not give up: let any man who wants her
make trial of me now in a hand-to-hand engagement."

So he spoke, and swift-footed noble Achilles smiled,[6]
enjoying Antilochos, since he was his dear companion,
and in response addressed him with winged words:
"Antilochos, if you want me to find from my own possessions
some extra gift for Eumēlos, I'll be glad to do so.
I'll give him the corselet I stripped off Asteropaios—
it's of bronze, with an inlay of shining tin all round it
in circles: this will be a most valuable gift for him."

With that he commanded his dear comrade Automedōn
to fetch it out of the hut: he went off and came back with it,
and presented it to Eumēlos, who received it with pleasure.

Now there also stood up among them Menelaös, sore at heart,
with implacable rage at Antilochos. A herald placed the scepter
in his hand, and called out for silence among the Argives.
Then Menelaös, that man of godlike mien, addressed them:
"Antilochos, once so sensible, consider what you've done!
You insulted my manhood, and you thwarted my horses
by driving your own ahead, though they're far inferior.
Come now, you leaders and rulers of the Argives,
make a fair judgment between us, not favoring either man,
lest one day some bronze-clad Achaian may declare:
'Menelaös defeated Antilochos with his lies, went off
taking the mare, because, while his own horses were nags,
he himself carried all the weight in prestige and power.'
I myself will offer a ruling, and I don't think any other
Danaän will find fault with it: it will be rightful.
As is the proper custom, Antilochos, Zeus's nursling,
come here, and, standing before your horses and chariot,
take the lithe whip with which you were lately driving,
and, touching your horses, by the Earth-Encircling Earth-Shaker
swear that you never meant to block my chariot by deceit."

To him then astute Antilochos offered this response:
"Wait a moment! Remember that I'm a good deal younger

6. Richardson notes (229) that this is the only time in the whole of the *Iliad* when Achilles is reported as smiling. He is, we are led to believe, delighted by his young aristocratic friend's frankness. What are we meant to infer from this unique instance? More, surely, than pleasure at the smart discomfiture of Agamemnōn's brother? But just what remains obscure.

than you, my lord Menelaös: you're my elder and better,
you know what a young man's transgressions are likely to be—
his mind's over-hasty, his judgment lacks real substance.
So bear with me in your heart: the mare that I won
I'll willingly give you, and if you want something better
from my house, I'd be only too glad to provide that as well,
here and now, Zeus's nursling, rather than spend my life
out of favor with you, and at fault in the eyes of the gods."

With that, great-hearted Nestōr's son now led up the mare,
and gave her to Menelaös, whose heart grew warm
and melted like morning dew that coats the ears of grain
where the plowland bristles with its ripe crop of tall wheat:
just so, Menelaös, did the heart melt in your breast.
Then he addressed him, speaking in winged words:
"Antilochos, now I myself will yield, and freely abandon
the anger I felt, since you were neither deranged nor foolish
before, though this time your youth outweighed your sense.
From now on take care to avoid outwitting your betters!
Indeed, no other Achaian would so soon have won me over,
but you've suffered much and done a great deal of work—
you, your excellent father, your brother—on my behalf;
so I'll yield to your entreaties—and, though the mare is mine,
I'll give her to you, so those present may recognize
that my spirit is never arrogant or unbending."

With that
he gave the mare to Noēmōn, Antilochos's companion,
to lead away, and then himself took the gleaming cauldron,
while Mērionēs, for fourth place, picked up the two gold
talents,
just as he'd driven. But the fifth prize went unclaimed—
the two-handled bowl: this Achilles gave to Nestōr,
took it over to him through the Argive assembly, and said:
"Something, old sir, for you too: let this bowl be your keepsake,
a memento of the funeral of Patroklos, whom nevermore
will you look on among the Argives. I give you this prize
without contest, for never again will you box or wrestle
in competition, or hurl the javelin, run a footrace,
since oppressive old age now weighs heavily upon you."

So saying, he gave it to Nestōr, who received it with pleasure,
and addressed him, speaking with winged words: "Yes, indeed,
all you just said, my child, was right and proper:
my limbs are no longer strong, friend, nor can my arms
still thrust out lightly and fast from either shoulder.
Would I were as young again, my strength still undiminished,
as on that day when the Epeians were burying lord Amarynkeus
at Bouprasion, and his sons gave prizes in the king's honor!
Then no man was my equal, neither of the Epeians,
nor of the great-hearted Aitōlians, nor of the Pylians themselves.
In boxing I beat Klytomēdēs, the son of Ēnōps,
and at wrestling Ankaios of Pleurōn, who stood against me;
in the footrace I outran Iphiklos, fine athlete though he was,
and at spear throwing I defeated both Phyleus and Polydōros.
In the chariot race alone did Aktōr's two sons[7] defeat me,
overtaking by force of numbers, begrudging me victory
because the best prizes were kept for this last contest.
Twin brothers they were: the one held the reins full-time—
held the reins full-time!—while the other drove with his whip.
That's how I once was; now it's time for younger men
to take on such tasks, while I must resign myself to wretched
old age, though then I stood out among the heroes.
So now honor your comrade too with funeral rites and contests!
This gift I accept with pleasure: my heart rejoices
that you think of me still as a friend, and do not forget
the honor that's proper for me to receive among the Achaians.
May the gods in return for this grant you bountiful favors."

So he spoke. Back through the great crush of the Achaians
Pēleus's son now went—after hearing out this discourse
by the son of Nēleus—to set out prizes for painful boxing.
He brought to the place of assembly a working mule, tethered it there,
an unbroken six-year-old hinney, the toughest kind to break,
and for the loser set out a two-handled cup. This done
he stood up and spoke as follows among the Argives:

7. These were the twins Kteatos and Eurytos: officially Aktōr's offspring, but in fact sired by Poseidōn. They are also sometimes identified as descendants of Molos, their maternal grandfather (11.709 and note, 750—again, in a reminiscence of Nestōr's). In late tradition (*HE* 1: 28), they were pictured as Siamese twins.

"Son of Atreus, and all you other well-greaved Achaians,
we call on two men, the best, to compete for these prizes,
putting up their fists: the one whom Apollo endows
with strength to endure—something all the Achaians recognize—
can then return to his hut leading off the hardy mule,
while the loser will carry away the two-handled cup."

So he spoke;
and at once there stood up a tall and powerful man,
well skilled in boxing, Panopeus's son Epeios,
who, one hand on the working mule, now addressed them, saying:
"Come on then, the man who'll collect that two-handled cup!
But the mule, I declare, no other Achaian will carry off
by defeating me with his fists, since I tell you, I'm the greatest!
Does it not suffice that I fall short in battle? There's no way
a man can make himself expert in every activity!
For this I declare, and it will certainly be fulfilled:
Utterly will I both mangle his flesh and shatter his bones!
So it would really be best if his kinsmen all remain here,
to carry him out after he's been broken up at my hands."

So he spoke, and they all fell silent: in the hush
only Euryalos rose, a godlike man, to confront him—
the grandson of Talaös, the son of king Mēkisteus,
who long ago came to Thēbē when Oidipous had fallen,[8]
for his funeral, and there defeated all the sons of Kadmos.
As his second Euryalos had Tydeus's son, the famous
spearman, to cheer him on, very keen that he should win.
First he laid out a loincloth for him, and then produced
some well-cut leather thongs[9] from the hide of a field ox.
So the two of them girded themselves, stepped out in the center
of the place of assembly, put up their mighty fists,
and went at each other: their strong hands intermingled,

---

8. That Oidipous (Oedipus) died at Kolōnos, outside Athens, seems to have been an Athenian invention, perhaps by Sophoklēs; other sources, including the *Odyssey* (11.275–80) have him living on in Thēbē after the suicide of his mother and wife Epikastē (Jocasta) and dying a wealthy landowner (Hes. *WD* 162–63). Most of the best-known stories about him are of late occurrence. See *HE* 2: 594, Richardson 243.

9. Such supple leather thongs were worn by ancient boxers well into the classical period to protect their hands. Later they were replaced by *sphairai*, a harder type of glove, more liable to cause damage to one's opponent; thus the thongs (ἱμάντες, *himantes*) were known as "softer" or "gentle" (Richardson 244).

and fearsome the grinding of jaws, while the sweat streamed down
everywhere from their limbs. As Euryalos looked for an opening,
noble Epeios moved in, uppercut him. No time did he stay
on his feet: there and then his bright limbs gave beneath him.
As, caught by the ruffling north wind, a fish will leap up
from the wrack-strewn shallows, and then a dark wave hides it,
so, when struck, he jerked skyward; but great-hearted Epeios
grabbed him, set him upright. His comrades crowded round him,
led him off through the place of assembly dragging his feet,
spitting out blood clots, head lolling on one side.
They brought him, still dazed, sat him down there in their midst,
and themselves then went off to collect the two-handled cup.

Pēleus's son now displayed other prizes to the Danaäns,
for a third contest, that of painful wrestling. The winner
would get a great tripod, made to stand on the fire—
twelve oxen's worth, the Achaians figured amongst themselves;
while for the loser Achilles set in their midst a woman,
well skilled in much handiwork. Four oxen they priced her at.
Then he stood up among the Argives, and addressed them, saying:
"Up now, those who'd compete in this contest too!" So he spoke,
and thereupon there arose huge Aias, Telamōn's son,
and resourceful Odysseus also, that expert in crafty skills.
So these two girded up, strode out into mid-assembly,
and gripped each other's arms with their brawny fists,
like crossbeams that some skilled carpenter dovetails together
in a high house, with a view to resisting the gale-force winds.
Their backbones cracked under the violent to-and-fro tugging
of their powerful hands, their sweat poured down in streams,
clustering welts sprang up along their ribs and shoulders,
reddened with blood. They never let up the pressure
as they battled for victory and the well-wrought tripod:
Odysseus could not trip Aias and pin him to the ground,
nor Aias him, for Odysseus's great strength held firm.
But when this began to weary the well-greaved Achaians, then
to Odysseus huge Aias, the son of Telamōn, said:
"Zeus-sprung son of Laertēs, resourceful Odysseus,
you lift me, or I you: for the rest, let Zeus decide."

With that, he tried to lift him; but Odysseus had not forgotten
his cunning, and struck him sharply behind the knee joint,

loosened his limbs, threw him backward, and dropped on his chest,
so that those watching were struck with amazement; and then
much-enduring noble Odysseus attempted to lift him,
raised him just off the ground, yet couldn't heft him up.
He hooked his knee inside Aias's, and the two dropped back,
close-entwined, on the ground, and all begrimed with dust.
Then for the third time they'd have sprung to their feet and wrestled,
had Achilles himself not got up and restrained them:
"Break it up now! Don't strain till you hurt yourselves!
You're both the victors. You'll both get the same prizes.
Off with you now—so that other Achaians can compete."
So he spoke, and they listened, and were glad to obey:
they wiped off the dust, and got back into their tunics.

Pēleus's son now set out other prizes, for speed of foot:
a finely worked silver mixing bowl, of six measures only,
yet for beauty it far exceeded every last one on earth,
having been cunningly fashioned by Sidonian craftsmen.
Phoenician merchants ferried it over the misty deep,
and brought it to harbor, and made a present of it to Thoas;
and as ransom for Priam's son Lykaōn it was surrendered
by Eunēos, the son of Jason, to the hero Patroklos.
This bowl Achilles set out, in honor of his comrade,
for whoever might prove the speediest in the footrace.
For the runner-up he provided a big ox, rich with fat,
and for the contestant in last place a half-talent of gold.
Then he stood up and spoke among the Argives, saying:
"Up now, those who are ready to compete in this contest too!"
So he spoke: there then arose swift Aias, the son of Oïleus,
and resourceful Odysseus, and after them Nestōr's son
Antilochos, who as a runner beat all the youngsters.
They all lined up, and Achilles showed them the turning point.
Right from the start they ran at full stretch, but quickly
Oïleus's son moved ahead, with noble Odysseus behind him,
very close—as close as a weaving rod comes to the breast
of a fine-sashed woman, who deftly draws it tight with her hands,
pulling the spool past the warp, and holding the rod
right by her breast—so close ran Odysseus: his own feet
trod in Aias's footsteps before the dust had settled on them,
while down on Aias's head came Odysseus's panting breath

as he kept up the fast pace: all the Achaians were cheering
his struggle to win, urged him on to yet greater efforts.
But when they were running the final stretch, then Odysseus
made a quick prayer in his heart to grey-eyed Athēnē:
"Hear me, goddess! Come as a good helper to my feet!"
So he spoke in prayer, and Pallas Athēnē heard him,
and lightened his limbs, both his knees and his arms above them.
But as they went into their final sprint for the prize,
then Aias slipped as he ran—for Athēnē tripped him—
where the dung was spread from the slaughter of the bellowing
oxen killed for Patroklos by swift-footed Achilles,
and his mouth and nostrils were filled with this cattle dung.
So the bowl was won by noble and much-enduring Odysseus,
who came in first, and the field ox went to illustrious Aias.
He stood there, with one hand clutching his beast by its horn,
and spat out the dung, and addressed the Argives, saying:
"Oh, my, that goddess for sure tripped my feet—she always
stands by Odysseus and helps him, just like a mother."

So he spoke, and they all had a hearty laugh at him.
Antilochos then collected the prize for the last contestant,
smiling, and spoke among the Argives, saying:
"Something, my friends, you all know, but I'll say it now
just once more: even today the gods honor older men!
Aias may be only a little older than I am,
but Odysseus here belongs to an earlier generation—
men call his a green old age—yet it's hard for any
Achaian to match him at running, save only Achilles."

So he spoke, with a flattering word for Pēleus's swift-footed son.
To this Achilles responded, addressing him as follows:
"Antilochos, not in vain shall your praise have been expressed!
I shall add to your prize another half-talent of gold."

So saying, he handed it to him, and he took it with pleasure.
Then Pēleus's son brought out a far-shadowing spear,
set it down in the place of assembly, with a shield and helmet—
the battle gear of Sarpēdōn, that Patroklos took from him—
then stood up among the Argives, and addressed them, saying:
"We call on two men, the best, to compete for these prizes,
to put on their armor, to take the flesh-cutting bronze,

and make trial of each other in front of the troops assembled.
Whichever one's first to touch the other's handsome flesh,
gets through armor and black blood, pricks the body within,[10]
to him shall I give as prize this silver-studded sword,
a fine Thracian weapon I took from Asteropaios.
As for the armor, let the two men share it between them,
and we'll give them a splendid banquet here in the huts."

So he spoke. There then arose huge Aias, Telamōn's son,
and the son of Tydeus stood up, the mighty Diomēdēs;
and after arming themselves, on either side of the throng,
they converged at the midpoint, eager to start their fight,
exchanging fearsome glances: the Achaians were astonished.
So when, advancing, they closed in, the one on the other,
three times they attacked, three times fought hand to hand.
Then Aias, faced with that balanced buckler, thrust hard,
yet missed the flesh, for the corselet protected it, while
Tydeus's son kept aiming over Aias's great tower shield
with his gleaming spear point, going for his opponent's neck.
At this point the Achaians, in great alarm for Aias,
commanded them to break off, accept equal prizes.
But to Tydeus's son the hero presented the great sword,
complete with its matching scabbard and its well-cut baldric.

Next Pēleus's son set out a great mass of pig iron,
that Ēetiōn, with his great strength, once used as a throwing
weight;
but him swift-footed noble Achilles had killed, and carried
this lump off aboard his ships with his other possessions.
Now he stood up and spoke as follows among the Argives:
"Up now, those who'd compete in this contest too! Even if
the winner's rich fields are far distant, he'll still enjoy
five full revolving seasons to satisfy his requirements—

10. The word I translate as "the body within" (ἐνδίνων, *endinōn*) occurs only here in surviving Greek literature, and from antiquity on there has been debate as to whether it means this, or, more specifically, the vitals or innards: see Richardson 260. Was there in fact a time when such a competitive fencing match was determined by a potentially fatal wound? Both Leaf (2: 429) and, more hesitantly, Richardson, think so. I am inclined to doubt this, not least since both verbs used, ὀρέγω (*oregō*) and ψαύω (*psauō*), are limited to touching, or at most pricking the surface. What we have here is a very slight modification (blood must be drawn) of the normal fencing "hit": so one scholiast. I translate accordingly.

it won't be for lack of iron that his shepherd or plowman
will need to go to the city: this will provide for them."

So he spoke: up jumped Polypoitēs, that staunch fighter,
and godlike Leonteus, a man of mighty strength,
and Aias, Telamōn's son, and noble Epeios.
They stood in line: noble Epeios first took up the weight,
swung it round, and let fly. The Achaians all laughed at him.[11]
Leonteus, scion of Arēs, was the next to take his shot,
and third to throw was huge Aias, Telamōn's son:
with his brawny fist, he got beyond both their marks.
But when Polypoitēs, staunch fighter, got the mass in his hands,
then—as far as an oxherd can fling his throwing stick,[12]
and away it flies, whirling, over the heads of his cattle—
so far, beyond the assembly, he cast it, to great cheering,
and the comrades of strong Polypoitēs rose to their feet
and bore off the prize of their king to the hollow ships.

Then for the archers Achilles offered dark iron:
ten double axes he brought and set out, and ten single,
and some way off set up the mast of a dark-prowed vessel
in the sand, and tethered a fluttering pigeon to it
by a thin cord attached to its foot, then told them that this
was their target. "Whoever hits the fluttering pigeon
will get all the double axes to take back home as prizes,
while the man who misses the bird, but hits the cord,
will win the single axes, since his shot's the less accurate."

So he spoke: up sprang lord Teukros, great in his strength;
up, too, Mērionēs, Idomeneus's worthy henchman.
They took the lots, shook them up in a bronze helmet,
and Teukros drew first place. He promptly let fly
a powerful shot, but had not promised to offer
a fine sacrifice of firstling lambs to the lord Apollo,
so missed the bird—Apollo begrudging him that—

11. From 670–72 it seems clear that shot-putting was yet another area in which Epeios's strength was not equaled by his skill.

12. Richardson (265) cites ancient commentators for the information that such a throwing stick "was equipped with a string for holding it, and a weight at the other end." A modern comparison (J. L. Myres, cited in *JHS* 27 [1907]: 5) is with "the *bolas*, a weapon consisting of a string with one or more stones attached to it, which is used in Spanish America for throwing at and catching cattle."

but struck the thin cord by the bird's foot, where it was tethered,
and the bitter shaft cut it clean through. The pigeon fluttered
high up into the sky, with the cord still hanging loosely
earthward, and all the Achaians gave a loud cheer.
Mēriones then quickly snatched the bow from Teukros's hand—
he'd been holding an arrow ready while Teukros aimed—
and vowed on the spot to Apollo the deadly archer
that he'd make him a fine sacrifice of firstling lambs.
High up under the clouds he spotted the fluttering pigeon,
and as she circled he hit her in mid-breast under the wing.
The shaft passed clean through, dropped earthward, fixed itself
in the ground in front of his feet, while the bird alit
on the mast of the dark-prowed vessel, and huddled there,
her head hanging down. Her beating wings now drooped
as the life left her limbs, and then, far from the mast
she fell, as the crowd, in rapt amazement, watched.
So Mēriones collected all ten of the double axes,
while Teukros took the single ones back to the hollow ships.

Then Pēleus's son brought out a far-shadowing spear,
and a flower-embossed cauldron, unfired still, worth an ox,
and set them by the arena, as javelin throwers stood up,
the son of Atreus among them, wide-ruling Agamemnōn,
along with Mēriones, Idomeneus's worthy henchman.
Then swift-footed noble Achilles spoke up among them:
"Son of Atreus, since we know how far you excel us all,
how much stronger you are, as a spear thrower without rival,
take this prize now, bear it off to the hollow ships;
and the spear let us give to the hero Mēriones—
that is, if you wish it: this is my suggestion only."

So he spoke: no dissent from the lord of men, Agamemnōn.
To Mēriones the hero then gave the bronze spear; but his own
splendid prize he handed to the herald Talthybios.

Book 24

Then the assembly broke up. The troops now scattered, each man
off to his own swift ship, their minds on the evening meal
and the joy of a full night's sleep. But Achilles wept and wept,
thinking of his dear comrade, so that sleep the all-subduing
got no hold on him: he kept tossing this way and that,
missing Patroklos—his manhood, his splendid strength,
all he'd been through with him, all the hardships he'd suffered,
facing men in battle and the waves of the cruel sea.
Recalling these things he shed large tears, lying now
stretched out on his side, but, restless, sometimes again
on his back, or prone. Then again he'd rise to his feet
and wander, distraught, by the seashore: the rising dawn
never brought light to sea and to beaches but he was there.
Then he would yoke his swift horses to the chariot,
and tie on Hektōr behind it, to be dragged; and when
he'd trailed him three times about Menoitios's dead son's mound
he'd go back and rest in his hut, leaving Hektōr's body
stretched out prone in the dust. But Apollo, pitying Hektōr,
preserved his flesh, though mortal, from all unseemly decay
even in death, wrapped the golden aegis round his whole body
to save the dragged corpse from disfigurement by Achilles.

So Achilles in his fury aimed to mutilate noble Hektōr;
but the sight of him stirred compassion among the blessed gods,
and they urged Argos's sharp-sighted slayer, Hermēs, to steal the corpse.
This plan pleased the rest of them, but neither Hērē
nor Poseidōn liked it, nor the grey-eyed virgin goddess,[1]

1. This is the sole reference in the *Iliad* to the famous, or notorious, Judgment of Paris (Aléxandros) in the beauty contest between Hērē, Athēnē, and Aphrodītē. By giving the prize to Aphrodītē, Paris earned her reward to him: she made Helen irresistible to his advances, and by so doing precipitated the events that led to the Trojan War. The genuineness of the passage was long debated, but it is now (and rightly, I think) accepted. Even so, problems remain: if this was the casus belli, why delay its mention so long, and then make it so brief? Embarrassment at such petty motivation? But similar examples of personal divine spite are frequent in Homer: I suspect the reason may simply have been that the incident was so well known that any ancient audience would take it for granted. See Richardson 278–80 for a good survey of the debate.

who still nursed the hatred they'd conceived for sacred Ilion,
and Priam, and Priam's people, through Aléxandros's blind delusion:
for when these goddesses came to his courtyard he despised them,
but had praise for the one who furthered his fatal lust.
So now, on the twelfth morning after Hektōr's death,
Phoibos Apollo spoke his mind among the immortals:
"A hard-hearted lot, you gods, and destructive! Did Hektōr never
burn for you thighs of oxen, then, or of unblemished goats?
Yet you couldn't be bothered to save him, dead though he is,
for his wife to look on, his mother and his child,
his father Priam, the Trojans—who would all promptly
burn his corpse in the fire, give him proper funeral rites.
No, gods: it's the ruthless Achilles you're bent on supporting,
though his mind's out of proper order and the will in his breast
inflexible—his nature's turned savage, like a lion
that in thrall to its huge might and its daring spirit
makes for the flocks of men to capture itself a feast:
so Achilles has lost all pity, and has no respect in him—
a great source to a man of both harm and benefit.
Any man may well have lost someone even dearer than he has—
a full brother, say, or even a son; yet when
he's wept and lamented the loss, he lets him go,
for it's an enduring heart the Fates have given to mortals.
But this man, after robbing noble Hektōr of his life,
ties him behind his chariot and then drags him about
his dear comrade's mound: nothing fine or decent there.
Great though he is, he should watch out for our anger:
through this fury of his he's outraging the silent earth."[2]

Then angrily white-armed Hērē addressed him, saying:
"What you say might even be true, lord of the silver bow,
if indeed you all grant equal honor to Achilles and Hektōr.
Hektōr is mortal, was suckled at a woman's breast; but Achilles
is the offspring of a goddess, one whom I myself
nurtured and reared, and gave to a mortal as his wife—

2. Both Leaf (2: 440) and Richardson (282) assume that the reference is solely to the mutilation of Hektōr's body, now dumb or senseless clay—as both point out, a traditional metaphor; but surely (and still more strikingly) what we have here is the sense of the earth itself (which cannot complain) being outraged by what is taking place, very directly, on its surface?

to Pēleus, a man who was dear to the hearts of the immortals;
and all of you gods were guests at their wedding—yes, you too[3]
sat at that feast, lyre in hand, ever faithless, friend of the wicked!"

Then Zeus the cloud-gatherer responded to her, saying:
"Hērē, no need to rage so vehemently at the gods!
The honor of these two will not be the same; yet Hektōr
was more dear to the gods than all other mortals in Ilion!
To me at least, for he never failed me with gifts I enjoyed—
Not once did my altar lack its fair share of the feasting,
the libations, the burnt fat, our accepted privileges!
We'll forget about stealing bold Hektōr—no way to do it
with Achilles not finding out: his mother is constantly
around him both day and night. In fact I wish
that one of you gods would tell Thetis I want her here,
to give a wise message to her, to make Achilles
accept ransom from Priam, and give Hektōr's body back."

So he spoke: storm-footed Iris hastened to take his message.
Midway between Samothrakē and rocky Imbros
she plunged into the dark sea with a loud splash of water,
and plummeted down to the depths like a lead weight
attached to the horn of a field ox on a fisherman's line
that brings death in its descent to the ravenous fishes.
Thetis she found in her hollow cave, and round her other
sea goddesses gathered, while she in the midst of them
wept for the fate of her peerless son, who was destined
to perish in rich-soiled Troy, far off from his own country.
Standing beside her, swift-footed Iris now said:
"Move yourself, Thetis: Zeus, the eternal planner, wants you."
Then the goddess, Thetis the silver-footed, answered her:
"What does that great god want with me? I'm embarrassed,
going among the immortals, with this endless grief at heart.
Still, I'll go. Whatever he says, it won't be pointless."

So saying, she, brightest of goddesses, put on her blue-black
veil, than which no garment she had was darker,
and set out to go, wind-footed swift Iris ahead of her

3. Apollo played at the wedding feast of the future Achilles' parents, but went on (as a fragment of Aeschylus, spoken by Thetis, alleges: Richardson 283) to be responsible for their famous son's death.

leading the way: the sea's waves parted before them.
They stepped out onto the beach, then darted up skywards
and found Kronos's far-seeing son, with all the other
blessed gods who exist forever around him. Thetis
sat down by Zeus the Father—Athēnē yielded her seat—
and Hērē put in her hand a splendid golden cup,
with a friendly greeting. Thetis drank, and returned it.
The Father of men and gods now began their discussion:
"Thetis, goddess, you've come to Olympos, despite your distress,
and the ceaseless grief in your heart: this I know myself.
Even so, I shall tell you the reason I brought you here.
For nine days there's been a quarrel among the immortals
about Hektōr's corpse and Achilles, sacker of cities.
They're urging Argos's sharp-eyed slayer to steal the body,
but this is an honor that I'm reserving for Achilles,
to preserve your respect and friendship in the days ahead.
Go quickly, then, to the camp, and give your son this message:
Say that he's angered the gods, that I, above all other
immortals, am filled with rage, because in his maddened heart
he's kept Hektōr by the curved ships, won't give him up.
It may be, through fear of me, he'll return Hektōr's body;
but I'll send down Iris to great-hearted Priam, who must
offer ransom for his dear son, go to the Achaians' ships
in person, with gifts for Achilles that will soften his heart."

So he spoke,
and Thetis the silver-footed, the goddess, did not ignore him,
but went on her way, darting down from the peaks of Olympos,
and arrived at her son's hut. It was there that she found him,
making ceaseless lament, while round him his dear comrades
were busy about their tasks, preparing their morning meal:
a big shaggy ram had been killed for them, there in the hut.
So now his lady mother sat down close by Achilles' side,
caressed him with her hand, then spoke to him, saying:
"My child, how long will you go on eating your heart out
with weeping and lamentation, thinking neither of food
nor of bed? A good thing it is to lie with a woman,
to make love: for you've not long to live—even now, already,
death and all-mastering destiny are there beside you.
But now listen well: I bring word to you from Zeus.

He says that you've angered the gods, that he, above all other
immortals, is filled with rage, because in your maddened heart
you've kept Hektōr by the curved ships, won't give him up.
So come now, let him go, accept ransom for his corpse."

In answer to her swift-footed Achilles declared:
"So be it: he who brings ransom can take the corpse—if indeed
the Olympian himself, of his own free will, so orders."

Thus they, where the ships were drawn up now, mother and son,
conversed together, exchanging many a winged word;
and Kronos's son meanwhile dispatched Iris to sacred Ilion:
"On your way now, swift Iris, leave the seat of Olympos
for Ilion, take this message to great-hearted Priam. He must
offer ransom for his dear son, go to the Achaians' ships,
in person, with gifts for Achilles that will soften his heart—
alone: no Trojan warrior should accompany him,
just a herald, well on in years, to drive the mules
and a smooth-running wagon, to carry back to the city
the corpse of the man whom noble Achilles killed.
Let death not be on his mind, nor any such fear,
such a guide we'll provide him with, the slayer of Argos,
who'll be his leader, convey him safely to Achilles;
and when he's brought him into Achilles' hut,
Achilles himself will not kill him, and will restrain all others,
being neither senseless nor careless nor malicious:
with compassion, rather, he'll spare a man who's a suppliant."

So he spoke: storm-footed Iris sped off with his message.
She reached Priam's house, and found there wailing and sorrow:
sons sitting around their father in the courtyard,
tears marring their garments, the old man in their midst
wrapped tight in his cloak, and round him an abundance
of dung all smeared on his aged head and neck
that he'd scraped up in his hands as he rolled on the ground.
In the house were his daughters and his sons' wives, keening,
their thoughts on the warriors, so many and so warlike,
lying dead now, those who'd lost their lives to the Argives.
Zeus's messenger stood close to Priam now, and addressed him,
speaking softly, yet shivering still invaded his limbs:
"Take heart, Priam, scion of Dardanos: no need to be scared—

I've not come here to foretell some disaster for you,
but rather with good intent. I'm a messenger from Zeus,
who, remote though he is, both pities and cares for you greatly.
The Olympian commands you to ransom noble Hektōr,
taking gifts to Achilles that will soften his heart—
alone: no other Trojan warrior should accompany you,
just a herald, well on in years, to drive the mules
and a smooth-running wagon, on which to take back to the city
the corpse of the man whom noble Achilles killed.
Let death not be on your mind, nor any such fear,
such a guide we'll provide you with—the slayer of Argos,
who'll be your leader, convey you safely to Achilles;
and when he's brought you into Achilles' hut,
Achilles himself won't kill you, and will restrain all others,
being neither senseless nor careless nor malicious;
with compassion, rather, he'll spare a man who's a suppliant."

So speaking, swift-footed Iris went on her way,
and Priam ordered his sons to make ready the smooth-running
mule wagon, and strap the wickerwork basket on it.
He himself went down to his storeroom—fragrant it was
with cedar wood, and high-ceilinged—where many treasures lay,
and sent for his wife Hekabē, and spoke to her, saying:
"Dear wife, an Olympian messenger's reached me from Zeus—
I'm to go to the ships, offer ransom for my dear son,
in person, with gifts for Achilles that will soften his heart.
So tell me, what's your reaction to this, how does it strike you—
since my own whole passionate instinct is terribly set
on going to the ships, to the broad camp of the Achaians."

So he spoke: but his wife cried out aloud, and responded:
"Oh my lord, what's become of that good sense for which
you were famous once, both abroad and with those you rule?
How can you want to go to the Achaians' ships, alone,
into the sight of the man who's slaughtered so many
of your noble sons? You must have a heart of iron.
For once you are in his power, once he sets eyes on you,
that treacherous raw flesh eater will show you no pity,
nor any respect! Let us rather lament far from him,
sitting here in our own home. All-mastering Destiny

surely spun a thread at his birth, when I myself bore him,
that far from his parents he'd glut quick scavenging dogs
after meeting a stronger man—whose whole liver I wish
I could get in my jaws and devour! A fair requital, that,
for my son, who was not playing the coward when he killed him,
but in defense of Troy's men and deep-bosomed women,
standing firm, with no thought of panic, or of fleeing the foe."

In answer to her the old man, Priam the godlike, said:
"Don't try to stop me when I want to go; do not yourself
prove a bird of ill omen here in our home: you won't persuade me.
If anyone else on earth had been urging me thus—
whether seers divining from sacrifices, or priests—
we'd call it a lie and have nothing to do with it!
But now, since I heard the goddess and saw her face myself,
I'm going—her word won't be wasted. And if it's my fate
to end up dead beside the bronze-clad Achaians' ships,
I'm ready. Achilles is welcome to slaughter me there and then
once I've held my son in my arms, and had my fill of mourning."

With that he opened up the fine lids of the clothes chests,
and from them took out a dozen most elegant robes,
a dozen plain cloaks, the same number of rugs and blankets,
and of white linen mantles, as well as tunics to match them;
and of gold he weighed out and took ten talents in all,
with four cauldrons, and two brightly gleaming tripods,
and an exquisite cup, that was given him by some Thracians
when he went there on a mission, a great treasure: not even this
did the old man keep in his home, so strong was his passion
to ransom his dear son. Then he drove all the Trojans away
from his colonnade, upbraiding them with abusive insults:
'Get out, you worthless no-goods! Do you not have your own
mourning to do at home, that you've come here to double mine?
Or is the grief nothing to you that Zeus the son of Kronos
has laid on me: the loss of my best son? You too will learn—
you'll be that much easier for the Achaians to slaughter
now that he's dead! As for me, before I'm forced
to see the downfall and sacking of this city
with my own eyes, may I go down into Hādēs' realm."

That said, he went after the men with his staff, and they
ran off from the old man's assault. Then he yelled at his own sons,
abusing them—Helenos, noble Agathōn, Paris,
Pammōn and Antiphōn, Politēs of the great war cry,
Deïphobos and Hippothoös and illustrious Dios:
To these nine the old man now shouted his harsh orders:
"Get moving, you wretched children, you downcasts—how I wish
all of you, rather than Hektōr, had been killed at the swift ships!
Alas, I'm wholly ill-fated—I sired sons who were the best
in the broad land of Troy, yet of them not one, I tell you,
is left—neither godlike Mēstōr, nor Trōilos, charioteer,
nor Hektōr, a god among men, who never did seem
a mortal man's son, but the offspring of a god!
These Arēs destroyed: what's left are all the no-goods—
the liars, the dancers only expert at matching the beat,
the lifters of lambs and kids from those in your own country![4]
So at least make me ready a wagon, and do it quickly,
and load all this stuff aboard it, so we can be on our way."

So he spoke, and they, alarmed by their father's reproof,
went and brought out for him the smooth-running mule wagon—
a fine one, newly made—strapped the wickerwork basket to it,
and down from its peg took the yoke for the mules, of boxwood,
with a boss on it, well equipped with guide rings for the reins.
Then they fetched the nine-cubit yoke strap, and the yoke itself,
which they settled down firmly upon the well-polished pole
at its front end, set the ring on the peg, then fastened
the strap three times each side of the boss, made it tight
in a series of turns, and twisted it under the hook. They brought
from the storeroom and stacked up aboard the polished wagon
the boundless ransom to offer for the head of Hektōr;
they yoked the strong-hoofed mules, broken to work in harness,
that the Mysians had given to Priam, a splendid gift; while for him
they harnessed up the horses that the old man kept on
for his own use, and cared for, there in his polished stalls.

4. As Thucydides observed (1.5.1) and Richardson duly notes (300–301), "robbing livestock outside one's community was no disgrace in heroic society." Modern Greece and the Scottish Highlands offer good parallels.

So these two[5] in the high palace, while their teams were harnessed,
the herald and Priam, had much to meditate on;
and Hekabē now approached them, heavy-laden at heart,
carrying in her right hand wine sweet to the mind
in a golden cup, for libation before they departed.
Standing in front of the horses, she spoke to Priam, saying:
"Here, pour a libation to Zeus, the Father, and pray that you
get back home safe from these hateful men, since your heart
impels you
to go to the ships, even though I'm set against it.
Then pray to Kronos's son, lord of the dark clouds,
who from Ida looks down on all the country of Troy.
Ask him for a bird of omen—the swift messenger that's
the dearest of birds to him, and its power is the greatest—
on your right hand, so that, after seeing it for yourself,
and trusting it, you can go to the swift-horsed Danaäns' ships.
But if far-seeing Zeus does not grant you his messenger,
then I at least would not encourage you to go out
to the ships of the Argives, however much you may want to."

In answer to her, godlike Priam then declared:
"My wife, in this I shall not disregard your wishes:
it's good to raise hands to Zeus: he always might show pity."

So saying, the old man asked a servant, the housekeeper,
to pour pure water over his hands; the servant stood
beside him, with in her hands both ewer and wine jug.
When he'd washed his hands he took the cup from his wife,
and stood in the forecourt and prayed, poured out the wine
eyes upturned to heaven, and spoke aloud, in these words:
"Zeus, Father, ruling from Ida, most glorious, greatest,
grant that Achilles receive me with both friendship and pity—
and send me a bird of omen—the swift messenger that's
the dearest of birds to you, and its power is the greatest—
on my right hand, so that, after seeing it for myself,
and trusting it, I can go to the swift-horsed Danaäns' ships."

---

5. This is the first we are told of a herald actually being found (at short notice, at night) and brought to the palace. It is only later (325), and equally casually, that we learn that his name is Idaios (cf. 3.248, 7.276, and elsewhere).

So he spoke in prayer, and Zeus the Counselor heard him.
He at once dispatched an eagle, of winged life the surest omen,
dark hunter, sometimes known to men as the black falcon.
Wide as the door is built to fit some wealthy man's
high-ceilinged treasure chamber, a door well-equipped with bars,
so wide the spread of its wings on either side. It appeared
on their right, swooping over the city, and seeing it they
rejoiced, and the hearts in the breasts of all were cheered.

Briskly now the old man stepped into his chariot,
and drove out through the forecourt and the echoing colonnade.
In front of him went the mules, that drew the four-wheeled wagon
driven by skillful Idaios, and following after them
the horses, that the old man smartly whipped on
at speed through the city, his kinsfolk all following behind
with great weeping and sorrow, as for one going to his death.
When they'd come down out of the city, and reached the plain,
these last turned and went back into Ilion—Priam's sons,
and his daughters' husbands. Far-seeing Zeus did not fail
to notice the two as they entered the plain, and, seeing Priam,
felt pity, and spoke at once to Hermēs, his own dear son:
"Hermēs, it gives you much pleasure to act as a man's
companion; you're glad to listen to those whom you enjoy!
So, off with you now, escort Priam to the Achaians'
hollow ships—but make sure he's not seen or recognized
by the other Danaäns before you get to Pēleus's son."

So he spoke: the guide, Argos's slayer, did not ignore him,
but at once strapped under his feet the beautiful sandals,
golden, immortal, that carried him over water
or boundless land, as swift as the wind's blast,
and took the wand with which he bewitches the eyes
of those he chooses, while others he rouses from their sleep.
With this in his hand the mighty slayer of Argos
took to the air, quickly reaching the Hellespont, and Troy,
where he set off to walk in the likeness of a young prince
with the first down on his chin, youth's most charming age.

When the two had driven past the great burial mound of Ilos,
they halted their mules and horses to let them drink
at the river: by this time darkness had fallen over the land.

Looking around, the herald caught sight of someone nearby—
Hermēs—and turning to Priam said: "Think quickly,
scion of Dardanos—we need a smart decision!
I see a man—I'm afraid we may soon be cut to pieces!
Let's run for it in the chariot, or else perhaps
clasp his knees and entreat him—he might take pity on us."

So he spoke: the old man was terrified, his mind
in turmoil, on his bowed limbs the hairs rose up,
and he stood in a daze: but the Helper himself approached,
took the old man's hand in his, and questioned him, saying:
"Where are you off to, father, driving horses and mules
through the fragrant night, when other mortals are sleeping?
Aren't you scared of the Achaians, your implacable enemies,
whose breath is fury, who are very near around you?
Should one of them see you coming, through the swift dark
night,
conveying all that treasure, what answer would you have then?
You're not young yourself, and your attendant here's old too:
how stand off any man who decides to attack you? Myself,
I shan't harm you in any way, in fact I'd defend you
against anyone else: you're so like my own dear father."

Then the old man, Priam the godlike, made him this answer:
"These things, dear child, are indeed correct as you state them—
but one of the gods must still have had a protective hand
over me, to have put a traveller like you in my path,
so happily met, so handsome, of so fine a demeanor,
and sensible too: your parents are truly blessed!"

Then the guide, the slayer of Argos, gave him this reply:
"All this indeed, old sir, you have fittingly spoken.
But tell me now, please, and make a true declaration:
all these splendid treasures—are you shipping them out
to foreign people abroad, to be kept in safety for you?
Or is it that you're all abandoning sacred Ilion
out of fear now, since your finest warrior's perished—
your son? *He* never shrank from battling the Achaians."

Then the old man, Priam the godlike, made this answer to him:
"Who are you, most noble sir, and who, pray, are your parents,
that you speak so well of the fate of my unlucky son?"

Then the guide, the slayer of Argos, made him this reply:
"You're testing me, old sir, when you ask about noble Hektōr.
Him I have often seen, in battle, where men win honor,
with my own eyes, and when, after driving them to the ships,
he would slay Argives, cut them down with the sharp bronze.
We would stand there and marvel, because Achilles
would not let us fight, being embittered at Atreus's son.
His henchman am I: the same well-built ship brought us here.
From the Myrmidons I am sprung; my father is Polyktōr,
a wealthy man—and an old one, just as you are.
Six other sons he has, and I myself am the seventh.
We cast lots, and I was chosen to serve out here;
and now I've come to the plain from the ships, for at first dawn
the sharp-eyed Achaians are going to attack around the city.
Sitting idle has made them impatient: the Achaians' princes
can no longer restrain them, so eager they are for battle."

Then the old man, Priam the godlike, made him this answer:
"If you indeed are a henchman of Pēleus's son Achilles,
then please recount to me the whole truth of the matter:
does my son remain by the ships, or has Achilles already
hacked him to pieces, and thrown them out for his dogs?"

Then the guide, the slayer of Argos, made him this reply:
"Old sir, not yet have dogs or birds of prey devoured him;
the man is still lying there beside Achilles' ship,
among the huts, just as he was; though this is the twelfth day
he's been there, his flesh has not rotted, nor have maggots
devoured it—the kind that feed on mortals killed in battle.
Achilles indeed now drags him around his dear comrade's tomb,
ruthlessly, daily, as soon as the light of dawn appears—
yet does not disfigure him: go look, and you'd be amazed
how dew-fresh he lies there, washed quite clean of blood
and nowhere befouled. All the wounds that he was given
have closed—and many there were who thrust the bronze into him!
This is how the blessed gods take good care of your son,
corpse though he is, since he was dear to their hearts."

So he spoke: the old man rejoiced, and answered in these words:
"My child, it's a good thing indeed to make proper offerings
to the immortals: my son—if he ever truly existed—

never forgot in his halls the gods who possess Olympos,
so now they've remembered him, even in his destined death.
But come, accept from me this beautiful drinking cup,
and be my protector, and in company with the gods
escort me, until I arrive at the hut of Pēleus's son."

Then the guide, the slayer of Argos, made this reply:
"You're testing my youth, old sir, but you'll not persuade me,
when you ask me to take gifts from you behind Achilles' back!
Him I fear and respect too much at heart to ever
defraud him—I wouldn't want to get into trouble later!
But as your guide I'd go with you as far as famous Argos,
protecting you carefully, in a swift ship or on foot,
nor would any man, scorning your escort, dare to attack you."

So saying, the Helper took charge of chariot and horses,
quickly got his hands on the whip and the reins, and breathed
potent strength into horses and mules alike; and when
they reached the ditch and the battlements protecting the ships,
where the guards were still busy preparing their evening meal,
on all these the guide, the slayer of Argos, shed sleep,
then opened the gates, drew back the bars, and brought
Priam inside, along with the splendid gifts on the wagon.
But when they arrived at the hut of Peleus's son—
that high cabin built by the Myrmidons for their king,
with rough-cut fir-wood beams, and a roof set up over it,
made of bristling thatch that they'd harvested from the meadows,
and around it enclosed a large courtyard for their king
with a close-set palisade, the entrance to which was secured
by one single fir beam: to close it took three Achaians,
and three to haul open this huge cross-bar on the doors
(except for Achilles, who'd ram it home single-handed)—
then Hermēs the Helper opened the entrance for the old man,
and fetched in the splendid gifts for Pēleus's swift-footed son,
and stepped down to the ground from the chariot, and declared:
"Old sir, I who have come to you am an immortal god,
Hermēs, sent here to escort you by my father.
But now I must hasten back, and not come in where Achilles
can see me: it would be most improper for an immortal
god to be entertained by mortals, face to face! But you
must go in there now, embrace the knees of Pēleus's son,

and in the name of his father and of his fine-haired mother—
and of his child[6]—entreat him, attempt to touch his heart."

Having so spoken, Hermēs then departed to high Olympos,
while Priam stepped from his chariot to the ground,
leaving Idaios there, to stay behind and look after
the horses and mules. He himself went straight to the dwelling
where Achilles, dear to Zeus, was sitting; entered, and found
the man himself, but his comrades were sitting elsewhere—
two only, the hero Automedōn, and Alkimos, scion of Arēs,
were in busy attendance on him. He was through with his meal,
with eating and drinking: the table still stood by him.
Unnoticed, great Priam came in, approached Achilles,
embraced his knees, and kissed his hands—those terrible
murderous hands, that had killed so many of his sons.
As when blind delusion possesses a man to murder
someone in his own country, and he flees to an alien people,
to some wealthy man's house, and wonder grips those who see him—
so Achilles was amazed at the sight of godlike Priam,
and the rest were likewise amazed, and looked at one another.
Then Priam addressed Achilles, entreating him in these words:
"Remember your own father, godlike Achilles,
whose years equal mine, on old age's deathly threshold:
him too, it may well be, those dwelling on his frontiers
are harassing, with no one to ward off ruin from him.
But he at least, while he hears that you're still living,
is happy at heart, and hopes from day to day
that he'll see his dear son returning from the land of Troy—
whereas I am wholly ill-fated: of the best sons I sired,
in the broad land of Troy, not one, I tell you, is left:
fifty I had, when the Achaians' sons first came;
nineteen were born to me from one single womb, the rest
other women bore in my halls. But most of these, though many,
had their limbs unstrung by impetuous Arēs. The one
true son I had left me to guard the city and its people

6. Achilles' only son, by Deidameia, was Pyrrhos, also known as Neoptolemos. There is grim irony here, since according to one tradition (*Little Iliad* fr. 18 = West 2003 [A]: 136–37), it was Neoptolemos—one of the warriors in the Wooden Horse—who during the sack of Troy killed Priam, while the latter was seeking sanctuary at the altar of Zeus. For this outrage Neoptolemos was later slain at Delphi (*HE* 2: 569).

you slew untimely as he fought in defense of his country—
Hektōr! It's for his sake I've come, now, to the Argives' ships,
to recover him from you. I bring with me ransom past counting.
Revere the gods, Achilles, and to me show pity,
remembering your own father: but I'm the more pitiable,
for I've borne what no other mortal on earth has yet endured:
I've brought to my lips the hand of the man who killed my son."

So saying, he stirred in Achilles the urge to weep for his father:
he took the old man by the hand, gently pushed him away.
Both had their memories: Priam of Hektōr, killer of men,
as, bitterly weeping, he crouched at Achilles' feet,
while Achilles wept, now for his own father, now again
for Patroklos: their joint mourning resounded throughout the hut.
But as soon as noble Achilles had had his fill of weeping,
and the urge for it had departed from his heart and limbs,
he rose from his chair, took the old man by the hand,
and raised him up, pitying his grey hair, his grey beard,
and then addressed him, speaking with winged words:
"Unhappy man, your heart's indeed endured many sorrows!
How could you bear to come to the Achaians' ships, alone,
to look me straight in the face, the man who slaughtered so many
of your noble sons? You must have a heart of iron.
Come then, sit down on this chair, and let's allow our distress
to lie at rest in our hearts, for all our grieving,
for there's no profit accrues from numbing lamentation:
that's how the gods spun life's thread for unhappy mortals—
to live amid sorrow, while they themselves are uncaring.
There are two great jars, sunk down in the floor of Zeus's abode,[7]
full of gifts he hands out, one of ills, the other of blessings;
and the man who gets a mixed handout from thundering Zeus
will sometimes encounter trouble, and sometimes good luck;

7. The jars (πίθοι, *pithoi*) of Zeus are generally treated as a moral allegory, but there is something more practical, more physical and earthy, about the image (Leaf, 2: 467; Onians 395–97, 404, 409; Richardson 330). These are the great clay *pithoi* familiar from Minoan and Mycenaean excavations, which were indeed sunk in the floor of the storeroom. Like words, that are winged, and escape the barrier of one's teeth, evils were in the beginning thought of as physical entities, to be stored, like anything else, in jars. As Leaf says, what we have here is early thinking applied to what we (and indeed already Plato, who for "gifts" substituted κῆρες (*kēros*), "fates", *Rep.* 2.379D) think of as a moral abstraction.

whereas he who gets only ills Zeus renders an outcast,
driven by evil hunger to wander across the face
of the sacred earth, with respect from neither gods nor mortals.
So the gods bestowed on Pēleus the most splendid gifts
from his birth onward, for he outstripped all mortal men
in wealth and prosperity, ruled as lord of the Myrmidons,
and though he was mortal they married him to a goddess.
Yet even on him the god laid evil: no family
of lordly sons was born to him in his halls, but only
the one short-lived male child. Nor am I able
to care for him as he ages, but sit here, far from my country,
in Troy, bringing grief to you and to your offspring.
Yet you too, old sir, were once, we hear, fortunate.
Everywhere southward as far as Lesbos, seat of Makar,
or Phrygia inland, with the vast Hellespont—here, they say,
through your wealth and sons, old sir, you were preeminent.
But since the heavenly gods brought this trouble upon you,
round your city the fighting, the killings have never stopped.
Bear up then, don't nurse unending grief in your heart:
you'll gain nothing by mourning your son, you won't
bring him back to life; before that you'll have other troubles."

Then the old man, Priam the godlike, answered him, saying:
"Zeus's nursling, you'll not make me sit, so long as Hektōr lies
uncared-for among the huts! So, waste no time,
release him—let me see him myself—and accept the ransom,
the very great ransom, we bring you! Enjoy it, and go back home
to your own country, now that you've spared me
[to live myself, and to gaze on the light of the sun].[8]

Eyeing him angrily, swift-footed Achilles exclaimed:
"Provoke me no further, old man: I myself am minded
to give you back Hektōr, since a messenger's reached me from Zeus—
the mother who bore me, daughter to the Old Man of the Sea.
What's more, I am well aware, Priam—you do not deceive me—
that it was some god brought you here to the Achaians' ships:
no mortal man would dare, however youthful and strong,

8. Line 558 is missing in some MSS, and the scholiasts do not refer to it. It may have been interpolated in the belief that "spared" (ἔασας, *eāsas*) needed an explanatory phrase to complete the predicate (Richardson 335), though it stands on its own elsewhere in the same book (569, 684).

to enter the camp, or could make his way past the guards,
or easily thrust back the great bar on our gateway.
Stop working on my emotions amid my sorrows, old sir,
lest I might not spare even you, while you're here in my hut,
suppliant though you are, and break Zeus's ordinances."

So he spoke: the old man was frightened, and heeded his words.

Now the son of Pēleus strode out of the hut like a lion:
not alone, but two of his henchmen accompanied him,
the hero Automedōn and Alkimos, those whom Achilles
most honored of all his comrades now Patroklos was dead.
Together they unyoked both the mules and the horses,
brought in the herald, the old man's public crier,
sat him down on a chair, and from the smooth-running wagon
took the boundless ransom for Hektōr's head, but left there
two robes and a fine-woven tunic, in which Achilles
would wrap the corpse before yielding it to be carried home.
Then he summoned the handmaids, told them to wash and anoint it—
having first moved it away, to stop Priam seeing his son,
lest, heartbroken, he failed to restrain his wrath at the sight,
and Achilles' own heart should be stirred to fury, so that
he murdered Priam, thus breaking the ordinances of Zeus.
So when the handmaids had washed it and anointed it with oil,
and shrouded it in a fine robe and a tunic besides,
Achilles himself raised the body and placed it upon a bier,
which he and his comrades lifted onto the polished wagon.
Then he heaved a sigh, and addressed his dear comrade by name:
"Don't be angry with me, Patroklos, if you chance to hear,
even in Hādēs' realm, that I've given back noble Hektōr
to his dear father: the ransom he offered was not unfitting—
and of this I'll allot to you all that's your proper due."

That said, noble Achilles went back inside his hut,
sat down on the richly worked chair from which he'd arisen,
against the opposite wall, and then addressed Priam, saying:
"Your son, old sir, has been released to you as you wanted,
and is lying on a bier: at daybreak you shall yourself
see him as you take him, but for now let's turn to supper—
for even fair-haired Niobē was minded to eat,
though all her twelve children had perished there in her halls,

six daughters and six sons in the prime of their youth!
The sons were slain by Apollo with shafts from his silver bow,
out of anger against Niobē; the daughters by Artemis
the huntress—Niobē had praised herself over fair-cheeked Lētō,
who, she said, bore two only, whereas she was mother to many.
Her brood Lētō's twins then slaughtered, every last one.
Nine days they lay in their blood, nor was there anyone
to bury them: Kronos's son turned their people to stones.
But on the tenth day they were buried by the heavenly gods,
and Niobē's mind turned to food, since she'd tired of weeping.
Now somewhere among the rocks, in those lonely mountains,
on Sipylos—where, they say, goddesses have their abodes:
the nymphs who move nimbly, dancing round Achelōïos—
there, though stone, she broods on the woes that the gods dealt her.
So come, let the two of us likewise, noble old sir, take thought
for food: after that you can mourn your dear son, when
you've returned him to Ilion: much wept over he will be."[9]

With that swift Achilles sprang up, and cut the throat
of a white sheep: his comrades skinned it, butchered it neatly,
cut up the meat with skill, threaded the bits on skewers,
grilled them with care, then drew them all off. That done,
Automedōn brought bread and put it on the table
in handsome baskets, while Achilles shared out the meat.
So they reached out their hands to the good things ready for them;
but when they'd satisfied their desire for food and drink,
then Priam, scion of Dardanos, gazed in wonder at Achilles,
his stature and beauty, how like the gods he appeared;
while at Priam, scion of Dardanos, Achilles gazed in wonder,
observing his noble features, listening as he spoke.

---

9. Achilles suggests a meal even though he has himself recently eaten (475–76): as Graziosi 2011 says (449) "he is now imparting a lesson he has only just learned" (cf. 19.205–14 and 314–55). The use of the myth of Niobē as a recommendation for this is odd, since Niobē was an example of never-ending sorrow, even when petrified (a vaguely human-looking rock formation on Mt. Sipylos dripping with tear-like water gave rise to this aspect of the myth). Other details, not extant elsewhere, seem to have been introduced in the Homeric narrative for symbolic effect: the nine days before burial match both the time Hektōr's body lies in Achilles' hut and the mourning period in Troy (664–65, 784–87; Richardson 340), while the gods' personal care for the burial of Niobē's offspring foreshadows divine concern for Hektōr's obsequies. The Achelōïos is a local river: there were several of that name, and Achelōïos can be "a generic name for rivers or water in general" (Richardson 342).

But when they'd had their pleasure of looking at one another,
then the first to speak was the old man, Priam the godlike:
"Let me bed down now, Zeus's nursling, so that at last
we may take our rest and get our fill of sweet slumber:
for never yet have my eyes closed under my eyelids
since at your hands my son was bereft of life—I've been
lamenting ceaselessly, nursing my countless sorrows,
rolling about in the dung in my courtyard's enclosure.
But now I've tasted food, permitted fire-bright wine
to pass down my throat: before that I'd taken nothing."

Thereupon Achilles instructed his comrades and the handmaids
to set bedsteads under the colonnade, and lay upon them
fine purple wool throws, and over these to spread blankets,
topped off with fleecy cloaks to serve as coverlets.
Out from the hall went the handmaids, each holding a torch,
and quickly made up two beds. In a teasing voice
swift-footed Achilles then had this to say to Priam:
"Best sleep outside, good old sir! Some Achaian counselor
might come over here—they're always having sessions with me,
seeking advice in their planning, a common practice—
but if one of them saw you, during the swift black night,
he might go and tell Agamemnōn, the people's shepherd,
and then there'd be, ah, delay in the release of the body.
Now, tell me this, and be honest: how many days
do you have in mind for the funeral of noble Hektōr,
so I hold off that long, and restrain the troops as well?"

Then the old man, Priam the godlike, answered him, saying:
"If you truly mean that I can complete noble Hektōr's burial,
you'd be doing me a great kindness by acting thus—you know
how we're shut up inside the city, and firewood has to be fetched
a long way from the mountains, and the Trojans are really scared.
Nine days we would mourn him in our halls, and then
on the tenth we'd inter him, and there'd be public feasting;
on the eleventh we'd raise the funeral mound over him—
and on the twelfth, if we have to, we'll join battle once again."

Then noble swift-footed Achilles answered him, saying:
"All these things, aged Priam, shall be as you propose:
I shall hold back the attack for the time that you've requested."

So saying, he took hold of the aged man's right hand
by the wrist, to allay any fear that might be in his heart.
Then they lay down to sleep there, in the dwelling's forecourt,
the herald and Priam, with a great deal to think about;
but Achilles himself slept at the back of the well-built hut,
with the fair-cheeked Briseïs now lying there by his side.[10]

All others, both gods, and mortals, chariot marshals,
slept the night through, overcome by gentle slumber;
but on Hermēs the Helper sleep could get no hold
as he pondered on how he was going to escort King Priam
away from the ships unseen by the watchful gate guards.
So he stood close, above his head, and addressed him, saying:
"Ah, old sir, you're not bothered by danger, still fast asleep
among enemies as you are, since Achilles has spared you!
Now you've ransomed your son, and a great deal you gave
  for him;
yet to get you back alive would cost your surviving sons
three times that amount in ransom, were Atreus's son
Agamemnōn or all the Achaians to learn you were here."

He spoke,
and the old man, badly frightened, made the herald get up,
while Hermēs himself yoked the mules and the horses for them,
and briskly drove them out of the camp. No one noticed them.
But when they came to the ford of the swift-flowing river,
eddying Xanthos, begotten by immortal Zeus,
then Hermēs went on his way to lofty Olympos,
as saffron-robed Dawn was spreading across the entire earth,
and the others, weeping and wailing, drove the horses to the city,
while the mules drew the dead body. Once more no man,
nor any fine-sashed woman, recognized them now,
save only Kassandrē, as lovely as golden Aphroditē,
who'd gone up onto the citadel, and recognized her dear father
as he stood in the chariot, and the herald, the city's crier—
and him she saw stretched on a bier in the mule-drawn wagon.
Then she shrieked aloud, and went screaming throughout the city:
"Go look, men and women of Troy! Go now and see Hektōr,

10. Achilles, having eaten, now fulfills the second part of his mother Thetis's advice: see above, 128–32.

if ever while he yet lived you were happy to see him coming
home from the battle, great joy to our city and all its people!"

So she spoke: not one man was left behind in the city,
nor any woman: upon them all came sorrow past bearing.
It was near the city gates they encountered the dead man's escort.
His dear wife and his lady mother were the first to fling themselves
aboard the smooth-running wagon, tearing their hair,
to cradle Hektōr's head: the thronged bystanders all wept,
and from then all day long until sunset, there by the gates,
they'd have gone on shedding tears and mourning for Hektōr
had the old man not called out to the crowd from his chariot:
"Make way for the mules to come through! You'll get your fill
of lamenting later, as soon as I've brought him home."

So he spoke: they stood to one side, made way for the wagon.
When Hektōr's body reached Priam's famed palace, they moved it
to an inlaid bedstead, and by his side placed minstrels,
leaders of dirges: these chanted the song of lamentation
while the women in chorus added their lament to the dirge.
Of these it was white-armed Andromachē led the mourning,
cradling in her arms the head of Hektōr the killer:
"Husband, perished too young, you're leaving me a widow
here in our home, and the son's still only an infant
that we, both ill-fated, made: nor do I believe he will
ever come to the years of manhood—before then this city
will be leveled, since you, its guardian, have perished,
who protected it, kept safe its devoted wives, its children.
Soon enough these'll be cargo aboard the hollow ships,
and I among them; and you, my child, will go with me
to a place where you must labor at unseemly tasks,
slaving for a rough master, or else some Achaian
will strong-arm you down from the battlements, a grim death,
angered maybe because it was Hektōr killed his brother—
or father, or son, since there are so many Achaians
have bitten the boundless dust at Hektōr's hands,
for in grim warfare your father was far from gentle.
So there's public mourning for him throughout the city—
and unspeakable grief and sorrow you've brought on your parents,
Hektōr: to me, above all, there's left this bitter loss,
for you never, dying, reached out to me from your bed,

you never uttered for me some enduring last word
that I could have recalled, night and day, as I shed my tears."

So she spoke, weeping: the women added their own lament,
and among them now Hekabē led the passionate mourning:
"Hektōr, of all my children far the dearest to my heart,
while you still were living you were beloved of the gods,
they cared for you even in your destiny of death:
those other sons of mine swift-footed Achilles, whenever
he took one, would sell abroad, beyond the unharvested sea,
to Samos or Imbros or mist-enshrouded Lēmnos;
but you—though he'd robbed you of life with the keen-edged bronze,
and often dragged you around the tomb of his comrade,
Patroklos, whom you slew—yet never could bring him back to life—
you lie now in my halls as though new-slain, dewy-fresh,
like one whom lately Apollo, he of the silver bow,
has assailed with his gentle shafts, and put to death."

So she spoke, weeping, and stirred up unending lamentation.
Then, third in line, to lead the mourning came Helen:
"Hektōr, most dear to my heart of all my husband's brothers!
Yes, indeed, my husband is Aléxandos the godlike,
who brought me hither to Troy—ah, would that I'd died first!
This is now the twentieth[11] year that's passed since I
ran off from home, abandoning my own country;
yet from you I've never had one mean or degrading word,
and if anyone else reviled me here in these halls,
one of your brothers or sisters, or a brother's well-dressed wife,
or your mother—your father could have been mine, he was
always so gentle—then you'd talk them round and restrain them
with your gentleheartedness and the gentle things you said.
So I weep, sad at heart, for both you and my ill-starred self,

11. This is the tenth year of the war, and whatever allowances we make for such things as the time taken to assemble the expedition, the delay of the Greek fleet setting out from Aulis, or Paris's travels with Helen en route to Troy, the figure Helen gives is simply incompatible with the accepted chronology (e.g., with the return of Odysseus, likewise placed in the twentieth year). It is now generally argued (e.g., by Richardson 358) that "twenty" is a rough Homeric equivalent for any time more than "ten", thus eliding both Helen's and Odysseus's dates to a vague extension beyond the canonical ten years of the war; but how likely is it that any poet or rhapsode would, at this point, choose a figure so certain to provoke dissent? For the same reason, textual corruption is highly unlikely. The problem remains.

for no more in all broad Troy is there anyone left
who's gentle or loving to me: all regard me with horror."

So she spoke, weeping, and the countless throng lamented.
Then the aged Priam addressed his people, saying:
"Fetch in firewood now to the city, don't be scared at heart
lest the Argives set up some smart ambush: for Achilles,
when sending me back from the black ships, guaranteed
that he'd do us no harm until the twelfth day's dawn from now."

So he spoke, and at that they harnessed both oxen and mules
to wagons, and quickly assembled outside the city.
For nine days they carted back timber in abundance;
But when the tenth dawn came, bringing light to mortals,
Then, shedding tears, they carried out bold Hektōr,
laid his corpse on top of the pyre, and set it ablaze.

But when Dawn appeared, lately born, with her rosy fingers,
then a crowd collected around illustrious Hektōr's pyre,
and when they were all assembled and gathered together,
first they quenched the still-smoldering pyre with fire-bright wine
in each part that the fire's force reached, and next
his brothers and comrades gathered up the white bones,
still mourning, with great tears streaming down their cheeks,
took them and laid them away in a golden casket,[12]
wrapped in a soft purple cloth, and at once after that
put the box in a dug-out grave, and covered it over
with great close-set stones, and last, very quickly,
heaped up the burial mound, with lookouts all round it, in case
the well-greaved Achaians attacked them before the stated time;
and when they'd raised the mound, they all went back,
then sat down together and shared a glorious feast
in the palace of Priam, the king who was Zeus's nursling.

Such were the funeral rites for Hektōr, breaker of horses.

12. There is a remarkable parallel to this golden container (λάρναξ, *larnax*) in the actually surviving gold *larnax* from the Macedonian royal tomb at Vergina, with the bones of the tomb's occupant still in it.

Synopsis

BOOK I

1–7: The theme of the work stated: the destructive wrath of Achilles, and its effects, including the fulfillment of Zeus's plans for mankind.

8–42: Chrysēs, priest of Apollo, comes to the ships of the Achaians offering ransom for the return of his daughter Chryseïs, at present the captive prize of the commander in chief, Agamemnōn, who—against the general wishes of the assembled Achaians—rebuffs him discourteously. Dismissed, Chrysēs prays to Apollo.

43–100: Apollo hears his prayer and visits the Achaian army with plague. After nine days of his deadly arrows, an emergency Achaian assembly is called, and Achilles invites the priest Kalchas to offer an explanation of why Apollo is offended. Kalchas claims that it is because of Agamemnōn's act in refusing to ransom Chryses' daughter.

101–305: Agamemnōn, furious with Kalchas, nevertheless offers to release Chryseïs, but only if he is awarded a comparable woman as prize to replace her loss. How, asks Achilles, can we do this? The prizes have been distributed. Give her up, and we'll recompense you three- or fourfold when Troy falls. No, cries Agamemnōn, it must be now, and if the Achaians don't find me another woman, I'll take yours, or Aias's, or that of Odysseus, by force if necessary. He then makes arrangements for the return of Chryseïs. At this Achilles announces he will withdraw from the fighting and take his troops home. Agamemnōn remains obdurate: Achilles can go, but he, Agamemnōn, will take his woman Briseïs regardless. Achilles is about to draw his sword and kill Agamemnōn, but is restrained by the invisible goddess Athēnē. Old Nestōr of Pylos tries to calm both of them down in a long rambling speech, telling Achilles to respect his sceptered king, and Agamemnōn to give over his wrath against their best warrior. Both stand firm, and the assembly breaks up.

306–427: The ship with Chryseïs aboard leaves. The Achaian troops purify themselves. Two heralds are sent by Agamemnōn to remove Briseïs from Achilles' hut, and they do so without incident. Achilles prays to his mother, the sea nymph Thetis, telling her of the incident. She comes up from the sea to comfort him, and he relates the whole story. He then begs her to seek solace for him by persuading Zeus to favor the Trojans and to pen up the Achaians by their ships to teach Agamemnōn a lesson. Thetis bemoans the short life that is her son's destiny, but promises to do what she can with Zeus—"and I think I shall persuade him." On that note she leaves him.

428–92: Meanwhile Chryseïs is returned to her father by Odysseus, a rich sacrifice is made to Apollo, and Chrysēs prays Apollo to call off the plague on the Achaians. Apollo takes note. A celebratory feast of offering meat follows. Odysseus and his crew sleep by their ship. Next morning they have a fair wind sailing back to the Achaian camp. Achilles meanwhile settles into a miserable withdrawal from the action.

493–611: The gods have been absent feasting with the remote Aithiōpians but now return. Thetis fulfills her promise to Achilles by petitioning Zeus to favor the Trojans until the Achaians make proper amends to him. Although admitting this will get him in trouble with his sister-wife Hērē, Zeus bows his head in avowal that he will do as Thetis asks. Zeus then returns to his palace, where the other gods are. Hērē has indeed noted his conference with Thetis, guesses its substance, and challenges him with it. A barbed exchange ends with a threat of violence from Zeus, and Hērē backs off in fear. Her lame son Hēphaistos, the smith god, smooths things over, warns Hērē to behave, and pours out drinks all round. The other gods laugh at him hobbling about. The day ends in feasting. Finally all retire to their own dwellings, and Hērē duly sleeps beside Zeus.

BOOK 2

1–34: Zeus is insomniac with worry (the war, Achilles), and sends Agamemnōn a destructive Dream, with the message that the gods are now in agreement and the Achaians will conquer Troy. The Dream duly comes to Agamemnōn and delivers this message.

35–83: Convinced that he can indeed take Troy, Agamemnōn gets up and orders the Achaians to assembly. But first he calls a meeting of the elders, to report the Dream's message, and to propose testing the spirit of the troops by telling them to board their ships and pull out: the elders are to stop those who might fall for the ruse. Tactful Nestōr gets up and says that if anyone else had reported this dream, he wouldn't have been believed, but since it was the commander in chief, they should set about arming the Achaians. No reference to the testing of the troops.

84–210: The troops gather, urged on by Rumor. Agamemnōn addresses them, saying that Zeus has told him to pull out the troops and go home. He agrees. They've been at it nine years, have lost men, have got nowhere. Their ships are rotting. They will never take Troy. So, he says, let's go home. The result is a stampede for the ships, like the Aegean whipped up by the wind, and the men begin knocking the props from under the hulls prior to launching.

For the first time, the Achaians seem to be doing something "beyond what was fated", and this stirs action on Olympos. To stop the flight, Hērē sends down Athēnē, who delegates the job to Odysseus. Grabbing Agamemnōn's scepter, he sets about it, arguing politely with the officers, but savagely upbraiding the rank and file. The rout stops, and the men return to their seats, noisily, like waves thundering on a beach.

211–393: Thersītēs, an ugly, rabble-rousing soldier, gets up and urges them to go, leaving Agamemnōn, who's dishonored a better man in Achilles, behind with his prizes. Odysseus rebukes Thersītēs for gross insubordination and strikes him with the scepter. The men all laugh at the sight and praise Odysseus, who now addresses them.

Yes, it's been a long war, he says. But to go on so long and then return empty-handed would be shameful. He reminds them of the omen at Aulis, the snake that ate the sparrow and her eight chicks, but was then turned to stone by Zeus—meaning, a nine-year war and victory in the tenth!

Loud cheers from the troops. Next Nestōr speaks: Yes, Zeus promised us victory. And don't let's forget our oaths! And you, Agamemnōn, sort the troops by tribe and clan: that way you'll know who's brave and who's a coward. Yes, says Agamemnōn, all true—but Zeus has brought me trouble, led me into a quarrel with Achilles over a girl. Once we all agree, the Trojans are done for. All right, break for now: prepare arms, have a bite to eat, and death to shirkers!

394–483: The Argives eat a meal, and sacrifice to the gods, as does Agamemnōn, praying for success in battle. (Zeus accepts the sacrifice, but plans to increase the hazards of war.) He and the leaders then feast. Nestōr proposes that they go through the ranks encouraging and marshaling the troops. Agamemnōn agrees. The troops are drawn up and march out to the plain.

484–759: The poet appeals to the Muses to list the commanders and princes of the Achaian forces, while conceding that the main mass of troops is a multitude beyond reckoning. What follows, city by city, is the so-called Catalogue of Ships. Here and there the strict Catalogue is interspersed with personal details: e.g., Aias son of Oïleus (529–30) is described as being short but a great spearman; Menelaös (589–90) is hot to revenge himself for all the trouble and sorrow over Helen; Achilles (689–91) won Briseïs at the sack of Lyrnessos; Prōtesilaös (700–702), who would be the first Achaian killed when he jumped ashore at Troy, had left behind a bride and a half-built house.

760–877: The best horses are those of Eumēlos; the best warrior, while Achilles continues withdrawn in his wrath, is Aias son of Telamōn. Zeus sends Iris (in the likeness of a son of Priam) to alert the Trojans, and instruct Hektōr, similarly, to marshal Troy's own great international host, which is listed far more briefly.

BOOK 3

1–75: The Trojan and Achaian armies approach each other, and Paris Aléxandros struts out ahead, challenging the Achaians to single combat. Menelaös springs down from his chariot to take up the challenge, but Paris starts back at the sight of him, and retreats to the ranks, where he gets a contemptuous scolding for his conduct from his brother Hektōr. Paris says, Yes, right, but don't despise the gifts of Aphrodītē, she's a goddess. And if you want me to fight, I'll take on Menelaös now in a duel—winner gets the woman and her goods, ends the war.

76–244: Hektōr, speaking between the two armies, announces this offer. Menelaös takes it up and calls for a sacrifice and a solemn oath, to be sworn by Priam in person, agreeing to the terms. In the likeness of Priam's daughter Laodikē, Iris meanwhile goes to Helen and invites her to come and watch the duel from the ramparts. She goes and is asked by Priam to identify some of the Achaian leaders below. Self-pitying, modest, and sorrowful, Helen nevertheless points out Agamemnōn (her husband's brother), Odysseus, and Aias, with vivid touches.

245–447: Down below Priam is briefed, brought to the sacrifice, and swears the oath, but cannot bear to watch the duel, and returns to the city. The two contestants arm themselves and engage. Menelaös's sword shatters on Paris's helmet: he then leaps and grabs the helmet, choking Paris on the leather chin strap, and starts dragging him off the field. But Aphrodītē, invisible, first breaks the chin strap, so that the helmet comes off in Menelaös's hand, then wraps Paris in a magical mist and wafts him away to Helen's boudoir; next she disguises herself as an old wool carder and lures Helen away from the ramparts to join him. Helen sees through the disguise and is angry. Aphrodītē threatens her, terrifies her into submission. Helen confronts Paris, furious but conflicted, wanting him to fight, scared that he'll be killed. Paris decides the issue by calling her to bed, and she follows him.

448–61: Menelaös searches everywhere for the vanished Paris but cannot find him. None of the Trojans or allies can help him (and they wouldn't have kept quiet had they seen him, says Homer, since they all detested Paris). At this point Agamemnōn announces that the victory clearly goes to Menelaös and demands the return of Helen and her property. The Achaians cheer his words.

BOOK 4

1–73: On Olympos, the gods are drinking and observing the scene in and around Troy. Zeus, needling Athēnē and Hērē, agrees that Menelaös has won the duel, but points out that while he's supported by these two goddesses, the unnamed Paris Aléxandros always has Aphrodītē on his side. What's to be done? Should the Olympians stir up war again or make a lasting peace? Do that, and Troy survives, while Menelaös gets Helen back.

How, Hērē demands, can Zeus undo all the work she's put in to make trouble for Priam and his city? All right, says Zeus, I'll give in on this one: clearly you'd eat Priam raw if you could. But Troy has done well by me, and there's no city I honor more, so next time *I* want to ruin a city, let me be! Right, says Hērē: *my* favorite cities are Argos, Sparta, and Mykēnai: sack any of them when you feel like it. But I'm a god too, and our Father's eldest daughter; so let's agree. And tell Athēnē to go down and see if she can get the Trojans to be the first to break their oath over the truce.

74–219: Zeus gives the order, and Athēnē darts down. Both sides see her. Is it to be peace or war? She finds Pandaros the archer, Lykaōn's son, and persuades him to launch an arrow at Menelaös. Pandaros does so, but Athēnē makes sure it only grazes its target. Nevertheless, it draws blood, greatly alarming Agamemnōn, who fears for his brother's life. Menelaös assures him that the wound is not a serious one, however, and Agamemnōn sends for Machaōn, son of Asklēpios, god of medicine, who sucks out the (perhaps poisoned) blood and applies healing herbs.

220–421: The Trojans advance, and Agamemnōn in person descends from his chariot and goes through the ranks exhorting the troops, praising the eager and chastising those hanging back. He lauds Idomeneus and his Krētans, the two Aiases (their dark forces like a gathering storm cloud), and old Nestōr (too old to fight, but mustering the Pylians, mounted and infantry, both in good order), but rebukes Menestheus and Odysseus, who are not yet engaged (Agamemnōn withdraws a reproof after a stinging response from Odysseus). Diomēdēs is treated to a harangue about the superior fighting ability of his father, Tydeus, but wisely says nothing, and shuts up his charioteer, Sthenelos, when he calls Agamemnōn a liar.

422–544: The Achaians move silently forward into battle rank upon rank. The Trojans and their various-tongued foreign allies are noisy: like bleating ewes waiting to be milked, says Homer. They are urged on by the war god Arēs, while the Achaians are encouraged by Athēnē. Strife (Eris) roams the battlefield making trouble. Various encounters are depicted in detail, with wounds inflicted by spear or sword vividly described, as well as the struggles to strip a fallen enemy of his gear. This is the first of many such battle scenes. Antilochos and Aias show their prowess as warriors. Apollo calls on the Trojans to rouse themselves, while Athēnē remains vigilant on behalf of the Achaians.

BOOK 5

1–94: Diomēdēs, strengthened and encouraged by Athēnē, begins his *aristeia* (display of excellence as a warrior: in effect a killing spree).

Athēnē leads Arēs out of the fighting and sits him down by the river, saying they should both stay out of the battle and let Zeus decide the issue. Menelaös, Idomeneus, and Mērionēs distinguish themselves, and Diomēdēs storms like a winter torrent that bursts walls and embankments.

95–317: Lykaōn's son Pandaros hits Diomēdēs in the right shoulder with a well-aimed arrow, and boasts over the shot. This does not stop Diomēdēs, who has his charioteer Sthenelos pull out the arrow (presumably against the barbs, which is why the blood spurts out: Diomēdēs shows no sign of pain, all part of the *aristeia*). He prays to Athēnē, who says, go to it, just don't tangle with any god—except Aphrodītē. Now he attacks the Trojans. Aineias sees him and teams up with Pandaros, who chatters on about himself till told to stop. Sthenelos warns Diomēdēs about them; Diomēdēs ignores the warning, kills the still-boasting Pandaros, and knocks Aineias out, shattering his hip with a huge rock. But Aphrodītē protects Aineias —he is, after all, her son—and starts carrying him off the battlefield.

318–453: Diomēdēs pursues Aphrodītē and wounds her in the wrist. She screams and drops Aineias. Apollo scoops him up and hides him in a dark cloud. Iris takes Aphrodītē out of the fighting. She borrows Arēs' chariot and horses, returns with Iris to Olympos, and runs, pain-racked, to her mother Diōnē, who hears her story, tells her to endure, and regales her with stories of other goddesses who've been similarly hurt. She then wipes off the ichor, and Aphrodītē, being divine, is at once healed and as good as new. Athēnē and Hērē go to Zeus and tattle maliciously about Aphrodītē's little accident. Zeus summons her and tells her to stick to love, marriage, and such, and to leave warfare to Arēs and Athēnē.

Diomēdēs meanwhile goes for Aineias three times, only to be beaten back by Apollo. On his fourth attempt, the god tells him to remember he's mortal, not a god, and to back off. He does. Apollo wafts Aineias away to Pergamon, where Lētō and Artemis heal him in their shrine. Meanwhile Apollo creates a phantom image of Aineias for Achaians and Trojans to fight over.

454–667: Apollo urges Arēs to take out Diomēdēs, but sits out the fight himself. Arēs, in the likeness of a Thracian leader, Akamas, urges on the Trojans. Sarpēdōn, leader of the Lycians (and a son of Zeus) accuses Hektōr of lackluster performance. Hektōr starts rallying the Trojans. Like blown chaff from a threshing floor, the dust from the horses' hooves whitens the Achaians, and Arēs brings darkness to aid the Trojans. Apollo brings the healed and fit Aineias back from Pergamon, and he rejoins the battle. Both Aiases, Odysseus, and Agamemnōn urge on the Achaians, who hold firm. Aineias's victims fall like felled firs. Hektōr enters the fray, accompanied by Arēs: Diomēdēs shudders and calls for a retreat: the man has a god with him, we can't fight gods. Tlēpolemos challenges Sarpēdōn (grandson of Zeus against Zeus's son). Much exchange of insults and rival genealogies and achievements: Tlēpolemos spears Sarpēdōn in the thigh; Sarpēdōn kills Tlēpolemos. Sarpēdōn is carried out of the battle with the spear still trailing from his thigh.

668–766: Odysseus attacks the Lycians. Hektōr (ignoring Sarpēdōn's appeal for assistance) advances, with Arēs, against the Achaians. Sarpēdōn's comrade Pelagōn pulls out the spear from his thigh. The Achaians, seeing Arēs, steadily give ground, and have many casualties. Hērē and Athēnē seeing this, decide to intervene themselves. Hērē readies the chariot; Athēnē arms herself, takes the aegis and a spear, and they drive out to Zeus, sunning himself on the mountain, and enquire whether he'll mind if they knock Arēs out of the fighting. No, says Zeus, let Athēnē do it; she's used to dealing with him.

767–908: Hērē and Athēnē drive to Troy, leave their chariot (hidden in a magical mist), and strut off, says Homer, like a brace of wild pigeons, to aid and encourage the Achaians, which Hērē does in the likeness of loud-voiced Stentōr to get maximum audibility. Finding Diomēdēs nursing his wound, Athēnē, like Agamemnōn earlier, compares him, to his disadvantage, with his father Tydeus (though assuring him of her support). Why, says Diomēdēs, I'm obeying your order: no fighting against gods (except for Aphrodītē)! We saw Arēs in action, so we pulled back. No problem, says Athēnē. Arēs promised me and Hērē he'd help the Achaians, but he's gone back on his word and is fighting with the Trojans! So let's at him! She takes over from Sthenelos as charioteer, and the chariot creaks under her great weight. They charge. Athēnē deflects Arēs' spear; Diomēdēs drives his own spear into Arēs' nether belly, and the god roars as loud as nine or ten thousand men. Like a black cloud he goes up into the sky to Zeus on Olympos, where he complains loudly about his treatment. Zeus, though contemptuous of Arēs, nevertheless tells Paiēōn the divine physician to heal his wound (he's family), and Paiēōn duly does so. Zeus's daughter Hēbē bathes and dresses him, and he returns to sit by Zeus, magically healed, self-confidence restored. Hērē and Athēnē, having stopped his pro-Trojan activities, now return to Zeus's abode themselves.

BOOK 6

1–118: Free of gods now on both sides, the battle rages on. Aias, Diomēdēs (despite his wound), Odysseus, and others press forward, killing as they go. Menelaös takes Adrēstos alive when his fleeing horses get entangled in a bush, and is on the point of agreeing to his prisoner's offer of ransom when his brother Agamemnōn storms up, calling for relentless slaughter, and kills Adrēstos himself. Old Nestōr calls for a continued advance—no stopping for armor-stripping or other booty!

On the Trojan side, Helenos the diviner tells Aineias and Hektōr to rally the troops for a stand, but also recommends that the women of Troy, en masse, petition Athēnē with sacrifice and prayer to hold back the raging Diomēdēs. Hektōr calls on the Trojans to hold firm while he returns to Troy to deliver this message.

119–236: Encountering Glaukos, a companion of the Trojan ally Sarpēdōn, on the battlefield, and fearing that he might be up against a god again, Diomēdēs asks him who he is (presumably Glaukos is wearing a helmet that conceals his identity). In reply, Glaukos begins with the famous simile comparing the generations of men to the generations of leaves and then proceeds to give an account of himself and his lineage at great length. On learning his identity, Diomēdēs realizes that through their respective families in Argos and Lycia, he and Glaukos are ancestral guest-friends and must not fight each other. Instead, they exchange armor in token of true friendship, but Homer says, in a rare authorial comment, Zeus must have stupefied Glaukos, for in exchange for bronze, he gave gold armor worth over ten times more.

237–311: Hektōr returns to Troy by way of the Skaian Gates, with no word for the women asking for news except that they should pray to the gods. In Priam's house he meets his mother, Hekabē, who asks why he's there, and offers him wine, which he refuses. He tells her to take the women to pray to Athēnē for respite from the fury of Diomēdēs, and indicates that he himself is going to see Paris Aléxandros, to shame him into fighting. Hekabē gathers the women and leads them to Athēnē's shrine, where the goddess's priestess, Theanō, wife of the Trojan elder Antēnōr, offers up the prayer and promise of sacrifice.

312–68: Hektōr finds Paris looking over his bow and armor, while Helen assigns tasks to her handmaidens. He upbraids his brother for his seeming lack of martial spirit. Paris explains the reason as sorrow (presumably for his poor showing in the duel, and subsequent magical disappearance). Helen, he says, has been urging him back to the fighting, and he thinks she's right. So, he says, either wait until I put on my battle gear, or go, and I'll catch you up later. Hektōr says nothing to this, but engages in conversation with Helen, who reproaches herself bitterly for the trouble she's caused, while at the same time inviting her brother-in-law in to sit and talk. No, says Hektōr, just stir up *this man* here to join in the fighting: I'm going to see my wife and son, perhaps for the last time.

369–493: Hektōr finds his wife Andromachē away from the house, on the walls, and meets her near the Skaian Gates, with his baby son Astyanax. She is scared of his being killed and leaving her a widow, and begs him to stay on the ramparts himself and station a defensive force by the wild fig tree, where three previous assaults have been attempted. Hektōr knows very well what her fate will be in the event of defeat, and he therefore insists on going out and fighting. He picks up his son, who is scared by the great crest on his helmet, so he takes it off, and prays for his son's future. Then he caresses his wife, tells her what's fated will be, and sends her back home.

494–529: Andromachē returns home, and she and her women mourn for Hektōr as though he were already dead, lamenting that he will never again return from battle. Meanwhile Paris Aléxandros, having armed himself, hurries down through the city, laughing and handsome, like some thoroughbred stallion in pursuit of mares, Homer says, and overtakes Hektōr, apologizing for being late. Hektōr grudgingly concedes his valor, but still complains of his hanging back. Finally he drops the argument, saying they can thrash problems like this out over drinks after victory.

BOOK 7

1–42: Hektōr and Paris Aléxandros charge out from the Skaian Gates and begin killing their enemies. Athēnē notices this, and hurries down from Olympos, to be met by Apollo, who suggests a time-out. They confer on how to stop the fighting. Apollo proposes encouraging Hektōr to challenge the Achaians to a one-on-one formal dual.

43–199: Helenos the seer senses this plan and encourages Hektōr to do it, reminding him that his fated time is not yet come, so he's safe. Athēnē and Apollo perch on the great oak tree disguised as vultures to watch. Hektōr makes his offer of a duel between the two armies: winner to give back the body of his opponent. There is a nervous silence. Finally Menelaös gets up and proposes himself, but is stopped by Agamemnōn, who knows he'd be slaughtered. Nestōr then makes a rambling speech about how things were in *his* day, and shame on everyone now. Nine men then stand up, and lots are drawn: Aias is chosen. All are much relieved. If anyone can take down Hektōr, he's the man.

200–312: The combatants arm, make challenging speeches to one another, and go to it. Evenly matched, they fight first with spears, then with rocks: it seems clear that

Aias has the advantage (his spear draws blood, he beats Hektōr down with a huge rock like a millstone, though Apollo at once raises him up again), but the umpires (one Achaian, one Trojan) say it's getting dark, and stop the duel. The two shake hands and exchange gifts. Honor is served. Aias, not surprisingly, rejoices in what he sees as his victory.

313–78: A feast is held, and Aias gets the winner's portion. Nestōr speaks again, recommending a truce to collect and bury the dead with proper funeral rites. He also proposes that the Achaians build a wall, with gates, and a deep ditch, to defend their ships. Meanwhile an assembly is also being held in Troy. Now that we've broken our oath [Pandaros shooting Menelaös], Antēnōr says, we should give Helen and her goods back to the Achaians. Paris Aléxandros is willing to return the goods, but not Helen. Priam proposes sending an envoy to the Achaians, reporting Paris's offer and asking for a truce to bury the dead.

379–482: Next day the envoy delivers the message. Diomēdēs says no, don't just accept the goods: everyone knows the Trojans are as good as beaten. Agamemnōn then accepts the request for a truce. Both sides at once go in search of wood to build funeral pyres; but the Achaians also busy themselves with constructing their wall, gates, and ditch. The gods observe this. Poseidōn points out that Achaians are not making proper sacrificial offerings, and complains that everyone will now forget the wall that he and Apollo built for Priam's father, Laomedōn. Don't worry, says Zeus, once the Achaians are gone, you can sweep everything here into the sea. Meanwhile both sides feast again, wine is brought in by sea for the Achaians, Zeus thunders enough to scare everyone into making drink offerings to him, the feasting ends, and all retire to sleep.

BOOK 8

1–52: Zeus calls an early morning assembly of the gods, issues a ban on their aiding either Trojans or Achaians, and makes graphic threats as to what any god who offends against it will suffer. Athēnē says, yes, we know you have the whip hand, and we won't *aid* the Achaians, but there's nothing to stop us giving them *advice*. To which Zeus gives the surprising answer, Don't worry, dear, I don't really mean it, and you I'm fond of (cf. 22.182–84). He then takes off in his chariot to Ida and settles himself on a mountaintop to watch the war.

53–166: Battle is joined in the morning and the outcome remains uncertain until midday, when Zeus put each side's fate (*kēr*) in his scales, and the Achaians' fate sinks down. Zeus thunders from Ida and sends lightning down into the Achaian army, causing terror. General retreat, except for Nestōr, who's had a horse shot by Paris Aléxandros. Diomēdēs comes to his rescue in his chariot. They attack Hektōr and kill his charioteer. Zeus spots this and thunders, sending a white-hot bolt down in front of Diomēdēs' horses. Nestōr, seeing that Zeus is against them, calls on Diomēdēs to retreat. Diomēdēs agrees, although knowing Hektōr will make mock of him if he does. Never mind, says Nestōr: the other Trojans know better—especially the wives of those you've killed. They turn and retreat, pursued by a shower of missiles and, sure enough, insults from Hektōr.

167–252: Diomēdēs thinks of going back and fighting Hektōr, but Zeus thunders, signifying a turn in the tide of battle, and Hektōr calls on Trojans and allies to breach the wall and fire the ships. He then calls on his horses to help him bring down and strip Nestōr and Diomēdēs. At this Hērē tells Poseidōn that although the Achaians honor and sacrifice to him, he's not doing a thing for them, that if all the gods who were pro-Achaian took action, they could drive the Trojans back, and Zeus would be left sitting miserably on Ida. Poseidōn is shocked and says don't tangle with Zeus, he's stronger than any of us!

Meanwhile, troops are crowding into the space by the ditch and the wall, and there's a real danger of Hektōr firing the ships. Hērē puts it into Agamemnōn's mind to rally the Achaians, and, weeping, he makes an impassioned speech. Zeus takes pity on him and sends an eagle as an omen that at least he and his army will not perish. The Achaians take heart and rally.

253–334: The Achaians, led by Diomēdēs, storm across the ditch, killing as they go. Teukros the archer advances behind Aias's great tower-like shield, popping out to pick off targets, then scuttling back like a child to its mother. Encouraged by Agamemnōn, he twice, unsuccessfully, shoots at Hektōr, the second time killing his charioteer.

Enraged, Hektōr hits him with a rock near the collarbone, snapping his bowstring and paralyzing his arm. Teukros collapses and is carried out of the battle.

335–437: Hektōr goes after Achaians like a hunting hound after a lion or boar. But they halt and make a stand before their ships, hard pressed by the Trojans. Hērē calls on Athēnē to join her in stopping Hektōr. She agrees. Hērē gets the chariot ready while Athēnē arms herself. The two of them drive out from Olympos, ready for action. But Zeus sees them, and sends Iris to stop them, with fearful threats of punishment. When she gets the message, Hērē backs down. Let the mortals fight on, she says. Zeus will decide the issue. Back they go, and sit with the other gods, dispirited.

437–565: Zeus now returns from Ida. What's wrong with you two? he asks Hērē and Athēnē. You couldn't have won, you were scared stiff before you got anywhere near the fighting, and I'd have flattened you anyway. Hērē says, Yes, we know you're too strong for us, but we're sorry for the Achaians. Like Athēnē earlier, she proposes to offer them good advice. So what, Zeus replies: tomorrow you can watch me wreaking havoc on the Achaians, and Hektōr won't stop until Achilles rejoins the battle when they're fighting over dead Patroklos: that's how it's fated, that's how it will be. I don't give a rap for your anger. Night falls, the fighting stops, and Hektōr calls an assembly. Tomorrow we'll make a great assault, he says. We'll leave the women to burn watch fires and look out for a surprise attack while we fight Diomēdēs and the Achaians at the ships! So they feast and sacrifice—but the gods reject their offering. They sit around their fires, and their horses stand by their chariots, waiting for morning.

1–88: The Achaians are now fearful and depressed, despairing of ever taking Troy. Agamemnōn calls an assembly. Weeping, he proposes that they give up the struggle and go home.

Diomēdēs responds: Agamemnōn, you questioned my courage. But Zeus made you a king without courage, the true source of authority! The Achaians aren't such cowards as you think. If you want to leave, go! They'll stay and fight. And even were they to go, Sthenelos and I will stick it out till victory: a god brought us here.

Next, Nestōr speaks, saying: Diomēdēs, you're a great warrior and a wise counselor, but you haven't said the last word here. Let's post sentries at the trench. Meanwhile, ask the elders advice, Agamemnōn, make a feast, with wine for the elders. Solicit their advice. Tonight presents a make-or-break situation for the Achaians.

There is general agreement.

89–181: Agamemnōn holds a feast for the elders. Nestōr directly addresses him, both as commander in chief, and as the cause of Achilles' persistent wrath at Agamemnōn's having seized Briseïs, *against the will of the assembly*. Now he must consider how to make amends. Agamemnōn responds: Yes, I was deluded in doing so: I'll compensate him. He will offer Achilles, among other things, marriage to one of his daughters and rule over seven cities. In return, he says, Achilles must renounce his anger and submit to Agamemnōn, who outranks him and is older.

Good, says Nestōr: now we need to send an embassy to persuade him to accept your terms. Phoinix, Odysseus, Aias, and two heralds are chosen, advised by Nestōr, and promptly leave.

182–306: They find Achilles singing warrior lays and accompanying himself on the lyre: he welcomes them hospitably as good friends. After they have eaten, Odysseus tells Achilles: There is a real danger that without you the ships will be lost: we need you to rejoin us! Remember your father's lesson: strife breeds dissension and trouble. Put an end to your obstinate wrath. Agamemnōn is offering rich amends [he lists them]. If they don't persuade you, think of the worn-down Achaians—you might kill Hektōr, and they'd honor you like a god!

307–429: Achilles dismisses the offer: I must speak straight out, he says. I hate anyone who says one thing but thinks another. Neither Agamemnōn nor you and the other Achaians will persuade me. The shirker and the fighter get equal treatment. Cowards are honored like heroes. Death comes to all alike, the idle and the hard-working. I fought endlessly but got little for it. Agamemnōn sits by the ships, collects our booty, throws us a few scraps, and keeps the rest—he even takes back the woman who was given to me! So, let him keep her! Why are we fighting the Trojans? What did he bring this army here for? Helen! Does he think he and his are the only men who love their wives? He's taken my woman, he's deceived me, he won't persuade me, and that's that. He and you need to work out a plan of defense, Odysseus. Yes, he's got a wall and a ditch in place. But that won't stop Hektōr! I could, and he knows it, but tomorrow

I and my men are sailing home. Tell him this. He dared not confront me in person, and I won't fight for him or work or plan with him. And Zeus has addled his mind! His gifts are nothing to me: if he offered me ten times as much it'd make no difference. Nor will I wed his daughter—Pēleus will find me a fine wife if I get home. Life is worth more than all the wealth in the world! My mother's told me my fate: I can stay here and fight, win immortal glory, but die young; or I can go home, live long, and forfeit my renown—and you should all go home, for you'll never conquer Troy! Tell the elders they'd better think up a new plan to save their ships. And Phoinix can stay and sleep here, and if he wants to sail with me tomorrow, he's welcome to do so, but I won't make him.

430–605: A hush, and then old Phoinix, Achilles' early mentor, speaks up in a long and rambling speech about his own youth: how, leaving home after a quarrel with his father (also over a concubine), he came to Pēleus in Phthiē, who took him in and treated him like a son, gave him a fief to rule, and made him rich. Phoinix was also put in charge of the child Achilles, whom he treated as a surrogate son (because of his father's curse he had no sons of his own). So, Achilles, he says, conquer your obstinacy: even the gods, for all their high honor, can do that. Prayers are Zeus's daughters, and they follow the obstinate: those who persist are afflicted by Zeus with Blind Delusion and pay a heavy price. Agamemnōn is not obstinate; he's offering you rich compensation: don't scorn him or his embassy. Great men of old could be turned from their anger by gifts.

As an example, Phoinix recounts a tale about Meleagros refusing to aid the Aitōlians against the Kourētes. Miffed at his lack of sacrifices, Artemis had sent a huge wild boar against Oineus, king of Kalydōn in Aitōlia: Meleagros killed it, and Artemis then stirred up trouble between the Aitōlians and the Kourētes. When the latter were getting the better of it, Meleagros was appealed to, and to begin with fought for them. Then, like Achilles, over a matter of unjustly sequestered spoils, he withdrew in rage; finally, after being offered a prize estate, he came back at the last minute and saved the day for the Aitōlians. Achilles should do likewise, and soon: it would be harder to rescue the ships when they were burning.

606–713: Achilles stands firm, urging Phoinix not to back Agamemnōn or to try and confuse Achilles by weeping, which might change his love for the old man to hate. The embassy is sent back to convey Achilles' implacable message: he won't move till Hektōr is burning the Achaian ships and threatening the Myrmidons. When Odysseus delivers Achilles' refusal to the Achaians, Diomēdēs responds: You shouldn't have offered that arrogant man gifts—it just makes him even more arrogant. Forget him.

BOOK 10

1–71: Unable to sleep because worrying about the Achaians' plight (he sees the Trojan fires on the plain, hears their fifes and pipes), Agamemnōn decides to seek advice, and some kind of plan, from Nestōr. He gets up, dresses, and goes out into the darkness. Menelaös too decides to rouse his brother, and finds him up and arming. Is Agamemnōn, he asks, planning to send out a spy to investigate the Trojans? No one is likely to have the courage. Agamemnōn doesn't answer directly, but tells him to fetch Aias and Idomeneus, while he himself gets Nestōr to give instructions to the sentries (but doesn't say what he's proposing they should be told). Menelaös should not try to return, he says, lest they miss each other on the camp's crisscross paths.

72–179: Agamemnōn identifies himself to Nestōr, who is not asleep, explains his insomnia, and suggests that they go check on the wakefulness of the sentries. Nestōr agrees, hopes Achilles will yet abandon his wrath and rejoin the fight, and proposes also rousing Odysseus, Aias, and Idomeneus. Also Menelaös, who, he assumes, has left his brother to do the work. Yes, he can be slack, Agamemnōn agrees, but not this time, and he tells Nestōr where Menelaös has gone. Together they wake Odysseus and Diomēdēs (who twits Nestōr about being so active at his age) and visit the sentries.

180–271: After finding the sentries awake and watching the plain for any Trojan advance, they hold a council meeting, attended by Mēriones and Antilochos. Nestōr proposes that a volunteer go by night to spy out the enemy camp and learn what he can of the Trojans' intentions. He will be well rewarded. Diomēdēs offers to go but wants a companion: two are better than one. Agamemnōn agrees but tells him to choose the best man, rather than, out of respect, the highest-born (he's afraid for Menelaös). How, says Diomēdēs, can I not choose Odysseus? He's not only good; he's loved by Athēnē. Spies need the gods on their side. Odysseus agrees but urges hurry: with two-thirds of the night already gone, they've very little time. They arm with helmets, swords, and—in Odysseus's case—a bow and arrows.

272–337: Diomēdēs and Odysseus leave on their mission and are encouraged by a heron on the right, an omen sent by Athēnē. Both pray to the goddess. Odysseus asks to count on her love for him. Diomēdēs offers to sacrifice a heifer if they return safely. Meanwhile Hektōr, too, is asking for a volunteer to spy on the Achaian camp and ships and find out whether they mean to fight or pull out. Achilles' own horses and chariots are offered as a reward, after they're taken. Dolōn, an unprepossessing character, the one son among five sisters, makes Hektōr swear to the this reward, takes a bow and a javelin, puts on a ferret-skin cap, and leaves.

338–464: Odysseus and Diomēdēs spot Dolōn coming, hide, let him pass, then pursue and corral him. Scared, he offers ransom. Cheer up, says Odysseus, and proceeds to debrief him about the Trojans. Dolōn tells all. Hektōr and the elders are in council. The Trojans are keeping watch, the allies are asleep (*their* wives and children aren't at risk!). He tells where everyone's camped, and adds that those on the perimeter, newly arrived, are the Thracians, led by King Rhēsos, with his famous white horses. Now, he finishes, tie me up and leave me! No way, says Odysseus: if we do that, you'll come spying again! Diomēdēs beheads him and they hang the ferret-skin cap and the rest of Dolōn's gear on a bush to pick up on their return.

465–514: They then, following Dolōn's instructions, find the Thracian camp. Everyone is asleep. They locate Rhēsos and his lords, asleep, with their horses tethered by them. Diomēdēs systematically starts killing them, while Odysseus hauls the bodies out of the way so as not to scare the horses. It's now very near dawn. Athēnē tells Diomēdēs that they should be on their way. They mount and take off with the royal horses.

515–79: Apollo sees it all, arouses Rhēsos's kinsman Hippokoōn, who gives the alarm. Meanwhile, Odysseus and Diomēdēs recover Dolōn's equipment from the bush and hurry back to camp. How did you get such horses? cries Nestōr. By battling the Trojans? No, some god must have given them to you! No, says Odysseus, brave Diomēdēs killed their lord and a dozen of his comrades too; and we also killed a man the Trojans had sent out to spy on our camp. They then stable the horses with those of Diomēdēs, hang up the spoils, wash off in the sea, take a bath, and sit down to eat—with a thank-offering of wine to Athēnē.

BOOK 11

1–83: Zeus sends the spirit Strife to the Achaians to stir up the urge to battle. Agamemnōn arms himself, and Athēnē and Hērē make it thunder in his honor. The charioteers get ready. Hektōr glints among the Trojans like a destructive star [Sirius], or the lightning of Zeus. Trojans and Achaians face up like two rows of reapers in a field of wheat or barley. They rage like wolves. Strife watches and rejoices. The other gods all blame Zeus, who sits apart, a spectator of the fighting.

84–162: Till noon the fighting continues evenly. But about noon Agamemnōn and the Achaians make a breakthrough. Agamemnōn kills Biēnōr, Oïleus, Isos, Antiphos, Peisandros, and Hippolochos, and presses on, killing like an out-of-control forest fire. Horses rattle around with empty chariots.

163–283: Zeus pulls Hektōr out of the conflict. Agamemnōn continues the pursuit as far as the Skaian Gates. Both armies halt there, though many Trojans are still in flight; Agamemnōn continues to harry the hindmost. Zeus now sends Iris to Hektōr with a message: he can fight, but only to hold position until/unless Agamemnōn is wounded and retires. But then he can attack till he reaches the ships and darkness falls. The Muse is asked to list those who faced, and were killed by, Agamemnōn. As his wound dries, Agamemnōn begins to hurt, boards his chariot, and is driven out of the fighting.

284–367: Hektōr sees this, and calls on the Trojans to launch a charge. He himself kills nine leading Achaians in short order and then goes for the rank and file. Odysseus calls to Diomēdēs, and the two try to stem the advance. They turn and stand against the charge, killing and stripping the sons of Merōps the seer. Zeus balances his scales over the conflict. Diomēdēs kills Agastrophos, but then Hektōr comes against him and Odysseus. Diomēdēs half-stuns him with a spear cast to the head, but he recovers and retreats into the ranks. Diomēdēs shouts threats after him.

368–471: While Diomēdēs is stripping Agastrophos, Paris Aléxandros shoots him through the foot, and boasts, laughing. Diomēdēs dismisses him as a dandified skirt-chasing fop and pooh-poohs his bowmanship. Odysseus protects Diomēdēs as he tears out the arrow. Then he boards his chariot and is driven out of the fighting. Odysseus is left alone, wondering whether to fight or run for it. The Trojans hem him in like hounds and hunters round a fierce old boar. He kills five, and then the brother of the fifth, Sokos, drives a spear through his shield, slices flesh off his flank, and turns to retreat. As he does so Odysseus plants his own spear between Sokos's shoulder blades; the point comes out of his chest. The Trojans see Odysseus's blood, and press him hard. Menelaös calls on Aias to help him.

472–595: Aias and Menelaös find Odysseus at bay, but the Trojans scatter before Aias with his great shield. Menelaös escorts Odysseus out of the fighting. Aias charges. Hektōr meanwhile is away on the left flank by the river.

The Achaians hold firm. But Paris shoots Machaön in the shoulder, and Nestōr drives him out of the fighting. Then Hektōr gets words of Aias routing Trojans on the right and redoubles his efforts, ranging along the ranks, but avoids Aias. Zeus dazes Aias, makes him stop and retreat. Eurypylos goes to his aid, but is hit in the thigh by an arrow from Paris while stripping Apisaön, and withdraws, urging the Achaians to stand firm. Aias is covered while he retreats into the ranks.

596–803: Achilles, watching the battle and figuring the Achaians will be wanting him now, tells Patroklos to ask Nestōr who he's bringing out—from the back it looks like Machaön. At Nestōr's hut Hekamēdē, a captive, makes drinks for him and Machaön. Patroklos comes, recognizes Machaön, but can't stay, he says—Achilles is so quick-tempered. Agamemnōn, Odysseus, Diomēdēs, Eurypylos, Nestōr exclaims—all wounded and out of action! Achilles doesn't care! Is he waiting for the ships to be burned? There follows a long wandering rigmarole about conflict between the Epeians and the men of Pylos. Then Nestōr reminisces about when he and Odysseus were in Pēleus's house and their fathers were giving their sons, Achilles and Patroklos, instructions about how to conduct themselves in the war. And how Patroklos's father reminded him that while Achilles was nobler, he, Patroklos, was the older man, and should advise Achilles with words of wisdom. So, now, work on him!

803–48: Off goes Patroklos, to be met en route to Achilles' hut by the limping Eurypylos, the arrow still in his thigh, blood dripping from the wound. Patroklos asks him whether the Achaians will be able to hold off Hektōr. Unlikely, Eurypylos says, and asks Patroklos to extract the arrow and dress his wound. Patroklos has to relay Nestōr's message to Achilles, but he'll take care of Eurypylos first, and does so, cutting out the arrow and dressing the wound with painkilling styptic herbs.

BOOK 12

1–33: The Achaians and Trojans fight on. Digression concerning the Achaians' wall and ditch, which are to last as long as the war. But after Hektōr and Achilles have been killed, Troy has been sacked, and the Achaians (those who have survived) have sailed home, Poseidōn and Apollo will sweep the stones and timbers of the wall out to sea, restore the beach, and return the rivers to their original courses.

34–174: Battle continues round the walls. Hektōr urges his troops to cross the ditch, yet his own horses baulk at doing so: its sheer banks are bristling with sharp stakes. The Trojan infantry are eager to charge, and the charioteers face impossible odds. Poulydamas suggests to Hektōr that they all leave their chariots and attack on foot. Hektōr agrees. They marshal themselves in five companies, under, respectively: (1) Hektōr and Poulydamas; (2) Paris, Alkathoös, and Agēnōr; (3) Helenos and Deïphobos; (4) Aineias, Archelochos and Akamas; and (5) Sarpēdōn, Glaukos, and Asteropaios. These now advance on the Achaians. But Asios refuses to abandon his chariot and charges the ships where a gate has been left open for stragglers. Two Lapiths, Polypoitēs and Leonteus, block their advance, while Achaians hurl down rocks from the walls. Asios cries that Zeus must be a liar—the Achaians are holding out like wasps protecting their young and won't budge. Zeus takes no notice: he will give Hektōr glory, whatever happens.

175–289: Battle continues fiercely. Polypoitēs and Leonteus continue to claim victims. Meanwhile the Trojans, led by Hektōr and Poulydamas, have been brought up short by an omen—an eagle has flown over clutching a blood red snake in its claws, which bit the bird, causing it to drop its prey and fly off. Poulydamas sees this as a warning from Zeus that the Trojans will be driven back with heavy losses if they attack. Hektōr rejects this notion, however, and they advance. Zeus sends a dust storm against the ships, and the Trojans begin to break down the wall. The Achaians hold firm and mend the gaps with hides. Both Aiases urge on the defenders. Stones rain from both sides and a vast clamor goes up.

290–369: Still the Trojans can't break through the gates. Zeus rouses his son Sarpēdōn against the Achaians. Sarpēdōn arms himself and reminds Glaukos that why the two of them get special perks and treatment from the Lycians is in return for protection. If they were immortal, he for one wouldn't ever fight again. But they're not, so they might as well kill or be killed. He and Glaukos advance against the stretch of wall defended by Menestheus, who sends a message asking for Aias son of Telamōn and Teukros the archer to come help him. Aias with Teukros and Pandiōn answer the call.

370–471: The Trojans are climbing the battlements. Aias kills Sarpēdōn's comrade Epiklēs with a huge rock. Teukros shoots Glaukos in the arm. Glaukos unobtrusively withdraws to avoid his having been wounded being noticed. Sarpēdōn tears out part of the battlement but gives ground when assaulted by Aias and Teukros: his father Zeus ensures he isn't wounded. He upbraids the Lycians for sluggishness. But the Lycians and Achaians are in a dead heat: the first can't break through, the second can't repel them. Then Hektōr, helped by Zeus, lifts a huge stone, smashes in the double gates with it, and charges irresistibly in. He rallies the Trojans, who swarm in at the gates and over the wall, while the Achaians are routed among their ships.

1–38: Zeus, having seen Hektōr to the ships, goes off, not thinking that any immortal will now help either Trojans or Achaians. But Poseidōn is up on a peak on the island of Samothrâkē, furious with Zeus and sorry for the Achaians. He goes to Aigai, harnesses his chariot, and skims over the waves towards the Achaians' ships, leaving his chariot in a submarine grotto between the islands of Tenedos and Imbros.

39–135: While the Trojans press on after Hektōr, Poseidōn comes up from the sea and encourages the Achaians in the likeness of Kalchas the priest, urging the two Aiases to stand firm, and infusing them with strength. Then he takes off, and Aias(2) recognizes that this was a god. Both are hot to fight. Meanwhile Poseidōn is upbraiding Teukros and the other Achaians, who gather round the Aiases, eager to fight.

136–205: Hektōr and the Trojans thrust forward, but faced with solid Achaian resistance Hektōr gives ground, calling for support. Deïphobos advances; Mērionēs breaks a good spear on his shield and trails back to the huts for a new one. Teukros kills Imbrios. Hektōr aims at Teukros, who is stripping off Imbrios's armor, but Teukros dodges the spear, which kills Amphimachos. As Hektōr is tearing off his helmet, Aias hits his shield and forces him back. The two Aiases sweep away Imbrios, strip him, decapitate him, and send his head rolling at Hektōr's feet.

206–329: Angry at his grandson Amphimachos's death, Poseidōn visits the huts and ships disguised as Thoas the Aitōlian to arouse the Achaians, while thinking up trouble for the Trojans. He meets Krētan Idomeneus, and asks him what's become of the Achaians' threats? We're all fighting well, Idomeneus replies: it must be the will of Zeus. Idomeneus then encounters Mērionēs going to get a fresh spear, and offers him one of his. Where should they enter the fighting? Right, center or left? Deciding that the right and center are well manned, they move to the left.

330–454: The Trojans go for Idomeneus. A rare comment here by Homer: "Hardhearted would that man be / who seeing this scene, experienced joy, not grief." Zeus and Poseidōn, in opposition, make trouble for both sides: Zeus backing the Trojans, to bring glory (eventually) to Achilles and satisfy Thetis, yet not planning final defeat for the Achaians; Poseidōn secretly (in a mortal's likeness) encouraging the Achaians, but always conscious of being Zeus's younger brother, and therefore avoiding open support. The two of them thus tighten the noose of war around both armies. Idomeneus first kills Othryoneus (engaged, with Priam's approval, to Kassandrē) and exults over his corpse; then Asios. Meanwhile Antilochos knocks off Asios's charioteer and corrals his horses. Deïphobos aims at Idomeneus, misses, but hits Hypsēnōr, and claims revenge for Asios (though Hypsēnōr is removed, still alive, from the fighting). Anchīsēs' son-in-law Alkathoös is frozen in place by Poseidōn and made an easy target for Idomeneus. Idomeneus, citing his ancestry, challenges Deïphobos.

455–539: Deïphobos ducks the challenge and goes to find Aineias to help him rescue Alkathoös's body. Awaiting his attack Idomeneus calls on Mērionēs and Antilochos, among others, to help him against Aineias. They rally to him. Aineias calls on Deïphobos and Agēnōr, who come, followed by their troops. Battle is joined over Alkathoös's body. Aineias misses Idomeneus, who spears Oinomäos in the belly, then retreats slowly, feeling his age, too hard pressed by missiles to strip the corpse. Deïphobos misses him, but hits and kills Ares' son Askalaphos. In the struggle over Askalaphos, Deïphobos gets his helmet, but is wounded in the arm by Mēriones and taken out of the fighting by his brother Polītēs.

540–672: The struggle continues. Aineias kills Aphareus. Antilochos kills Thoön, and begins to strip his body, protected by Poseidōn from the surrounding Trojans. Adamas thrusts at him, but the god weakens the blow, and Mēriones spears Adamas in the nether belly: he writhes like a roped bull, but not for long. Helenos kills Dēïpyros; Menelaös and Helenos let fly at each other simultaneously. Helenos's arrow bounces back off Menelaös's corselet, but Menelaös's spear pierces clean through Helenos's bow hand, and he backs into the ranks. Menelaös then is attacked by Peisandros, axe against sword, and drives his sword into Peisandros's forehead, killing him, and strips off his armor. Moving back, he's thrust at from close quarters by Harpaliōn, who's shot dead by Mēriones. Enraged at this—Harpaliōn was his guest-friend—Paris lets fly an arrow, killing the Korinthian Euchēnōr.

673–754: Hektōr is still pressing on inside the gate and wall, unaware that on the left, with Poseidōn's powerful assistance, the Achaians are overwhelming the Trojans. Hektōr's attack is opposed with difficulty by the Boiōtians, Ionians, and others. The two Aiases fight side by side, and the Lokrians throw the Trojans off balance with a shower of arrows. Had Poulydamas not brought Hektōr to the rescue, the Trojans would have been driven off the ships and back to Ilion.

755–837: Hektōr is furious to find so many of the Trojan leaders wounded and hors de combat. We've been fighting here since this attack started, Paris tells him. Deïphobos and Helenos are wounded and out of it. But lead on and we'll follow. Spurred on by Zeus, they plunge into the thick of the fighting, with Hektōr leading. He's faced by Aias, and as Aias speaks an eagle flies by on the right, a good omen for the Achaians. The two armies face each other shouting battle cries.

BOOK 14

1–134: Nestōr hears sounds of battle, leaves Machaōn to be cared for by Hekamēdē, and sees the Achaians being routed. He's torn two ways: shall he join the throng or go and find Agamemnōn? He decides to find Agamemnōn, and leaves the cut-and-thrust behind. He meets the trio of wounded heroes—Odysseus, Diomēdēs, and Agamemnōn—coming from the fray, still watching the battle. Why, asks Agamemnōn, has Nestōr come here? Hektōr seems to be carrying out his threats. It seems the Achaians are as angry with me as Achilles is, and have no wish to fight for the ships. Yes, says Nestōr, the wall's breached, and the Achaians are routed. We need to confer, think up a plan. But not to fight: the wounded can't fight. Agamemnōn replies: You're right, the wall and ditch are breached, they're fighting at the ships—Zeus must mean the Achaians to perish here! So, we should launch the ships overnight and run for it: better that than being captured. Odysseus is scathing: You should be leading some third-rate army, not be king over us! Shut up, and don't let the Achaians see or hear you! Once they see the ships being hauled beachwards, they'll *never* fight! Oh, says Agamemnōn, I'm not urging retreat against the army's will! Is there anyone with better advice?

Yes, says Diomēdēs. Let's go to the fighting and encourage the others. They agree, and go off, Agamemnōn leading.

135–52: Poseidōn, watchful, goes along with them in the likeness of an old man, telling Agamemnōn that Achilles must be rejoicing in the Achaian rout. But the immortals aren't angry with you, he says, and very soon, I think, you'll see the Trojans in flight in their turn. Then he speeds off across the plain, giving a tremendous war shout as he goes, raising the hopes and fighting spirits of the Achaians.

153–223: Hērē wonders how to distract Zeus? Why not pretty herself up, get him to have sex with her, and then leave him sound asleep while she and Poseidōn take care of the war? She asks Aphroditē for the aphrodisiac that works on mortals and immortals alike. Ocean and Tethys have been quarrelling, she says. I want to reconcile them. Well, says Aphroditē, who (one suspects) sees through this story: I can't say no to you—*you sleep with Zeus!* She unfastens and gives Hērē her embroidered breast band, which contains all desire and allurements. Hērē smiles, and tucks it in her cleavage. Aphroditē goes home.

224–351: Hērē next flies over to Lēmnos, where she seeks out Sleep and tries to bribe him to keep Zeus sound asleep for a while after she's made love with him. But Sleep has done a similar job for her once before, incurred Zeus's wrath, and had to be rescued by Night. Hērē then offers him Pasithēē, the youthful Grace he's always longed for, as his wife. He accepts, but makes her swear a great oath that she'll keep her word. Then they fly to Ida, and Sleep hides up in a tall fir tree, while Hērē goes off to find Zeus, who takes one look at her and is consumed by desire. Hērē spins him the story of visiting Ocean and Tethys, but says she's come to let him, Zeus, know what she's doing first. Oh, says Zeus, you can go there later! I haven't wanted anyone so much—a list of conquests follows—as I want you now! Now now, says Hērē, not here in the open! What if some god saw us? Let's rather go to the bedroom Hēphaistos made for me. No need, says Zeus I'll envelop us in a golden cloud. He does so, and a bed of flowers springs up under them, while the cloud sprinkles them with dew.

352–432: While Zeus sleeps, Sleep goes to the ships, to Poseidōn, and tells him to aid the Achaians while Zeus remains unconscious. Poseidōn at once goes down among the Achaians. Are we to let Hektōr get the glory just because Achilles is sitting it out? he cries. Arm the best men with the finest weapons and helmets and I'll lead the attack! The three wounded Achaian leaders—Agamemnōn, Odysseus, and Diomēdēs—

spread this word through the ranks. Poseidōn leading, the Achaians face Hektōr's forces. Hektōr lets fly at Aias, but the spear hits where two baldrics cross on his chest, and drops harmlessly. As Hektōr, vexed, draws back, Aias hurls a huge rock at him and hits him in the neck above his shield. The blow spins him round and floors him. The Achaians run up, but the best Trojan fighters—Poulydamas, Aineias, Agēnōr, Sarpēdōn, and Glaukos—cover Hektōr till he can be lifted, carried unconscious to his chariot, and driven off the battlefield.

433–522: By the Xanthos river they lift Hektōr out and dash water over him. He comes to, kneels, vomits up black blood, then relapses into unconsciousness. His withdrawal from battle encourages the Achaians even more. Aias (2) floors Satnios, spearing him in the side. Poulydamas responds by spearing Prothoēnōr and boasts over his body. Aias (1) has a shot at him, but misses, and hits Archelochos at the top of the spine. Archelochos's brother Akamas, a high Trojan leader, kills the Boiōtian Promachos as he tries to drag Archelochos off. His boasting angers the Achaians further, and Pēneleōs attacks him. Akamas dodges, and Pēneleōs instead spears Ilioneus in the eye, then draws his sword and beheads him.

The Trojans are scared. The Muses are invoked to give a list of those Achaians who carried off an enemy's armor after Poseidōn turned the tide of battle. The victims of Aias, Antilochos, Mēriones, Teukros, Menelaös, and Aias (2) (who accounted for most deaths) are duly listed.

BOOK 15

1–112: Zeus wakes on Ida and sees the Trojans routed, Hektōr lying disabled, and Poseidōn rallying the Achaians. Angrily he rounds on Hērē, at once blames her wiles for what's happened, and reminds her—to make her stop her deceptions—of the time he hung her on high with anvils tagged to her feet after she and the north wind spirited Hēraklēs away to Kōs. Hērē shudders and swears that Poseidōn is doing all this of his own accord, having taken pity on the beleaguered Achaians. She adds that she'd advise him to do whatever Zeus told him to. Zeus, not taken in, smiles, and says, if you're being honest, bring Iris and Apollo here: she's to tell Poseidōn to stop it and go home, while he's to go patch up Hektōr, fill him with strength, have him drive the Achaians back among Achilles' ships. Then Achilles will send Patroklos into battle, and after Patroklos has killed many Trojans, including my son Sarpēdōn, Hektōr will kill him, and Achilles, will be drawn back into the war out of rage and kill Hektōr. Then I'll have the Trojans in retreat, until Troy's taken through Athēnē's advice. But till then, till Achilles gets his wish, I'll not let any god aid the Achaians, as I promised Thetis. Hērē says nothing, but leaves swiftly and returns to Olympos. Themis greets her, saying she looks scared. We're fools to tangle with Zeus, Hērē says: he's stronger than any of us; he sits apart and couldn't care less! Meanwhile, Arēs' son has been killed in battle.

113–219: Arēs cries out: Don't blame me if I now help the Achaians, even if Zeus blasts me with his thunderbolt! He arms himself and orders Terror and Rout to harness up his chariot. But then Athēnē comes out, takes away his helmet and spear, and upbraids him fiercely: you're mad, you don't listen, or understand, she exclaims. Didn't you hear what Hērē just said, who's come straight from Zeus? Do you want to bring great trouble on all of us, not just yourself? Zeus would surely come to Olympos and wreak havoc on all the gods, innocent and guilty alike. So, forego your anger! Better men have been, and will be, killed: it's hard to preserve every mortal line! After getting Arēs to sit down again, Hērē then calls Iris and Apollo out of the hall and tells them to go to Ida and follow Zeus's orders. They duly find Zeus, who first briefs Iris: she's to go to Poseidōn, and tell him to desist, and either come to Olympos or go down into the sea—and remind him that he, Zeus, is the older and more powerful!

Iris flits off, delivers the message, and adds that if Poseidōn disobeys, Zeus will come in person and fight him. Poseidōn, nothing fazed, replies that he, Zeus, and Hādēs shared out power in equal thirds. Let Zeus stick to his third, and stop trying to strong-arm his equals! Iris says: You want me to report this? You don't want to soften the message a little? Don't forget: the Furies back the older in a dispute! You're right, says Poseidōn. A good thing when the messenger knows what's what! So, I'm furious, but I'll yield for now. But tell him this: if despite me, and Athēnē, and Hēphaistos, he spares Ilion, then he has a quarrel on his hands that's past mending. With that Poseidōn leaves the Achaians and goes back down into the sea.

220–305: Having seen Poseidōn depart, Zeus instructs Apollo to go to Hektōr. Take the aegis, he says, shake it over the Achaians and scare them! Take care of Hektōr and strengthen him: let the Achaians flee to their ships and the Hellespont. I shall make sure they get respite after that. Apollo goes down, approaches Hektōr, and asks what the trouble is. Which god are you? Hektōr says. I was crushed by a rock from Aias: I thought I'd die. Take heart, Apollo says: Zeus has sent me, Apollo, to help you. Prepare your chariots to go against the ships and I'll smooth the way for them. Then he breathes great power into Hektōr, who gets up and urges on his charioteers. The Achaians are still pressing forward, but when Hektōr appears, they are scared. Thoas the Aitōlian addresses them, saying: Amazing how Hektōr has recovered when we thought he was dying! Some god must have saved him. So, let's send the rank and file back to the ships, while the best of us stay and face him! He won't charge our levelled spears! The Achaian rank and file return to the ships, while Aias, Idomeneus, Teukros, Mēriones, and Megēs remain there with their companies.

306–89: The Trojans advance, led by Hektōr, with Apollo carrying the aegis. Arrows and spears fly. But when Apollo shakes the aegis and utters his war cry, the Achaians are unnerved. Hektōr and Aineias kill two opponents each. Poulydamas, Polītēs, and Agēnōr all claim victims. Paris spears one fleeing Achaian from behind. The Achaians are in rout, inside the wall and in the ditch. Hektōr yells out to the rest to leave the armor-stripping, on pain of death, and press on to the ships. Apollo throws down the banks of the ditch to make a bridge for the Trojan chariots to cross on. He destroys the wall as easily as a child knocking down a sandcastle. The Achaians, led by Nestōr, offer desperate prayers to the gods. Zeus hears them and thunders. But this only encourages the Trojans more. They come on, fighting from their chariots, and are fended off by Achaians from the decks of their ships with long naval pikes.

390–483: Patroklos, tending Eurypylos, sees the Trojan attack and Achaian retreat, and leaves Eurypylos's hut with the intention of persuading Achilles to rejoin the fighting, which is stalemated. The Trojans can't break through to the ships and huts, and Aias can't drive Hektōr back. Aias spears Kalētōr, Hektōr's cousin. Hektōr, enraged, shouts orders to stop his body being stripped. He hurls his spear at Aias, but misses him and hits his attendant, Lykophrōn.

Aias tells Teukros to use his bow. Teukros shoots Kleitos the charioteer, and he falls from his chariot. Poulydamas rounds up the horses. Teukros then aims at Hektōr, but Zeus breaks his bowstring and knocks the bow from his hand. A god's done it, Teukros exclaims. So, says Aias, leave your arrows, take shield and helmet, and fight like the rest. Teukros arms himself, and stands by Aias.

484–591: Hektōr sees Teukros's bow disabled, guesses Zeus is responsible, and calls on the Trojans to press their attack. If a man dies, so be it; if the Achaians are driven out, his family's safe. Across from him Aias encourages his comrades: If Hektōr burns their ships, do they think they'll walk home? Die or win, let's go for it, not stay stuck here by the ships fighting inferior opponents! A murderous scrimmage develops.

Hektōr and Aias both kill opponents. Apollo protects Poulydamas.

Dolops attacks Megēs as he's stripping a corpse, but is killed by Menelaös. Hektōr calls on Melanippos to join the fray, and they advance together. Aias urges on the Achaians, and they form a bronze fence defending the ships. Zeus encourages the Trojans. Menelaös urges young Antilochos to attack a Trojan. Antilochos spears Melanippos in the chest. Hektōr comes after Antilochos, who flees back to the ranks, pursued by a shower of missiles.

592–695: The Trojans keep pressing on to the ships, as Zeus wills, planning to let Hektōr fire them, and fulfill Thetis's prayer. That done, Zeus plans to reverse his support and let the Achaians drive back the Trojans. Hektōr is being granted glory by Zeus, but already Athēnē is planning his death at Achilles' hands. And the Achaians are holding firm against his assault. Hektōr attacks and the Achaians give way but he kills only one man, Periphētēs of Mykēnai, who trips over his own shield and offers an easy target. They are now among the outermost ships. The Achaians rally before their huts, and are urged to stand firm by Nestōr. Athēnē disperses the cloud of mist that has hung over them. The scene is now bright. Hektōr and his supporters are clear in view. Aias strides up and down the ships' decks wielding a long, jointed naval pike. Hektōr, backed by Zeus, charges Prōtesilaos's ship.

696–746: A furious hand-to-hand struggle with swords, axes, and javelins develops. Hektōr lays hold of the ship's stern and calls for fire. Although hard pressed by missiles, Aias stands ready to ward off any Trojan bringing fire, and rallies the Achaians, reminding them that their backs are to the sea now—they've reached their last line of defense. He wards off twelve Trojans in turn who come with flaming torches.

BOOK 16

1–100: Patroklos approaches Achilles, weeping. Achilles asks him why the tears? Is it a death in the family? Or is it because of the Achaians' dying by the ships as a result of their own presumption? Patroklos answers: Don't be angry: the Achaians are indeed hard hit. Their best men are wounded and out of it—Diomēdēs, Odysseus, Agamemnōn, Eurypylos. You're impossible, Achilles! I hope I never feel such wrath as yours! What profit from you for future mortals if you don't now rescue the Achaians? You were born not of Pēleus and Thetis but of grey sea and sheer rocks, so set is your mind! If you're avoiding some oracle your mother's told you of, at least let me use your armor—the Trojans may take me for you and give the Achaians some respite: we might even drive them back from the ships! *Such his entreaty, the great fool: but as fate decreed, / his own ghastly death and destruction it was for which he prayed*, says Homer, in one of his rare comments.

Achilles, much troubled, replies: No, no oracle: just the keen pain of being robbed by an equal with greater power! The girl I was granted as a prize for my achievements has been snatched away again! But let this be! If the Trojans are at the ships, yes, take my armor, lead out the Myrmidons! The voice I hear is Hektōr's. But when you've driven him and his back from the ships, come back: don't press on to Ilion!

I wish just the two of us could, from both sides, survive to take the city!

101–256: Tiring and hard-pressed, Aias gives ground. Hektōr shears off the head of Aias' spear with his sword, and he withdraws. The Trojans fire the ship. At this Achilles urges Patroklos to arm quickly, while he, Achilles, rouses the Myrmidons to action. Patroklos arms himself with Achilles' gear, except for the great spear of Pēlian ash that only Achilles can wield. Automedōn, Achilles' charioteer, harnesses his immortal horses, Xanthos and Balios, with the mortal Pēdasos as trace horse.

Meanwhile Achilles rouses the Myrmidons, who charge out like ravening wolves. There are fifty ships, each with fifty men, divided into five companies, led by Menesthios, Eudōros, Peisandros, Phoinix, and Alkimedōn. To them Achilles says: Don't forget your threats against the Trojans—nor your accusations against me, for keeping you here! Go to it! Achilles brings out a cup and makes libation, with a prayer to Zeus of Dōdōna for Patroklos's success and safe return.

257–357: The Myrmidons, with Patroklos at their head encouraging them, pour out. The Trojans believe it's Achilles attacking them and look round for a way of escape. Patroklos spears Pyraichmēs, leader of the Paiōnians, and drives off his followers. The fire on the half-burned ship is put out, and the Achaians, once the fire's out, catch their breath, but there's no rout; the Trojans are just forced slowly back. Patroklos kills Areïlykos, Menelaös kills Thoas, Megēs kills Amphiklos, Antilochos kills Atymnios, whose brother Maris is killed by Thrasymēdēs. Aias (2) kills Kleoboulos. Pēneleōs kills Lykōn, Mēriones kills Akamas, Idomeneus kills Erymas.

358–507: Aias wants to spear Hektōr, but Hektōr is constantly watching out for missiles from behind his shield: he knows the tide is turning, but still stays to help his comrades. The Trojans straggle back across the ditch, and Hektōr too now withdraws. Many chariots and horses are entangled in the ditch. Patroklos leads the pursuit, his divine horses leaping the ditch. Patroklos turns the retreat away from the city, rounds it towards the ships, and kills many: Pronoös, Thestōr, Erylaös, Erymas, Amphoteros, Epaltēs, Tlēpolemos, Echios, Pyris, Ipheus, Euippos, and Polymēlos. Sarpēdōn, seeing this slaughter, upbraids the Lycians, and he and Patroklos go for each other. Zeus, watching, tells Hērē he's debating whether to save Sarpēdōn, his son, or let him be vanquished as Fate decrees. Hērē is shocked at the idea of Zeus overriding Fate. If you set a precedent, other gods will follow your lead, she says. Let Sarpēdōn die if Fate wills it, but send Death and Sleep to carry him home to Lycia for family burial. Zeus agrees, but sends a rain of blood to show honor for Sarpēdōn. Patroklos kills Sarpēdōn's charioteer, Thrasymēlos. Sarpēdōn fatally wounds Patroklos's mortal trace horse Pēdasos, but Automedōn cuts it loose from the chariot. Sarpēdōn misses again, and Patroklos spears him in the midriff. He falls with a final appeal to his comrade Glaukos to hold firm and protect his corpse.

508–631: Glaukos hears and grieves. Still hurting from Teukros's arrow, he prays to Apollo for relief: Sarpēdōn is dead, heal my wound, let me fight! Apollo hears, dries the blood, stops the pain, and fills Glaukos with strength. He urges on the Trojans, calling on Hektōr in particular to protect Sarpēdōn's body. They advance. Patroklos calls on the Aiases to seize and strip Sarpēdōn. The two sides clash. Zeus plunges the engagement into darkness. At first the Trojans prevail: Hektōr kills Epeigeus as he lays hands on Sarpēdōn's corpse. In grief for his comrade, Patroklos charges through the ranks and kills Sthenelaös. Hektōr and the Trojans give a little ground, but Glaukos turns and kills the Myrmidon Bathyklēs. Mērionēs kills the priest Laogonos: Aineias tries to spear Mēriones, but he ducks. If I'd hit you, I'd have killed you, Aineias says. Mēriones replies: Mighty you may be, but you can't score every time: you too are mortal. If I hit you squarely. you'd be finished too. Why bluster like this, says Aineias: the Trojans aren't giving ground to mere words. Don't talk, fight.

632–711: The battle rages over Sarpēdōn's body, made unrecognizable by blood and dust. Zeus watches, debating the killing of Patroklos: should it be now, or should he, Zeus, let Patroklos drive the Trojans and Lycians citywards? He decides on the latter course: Hektōr recognizes the scales of Zeus, and calls for a retreat. The Myrmidons strip Sarpēdōn, and carry back his arms to the ships. Zeus instructs Apollo to waft Sarpēdōn's body away, clean and bathe him, and have Sleep and Death take him home to Lycia. Apollo obeys, and all this is done. Patroklos now presses on—stimulated to do so by Zeus—in pursuit of the Trojans and Lycians, ignoring Achilles' instructions. (Had he obeyed them, Homer comments, he'd have avoided death.) He kills Adrēstos, Autonoös, Echeklos, Perimos, Epistōr, Melanippos, Elasos, Moulios, and Pylartēs. Then he starts climbing the city wall. Three times he's flung back by

Apollo: the fourth time the god cries out to him to stop: Troy's not fated to be taken either by him or by Achilles. Patroklos duly backs off to avoid the god's wrath.

712–867: Hektōr at the Skaian Gate is uncertain whether to drive to battle or recall the troops inside the wall. He's approached by Apollo in the likeness of his mother's brother Asios, urging him to fight Patroklos.

Hektōr tells Kebrionēs, his charioteer, to join the fray. Apollo panics the Achaians, granting glory to the Trojans. Hektōr ignores all other Achaians and makes straight for Patroklos. Patroklos springs down and kills Kebrionēs. He and Hektōr fight over the corpse. Hektōr seizes the head, Patroklos the feet. Round them Trojans and Achaians fight, evenly matched till evening. Then the Achaians strip Kebrionēs, and Patroklos makes three assaults on the Trojans. But the fourth attack is met by Apollo, shrouded in mist, who slams him from behind with the flat of his hand, dizzying him, breaking his spear, and knocking off his helmet. While he's dizzy, Euphorbos spears him in the back, and Hektōr hurries up and spears him in the underbelly as he's retreating. Dying, Patroklos says: It was the gods and Fate that destroyed me, twenty like you alone would not have done it. And your own fate at Achilles' hands will very soon follow. Hektōr says: Who knows? It may well be that I kill Achilles. Then he pulls out the spear and goes after Automedōn the charioteer, but he, and Achilles' immortal horses, are gone.

BOOK 17

1–81: Seeing Patroklos struck down, Menelaös stands protectively over his body. Euphorbos calls on him to withdraw: let me win renown, or I'll kill you too. You'll pay for the death of my brother—the least I can do for his widow is to bring her your head! He throws, but his spear's stopped by the shield, and Menelaös stabs him in the throat. Menelaös strips him, and no one dares come against him. But Apollo grudges him the arms, and, in the likeness of Mentēs, urges Hektōr to leave off his pursuit of Achilles' horses and tackle Menelaös.

82–139: Hektōr sees the corpse and shouts. Menelaös hears him and knows who it is. He thinks: The Achaians will blame me if I back off. But if I try to fight Hektōr and all the Trojans, I'm done for. But, ah, Hektōr has a god fighting for him: the Achaians know that, and wouldn't blame me . . . perhaps I should try to find Aias and get him to help me. The Trojans advance, led by Hektōr. Menelaös slowly retreats, turning back as he goes, like a lion cornered by dogs and hunters. Back in the ranks, he sees Aias, asks for his help in saving Patroklos's corpse for Achilles—Hektōr has his armor. Aias agrees and comes with him. Hektōr is dragging Patroklos's body away, planning to behead it, but retreats quickly on seeing Aias, boards his chariot, and gives Patroklos's armor to others to take back to the city. With Menelaös beside him, Aias covers Patroklos's corpse with his shield.

140–97: Glaukos upbraids Hektōr as a coward. Save Ilion with Trojan help alone—you'll get no help from the Lycians! How will you save a lesser man when you deserted Sarpēdōn, who was your guest and comrade? If it were up to me, the Lycians would go home. If we had some brave Trojans, we could drag Patroklos to Ilion: then the Achaians would give back Sarpēdōn's body and armor! But you hadn't the courage to face Aias, who's a better man than you. Angry, Hektōr replies: Glaukos, why this arrogance? I thought you wise, but you're senseless. I'm not afraid of battle, but who can resist Zeus? So come and fight beside me and see if I'm a coward or not. He shouts to the Trojans and their allies to hold firm. Then, having retrieved Achilles' armor from the men taking it to the city, he dons it.

198–318: Zeus watches him, reflects that he's nearer death than he knows, that he's improperly wearing the gear of a better man. Still, muses Zeus, knowing that Hektōr will never come back home from the battle, he can have a little glory now. Hektōr is filled with warlike ardor, makes a rousing speech to the allies—whoever gets Patroklos's body from Aias will share the spoils and the glory with Hektōr! They charge Aias and Menelaös, who resist under pressure, but need help. Menelaös calls out, and Aias son of Oïleus and Idomeneus and Mērionēs come running, with a whole mass of men at their heels. Hektōr and the Trojans advance, but the Achaians stand firm and Zeus covers them with darkness. Zeus did not dislike Patroklos when he was alive and Achilles' comrade, and he has no wish now for his corpse to be thrown to Trojan dogs, so he puts strength into his comrades to defend his body. Even so the Trojans drive back the Achaians and begin to drag off Patroklos's body. But Aias rallies the Achaians, charging the foremost Trojans and scattering those around Patroklos's body. He kills Hippothoös, who's dragging the corpse with a belt tied round its ankles. Hektōr tries to spear Aias, but misses him and hits Schedios. Aias meanwhile disembowels Phorkys. Hektōr and the Trojans give ground. The Achaians drag off Phorkys and Hippothoös and start stripping them.

319–422: Despite Zeus, the Trojans would have been beaten, and the Achaians would have won more glory, had Apollo, taking on the likeness of Periphas the herald, not encouraged Aineias. If a god were against you, you might not save Ilion, he says, but Zeus wants the Trojans to win more than he does the Achaians, so why hold off? Aineias knows it's Apollo and calls out to Hektōr and the rest: To be driven back is disgraceful! A god tells me Zeus is for us, so let's fight, and stop them getting Patroklos away to the ships! The Trojans rally, but the Achaians stand firm over Patroklos, while Aias ranges to and fro, attacking the Trojans and urging his comrades to stand firm. Unaware that Patroklos is dead, Thrasymēdēs and Antilochos are still fighting, and Achilles does not know yet either. Both sides meanwhile desperately hold firm in the struggle for the corpse: better to die, they say, than give in.

423–542: Achilles' divine horses weep when they realize that Patroklos is dead, Despite all Automedōn's efforts, they remain fixed by their chariot, like the marker on a burial mound. Zeus, seeing them, is touched by pity, regrets having bestowed them, immortal as they are, on a mortal, with all the consequent sorrows, and promises that Hektōr won't get them, that Automedōn will bring them back to the ships, but that the Trojans will have the better of it till they reach the ships and darkness falls. He breathes strength into the Achaians, and Automedōn leads them into battle. But—as Alkimedōn reminds him—he can't drive and fight at the same time. Automedōn takes Alkimedōn as his charioteer, and steps down to fight. Hektōr and Aineias see them, and, with Chromios and Arētos, go after the immortal horses. Automedōn sees them coming, tells Alkimedōn to stick close behind him, and calls to the Aiases and Menelaös for support. He spears Arētos. Hektōr tries to spear Automedōn, but he ducks. The arrival of the Aiases stops an imminent sword fight: Hektōr, Aineias, and Chromios prudently withdraw. Automedōn strips Arētos of his armor and returns with it to his chariot.

543–647: The fight for Patroklos's body continues. Zeus, having changed his mind, sends Athēnē down to encourage the Achaians: she appears, wrapped in a cloud, and addresses Menelaös, in the likeness of old Phoinix, urging him into action: it would be shameful for Achilles' comrade to become prey to Trojan dogs! Menelaös replies: Hektōr is dangerous, and Zeus is backing him! If only Athēnē would strengthen me, protect me from missiles, I'd stand firm over Patroklos! Delighted that he has picked her to appeal to—we're not told whether or not he has recognized her—Athēnē invigorates him. Menelaös at once spears Podēs and drags off his body. Then Apollo approaches Hektōr in the likeness of Phainōps and upbraids him for yielding to Menelaös, reckoned a poor warrior. Furious, Hektōr goes to the front. Zeus clouds up Ida, thunders and lightens, and shakes his aegis as token of giving the Trojans the upper hand. Poulydamas disables Pēneleōs, Hektōr wounds Lēïtos, Idomeneus breaks a spear on Hektōr, and Hektōr in return misses him, but kills Mērionēs' charioteer Koiranos, who's just come to pick up Idomeneus, who's on foot. At Mērionēs' urging, Idomeneus grabs the whip and drives back to the ships. Aias and Menelaös see that Zeus has turned the tide of victory. Aias exclaims that he wishes there was someone to take the bad news to Achilles, but they're all in darkness—Zeus, he prays, clear the sky! If you're going to kill us, do it in sunlight!

648–761: Zeus pities him and disperses the dark mist. The sun shines. Aias tells Menelaös to find Antilochos and send him to Achilles with the news of Patroklos's death. Menelaös goes reluctantly, like a lion frustrated by a blizzard of missiles, afraid that the routed Achaians will leave him a victim to the Trojans: he urges the Aiases and Mērionēs to remember how kind Patroklos was when alive. Then he moves off looking for Antilochos. He finds him and breaks the news of Patroklos's death, urging him to go and tell Achilles—perhaps he'll be able to rescue the body. But Hektōr has his armor. Antilochos, horrified and weeping, sets off to tell Achilles. Menelaös sends Thrasymēdēs to replace him in the line, and himself goes back to the conflict over Patroklos's body, pessimistic about Achilles joining the fight and urging the Achaians to make a great effort to get the body away now. When they see Patroklos's body being moved, the Trojans attack, with Aineias and Hektōr in the vanguard, but the two Aiases fight them off. Meanwhile, most of the Achaians flee, discarding their armor around the ditch as they run.

BOOK 18

1–147: Antilochos finds Achilles by his ships, worried at the rout of the Achaians, and suspecting that Patroklos must be dead, despite the orders he had to return after saving the ships. Antilochos confirms his fears, says they're fighting over Patroklos's stripped body, and that Hektōr has his armor. Achilles is consumed with grief, weeps, tears his hair, grovels in the dust. The two women captives join the mourning. Thetis hears her son's groans, shrieks aloud, and laments to the gathered sea nymphs: I sent my splendid son to Ilion, but I'll never welcome him home—I must go comfort him now, though there's no real way I can help him. She and the nymphs then go to Troy. Thetis embraces Achilles and says: What's your grief? Zeus has given you what you wanted! The Achaians are in disarray by the ships! What's that to me? asks Achilles. My dear comrade is dead, and Hektor has the armor the gods gave Pēleus at his wedding. I wish you'd stayed a sea nymph, that Pēleus had married a mortal! I've no wish to live unless I can kill Hektōr first for destroying Patroklos! That means, says Thetis, that your own death will follow: it's fated that you will die very soon after Hektōr. Let me die now then, Achilles responds: I wasn't there to help my comrade! I sit here a useless burden! I'll go after Hektōr and accept my death when the gods want it. For now, I'll seek renown in battle. Don't try to stop me. Fine, says Thetis, but Hektōr has your armor. Don't go into battle till I return tomorrow with new armor for you from Hēphaistos. She then sends her nymphs home, telling them she's going to Olympos to persuade Hēphaistos to make arms for Achilles. They, and she, then take off.

148–243: The fighting is at the ships. The Achaians can't drag Patroklos's carcass clear: the Trojans are pressing too hard. Hektōr has Patroklos by the feet: the Aiases stand him off three times, but he gives no ground. At this point Iris reaches Achilles with a private message from Hērē, that he should arm himself and protect Patroklos's body from the shame of mutilation. Who sent you? asks Achilles. Hērē, says Iris: Zeus and the other gods don't know. Then Achilles says: How can I fight? They have my armor. No other man's armor would fit me. My mother says Hēphaistos is making me a new set. Aias's great shield would do, maybe, but he's in action with it.

Iris says: We know about your armor. Just go to the ditch and show yourself to the Trojans! It may scare them and give the Achaians some respite. She then leaves. Achilles gets up. Athēnē puts the aegis round his shoulders, a golden cloud over his head, and has a flame blaze out from him. He goes to the ditch, but doesn't join the Achaians. Then he shouts three times, and Athēnē echoes his cry. The Trojans are panic-stricken, and a dozen of them drop dead, though safe among their own people. The Achaians drag Patroklos clear, put him on a bier. They stand round him weeping, Achilles among them. The sun goes down and there's a break in the fighting.

243–355: The Trojans hold an emergency assembly before the evening meal. The first speaker is Poulydamas, Hektōr's coeval and comrade: Go back to the city! Don't stay by the ships! he says. While Achilles was out of the fighting, that was all very well. But now, with Achilles in action, things are very different! He'll be attacking the city, and many

Trojans will die. So let's withdraw and man the walls: that will stop him. Angrily, Hektōr responds: Poulydamas, I don't like what you're saying! Aren't you tired of being cooped up in the city? And Priam's city used to be wealthy, but no longer! Look, Zeus is granting me glory over the Achaians by the ships, and now you call for retreat! No one's going to obey you, I'll make sure of that! Rather now eat by companies, keep strict watch all night, and be ready in the morning to fight by the ships! And if Achilles wants a battle, I'll be ready for him then! The Trojans shout assent. (Homer comments: Athēnē addled their wits! They praised Hektōr's bad advice, and ignored the good sense of Poulydamas.) Meanwhile the Achaians, led by Achilles, are collectively mourning Patroklos. Achilles is like a furious lion tracking a hunter who's taken its cubs. Vain was the promise I gave Menoitios, that I'd bring back his son laden with spoils, when Troy was down, he cries. Zeus has chosen otherwise—we're both going to die here! But I won't rest, Patroklos, till I have the head and armor of Hektōr and a dozen young Trojans to sacrifice at your pyre! He has water heated, and his comrades wash Patroklos's body, anoint his wounds, and lay him out. The Myrmidons mourn him all night long.

356–467: Zeus to Herē: Well, you got your way: you've roused Achilles! The Achaians must be your own flesh and blood! Hērē replies: I'm the top goddess—how could I fail to make trouble for the Trojans? Meanwhile Thetis goes to Hēphaistos's house. Hēphaistos recalls how Thetis and Ocean's daughter Eurynomē rescued him when he was thrown out of Olympos by his mother Hērē: he owes much to Thetis.

He puts away his tools, washes, and asks Thetis what he can do for her. She replies: Is there any goddess with as many troubles as I have? Zeus married me off against my will to a mortal, who's now old and weak. And the son I bore I sent to Troy, but I shall never welcome him home again. Because Agamemnōn took his prize woman back, he held back from the fighting; but when the Achaians were backed up by the Trojans against their ships, he sent Patroklos in his own armor, with the Myrmidons, to help them. They would have taken the city had Apollo not killed Patroklos and granted glory to Hektōr. So I'm here to beg you to make new armor for my ill-fated son—that which he had was stripped from Patroklos by the Trojans. Hēphaistos says: I wish I could save him from death! But fine armor he shall indeed have.

468–617: Hēphaistos sets to work making a five-layered shield with a silver shield strap. Heavenly bodies and two cities decorate it. In one city a wedding is taking place and a dispute is under arbitration. The other city is besieged. With the walls manned by women and children, the men march out, led by Arēs and Athēnē, to ambush the besiegers' herdsmen and capture sheep and cattle. Strife, Tumult, and the Death Spirit all join in the fighting. Plowing is depicted too, and a wheatfield, with reapers using sickles and sheaves being bound. There is also a golden vineyard, with the vines supported on silver poles and grapes in abundance, surrounded by a cobalt enamel ditch and a fence of tin. A queue of boys and girls with baskets full of grapes dance to a boy singing and accompanying himself on a lyre. A herd of cattle is fashioned from gold and tin, with golden herdsmen. Two lions are dragging off a bellowing bull, with dogs and men in pursuit. The dogs bark at the lions but stay clear of them. A pastoral scene shows a flock of white sheep and huts and sheepfolds, and elsewhere young people dance, led by two tumblers. In conclusion, Hēphaistos sets Ocean all round the rim of the shield. Then he fashions a corselet, helmet, and greaves. All these marvels he gives to Thetis.

BOOK 19

1–144: Thetis brings this new battle gear to the mourning Achilles. The Myrmidons are astounded by it; Achilles' fury swells along with his pleasure as he examines it. He will arm himself, he says—but he is also worried that Patroklos may rot and be consumed by flies and maggots. No, says Thetis, I'll keep his flesh sound! Now you call an assembly and make your peace with Agamemnōn: after that, arm yourself. She then drips nectar and ambrosia through Patroklos's nostrils to preserve his body unchanged. Achilles goes down the beach calling everyone to assembly. Because it's Achilles, they all, even the pilots and stewards, now show up: Diomēdēs, Odysseus, and Agamemnōn come limping in with their wounds. Achilles says: I wish Briseïs had died in Lyrnessos! Far fewer Achaians would then have died because of my wrath! That profited Hektōr and the Trojans, and the Achaians won't forget it in a hurry. But we need to put all this behind us: I must quench my wrath and we must rouse the Achaians to battle and see whether the Trojans continue attacking the ships. Those who escape may count themselves lucky! The Achaians rejoice to hear this. Agamemnōn then speaks: I'm not at fault, he says; the fault lies with Zeus and Fates and the Furies, who deluded me. Zeus robbed me of good sense, but now I'm ready to make amends—so prepare for battle!

145–237: The troops shouldn't have to go into battle hungry, Odysseus says. The fight will be a long one. Let them eat and drink first. Meanwhile, Agamemnōn should display the gifts to be given to Achilles and swear on oath that he's never had sex with Briseïs. Agamemnōn agrees and asks Odysseus to display of the gifts. But Achilles demurs: You can do all that another time, he says. Men are lying dead and unavenged and you want us to eat! I shan't eat till I'm avenged and the sun goes down. You're the great fighter, Odysseus replies, but my advice makes more sense. Those who eat regularly fight better.

238–339: Odysseus takes a group of warriors to Agamemnōn's hut to fetch the gifts, which include eight captive women, Briseïs among them, and weighs out the ten talents of gold. Agamemnōn swears that he has not slept with Briseïs, and a boar is sacrificed. Achilles accepts the argument that Agamemnōn was deluded by Zeus and dismisses the assembly. The Myrmidons take the gifts to Achilles' hut. Briseïs mourns over Patroklos's body: her husband and her brothers have all been killed, but Patroklos promised that she would wed Achilles, and she mourns him for his kindness. The other women join in the lamentation—officially for Patroklos, but each one for her own sorrows. The Achaians beg Achilles to eat, but he steadfastly refuses. A few leaders, including Agamemnōn, Menelaös, and Odysseus, stay and try to comfort him. But he remembers the meals Patroklos prepared for him, and won't eat. Nothing, he says, could be worse, not even the deaths of his father Pēleus or his son Neoptolemos—whom he'd hoped Patroklos would take back to Phthiē. Those with him join the weeping, remembering those they too have left behind.

340–424: Zeus sees and pities them. Achilles is fasting while the rest of them eat, he tells Athēnē. We mustn't let hunger make him weak, so go and feed him with nectar and ambrosia. She flies down and does so. The Achaians arm themselves and pour out from their ships. Achilles is shown donning his new armor in a state of murderous rage. It fits perfectly. Automedōn readies his chariot, and Achilles exclaims to his immortal horses: Bring your charioteer back safely; don't let him be killed, as you did Patroklos. One horse, Xanthos, on which Hērē has bestowed speech, responds: This time we'll save you, though your end is near! The stripping of Patroklos wasn't our fault: we can run as fast as the west wind! Fate and the gods so decreed, just as your own death is decreed! Achilles replies: Xanthos, you don't need to foretell my death. I know that myself. But I won't stop until I've given the Trojans their fill of war! And with that he drives off to battle.

BOOK 20

1–74: While both sides prepare for battle, Zeus sends out Themis summoning all the gods to assemble on Olympos. All come, except Ocean. Poseidōn asks why they've been called. Something perhaps to do with the Achaian and Trojan preparations for battle? Zeus says: You have it: I'm concerned for them. I shall simply watch, but you gods can help whichever side you like. With Achilles back fighting, and furious over Patroklos's death, I fear he may storm the walls, doing more than what's fated. The gods divide: Hērē, Poseidōn, Athēnē, Hermēs, and Hēphaistos go to support the Achaians; Arēs, Phoibos Apollo, Artemis, Lētō, Xanthos, and Aphrodītē will back the Trojans. Meanwhile, the Achaians have the edge because of Achilles' presence in his new armor. When the gods join in, Strife goes to work, and Athēnē (by the ditch) and Arēs (on the ramparts) urge each side on with great war cries. Zeus thunders; Poseidōn makes the earth quake—so violently that Hādēs fears that his subterranean realm may be exposed. Apollo confronts Poseidōn; Athēnē takes on Arēs; Hērē is faced by Artemis; Lētō by Hermēs; Hēphaistos by Xanthos/Skamandros.

75–155: Achilles is determined to fight Hektōr. Apollo, disguised as Priam's son Lykaōn, urges Aineias to attack Achilles, but Aineias is not eager to do so. Still, he adds, if a god were to fix things, that might be different. Pray to the gods, says Apollo, and don't forget: your mother was Aphrodītē, his was only a nymph. He infuses great strength into Aineias, who decides to challenge Achilles after all. Hērē notices, and addresses the gods, Poseidōn and Athēnē in particular. Aineias should be turned back, or one of us should encourage Achilles with our support! We're here to make sure Achilles suffers no harm today, whatever his ultimate fate may be. If he isn't reassured about this by a god, he'll take fright when a god comes against him in battle. Poseidōn says: Gods shouldn't fight gods anyway. We all should sit this out and leave the fighting to mortals. But if Arēs or Apollo should try to block Achilles in battle, then we should all weigh in and stop them. With that Poseidōn leads most of the gods to Hēraklēs' wall, while Apollo and Arēs station themselves on a hill—both sides plotting, but reluctant, despite Zeus's permission, to involve themselves directly.

156–352: The two sides advance. Aineias and Achilles approach each other. Achilles calls out to Aineias: Why are you doing this? Even should you kill me, Priam wouldn't recognize your status. Have you forgotten, too, how I beat you once before, and only Zeus saved you? So stand down before you're hurt. Aineias replies: Don't try to scare me as though I were a child. We both know each other's lineage. But why stand here bickering like a pair of women? Rather, let's fight. His spear is stopped by Achilles' shield; Achilles' spear pierces through Aineias's shield, but fails to hit him. Then Achilles comes at him with drawn sword, while Aineias hefts a great rock to throw at him. Poseidōn prepares to intervene: Aineias has been egged on by Apollo, who won't save him from being killed, which will infuriate Zeus, since it's his fate to survive and lead the Trojans. Hērē says he'll have to decide whether to save Aineias, reminding him that she and Athēnē have sworn not to save Troy. Poseidōn blinds Achilles with mist and pulls his spear out of Aineias's shield, setting it down by its owner. He then heaves Aineias to the furthest edge of the conflict, telling him: Don't fight Achilles; he's a better man than you and the gods love him. But when he's dead, fight: then no other Achaian will be able to match you.

353–454: Achilles urges on the Achaians—good though he is, he can't handle all the Trojans alone! Hektōr says: We can fight the gods with words: with spears it's harder. I'll battle Achilles, however powerful he is: he may fulfill some of his threats, but not all. The two sides clash. Apollo tells Hektōr to await Achilles in the ranks, not challenge him solo. Hektōr, scared by the god's voice, obeys. Achilles attacks the Trojan ranks. He kills Iphitiōn, and the Achaian chariots roll over his body. Then he kills Dēmoleōn, Hippodamas, and Hektōr's brother Polydōros. Furious, Hektōr makes for Achilles, who beckons him: Come close, and die the sooner! Hektōr says: Don't try to scare me like a child. Yes, I'm a lesser warrior than you. But these things lie in the lap of the gods. He hurls his spear, only to have Athēnē turn it back and drop it at his feet. Achilles springs at him, shouting. Apollo then snatches up Hektōr and hides him in mist. Achilles tries to get at him in the mist three times, but fails. Guessing that Apollo has saved him, he turns in search of other victims.

455–503: Achilles kills Dryōps, Dēmouchos, Laogonos and Dardanos, Trōs, Moulios, Deukaliōn, and Rhigmos and Areïthoös. He charges on, spattered with blood.

BOOK 21

1–135: The rout reaches the Xanthos (Skamandros) river. Achilles has chivvied the retreating Trojans into two groups: one making for the city, the other, men and chariots together, diving into the stream, like locusts fleeing a fire. Achilles leaves his spear by a bush, and plunges in armed with his sword alone, attacking indiscriminately: the Trojans cower like small fish chased by a dolphin. Achilles now captures twelve young Trojan warriors, ties their hands, and turns them over to his comrades to be kept as a blood offering for Patroklos. Now he's confronted by Priam's son Lykaōn, whom he'd earlier captured and sold into Lēmnos: but he's escaped, and is now once again at Achilles' mercy. He begs to be taken alive, in a long and detailed plea—he doesn't, he emphasizes, have the same mother as Hektōr—but Achilles is adamant. Till Patroklos was killed, he says, he ransomed quite a few Trojans. But no more now! Patroklos died, who was a better man than you are: why should you survive? I'm a fine warrior, but I too face death. With that he plunges his sword in, seizes the corpse by one foot, flings it into the river, and apostrophizes it: Lie there with the fishes! All of you, till I pursue you to Troy! Not even Xanthos will save you now—you'll pay for the deaths of Patroklos and all the other Achaians you've slaughtered!

136–227: The River, angered, plots how to stop Achilles. Meanwhile Achilles charges Asteropaios (a Paiōnian, son of the Axios, another river), who is filled with strength by Xanthos. He is also ambidextrous, and he throws two spears at once at Achilles: one hits his shield, the other grazes his forearm before grounding itself in the earth. Achilles' spear misses, and buries itself half its length in the riverbank. Asteropaios can't pull it out, and Achilles finishes him off with his sword, boasts over him of superior lineage, leaves him there to be eaten by eels and fishes, and goes after more Paiōnians: kills seven, and would have killed more, had the River not addressed him: If Zeus is allowing you to kill Trojans without number, at least do it in the plain, don't choke my waters with blood and corpses! Lay off! Very well, Achilles says. But I shan't stop killing Trojans till I've driven them back into their city and seen whether Hektōr will fight me or not.

227–382: Achilles keeps on after the Trojans. The River now reproaches Apollo, saying that he hasn't done as Zeus asked, namely, protect the Trojans until darkness fell. Achilles now leaps into mid-stream: Xanthos surges against him in a huge wave, sweeping corpses along, hiding living survivors in his eddies, bellowing like a bull. Achilles grasps a tree, swings himself ashore, but the River follows, flooding after him over the plain with a great roar. It chases him like an irrigation stream that gets up speed when all the dams are removed from a channel: the River is a true match for him in both speed and violence. He prays, desperate, to Zeus: Save me, but do what you will after! I'd rather have been killed by Hektōr! But now I'm going to be drowned like a young swineherd trying to cross a winter torrent! Poseidōn and Athēnē appear by him in mortal form: Poseidōn reassures him—it's not his fate to be killed by a river: Xanthos will soon let up! Keep attacking, they tell him, until you've driven the Trojans back into Ilion. But when you've slain Hektōr, then return to the ships: so far do we promise you glory! They take off and leave him. Achilles moves on over the flooded plain, thick with corpses and abandoned weapons: he now has the strength to defy the rolling river. But Xanthos doesn't let up, calls to Simoeis, the other river of the plain, to join with him in stopping this wild madman: he, Xanthos, will drown him, bury him and his armor deep! With that his surging wave, all blood and corpses, towers over Achilles. Hērē, watching, scared that the wave will wash him away, calls to Hēphaistos to stop Xanthos with consuming fire, which she'll speed with gales, and only to stop when she tells him, not before! Hēphaistos at once gets to work. He dries the plain with a front of fire that consumes the dead and their gear, trees, rushes, and bushes and torments the fishes and eels, and the River himself. Xanthos says, his water seething, like a cauldron as its water boils and melts hog fat: I won't fight you, Hēphaistos! Let Achilles drive them out of Troy! What's it to me? He stops his pursuit, and asks Hērē why her son has picked on his stream to attack? He'll stop now, and tell Hēphaistos to stop too! And he'll swear an oath never to ward off the day of doom from the Trojans, even when the city's ablaze.

At this Hērē tells Hēphaistos to stop: it's not right to harry a god on behalf of mortals. Hēphaistos quenches his fire, and the river flows back.

383–434: These two gods stop, but the others are in noisy conflict: Zeus sitting on Olympos laughs to see them at it. Arēs attacks Athēnē, spears her aegis; Athēnē hefts a huge boundary stone and knocks Arēs down with it, exclaiming: You still haven't learned how much more warlike I am than you! This will keep your mother happy—she's furious at you for deserting the Achaians for the Trojans! Aphrodītē now leads Arēs away, groaning and short of breath. Hērē sees them, and calls to Athēnē to go after them. Athēnē does, and hits Aphrodītē in the chest: she collapses, and both she and Arēs lie there. Athēnē exclaims: May all Trojan supporters be as bold and resolute as Aphrodītē! We'd have won the war long since if they had been! Hērē smiles . . .

435–514: Poseidōn addresses Apollo: Why are we holding back? Shame on us if we return to Olympos without fighting! You begin: you're the younger. And you're a fool: have you forgotten how Zeus made us serve Laomedōn for a year? I built Ilion's ramparts, you herded Laomedōn's cattle, and then he cheated us of our agreed hire, threatened us physically? Yet you now support his people, you don't want to destroy the Trojans! Apollo replies: Earth-Shaker, if I quarreled with you over mere transient mortals you'd say I was crazy. Give over this involvement, leave them to battle on their own! Apollo says this being ashamed to fight with his own uncle. But his sister Artemis upbraids him: Running away, are you? What use is your bow now ? Don't let me ever hear you boasting again that you'd fight with Poseidōn! Apollo says nothing, but Hērē has an angry outburst at her: Want to fight me, do you? I'm no easy opponent, never mind your bow—it was women against whom Zeus made you a lion: better for you to be hunting wild beasts than fighting those stronger than yourself! Now, learn how much stronger I am than you! Hērē then grabs her wrists with one hand, and with the other beats her about the ears with her own bow and quiver. Weeping, Artemis flees, like a dove from a hawk, leaving her bow and arrows behind. At this Hermēs prudently tells Lētō that fighting Zeus's wives is unrewarding, and if she wants to say she beat him, that's fine. Lētō gathers up her daughter's archery gear, while Artemis herself runs to Zeus ("Your wife beat me!") who's highly amused.

515–611: Apollo meanwhile goes to Ilion, concerned lest the Achaians defy fate by storming the city now. The other gods join Zeus as spectators of the conflict. Achilles, like smoke from a burning city, fuelled by angry gods, continues his attack. Priam watches the rout from the walls of Troy, and calls to the gatekeepers to let the fugitives in, but to shut the gates again before Achilles can enter. They do so. Apollo, invisible by the oak tree, rouses Agēnōr to face Achilles. Agēnōr is in an agony of indecision. Shall he flee from Achilles? Then Achilles will overtake and kill him. Shall he run off to the thickets of Ida, cool off in the river, and return to Ilion in the evening? But what's the chance of Achilles not noticing and overtaking him? Oh, he reflects, what am I thinking about? Best to face him: he's human, can be wounded, is in fact mortal, even if Zeus favors him. With that he crouches ready, like a leopard that, even when speared, is ready to fight to the death. You thought you'd sack Troy today, he shouts at Achilles, but there are plenty of us here to stop you! You're the one who'll die! He throws his spear, hits Achilles' shin.

Achilles comes for him, but Apollo whisks Agēnōr to safety, hidden in mist, himself takes on Agēnōr's semblance, and leads him away in a chase over the plain, thus giving the fleeing Trojans a chance to get safely into the city.

BOOK 22

1–89: Trojans are cooling off and quenching their thirst on the battlements; Achaians are coming up to Troy, shields on their shoulders.

Hektōr is still outside Ilion, beyond the Skaian Gates. Apollo now asks Achilles why he, a mortal, is chasing him, Apollo, a god—not having recognized him as such—rather than keeping an eye on the Trojans: anyway he can't kill him. Achilles replies: You've fooled me: I'd have killed many more had it not been for you. If I had the power, I'd take my revenge on you. Achilles now moves at full speed to the city. Priam sees him first: he comes gleaming across the plain like that bright but malign harvest star called Orīōn's Dog. Priam then makes an urgent plea to Hektōr: Don't face Achilles alone, or you'll be killed! I wish *he* was dead, he's killed or sold off so many of my sons! And two more, Lykaōn and Polydōros, I don't see anywhere—if they're alive we'll ransom them, if dead, the more sorrow for us! Come inside, defend the city from here, on the ramparts! Take pity on me—Zeus will give me a bad enough death when the city falls and my sons are dead, my daughters and daughters-in-law raped, my children killed, my treasure gone: I'll be torn to pieces, an old man, by my own dogs! Nothing could be more shameful! His wife adds her own pleas; but Hektōr remains unmoved.

90–187: Achilles advances, huge and formidable. Hektōr holds his ground like an angry serpent in front of its lair. But he debates to himself: If I go inside, Poulydamas, who urged me to do just that when Achilles first rose up, will rebuke me! I should have listened to him. Now someone may say that I caused disaster by relying on my own strength. Better, then, to fight Achilles now, kill or be killed? Or should I lay aside my arms, go to him, promise to give back Helen and her possessions?

To divide up the wealth of the city? Have the Trojan elders swear to this? No, I can't approach him as a suppliant—if he doesn't pity me he may kill me, unarmed as I am, like a woman! Talk with him like a lover I can't: better to fight him, take my chances. Achilles approaches, spear in hand, bronze flashing like the sunrise. Hektōr, terrified, runs for it. Achilles pursues him like a hawk after a dove: past the fig tree and the two springs with their washing tanks, three times round the walls of Troy, running for Hektōr's life, with the gods all watching. Zeus exclaims: I'm sorry for Hektōr, who's always honored me, but with Achilles chasing him, the question is, shall we save him from death, or leave Achilles to kill him? Athēnē says: What? Rescue a mortal from his fate? If you choose to do that, you can; but we gods do *not* assent to it! Zeus replies: I'm not serious about this, and I want to be kind to you: do what you will about it. Athēnē flies down from Olympos.

188–272: Achilles continues hard in pursuit of Hektōr, who, like a deer chased by hunting dogs, isn't caught but can't get away. As in a dream, the pursuer can't catch his quarry or the quarry escape. Round they go three times, with Achilles keeping Hektōr in the plain, away from the walls. On the fourth round Zeus puts their two fates in his scales, and Hektōr's side plummets. Apollo, who's been helping him run fast, now leaves him. Athēnē comes to Achilles and says: He can't escape us now! Get your breath; I'll talk him into fighting. She then goes to Hektōr in the guise of his brother Deïphobos and says: Achilles is pressing you hard; let's both make a stand here! Achilles says: You were always my favorite brother: even more so now for daring to come outside with me. Athēnē says: Everyone begged me to stay inside! But now let's attack him! The warriors approach each other. Hektōr says: No more running away! And I swear to return your body if I win; so too do you. Achilles exclaims: We have no bond of friendship, any more than lions and men, wolves and lambs! Now you'll pay with your life for my comrades whom you killed.

273–366: Achilles throws his spear, Hektōr dodges it, Athēnē covertly picks it up and returns it to Achilles. Hektōr says: You missed! You didn't know my fate through Zeus after all. Hektōr's spear then rebounds from Achilles' shield. With no second spear, he calls to Deïphobos for one, but Deïphobos is nowhere to be seen. Hektōr instantly realizes the gods have doomed him, but determines not to die without a fight. He draws his sword and swoops like an eagle. Achilles charges him, spots a gap by the collarbone in the armor that Hektōr stripped from Patroklos, and drives his spear clean through. Hektōr falls, and Achilles boasts over him. Hektōr (the spear missed his windpipe) begs for his body to be returned home for burial, not left for the dogs to devour. Achilles says: Don't beg me! I wish I were mad enough to eat you raw myself! You're for the dogs and birds! No ransom will save you, however great. Dying, Hektōr says: I know you well. Perhaps it will be I who cause the wrath of the gods that day when Apollo and Paris kill you by the Skaian Gates. With that he dies. Achilles says: Lie dead! I'll accept my own death when the gods so say.

367–515: He pulls out his spear and starts stripping the corpse. The Achaians gather round and admire it, each one giving it a fresh wound. Hektōr's easier to deal with now than he was by the ships, they joke. When he's got off the armor, Achilles says: Now Hektōr is dead we should find out whether the Trojans still plan to hold out. And Patroklos is still unmourned, unburied! But for now we can go back to the ships with Hektōr's body, singing our victory paean! Then he lashes the body behind his chariot by its pierced heels and drags Hektōr off in the dust.

Priam and Hekabē see this; Priam, weeping, announces his determination to beg Achilles for the body; Hekabē leads the women in lamentation. Hektōr's wife, Andromachē, hears, from her loom, the sounds of mourning and rushes out: she too sees Hektōr being dragged in the dust, and she faints. When she recovers she laments the fate in store for their baby son Astyanax, robbed of a father, and cries that she'll burn all his fine clothes now, since he'll never wear them again.

BOOK 23

1–107: The rest disperse at the ships, but Achilles keeps back the Myrmidons, with their harnessed chariots, to drive three times round the body of Patroklos in mourning. The corpse of Hektōr is laid in the dust before him. Then they sit down to a funeral feast. After it the chiefs take Achilles to the hut of Agamemnōn. He refuses to wash off the blood and filth from his person until Patroklos has had formal burial.

Feasting in the evening; in the morning Agamemnōn should order men out to gather firewood and make all other preparations for Patroklos's funeral. After feasting, Achilles sleeps by the sea among his Myrmidons, and is visited by the ghost of Patroklos, who begs for proper burial, so that he can have proper admission to Hādēs, and for their bones to be buried together. Achilles tries to embrace him, but he vanishes like smoke, leaving Achilles with the reflection that yes, something survives in Hādēs, but it's terribly insubstantial.

108–248: The mourning continues all night. Men and mules go out to the forests to fell trees for the funeral pyre. Mourners cover Patroklos with their shorn hair. Achilles plans a great burial mound for both of them. The pyre is raised, sheep and cattle are sacrificed and the body wrapped in their fat. Achilles prays to the Spercheios river, dedicates his own hair, sacrifices Patroklos's own dogs and the twelve Trojan youths.

He threatens to turn Hektōr's corpse over to the dogs, but Aphrodītē and Apollo keep it undecayed and untouched by scavengers. He lights the pyre, but it refuses to kindle. He prays to the Winds for help, and Iris takes his message to them: they come and fire the pyre with a sustained gale. The blaze rages all night, while Achilles pours libations, and dies down at dawn, and the Winds go home. Achilles sleeps, but is woken by the leaders. He tells them to gather Patroklos's bones and ashes, put them in a golden casket, and bury them under a modest mound.

249–361: They do all this. When it is done, Achilles brings out prizes for the funeral games: cauldrons, tripods, horses, mules, oxen, women, pig iron, gold. First comes the chariot race. Achilles would himself have won it, he says, with his immortal team, had he competed. But now others must try. Eumēlos, Diomēdēs, Menelaös, Antilochos, and Mērionēs all come forward. Nestōr advises his son Antilochos, whose horses are not the best there, to keep close to the marker at the turning point, and drive cleverly. They draw lots for positions at the start.

362–538: The race takes place. As they near the turn by the sea Eumēlos moves into first place, with Diomēdēs close behind and threatening to overtake him. But Apollo knocks the whip from Diomēdēs' hand. Athēnē gives the whip back to him, strengthens his horses, then wrecks Eumēlos's chariot. Diomēdēs and Menelaös drive on past. Antilochos urges on his horses, passes Menelaös off-track, dangerously, despite Menelaös's enraged objections. Back at the finishing line Idomeneus says he thinks he's seen Diomēdēs leading the pack. Aias (2) says, No way, big mouth, it has to be Eumēlos. Achilles stops them quarrelling. Then Diomēdēs indeed comes in first, followed by Antilochos, with Menelaös close behind, Mērionēs trailing a spear cast behind him, and Eumēlos last of all, on foot and dragging his chariot. Achilles tells them to give Eumēlos the second-place prize, since he's by far the best.

539–650: General agreement, but Antilochos objects: I came in second, he may be good but he overturned. Give him a special prize if you like, but the mare for second place is mine. Achilles smiles, and agrees to do that. He gives Eumēlos a corselet he won. But now Menelaös raises his own objection, and calls for a judgment: Antilochos, he says, got ahead of him with inferior horses by trickery and cheating. Let him declare on oath whether he did or not! Antilochos says: I'm younger than you: you know what a young man's offenses can be! I'll give you the mare, and more of my own if you want, rather than be estranged from you and the gods! Menelaös, warmed and touched, says: I give up my anger! Just don't try to con your betters! And though the mare is mine, I'll let you keep it! Mērionēs now takes fourth-place prize; the fifth is unclaimed, and Achilles gives it to Nestōr as a memento. Nestōr thanks him with a long rambling anecdote about his one-time prowess at the games.

651–739: Achilles now sets out prizes for boxing. Epeios admits inferiority as a warrior, but asserts that no one will beat him as a boxer, and that the next of kin should be on hand to carry his victim out. Euryalos stands up, who'd once defeated all the sons of Kadmos at the funeral of Oidipous (Oedipus), with Diomēdēs as his backer. Epeios knocks him out and claims the prize. The next prizes are for wrestling: Aias takes on Odysseus, and the two struggle mightily, close gripped like a high house's cross-beams carpentered to resist gales, but neither can gain the mastery, and Achilles declares the bout a draw, with equal prizes.

740–897: Next comes the footrace, with a silver mixing bowl, a fat ox, and a half-talent of gold as prizes. Aias son of Oïleus, Odysseus, and Antilochos compete. Aias leads, with Odysseus as close behind him as a weaving rod is to the weaver's breast at the loom. Odysseus prays to Athēnē, who both gives him extra strength and tips Aias headlong in the cattle dung from Achilles' bull sacrifice. Aias knows, and says, spitting out dung, that Odysseus has had Athēnē's help, but everyone laughs at him. Antilochos gracefully compliments the older Odysseus—only Achilles could have beaten him. Achilles, flattered, adds another half-talent of gold to his third prize. Then it's the turn of the armed warriors' duel, and here Aias son of Telamōn and Diomēdēs compete. They fight violently; the Achaians, scared for Aias, stop the fight. Both get armor, but Diomēdēs is also given the sword that was the original prize. For the shot-putters, the prize is a great mass of pig iron, which also serves as the shot. Polypoitēs, Leonteus, Epeios, and Aias son of Telamōn compete. Everyone laughs at Epeios's effort. Polypoitēs far out-throws all the rest, and wins the prize. For archers, the target is a live dove tied to a cord that's attached to a ship's mast: prizes, ten double and ten single iron axes. Teukros and Mēriones compete. Teukros forgets to vow Apollo a sacrifice, misses the dove but severs the cord. Mēriones has an arrow ready, snatches the bow from Teukros, offers Apollo a sacrifice, and hits the dove in midair. He gets the double axes. Finally, for the spear throwing, Achilles gives the first prize, a cauldron, without competition to Agamemnōn, on reputation alone. Mēriones gets the second prize, a bronze spear.

BOOK 24

1–119: All the others eat and turn in for the night, but Achilles remains sleepless, tossing and turning, then wanders along the shore, till dawn, mourning Patroklos. He ties Hektor behind his chariot again, drags him three times around the burial mound, and leaves him lying there when he goes back to rest. But Apollo keeps his flesh undecayed, wrapped in the aegis. The gods pity Hektōr and urge Hermēs to steal his body. All, that is, except Poseidōn and Hērē and Athēnē, who still hate the Trojans because of the insult to them in the Judgment of Paris. On the twelfth day Apollo upbraids them as hard-hearted: Did Hektōr never sacrifice to you? Why do you support Achilles now? He's mad, obsessional, pitiless. Most mourners weep and that's that. But this man trails the corpse round his comrade's tomb—no honor in that! He should beware: we could grow angry with him. He's outraging the earth!

Hērē says to Apollo: Yes, if you grant Hektōr and Achilles equal honor: but while Hektōr's mortal, Achilles is the son of a goddess, and we were all at the wedding—you too! Zeus says: These two don't have equal honor, but Hektōr was dear to the gods, certainly to me, to whom he always sacrificed. And let's hear no more about stealing his corpse—Achilles would know at once because of Thetis his mother. So, call Thetis here: I want to have her persuade Achilles to return Hektōr's body to Priam for ransom. Iris fetches Thetis from the deep sea, and she joins the gods' assembly. Zeus tells her the gods want to remove the body, and that she must persuade her son to give it back to Priam; Iris meanwhile must tell Priam to go to the ships with an offer of ransom.

120–264: Thetis goes back to Achilles, who is still lamenting, while his companions prepare the morning meal. She says: How long will you go on like this? You need to eat, to have a woman—you're not long for this life! Zeus and the gods are angry with you for not returning Hektōr's body. Give him up, accept ransom! Achilles says: If that's so, if Zeus so orders, then whoever brings ransom can have him. Meanwhile Zeus sends Iris to Troy to tell Priam to amass ransom and go alone to the ships, with just a elderly herald to drive the loaded mule wagon and return with the body. Hermēs will guide him, and Achilles won't kill him, or let anyone else do so: he respects suppliants. Iris goes and finds Priam, filth-stained, mourning with his family. She passes on Zeus's message and leaves. Priam tells his sons to ready the wagon. He then goes to his treasure chamber, telling his wife Hekabē what he's planning. She screams and tries to deter him—so ruthless is Achilles: were it possible she would eat his heart raw! Priam says: Don't try to stop me; a goddess it was gave the orders. If I can have my son back, then Achilles can kill me if he so chooses. He then picks out the ransom: fine robes, rugs, ten talents of gold, tripods, cauldrons, a beautiful Thracian cup. With his staff he drives the Trojans away from his courtyard. Then he calls on his sons, with many insults—all the best are dead—to hurry up and get the wagon ready, and load the ransom onto it.

265–439: Priam's sons bring out the wagon, yoke the mules, and load the treasure. Hekabē tells Priam to make libation and pray to Zeus for a favorable sign. He does so, and Zeus sends a black eagle on the right. Seeing it, they rejoice. The wagon then leaves Troy, driven by Idaios the herald: the family members seeing them off now turn back. Zeus now tells Hermēs to accompany them as a guide and helper. Hermēs puts on his winged sandals, takes his wand of sleep, and goes, disguised as an aristocratic youth. He finds the mules being watered at the river. Priam and Idaios are scared. Hermēs puts them at ease, offers to help and defend them. Priam says the gods must be looking out for them to send such a fine youth their way. Where are you taking this treasure, Hermēs asks. Are you fleeing the city, or storing your goods now your son Hektōr is dead? Who are you, Priam asks. An attendant of Achilles, Hermēs says. At dawn the Achaians plan to attack the city. Priam asks: Is my son still there by the ships or has he been given to the dogs? No, Hermēs says, he's not devoured, he's still by the ships, and his flesh hasn't rotted after twelve days, nor have maggots got into it! He's still fresh, he's free of bloodstains, his wounds are closed—he was dear to the gods, they're taking care of him. Priam says, that shows how right my son was always to remember what was due to them! So, here's this cup I'll give you, if you'll be our guide till we reach Achilles' hut. Hermēs says: You're testing me, trying to make me take gifts behind Achilles' back! I'll gladly be your guide, though, on land or at sea.

440–558: With that Hermēs takes over the driving of the wagon. He puts the meal-busy guards at the wall to sleep, then slides back the bar and opens the gates. They then drive in, and Hermēs also opens the gateway to the palisaded enclosure the Myrmidons built for Achilles, drawing back the bar it took three men (except for Achilles) to shift. He then brings in the ransom and leaves for Olympos, saying he is Hermēs, and that it's improper for a god to be entertained by mortals. Priam leaves Idaios with the horses and mules, and goes into the hut, where Achilles has just eaten, and is being attended by Automedōn and Alkimos. Priam clasps Achilles' knees, and kisses his slaughterer's hands. All are amazed. He begs Achilles to think of his own father, and rehearses his own miseries, not least the death of Hektōr, announces he's come with ransom for the body, urges Achilles to respect the gods and pity him. They both weep: Priam for Hektōr, Achilles for both Pēleus and Patroklos. Finally Achilles, astonished that Priam has dared come, calls for a truce to mourning: men get whatever Zeus gives, good and bad: Pēleus too. Priam too was once fortunate, but now—! Give over; you won't bring your son back that way. Don't grovel, get up, take a seat. Priam refuses to sit while Hektōr remains untended. Return the body, he says, and quickly: accept my ransom.

559–676: Don't provoke me, Achilles says. My mother brought me Zeus's fiat: I intend to return Hektōr to you! And I know some god brought you here: you'd never have made it otherwise! So annoy me no further—I might ignore your suppliant status, and Zeus's fiat! Priam obeys. Automedōn and Alkimos unyoke the horses and mules and bring in the herald, along with the ransom, except enough apparel to shroud the corpse in. Achilles orders the handmaids to wash and dress the body elsewhere, to avoid arousing Priam's wrath so that Achilles would be driven to kill him. The body is then set on a bier and the bier on the wagon. Achilles apologizes to the ghost of Patroklos for what he is doing. He then goes back in, tells Priam his son is ready on a bier to be removed in the morning. But for now, you should eat, he says: even Niobē took food after her children were all killed by Apollo and Artemis! Keep your mourning for when you're back in Ilion. So they eat supper, and eye each other, marveling. Priam says: I need to sleep. This is the first I'll have eaten or slept since my son's death. Achilles has beds made up out in the portico, explaining to Priam that he sometimes gets late-night visitors from among the Achaians, who might, seeing Priam, tell Agamemnōn, who might well be less accommodating over the body. He then asks: How many days do you need for Hektōr's proper funeral? Priam says: Nine days to gather wood for the pyre and to mourn him. Funeral and feast on the tenth; actual burial on the eleventh. Back to warfare, if we have to, on the twelfth. Agreed, Achilles says, and clasps hands on it. Then they both sleep, Priam outside, Achilles with Briseïs.

677–804: Hermēs now ponders how to get Priam and the body away unnoticed. He stands over Priam and tells him: Get up and be on your way now you've ransomed your son! If Agamemnōn or the others find out you're here, it'll cost three times as much to ransom you yourself! Priam wakes, terrified, and rouses Idaios the herald. Meanwhile Hermēs yokes up horses and mules, and drives them out unseen as dawn breaks, leaving them for Olympos when they reach the Xanthos river. Priam and Idaios then drive chariot and wagon back to Troy. Only Kassandrē sees them, but she then arouses the Trojans, and a crowd gathers at the gates to welcome Priam, led by Andromachē and Hekabē. Andromachē laments: Hektōr, you leave me a young widow, with a baby son. Who will save Troy now? The city will be destroyed, I shall be sold into servitude, and my son will either go likewise or be murdered!

Then Hekabē: Hektor, dearest of my sons, the gods looked after you! My other sons Achilles sold abroad; but though he dragged you round Patroklos's tomb, that still didn't bring Patroklos back, and despite it all your body's still fresh! Then it was Helen's turn: In all the time I've been in Troy, Hektōr, I've never had anything but kindness from you, and you stopped the unkindness of others as well. So I weep for you and myself: everyone here now hates me! Priam then gives orders for fetching timber, since Achilles has guaranteed a truce. For nine days they collect it. On the tenth they set Hektōr on the pyre, and light it. On the eleventh they gather the bones in a golden urn, and bury them. Finally they celebrate a funeral feast in Priam's home. Hektōr's burial is complete.

Select Glossary

NOTE: This glossary is mostly limited to the names of people and places that play a sufficient part in the narrative of the *Iliad* to arouse the reader's or listener's interest. It does not include all the many victims slaughtered on both sides, who for the most part exist only as names, sometimes with a brief biography attached. The same is true of a host of attendant nymphs. In general, main characters excepted, I ignore any name for which the evidence comes only from the poem itself.

ABANTES A people of the island of EUBOIA, they are skilled at hand-to-hand fighting and notable (2.542) for wearing what are apparently long pigtails.

ACHAIA (AHHIYAWA), ACHAIANS Achaia seems to have been originally the northern Achaia in PHTHIŌTIS, home of ACHILLES. For Homer, "Achaians", like ARGIVES and DANAÄNS, has become a term loosely equivalent to "Hellenes", that is, Greeks, in historical times. To the Hittites, Ahhiyawa was a powerful kingdom; it was seemingly located on the Greek mainland and is now generally agreed to be identical to Achaia (Latacz 2004, 121–28). How far south this kingdom extended is uncertain.

ACHELŌÏOS Both a river and a river god (21.194), the offspring of OCEAN and Tethys. Homer mentions two rivers of this name: the more important one (though not located) in Akarnania (a mountainous district in northwestern Greece), and the other in Asia Minor, near Sipylos.

ACHILLES Son of PĒLEUS and the divine sea nymph THETIS, unrivalled ACHAIAN warrior from PHTHIĒ in THESSALY, leader of the MYRMIDONS, and the central figure in the drama of the *Iliad*. Early details about him known from other sources such as his physical invulnerability and his posthumous translation by THETIS to immortality on the White Island (Leukē) are not mentioned in the *Iliad* (*Aethiopis* arg. 4 = West 2003 [A], 112–13). His rage or wrath (*mēnis*) is appropriate given the divine element in his blood, since it is a kind of intense fury most often found elsewhere among the gods. Disillusioned with the whole epic notion of heroism, of fighting for honor and *kléos* (glory), since heroes and cowards now, he argues (9.318–20) get equal honor and all die anyway, he toys with the idea of going home to PHTHIĒ and leading a long peaceful life. It is the death of his beloved comrade PATROKLOS that spurs him on to embrace the short glorious life that is fated for him, and now his motive is simply revenge, exemplified by his abuse of Hektōr's corpse (22.395–404). It takes his confrontation with HEKTŌR's father PRIAM, come to ransom his son's body (24.477–551), to make him recognize their common humanity and sorrow; and even this encounter has to be organized—and insisted on—by ZEUS (24.103–19). His death at the SKAIAN GATES, shot by PARIS ALÉXANDROS at the instigation of APOLLO, is prophesied by the dying HEKTŌR (22.359–60) but takes place (*Aethiopis* arg. 3 = West 2003 [A], 112–13) after the conclusion of the *Iliad*.

AEGEAN SEA The extension of the Mediterranean delimited to the west by the Greek mainland, to the south by the great island of KRĒTĒ (CRETE), to the east by the coast of Asia Minor, from the AEOLIS down to CARIA, and in the north by Macedonia and the Chalcidic peninsula (see map), and enclosing numerous islands, in particular those of the archipelago in the southern Aegean known as the Cyclades.

AEGIS A magical object, possessed by ATHĒNĒ and ZEUS (who lends his to APOLLO, 15.219–30) of which the exact appearance is never fully clarified. It is made of material, most probably goatskin, and has been likened to a large bib or shawl, draped round the shoulders (5.738). It is ageless, immortal, fringed with gold tassels, and of great value (2.447–49). It is decorated with the Gorgon's head and with allegorical figures such as Valor and Rout, appropriate for the battlefield, where it is most frequently used in the *Iliad*, being shaken out like a standard (15.229–30, 17.593–96) to encourage the side the god favors, to terrify their enemies, and to protect individuals. In this last capacity Apollo uses it (24.18–21) to cover HEKTŌR's dead body and keep it from defilement as ACHILLES drags it behind his chariot: just how, we are not told, nor whether Achilles can see it. See also book 2, note 2.

AEOLIS That portion of the Asia Minor coast from the entrance of the HELLESPONT south as far as the Hermos river (thus including the TROAD, q.v.).

AGAMEMNŌN Son of ATREUS and brother of MENELAÖS: married to HELEN's sister KLYTAIMNĒSTRA, and the father of ORESTĒS and at least three daughters, including IPHIGENEIA. The commander in chief of the ACHAIAN expedition to TROY, and thus characterized as "lord of men" (*anax andrōn*), he is by turns arrogant, clumsy, aggressive, insulting, and panic-stricken, characteristics that determine his actions throughout the *Iliad*. Despite this, and accusations of cowardice, he proves himself (11.91–263) a fine warrior in battle and an expert spearman. Much of the trouble he incurs is due to his excessive concern for his own aristocratic status. The nervous apologia he makes for his own behavior (19.78–144) is typical. Impulsive and tactless, given to fits of despair, he nevertheless recognizes his own faults in the quarrel with ACHILLES, and he more than once (e.g., at 9.115–61) at length declares himself willing to make ample amends. The notorious deed that eventually leads to his murder by his wife after his return home (*Od.* 11.405–35), the sacrifice of

IPHIGENEIA to appease ARTEMIS, is not mentioned in the *Iliad*, although his anger at KALCHAS the priest (who called for the sacrifice) as having never brought anything good to pass, only disasters (1.108–9) may hint at this episode.

AGĒNŌR A leading Trojan warrior, the son of ANTĒNŌR and the priestess Theanō, he scores the first kill recorded (4.469) for the Trojans, and alone stands up to ACHILLES in the great battle by the SKAMANDROS river. He is unsuccessful, but APOLLO wafts him off the battlefield, and then, assuming his likeness, lures Achilles away from pursuit of the routed Trojans (21.544–611).

AHHIYAWA See s.v. ACHAIA.

AIAKOS Father of PĒLEUS and TELAMŌN, and thus grandfather to ACHILLES. He himself was a son of ZEUS by a nymph, Aigina, daughter of the ASŌPOS river; according to one tradition he was connected with AIGINA the island before it was inhabited, and ZEUS supposedly created a population for his benefit (Hes. *Cat.* fr. 145 Most 2.212–13) from the local ants (*myrmēkes*), which became the MYRMIDONS (q.v.) and accompanied the family to PHTHIĒ in THESSALY, where it was well established by Pēleus's day.

AIAS (1) Son of TELAMŌN, known as "the Greater" to distinguish him from AIAS (2), together with whom he frequently fights; they are a kind of double turn (bracketed by Homer through the use of the dual to describe them as a pair). He is notably huge and strong, and carries a large (anachronistic) shield, which he uses (17.128–38) to protect the body of PATROKLOS. As a warrior he is regarded as second only to ACHILLES, and perhaps on that account, he is also part of the diplomatic embassy (9.182–655) that attempts to bring ACHILLES back into the war. His end takes place beyond the time frame of the *Iliad*. After ACHILLES' death, AIAS and ODYSSEUS rescue his body and bring it back to the ACHAIAN camp; but at the funeral games the prize for bravery, consisting of the arms of ACHILLES, is awarded to ODYSSEUS rather than to him; as a result he goes mad and commits suicide (*Little Iliad*, arg. 1 = West 2003 [A], 120–21). He never forgives his rival even in the underworld (*Od.* 11.543–64).

AIAS (2) Son of OÏLEUS, LOKRIAN hero, known as "the Lesser" to distinguish him from the son of Telamōn, AIAS (1), but a member of AGAMEMNŌN'S council of war and a formidable warrior in his own right. He emerges with the highest headcount of slain Trojans in the *Iliad* (Polinskaya, *HE* 1: 26). His rape of KASSANDRĒ at the sack of Troy (*Sack of Ilion* arg. 3 = West 2003 [A], 146–47) is not referred to. He dies at the hand of POSEIDŌN on the way home from Troy (*Od.* 4.99–511, *Returns* arg. 3 = West 2003 [A], 154–55).

AIGINA Island in the Saronic Gulf, roughly halfway between Attica and Epidauros. In the CATALOGUE OF SHIPS (2.559–64) it figures as part of the ARGOLID controlled by DIOMĒDĒS.

AINEIAS Son of ANCHĪSĒS by the goddess APHRODĪTĒ, and (like his second cousin PRIAM) descended from Dardanos and the Trojan royal line, though through Kapys rather than LAOMEDŌN. He bears a permanent grievance at not receiving from PRIAM the honor that he feels is his due (13.460–61, cf. 20.178–83). Despite his reputation as a warrior second only to HEKTŌR (6.78–79 and elsewhere) he does not figure very impressively in battle (e.g., 5.297–318, 20.86–102): on the other hand, his standing with the gods is marked by the number of times they rescue him when he is in trouble: his mother saves him from DIOMĒDĒS (5.311–17), and so does APOLLO (5.431–47); POSEIDŌN spirits him away through the air from ACHILLES (20.318–39), prophesying that he will rule over the TROJANS. He escapes from TROY at the time of its sack. His lasting fame is owing, not so much to the *Iliad*, as to the Roman tradition, promoted by Virgil in the *Aeneid*, of his emigration to Italy and foundation there of the port city Lavinium and the *gens Iulia* (thus figuring as the ancestor of Caesar and Augustus), leading eventually to the foundation of Rome itself.

AITŌLIA A rugged, mountainous area of west central Greece, adjacent to Akarnania, the Gulf of Corinth, and the ACHELŌÏOS RIVER. The Aitōlians are listed in the CATALOGUE OF SHIPS (2.638–44) as contributing forty vessels to the expedition against TROY, and their battle with the Kourētes is described at length by PHOINIX (9.529–99).

ALÉXANDROS See s.v. PARIS/ALÉXANDROS.

ALKMĒNĒ Daughter of Elektryōn, married to Amphitryōn, mother of Iphiklēs, and (by ZEUS, who seduces her disguised as her husband) of HĒRAKLĒS (14.323–24). HĒRĒ, determined to thwart Zeus's plan for Hēraklēs to become king of the Argolid, holds up his birth until after that of his cousin EURYSTHEUS (19.95–125); as an adult Hēraklēs (about whom the *Iliad* displays more knowledge than it does about most of the earlier generation of mythical heroes) is indentured to Eurystheus to perform the Twelve Labors (variously referred to at 8.363, 367–69; 15.30, 639; 19.114–24, 133).

ALPHEIOS The largest river in the PELOPONNESE: rising in the mountains of ARCADIA it flows west-northwest past Olympia and Elis, forming the northern boundary of NESTŌR's kingdom of PYLOS and discharging into the IONIAN SEA. Also recognized by Homer (11.727) as a river god.

ALTHAIĒ Daughter of Thestios, married to Oineus, king of Kalydōn, and mother of MELEAGROS, whom she curses for the killing of her brother in a fight over the Kalydōnian boar; her curse is heard by the FURIES (9.567–72).

AMAZONS A mythical race of warrior women, traditionally descended from ARĒS, and located in Anatolia, near the Sangarios river, which was where PRIAM (3.186–89) fought them in his youth. BELLEROPHŌN also defeated them (6.186). In both cases Homer describes them as *antianeíras*, "a match for men".

ANCHĪSĒS Son of Kapys, descendant of TRŌS, and by APHRODĪTĒ father of AINEIAS. During the TROJAN WAR he is an elderly man (17.324); the tradition regarding his escape at the time of the city's sack is familiar from Virgil's *Aeneid*. Homer has a reference to his mortal wife (13.429–33) and to a daughter, Hippodameia.

ANDROMACHĒ Daughter of ĒETIŌN, king (6.396–97) of THĒBĒ (2); married to HEKTŌR (22.468–72), with whom she comes to TROY, and mother of a baby son, called by his parents Skamandrios, but known to the Trojans as Astyanax, "lord of the city" (6.402–3). Her fear, after Hektōr's death, that the child will be flung from the battlements when the city is captured (24.726–38) is all too prescient (*Little Iliad*, fr. 29 = West 2003 [A], 140–41): this scene (with ACHILLES' son NEOPTOLEMOS—who also got Andromachē as war booty—doing the deed) is a favorite with both black- and red-figure Athenian vase-painters (Anderson, *HE* 1: 107). The strong and loving relationship between husband and wife is wonderfully conveyed in their all-too-brief meeting with their son (6.390–493) near the gates of Troy. The scene (22.437–516) in which Andromachē first learns of Hektōr's death is equally powerful and moving.

ANTĒNŌR A Trojan elder, married to the priestess Theanō (6.295–300); he is most notable for unsuccessfully advocating the return of HELEN to the ACHAIANS (7.347–53).

ANTILOCHOS A son of NESTŌR, an aristocrat who distinguishes himself, though comparatively young, among the various ACHAIAN warriors. He comes into dramatic prominence relatively late. It is he who brings news of the death of PATROKLOS to ACHILLES (18.2–21). At Patroklos's funeral games, he is carefully coached for the chariot race by his father (23.306–48), interprets the advice in a somewhat questionable way, and wins (23.373–447). Challenged by MENELAÖS, he backs down charmingly, and ends by keeping his prize. Last in the foot-race, he elegantly flatters Achilles, who doubles his consolation prize (23. 785–97). He is also, famously, the only character in the entire *Iliad* who, just once (23.555), makes Achilles smile. He is killed (after the close of the *Iliad*) by Memnōn, son of the DAWN (*Od.* 4.186–87; *Aethiopis* arg. 2, 4 = West 2003 [A], 112–13).

APHRODĪTĒ Goddess of erotic desire, well established in the Hellenic pantheon by Homer's time. Neither her birth nor her origins are certain. According to Homer, she was the child of ZEUS by Diōnē; in Hesiod (*Th.* 190–206) she is sired by the foam (*aphros*) round the genitals of Ouranos, thrown into the sea by his son KRONOS after the latter had cut them off, which suggests an older, more primitive tradition, against which Homer may be reacting. The *Iliad* knows about her affair with ANCHĪSĒS (which produced AINEIAS), and of her calamitous role in the JUDGMENT OF PARIS (not least her having made HELEN unable to resist Paris's advances in return for his vote rating her beauty above that of HĒRĒ and ATHĒNĒ, thus precipitating the TROJAN WAR). Cf. 2.819–21, 24.25–30.

Throughout the *Iliad* Aphrodītē is viewed, not unreasonably, as a disconcerting mixture of dangerous power and adolescent silliness. She uses her magic to rescue PARIS when he's about to be killed in a duel by MENELAÖS, and wafts him back home to have sex with Helen—who still, clearly, can't resist him, and hates herself for it (3. 377–448). Aphrodītē rescues her bastard son AINEIAS from DIOMĒDĒS, and starts to carry him off the battlefield; but Diomēdēs attacks and wounds her, with loud insults, so that she drops Aineias (who is rescued by APOLLO), borrows ARĒS' chariot, and drives home to OLYMPOS to seek comfort from Daddy (Zeus) and Mommy (Diōnē), like any teenage girl, while Athēnē and Hērē mock her (5.311–429: so much for the Judgment of Paris!). Both silliness and power are to the fore when Hērē borrows Aphrodītē's magic to produce (for her own nefarious purposes) an irresistible urge for sex in Zeus (14.187–223). In the Battle of the Gods, Aphrodītē is rudely beaten up by Athēnē (21.415–26). To Homer, it is her childishness that makes her enormous power (through the ability to manipulate the male sexual drive) so perilous: this, after all, is what, in the last resort, underlies the unstoppable waste and futility of the Trojan War—this, and the PLAN OF ZEUS. In an unlooked-for sense, Aphrodītē is very much her father's daughter.

APOLLO The son of ZEUS and Lētō, who bore him on the AEGEAN island of Dēlos, which, like Delphi, became one of his major sanctuaries. The *Iliad* makes clear that by Homer's time, Apollo's cult was widespread (though his name, unlike those of several other Hellenic deities, does not figure in the MYCENAEAN LINEAR B tablets). The main myths regarding him are well known. He is regularly portrayed as young, handsome, and beardless. His many special powers and interests include archery, disease and healing, and music and poetry: he is associated with the lyre, rather than with the wilder wind and percussion instruments. Yet his civilization has its limits. His first introduction in the *Iliad* shows him (1.8–53) physically shooting arrows bearing plague into the ACHAIAN troops (a nice instance of the way Homer retains an archaic reified concept of things later regarded as no more than immanent if not actually abstract), in reprisal for the insulting dismissal by AGAMEMNŌN of Apollo's priest CHRYSES.

Throughout the poem, in fact, Apollo remains consistently on the side of the TROJANS. On the battlefield he rescues AINEIAS, and takes him to his own Trojan shrine, where Lētō AND his twin sister ARTEMIS (who are as pro-Trojan as he is) magically nurse him back to health (5.344–45, 431–48). He is directly responsible for the death of PATROKLOS, dealing him a dizzying blow from behind (16.786–805) that leaves him helpless and vulnerable (cf. also 700–711). He keeps HEKTŌR's dead body free from decay and mutilation (24.18–21), and fulminates against the other gods (24.33–54) for standing by during the abuse of the corpse by ACHILLES—a tirade that indirectly leads (Graf, *HE* 1: 66) to the ransoming of Hektōr by PRIAM. His main opponent on OLYMPOS is ATHĒNĒ, whose pro-Achaian stance is still seemingly fuelled by resentment at the long-past JUDGMENT OF PARIS. Graf (ibid.) goes on to point out that since LAOMEDŌN cheated both Apollo and his uncle POSEIDŌN of their due hire for building the walls of TROY and guarding his cattle during the building, Apollo should logically be anti- rather than pro-Trojan (as Poseidōn reminds him, 21. 444–60). However, he draws the line at actual combat with his uncle (21.461–66).

ARCADIA A mountainous and poverty-stricken inland region of the north-central PELOPONNESE. Arcadians were traditionally regarded as pre-DORIANS, and their dialect differed sharply from that of other Peloponnesians. No seafarers, they nevertheless brought sixty ships to Troy (supplied them by AGAMEMNŌN: 2. 603–14).

ARĒS Son of ZEUS and HĒRĒ, but essentially marginal (indeed, almost mortal: 5.388–91), and thoroughly disliked by his divine father (5.887–93), Arēs is the god of the more brutal and thuggish aspects of warfare (in contrast to his opponent ATHĒNĒ, "who represents the intelligent and orderly use of war to defend the *polis*" (Graf, *OCD*[3] 153). In the *Iliad* he fights—by no means always successfully—on the side of the TROJANS. Wounded by DIOMĒDĒS, he bellows "as loud as the war-cry of nine thousand—no, ten thousand—fighting troops" (5.859–61). Hit in the neck by a well-aimed rock from Athēnē, he sprawls out over seven furlongs in the dust (21.406–14), and she laughs at the sight. There is something inherently ridiculous about Arēs. He goes whining to Zeus like a child (5.867–86); when, in the *Odyssey*, he's snared in bed with APHRODĪTĒ by her outraged husband HĒPHAISTOS, all the gods come and mock the guilty pair (*Od.* 8.266–343). Yet he is described as "a glutton for war" (5.388) or, regularly, as "ruin of mortals"; he is accompanied in battle(4.440, 11.37, 15.119) by *Deimos* (Terror) and *Phobos* (Rout), the surprisingly abstract offspring from his coupling with Aphrodītē; his very name is used as shorthand for "war frenzy", while the *mōlos Arēos* (perhaps literally Arēs' mill) is the "grind of battle" (2.401).

ARGOLID, THE Extended peninsula south of CORINTH (KORINTHOS) and west of the Saronic Gulf, mostly mountainous except for its coastline and the large and fertile ARGIVE plain at the head of the Gulf of ARGOS. This plain was the site of several major Mycenaean sites, including MYKĒNAI (MYCENAE) and TIRYNS. In the *Iliad* the Argolid is divided between two dominant kingdoms, that extend beyond its boundaries: those of DIOMĒDĒS and AGAMEMNŌN. The first, based on Argos, includes most of the Argolid, including Troizēn and Epidauros; the second, ruled from Mykēnai, extends northward into Corinthian territory. See the CATALOGUE OF SHIPS, 2.559–61, 569–75. Both suggest Dorian manipulation in the Archaic Age (Finkelberg 2005, 171).

ARGOS, ARGIVES The pre-DORIAN MYCENAEAN city of Argos, at the southern end of the Argive plain in the northeastern PELOPONNESE, flourished c. 1350–1200 B.C.E., and in the *Iliad* forms the capital of the kingdom of DIOMĒDĒS. The later Dorian occupants seem to have appropriated some of this Mycenaean tradition. To complicate the picture further, "ARGIVES" is one of the three generic terms (the others being "ACHAIANS"—the most popular—and "DANAÄNS") used in the *Iliad* to describe members of the force attacking TROY, which is to say, in the loosest sense, Homeric Greeks. Indicative of a more limited geographical sense are phrases such as "ACHAIAN Argos" (the Argolid or Argive valley) and "Pelasgian Argos" (southern THESSALY, the home of ACHILLES: Finkelberg, *HE* 1: 87).

ARISTEIA The concentrated formal description, sometimes at considerable length, of the arming, military successes, and climactic crisis of a single warrior performing at his best (from Greek *aristos*, "best"). Mueller (*HE* 1: 89) well compares the aristeia to "a solo in a concerto." The four major aristeias are those of DIOMĒDĒS (5.1–8, 84–352,

431–44), AGAMEMNŌN (11.15–46, 84–180, 218–83), PATROKLOS (16.130–54, 364–507, 553–87, 684–857), and ACHILLES (20.156–503; 21. 17–382, 520–611).

ARTEMIS Daughter of ZEUS and Lētō, and twin sister of APOLLO, Artemis has signs, even in Homer, of great antiquity: not least the title "Lady of Beasts" (*Potnia Thērōn*, 21.470), which suggests MYCENAEAN, even possibly MINOAN, antecedents. Despite this, she does not figure prominently in the *Iliad*. Like her mother and brother, she is very much on the TROJAN side. She helps nurse the wounded AINEIAS (5.445–48). When her brother chooses not to fight his uncle POSEIDŌN she angrily accuses him of cowardice (21.468–77) and gets banged around the ears by HĒRĒ for her pains with her own bow and arrows (21.479–504). This hardly enhances her tradition in myth as virgin huntress, protector of women in childbirth, and presider over their various *rites de passage*, not least that from maidenhood to marriage. Homer rather emphasizes her role as a death-bringing deity: like her brother, Artemis is a "deadly archer". Together the two of them (as ACHILLES recalls, 24.602–9) shot to death the numerous brood of Niobē's children, Artemis taking care of the girls while Apollo did away with the boys. She is also on record (without explanation) as having killed the mothers of both SARPĒDŌN and HEKTŌR's wife ANDROMACHĒ (6.205, 428). See also s.v. ASKLĒPIOS.

ASINĒ A MYCENAEAN and Archaic site in the Argolid, on a rugged promontory near Tolō and Nauplion: given modern prominence by George Seferis's famous poem "The King of Asine" (Seferis 259–65), where it is referred to as "only one word in the *Iliad* and that uncertain" (in the CATALOGUE OF SHIPS, 2.560). Conquered by ARGOS c. 700, it survived into the Hellenistic period.

ASKLĒPIOS Homer knows him only as a "peerless healer" (4.194, 11.518), taught by the Centaur CHEIRŌN (4.219), and the father of two noted healers at TROY, Machaōn and Podaleirios (2.731–32), from THESSALY (2.729–33). The *Iliad* has no mention of his parentage (APOLLO and the nymph Korōnis), of his dramatic birth (snatched from his mother's womb on her funeral pyre: Apollo had sent ARTEMIS to kill Korōnis for suspected infidelity), or of his death by ZEUS's thunderbolt (he had become so famous a healer that he even attempted to raise the dead: Zeus killed him for trying to nullify inexorable FATE: see Gantz 91 with ref.)

ASŌPOS The main river of BOIŌTIA, flowing eastward from Thespiai through a gorge near Tanagra and discharging into the river Euripos near Orōpos (4.383, 10.287). Homer's description of it as reed-thick with grassy banks still holds good.

ATHĒNĒ Favorite daughter of ZEUS, born from his head (though this is never specifically stated in the *Iliad*, frequent though her presence is throughout) without any mother (Gantz 51–52 with ref.). ARĒS, when remonstrating with Zeus about her encouragement of DIOMĒDĒS' killing spree (5.871–86) nevertheless comes very close when he says (874–75): "We're all at war with you, for *you bore* [*tékes*] this mad accursed / daughter of yours . . ." She is early established: in the MYCENAEAN LINEAR B tablets there is an *a-ta-na po-ti-ni-ja* who may well be *Athēnē Potnia*, Lady Athēnē. Several of her epithets are of doubtful meaning: again, a sign of antiquity

(Is *glaukōpis* "grey-eyed", "bright-eyed", or "owl-eyed"? All are possible). More formidable on account of her close, and indeed unique, relationship with Zeus, Athēnē is a virgin warrior goddess, who wears armor as well as her terrifying AEGIS, and stands, sometimes disguised, as helper and ally, beside those mortal men whom she favors (e.g., DIOMĒDĒS and ODYSSEUS), and over whom she watches carefully (e.g., in the night-raid on the Thracians, 10.278–91). Having not experienced normal childbirth, she undertakes masculine actions with no hesitation; yet she also possesses female skills. Besides making clothes (5.733–37) she is an expert in, and patron of, skills such as weaving, pottery, carpentry, and metalworking. Both sides are to the fore in her role as city protector, Athēnē Polias.

Her relationship to ATHENS is more ambiguous than might be supposed. Though her name and that of the city are virtually identical, and the CATALOGUE OF SHIPS insists (2.546–51) that she nurtured Athens's early earth-born mythical king ERECHTHEUS, the Athenians are considerably more interested in her than her own mythical and religious tradition is in them. This is very noticeable in the *Iliad*, where Athēnē is more prominent than any other god aside from Zeus, yet the ATHENIANS are barely mentioned. Her Athenian association with the owl reminds us of her reputation for wisdom and good judgment, and her first entry in the *Iliad* (1. 188–222) is to stop the furious ACHILLES from drawing his sword on AGAMEMNŌN.

However, this action of hers, it turns out, is not characteristic. Throughout the action she is a committed supporter of the ACHAIANS, not only continually urging them on to fight, armed with her AEGIS (2.445–52, 5.793–834), but on occasion more than ready to join the battle herself (5.835–63, 21.391–433). When Achilles renounces his wrath and is ready to return to the fray, Athēnē (18. 203–6) wraps him in her aegis, sets a golden cloud over his head, and makes a bright flame blaze from his head (how metaphorical this last is Homer deliberately does not make clear). It is not until the very last book (24.25–30), and then in a casual aside, that we are reminded of the earliest, and most rankling, reason for Athēnē's and HĒRĒ'S implacable hatred of TROY and the TROJANS (4.30–68, 20.313, and throughout): their dismissal, in a beauty contest, by PARIS in favor of APHRODĪTĒ. Homer's placing of this reminder, after all the slaughter and heartache, was surely no accident.

ATHENS, ATHENIANS Like CORINTH (KORINTHOS), Athens notably fails to live up to its later fame in the *Iliad*, rating only a brief mention in the CATALOGUE OF SHIPS (2.545–54), where it figures as "a well-built citadel" but the ATHENIANS receive only four other glancing references (4.32; 13.196, 689; 15.337).

ATREUS Son of Pelōps and Hippodameia, brother of Thyestēs, father of AGAMEMNŌN and MENELAÖS by his wife Airōpē, and king of MYKĒNAI. At 2.100–108 we are given a dynastic list of Agamemnon's predecessors as inheritor of the royal scepter: from Atreus it passes without incident to Thyestēs, and Thyestēs similarly passes it on to Agamemnōn. But (as scholars not been slow to point out) this completely ignores, and rewrites, a more then usually lurid sequence of mythical dynastic infighting, involving murder, treachery, adultery, incest, and unwitting cannibalism (details in Gantz 540–56), in which Atreus and Thyestēs figure as deadly enemies. One of the last acts in this sequence is the murder of Agamemnōn by Thyestēs's son Aigisthos, in collusion with Agamemnōn's wife Klytaimnēstra. Since this is repeatedly referred to throughout the *Odyssey*, Homer was clearly aware of the tradition, and carefully cherry-picked what he used from it, ignoring the rest, and censoring the Atreus-Thyestēs quarrel. This is not the only occasion on which the author of the *Iliad* shows himself sensitive to the more embarrassing features of archaic myth.

ATTICA The land surrounding, and ultimately controlled by, ATHENS: a roughly triangular domain extending from the Parnēs range in the north down to the Sounion promontory in the south. According to myth the Athenian unification of Attica's settlements (*synoikismos*) was carried out by Thēseus: unusually, there is clear evidence of more or less uniform continuity from MYCENAEAN times through to the Archaic and Classical eras.

AULIS A small harbor on the coast of BOIŌTIA, facing EUBOIA, below a promontory near Tanagra: famous—from the Epic Cycle (*Cypria* arg. 6, 8 = West 2003 [A], 72–75) and plays by Aeschylus and Euripides—as the assembly point for the ACHAIAN armada that sailed against TROY, and the site of the sacrifice of IPHIGENEIA to placate ARTEMIS and obtain a favorable wind. This episode is not directly referred to in the *Iliad*.

AUTOMEDŌN Son of Diōrēs; the charioteer of ACHILLES (9.209, 24.474) and PATROKLOS (16.145–47, 472–75), and also a notable warrior in his own right (17.359–542). After the death of PATROKLOS, ACHILLES honors Automedōn most highly of all his comrades (24.574–75). In Roman times, his name, used alone, came to mean "charioteer."

BELLEROPHŌN More properly, in Homer, Bellerophontēs. He appears in the *Iliad* solely as part of the long speech by GLAUKOS (6.144–211) describing his ancestry in the royal Corinthian dynasty of Ephyrē. Bellerophōn is the grandson of Sisyphos and grandfather to the brothers Glaukos and SARPĒDŌN. The account of Bellerophōn's adventures given by Glaukos is remarkable for two things: the one reference to writing in the Homeric poems and the absence of any mention of the winged horse Pegasos, elsewhere a key figure in Bellerophōn's ARISTEIA, when he successfully accomplishes the tasks given him by the king of LYCIA, whose spurned wife has falsely accused him of raping her.

BOIŌTIA, BOIŌTIANS Boiōtia is the region of Greece immediately to the north of Attica, from which it is divided by the mountain ranges of Kithairōn and Parnēs: like Attica, it faces the island of EUBOIA on the east. The Boiōtians form the first, and very sizable, item in the CATALOGUE OF SHIPS (q.v. for some of the puzzling Boiōtian omissions and inclusions of townships), providing fifty ships each with a crew of 120; only AGAMEMNŌN's contingent is larger. Yet they do not perform well or often at TROY: in the battle over PATROKLOS's body, "First to panic and flee was Boiōtian Pēneleōs" (17.597); wealthy Helenos is mentioned only to fall victim to HEKTŌR (5.707–9, cf. 15.330).

BRISEÏS As ACHILLES' war prize—whose arbitrary seizure by AGAMEMNŌN triggers the whole plot of the *Iliad*, from Achilles' wrath and withdrawal from the campaign to his return to avenge the death of his comrade PATROKLOS—Briseïs is far from a talkative heroine. In fact she has nothing to say at all till the fourteen lines she gets to mourn Patroklos (19.287–300). We hear that she was captured by Achilles at the sack of Lyrnessos (2.688–93), where he also killed her husband (19.291–96); yet when, at his reconciliation with Achilles, Agamemnōn swears he never had intercourse with Briseïs (19.258–65), he speaks as though he had respected her virginity. There is also one tradition that her name was Hippodameia. Dué (*HE* 1: 145, with citation of his earlier work) suggests plausibly that there are two victim stories conflated here, both to do with the death of a king at the sacking of his city: in one it is his unmarried daughter who is captured (and falls in love with his enemy), in the other, his wife.

CARIA, CARIANS A mountainous coastal region in southwestern Asia Minor, adjacent to IONIA. The Carians are the only contingent in the TROJAN CATALOGUE (2.867–75) described as "of barbarian speech" (*barbarophōnoi*); this was in fact "an Anatolian language related to HITTITE" (Rutherford, *HE* 1:149), recently deciphered.

CATALOGUE OF SHIPS, THE List of local contingents in the expedition to TROY, together with the numbers of ships each provides (2.494–759). Few aspects of the *Iliad* have occasioned more fractious scholarly debate. One of the rare points generally agreed is that catalogues as such are an accepted feature of Greek epic: see, e.g., *Il.* 2.816–77; *Od.* 11.225–330, and the fragmentary Hesiodic *Catalogue of Women* (Most, 2, 40–261). But otherwise consensus is rare. Did Homer compose the Catalogue as we have it? In any case does it reflect some kind of pre-Homeric memorized document, and if so was this a product of Geometric / Dark Age Greece or a surviving tradition from the Mycenaean Bronze Age?

The first thing to remember is how large, in the statistical sense, this Catalogue is. There are twenty-nine major entries, each one detailing the cities of the region concerned, the names of their captains, and the numbers of ships and men involved. The total comes to over a thousand ships with a hundred or so troops allotted to each. We know of such lists generally in antiquity, but they tend, unsurprisingly, to be a very practical part of the business of warfare: borrowed from by bards to commemorate local participation in great deeds, but seldom as long and detailed as the Catalogue of Ships (Latacz 2004, 219–23). Literally one-third of the Catalogue consists of place-names, 178 in all. As far as we can tell, all are genuine, not fictional, and none turn up in the wrong region. The idea that Homer, or some earlier bard, went round identifying them like a modern research scholar is, as Latacz says (225), prima facie "quite unrealistic". So the list must have been compiled earlier, an appropriate general preface to the great maritime expedition against TROY. But the *Iliad* takes place in the ninth to tenth year of that expedition, so Homer simply borrowed such a list, emending details where necessary to allow for altered circumstances; and sure enough, we find the absence of leaders like PROTESILAÖS (killed) and PHILOKTĒTĒS (left behind on LĒMNOS with a suppurating wound) having to be accounted for (2.695–99, 716–23).

So the Catalogue was a pre-existent entity: but can we date it? Here several factors are crucial. (i) Almost a quarter of the names listed were unlocatable by historical times, and had therefore at some point beyond the general reach of memory been abandoned or undergone a name change. (ii) The names show no awareness of the so-called Dorian invasion during the Geometric period. (iii) Likewise, there is no notion of Greeks inhabiting the Anatolian coastline, which again points to a period prior to the great years of colonization that began c. 1050. (iv) The actual structure of the entries to the Catalogue bears a remarkable resemblance to the bureaucratic records of the LINEAR B TABLETS. Thus a Mycenaean origin for the Catalogue is highly probable. (The best analysis of these arguments known to me is Latacz 2004, 219–49, to which I am heavily indebted.)

Nevertheless, skepticism remains widespread, and the best summing-up of the difficulties remaining in the Catalogue is Oliver Dickinson's article on it in the *Homer Encyclopedia* (*HE* 1: 150–55, though many of his criticisms (e.g., the surprising prominence given to the BOIŌTIANS) do not take sufficient account of the likelihood that the Catalogue was not originally designed for the *Iliad*). Significant Mycenaean names are missing (but the Catalogue states specifically (2.492) that it only lists *those who went to Troy*). And so on. The debate continues.

CENTAURS See s.v. CHEIRŌN.

CHEIRŌN The Centaurs, mythical beings, horses, but human down to the waist above their forelegs, embodied the notion of humans before the advent of restraining civilization. Wild, violent, greedy (especially for liquor), and indiscriminately lecherous, they traditionally occupied the mountains and forests of northern Greece. The virtuous exception to this pattern of uncontrolled excess was Cheirōn, a kind of demi-equine Socrates, who was not only, like most Centaurs, versed in herbal medicine and many basic crafts, but wise and just (11.832), a renowned teacher and mentor, who was traditionally supposed to have educated not only ACHILLES, but also ASKLĒPIOS and Jason (of Argonaut fame).

Homer somewhat downplays Cheirōn's traditional role in the upbringing of Achilles: he instructs the boy in herbal medicine (11.829–32), and is mentioned as being close to his father PĒLEUS (to whom he gave the great ash spear that Achilles inherited, 16.141–44, 19.388–91), but Achilles' prime teacher—and much cherished by him as such—is the elderly PHOINIX (9.438–43, 485–91). This variation is in line with Homer's general avoidance of the wilder aspects of early traditional myth.

CHIMAIRA A composite tripartite fire-breathing mythical monster— a lion in front, a serpent behind, a goat in the mid-part" (6.181)—killed by BELLEROPHŌN as the first of the ordeals laid on him by the king of LYCIA (6.179–83).

CHRYSEÏS Daughter of the priest of APOLLO, Chrysēs, she is captured at the sack of Cilician THĒBĒ (2), and awarded in the share-out of spoils to AGAMEMNŌN, who at first rebuffs her father's offer to ransom her. However, after Apollo vents his anger on the ACHAIANS, they override Agamemnōn and insist on Chryseïs being returned to her father. Agamemnōn's arbitrary seizure of ACHILLES' prize, BRISEÏS, as compensation for his loss, leads directly to Achilles' wrath and withdrawal from combat, thus precipitating the *Iliad*'s central theme. Dué (*HE* 1: 165) argues that since Chryseïs was captured from Thēbē, rather than her parental home, she was already married—in fact, a widow, Achilles having most likely killed her husband.

CILICIA, CILICIANS See s.v. THĒBĒ (2).

CORINTH (KORINTHOS) Controlled by AGAMEMNŌN and mentioned in the CATALOGUE OF SHIPS (2.570) as "wealthy"; also referred to (6.152, 210) as Ephyrē, but otherwise giving no hint in the *Iliad* of its later importance.

CRETE, CRETANS See s.v. KRĒTĒ (CRETE).

DANAÄNS One of the three regular names, together with ACHAIANS (the most common) and ARGIVES, used to identify participants in the mixed Greek expeditionary force that sailed against TROY. The derivation of the name is uncertain, though ancient: references from Egypt date back to the fifteenth and fourteenth centuries B.C.E. (Lopez-Ruiz, *HE* 1: 192). The most likely connection is with the Danuna, known to the Egyptians as one of the SEA PEOPLES (Latacz 2004, 130ff.)

DARDANOS, DARDANIA/NS Dardanos in the *Iliad* (20.215–40, 304–5), as AINEIAS informs ACHILLES, is recalled as the favorite son of ZEUS by any mortal woman (by Elektra, daughter of Atlas, in this case). He founds Dardania, near the site of TROY, before Troy itself is built, and becomes the founding ancestor (through Erichthonios and Trōs) of the Trojan kings, so that both Aineias (son of Kapys) and PRIAM (son of LAOMEDŌN) are his descendants. But it is POSEIDŌN who guarantees (20. 302–4) that the dynasty founded by Dardanos will not die out. The Dardanians in the *Iliad* are related to the Trojans, but not yet, as they became later (e.g., in Virgil's *Aeneid*), identical with them. Historically, the Dardanians occupied a region near the IDA range in the TROAD (Strab. 13.1.33, cf. Dueck, *HE* 1: 194).

DAWN (Eōs) Dawn, or Eōs, daughter of the sun god Hyperiōn, is barely anthropomorphized at all in the *Iliad:* she is regularly described as "saffron-robed" or "rosy-fingered" and she does, once (11.1), rise from the bed of Tithōnos, but her sole function is to herald the morning, and quite often the context makes clear that this is simply the dawn, small *d*, with no personality. Yet elsewhere she displays a strong mythological character. By the beautiful boy Tithōnos (PRIAM'S brother, no less) she is the mother of MEMNŌN, on whom she persuades ZEUS to confer immortality (*Aithiopis* arg. 2 = West 2003 [A], 113): Tithōnos too is granted immortality, but in his case Dawn forgets to ask for eternal youth as well, so that he ends up as a dry, piping husk, a kind of human cicada (*HHAphr.* 218–38) She pursues mortal lovers with zest, including the hunters Orīōn (*Od.* 5.121–24) and Kephalos (Hes. *Th.* 986–87). She also (Hes. *Th.* 378–823) is reported as giving birth to winds and stars, a wonderful chance, I've always thought, for some inspired graphic-book illustrator.

DEATH In personified form (Thanatos) represented as the brother of SLEEP, both being sent by APOLLO to convey SARPĒDŌN's body to LYCIA (16.676–83). Hesiod (*Th.* 212–13, 756–59) makes Death and Sleep the offspring of Night and Erebos.

DEATH-SPIRIT The Homeric *kér* (not to be confused with *kēr*, heart, mind, feeling) was thought of as in some way akin to FATE (*moira*)—each individual got his or her own *kér* at birth—but also figured as a quasi-physical agent, more than capable of swallowing a victim (23.78–79). This death-spirit was "personal and dangerous" (Vermeule 39), "a sister of sleep, death, and the furies." Cf. Onians 399–400.

DEÏPHOBOS Son of PRIAM and HEKABĒ and (22.233–34) HEKTŌR's best-loved brother—though Priam (24.251) scolds him as a no-good. ATHĒNĒ therefore assumes the likeness of Deïphobos to persuade Hektōr to halt his flight and face ACHILLES in battle, well aware, anti-TROJAN as she is, that this will mean his death (22.228–47). After PARIS/ALÉXANDROS is killed by PHILOKTĒTĒS, Deïphobos marries Helen (*Little Iliad*, arg. 2 = West 2003 [A], 121–23), perhaps by a leviratic-style obligation to wed a dead brother's childless widow. He is subsequently killed by MENELAÖS, who thus recovers HELEN (*Sack of Ilion*, arg. 2 = West 2003 [A], 145; cf. *Od.* 8. 516–20).

DELUSION (Atē) The Greek *atē*, which I and others translate as "Blind Delusion" or simply "Delusion"—most often capitalized thus in view of its dramatic personification by PHOINIX (9.496–514), but sometimes lowercase, where it seems recognized simply as a psychological force—is a compulsive urge, originally seen as external, to behave in a fashion leading to disaster. It is Delusion, but it also can characterize the fatal consequences of that Delusion. Most notably, AGAMEMNŌN uses it (19.85–138) to disclaim responsibility for his actions regarding ACHILLES and BRISEÏS, exactly in the way a modern defendant in court may offer insanity as an excuse. In modern scholarship, Homer's often ambiguous use of *atē* has increasingly come to be seen as an early step toward the internalization of emotional motives, rather than objectifying these as external visitations inflicted by some (generally malevolent) deity.

DĒMĒTĒR This famous goddess of agriculture (and the mystery cults connected with agriculture) is strikingly absent from the Homeric OLYMPIAN pantheon, though casual references (2.696, 5.499–502, 13.322,14.326, 21.76) show full awareness of her functions and precincts, and other epic poetry such as the *Homeric Hymn to Demeter* and Hesiod's *Works and Days* stress her importance. The exact reason for her suppression by Homer has never been satisfactorily explained (for theories advanced, see Currie, *HE* 1: 201–2).

DESTINY See s.v. FATE.

DIOMĒDĒS Son of TYDEUS, one of the Seven at THĒBĒ (1), with whose great reputation as a warrior AGAMEMNŌN compares Diomēdēs very much to his disadvantage (4.365–98): Diomēdēs shows his maturity by ignoring the slur, and attributing it to stress (4.402–18). He is, in fact, among the leading, and most aggressive, ACHAIANS at TROY, and has his own ARISTEIA (q.v.). Though young, he is listed among the elders, and speaks with authority (2.406, cf. 7.399–402, 9.31–49, 14.109–32); he has brought a large contingent of eighty vessels to Troy, from known MYCENAEAN strongholds in the Argolid such as ARGOS and TIRYNS (2.560–68). Exactly where his domain ends and that of AGAMEMNŌN begins is never entirely clear in the *Iliad*. He is a favorite of ATHĒNĒ, who frequently protects him (5.1–8, 121–32, 794–861; 10.503–14). After the fall of Troy he has a safe return to Argos (*Od.* 3.180–82).

DIONYSOS Like DĒMĒTĒR, another powerful agricultural deity (presiding over grapes as Dēmētēr over grain) who is barely referred to in the *Iliad*, though Homer is well aware of the myths surrounding him, including his curious birth to Semelē and ZEUS (6.129–37, 14.325).

DŌDŌNA Described in the CATALOGUE OF SHIPS as "hard-wintered" (2.750), and referred to (16.233–35) in ACHILLES' prayer to ZEUS on behalf of PATROKLOS, Dōdōna (*BA* 54 C2), site of the famous and ancient oracle of Zeus, is situated in northwestern Greece, near modern Ioannina. ODYSSEUS (*Od.* 14.327–30) was said to have consulted "the high-leafed oak" there, the rustling of its leaves interpreted by the ascetic Selloi (16.235), who went barefoot and slept on the ground (but by historical times had been replaced by three priestesses: Hdt. 2.55–57, Strab. 7.7.12, cf. Finkelberg, *HE* 3: 788).

DOLŌNEIA The "Lay of Dolōn", or *Dolōneia*, is the scholarly name for book 10 of the *Iliad*. From antiquity on, it has always found critics eager to dismiss it as a later addition to the rest of the text: Martin West, indeed, confidently omits it in toto from his Teubner text (*Homeri Ilias*, 2 vols., Stuttgart 1998–2000), and one recent translator, Stephen Mitchell, has followed his example, dismissing it as a "baroque and nasty episode" (Mitchell lvii). Several reasons have been given down the centuries for its alleged inauthenticity. It is singularly lacking in the *Iliad*'s high military code of honor. It is, uniquely, a night operation, and a fairly ruthless one. Its vocabulary has unusual features. It could be excised without any damage to the overall plot.

All this is true, but still does not add up to proof; and there can be no doubt that the primary driving force has always been the fact that, for various reasons, many people found it, and still find it, decidedly unpleasant. Yet it comes at a very apposite point. The two warriors, DIOMĒDĒS and ODYSSEUS, who at the end of book 9 are most impatient with the honor-bound, militarily disastrous, grandstanding of ACHILLES (and, by implication, with the aristocratic code that has prolonged the war for nine long years) are also the two who at once follow up their fruitless embassy to the grandstander with a highly successful nocturnal guerilla raid on the enemy camp. They wipe out the leaders of the newly arrived THRACIAN contingent, including its king, RHESOS; they take his famous team of horses as spoils of war; they capture, and extract valuable information from, a would-be TROJAN spy, DOLŌN; they get back to camp safely. *This*, they imply, *is how it should be done*. It all foreshadows the warfare of the future: they lie to Dolōn, then behead him; they kill Rhēsos and his warriors while they are asleep; the end justifies the means. We don't know when, or if, the *Dolōneia* was in fact added to a putative canon. More to the point, it's not even certain whether there ever was a canonical Ur-text by Homer to which it could be attached. There are rather more good reasons for keeping than for excising it.

DORIANS The third main ethnic division of the Hellenes (ancient Greeks), the other two being the IONIANS and the Aeolians (see AEOLIS). According to both mythic tradition and actual historical probability, the Dorians only migrated from Epiros in the northwest to the southern Homeric world of the ARGOLID and the PELOPONNESE after the TROJAN WAR; and the *Iliad*, in confirmation of its MYCENAEAN antecedents, makes no mention whatsoever of them.

ĒËTIŌN Father of ANDROMACHĒ, and king of Cilician THĒBĒ (2), at the capture of which he was killed, along with all his sons, by ACHILLES (6.395–98, 416–28). Notably, several of his captured possessions—a lyre (9.186–88), a chariot horse (16.152–54), and a mass of pig iron (23.826–27)—are paraded by their captor in the course of the *Iliad:* Achilles plays the lyre, the horse joins his immortal team when PATROKLOS goes to fight on his behalf, and the pig iron features as a prize at Patroklos's funeral games. Not to be confused with minor homonyms at 17.675 and 21.43.

EILEITHYIA Ancient goddess of childbirth (16.187–88), mentioned in the LINEAR B tablets: daughter of HĒRĒ (11.270, 19.119) and ZEUS (Hes. *Th.* 922). ODYSSEUS refers to her famous cave at Amnisos on KRĒTĒ (CRETE). She was widely worshipped in Greece: see Lyons, *HE* 1: 242.

ELYSIUM, THE ELYSIAN FIELDS Nicely described by Mackie (*HE* 1: 246) as "a kind of paradise for heroes in Greek eschatology". Such eschatology is notably rare in Homer: Elysium gets one mention only (*Od.* 4.561–69), where its main attraction is its idyllic climate. Most dead warriors, HEROES or not—even a son of ZEUS such as SARPĒDŌN—seem, even after special treatment (16.433–38, 667–83) to end up as sad wraiths in the dreary realm of HĀDĒS. Yet, arbitrarily, MENELAÖS, as husband of HELEN and Zeus's son-in-law, is promised entry to Elysium after death (*Od.* 4.561–64). A more promising destination for the elect seems to be evolving.

ENYALIOS An ancient war god mentioned in the LINEAR B tablets: in the *Iliad* mostly an epithet attached to the courageous, such as MĒRIONĒS (7.166, 8.264), who are described as "a match for" him; in a couple of places (17.211, 20.69), he has become no more than an epithet for ARĒS (q.v.).

ERECHTHEUS An early mythical king of ATHENS: mentioned in the CATALOGUE OF SHIPS as supposedly autochthonous (2.547–51), and set by ATHĒNĒ in her own shrine (i.e., the Erechtheion), he was also closely associated with POSEIDŌN.

ERIS See s.v. STRIFE.

EUBOIA The large island, second only to KRĒTĒ (CRETE) in the AEGEAN, long and narrow, lying very close along the east coast of mainland Greece opposite BOIŌTIA and ATTICA. Though only briefly mentioned in the CATALOGUE OF SHIPS (2.535–36), Euboia is notable for having, as an island of seafarers, in contrast to the isolated and impoverished mainland, preserved its wealth, its links to the East (Powell, *HE* 1: 268–69), and some of its old MYCENAEAN traditions (one famous burial, at modern Lefkandi, is truly Homeric) right through the Dark Age.

EUMĒLOS Son of Admētos and Alkēstis, and married to Iphthimē, the sister of ODYSSEUS'S wife Penelope (*Od.* 4.797–98), Eumēlos is a leading commander (*anax andrōn*), and brings eleven ships to TROY from southern THESSALY (2.711–15). His horses, bred by APOLLO. are by far the best (2.763–67), and he himself a skilled horseman (23.289). In the chariot race at the funeral games of PATROKLOS he is expected to win, but when Apollo attacks DIOMĒDĒS, who looks like overtaking Eumēlos (23.382–84), ATHĒNĒ retaliates by snapping Eumēlos's yoke, so that he is thrown from his chariot and injured (23.391–97). He limps in last on foot, dragging his chariot, but ACHILLES gives him, on reputation alone, a rich consolation prize (23.532–65). A later meliorizing tradition (Apollod. *Epit.* 5.5, cited by Polinskaya, *HE* 1: 271) has Eumēlos winning the race for Achilles.

EURYSTHEUS Son of Sthenelos, and thus great-grandson of ZEUS, who was forced to grant him, rather than his cousin HĒRAKLĒS, rule over the ARGOLID by a trick of HĒRĒ (see 19.91–133, and s.v. ALKMĒNĒ). It was also Eurystheus who later imposed the Twelve Labors on Hēraklēs, probably as a penalty for the murder of his children (cf. Gantz 382–83).

FATE The idea of Fate (*moira, moros, aisa*) as a determining power, independent of divine will, is one of common occurrence throughout the *Iliad*. It is particularly associated with the time, and manner, of an individual's death. Etymologically these terms are all based on the notion of due measure, a proper share or portion. How that measure is to be assessed in each individual case is never made entirely clear. When ZEUS weighs the relative fates of mortals in his scales (8.68–77, ACHAIANS and TROJANS; 22.209–13, ACHILLES and HEKTŌR), he is not the arbiter, but merely assessing what is already predetermined. The same applies to his general predictions concerning the war (8.473–77, 15.61–71). Yet there is at least one occasion (the battle during which his mortal son SARPĒDŌN is fated to be killed by PATROKLOS, 16.431–61) on which Zeus would seem seriously to consider the possibility of overriding Fate, but is talked out of it by HĒRĒ (unless this is simply a clever ploy to leave open the determination of whether in fact he could, or could not, do it.) By Homer's day the notion of predestined Fate was becoming at least debatable. The gods worry about the possibility (20.30, 21.517) or work to prevent it (2.155, 17.231), as Edwards (*HE* 1: 286–87) rightly reminds us. He also points out that it is, precisely, the existence of firmly determined individual fates that facilitates their prediction, as that of Hektōr by Patroklos (16.851–54) or that of Achilles by Hektōr (22.358–60).

FURIES, THE Female chthonian (19.259–60) deities known as the Erinyes (as far back as the LINEAR B tablets), the Furies are particularly concerned with ensuring retribution for offenses, more often than not those involving blood-guilt, within the family. They are invoked by parental curses, and generally fulfill them (9.454–57, 571, 21.412, *Od.* 11.279–80). They protect elders' rights in particular (15.204). They uphold the sanctity of oaths (19.259–60, 3.279). They can, or so AGAMEMNŌN claims, blind a man's reason (19.86–89, cf. *Od.* 11.234). They remain most famous as the black-garbed, snake-haired, sinister avengers, daughters of Night, brought on stage by Aeschylus in his *Eumenides*.

GANYMĒDĒS In the *Iliad* (20.231–35) the beautiful son of TRŌS, whom the gods raise up to OLYMPOS to be ZEUS's wine server; Zeus by way of recompense gives Trōs a team of immortal horses, which are in due course inherited by his grandson LAOMEDŌN (q.v.).

GARGAROS See s.v. IDA, MT.

GLAUKOS Son of Hippolochos, and cousin to SARPĒDŌN, his co-commander of the LYCIAN contingent (2.876–77), Glaukos is descended from SISYPHOS, and BELLEROPHŌN is his grandfather. At his famous battlefield meeting with DIOMĒDĒS (6.119–236) it transpires that the latter's grandfather Oineus once entertained Bellerophōn, making Diomēdēs and Glaukos official guest-friends: instead of fighting they therefore exchange armor (6.232–36). Glaukos is generally a distinguished warrior (e.g., 7.13, 14.426, 16.593) and abuses HEKTŌR for failing either to secure Sarpēdōn's body or to recover that of PATROKLOS. With Sarpēdōn, he is one of the very few TROJAN allies (or indeed Trojans) who is more than a name in the *Iliad*. The *Aithiopis* (arg. 3 = West 2003 [A], 112–13) and Apollodorus (*Epit.* 5.4) both have him killed by AIAS (1) during the battle over ACHILLES' body.

GORGON In myth, Perseus decapitates the Gorgon Medousa (Hes. *Th.* 280), whose gaze retains the power of petrification, and gives her head to ATHĒNĒ: it duly appears on the goddess's AEGIS in battle (5.741–42). "In the Homeric epics, the Gorgon's (Medousa's) head is already detached from her body, and it has become a potent symbol of fear and death" (Ebbott, *HE* 1: 323). AGAMEMNŌN similarly has a Gorgon's face on his shield to inspire terror in his opponents (11.36–37); HEKTOR's eyes when fighting are compared to the Gorgon's gaze (8.348–49).

GRACES The number of these minor goddesses of charm, grace, and beauty, known as Charites, is uncertain. Hesiod (*Th.* 907–9) mentions three, Euphrosynē, Aglaia, and Thalia, the daughters of ZEUS and Euronomē, and various others crop up, such as Pasithëē (*Il.* 14.269, 276), who is given in marriage to SLEEP (Hypnos) as a bribe by HĒRĒ.

HĀDĒS The third son of KRONOS and Rhea, his brothers being ZEUS and POSEIDŌN, who in the *Iliad* (15.185–93) tells how their respective domains were determined by lot: Zeus got the heavens, Hādēs the underworld, and Poseidōn himself the sea, the earth and OLYMPOS being shared by them all in common. Hādēs is described as "unbending, implacable" (9.158–59), and, as the god of death, the one most hated by mortals (5.158–59), but plays no direct role in the *Iliad*, where references to Hādēs are normally not to the god himself, but to his subterranean realm of the dead, the UNDERWORLD. This is never clearly described in the poem, though apparently separated from the upper world by both a gate and the waters of Styx (8.366–68, cf. 23.71–74). It seems to be above TARTAROS (8.13–16, 478–81), and is a constant reminder of the ultimate fate of all HEROES, whether ACHAIAN or TROJAN. It is also very different from the afterlife visited in the furthest west by ODYSSEUS, with its fields of asphodel, more reminiscent of ELYSIUM (*Od.* 11, passim).

HEKABĒ (Hecuba) In the *Iliad*, daughter of King Dymas of Phrygia (16.718–19)—unsurprisingly, her name, like her husband's, is non-Greek—and wife of PRIAM, to whom she bears nineteen of his fifty children (24.496), including HEKTŌR, KASSANDRĒ, and PARIS/ALÉXANDROS (about whom in later tradition she has a dream, while pregnant with him, that she will bear a torch fated to burn TROY, and therefore had him exposed: see s.v. PARIS/ALÉXANDROS, and Roisman, *HE* 2: 335 with ref.). Homer presents her (ibid.) as "a caring mother and wife whose wishes are always thwarted" (6.254–68, 286–311; 22.79–89, 24.197–227). Because of her fecundity and the rate of TROJAN casualties, she is in perpetual mourning for her various sons. But Hektōr is her favorite, and her lamentation at his passing knows no bounds (22.431–36, 24.710–12, 747–59). Later tradition, especially as used by Euripides in his *Hecuba* and *Trojan Women*, envelops Homer's dignified matriarch in lurid melodrama.

HEKTŌR Son of PRIAM and HEKABĒ, married to ANDROMACHĒ, and father of the child Skamandrios/Astyanax (6.394–403), Hektōr is the leader and emblem of TROY's defense against the ACHAIANS: his death at the hands of ACHILLES foreshadows the city's fall; it is as though "all towering Ilion, top to bottom, were left smoldering with fire" (22.410–11). Troy's noblest warrior, he is never (in this unlike the most distinguished ACHAIAN warriors) given a formal ARISTEIA of his own, nor does he kill any of his leading opponents who are so honored. His backing by ZEUS is of a generalized nature: he is empowered to break through the Achaians' wall and to set fire to their ships—but this leads, inevitably, to the involvement, first, of PATROKLOS, and then, after Hektōr himself kills Patroklos, of Achilles, following which the sequence of events leading to the inevitable fall of Troy is determined by FATE. Though he is as conscious as Achilles of his reputation and his claim to military glory (*kléos*), unlike Achilles he is not battle-hungry by nature, but rather driven by a sense of social shame (*aidōs*), the fear of his society's censure if he fails to live up to the HERO's ideal (6.442; Redfield 118 and elsewhere). He is more defined by his strong sense of social responsibility than by any conscious pursuit of military prestige, though it is his *aidōs* that makes him insist, fatally, on meeting Achilles in single combat, rather than pursuing a more sensible defensive policy from inside the city's walls (6.429–46, 22.38–93). As the narrative progresses, he becomes gradually more nervous, stressed, abrupt, and angry (with himself at least as much as with others), ignoring warnings (12.223–27, 18.267–72) and wildly boasting (18.308–9) of his chances against Achilles. We remember this when, faced with Achilles in fact, he has a total failure of nerve, and runs for it (22.131–66, 188–207). His weaknesses are all too human; his brief moment of domestic happiness with his wife and baby son (6.399–493), shot through with foreboding about their future when the city falls, is one of the most unforgettable scenes in the *Iliad*.

HELEN Daughter of ZEUS—though her official father was Tyndareus—by Lēdē; sister to KLYTAIMNĒSTRA, Kastōr, and Polydeukēs (3.236–44), and married to MENELAÖS. Tyndareus made all the suitors for her hand swear an oath that, were she ever abducted—which in fact happened twice, the first time by Thēseus—they would, all of them, combine to recover her (Hes. *Cat.* fr. 155 = Most 2: 231–33). Homer refers only briefly and late (24.25–30) to the JUDGMENT OF PARIS, as a result of which PARIS/ALÉXANDROS, having duly assigned the prize for beauty to APHRODĪTĒ, was rewarded by her by being made irresistible to Helen, thus in effect triggering the TROJAN WAR. It is stressed (3.282, 458; 13.626) that when Helen eloped, she took much property with her (though how this was done secretly is never explained). The comparatively few times she appears in the *Iliad* (3.121–244, 383–447; 6.343–69; 24.761–76), she is filled with shame, not least by her inability to resist Paris sexually (reified in a personal clash with Aphrodītē, 3.380–420), and is touching in her posthumous tribute to HEKTŌR, who alone of her TROJAN relatives, except for PRIAM, was unfailingly kind to her. One account has her baring her breasts (successfully: he drops his sword) to a furious Menelaös at the sack of Troy (*Little Iliad*, fr. 28 = West 2003 [A], 138–39), and she and Menelaös (both now comfortably middle-aged, if not elderly) later entertain Tēlemachos with reminiscences of the Trojan War in Sparta (*Od.* 4.219–303). The post-Homeric countertradition that Helen never in fact went to Troy (it was a phantom, an *eidōlon*, that did so) reminds us of the new middle-class morality exemplified by Xenophanes, who complained about Homer (and Hesiod) attributing immoral behavior to the gods, when in fact they were simply reporting traditional (but now embarrassing) ancient myths.

HELLAS In the *Iliad* restricted to a small region in southeastern THESSALY, neighbor to PHTHIĒ (9.478), and (like its neighbor) home to MYRMIDONS (16.594–96). Both formed part of the kingdom of PĒLEUS and ACHILLES (2.683–85). In the *Odyssey* (1.344, 4.726, etc.), Hellas is northern Greece, as opposed to the PELOPONNESE, there called "Argos"; for Hesiod (*WD* 653), "Hellas" and "Hellenes" referred respectively to the whole of Greece and Greeks generally, as they do today. Between Homer and Hesiod, "Panhellenes" undergoes an identical extension (*Il.* 2.530, Hes. *WD* 528, cf. Fowler, *HE* 2: 339.)

HELLESPONT, THE The strait (today known as the Dardanelles) dividing Europe from Asia, and connecting the Black Sea with the AEGEAN.

HĒPHAISTOS The Greek god of fire (strikingly exemplified in the *Iliad* by his napalm-like attack on the aggressive waters of the SKAMANDROS RIVER (21.342–56), and—uniquely among the OLYMPIANS—a highly skilled divine blacksmith, artisan, and architect, the "famed craftsman" (1.571, 18.143, 391) various creations of whose, some disconcertingly modern, are scattered through the Homeric poems: for ZEUS (recognized as his father in the *Iliad*), a scepter and AEGIS (2.100–102, 15.307–10); for his mother HĒRĒ, a throne and a private bedchamber (14.238–40, 166–67); self-moving tripods (18.373–79), golden robots that can speak and think (18.417–21), and, above all, the marvelous new armor he fashions for ACHILLES (18.469–613). His position on OLYMPOS is decidedly ambiguous. His aristocratic fellow deities deride both his lameness and his plebeian skills; when he traps his wife APHRODITE in bed with ARĒS (*Od.* 8.266–333), the mockery is directed against the comic vulgar cuckold no less than the aristocratic adulterous couple. Yet the Olympians are more than ready (in this like their human counterparts) to exploit those skills when needs be; while Hēphaistos's deliberate invitation of that laughter (by hobbling round in imitation of the beautiful cup bearer Ganymēdēs) in order to defuse a difficult situation (1.595–600, cf. Rinon, *HE* 2: 341) suggests a more sophisticated social sense than his audience is aware of. Tradition has it that he was twice thrown headlong out of Olympos. The first time was by Zeus (when he took his mother's side in a quarrel): he landed on LĒMNOS, and lamed both legs in the fall (1.590–94). The second time was by HĒRĒ herself, who (he alleged) found his lameness an embarrassment (18.395–97). On this occasion THETIS saved and looked after him, so that his readiness to forge armor for her son ACHILLES is in repayment for her kindness. Overall, one is more conscious with Hēphaistos than with most characters in the *Iliad* of Homer carefully cherry-picking only what he needs from a large and variegated mythic tradition.

HĒRAKLĒS The greatest of all Greek HEROES, and (like so many of the best of them) sired by a god (ZEUS) on a human woman (ALKMĒNĒ, q.v.). He belongs to an earlier generation than that of the TROJAN WAR and so plays no direct part in the *Iliad*—though his son Tlēpolemos, later killed by SARPĒDŌN (5.628–59) is listed as a Rhodian leader in the CATALOGUE OF SHIPS (2.653–69), as are two grandsons (2.678–79), while the narrative shows broad familiarity with the various myths concerning him. Homer has several indirect allusions to the Twelve Labors (e.g., 8.363, 19.132–33); but *Od.* 11.620–26 is the only place where a specific Labor—the fetching up of Kerberos—is mentioned. He has an implacable enemy in HĒRĒ, literally from the time of his birth (19.104–24, see s.v. ALKMĒNĒ and EURYSTHEUS); for later harassment, cf. 14.253–56, 15.26–28 (though he gets his own back, probably during his attack on PYLOS, by shooting her in the breast with a three-barbed arrow: 5.392–94, cf. 11.690–93). Hērē is also involved in his death: 18.115–19, a passage where ACHILLES, while resigning himself to a brief life, reminds his mother, THETIS, that even Hēraklēs, though a glorious HERO, was mortal and had to die. The most ironic reference to him comes at 5.635–42, where his son Tlēpolemos is boasting to Sarpēdōn (who is about to kill him) that they don't make warriors now like those of former times: why, Hēraklēs, with only six ships and a few men, was able to reduce and sack TROY after being cheated by LAOMEDŌN (q.v.)! So much for an expedition of over a thousand ships and some hundred thousand men, after nine years of inconclusive warfare (there is a second reminder of Hēraklēs' achievement at 14.249–51).

HERALDS These ever-useful officials (e.g., AGAMEMNŌN's herald Talthybios) are prominent throughout the *Iliad*, where they perform a wide variety of services. They carry a special staff of office (the caduceus), their persons are inviolable, and they are under the protection of HERMĒS. Thus, apart from civic functions such as making public proclamations, summoning individuals to (and moderating their conduct at) assembly (2.50–52, 18.503–5) or warfare (2.442–44), and presiding at festivals and religious sacrifices (18.558–59, 3.116–20, 9.174), they are present on missions involving risk, where their sacrosanct character should guarantee safety: most notably with PRIAM on his mission to ACHILLES (24.149–51, 281–82). But as Thalmann says (*HE* 2: 346), "their status is hard to pin down". Sometimes they are referred to as henchmen or attendants, yet they can have noble personal epithets. Their special inviolable status is perhaps, like that of the seer, best seen as a religious aspect of their quasi-diplomatic profession.

HĒRĒ Self-styled eldest daughter of KRONOS and RHEA (4.58–61), and wife (as well as sister) of ZEUS, with whom the LINEAR B tablets already associate her in the Bronze Age. She is constantly treated, in myth and cult, as a goddess of marriage: somewhat ironically, seeing that her own marriage is not only incestuous but also, to say the least, difficult—on one occasion her irate spouse leaves her dangling in midair from a golden chain with a couple of anvils tied to her feet, as punishment for her persecution of HĒRAKLĒS (15.18–30). With ATHĒNĒ, and seemingly for the same reason (cf. JUDGMENT OF PARIS), she is strongly pro-ACHAIAN and anti-TROJAN throughout the *Iliad* (4.64–72, 5.711–861, 907–9, 8.198–219, 16.439–58, 18.168–84, 20.32–37, 21.328–39, 24.22–30). However, she remains very cautious—perhaps with those anvils in mind—of offending Zeus too directly: see 8.397–432, though she has no compunctions about seducing him so that POSEIDŌN can help the ACHAIANS during his postcoital slumber (14.153–360). With Athēnē and Poseidōn, she has even made an attempt (defeated by THETIS) to dethrone and imprison Poseidōn (1.396–404). She claims (4.50–52) that the cities dearest to her are ARGOS, SPARTA, and MYKĒNAI (MYCENAE). She is referred to as "Argive Hērē" (4.8, 5.908), and Argos continued to be her main cult center in historic times.

HERMĒS A minor deity in the OLYMPIAN pantheon, the son of ZEUS by a nymph, Maia. Known in the LINEAR B tablets from MYCENAEAN times. Right from birth, he is said to be "resourceful and cunning, a robber, a rustler of cattle, a bringer of dreams, a nightwatcher, a gate-lurker . . . by mid-day he was playing the lyre, and in the evening he stole the cattle of far-shooting Apollo" (*Homeric Hymn to Hermes* 13–18 = West 2003 [B], 112–59). He is, in fact, a classic trickster, sharing the epithet *polytropos* ("resourceful", "of many wiles") with ODYSSEUS. But in the *Iliad*, characteristically, this side of his nature is not emphasized (though when there is a divine scheme proposed to hijack HEKTŌR's body from ACHILLES (24.22–24), it is Hermēs who is chosen for the job). For Homer it is Hermēs' functions as a messenger of Zeus and a guide to mortals that are prominent. He delivers the royal scepter from Zeus to Pelōps (2.104). He rescues ARĒS from imprisonment by the Titans (5.385–91). He is pro-ACHAIAN, (20.34–35, 72) but refuses to fight (21.497–501). Most important, Zeus chooses him to escort PRIAM safely on the nocturnal journey to ransom his son from Achilles, and return him safely afterwards (24.153–54, 330–468, 677–94). Hermēs escorts him in the likeness of a young aristocrat, with great tact and skill. He uses his magic wand to lull sentries to sleep, open the gates, and unbar the entry to Achilles' hut (440–67). He takes care to wake Priam before dawn and drives him clear of the Achaian camp (683–94). In the *Odyssey*, similarly, he is twice dispatched to help Odysseus (1.38–43, 5.29, 10.275–307). At the end of the *Odyssey* (24.1–202), he performs one of his most famous functions, that of *psychopompos*, the conductor of the souls of the dead, when he leads the ghosts of the slaughtered suitors down to Hādēs. The exact meanings of his ancient epithets (e.g., "slayer of Argos") remain uncertain.

HEROES, HEROIC AGE In *Works and Days* (143–73), Hesiod describes the last two ages before his own in mythic terms, as an "age of bronze" (150–51) and an "age of mortal heroes, called demigods" (159). The end of this last, the era preceding his own, he specifically correlates with the THEBAN and TROJAN WARS. The men of it were superhuman in that they had divine blood in their ancestry, and they thus far outclassed, both physically and in prowess, the men of his own "iron age"; yet they nevertheless remained mortal, and all perished in "vile war and grim battle" (161). Their glory was their strain of divinity and the warrior code that they upheld (on which see the disquisition of SARPĒDŌN, 12.310–28, foreshadowing the creed of aristocrats everywhere up to and including 1914); their tragedy was that they could not escape death. Those who grew up in the aftermath of the Trojan War were the last of their breed: gods were never again to have direct intercourse (sexual or of any other kind) with mortals. That all this was an enhanced mythic recreation of the events leading to the final collapse of the historic MYCENAEAN palace culture has become increasingly clear with the advance of recent research into the Bronze Age.

Homer never spells out this scenario in detail, but both *Iliad* and *Odyssey* show acute awareness of a complete break between the world of heroes and that of ordinary mortals. In his remarkable speech to ODYSSEUS and DIOMĒDĒS rebuffing attempts to bring him back into the war (9.308–429), ACHILLES reveals total disillusion with the heroic code: a disillusion savagely emphasized by the profoundly unheroic, yet highly successful, night raid that Odysseus and Diomēdēs proceed to carry out that same night (bk. 10: cf. DOLŌNEIA). In the *Odyssey*, glory (*kléos*), if necessary at the price of death, is no longer the ideal: the goal is now survival.

The heroic age has died with its final generation of heroes. There is one striking proleptic image of this in the *Iliad:* the postwar flooding by POSEIDŌN and APOLLO of the ACHAIAN defense wall by the ships (12.17–33), which will destroy every last trace of these Achaian demigods' presence, and signal the end of the heroic era in which the *Iliad* is set.

IDA, MT. A mountain range in the southern TROAD, immediately north of the Gulf of Adramyttion (*BA* 57 E2), today called the Kaz Dag. Its main peaks, including GARGAROS, rise to nearly six thousand feet and offer a panoramic view of TROY and its environs, which lends plausibility to ZEUS's being seen throughout the *Iliad* (e.g., 3.276; 8.47–52, 75, 170–71,397; 11.181–94, 336–37; 12.252–53; 14.157; 15.5–12,151–53; 17.593–96; 20.56–57; 24.308) as either ruling from Ida, or using it as an observation post for keeping an eye on the progress of the war and giving signs by thunder (POSEIDŌN uses SAMOTHRAKĒ in the same way: 13.10–15). Ida was, and still is, "spring-rich" (*polypidax*, cf. 12.18–21 for its numerous rivers) and heavily wooded (23.117–20). Most notably, the summit of Ida is the scene of Zeus's al fresco lovemaking with HĒRĒ (14.292–353), despite her hope (327–40) for indoor privacy; for other couplings there, see 2.280–81, 4.475.

IDOMENEUS A leading older (13.361, 510–13) HERO, son of Deukaliōn, and captain of the contingent from KRĒTĒ (CRETE) (2.645–50), Idomeneus is distinguished enough to have been the guest of MENELAÖS in SPARTA (3.230–33), to receive praise from AGAMEMNŌN (4.257–64), and to have his own small ARISTEIA (13.361–454). He is regularly grouped with the best of the ACHAIANS: 2.404–5, 6.435–37, 7.165, 19.309–11, etc.).

ILION See s.v. TROY.

IONIAN ISLANDS/SEA A group of islands off the west coast of mainland Greece, and south of Kerkyra (Corfu), in the Ionian Sea. The main ones known to Homer are Leukas, ITHÁKĒ, Kephallenia/Samē, Zákinthos, Doulichion, and the Echinades. In the CATALOGUE OF SHIPS (2.625–30) the last two are ruled by Megēs of Doulichion, whereas the rest (2.631–37) are under ODYSSEUS.

IPHIGENEIA See s.v. KALCHAS.

IRIS Originally the rainbow, and as such (like the DAWN) not fully personalized in the *Iliad* (11.27, 17.547). More often (e.g., 2.786–806, 3.121–40, 11.185–210) she appears as a regular messenger of ZEUS (and once, 18.166–202, of HĒRĒ): she has the virtue of being "wind-footed". At one point, interestingly (15.159), Zeus warns her not be a "false messenger" (*pseudangelos*): there are in fact at least two occasions (8.423–24 and 15.179–81, the second directly following that warning!) on which she does insert some very tart and strongly worded additions of her own to the more diplomatic message she is sent to carry. Zeus clearly knows his messenger. Her two most important missions both take place in book 24: she summons THETIS to OLYMPOS (24.77–92) to be briefed on making ACHILLES accept ransom for the body of PATROKLOS, and also takes an encouraging message to PRIAM (24.147–88) to make him approach Achilles with the offer of that ransom.

ITHÁKĒ (ITHACA) One of the Ionian islands (whether modern Itháki or not is disputed: a plausible recent suggestion is that it was the—then separate—Palē peninsula of Kephallenia). The center of ODYSSEUS's kingdom, which probably extended to the islands of Samē (= Kephallenia) and Zákynthos, as well as part of the mainland (*Il.* 2.631–35; *Od.* 1.245–48). In sharp contrast to the *Odyssey*, the *Iliad* barely mentions Ithákē: HELEN (3.201) describes it as "a rugged dominion".

JUDGMENT OF PARIS, THE This famous episode, though apparently a major cause of the TROJAN WAR, is only once mentioned in the *Iliad*, and then very briefly, in the last book (24.22–30), where—as an explanation for the refusal of HĒRĒ and ATHĒNĒ to support a plan whereby HERMĒS would rescue HEKTŌR'S dead body from its abuse by ACHILLES—their hatred for all things Trojan is attributed to the fact that "when these goddesses came to [Paris's] courtyard he despised them / but had praise for the one who furthered his fatal lust."

To get the full picture we must turn to Proclus's synopsis of the *Cypria* (arg. 1 = West 2003 [A], 68–69), supplemented by Apollodorus (*Epit.* 3.2). Here we find ZEUS conferring with THEMIS about a prospective Trojan conflict (see s.v. PLAN OF ZEUS). In furtherance of this, at the wedding of PĒLEUS and THETIS, STRIFE mischievously throws a golden apple inscribed "For the fairest", to be competed for by HĒRĒ, ATHĒNĒ, and APHRODĪTĒ. Zeus then orders HERMĒS to conduct the three goddesses to the shepherd's steading of PARIS/ALÉXANDROS on MT. IDA, where this young herdsman (in fact a Trojan prince exposed at birth, because of an ill-omened dream by his mother: see s.v. HEKABĒ) will award the beauty prize to the goddess of his choice. All three goddesses try to bribe him. Hērē promises him kingship, Athēnē victory in war, and Aphrodītē sexual irresistibility to the most beautiful mortal woman in the known world, HELEN, who happens already to be married to MENELAÖS. He chooses Aphrodītē, who is as good as her word. While a guest of Menelaös, Paris duly absconds with Helen (and much of her property) during his host's absence at a funeral on KRĒTĒ (CRETE). Since Helen's prenuptial suitors have all sworn an oath to her father to rescue her if ever abducted (see s.v. HELEN), the result is the Trojan War, exactly as Zeus had planned.

KALCHAS Son of Thestōr, chief priest and seer of the ACHAIAN expeditionary force, who "knew events present and future as well as from the past" (1.70–72) and has brought the fleet safely to TROY with the aid of APOLLO. Though important, he is only prominent early in the *Iliad*. He explains the reason for Apollo's wrath (the refusal of ransom to the Apolline priest CHRYSES for his daughter) that has led to a visitation of plague on the troops (1.74–100), and, indirectly, to the rage of ACHILLES at AGAMEMNŌN (1.106–244). In a flashback narrated by ODYSSEUS (2.299–332) we learn of a portent at AULIS at the outset of the campaign, which Kalchas interpreted to mean that the war would last ten years. Outside the *Iliad*, Kalchas figures in several crucial episodes (e.g., the building of the WOODEN HORSE), the most important (*Cypria* arg. 8 = West 2003 [A], 74–75) being his explanation to Agamemnōn at Aulis that the contrary winds preventing the fleet from sailing are due to the wrath of ARTEMIS at Agamemnōn claiming to outperform her as a hunter, and that only atoning for this with the sacrifice of his daughter IPHIGENEIA will change the winds. He duly sends for Iphigeneia on the pretense that she is to marry Achilles: the sacrifice takes place (later tradition euphemizes this by the substitution of a deer; Aeschylus in the *Agamemnon* knew better), the prevailing wind changes, and the fleet duly sails. Ten years later, when Agamemnōn finally comes home to MYKĒNAI (MYCENAE), Iphigeneia's death is a major factor in his murder by his wife, KLYTAIMNĒSTRA. Some have seen a hint of this never-forgotten business in Agamemnōn's initial simmering distaste for Kalchas (1.105–8), but Homer never refers to it directly.

KASSANDRĒ The most beautiful (13.365–66, 24.699) daughter of PRIAM and HEKABĒ, briefly betrothed (13.368–69: her fiancé is killed), and the first person to see her father returning, with HEKTŌR'S corpse, from his momentous encounter with ACHILLES (24.700–706). This is all that the *Iliad* tells us about her. We hear nothing about her capacity for prophecy (*Cypria* arg. 1), bestowed on her by APOLLO in the hope of seducing her: when she refuses him, he cannot undo his gift, but adds the rider that no one will ever believe her predictions (Aesch. *Ag.* 1202–12). Nor does Homer mention her rape by AIAS (2) at the sack of TROY (*Sack of Ilion* arg. 3 = West 2003 [A], 146–47). In the *Odyssey*, however, we do learn briefly of how she, like AGAMEMNŌN (who has brought her to MYKĒNAI as his prize), is killed by KLYTAIMNĒSTRA (*Od.* 11.421–23).

KLYTAIMNĒSTRA Daughter of Lēdē and Tyndareus, married to AGAMEMNŌN, sister of HELEN, and mother of several daughters (including IPHIGENEIA) and one son, Orestēs. The only reference to her in the *Iliad* is at 1.113–15, where Agamemnōn compares her unfavorably to his prize of war CHRYSEÏS. In the *Odyssey*, however, the full story of her adultery with Aigisthos, and her subsequent murder of Agamemnōn, is related in detail, (3.263–72, 11.409–34, 24.199–202), primarily in the UNDERWORLD, to ODYSSEUS, by Agamemnōn's ghost. See also s.v. KALCHAS.

KRĒTĒ (CRETE) The "great island" (still known as such to modern Greeks) that lies like a rugged mountainous bar, about 160 miles in length, across the southern entry to the Aegean Sea, has always played a major part in Greek history as fortress and trading center. Paradoxically, we know a good deal more about its pre-MYCENAEAN Bronze Age "Minoan" culture than Homer did. In the *Iliad* —consonant with modern research positing a Mycenaean takeover of the island c. 1450—we find a major contingent of eighty ships, led by IDOMENEUS (q.v.), joining the expedition against TROY (2.645–52). There is mention of well-known cities—Knossos, Phaistos, Gortyn—under Idomeneus's rule. He himself is proud of his heroic lineage: son of Deukaliōn, and grandson of MĪNŌS (q.v.), whom ZEUS sired, and set as guardian over Krētē (13.448–54). We get one fleeting glimpse only of the island's legendary past, when, on the shield he is forging for ACHILLES, HĒPHAISTOS sets "a dancing floor like the one in spacious Knossos / that long ago Daidalos fashioned for fair-tressed Ariadnē" (18.590–92).

KRONOS Youngest of the TITANS, son of Ouranos (Heaven/Sky) and Gaia (Earth). By his sister Rhea he sires the OLYMPIAN family of gods: Hestia, DĒMĒTĒR, HĒRĒ, HĀDĒS, POSEIDŌN, and ZEUS. In the *Iliad* he is chiefly (and frequently) mentioned simply as these deities' progenitor, but there are brief allusions to Zeus's rebellion against him (14.203–4) and his subsequent defeat and imprisonment in TARTAROS (8.478–81, 14.203–4, 274–79). The full, and grisly, creation myth, avoided by Homer, is given by Hesiod in his *Theogony*, 137–38, 154–210, 453–506, 617–735.

KYPRIS In book 5 of the *Iliad* only, a title or alternative name ("the Kyprian /Cypriot") for APHRODĪTĒ, Kypros/Cyprus being both the place of her birth (Hes. *Th.* 199) and her cult center (*Od.* 8.362).

LAKEDAIMŌN Known in historical times as Lakōnia, Lakedaimōn (already so named in the LINEAR B tablets) comprises the area of the Eurōtas river valley, flanked east and west by the mountain ranges of Parnēs and Taÿgetos, that formed the basic territory of ancient SPARTA. It is described, accurately, in the CATALOGUE OF SHIPS (2.581) as "hollow ravine-scored", and is the domain of MENELAÖS (and, thus, by marriage as well as by birth, the home of HELEN). It furnishes sixty ships to the expedition against TROY (2.582–87).

LAOMEDŌN Father of PRIAM (20.237), and former king of TROY, the main reference to whom in the *Iliad* (21.441–57) concerns his not only defrauding POSEIDŌN and APOLLO out of wages due them for labor done at ZEUS's bidding on his behalf, but threatening to sell them as slaves and cut off their ears. Poseidōn in revenge sends a sea monster to ravage Laomedōn's lands, and he appeals to HĒRAKLĒS for help, promising him his immortal horses (inherited from his grandfather TRŌS, q.v.: 5.265–67) as a reward. Hēraklēs obliges (20.145–48), but, true to form, Laomedōn fobs him off with mortal horses, and in furious retaliation (5.638–42) Hēraklēs captures and sacks Troy.

LĒMNOS Island in the north Aegean. The *Iliad* refers to it (i) as a source of wine—perhaps in exchange for slaves (21.29–31)—for the ACHAIANS during their campaign (7.67–69); (ii) as where PHILOKTĒTĒS was left behind during the voyage to TROY, because of a foul-smelling wound caused by a bite from a water snake (2.721–24), and (iii) where HĒPHAISTOS was flung by ZEUS in anger during a domestic dispute (1.590–94): the association of the blacksmith god with this island has been plausibly linked to its fumaroles, and the volcanic gas and smoke rising from them.

LESBOS Large island in the northeastern Aegean, close offshore in the Gulf of Adramyttion to the TROAD, with long-standing connections to the area associated with Homeric TROY. Its capture by ACHILLES is mentioned in the *Iliad* (9.128–30), as is the woman Diomēdē whom he won there as a prize of war (9.663–65).

LINEAR B A MYCENAEAN syllabary in use between c. 1450 and the collapse of Aegean Bronze Age culture c. 1200, and surviving for the most part on clay tablets baked hard in destructive fires at Knossos on KRĒTĒ (CRETE) and in mainland Greece at PYLOS, THĒBĒ (1), TIRYNS, MYKĒNAI (MYCENAE), and LAKEDAIMŌN: named thus to distinguish it from Linear A, the still undeciphered earlier (1750–1400 B.C.E.) MINOAN syllabary on which it was based. The tablets (both A and B) were first discovered and categorized by Sir Arthur Evans (1851–1941); Linear B was deciphered as a form of proto-Greek in 1952 by the young architect and cryptographer Michael Ventris (1922–56). The Linear B tablets consist largely of bureaucratic records of personnel, livestock, and goods, and two major conclusions have been drawn from them. (i) The old theory, supported by Evans, that Mycenaean culture was throughout a minor (perhaps colonial) dependency of that of Minoan Krētē has been completely discarded. Indeed, it seems clear that the reverse was true from about 1450 on: the Mycenaeans established their own rule over Krētē, and the adaptation of Linear A to transcribing Mycenaean Greek was a direct consequence of this. (ii) The second conclusion, in essence that of Moses Finley, and still dominant in too many places, argued that the bureaucratic world of the tablets was so different from the one portrayed by Homer that the poet's picture must rather have been drawn in essence from the later, Archaic world, with which he was more familiar. But in fact what Linear B revealed was a world that medievalists already knew very well: while an illiterate aristocracy fought wars, pursued honor, and patronized the bards, a lettered clerisy kept the economic network on which they depended running smoothly and invisibly, leaving their masters to the pleasures of guest-friendships and the exchange of rich gifts and genealogies. Linear B, far from disproving the Mycenaean roots of Homeric society, in fact confirms them, by providing a key feature missing from the medieval comparison.

LOKRIS, LOKRIANS In the *Iliad*, we have to do only with eastern (Epiknēmidian and Opuntian) Lokris, on the coast north of Phōkis and BOIŌTIA, across from the island of EUBOIA (*BA* 55 D3). The Lokrian contingent is forty ships (2.527–35) and mainly notable for the important role assumed by its leader, AIAS (2), q.v. One of its towns, Opoeis, was the birthplace of PATROKLOS (23.84–88).

LYCIA, LYCIANS A region of southwestern Asia Minor, between CARIA and Pamphylia. In the Late Bronze age, Lycia and Pamphylia constituted a historical entity known to the Hittites as Lukka. The Lycians form the last entry (2.876–77) in the brief TROJAN CATALOGUE. Their leaders are SARPĒDŌN and GLAUKOS (q.v.).

MELEAGROS Son of Oineus, king of Kalydōn in AITŌLIA, and ALTHAIĒ (q.v.). Though the commander-designate of the Aitōlian contingent (2.638–44), he is dead before the expedition's departure. He is best known in myth for his role in the great Kalydōnian boar hunt, an episode related at length (9.529–99) by PHOINIX during the embassy to ACHILLES as an example that might induce him to be reconciled to AGAMEMNŌN and return to the fighting. ARTEMIS, angered by Oineus's failure to make due sacrifice to her, sends a huge boar to ravage his crops and orchards. It causes many deaths, but finally is killed by Meleagros. Still riled, Artemis then stirs up trouble between Aitōlians and Kourētes (a nearby tribe) over the boar's head and hide as trophies, during which Meleagros kills his mother's brother. Althaiē thereupon prays for his death, and the great warrior retires from the struggle, only being persuaded to rejoin the fight when losses to the Kourētes leave the enemy literally hammering at his and his wife's bedroom door. Let Achilles take heed! (Though sympathetic to his old tutor Phoinix, Achilles remains unconvinced.)

MENELAÖS Son of ATREUS; younger brother of AGAMEMNŌN, married to HELEN, and king of SPARTA. In the *Iliad* he is a brave warrior, but older than many and never considered in the top rank: Agamemnōn is worried that he may be killed (4.169–82, 7.107–16). Yet with good assistance he does well: for example, he and AIAS (1), helped by MĒRIONĒS, successfully rescue, and make off with, the corpse of PATROKLOS (17.90–261, 705–61). Furious when wronged—his anger at being cheated out of his victory in the chariot race at the funeral games for Patroklos (23.425–41, 566–85) is typical—he is easily flattered into a good mood by the offender (23.586–615). But at one crucial moment, during his enraged duel (3.21–29, 338–72) with PARIS/ALÉXANDROS, the man who, by cuckolding him and levanting with his wife, has precipitated the TROJAN WAR, Menelaös, on the point of victory, and about to strangle his opponent with the chin strap of his own helmet (3.369–76), is made to look a comic fool. APHRODĪTĒ, always protective of Paris, snaps the strap and magically wafts Paris away to Helen's boudoir for sex, leaving his puzzled opponent to storm frantically through the ranks in search of him, while he and Helen bed down (3.448–54). Menelaös is again captivated by Helen at the fall of Troy (*Little Iliad* fr. 28 = West 2003 [A], 138–39); see above s.v. HELEN on how the two of them later entertain Tēlemachos in Sparta (*Od.* 4.219–95). This is not the only occasion in the *Iliad* when we are—deliberately, I would argue—left wondering what, if anything, the Trojan War achieved.

MĒRIONĒS A CRETAN, son of Molos (13.249), and IDOMENEUS's henchman and second-in-command (2.650–51). A fine warrior (5.59–68, 13.156–68, 526–39), he offers to fight HEKTŌR (7.166) and is several times (e.g., 7.166, 8.264) likened to ENYALIOS. This, and his offer to ODYSSEUS (10.260–71) of a boar's-tusk helmet (such as went out of use several centuries before the putative date of the TROJAN WAR) hint at his great antiquity in the epic tradition. He is also a talented archer (13.650–56) who wins the archery contest at PATROKLOS's funeral games (23.850–83).

MINOAN CIVILIZATION The term "Minoan", derived by Sir Arthur Evans from the mythical king MĪNŌS (q.v.) was coined by him to describe the early palace culture (c. 1700—c.1400) of KRĒTĒ (CRETE), to distinguish it from the mainland MYCENAEAN culture then being explored by Heinrich Schliemann. In fact we do not know the real name of the colorful and highly sophisticated people, with their bull-leaping frescoes and parabolic drains, that Evans and his successors so successfully popularized: the Egyptians called them the Keftiu, and this name may be connected with biblical Kaphtor. There seem to have been major disasters c. 1650 and 1490–50—perhaps seismic and volcanic, with probable human intervention in the latter case, when it seems likely that the mainland MYCENAEANS profited by a natural disaster to take over the island (cf. LINEAR B). Thus for at least two centuries, until c. 1200, the KRĒTĒ known to the epic tradition would have been one dominated by Mycenaeans, and this would explain the island's participation in the TROJAN WAR.

The main Homeric reference to KRĒTĒ comes in the *Odyssey* (19.172–89), in one of the traveller's tales fabricated by ODYSSEUS for his wife Penelope, but so designed as to "make all his lies sound like true facts" (19.203). The island is thickly populated, with some ninety cities. They do not all speak the same language: there are native islanders, Dorians, and others. The main city is Knossos, and it was from there that King Mīnōs ruled. It has a difficult harbor at Amnisos. All this agrees well with the archaeological and linguistic record. Over forty sizable settlements have been excavated, and more are known. The architecture is advanced, offering maze-like rooms constructed, with light wells, around a central courtyard. Under the Mycenaeans many previously independent towns seem to have come under the central administration of Knossos. Like other Mycenaean centers, Knossos suffered in the general eclipse of palatial Bronze Age culture c. 1200.

Homer reveals little knowledge of Minoan life and society, but there are occasional flashes in the *Iliad* of familiarity with Minoan myth (e.g., of Ariadne's dancing floor built in Knossos by Daidalos, 18.592: cf. s.v. HĒPHAISTOS). Characteristically, given its nature, Homer does not mention the famous myth of the Minotaur, though clearly (*Od.* 11.321–25) well aware of it.

MĪNŌS Famous early legendary king of KRĒTĒ (CRETE), "where Mīnōs's line is," says Eumaeus (*Od.* 17.523), he is the subject of numerous (often conflicting) myths in later Greek tradition, but is mentioned only briefly by Homer. He is, by Eurōpē, the son of ZEUS, who sires him "to be Krētē's guardian" (*Il.* 13.450), and with whom he is intimate (*Od.* 19.178); the brother of RHADAMANTHYS (*Il.* 14.321–22), and the father of Deukaliōn (*Il.* 13.451, *Od.* 19.178) and Ariadnē, whose connection with Thēseus Homer knows but does not stress (*Od.* 11.321–25, cf. Diod. Sic. 4.61.4–5). He sits with a gold scepter in the underworld as judge of the dead (*Od.* 11.568–71). The only hint of his less savory activities—this in connection with Ariadnē—is that he has a "malign" mind (*Od.* 11.322). From other sources (e.g., Hdt. 1.171, Thuc. 1.4, Diod. Sic. 4.60.3), we know that Mīnōs was regarded as the first thalassocrat, with rule extending into the Cycladic islands of the Aegean: this tradition agrees with archaeological findings on Thēra (Santorini), for example. It is also possible that "Mīnōs" was a dynastic title rather than a name (cf. Diod. Sic. 4.60.2–3).

MUSES OLYMPIAN goddesses of song and creative inspiration, children of ZEUS and Mnēmosynē (Memory), and nine in number, each attached to a specific area (*Od.* 24.60–62, Hes. *Th.* 53–67), the best-known being Kalliopē (epic), Eratō (lyric), Melpomenē (tragedy) and Thalia (comedy). On Olympos they sing in chorus, accompanied by APOLLO on the lyre. They are regularly invoked, including at the opening of both *Iliad* and *Odyssey*, to provide knowledge and inspiration. However, as Ruth Scodel well points out (*HE* 2: 531) they do not themselves do the narration, but merely feed the poet with material, since Homer several times thereafter appeals to them for specific facts: for example, to name the ACHAIAN leaders in the CATALOGUE OF SHIPS (2.484–92), to identify the best warriors and chariot horses (2.761–62), or to explain (16.112–13) "how fire first came to be flung on the Achaians' ships." Their gifts could come dear: Dēmodokos in the *Odyssey* gets his skill from the Muse (who loves him dearly!) only in exchange for his sight (*Od.* 8.62–64); and when Thamyris unwisely boasts that he can sing and play better than the Muses themselves, they not only strip him of his talent, but "maim" him (*Il.* 2.594–600): this, as we learn elsewhere (Apollod. 1.3.3) likewise involved blinding. Inspiration, then as now, could, it was clearly felt, be dangerous.

MYCENAEAN CIVILIZATION The Late Bronze Age culture of mainland Greece, from c. 1550 to the approximate date (c. 1200) of the end of the palatial regime in such cities as MYKĒNAI (MYCENAE), TIRYNS, ARGOS, and PYLOS. It is the last century or two of this period, ending with the TROJAN WAR and its immediate aftermath, with which the Homeric epic tradition is primarily concerned. From southern THESSALY to the PELOPONNESE, we find a series of wealthy, powerful, and increasingly competitive elite groups: warrior kings based on strong-walled citadels, both served by and protecting the largely rural population surrounding them. Their burial goods (in particular those of the shaft graves at Mykēnai were resplendent, their beehive *tholos* tombs and their huge "Cyclopean" walls both costly and impressive: these were men who set out to leave their mark, whose legacy was calculated to suggest that they were indeed, as epic tradition repeatedly maintained, stronger and larger than the latter-day mortals who succeeded them.

It was long believed that, especially after the takeover of MINOAN KRĒTĒ (CRETE) c. 1450, these Mycenaeans were invaders. Today, however, the cumulative evidence suggests a slow cultural evolution of local clans. The basic features of this era, from its monumental strongholds to its battle-minded aristocracy, may well have furnished some fundamental elements of the Homeric (and Hesiodic) HEROIC AGE (q.v.). It seems probable that either Mykēnai or THĒBĒ (1) was in some sense (as the role of AGAMEMNŌN in the *Iliad* suggests) the capital of these largely independent fiefdoms, which collectively must have constituted the kingdom of AHHIYAWA (?ACHAIA).

For the economic functioning of these principalities see s.v. LINEAR B. With the collapse of the palace-centered system c. 1200, endemic warfare continued (as vase illustrations suggest), but all sophisticated aspects of this remarkable culture, from its writing system and its jewelry to its monumental architecture, were lost, and only fractionally preserved in memory.

MYKĒNAI (MYCENAE) Closely associated in the *Iliad* with AGAMEMNŌN, Mykēnai is strategically situated on a rocky eminence, protected on two sides by ravines, at the northeastern edge of the ARGIVE plain (cf. *Od.* 3.263). It looks toward ARGOS, and is linked with most other neighboring areas by traceable roads. Today, of course, with its great "Cyclopean" Lion Gate, its shaft-grave tombs, and its unforgettable gold burial masks ("golden Mykēnai" indeed, 11.46, *Od.* 3.304), it is, as Wiener says in his lapidary article (*HE* 2: 535–38), "inextricably linked" in public perception with Heinrich Schliemann. Everyone remembers how Schliemann believed, on first seeing the gold masks, that he had "gazed on the face of Agamemnōn". It is less often recalled that what he had seen in fact antedated any plausible date for Agamemnōn (cf. TROJAN WAR) by at least two centuries.

However, it was indeed around, or shortly before, the likeliest date for that war that much of Mykēnai as we know it came into being. The great palace, as well as the circuit walls, with their giant limestone slabs (dubbed "Cyclopean" in antiquity, since it was thought only giants such as the Cyclops could have built them) were erected c. 1350: "well-wrought citadel"(2.569) is right. The huge *tholos* tomb known as the "Treasury of Atreus" followed, soon after 1300. The Lion Gate itself was added c. 1270. Mykēnai was now at the very zenith of its wealth and power. How far did that power extend? At 2.108 Agamemnōn is "lord over many islands and the whole of Argos"; 9.149–53 suggests even wider Peloponnesian holdings. Yet in the CATALOGUE OF SHIPS (2.569–77), even though his is the largest contingent (100 ships), his holdings are largely limited to the area round CORINTH, while Argos and other sites are held by DIOMĒDĒS (2.559–66): this suggests a later date, and perhaps some Dorian manipulation (cf. s.v. ARGOLID).

MYRMIDONS In general, the inhabitants of PHTHIĒ and HELLAS, two regions in southeastern THESSALY, near the SPERCHEIOS RIVER (*Il.* 2.681–85, 9.395, *Od.* 11.496). See also s.v. HELLAS above.

The Myrmidons are the subjects of ACHILLES' father PĒLEUS (*Il.* 7.126, 16.15, 155; 21.188, 24.536); in a more restricted sense they are the picked warriors, the companions (*hetairoi*) who accompany Achilles to TROY, and it is in this sense that they are most frequently mentioned throughout the *Iliad* (1.180, 328; 9.185, 652; 11.796–97, 16.12–13, 68–220, 257–83; 18.69, 323–55; 19.14, 278, 299; 23.4–6, 60, 129; 24.449). They are "war-loving" (16.65, 23.129), a quality illustrated by similes comparing them to angry wasps (16.259–65) and thirsty wolves after a kill (16.155–67). For their early connection to AIGINA see s.v. AIAKOS.

NEOPTOLEMOS Also known as PYRRHOS (i.e., "redhead"): ACHILLES' sole son. PĒLEUS, knowing from THETIS that Achilles was fated to die at TROY, had sent him as a boy to Lykomēdēs, king of the island of Skyros, to be brought up secretly, disguised as a girl (*Cypria* fr. 19 = West 2003 [A], 96–97). While thus closeted Achilles made love to the king's daughter Deïdameia. Neoptolemos, the result of this union, was fetched to Troy after his father's death by ODYSSEUS, and given Achilles' armor. He proved a savage warrior. He was one of the picked fighters in the WOODEN HORSE (*Od.* 11.504–37: this tactful account by Odysseus, in HĀDĒS, to the shade of Achilles, of his son's actions during the sack of Troy omits his slaughter of PRIAM (*Sack of Ilion* arg. 2 = West 2003 [A], 144–45) and his getting ANDROMACHĒ as a prize of war after hurling her baby son Astyanax from the battlements (*Little Iliad* frs. 29–30 = West 2003 [A], 138–41).

NĒREÏDS Marine nymphs, daughters of the old sea god Nēreus, with whom they reside in the sea (generally the AEGEAN). They are of large but indeterminate number (estimates range from the thirties to the fifties): named, but—with few exceptions, such as THETIS—not individualized. In the *Iliad* their sole mention, and function, is as a funerary chorus of mourners, led by Thetis (18.35–69), for PATROKLOS and, beyond him, for the doomed ACHILLES. Their keening at Achilles' actual funeral (*Od.* 24.47–62) is so intense that it scares the ACHAIANS, who have to be calmed by NESTŌR.

NESTŌR Youngest son of Nēleus, king of PYLOS, and Chlōris, and grandson of POSEIDŌN. He and his father are the only survivors of the raid on Pylos conducted by HĒRAKLĒS (11.687–93). In the *Iliad* he is noted for two outstanding characteristics: his great age, and the wise persuasiveness with which age has endowed him (2.247–52). He has outlived two generations and is king among the third; he is a honey-sweet orator. He has three sons: ANTILOCHOS, Thrasymēdēs (10. 255–57, 16.317–25, 17.377–83, *Od.* 3.411–15) and Peisistratos (*Od.* 3.36–42, 4.155–67). He brings ninety ships to TROY (2.591–602) and despite his age helps out on the battlefield (8.80–121, 11.511–20, 15.559–66). But his chief role is that of ever-ready adviser: not always with success, as in his attempt to mend the initial rift between AGAMEMNŌN and ACHILLES (1.254–84). This speech is typical: it is long-winded, it calls upon ancient precedent, and it is careful to mention his own youthful achievement. Other such occasions include the embassy to Achilles (9.111–12, 162–73, 179–81, where he "kept giving them instructions"), the night raid on the TROJAN camp (10. 204–17), and rambling tips on chariot racing to Antilochos (23.305–48). Notable examples of his nostalgic ("I'm not so strong as I was") bragging are his battles with the Epeians (11.668–762) and his prowess as an athlete at long-ago funeral games (23.626–50). Despite his anecdotal loquaciousness he is invariably treated with the greatest courtesy and respect. In the *Odyssey* he is the first source of information to Tēlemachos about his father ODYSSEUS (*Od.* 3.118–29).

(Tēlemachos, incidentally, is the only character in either epic who is driven to dodge his relentless longwinded hospitality, conspiring with Peisistratos to avoid another stay at Pylos on his homeward journey: *Od.* 15.195–201).

OCEAN An extreme example of the archaic personification of natural phenomena. Ocean is the circular remote (3.5) stream thought to encompass the frontiers of a disc-shaped world, (14.200–201, 18.607–8, cf. Hes. *Th.* 790–91), and neighbor to distant, little-known, and thus fantasized peoples: Aithiōpians (1.423, 23.206), Pygmies (3.4–6), and Kimmerians (*Od.* 11.14–19). When rescued by THETIS after being thrown out of OLYMPOS by HĒRĒ, HĒPHAISTOS hides near Ocean (18.393–405). But Ocean is also the son of Ouranos (Sky) and Gē or Gaia (Earth), married to Tethys (14.201–2), and the progenitor of all the gods (14.246), as well as of every sea, river, and spring (21.195–97). He has a house, and Hērē proposes to visit him and Tethys there (14.301–11). With the rapid development of exploration, however, this always improbable personification was soon dropped; and by Herodotus's day the very idea of a circumambient stream embracing the world was challenged (Hdt. 2.23, 4.36).

ODYSSEUS Son of Laertēs and Antikleia (daughter of the thievish trickster Autolykos, *Od.* 19.392–466, Shakespeare's "snapper-up of unconsidered trifles"); married to Penelopē, father of TĒLEMACHOS, and lord of a small kingdom centered on the IONIAN island of ITHÁKĒ (q.v.). Despite this marginal background and dubious ancestry he is one of the most distinguished leaders at TROY (and, of course, the central hero of the subsequent *Odyssey*). Though his reputation for deviousness is several times mentioned in the *Iliad*—HELEN says that "he knows all manner of wiles and sharp devices" (3.200–202), while the angry AGAMEMNŌN addresses him as "you, skilled in vile deception, mind set on crafty profit!" (4.339)—it is only in his dealing with DOLŌN (10.371–458) that this side of his character shows itself (Stanford 14–19, who suggests, plausibly, that "in the *Iliad* the poet intended his hearers to enjoy the spectacle of a wily, sensitive, and self-controlled man disciplining his personality to fit into a rigid code of heroic conduct."

Elsewhere he displays fine courage as a warrior (11.310–488); his tough decisiveness and sharp words save the day when the Greek army is on the verge of breaking up (2.269–335); his persuasive tongue is put to good diplomatic use during the embassy to ACHILLES (9.223–306: yet even here Achilles in response expresses his hatred for a man "who hides one thought in his mind, but speaks another" (313).

It is surely significant that in the *Iliad* we hear nothing of Odysseus's extraordinary skill (*Od.* 21.366–430) with the bow: he does not even compete for the archery prize at the funeral games of PATROKLOS (23.850–83). The reason is clearly because this weapon was shunned by aristocratic HEROES as operating at a safe distance, and thus not encouraging true hand-to-hand valor. If so, in the post-*Iliadic Odyssey*, Homer must have enjoyed throwing off all restraints and portraying his much-travelled hero as the finest trickster of them all, in a world where survival mattered far more than aristocratic honor. Perhaps the most sharply etched portrait of him in the *Iliad* is delivered by the Trojan elder ANTĒNŌR (3.209–24), recalling his prewar diplomatic visit to TROY; short, but massive and broad-shouldered, the great voice booming from his chest as he makes his speech, "the words resembling some driving wintry snowstorm."

OLYMPOS, OLYMPIANS In one sense Olympos is a very tangible limestone mountain—at nearly ten thousand feet, it is the highest peak in the Greek mainland, and, straddling as it does the frontier between THESSALY and Macedonia, an impressive natural landmark, often veiled in clouds, and snow-capped annually from late fall to spring. But in Homer, notably in the *Iliad*, it is also the abode of the Olympian gods, a part of their heaven, and thus, inevitably, removed from its physical presence. Originally, in the far distant past, the two had been identical

(Olympos's regular epithets are all appropriate for a real mountain), and their one-time congruence manifests itself throughout the *Iliad*. The gods not only use Olympos (and IDA) as a vantage point to observe goings-on on earth; they have houses and workshops there, built by HĒPHAISTOS; Olympos is their home, most of them feast and sleep and quarrel there, as Purves nicely puts it (*HE* 2: 600–601) "in a kind of rowdy extended family," that contrasts sharply with the human heartbreak and slaughter going on below. This being the HEROIC AGE, the Olympians still have close contact with mortals; but, too, their high places are still sacrosanct. Some of the resultant discrepancies bothered the Greeks of historical times: ZEUS, for example, at one point (8.23–27) threatens to hang gods, sea, and earth on a golden cord from Olympos (mountain or heavenly sphere?), which led the commentator Aristarchos to observe, tartly, that he couldn't hang the earth from Olympos if Olympos was part of earth.

ORESTĒS Son of KLYTAIMNĒSTRA and AGAMEMNŌN, who refers to him, when making his offer of compensation to ACHILLES (9.142–43), as *tēlygetos*, probably meaning "late-born" and so "cherished" (Hainsworth 76), an epithet that would surely have been relished by Homer's audience, who knew, all too well, what was to come: Agamemnōn's murder by his wife, at least partly in revenge for the sacrifice at AULIS of his daughter IPHIGENEIA, and the subsequent killing of both Klytaimnēstra and her lover AIGISTHOS, after seven years, by Orestēs himself (*Od.* 3.193–98, 304–8, Hes. *Cat.* fr. 19.27–30 = Most 2.70–71). From Agamemnōn's viewpoint, a cherished son indeed.

PAIËŌN, PAEAN Paiëōn, alluded to by Homer at *Il.* 5.401, 899, 900 and *Od.* 4.232, is the name of an ancient god of healing, known from the LINEAR B tablets, later diminished to an epithet of APOLLO. The name is cognate with the Apolline paean, a cult song addressed to the god as an appeasement after the return of CHRYSEÏS (1.472–74) and urged by ACHILLES as a victory chant when escorting HEKTŌR's body back to the ships.

PANDAROS A wealthy Trojan, son of Lykaōn (whose name may have occasioned his false association with LYCIA at 5.105 and 173): leader of a contingent from the foothills of MT. IDA, and a famous archer favored by APOLLO (2.824–27). His most notable act in the *Iliad* is when—flattered and encouraged by a disguised ATHĒNĒ (4.86–103), because of her anxiety for the war to continue—he shoots and wounds MENELAÖS (4.104–47), thus breaking the sworn truce previously established (3.84–120, 245–301). When battle is rejoined, he also shoots DIOMĒDĒS in the shoulder (5.95–105). Called to action by AINEIAS, he makes a long, nervous, self-exculpatory speech (5.179–216), and shortly afterwards, boastful to the last, is killed by Diomēdēs (5.280–96). Many readers may well connect him with the Pandarus of Boccaccio, Chaucer, and Shakespeare's *Troilus and Cressida*—the cousin or uncle of the latter and the go-between facilitating her romance with Troilus—which, they may be surprised to learn, is a medieval invention, taking off from the increasingly anti-Homeric tradition in antiquity that culminated in the invented narratives of the TROJAN WAR (probably of the first century C.E.) ascribed by their anonymous authors to "Dictys of Crete" and "Dares the Phrygian" (see Frazer, R. M., 3–7, who provides the only available translation of both).

PARIS/ALÉXANDROS Son of PRIAM and HEKABĒ, younger brother of HEKTŌR, and—through his abduction of HELEN, the wife of MENELAÖS, together with her (no less important) possessions (3.70–72, 458; 7.361–64, cf. *Cypria* arg. 2 = West 2003 [A], 68–69, Strauss 20–21)—the direct cause of the TROJAN WAR. Of the two names by which he is variously known, "Paris" has no basis in Greek, while "Aléxandros" (which of course does) may well indicate a connection, if not identity, with an Alaksandu, prince of Wilusa (? = Ilion) who made a treaty with the Hittites (Latacz 2004, 103–10, 117–19) c. 1290–70. The two names have often been thought to indicate a melding in the epic of two separate characters: suggestive of this is the fact that although Aléxandros fights exclusively as an archer in book 11 (370–83, 504, 581), elsewhere Paris fights only as a spearman (12.93, 13.660–72, 15.341–42). Homer tells us neither of his exposure because of an ill-omened dream (on this see HEKABĒ), and its implications for his role in the JUDGMENT OF PARIS (q.v.), nor of the full significance of the PLAN OF ZEUS for this whole sequence of events.

We first meet him in book 3 (15–32), where his character is indelibly established: he comes prancing out ahead in a panther skin, carrying a bow as well as his spears, and challenging any ACHAIAN to fight him, but at the sight of MENELAÖS he panics and scuttles back in among the ranks, earning the first of several stinging descriptions by his brother HEKTŌR as a sex-mad, lyre-playing, long-haired, good-looking cheat and coward (3.39–57). His success at bedding women is seen, by the oh-so-happily married Hektōr, as an integral part of his cowardice: an all-too-familiar collocation that suggests (and was probably meant to suggest) a tinge of jealousy. There is always something a shade ridiculous about Homer's Paris: Menelaös dragging him off the field by his chin strap (3.369–82) is bad enough; his rescue from this predicament by APHRODĪTĒ, who wafts him magically home for (irresistible) sex with Helen is plain embarrassing, the more so because Paris himself—as narcissistic as they come—unlike the guilt-ridden Helen, isn't embarrassed at all, but takes the whole thing in his stride (3.421–48). Even when he finally joins Hektōr, laughing, in his fine armor, Homer likens him (6.503–29), in a fine simile (the point of which sometimes eludes translators), to a thoroughbred stallion galloping over the plain in search of "*the haunts and pastures of mares.*" The very last mention of him in the *Iliad*, by the dying Hektōr (22.359), foretells his killing of ACHILLES, with APOLLO's support, at the SKAIAN GATES: the proudest HERO of them all is thus casually dispatched (*Aethiopis* arg. 3 = West 2003 [A], 112–13) by the coward's weapon, an arrow (which—to outrage the heroic code even further—is probably poisoned, since he dies at once, though only hit in his vulnerable heel or ankle).

PATROKLOS Son of Menoitios, of Opoeis, his birthplace, in LOKRIS. After losing his temper during a game of dice as a boy, he accidentally kills a playmate and is banished in consequence (23.85–88). Taken in and raised by PĒLEUS together with Pelēus's own son ACHILLES, he becomes the latter's close companion, and shares his education (see s.v. CHEIRŌN). When they both leave for TROY, Menoitios instructs him, as the elder of the two, to look after Achilles (11.785–90), and he becomes the younger, but nobler, warrior's squire. In this capacity he alone of the other leading warriors stays with Achilles and his MYRMIDONS when Achilles withdraws from the fighting. We see him twice only, and then very briefly, in the first half of the *Iliad* (1.337–38, 9.190–91, 201–20) when he is simply acting as Achilles' aide and manservant, and says not a word.

But he is nevertheless "as battle-minded as Arēs: so began his undoing" (11.604). Sent on an errand to NESTŌR by Achilles, he refuses to come in and sit down: "quick to censure", he says, "is he who sent me" (11.649). But Nestōr, like the Ancient Mariner—and clearly knowing a frustrated hero when he sees one—holds him at the door with an enormously long speech (11.656–803), reminding Patroklos of his sworn duty to give Achilles good advice, stressing the critical stage the war has reached, and urging him to make Achilles rejoin the fighting force—or, failing that, to lend Patroklos his armor to deceive the TROJANS, and let him go into battle with the Myrmidons. Homer's audience is then left hanging for four whole books (though these total little dramatic time) in anticipation of how Patroklos will handle his all-too-famous decision.

Then, however, things move fast (16.1–100). Patroklos, weeping (like a child running to its mother, Achilles says at first, 7–10), makes his impassioned plea, followed by one of Homer's rare narratorial interjections (46–47) "Such his entreaty, the great fool: but as fate decreed, / his own ghastly death and destruction it was for which he prayed." Armed in Achilles' battle gear, he sallies forth. Achilles strictly warns him: drive the enemy back from the ships, but then come back (80–100). What HERO engaged in his ARISTEIA would do so? Patroklos kills SARPĒDŌN (16.462–507), and presses on to the walls of TROY. Thrice thrown back and warned by APOLLO (16.699–709), he persists. Had he obeyed Achilles, he would have survived: but ZEUS drove him on to his destined fate (16.684–91). His death, at the hands of Apollo, Euphorbos, and, finally, HEKTŌR, is now inevitable (16.786–867). Book 17 is entirely taken up with the struggle over his body: only at the beginning of book 18 does ANTILOCHOS bring the news to Achilles, thus precipitating the last section of the *Iliad*, with Achilles' return to the battle, the death of Hektōr, the ransoming by Priam of his body, and Achilles' final ending of his wrath.

As all this suggests, the truth of the matter is that Patroklos dead is of much greater use to the epic than Patroklos alive. As a living character all we really know of him is that he wants to fight; even as a ghost he offers nothing except a series of peevish complaints and demands about his treatment in the underworld (23.68–92). BRISEÏS in her lament (19.295–300) says he was always kind to her, just as HELEN, with better evidence, says of HEKTŌR (24.771–75); we have to take her word for it. Achilles regards him as his dearest comrade (18.80–82), and certainly mourns him desperately, but seems to regret the loss of his armor at least as much (18.82–85); his order to Patroklos not to pursue the attack to the walls, far from being out of concern for his comrade's safety, is because "you'd diminish my honor" (16.90). But once dead, Patroklos not only is the instrument of Achilles' return to the battlefield, but, through the fact of his loss, of Achilles' softening of heart, and so, indirectly, it is argued, of his concession to PRIAM. Yet even here there is doubt. What finally stops Achilles in his tracks is a no-nonsense order from ZEUS and all the gods, delivered by THETIS, to quit outraging the body of Hektōr and accept ransom for it (24.107–19). In response (24.139–40), Achilles says, "So be it." The expert in force majeure has recognized his superior. Whatever one may think about Homer's tragic sense, he is never, in the last resort, less than realistic over motive.

PĒLEUS Son of AIAKOS (q.v.) and thus a grandson of ZEUS, Pēleus is the wealthy king of the MYRMIDONS in PHTHIĒ (9.479–80, 11.766–70, 24.534–36), married to the immortal nymph THETIS, by whom he is the father of ACHILLES. Not surprisingly, it is to this marriage and its resultant child that Pēleus owes his off-stage presence in the *Iliad*. We hear nothing about his own very lively earlier mythic career (e.g., on the Kalydōnian boar hunt and as an Argonaut), though his cheerful quasi-adoption of the youthful PATROKLOS, exiled after an accidental killing, gains a certain savor from the fact that he himself had previously been twice exiled as the result of a couple of murders and ritually purified (Apollod. 3.12.6–13.2 = Frazer, J. G., 1: 56–63). Achilles, who clearly inherited his temper, will have known what to think when advised by him to control his pride, and to avoid "strife that breeds trouble"(9.255–58), before he sets out for TROY.

Pēleus's marriage is not calculated to produce harmony. Both Zeus and POSEIDŌN covet Thetis; but a prophecy (Apollod. 3.13.5 = Frazer, J. G., 2: 66–67; about this Homer is silent) that the child Thetis bears will grow to be greater than his father effectively chills their ardor, leading Zeus to lose no time in marrying her off—very much against her will (18.430–34) and despite a furious burst of shape-changing, also not mentioned by Homer—to a mortal, Pēleus, "a man who was dear to the hearts of the immortals" (24.61).

The gods themselves attend the wedding (24.62–63), at which APOLLO plays the lyre, and the MUSES sing. Gifts include the armor that Achilles later lends to Patroklos (18.82–85), his immortal horses (23.277–78, from Poseidōn) and the great spear of Pēlian ash that will be too weighty for Patroklos (16.140–44, from CHEIRŌN). But by the time of the *Iliad*, as Thetis complains to HĒPHAISTOS (18.435–61), Pēleus is a broken old man, while their glorious son—her one compensation for a hated marriage—is fated to die young. Homer does not tell us (though all his listeners would have known) the tradition that Thetis secretly at night worked at burning away the mortal element in her child, but that, interrupted and stopped by the alarmed Pēleus, she abandoned both of them, returning to a submarine life among her fellow NĒREÏDS (Apollod. 3.5.6 = Frazer, J. G., 2: 68–69, with further ref.).

PĒLION, MT. Coastal range some five thousand feet high running along the Magnesian peninsula in southeastern THESSALY (*BA* 55 A–B2), between the AEGEAN and the Gulf of Volos (ancient Pagasai), with numerous mountain streams, lush vegetation, and forests (2.757) of chestnut and ash. Pēlion was the home of the CENTAURS, and the site of the wedding of Pēleus and THETIS (*Cypria* fr. 4 = West 2003 [A], 84–85).

PELOPONNESE, THE The southern half of Greece, below the Isthmus of CORINTH: literally, the "island of Pelōps" (the father of ATREUS and the grandfather of AGAMEMNŌN and MENELAÖS): a patterned complex of mountain ranges and alluvial valleys that has always encouraged political separatism, the most famous case being that of SPARTA.

PHOINIX Son of Amyntōr (9.448), one of the five MYRMIDON captains at TROY (16.196), and the former tutor of the young ACHILLES. Cursed when young with sterility by the gods after (at his mother's urging) seducing his father's concubine, he fled to PĒLEUS, who took him in and established him (9.447–84). As Alden well stresses (*HE* 2: 662), this makes him "a dependent of Achilles' family, with no other loyalties", who treats the child Achilles as the son he himself never had. But Phoinix is thus also, in Achilles' family-conscious eyes—however close their personal relationship—an "unhonored refugee" (9.648) rather than the surrogate father he considers himself to be, who presumptuously attempts, in his long speech (9.434–605) during the embassy to Achilles, to talk his former pupil into a similar subordinate position, as prospective son-in-law, to AGAMEMNŌN. The aristocrat's rebuke to his vassal (9.611–14) is polite but sharp, and the embassy is not a success. It is notable that Phoinix from then on plays no real role in the *Iliad's* narrative.

PHTHIĒ, PHTHIŌTIS The kingdom, together with HELLAS (q.v.), of ACHILLES and the MYRMIDONS (q.v.), north of the Malian Gulf in southeastern THESSALY, by the SPERCHEIOS river. Its exact extent is never made clear in the *Iliad*.

PLAN OF ZEUS, THE First referred to at the very opening (1.5) of the *Iliad*, this "plan" or "will" seems to have three separate but related senses: (i) in general, Zeus's determination to reduce the overpopulation of the world, and end the HEROIC AGE (*Cypria* fr. 1 = West 2003 [A], 80–83; Hes. *Cat.* fr. 155.95–120; Most 2: 232–35), by causing first the THEBAN and then the TROJAN WAR; (ii) The various means by which he did so: the marriage of PĒLEUS and THETIS, which produced ACHILLES; the birth of HELEN; and, especially, the JUDGMENT OF PARIS (q.v.), leading to the cuckolding of MENELAÖS, the lasting hatred of TROJANS engendered in HĒRĒ and ATHĒNĒ, and the ten-year expedition against TROY; and (iii) his promise, in response to the prayer of THETIS, that he would compensate Achilles for AGAMEMNŌN'S insulting treatment of him by letting the TROJANS gain the upper hand in the war until the ACHAIANS made him proper amends (1.503–30). The numerous manipulative actions on Zeus's part scattered through the epic narrative all, in one way or another, form part of this overall scheme—including the peremptory order to Achilles to accept ransom and surrender HEKTŌR's body (24.107–19).

POSEIDŌN Second of KRONOS's three sons by Rhea (the other two being ZEUS and HĀDĒS (q.v.), with whom he shares earth and OLYMPOS, while having the sea as his personal realm (Zeus gets the sky and Hādēs the underworld). Poseidōn is an ancient deity, mentioned in the LINEAR B tablets: besides the sea, he is particularly associated with earthquakes (as the "Earth-Shaker") and horses (he is "dark-maned"). Both the tablets and Homer (*Od.* 3.4–66) associate him with PYLOS. In the *Iliad* he is consistently anti-TROJAN (even objecting to the rescue of HEKTŌR's body, 24.26) and pro-ACHAIAN, because of the way LAOMEDŌN (q.v.) cheated him over his recompense for building the walls of TROY (21.441–57). He is also resentful at the building of the Achaian Wall (7.445–53) and his postwar destruction of it is foretold (12.10–33). He has a past record of opposition to Zeus (1.396–406), but carefully avoids direct confrontation with him (8.198–211, 13.356–57, 15.205–19). Nevertheless, he persistently encourages the Achaians, and, when he sees the opportunity (e.g., when Zeus is somnolent after his love-making with HĒRĒ, 14.383–87), backs them more actively: 13.10–38, 43–75, 83–125, 206–38, 351–60, 676–78; 14.357–60). Sometimes he uses magic to this end (13.434–38, 562–63). He is careful, nervous, and cautious, especially when FATE is involved: at 20.290–308, for example, he is anxious to spare AINEIAS, whose destiny it is to secure Troy's future via "the line of Dardanos" (20.303), and—as APHRODĪTĒ does with PARIS—wafts him safely off the battlefield (20.318–40). Undecided about the gods fighting, he first keeps out of it (20.132–43) but has second thoughts until apparently dissuaded by APOLLO's scorn for fighting with mere mortals (21.436–60). How far this is, as often alleged, proof of his "prudence, circumspection and dignity" (Friedrich, *HE* 2: 688) is a matter for debate.

PRIAM Son of LAOMEDŌN, king of TROY, and married to HEKABĒ, by whom he has nineteen of his fifty offspring, including HEKTŌR, PARIS/ALÉXANDROS, DEÏPHOBOS, and KASSANDRĒ (Apollod. 3.12.5 = Frazer, J. G., 2: 44–47). He does not appear often in the *Iliad*, but leaves a strong impression whenever he does, not least because of his considerable age, which makes him the TROJAN equivalent of NESTŌR. He is a sensible, honorable man, as even his enemies MENELAÖS and ACHILLES concede (3.105–10, 20.179–83). He treats HELEN with kindness and sympathy (3.161–70), deploring the war, but blaming it on the gods rather than her (for which a convincing case could be made: see, e.g., JUDGMENT OF PARIS and PLAN OF ZEUS). When a peace treaty is concluded (soon to be broken by PANDAROS at ATHĒNĒ's urging, 4.93–140), it is Priam who swears to it for the TROJANS (3.250–302), but also, characteristically, is too tender-hearted to stay and watch his son Paris duel with Menelaös for Helen and her possessions (3.303–13).

It is in book 22 that Priam's quality as the embodiment of humanity and common sense fully emerges, when he desperately challenges Hektōr's (equally desperate) upholding of the HEROIC, and essentially egotistical, rule of life: "always to be the best, pre-eminent over others" (6.208, 11.784). Hektōr remains outside the SKAIAN GATES, determined to face Achilles, when the rest of the Trojans have taken refuge inside the walls. Priam, very sensibly, and for good practical reasons, begs him to come in: he is Troy's best champion, a defensive campaign makes sense, his death would be an irreparable loss, and well might result in the horrors of defeat (22.33–76). But Hektōr stubbornly refuses to budge; his mother HEKABĒ's pleas on personal grounds likewise fail to move him. Even so, his inner reflections (22.90–130) are conditioned, not by practicalities, humanity, or common sense, but rather by his sense of heroic self-respect—what will his fellow warriors think if he acts otherwise than a HERO would? Yet, ironically, faced with the fearful Achilles, his nerve snaps, and he runs for it. His inevitable death at Achilles' hands follows.

Priam has now suffered the worst that this war can inflict on him. He, who could not bear to watch his errant son PARIS/ALÉXANDROS fight a duel, now sees his beloved Hektōr stripped and dragged in the dust behind his killer's chariot (22.395–409). He then gives voice to what will be the main theme of the *Iliad*'s final book: his determination to confront the killer of his sons, to appeal to his humanity as a son himself (22.414–28). Yet even now it is ZEUS who (to the horror of Hekabē, 24.200–16) effectively sends Priam to the ACHAIAN ships and orders the hitherto unmovable Achilles to surrender Hektōr's body for ransom (24.64–186). So the stage is set—by the gods—for Priam's famous appeal to Achilles, when he kisses the murderous hands that have killed his sons (24.477–80) and the two finally share their mourning for what each has lost and recognize their common lot (24.485–512).

PYLOS In Homer, the extensive coastal kingdom of NESTŌR, son of Nēleus, in western Greece, stretching from the Gulf of Messēnia in the south northward through Triphylia as far as the natural boundary close to Olympia created by the ALPHEIOS river (9.153, 1.712). The size of this realm matches the large Pylian contingent (ninety vessels) listed in the CATALOGUE OF SHIPS (2.591–602). Whether the MYCENAEAN palace excavated by Navarino Bay in southern Messēnia (*BA* 58 B4) is the true site of Nestōr's capital city of Pylos (there were several cities of that name known in Greece) remains uncertain; it is certainly the best candidate for Pylos's Homeric epithet "sandy" (9.153, 295, etc.).

PYRRHOS See s.v. NEOPTOLEMOS.

RHADAMANTHYS In the *Iliad* (14.322) mentioned as the offspring of ZEUS and Eurōpa, and the brother of MĪNŌS. His name is pre-Greek, and his associations suggest a CRETAN origin. In the *Odyssey* (4.564) he is immortalized in the ELYSIAN FIELDS, and later tradition makes him a famous judge in the UNDERWORLD, together with Mīnōs and AIAKOS.

RHĒSOS See s.v. DOLŌNEIA.

SALAMIS Offshore island in the Saronic Gulf between Megara and ATHENS, the home OF AIAS (1) (2.557–58). This passage is of interest chiefly because of the number of ancient authors, including Aristotle, Plutarch, and Strabo, who allege that it was a forgery, inserted by the Athenians to support Solon's claim on the island as the property of Athens.

SARPĒDŌN The son of ZEUS and (in the *Iliad*) BELLEROPHŌN's daughter Laodameia (6.198–99), Sarpēdōn is, together with GLAUKOS, commander of the LYCIAN contingent allied with the TROJANS (2.876–77). He is one of the most outstanding warriors on the Trojan side: he kills Tlēpolemos, a son of HĒRAKLĒS (5.627–59); he upbraids HEKTŌR (5.471–92) for leaving the hard fighting to others; he leads one of the teams that assaults the ACHAIANS' wall (12.101–4), and makes a breach in it (12.397–99). He and Glaukos (q.v.) have a famous discussion (12.310–28) about the rewards, and matching responsibilities, of an aristocratic HERO. Zeus, who cares greatly for Sarpēdōn, protects him in combat (5.662, 12.400–403), but is dissuaded by HĒRĒ (16.433–57) from overriding his predestined FATE, to be killed by PATROKLOS (16.462–505). However, he does have APOLLO step in (16.666–83) to rescue the corpse, clean and dress it, and hand it over to SLEEP and DEATH to be returned to Sarpēdōn's family home in Lycia for burial.

SEA PEOPLES, THE A still mysterious group of migratory and predominantly naval piratical raiders operating from the late thirteenth century until well past the collapse of Mycenaean civilization, with which they seem to have been closely connected. Names associated with them include Lycians, Philistines, and the possibly Cretan Danuna (? Danaäns): they were a force to be reckoned with, and only Rameses III of Egypt seems to have managed to stand them off.

SIMOEIS One of the many streams flowing from IDA (12.20–22) into the TROJAN plain, where it joins the SKAMANDROS/XANTHOS (5.773–74). Personified during the latter's battle with ACHILLES (21.305–23).

SISYPHOS Son of Aiolos, and, like Autolykos, a famous trickster. In the *Iliad* he appears as part of GLAUKOS'S ancestry, by way of BELLEROPHŌN (6.152–55); in the *Odyssey* we catch a glimpse of him in HĀDĒS, doing what he has become most famous for—laboriously pushing uphill a boulder that invariably rolls back down to the bottom, so that he has to start all over again (*Od.*11.593–600), with one line (598) in Greek offering a notable example of onomatopoeia, echoing the boulder's bumping, clattering descent: *autis epeíta pedonde kylindeto lâas anaidēs* ("then again plainwards trundled the shameless boulder"). For a hilarious account of the misdeeds for which he was being punished, see Gantz 174.

SKAIAN GATES, THE Presumably the main entry into TROY; the Dardanian Gates (5.789, 22.194) are the only other gateway specifically mentioned in the *Iliad.* PRIAM leaves by the Skaian Gates to swear to the truce (3.261–63); HEKTŌR and ANDROMACHĒ meet there (6.390–97); a viewing point from the ramparts is close by (3.146–53), as is a landmark oak tree (9.354, 11.170). The struggle over PATROKLOS'S corpse (18.453) takes place in front of the Skaian Gates, and it is here that Hektōr obstinately persists in fighting outside the walls (22.5–6) and, dying, predicts that ACHILLES will die in the same place (22.358–60, cf. *Aethiopis* arg. 3 = West 2003 [A], 112–13).

SKAMANDROS /XANTHOS The chief river of the TROAD, flowing from the IDA range past TROY, where it joins the SIMOEIS, to the HELLESPONT, and "known to the gods as Xanthos, but as Skamandros by mortals" (20.74). The plain in its immediate vicinity forms the main battleground in the *Iliad*. It has sandy banks (5.36) and is fast-flowing (7.329) with deep eddies (21.124–25, 603, 22.148). The Skamandros is personified (as the nursling son of ZEUS, rather than, as with most rivers, of OCEAN) in book 21 (136–38), and given a voice to address both ACHILLES (214–21) and its fellow river the Simoeis (308–23). On the point of overwhelming Achilles (324–27), it is stopped by HĒPHAISTOS, who at HĒRĒ's request so scorches its seething waters with napalm-like blazing fire (342–82) that it abandons the attack.

SLEEP (HYPNOS) The twin brother of DEATH (Thanatos: 14.231, 16.672, 682), and "lord over all gods and all mankind" (14.233). Hesiod (*Th.* 212, 756–49) describes both gods as sons of Night and as "fearful deities". In the *Iliad*, however, Sleep, unlike his brother (iron-hearted and pitiless, Hes. *Th.* 764–66), is "soothing" (14.242, 354, 16.454). He features in two episodes: HĒRĒ bribes him to keep ZEUS unconscious while POSEIDŌN aids the ACHAIANS (14.231–91), and APOLLO enlists the services of both Sleep and Death to convey the body of SARPĒDŌN (q.v.) back home to LYCIA. The first of these contains two intriguing items: Sleep reveals (14.242–62) that Hērē had had him do something very similar before, which got him into deep trouble with Zeus; and, concealed in the top of a tree as a bird, he is apparently a voyeur during the al fresco divine coupling that Hērē has carefully set up (14.284–91).

SPARTA Situated in Lakedaimōn (2.581), the fertile region of the southern PELOPONNESE in the Eurōtas Valley between the north/south mountain ranges of Taÿgetos and Parnon, Sparta is the home of MENELAÖS (*Od.* 1.285–86, 4.1–19) and (in the *Odyssey*, with the TROJAN WAR over) of HELEN (4.120–305). Though archaeology has not revealed much from the MYCENAEAN era, there is a large Late Bronze Age building nearby, the so-called "Menelaion", which could be the remains of a "palace"; nearby is a small shrine dedicated to Menelaös and Helen. More than at most sites, the mythic tradition at Sparta was reshaped, after the collapse of the Mycenaean kingdoms, by energetic DORIAN newcomers who described their advent as "the return of the sons of HĒRAKLĒS".

SPERCHEIOS A river running eastward in the plain between PHTHIĒ (q.v.) and Mt. Oetē (Oeta), discharging into the Malian Gulf south of Lamia (*BA* 55 C3), the Spercheios was especially dear to ACHILLES as part of his own domain.

STRIFE (ERIS) In the *Iliad*, this personified abstract force is associated with the business of urging on (or, alternatively, scaring) troops in battle (4.439–45, 5.518, 11.3–14, 73; 18.535, 20.48). But Strife is best known (though not in Homer) for appearing, uninvited, at the wedding of PĒLEUS and THETIS, *Cypria* arg. 1 =

West 2003 (A), where she stirs up the dispute on beauty between HĒRĒ, ATHĒNĒ, and APHRODĪTĒ that is resolved by the calamitous JUDGMENT OF PARIS (q.v., and cf. Gantz 9–10).

STYX The most famous of the rivers connected with the UNDERWORLD (8.367–69, 14.271, *Od.* 10. 513–14) and invoked as the most powerful oath sworn to by the gods (2.755, 15.37–38, *Od.* 5.185). Unlike later writers who place the Styx in ARCADIA, Homer apparently (2.751–55) located it in THESSALY. Critics such as Kirk, 1: 236–37, offer no convincing explanation for the discrepancy.

TALTHYBIOS See s.v. HERALDS

TARTAROS An underworld realm even lower than HĀDĒS (8.13–16, 477–81) where the TITANS endure imprisonment (14.277–79): used by ZEUS as a threat to the recalcitrant. Cf. Hes. *Th.* 711–33.

TELAMŌN As Gantz (221) rightly points out, "Homer speaks of Telamon only as the father of Aias and Teukros, never as the son of anyone": understandably, because his lineage is confused and much debated. What seems probable is that he was a son of AIAKOS and brother to PĒLEUS; whether originally he was a native of AIGINA (see s.v. AIAKOS) or of SALAMIS (2.557, 7.199, cf. 2.562: see Gantz 222) is far less certain. He fathers TEUKROS by Hēsionē (daughter of LAOMEDŌN), won as a prize at HĒRAKLĒS' sack of Troy.

TEUKROS Son of TELAMŌN and his captive prize Hēsionē, and thus, though a half-brother of AIAS (1), illegitimate (8.284). Though he can use a spear or sword if needs be (6.31, 13.170–84, 14.515, 15.463–83), he is primarily a highly skilled archer (8.266–70, 273–334; 12.350, 387–400; 13.313–14), who only loses at the funeral games for Patroklos (23.859–83) through forgetting to sacrifice in advance to APOLLO: at the post-*Iliadic* games for ACHILLES (*Aethiopis* arg. 4 = West 2003 [A], 112–23), he is the victor. He operates in close cooperation with Aias (1), using the latter's great, tower-like shield as an observation post, from which he makes brief sorties to pick off his targets, quickly scurrying back (like a child fleeing to its mother, Homer remarks): 8. 266–72. ZEUS's refusal to let him bring down a leader, either SARPĒDŌN (12.400–403) or HEKTŌR (15.458–70: he snaps Teukros's bowstring) may have been dictated to the epic tradition by the requirements of FATE; but I suspect that the archer's bastardy, together with the idea of the bow as not quite a gentlemanly weapon, may also have been meant as factors contributing to the god's decision.

THEBAN WAR, THE The conflict (earlier than the TROJAN WAR) begun by OIDIPOUS (OEDIPUS) cursing his two sons Eteoklēs and Polyneikēs. This led to the latter's removal to ARGOS, and returning to attack THĒBĒ (1) (Thebes) with six other leaders (the "Seven Against Thebes"), including Adrēstos, king of Argos, the seer Amphiaraös, and Tydeus the father of DIOMĒDĒS, who earned notoriety by eating the brains of an enemy from his split skull while dying: *Thebaïd* fr. 9 = West 2003 (A). Adrēstos is the only survivor of this bitter, long-drawn-out war. The city finally falls to the sons of the Seven, the Epigoni ("Successors"), which is sometimes used to explain the absence of Thēbē (1) from the BOIŌTIAN contingent in the CATALOGUE OF SHIPS. Described by Homer (authorship often queried) in two lost epics, the *Thēbaïd* and the *Epigonoi*, each said to have been seven thousand lines long, brief fragments of which are reproduced in West 2003 (A), 42–59.

THĒBĒ/AI (1) This is the famous Thēbē (Thebes) on the BOIŌTIAN plain, associated with a whole group of early quasi-historical myths and characters: Kadmos, Semelē, Laïos, Oidipous (Oedipus: *Od.* 11.271–80, *Il.* 23.679–80), Polyneikēs, Eteoklēs, the expedition of the Seven Against Thebes, Antigonē, Amphiaraös (*Od.* 15.244–47), and Teirēsias (see Ganz, ch. 14, 467–530). Homer knows about this mythical background, but refers to the city only indirectly. It has a "fair crown of walls", which are "sacred" (4.378, 19.99), and is "seven-gated" (*Il.* 4.406; *Od.* 11.262–65). Its inhabitants are Kadmeians (5.804, 10.286–88), and it was founded by Amphiōn and Zēthos (*Od.* 11.262–65). Excavation has revealed a comparable site, which by the MYCENAEAN (Late Bronze Age) era was the palatial equal of MYKĒNAI (MYCENAE). The absence of Thēbē (1) from the BOIŌTIAN contingent in the CATALOGUE OF SHIPS (2.494–510) remains a puzzle.

THĒBĒ/AI (2) Known as CILICIAN Thēbē (Thebes), not because of its location (in the wooded foothills of Mt. Plakos, part of the IDA range in the TROAD) but through being inhabited by Cilicians (6.396–97). It features in the *Iliad* as the home of ANDROMACHĒ (q.v.), before she was married to HEKTŌR: she reminds him (6.414–28, cf. *Cypria* fr. 24 = West 2003 [A], 100–103) of how ACHILLES sacked it, killing her father, King Ēëtiōn, and all her brothers.

THĒBĒ/AI (3) This is Egyptian Thēbē/Thebes, modern Luxor, to which Homer refers twice only (*Il.* 9.381–84; *Od.* 4.126–27), on both occasions simply to give an example of vast wealth, a hint of how vague Greek knowledge of Egypt still was prior to c. 750 B.C.E.

THEMIS Daughter of Gaia (Earth) and Ouranos (Sky: Hes. *Th.* 135), and thus a TITAN. Appears only twice in the *Iliad*, both times as a minor goddess on OLYMPOS: once greeting and comforting HĒRĒ (15.87–91), once (like IRIS) acting as a messenger for ZEUS, calling the gods to assembly (20.4–6). There is no hint of her primary role as a goddess of law, justice, and right thinking and behavior—much less of the fact that she had been Zeus's second wife (Hērē was only his seventh), on whom he sired a whole string of personified abstractions: Good Order, Justice, Peace, the Seasons, and the three Fates, Klōthō, Lachesis, and Atropos (Hes. *Th.* 901–6).

THERSĪTĒS One of the most intriguing characters in the *Iliad*, though his appearance is limited to one scene in book 2 (211–77), immediately after ODYSSEUS has, with difficulty, checked the rush to the ships triggered by AGAMEMNŌN's foolhardy "test" of the troops' spirit. A quintessential barrack-room lawyer (seventy years ago a teacher of mine described him as "insubordination personified"), he is here attacking, not his favorite targets, Odysseus and ACHILLES, but Agamemnōn—and, indeed, borrowing Achilles' own main point against him, his greed for booty, from book 1 (149–71). It is easy to see why his rant has so often been attributed to class warfare: he sums up the Greek aristocrat's stereotypical view of the lower classes as, by definition, not only poor, but mean, cowardly, ignorant, vulgar, and *ugly*. Thersītēs' deformities, lovingly catalogued (2.216–19), are the first thing we learn about him. Nor is it any accident that his appearance is immediately preceded by Odysseus's demonstration of the niceties of social and military status: aristocrats and officers are reasoned with politely (2.188–97), but other ranks (2.198–206) are treated like dirt, beaten, and told to shut up and listen to their betters. In due course Odysseus hands out precisely this last treatment—beating included—to Thersītēs (2.243–75), and "[s]orry for him or not, the troops still found him comic" (270). The social order has not only been maintained but is endorsed from the bottom.

THESSALY The great central plain of northern Greece, south of Macedonia, surrounded by mountain ranges—OLYMPOS, Ossa, PĒLION, Othrys, and Pindos—and with its main access to the sea from the Gulf of Pagasai, modern Volos, an area famous as the departure point of the Argonauts, with many MYCENAEAN remains. Homer never mentions it by name, and is mainly concerned with its small southeastern regions of PHTHIĒ and HELLAS, in connection with ACHILLES, PĒLEUS, and the MYRMIDONS. A number of Thessalian towns, mostly now identified, are listed in the CATALOGUE OF SHIPS (2.681–759).

THETIS A more than usually privileged sea NYMPH, daughter of Nēreus, the Old Man of the Sea; married to (but mostly separate from) PĒLEUS (q.v. for details of, and the reason for, her engagement and forced wedding to a mortal); living in the depths of the sea with her fellow NĒREÏDS; and—most important by far for the *Iliad*—the mother of ACHILLES. As such, she is the only nymph who can come calling on OLYMPOS, let alone as, to HĒRĒ' s great annoyance and suspicion (1.517–21, 536–43), ZEUS'S one-time object of desire and current favorite and confidante. Not only that: as her son reminds her (1.396–406), she played a key role in saving Zeus during his generational war with his father KRONOS. Zeus owes her a big favor; and Achilles' getting Thetis to extract a promise from him to favor the TROJANS for so long as FATE permits, thus punishing AGAMEMNŌN for the insult Achilles has suffered at his hands, shapes the whole subsequent course of the *Iliad*.

One consequence of Thetis's marrying a mortal is that their child is mortal too (despite several attempts by Thetis—e.g., by fire and dipping in the Styx—to make Achilles immortal, of which Homer says nothing). Since he is fated to choose either a short and glorious life or a long one at home without the glory (as Thetis reminds him at 9.410–16), there is no real doubt as to which it will be. Indeed, Thetis is a striking early version of the *mater dolorosa:* her mourning for her son begins even before his actual death (18.52–64). Once PATROKLOS is dead, ACHILLES will kill HEKTŌR in revenge; and as Thetis well knows (18.88–96) her son's death is fated to follow close after Hektōr's. Immortal though she is, she cannot save him, even with HĒPHAISTOS'S marvelous armor; she can only commemorate him (Slatkin, *HE* 3: 873, is very percipient on this). It is not until the end of the *Odyssey*, in HĀDĒS (24.35–94), that we finally get closure, when the shade of AGAMEMNŌN recounts Achilles' funeral, with Thetis, silver-footed and immortal, leading MUSES and Nēreïds in the dirges, providing elegant gifts (including Achilles' armor) at the funeral games, and finally committing her son's ashes, mingled with those of Patroklos, to a golden urn—or, in an alternative version (*Aethiopis* arg. 4 = West 2003 [A], 112–13) snatching his body from the pyre and conveying it to the White Island (Leukē), in fact located at the mouth of the Danube, but in mythic tradition a kind of foreshadowing of Avalon.

TIRYNS A MYCENAEAN citadel situated on a rocky eminence in the ARGIVE plain: mentioned by Homer only once, as part of DIOMĒDĒS' domain in the CATALOGUE OF SHIPS (2.559) where it is described as "high-walled": its great "Cyclopean" battlements still survive.

TITANS The pre-OLYMPIAN generation of gods, twelve in number, offspring of Gaia (Earth) and Ouranos (Sky, Heaven), of whom the best-known is KRONOS (q.v.), overcome by his son ZEUS in the great mythical battle described in detail by Hesiod (*Th*. 664–735), known as the "Titanomachy". As so often, Homer knows this myth well, but refers to it only obliquely. We learn how THETIS helped Zeus during the conflict (1.396–406), and there are several references (8.477–81, 14.274) to the imprisonment of the defeated Titans in TARTAROS (q.v.). Some surviving Titans, e.g., OCEAN and THEMIS, are mentioned without identification as such.

TROAD, THE The northwestern massif of Asia Minor (*BA* E–F 1–2), largely mountainous (culminating in the IDA range in the south) but with an extensive coastal strip fronting successively on the Gulf of Adramyttion, the AEGEAN, the HELLESPONT, and the Propontis. On this coastal strip all the region's important cities are situated, TROY—near the Aegean entrance to the Hellespont—included.

TROJAN CATALOGUE, THE The record (2.816–77) of the TROJANS and those allied with them: it does not include the allies' ships and is far shorter and more perfunctory than the lengthy CATALOGUE OF SHIPS provided for the ACHAIANS. Its historical accuracy is dubious: it is probably most reliable, outside TROY and the TROAD, for LYCIA. As Rutherford suggests in an excellent up-to-date survey (*HE* 3: 890–92), its version of Bronze Age geography is very hit-and-miss. Interestingly, it carefully omits those places ACHILLES is reported as having already sacked, e.g., Lyrnessos and THĒBĒ (2) (2.691).

TROJAN WAR, THE "It is generally assumed that some residue of historical truth persists in the legends concerning the Trojan War, although how much and where is uncertain," the *OCD*[3] pronounced in 2003 (1557). Since then the problem has become even more knotty. The understandable popularity of Troy VIh as the scene of such a war (c. 1250; a city of undiminished greatness until its end) has been undercut by the recent excavations of Manfred Korfmann, which demonstrated, not only an unbroken continuity between Troy VI and Troy VII, but the hitherto unknown existence of a large outer suburb extending outside the walls.

What would this do to the Greek tradition of total destruction? But alternatively, if we the choose the later (revised) date of Troy VIIa's end as c. 1180, then the war postdates the collapse of MYCENAEAN palace culture, which, again, would come into direct conflict with the epic tradition. Nor does what has been termed the "Anatolization" of the problem espoused by Latacz 2004 (see 283–87 for a succinct summary) help. While the identifications of Wilusa with Ilion/Troy, and of the kingdom of AHHIYAWA with an ACHAIAN federation, are both plausible to the point of near-certainty, unfortunately, as Finkelberg reports (*HE* 3: 894), the relevant Hittite texts have been convincingly backdated a century and a half, so that no reference to Wilusa can predate c. 1230. While this fits admirably with the MYCENAEAN dating of the war to Troy VI and the mid-thirteenth century, it is incompatible with the now fashionable late date of c. 1180. (Also, by treating the war as largely an internal Anatolian affair, it severely undercuts the notion of a vast Achaian naval expedition.)

What conclusions can we draw from all this? It remains true that a date in the mid-to-late thirteenth century, say between 1250 and 1230, while the Mycenaean palace culture was still in existence, is a sine qua non for the epic tradition, and fits admirably with the new dating of the Hittite documents. The prevalence of the late dating owes a lot to the mistaken assumption that the LINEAR B (q.v.) documentation ruled out the society predicated in the *Iliad*, whereas in fact it confirmed it by adding a dimension familiar to medievalists: the lettered scribes who got on with the routine business of existence while their illiterate aristocratic superiors pursued glory according to a strict HEROIC code, exchanged gifts and genealogies, and enjoyed guest-friendships. For this, the Mycenaean palace society would form a natural background: anything after the collapse of that culture would not. As for the archaeological evidence, total destruction is both harder and much rarer than is often supposed. The survival of a site does not preclude the total destruction of the culture that had previously occupied it: TIRYNS offers a good case in point. There is still a case to be made for the epic tradition going back to, and in many ways reflecting, Bronze Age Mycenaean society, and the disasters that brought its HEROIC AGE to a close.

TROY, TROJANS From the viewpoint of the Homeric epics, the *Iliad* in particular, there is nothing problematic about the city of Troy, often given its alternative name of ILION, or the Trojans who inhabited it. Troy is a wealthy city in the TROAD, its famous walls built by POSEIDŌN and APOLLO (7.451–53, 21.441–60), and still ruled in the *Iliad* by the dynasty descended from DARDANOS (a son of Zeus) and the eponymous Trōs's sons Īlos and Assarakos, PRIAM being the current king in Īlos's line of descent, and AINEIAS the frustrated claimant (13.460–61) in that of Assarakos. This distinction is reflected in the TROJAN CATALOGUE (2.816–23), where the Trojans are led by Priam's son HEKTŌR, while Aineias is in command of the Dardanians, domiciled in the foothills of IDA (20.216–18).

How does this scene stand up in the light of the latest research? Fairly well, in fact. Nowadays (see Kelly, *HE* 3: 895–96) there is no real problem in identifying

Homer's citizens of Troy or Ilion with the inhabitants of Taruisa or Wilus(iy)a, and the Dardany appear in thirteenth-century Egyptian inscriptions; there is even a thirteenth-century ruler of Wilus(iy)a called Alaksandu, whom it is very tempting to identify either with PARIS/ALÉXANDROS himself or else with a homonymous relative. As for Homeric Troy itself, its identity with the much-excavated site of Hisarlik, though never formally proven (and in light of the ongoing debate between the respective proponents of an early and a late date for the TROJAN WAR, very probably unprovable) remains highly likely: it is by far the most important Bronze Age site of the whole region. If this was not Homer's Troy, what else, of comparable importance, could it have been?

UNDERWORLD, THE See s.v. HĀDĒS.

WOODEN HORSE, THE: The famous episode of the Wooden Horse—created by an ACHAIAN, Epeios (*Od.* 11.523), in the tenth year of the war, filled with an attack group of chosen warriors, and left behind for the TROJANS to consider—trap or offering to the gods?—while the main Greek expeditionary force hides out at the nearby island of Tenedos—goes back to earliest times, both iconically and in literature. Yet there is not a word about it in the *Iliad*, though it is the ruse that finally brings about the defeat and sack of TROY. On the other hand it is referred to several times in the *Odyssey*. MENELAÖS mischievously reminds his wife, HELEN, of how she tried, by imitating the voices of their wives, to make the warriors she was sure were hidden inside betray their presence by crying out (*Od.* 4.271–89). ODYSSEUS—himself the leader of the commando group (*Od.* 8.494–95, 11.524–25)—persuades the bard Dēmodokos to sing of the episode (*Od.* 8.492–515), and when visiting the dead, he recalls how cool the young NEOPTOLEMOS was inside the Horse (11.523–32). It is an integral element in the Trojan epic.

Yet the full narrative—including how, after heated argument, pro and con, the Trojans finally decide that it's a sacred object, to be dedicated to ATHĒNĒ, and haul it into the city, even breaking down part of the wall to do so—is only found, among the earliest sources, in the arguments and fragments of the *Little Iliad* (arg. 4–5, fr. 12 = West 2003 [A], 122–25, 132–33) and the *Sack of Ilion* (arg. 1–2, fr. 1 = West 2003 [A], 144–47). The number of warriors varies, from thirteen to fifty. The Horse itself is huge: 100 (or 130) feet long, 30 (or 50) feet wide, with movable tail, knees, and eyes. The advance party opens the gates to the main force, which meanwhile has returned from Tenedos under cover of darkness. The Trojans, who have been celebrating their apparent deliverance, are sleeping off their potations. The sack begins.

What nobody has decided, from antiquity to the present, is what, in origin, if it ever existed, the Wooden Horse really was. One of the earliest suppositions was a horse-headed battering-ram. More recently (1950) Fritz Schachermeyr thought it symbolized the destruction of Troy by earthquake, since the earthquake god POSEIDŌN was also the god of horses. Nobody, except the builders of modern Wooden Horses to attract tourists, seems happy with the idea that it might have been conceived exactly as what our ancient sources claim it was: a large siege engine decked out in the semblance of a horse, with a barrel body capable of holding a score or more commandos. In this connection Anderson (*HE* 3: 941) notes, interestingly, that the two earliest known representations (c. 700–650 B.C.E.) are both shown equipped with wheels.

XANTHOS See s.v. SKAMANDROS.

ZEUS For a modern reader coming to Homer for the first time, the nature of the OLYMPIAN gods, and their relationship to mortals, constitutes perhaps the largest stumbling block. Where, ask the uninitiated, is any recognizable morality? The problem is not new. As early as the sixth century B.C.E. the philosopher Xenophanes of Kolophōn in Ionia was complaining that the gods of Homer and Hesiod were guilty of all the worst human faults, including theft, adultery, and mutual deceit. New readers are often astonished by the solipsistic pettiness, as they see it, of so much divine motivation: not least the reason of POSEIDŌN (resentment at being bilked, see s.v. LAOMEDŌN) or HĒRĒ and ATHĒNĒ (sexual jealousy, see s.v. JUDGMENT OF PARIS) for their persistent and intense opposition to the TROJANS during this ten-year war. These gods are the immortal easy livers; they quarrel peevishly among themselves like the members of any privileged extended family who don't have to work for a living; and the only limitations on their actions (over and above what they can get away with for their own selfish ends) are provided by the quasi-deterministic rulings of FATE and the superior power and authority of Zeus, the original Indo-European divine patriarch. The ultimate winner in this divine world is not virtue but strength.

The degree to which mortal actions in the *Iliad* are dictated by what seem arbitrary, and always personal, decisions by Zeus, in counterpoint to the equally arbitrary, and inscrutable, requirements of Fate (mostly in the matter of human destinies) can be judged by a careful study of the PLAN OF ZEUS (q.v.), from which it becomes clear (i) that both the THEBAN and the TROJAN WARS were deliberately started by Zeus in order to reduce overpopulation and end the HEROIC AGE; (ii) that both the Judgment of Paris and the forced marriage of THETIS to PĒLEUS that produced ACHILLES were part of the mechanism involved; and (iii) that despite Zeus's various ploys during the Trojan War (e.g., his promise to Thetis that he will honor Achilles by giving AGAMEMNŌN and the ACHAIANS a hard time of it) the ultimate outcome—the destruction of Troy, the deaths of Achilles and HEKTŌR—is predestined. How far this is to be accomplished by the fiats of Zeus, and how far by the inexorabilities of Fate, is never made quite clear.

Nor, indeed, are the relative powers of Zeus and Fate ever put to a decisive test. A nice case is the (long fated) death in battle, at the hands of PATROKLOS, of Zeus's son SARPĒDŌN (16.431–61). Zeus considers saving him: this brings an instant response from HĒRĒ, who says, in effect: *Override fate, and we other gods will take it very badly! Besides, do it once and the habit'll catch on: we'll have every god saving his own son in this war!* Zeus, without arguing the point, agrees, and merely honors the dead Sarpēdōn with a shower of bloody rain, after which SLEEP and DEATH (qq.v.) are commissioned to return the corpse to LYCIA. Zeus's own implication here is that while he has the power to override Fate, he chooses not to exercise it. Centuries of counterarguments between the respective advocates of determinism and divine power suggest that Homer made him choose wisely.

Otherwise the Zeus of the *Iliad* behaves very much as a MYCENAEAN *wanax* (lord, prince) might be expected to if granted immortality and supreme authority. He also exercises his nature as a traditional weather god: he is the cloud gatherer, he sends rain, he hurls a nifty, and accurate, thunderbolt. It is his patronage that gives power to chosen princes and warriors on earth, who are "Zeus's nurslings" (1.176, 2.660, and often). He never tires of reminding his large and obstreperous divine family of the horrendous punishments that result from opposing him (e.g.,15.18–24); this does not stop them from regularly doing so whenever they have the chance, most notably Hērē (14.153–353) and POSEIDŌN (13.10–38, 59–79, 206–39). Despite Zeus's constant interference in human affairs, it is a striking fact (Strauss Clay *HE* 3: 953) that in the *Iliad*, alone among the Olympians, he has no direct dealing with mortals—despite his Leporello's catalogue of earlier sexual conquests (14.313–28)—but always sends a messenger. The most notable instance, of course, is his brief, and angry, command to Achilles, via Thetis, to release HEKTŌR's abused body for ransom (24.134–40). Achilles, hitherto obstinate to a degree, instantly bows to higher authority. One sometimes wishes that Zeus had issued a few other similar orders rather earlier in the epic; but that would have once more raised the always delicate problem of overriding Fate. The hard lessons in humanity that Achilles learns are still framed in a relentless pattern that was fixed before his birth.

Select Bibliography

NOTE: Basic texts apart, these titles, mostly in English, are chosen for beginners, the especially useful ones marked with an asterisk (*). Their bibliographies lead to further reading. A few advanced studies of particular value are also included, identified by a dagger (†).

My translation was made, basically, from Monro and Allen, together with regular consultation of van Thiel, West (1998-2000), and A.T. Murray in Wyatt's revised edition.

Alexander, C. *The War That Killed Achilles*. London, 2010.

Austin, N. *Helen of Troy and Her Shameless Phantom*. Ithaca, NY, 2008.

*Barker, E., and J. Christensen. *Homer: A Beginner's Guide*. London, 2013.

Blondell, R. *Helen of Troy: Beauty, Myth, Devastation*. Oxford, 2013.

Burgess, J. S. *The Tradition of the Trojan War in Homer and the Epic Cycle*. Baltimore, 2001.

———. *The Death and Afterlife of Achilles*. Baltimore, 2009.

Casson, L. *Ships and Seamanship in the Ancient World*. Princeton, NJ, 1971.

*Cline, E. H. *The Trojan War: A Very Short Introduction*. Oxford, 2013.

———. *1177 BC: The Year Civilization Collapsed*. Princeton, NJ, 2014.

Dalby, A. *Rediscovering Homer: Inside the Origins of the Epic*. New York, 2006.

Day Lewis, C., trans. *The Aeneid of Virgil*. 1952. Garden City, NY, 1953.

Edwards, M. W. *Homer: Poet of the Iliad*. Baltimore, 1987.

†———. *The Iliad: A Commentary*. Volume 5: *Books 17–20*. Cambridge, 1991.

Finkelberg, M. *Greeks and Pre-Greeks: Aegean Prehistory and Greek Heroic Tradition*. Cambridge, 2005.

*———, ed. *The Homer Encyclopedia*. 3 vols. Oxford, 2011. Cited as *HE*.

Foley, J. M., ed. *A Companion to Ancient Epic*. Oxford, 2005.

*Fowler, R., ed. *The Cambridge Companion to Homer*. Cambridge, 2004.

French, E. *Mycenae: Agamemnon's Capital*. Oxford, 2002.

Frazer, J. G. *Apollodorus: The Library*. 2 vols. Cambridge, MA, 1921.

Frazer, R. M., Jr. trans. and ed. *The Trojan War: The Chronicles of Dictys of Crete and Dares the Phrygian*. 1966. Bloomington, IN, 1990.

*Gantz, T. *Early Greek Myth: A Guide to Literary and Artistic Sources*. Baltimore, 1993.

Graziosi, B. *Inventing Homer: The Early Reception of Epic*. Cambridge, 2002.

———. Introduction and Notes (ix–xxviii, 410–50) to *The Iliad*, trans. A. Verity, ed. B. Graziosi. Oxford, 2011

*Griffin, J. *Homer on Life and Death*. Oxford, 1980.

†Hainsworth, B., ed. *The Iliad: A Commentary*. Volume 3: *Books 9–12*. Cambridge, 1993.

Hammer, D. *The Iliad as Politics*. Norman, OK, 2002.

Heath, M. ed. and trans. *Aristotle: Poetics*. Harmondsworth, UK, 1996.

**HE:* see Finkelberg above.

Hughes, B. *Helen of Troy*. New York, 2005.

†Janko, R. *The Iliad: A Commentary*. Volume 4: *Books 13–16*. Cambridge, 1992.

Kahane, A. *Homer: A Guide for the Perplexed*. London, 2012.

†Kirk, G., ed. *The Iliad: A Commentary*. Volume 1: *Books 1–4*. Cambridge, 1985.

———. *The Iliad: A Commentary*. Volume 2: *Books 5–8*. Cambridge, 1990.

*Latacz, J. *Homer: His Art and His World*. Translated by J. P. Holoka. Ann Arbor, MI, 1998.

———. *Troy and Homer: Towards a Solution of an Old Mystery*. Translated by K. Windle and R. Ireland. Oxford, 2004.

Lattimore, R., trans. *The Iliad of Homer*. Rev. ed. Edited and introduced by Richard Martin. Chicago, 2011.

†Leaf, W., ed. *The Iliad*. 2 vols. London, 1886.

Leigh Fermor, P. *Mani: Travels in the Southern Peloponnese*. London, 1958. New York, 2006.

Lynn-George, M. *Epos: Word, Narrative and the Iliad*. Atlantic Highlands, NJ, 1988.

Mackie, H. *Talking Trojan: Speech and Community in the Iliad*. Lanham, MD, 1996.

Martin, R. *The Language of Heroes: Speech and Performance in the Iliad*. Ithaca, NY, 1989.

*———. Introduction to *The Iliad of Homer*, trans. R. Lattimore, 1–65. Chicago, 2011.

Mitchell, S., ed. and trans. *Homer: The Iliad*. New York, 2011.

Monro D. B., and Allen, T. W., eds. *Homeri Opera*. 3rd ed. 2 vols. Oxford, 1920.

Most, G. W., ed. *Hesiod*. Vol. 1: *Theogony, Works and Days, Testimonia*. Vol. 2: *The Shield, Catalogue of Women, Other Fragments*. Cambridge, MA, 2006–7.

*Murray, A. T., trans. *Homer: Iliad*. 1924. 2 vols. 2nd ed., rev. William F. Wyatt. Cambridge, MA, 1999.

Murray, G. *The Rise of the Greek Epic*. 4th ed. Oxford, 1934.

Myrsiades, K., ed. *Reading Homer: Film and Text*. Madison, NJ, 2009.

Nagy, G. *The Best of the Achaians*. 1979. 2nd ed. Baltimore, 1999.

———. *Homer's Text and Language*. Urbana, IL, 2004.

Osborne, R. *Greece in the Making, 1200–479 BC*. London, 1996.

*†Onians, R. B. *The Origins of European Thought About the Body, the Mind, the Soul, the World, Time and Fate.* 1951. 2nd ed. Cambridge, 1954.

The Oxford Classical Dictionary. 3rd ed. rev. Edited by S. Hornblower and A. Spawforth. Oxford, 2003. Cited as *OCD*[3].

The Oxford Classical Dictionary. 4th ed. Edited by S. Hornblower, A. Spawforth, and E. Eidinow. Oxford, 2012.Cited as *OCD*[4].

*Powell, B. B. *Homer and the Origin of the Greek Alphabet.* Cambridge, 1996.

———. *Homer.* 2nd ed. Oxford, 2007.

Pulleyn, S., ed. and trans. *Homer Iliad I.* Oxford, 2000.

Radice, W. *The Translator's Art: Essays in Honour of Betty Radice.* Edited by B. Reynolds. New York, 1987.

Redfield, J. *Nature and Culture in the Iliad: The Tragedy of Hector.* Chicago, 1975. Expanded ed. Durham, NC, 1994.

†Richardson, N. *The Iliad: A Commentary.* Volume 6: *Books 21–24.* Cambridge, 1993.

Schachermeyer, F. *Poseidon und die Entstehung des griechischen Götterglaubens.* Munich, 1950

Schein, S. *The Mortal Hero: An Introduction to Homer's Iliad.* Berkeley, 1984.

Scodel, R. *Listening to Homer.* 2002. 2nd ed. Ann Arbor, MI, 2009.

Scott, W. C. *The Artistry of the Homeric Simile.* Hanover, NH, 2009.

Seferis, G. *Collected Poems, 1924–1955.* Translated, edited, and introduced by Edmund Keeley and Philip Sherrard. Supplemented ed. Princeton, NJ, 1969.

Shay, J. A*chilles in Vietnam: Combat Trauma and the Undoing of Character.* New York, 1995.

Slatkin, L. M. *The Power of Thetis: Allusion and Interpretation in the* Iliad. Berkeley, 1991.

Stanford, W. B. *The Ulysses Theme: A Study in the Adaptability of a Traditional Hero.* Oxford, 1954.

Steiner, G., ed. *Homer in English.* Harmondsworth, UK, 1996.

*Strauss, B. *The Trojan War: A New History.* New York, 2006.

Talbert, R. J. A. *Barrington Atlas of the Greek and Roman World.* Princeton, NJ, 2000. Cited as *BA.*

Taplin, O. *Homeric Soundings: The Shaping of the Iliad.* Oxford, 1992.

Thiel, Helmut van. *Homeri Ilias.* Hildensheim, 1996.

Thomas, C. G., and C. Conant. *The Trojan War.* Westport, CT, 2005.

*Vermeule, E. *Aspects of Death in Early Greek Art and Poetry.* Berkeley, 1979, 1981.

Vivante, P. *The Epithets in Homer: A Study in Poetic Values.* New Haven, CT, 1982.

*Wees, H. van. *Status Warriors: War, Violence and Society in Homer and History.* Amsterdam, 1992.

Weil, S. *The Iliad, or, The Poem of Force.* Translated by M. McCarthy. Wallingford, PA, 1956.

West, M. L. *Homeri Ilias.* Stuttgart/Leipzig, 1998–2000.

†*———. *Greek Epic Fragments from the Seventh to the Fifth Centuries BC.* Loeb Classical Library, Cambridge, MA 2003 (A).

———. *Homeric Hymns, Homeric Apocrypha, Lives of Homer.* Loeb Classical Library, Cambridge, MA, 2003 (B).

*†———. *The Making of the Iliad: Disquisition and Analytical Commentary.* Oxford, 2011.

———. *The Epic Cycle: A Commentary on the Lost Troy Epics.* Oxford, 2013

*Whitman, C. H. *Homer and the Heroic Tradition.* Cambridge, 1958.

Willcock, M. *A Companion to the Iliad.* Based on the translation by Richmond Lattimore. Chicago, 1976.

Wolf, F. A. *Prolegomena to Homer.* 1795. Translated with introduction and notes by Anthony Grafton, Glenn W. Most, and James E. G. Zetzel. Princeton, NJ, 1985.

Wood, M. *In Search of the Trojan War.* 1985. 2nd ed. Berkeley, 1996.

Index

NOTE

Some major entries consist of two sections: the first of events in order of occurrence, the second an alphabetically ordered selection of topics.

LOCATOR FORMATS AND SEQUENCE

Map: lowercase roman numerals, e.g., xii*map*

Introduction: italic typeface

Translation: plain typeface in book/line format, e.g., 1.111

Synopsis: italic typeface

Glossary: bold typeface